Studies in the Short Story

Studies in the Short Story

FOURTH EDITION

Virgil Scott
Michigan State University

David Madden
Louisiana State University

Holt, Rinehart and Winston
New York Chicago San Francisco Atlanta Dallas Montreal Toronto

to our students

Library of Congress Cataloging in Publication Data
Scott, Virgil, comp.
Studies in the short story.
First–3d ed. edited by A. H. Jaffe and V. Scott.
1. Short stories. 2. Short story. I. Madden, David, joint author. II. Jaffe, Adrian H., comp. Studies in the short story. III. Title.
PZ1.S429St8 [PN6014] 808.83'1 75–25515
ISBN: 0–03–089835–8

Printed in the United States of America
8 9 059 9 8 7 6 5 4

About the Cover

For the cover, we sought an illustration that would be far more than mere decoration, that would immediately express and become an integral part of the book's concept: its dual purpose of providing imaginary experiences and opportunities for interpretation of those experiences. Pavel Tchelitchew's *Hide-and-Seek* struck us as an unusually powerful visual metaphor of what writers create and what readers do when they interpret that creation.

Any painting generates in a single glance an impression of the whole image. The act of reading a story is different; one gets an impression of the whole only after one has read it line by line. But if one is to experience a painting fully, one must, to reverse the metaphor, reread it, line by line. And if one is to experience all a story's elements fully, one must reexamine it the way one discovers more faces, more figures, more colors, and more intricate relationships among all those elements the longer one scrutinizes *Hide-and-Seek.* A single look at *Hide-and-Seek,* a single reading of "The Garden of Forking Paths" provide one kind of experience; repeated viewings of *Hide-and-Seek,* repeated readings of "A Garden of Forking Paths" extend that first experience into something more complex, more satisfying, more lasting.

We imagine that even before you read the preface to this book, you will have enjoyed, emotionally, intellectually, and perhaps spiritually or mystically, more than one look at *Hide-and-Seek,* without having found everything hidden there (in plain sight, after all). And we do not need to convince you that reexamination in no way diminished, but rather obviously enhanced your enchantment. But because literature's finer qualities are not so immediately apparent, this book is necessary as a means of exercising your perceptions, as a way of persuading you that fiction too becomes more exciting the more you look at it; and as you discover for yourself elements you missed the first time you read a story, you experience emotional and intellectual delights quite similar to those stimulated by continued scrutiny of *Hide-and-Seek.*

And just as this painting may have shocked, frightened, confused, or even depressed you at first, and just as you gradually perceived that the beauty of its colors and its forms transcended those gloomier aspects, you will, we are convinced, come to see that these stories, many of which seem rather grim on first reading, have qualities of beauty and delight that only an increasing understanding and appreciation of the nature of fiction can reveal.

After you read a story—maybe even *as* you read—for the first time, look again at *Hide-and-Seek*. Use it as a way of developing your responses to the charged images writers create with words alone.

We offer *Hide-and-Seek*, then, as a symbol and a metaphor of the creative process itself and of the process of interpretation.

Preface to the Fourth Edition

As in earlier editions, our intent in this edition of *Studies in the Short Story* has been to provide a text-anthology that, by adapting the analytical approach to the abilities of college freshmen and sophomores, will help instructors broaden and deepen their students' understanding and appreciation of good modern fiction. With this in mind, we have followed five basic guidelines:

1. We have organized the book so that it will move from the simple to the complex, from the relatively obvious to the relatively subtle.
2. We have grouped our selections around a series of introductions designed to present to students, in language they can understand, certain fundamental critical principles that will give them a working basis for reading, understanding, and evaluating a variety of short stories.
3. We have followed each story with a set of study questions designed to focus attention on those aspects of a given story that we consider important.
4. In order to give students some practice in criticism through comparison, we have included some stories that are clearly inferior, either from the standpoint of method and effect or from the standpoint of significance.
5. We have tried to include as wide and as universal a selection of stories as possible; inclusion of stories as different in kind as those by Maugham and Hemingway, Collier and Borges, will, we hope, help lead students to an understanding and appreciation of as many kinds of stories as possible within the limits of six hundred pages.

A text is revised in order to improve it; our aim has been to do so here. The twenty-one stories we have carried over from the third edition are those that for many seemed to work best in classes. The twenty-two that are new will, we hope, freshen the text for many instructors, and the inclusion of such writers as Oates, Barthelme, Barth, and McPherson will update it.

Our critical apparatus has also undergone a number of changes. We have largely rewritten the introductions on the basic elements, point of view, and genres. We have added a section on style and another on avant-garde and experimental fiction; the section on symbol has been expanded to include other literary devices. Section 6, "Some Differences between Popular and Serious Fiction," deserves special mention because of its two-part format. In Part A, "Entertainment and Beyond," we hope to show the student that a modern mass-circulation magazine story can demonstrate as much skill as a quality story; many quality stories are not necessarily "better than" good commercial stories, only "different." Commercial stories vary in skill and significance in the same way that quality stories do. Part B, "Honesty and Dishonesty in Fiction," goes on, then, to show the student how and why.

We might add here one further word on these sections. Our original plan was to begin this revised text with "Entertainment and Beyond" as the opening section. But many readers of the manuscript felt that most students could better handle such a contrast-comparison section if they first had a few basic critical concepts to work with. For this reason we moved this section to its present position in the text. But given a relatively sophisticated class, instructors might well consider the possibility of beginning a course with this section rather than with a consideration of the basic elements of fiction.

In general, the introductory material tries to present as clearly and simply as possible those fundamentals that we feel a student must learn in order to read intelligently and perceptively serious, mature, and effective fiction. Our introductions make no claim to completeness; rather, they emphasize the problems involved in *reading* fiction. The beginning student can, we think, absorb only so much theory; beyond a certain point lies confusion rather than illumination. We have occasionally permitted ourselves certain oversimplifications because it has been our experience that the student new to criticism is usually bewildered by generalizations that are too carefully and judiciously modified. The situation is analogous to the study of grammar; first one learns the rules, *then* one learns when and how and why the rules may be broken or disregarded. In the main, therefore, early in the text we have discussed principles that are *generally* true and then, in later introductions or discussion questions, we have pointed out instances that show that these principles are neither necessarily nor universally true.

• • •

In the preparation of any text, editors contract more debts than they can hope to acknowledge, and this text is no exception. But we wish here to thank all those, students and teachers alike, who helped test our material in the classroom, and all those instructors who ripped from a busy day time to write us concerning their experiences with the third edition. And we owe a particular debt of gratitude to our editor, Harriett Nolte, whose patience and encouragement have seen us through a year of hard and exciting work.

V.S.
D.M.

East Lansing, Michigan
Baton Rouge, Louisiana
December 1975

Contents

5
GENRES: HUMOR, SATIRE, AND FANTASY 227

6
SOME DIFFERENCES BETWEEN POPULAR AND SERIOUS FICTION 273

A. Entertainment and Beyond 273

B. Honesty and Dishonesty in Fiction 304

7
AVANT-GARDE AND EXPERIMENTAL FICTION 343

8
MORE STORIES 387

Studies in the Short Story

To the Student

The preface to a recent anthology of short fiction opens with the question, "If one doesn't get pleasure out of reading fiction, then what's the use of it?" The question is, of course, rhetorical; few would argue with the person who says that anyone who sits down to a short story or a novel expects to enjoy the experience. But precisely what do we mean by pleasure? Can you derive different kinds of pleasure from different kinds of stories, and if so, what kinds? And, finally, there remain two other questions. This anthology-text has been designed for use in a classroom. Can the study of fiction in any way increase the pleasure you derive from reading fiction? Can it, further, show you how to enjoy fiction that you would not otherwise have enjoyed? *Studies in the Short Story* assumes that both of these questions can be answered affirmatively.

Most of you have been reading fiction for much of your lives. And if you think about it, you will realize that you have gone through a number of changes in your reading tastes. At one stage, you found stories in a first-grade reader interesting. At another, you graduated to adolescent fiction. At a third, you found "adult" fiction more rewarding. But at some point, your preferences probably stopped changing and became relatively fixed; you stopped climbing and sat down on a plateau. This book hopes to help you to discover that beyond this plateau are other mountains worth the ascent.

What is the nature of this plateau? Most of you are aware that at this moment you have certain preferences in fiction. If asked to define these, you would very likely come up with a list of characteristics that are to be found in that body of fiction which we call "popular" or "commercial." To begin with, you probably prefer fiction with a strong story line to fiction in which "nothing much happens." You probably prefer stories that end happily to those that leave you depressed. You may also have settled on what Robert Penn Warren has called "threshold interests" in fiction; you may read only sports or detective or love stories, or science fiction, or historical romance. Finally, you probably prefer "easy" stories to "difficult" ones; you prefer those stories whose meaning and intent are easily grasped.

We have described above what many critics call escape fiction. In general a story will either take us out of the life we know into a life we think we would prefer, or it will subject us more intensely than experience itself to the world we happen to live in. Many readers prefer the first kind of story to the second. And what needs emphasis at the outset is that one need not be apologetic or defensive about liking escape fiction; we all live in a world whose faults are more glaring than its virtues, and we can therefore appreciate an escape into a more perfect world. But sophisticated readers of fiction do not stop here; they have discovered that a different kind of fiction can also afford pleasure. If one kind of fiction offers us a vicarious escape from our world, our lives, our limitations, another kind increases our awareness of that same world, sharpens our understanding of those same limitations. Most readers new to such fiction may find their introduction to it an unpleasant experience. Since the stories in this anthology are predominantly of this second type, some of the reasons for this initial reaction merit attention.

To begin with, the writer of such stories is using fiction to interpret our lives or our world for us. Human nature and human experience tend to be, if not completely chaotic and senseless, at least so complex as to elude any comfortable and easy understanding of either. Writers of serious fiction are, among other things, trying to make us understand ourselves or our world better than we did before we read their stories. But such a "discovery" can, for the reader, be unpleasant. Serious writers are usually trying to tell us the "truth" about life insofar as they can perceive it, and truth is never completely pleasant or reassuring. Hence, some readers reject serious fiction on the grounds that life is depressing enough as it is. What these readers have not yet learned is that self-discovery and self-understanding can be at least as rewarding as self-delusion.

But there is a more immediate reason for studying serious fiction. The techniques and emphases of serious fiction are frequently not the same techniques and emphases of commercial fiction. If you have never learned to understand these differences in method, you may find some serious stories incomprehensible. Since various sections of this book are designed to introduce you to some of these differences, this is not the place to discuss them in any detail. But we should emphasize that by examining these techniques you may understand and appreciate stories that, at this moment, you might not like.

One final word about pedagogy. Fundamentally, the approach employed in this anthology-text is analytical. Such an approach to reading, you may discover, has its dangers as well as its advantages. For one thing, if the text is successful, it may help to change your reading tastes; you may discover that some fiction that you now like has been "spoiled" for you. Beyond this, you may feel that "tearing a story apart" is no superhighway to appreciation, that in fact analysis can (at least temporarily) take some of the pleasure out of reading fiction. It may take some time to convince you that such is not the case; but meanwhile, we can point out that probably the reader who derives the most enjoyment from reading is the critic, and the critic's approach to literature is primarily analytical. True, the analytical approach involves work, but those who have learned to employ it have almost invariably found the results worth the effort.

This said, let us begin with a brief consideration of the basic elements of fiction.

1 The Basic Elements of Fiction

Conflict

The first impulse of any reader of fiction is to ask, "What is the story about?" by which he usually means, "What happens in it?" The question betrays the feeling on the part of fiction readers that a story, before it can be anything else, must be a narrative of something that happens to somebody. Some recent critic-writers like Sherwood Anderson have complained that the notion of "plot" has "poisoned" storytelling. But it is as true today as it was in the beginning that to try to write a story without some kind of narrative action is analogous to trying to create a body without a skeleton.

At the same time, many readers are inclined to exaggerate the importance of narrative in fiction. The influence of De Maupassant and O. Henry, or the prevalence on newstands of "action-packed" slick fiction, still heavily affects reading tastes, and external action is still *all* that many readers ask from fiction. But even the devotee of suspense fiction realizes that some stories with comparatively little action are "better" than others with a great deal of action. Apparently there is more to this matter of "story" than at first meets the eye. What?

Let us first emphasize that this section is headed "conflict," not "plot." In the history of the story (drama, narrative poem, or prose fiction), the term *plot* has come to mean a very particular kind of story structure, a structure that has often been charted to show the entanglement, rising action, climax, and denouement of a story. While many stories do not have a plot in this sense of the word, all stories do have conflict. What is the distinction?

This. The term *plot* connotes a formal, relatively inflexible structure, one that originally described the structure not of prose narratives but of five-act plays. But the term *conflict* simply means that a story brings together two opposing forces, which we call a *protagonist* (that is, one who struggles for) and an *antagonist* (that is, one who struggles against), and then develops and resolves the struggle between these two forces. In most stories, these conflicts will assume one of two patterns. Either we will have an "accomplishment" story, in which the protagonist tries against opposition to achieve some goal (as in "The Rock Cried Out"), or we will have a "decision" story, in which a protagonist must choose between two things—two courses of action, say, or two sets of values (as in "The Last Day in the Field").

Now conflict is the backbone of a story; it is conflict that provides us with pattern and direction and gives us the sense of a story going somewhere. But conflict must be handled in certain ways if it is to be convincing and effective. What, then, are the basic principles that writers consider when they want to arouse and maintain a reader's interest in a story?

The conflict in a story must first be *significant*; it must be of obvious importance to the characters involved. All of us face constant conflicts in our daily lives, most of which are easily resolved. But we sometimes face conflicts that are not easily resolved. All of us from time to time experience conflicts that have a permanent effect upon us—that alter or modify our character, values, ideals, or concepts in some way. These are the kinds of conflicts we find in fiction, and because of their nature we call them *crisis situations.* We mean by this that as a result of a given conflict, the characters involved will never again be quite the same people they were before the incident occurred.

A second characteristic of effective fictional conflict is that the two opposing forces must be relatively equal in strength. In this respect, a skillful short story is like a good prize fight, where the outcome is in doubt until the final round. Hence, the skillful writer will balance opposing forces so that the outcome of a story remains in *suspense* until the end. To put it another way, conflict in effective stories is *developed.*

Third, a story must have *unity.* This is a comprehensive term; ultimately it means that everything—the conflict, the characters, the theme, the point of view, the incidental devices—must be functional, related to the story's basic purpose or effect. In the narrower terms of conflict alone, unity means that each development in the conflict of a story must follow logically from a preceding development.

A writer may manage all this and still fail to convince, for his conflict may lack the most essential characteristic of fiction, that of *plausibility*. Like unity, plausibility involves the *whole* story. There is, however, one general principle on which plausibility rests: the most convincing story will be one that most closely approximates life as the reader has experienced or observed it. This does not mean that the *initial situation* in a story must correspond to situations in our world; the skillful writer of fantasy, for example, can persuade us to accept a totally unfamiliar world. But it does mean that given a particular situation, the characters in a story will act and react according to familiar principles of human behavior. Or it means that the resolution of conflicts will adhere to basic facts of existence—that in a story as in life, for example, a stronger force will defeat a weaker force.

Writers may also employ other devices that are peculiarly associated with narrative handling. In story openings, for example, where a writer may have to establish time, place, character, or background before plunging us into the conflict, we may find *foreshadowing*—that is, the suggestion of conflict to follow. A writer may arouse our interest by arousing curiosity; or may intensify conflict by employing dilemma—that is, by placing his character in a situation in which the person is forced to choose between two equally undesirable alternatives. In these and other ways writers can increase the effectiveness of their story line.

But conflict is only one of several elements in fiction. And if it is the dominant element in some stories, in others it is simply one way to achieve quite another end than just suspense. Hence, the most crucial questions we can ask about conflict are, "What is its *function* in a given story? To what use is it put?"

Now the relationship between all the elements in a story is the subject of this entire text. But initially we can begin to see this relationship if we ask the following questions about a story's conflict.

1. Who is the protagonist? In most stories, the answer to this will be obvious. But in some it will not. In most stories, we can pinpoint the protagonist by asking, "On whom does this story have a maximum effect?" But if we discover that a story has no clear protagonist, we have through that discovery taken a step toward determining the story's purpose.

2. What seems to be the emphasized element in a story? Is it conflict,

or does conflict seem to be subordinated to some other element? Determining the dominant element is an important first step in discovering what a story's purpose is.

3. What is the focus of the conflict? In most accomplishment stories, the conflict is *external.* In most decision stories, the conflict is *internal.*

4. How is the conflict resolved? A story in which a protagonist wins says one thing. A story in which he loses says another. A story in which he wins but finds the winning tainted with some dissatisfaction says a third. A story in which the conflict remains unresolved says a fourth.

5. How is the conflict organized? Action may be organized in any of a number of ways, and frequently the purpose of the story is suggested by this organization. A writer who wants suspense will probably organize a story chronologically, or at least keep the resolution a secret until the end. But the writer may not be interested in creating suspense; he may want us to ask not "And then?" but "Why?" In this case he may invert his organization, giving us the resolution before giving us the events leading up to it. A great many stories are not organized chronologically, and if we ask why the "normal" organization is abandoned, we will often find the answer a help in determining a story's purpose.

Character

It was with considerable difficulty and little success that we tried above to discuss fictional conflict without constantly relating it to other story elements. All elements in fiction are closely related and constantly interact with and influence each other. This is particularly true of conflict and character, for a story has to happen to somebody. Indeed, in the effective short story the characters will in large part determine the nature, development, outcome, and effects of the conflict. And if we can therefore argue that character is at least as essential to fiction as conflict, we can also argue that it is as interesting. Unless we are interested in a fictional character, we are not going to be interested in what happens to him.

But if this is true, it is also true that characterization places certain demands upon a reader that conflict does not. In order to understand the whats and whys of these demands, let us briefly examine the basic nature of the reading process.

Most readers of fiction think of reading as a passive process in which the writer does most of the work and the reader reaps most of the reward. Such is not the case. A storyteller is trying to communicate experience, and this can be accomplished only as a joint enterprise. For vicarious experience can be communicated only in a very special way. Most of the elements of fiction cannot be handled directly, as a generalization in nonfiction is handled; rather they must be handled indirectly. Another way of putting this is to say that a writer *shows* rather than *tells*; much of a story's action and most of its characterization, its theme, its emotional effects are implied or suggested rather than stated. A storyteller does not tell us that a character is selfish, but shows the person acting selfishly. A storyteller does not write essays, but gives us a story from which we must deduce the theme. A storyteller does not tell us to feel sad, but places a sympathetic character in the kind of situation that will elicit sadness from us. The good writer knows that handling these elements in any other way will fail to convince and may fail to communicate at all. To illustrate, let us look at the opening of a very unsophisticated form of fiction, a "story" in a first-grade reader.

> This is Dick and Jane. Dick is nice. Jane is nice, too. Jane likes Dick. Dick likes Jane. Dick and Jane run and play. Oh, happy, happy Dick. Oh, happy, happy, Jane.

Clearly, no adult reader in his right mind would derive any esthetic pleasure from this passage because everything in it—what the characters are like, what they do, how they feel—is *told.* And if we compare this to any scene in, say, Bradbury's "And the Rock Cried Out," we will see the difference implication makes in a story. For here what the characters are like, how they feel, how we feel toward them, the meaning of what happens to them must be deduced from what they say, from how they act and react, even from such details as a cigarette left burning on a hotel table. The deductive process we go through when reading such an "adult" story is almost precisely the process we go through when we interpret and appreciate a joke; and, as with a joke, the pleasure we derive from a story is almost exactly proportional to the deductive demands made upon us. Hence we can generalize that the more sophisticated the story, the more the writer will rely on implication in order to accomplish his purpose and effects.

But implication is not enough. Beyond it, we must believe in the people in a story if we are to believe the story.

Plausible characterization, like plausible conflict, defies complete analysis. But again we can generalize that the most convincing fictional characters are those whose behavior most closely approximates the behavior of persons we have observed in life. This means, among other things, that fictional characters will be *consistent*; if a character is established as selfish, we expect him to behave selfishly throughout the story. On the surface, this may seem contradictory, for in actual life we have all known people to behave inconsistently. But this "acting out of character" is the exception, not the rule, and we accept it only because we actually observe it. And one important difference between fiction and life is that the behavior of people in stories imitates what people *usually* do, not what they *occasionally* do.

But how do we reconcile consistency with the principle of story as crisis, the principle that story involves some kind of character change? Here we meet with a second requirement, which is that plausible characters in fiction must be motivated; a story is concerned not only with what a character does but with why he does it. A character in fiction can change *if we are shown a convincing reason for that change*. Such a character will still be consistent.

Other kinds of fictional characters fail to convince a sophisticated reader. If we are to believe in a character, we must *know* him or her; one kind of character we do not know is the *shadowy* character, the mere name on a page. Similarly, mature readers will find *stock* characters—characters borrowed from other fiction, as the run-of-the-mill Western hero has been borrowed—implausible. Such readers will also reject the *oversimplified* or *flat* character, the character who is reduced to a single, one-dimensional character trait, and will ordinarily find the *round* or relatively complex character more plausible (an exception, of course, is the use of stock or flat characters in minor roles in short fiction).

Given convincing characterization, a reader must further remember that characters are only one element in a total story; the reader must be able to see the function of a character in a story. Again, as with conflict, we can offer no easy formula for understanding this function. But some of the questions we ask about conflict can with equal validity be asked about character. What happens to a character in a story? Why? If the conflict changes the character, how and why? If it teaches him something, what? If the conflict ends satisfactorily for the protagonist, why? If it does not, why not? Do you like, admire, respect this or that character in a story? If so, why? What are the dominant traits of the characters in a story? What are their values? Their drives? Their problems? Their dilemmas? The answers to such questions will usually provide significant clues as to a story's purpose or point.

The kind of character we have in a story can also help us understand a story's purpose. In general, fictional characters will fall into one of three categories. Probably the majority are what we call *typical*. The human race is subject to division and subdivision; these groupings are determined by such things as our occupation, our position on a socioeconomic ladder, our ancestry, our age. And because humans are mimics, our personalities tend to be stamped by the groups to which we belong. Thus, a typical character in fiction is one who represents a group, and we refer to him or her as a "typical" teacher, a "typical" advertising copywriter, a "typical" Italian.

But regardless of whether we are black or white, old or young, rich or poor, we share with all members of the human race certain characteristics, instincts, values. All languages share such abstractions as love, hate, pity, joy. All human beings share many of the same desires—the desire for wealth or power, for status, for love, for life, for comfort. Some stories concern themselves with problems common to all men, and some fictional characters share traits with their brothers and sisters everywhere. We call these characters *universal.* And in some stories we find universal characters pushed one step further into *allegorical* characters, characters who are not people but symbols of abstract human traits.

At the other extreme, characters in fiction can be *individual.* An individual character is one who is unique rather than representative. Such characters are comparatively rare in fiction, and ordinarily a writer who is using this type of characterization will deliberately use minor characters as *foils* (contrasts) to the individualized character. Thus, a story like Caroline Gordon's "The Last Day in the Field" contrasts an individual, unique character like Aleck to a typical youth like Joe.

Theme

Conflict and character are the two most basic and necessary elements of fiction, but all stories also have a third, which we call *theme.* We define theme as the application that the story has for the reader, the generalization that we can derive from the story, the comment that the story makes on some aspect of the human condition. In order to explain what we mean by this, let us briefly consider some of the reasons that lead to the writing of a story.

One impulse common to all of us is to generalize from experiences, real or vicarious. We read or hear of crimes committed and criminals punished, and we conclude that crime does not pay. We meet people who have made a lot of money and who have ulcers, and we gather that acquiring wealth is not necessarily a formula for happiness. Like the rest of us, the writer experiences and observes human existence, and he also comes to certain conclusions about human beings and their problems, conclusions that he feels impelled to communicate to others. One way to do this is by telling a story.

Theme, then, can be defined as the generalization, stated or implied, that lies behind the narration of a specific situation involving specific individuals; and theme exists in fiction because human beings live in the same world, share similar emotions, react in similar ways to similar stimuli, and face common problems. These generalizations tend to fall roughly into one of two categories. On the one hand, the writer lives in a particular, immediate world, a world of this time and this place; in some ways this world is unique, and the writer may comment on it in such a way that his observations apply to no other time or place. In such a story we say the theme is *topical.* On the other hand, there are many experiences or problems that mankind has faced from the beginning of time: Being born and dying. Loving and hating. Most of us mate, reproduce, share family relationships. Most of us speculate about the nature of good and evil, the existence of God, the kind of universe in which we live. When a writer deals with such subjects, we say the theme is *universal.*

So much for definition. And if all stories had titles like "War Is Stupid," or if they incorporated essays that interpreted the meaning of the story, theme would probably not present readers with the problems it does. But as in characterization, theme in fiction is usually handled by implication and must be deduced. That process is likely to involve analysis of conflict and character, consideration of a story's point of view, definition of symbols, recognition of allusions, interpretation of style and tone—to mention only some of the fictional elements that can have a bearing. Hence, one crucial question in regard to theme is: What are some of the things a reader looks for in order to arrive at a definition of a story's theme?

It will take us an entire text to answer this in any detail. But our first step will be to determine what the story is *about.* Every story concerns itself with some *subject*—materialism or justice or love or death or good and evil. But the subject of a story is not its theme; a story will make some statement about death, say. To determine what that statement is, look first at the characters. For a story to have meaning, the people in it must have something in common (character traits or attitudes or values), either with the reader or with people in the reader's world. In what ways, then, are the characters representative of people outside the story?

As with character, so with *situation.* The situation in which the fictional characters find themselves, the problem they face, will ordinarily parallel in some way situations in which we have found ourselves, problems we have faced or observed. Then, with character and situation analyzed, we consider how the characters react and what happens to them as a result. From this analysis of the specifics in a story, we can usually arrive at a generalization which will suggest that *if* we have this kind of character in this kind of situation, and *if* the character reacts thus, then this is what may happen to him or her.

This approach will not apply to all stories, for many stories employ other methods (point of view, symbol, allusion, irony, and so on) to arrive at theme. But when we are exploring the theme of a story, these are the first factors to be considered. At the same time, we should know that in translating something specific into something general, we are driving along a treacherous road and should therefore heed the warning signs along the way; for example—

1. In the terms in which we have already defined it, the theme of a story should not be confused with a story's subject; theme is, rather, a statement about that subject. The subject of "A Tree, A Rock, A Cloud," for example, is clearly "love." But ten stories on that subject can say ten different things about love. What exactly does Carson McCullers say about it here?

2. The idea of theme should not be equated with that of a "moral" or a "lesson." Although fiction can deal with ethical or moral problems or values, many stories do not, and those serious and intelligent ones that do are often concerned with challenging, not reaffirming, moral axioms or platitudes. Good stories do not *teach*, they *reveal*; they do not *preach*, they *interpret*.

3. In the truly intelligent and honest story, the theme cannot be reduced to a pat maxim like "Honesty is the best policy." Human experience is complex, and the thoughtful story illustrates a complexity that will be manifested in a number of ways. For one thing, no intelligent story will suggest that a given generalization is *always* true; it will only be true under certain circumstances. For another thing, the subjects and predicates of a story's theme will be constantly modified, or ambiguous, or ambivalent; good will never be totally good or evil completely evil. Finally, a story's theme will never apply to *all* human beings at *all* times. And if we are to state a story's theme at all accurately, we must account for these modifications.

4. We cannot approach a thematic story as we would a problem in physics, expecting to find only one correct interpretation. Art is not mathematics; a story will always mean something different to different readers, just as it will never mean to a reader *exactly* what the writer intended it to mean. This is because the writer brings to a story one set of experiences whereas the reader brings to that same story another set.

In some respects, these two backgrounds must be similar if the story is to communicate at all, but they will never be identical. Hence, no two interpretations of a story will ever be identical. This does not mean that the search for meaning in fiction is a speculative free-for-all, that a story can mean *anything* we choose to make it mean. Behind every story lies a specific intent, and the skillful writer selects and arranges his (or her) material in a way that will enable a reader to recognize that intent. For this reason, a reader, in discussing a given story, should be prepared not only to define *what* he thinks a story says but also to explain *why* he so thinks by relating *all* details to his conclusion. The phrase *all details* should be marked. A good story is, among other things, a unified story; unity means that everything is there for a purpose, that everything has bearing on a story's intent. Hence, if our interpretation of theme does not allow for, or is contradicted by, several details in the story, then we must question our interpretation. Or if we must go outside a story to substantiate our thesis, then we are again on the wrong track.

5. We have said that a story is, among other things, an interpretation of some aspect of the human condition. That interpretation is the essence of a story's theme. But regardless of how intelligent or skillful a writer is, a reader is under no obligation to *accept* a story's theme. Assign ten writers a story and you will get from them ten different and possibly contradictory themes. We explore theme in fiction not to *learn* about life but to *think* about it. The story that prompts us to examine critically our world or our ideas about the nature of human nature has done all that a story can be expected to do.

6. Above all else, we must constantly bear in mind that theme is only one of three basic elements in fiction; it is never the be-all and end-all of effective fiction nor can it by itself create an effective story. The elements of conflict and character are at least as important as that of theme, and the writer who fails to handle these skillfully will have written a poor story regardless of how profound or significant its meaning.

For the reader who thinks of fiction primarily as a "made-up" story written for the purpose of entertaining, the concept of the interpretative function of storytelling will be a new one. Serious fiction does not exist merely to entertain; indeed, the most effective fiction might be defined as that which interprets honestly and intelligently a genuine human problem. One statement we frequently hear is that "Fact is stranger than fiction." The statement was fathered by an article writer, and it is true because the article writer deals with the out-of-the-ordinary. To put this in another way, *factual* stories deal with what happens to 1 percent of the people 1 percent of the time. But the proper subject of fiction is the ordinary, the commonplace; fiction concerns itself with what happens to 99 percent of the people 99 percent of the time. The basic distinction between fiction and life is that fiction *interprets* life. Because it does so, and because it does so *emotionally*, by subjecting us vicariously to the ordered experience of a story, the fiction writer can reply, "Fiction is stronger than fact." In a large degree it is theme that is responsible for this strength.

RAY BRADBURY
And the Rock Cried Out

The raw carcasses, hung in the sunlight, rushed at them, vibrated with heat and red color in the green jungle air, and were gone. The stench of rotting flesh gushed through the car windows, and Leonora Webb quickly pressed the button that whispered her door window up.

"Good Lord," she said, "those open-air butcher shops."

The smell was still in the car, a smell of war and horror.

"Did you see the flies?" she asked.

"When you buy any kind of meat in those markets," John Webb said, "you slap the beef with your hand. The flies lift from the meat so you can get a look at it."

He turned the car around a lush bend in the green rain-jungle road.

"Do you think they'll let us into Juatala when we get there?"

"I don't know."

"Watch out!"

He saw the bright things in the road too late, tried to swerve, but hit them. There was a terrible sighing from the right front tire, the car heaved about and sank to a stop. He opened his side of the car and stepped out. The jungle was hot and silent and the highway empty, very empty and quiet at noon.

He walked to the front of the car and bent, all the while checking his revolver in its underarm holster.

Leonora's window gleamed down. "Is the tire hurt much?"

"Ruined, utterly ruined!" He picked up the bright thing that had stabbed and slashed the tire.

"Pieces of a broken machete," he said, "placed in adobe holders pointing toward our car wheels. We're lucky it didn't get *all* our tires."

"But *why*?"

"You know as well as I." He nodded to the newspaper beside her, at the date, the headlines:

OCTOBER 4TH, 1983: UNITED STATES,
EUROPE SILENT!

The radios of the U.S.A. and Europe are dead. There is a great silence. The War has spent itself.

It is believed that most of the population of the United States is dead. It is believed that most of Europe, Russia, and Siberia is equally decimated. The day of the white people of the earth is over and finished.

"It all came so fast," said Webb. "One week we're on another tour, a grand vacation from home. The next week—this."

They both looked away from the black headlines to the jungle.

The jungle looked back at them with a vastness, a breathing moss-and-leaf silence, with a billion diamond and emerald insect eyes.

"Be careful, Jack."

He pressed two buttons. An automatic lift under the front wheels hissed and hung the car in the air. He jammed a key nervously into the right wheel plate. The tire, frame and all, with a sucking pop, bounced from the wheel. It was a matter of seconds to lock the spare in place and roll the shattered tire back to the luggage compartment. He had his gun out while he did all this.

"Don't stand in the open, please, Jack."

"So it's starting already." He felt his hair burning hot on his skull. "News travels fast."

"For God's sake," said Leonora. "They can *hear* you!"

He stared at the jungle.

"I know you're in there!"

"Jack!"

He aimed at the silent jungle. "I see you!" He fired four, five times, quickly, wildly.

The jungle ate the bullets with hardly a quiver, a brief slit sound like torn silk where the bullets bored and vanished into a million acres of green leaves, trees, silence, and moist earth. The brief echo of the shots died. Only the car muttered its exhaust behind Webb. He walked around the car, got in, and shut the door and locked it.

He reloaded the gun, sitting in the front seat. Then they drove away from the place.

They drove steadily.

"Did you see anyone?"

"No. You?"

She shook her head.

"You're going too fast."

He slowed only in time. As they rounded a curve another clump of the bright flashing objects filled the right side of the road. He swerved to the left and passed.

"Sons-of-bitches!"

"They're not sons-of-bitches, they're just people who never had a car like this or anything at all."

Something ticked across the windowpane.

There was a streak of colorless liquid on the glass.

Leonora glanced up. "Is it going to rain?"

"No, an insect hit the pane."

Another tick.

"Are you sure that was an insect?"

Tick, tick, tick.

"Shut the window!" he said, speeding up.

Something fell in her lap.

She looked down at it. He reached over to touch the thing. "Quick!"

She pressed the button. The window snapped up.

Then she examined her lap again.

The tiny blowgun dart glistened there.

"Don't get any of the liquid on you," he said. "Wrap it in your handkerchief—we'll throw it away later."

He had the car up to sixty miles an hour.

"If we hit another road block, we're done."

"This is a local thing," he said. "We'll drive out of it."

The panes were ticking all the time. A shower of things blew at the window and fell away in their speed.

"Why," said Leonora Webb, "they don't even *know* us!"

"I only wish they did." He gripped the wheel. "It's hard to kill people you know. But not hard to kill strangers."

"I don't want to die," she said simply, sitting there.

He put his hand inside his coat. "If anything happens to me, my gun is here. Use it, for God's sake, and don't waste time."

She moved over close to him and they drove seventy-five miles an hour down a straight stretch in the jungle road, saying nothing.

With the windows up, the heat was oven-thick in the car.

"It's so silly," she said, at last. "Putting the knives in the road. Trying to hit us with the blowguns. How could they know that the next car along would be driven by white people?"

"Don't ask them to be that logical," he said. "A car is a car. It's big, it's rich. The money in one car would last them a lifetime. And anyway, if you road-block a car, chances are you'll get either an American tourist or a rich Spaniard, comparatively speaking, whose ancestors should have behaved better. And if you happen to road-block another Indian, hell, all you do is go out and help him change tires."

"What time is it?" she asked.

For the thousandth time he glanced at his empty wrist. Without expression or surprise, he fished in his coat pocket for the glistening gold watch with the silent sweep hand. A year ago he had seen a native stare at this watch and stare at it and stare at it with almost a hunger. Then the native had examined him, not scowling, not hating, not sad or happy; nothing except puzzled.

He had taken the watch off that day and never worn it since.

"Noon," he said.

Noon.

The border lay ahead. They saw it and both cried out at once. They pulled up, smiling, not knowing they smiled. . . .

John Webb leaned out the window, started gesturing to the guard at the border station, caught himself, and got out of his car. He walked ahead to the station where three young men, very short, in lumpy uniforms, stood talking. They did not look up at Webb, who stopped before them. They continued conversing in Spanish, ignoring him.

"I beg your pardon," said John Webb at last. "Can we pass over the border into Juatala?"

One of the men turned for a moment. "Sorry, *señor.*"

The three men talked again.

"You don't understand," said Webb, touching the first man's elbow. "We've *got* to get through."

The man shook his head. "Passports are no longer good. Why should you want to leave our country, anyway?"

"It was announced on the radio. All Americans to leave the country, immediately."

"Ah, *sí, sí.*" All three soldiers nodded and leered at each other with shining eyes.

"Or be fined or imprisoned, or both," said Webb.

"We could let you over the border, but Juatala would give you twenty-four hours to leave, also. If you don't believe me, listen!" The guard turned and called across the border, "Aye, there! Aye!"

In the hot sun, forty yards distant, a pacing man turned, his rifle in his arms.

"Aye there, Paco, you want these two people?"

"No, *gracias—gracias,* no," replied the man, smiling.

"You see?" said the guard, turning to John Webb.

All of the soldiers laughed together.

"I have money," said Webb.

The men stopped laughing.

The first guard stepped up to John Webb and his face was now not relaxed or easy; it was like brown stone.

"Yes," he said. "They always have money. I know. They come here and they think money will do everything. But what is money? It is only a promise, *señor.* This I know from books. And when somebody no longer likes your promise, what then?"

"I will give you anything you ask."

"Will you?" The guard turned to his friends. "He will give me *anything* I ask." To Webb: "It was a joke. *We* were always a joke to you, weren't we?"

"No."

"*Mañana,* you laughed at us; *mañana,* you laughed at our siestas and our *mañanas,* didn't you?"

"Not me. Someone else."

"Yes, you."

"I've never been to this particular station before."

"I know you, anyway. Run here, do this, do that. Oh, here's a peso, buy yourself a house. Run over there, do this, do that."

"It wasn't me."

"He looked like you, anyway."

They stood in the sun with their shadows dark under them, and the perspiration coloring their armpits. The soldier moved closer to John Webb. "I don't have to do anything for you any more."

"You never had to before. I never asked it."

"You're trembling, *señor.*"

"I'm all right. It's the sun."

"How much money have you got?" asked the guard.

"A thousand pesos to let us through, and a thousand for the other man over there."

The guard turned again. "Will a thousand pesos be enough?"

"No," said the other guard. "Tell him to report us!"

"Yes," said the guard, back to Webb again. "Report me. Get me fired. I was fired once, years ago, by you."

"It was someone else."

"Take my name. It is Carlos Rodriguez Ysotl. Go on now."

"I see."

"No, you don't see," said Carlos Rodriguez Ysotl. "Now give me two thousand pesos."

John Webb took out his wallet and handed over the money. Carlos Rodriguez Ysotl licked his thumb and counted the money slowly under the blue glazed sky of his country as noon deepened and sweat arose from hidden sources and people breathed and panted above their shadows.

"Two thousand pesos." He folded it and put it in his pocket quietly. "Now turn your car around and head for another border."

"Hold on now, damn it!"

The guard looked at him. "Turn your car."

They stood a long time that way, with the sun blazing on the rifle in the guard's hands, not speaking. And then John Webb turned and walked slowly, one hand to his face, back to the car and slid into the front seat.

"What're we going to do?" said Leonora.

"Rot. Or try to reach Porto Bello."

"But we need gas and our spare fixed. And going back over those highways . . . This time they might drop logs, and——"

"I know, I know." He rubbed his eyes and sat for a moment with his head in his hands. "We're alone, my God, we're alone. Remember how safe we used to feel? How safe? We registered in all the big towns with the American Consuls. Remember how the joke went? 'Everywhere you go you can hear the rustle of the eagle's wings!' Or was it the sound of paper money? I forget. Jesus, Jesus, the world got empty awfully quick. Who do I call on now?"

She waited a moment and then said, "I guess just me. That's not much."

He put his arm around her. "You've been swell. No hysterics, nothing."

"Tonight maybe I'll be screaming, when we're in bed, if we ever find a bed again. It's been a million miles since breakfast."

He kissed her, twice, on her dry mouth. Then he sat slowly back. "First thing is to try to find gas. If we can get that, we're ready to head for Porto Bello."

The three soldiers were talking and joking as they drove away.

After they had been driving a minute, he began to laugh quietly.

"What were you thinking?" asked his wife.

"I remember an old spiritual. It goes like this:

" 'I went to the Rock to hide my face
And the Rock cried out, "No Hiding Place,
There's no Hiding Place down here." ' "

"I remember that," she said.

"It's an appropriate song right now," he said. "I'd sing the whole thing for you if I could remember it all. And if I felt like singing."

He put his foot harder to the accelerator.

They stopped at a gas station and after a minute, when the attendant did not appear, John Webb honked the horn. Then, appalled, he snapped his hand away from the horn-ring, looking at it as if it were the hand of a leper.

"I shouldn't have done that."

The attendant appeared in the shadowy doorway of the gas station. Two other men appeared behind him.

The three men came out and walked around the car, looking at it, touching it, feeling it.

Their faces were like burnt copper in the daylight. They touched the resilient tires, they sniffed the rich new smell of the metal and upholstery.

"*Señor,*" said the gas attendant at last.

"We'd like to buy some gas, please."

"We are all out of gas, *señor.*"

"But your tank reads full. I see the gas in the glass container up there."

"We are all out of gas," said the man.

"I'll give you ten pesos a gallon!"

"*Gracias,* no."

"We haven't enough gas to get anywhere from here." Webb checked the gauge. "Not even a quarter gallon left. We'd better leave the car here and go into town and see what we can do there."

"I'll watch the car for you, *señor,*" said the station attendant. "If you leave the keys."

"We can't do that!" said Leonora. "Can we?"

"I don't see what choice we have. We can stall it on the road and leave it to anyone who comes along, or leave it with this man."

"That's better," said the man.

They climbed out of the car and stood looking at it.

"It was a beautiful car," said John Webb.

"Very beautiful," said the man, his hand out for the keys. "I will take good care of it, *señor.*"

"But, Jack——"

She opened the back door and started to take out the luggage. Over her shoulder, he saw the bright travel stickers, the storm of color that had descended upon and covered the worn leather now after years of travel, after years of the best hotels in two dozen countries.

She tugged at the valises, perspiring, and he stopped her hands and they stood gasping there for a moment, in the open door of the car, looking at these fine rich suitcases, inside which were the beautiful tweeds and woolens and silks of their lives and living, the forty-dollar-an-ounce perfumes and the cool dark furs and the silvery golf shafts. Twenty years were packed into each of the cases; twenty years and four dozen parts they had played in Rio, in Paris, in Rome and Shanghai, but the part they played most frequently and best of all was the rich and buoyant, amazingly happy Webbs, the smiling people, the ones who could make that rarely balanced martini known as the Sahara.

"We can't carry it all into town," he said. "We'll come back for it later. Later."

"But . . ."

He silenced her by turning her away and starting her off down the road.

"But we can't leave it there, we can't leave all our luggage and we can't leave our car! Oh look here now, I'll roll up the windows and lock myself in the car, while you go for the gas, why not?" she said.

He stopped and glanced back at the three men standing by the car, which blazed in the yellow sun. Their eyes were shining and looking at the woman.

"There's your answer," he said. "Come on."

"But you just *don't* walk off and leave a four-thousand-dollar automobile!" she cried.

He moved her along, holding her elbow firmly and with quiet decision. "A car is to travel in. When it's not traveling, it's useless. Right now, we've got to travel; that's everything. The car isn't worth a dime without gas in it. A pair of good strong legs is worth a hundred cars, if you use the legs. We've just begun to toss things overboard. We'll keep dropping ballast until there's nothing left to heave but our hides."

He let her go. She was walking steadily now, and she fell into step with him. "It's so strange. So strange. I haven't walked like this in years." She watched the motion of her feet beneath her, she watched the road pass by, she watched the jungle moving to either side, she watched her husband striding quickly along, until she seemed hypnotized by the steady rhythm. "But I guess you can learn anything over again," she said, at last.

The sun moved in the sky and they moved for a long while on the hot road. When he was quite ready, the husband began to think aloud. "You know, in a way, I think it's good to be down to essentials. Now instead of worrying over a dozen damned things, it's just two items—you and me."

"Watch it, here comes a car—we'd better . . ."

They half turned, yelled, and jumped. They fell away from the highway and lay watching the automobile hurtle past at seventy miles an hour. Voices sang, men laughed, men shouted, waving. The car sped away into the dust and vanished around a curve, blaring its double horns again and again.

He helped her up and they stood in the quiet road.

"Did you see it?"

They watched the dust settle slowly.

"I hope they remember to change the oil and check the battery, at least. I hope they think to put water in the radiator," she said, and paused. "They were singing, weren't they?"

He nodded. They stood blinking at the great dust cloud filtering down like yellow pollen upon their heads and arms. He saw a few bright splashes flick from her eyelids when she blinked.

"Don't," he said. "After all, it was only a machine."

"I loved it."

"We're always loving everything too much."

Walking, they passed a shattered wine bottle which steamed freshly as they stepped over it.

They were not far from the town, walking single file, the wife ahead, the husband following, looking at their feet as they walked, when a sound of tin and steam and bubbling water made them turn and look at the road behind them. An old man in a 1929 Ford drove along the road at a moderate speed. The car's fenders were gone, and the sun had flaked and burnt the paint badly, but he rode in the seat with a great deal of quiet dignity, his face a thoughtful darkness under a dirty Panama hat, and when he saw the two people he drew the car up, steaming, the engine joggling under the hood, and opened the squealing door as he said, "This is no day for walking."

"Thank you," they said.

"It is nothing." The old man wore an ancient yellowed white summer suit, with a rather greasy tie knotted loosely at his wrinkled throat. He helped the lady into the rear seat with a gracious bow of his head. "Let us men sit up front," he suggested, and the husband sat up front and the car moved off in trembling vapors.

"Well. My name is Garcia."

There were introductions and noddings.

"Your car broke down? You are on your way for help?" said *Señor* Garcia.

"Yes."

"Then let me drive you and a mechanic back out," offered the old man.

They thanked him and kindly turned the offer aside and he made it once again, but upon finding that his interest and concern caused them embarrassment, he very politely turned to another subject.

He touched a small stack of folded newspapers on his lap.

"Do you read the papers? Of course, you do. But do you read them as I read them? I rather doubt that you have come upon my system. No, it was not exactly myself that came upon it; the system was forced upon me. But now I know what a clever thing it has turned out to be. I always get the newspapers a week late. All of us, those who are interested, get the papers a week late, from the Capital. And this circumstance makes for a man being a clear-thinking man. You are very careful with your thinking when you pick up a week-old paper."

The husband and wife asked him to continue.

"Well," said the old man, "I remember once, when I lived in the Capital for a month and bought the paper fresh each day, I went wild with love, anger, irritation, frustration; all of the passions boiled in me. I was young. I exploded at everything I saw. But then I saw what I was doing: I was believing what I read. Have you noticed? You believe a paper printed on the very day you buy it? This has happened but only an hour ago, you think! It must be true." He shook his head. "So I learned to stand back away and let the paper age and mellow. Back here, in Colonia, I saw the headlines diminish to nothing. The week-old paper—why, you can spit on it if you wish. It is like a woman you once loved, but you now see, a few days later, she is not quite what you thought. She has rather a plain face. She is no deeper than a cup of water."

He steered the car gently, his hands upon the wheel as upon the heads of his good children, with care and affection. "So here I am, returning to my home to read my weekly papers, to peek sideways at them, to toy with them." He spread one on his knee, glancing down to it on occasion as he drove. "How white this paper is, like the mind of a child that is an idiot, poor thing, all blank. You can put anything into an empty place like that. Here, do you see? This paper speaks and says that the light-skinned people of the world are dead. Now that is a very silly thing to say. At this very moment, there are probably millions upon millions of white men and women eating their noon meals or their suppers. The earth trembles, a town collapses, people run from the town, screaming, *All is lost!* In the next village, the population wonders what all of the shouting is about, since *they* have had a most splendid night's repose. Ah, ah, what a sly world it is. People do not see how sly it is. It is either night or day to them. Rumor flies. This very afternoon all of the little villages upon this highway, behind us and ahead of us, are in carnival. The white man is dead, the rumors say, and yet here I come into the town with two very lively ones. I hope you don't mind my speaking in this way? If I do not talk to you I would then be talking to this engine up in the front, which makes a great noise speaking back."

They were at the edge of town.

"Please," said John Webb, "it wouldn't be wise for you to be seen with us today. We'll get out here."

The old man stopped his car reluctantly and said, "You are most kind and thoughtful of me." He turned to look at the lovely wife.

"When I was a young man I was very full of wildness and ideas. I read all of the books from France by a man named Jules Verne. I see you know his name. But at night I many times thought I must be an inventor. That is all gone by; I never did what I thought I might do. But I remember clearly that one of the machines I wished to put together was a machine that would help every man, for an hour, to be like any other man. The machine was full of colors and smells and it had film in it, like a theater, and the machine was like a coffin. You lay in it. And you touched a button. And for an hour you could be one of those Eskimos in the cold wind up there, or you could be an Arab gentleman on a horse. Everything a New York man felt, you could feel. Everything a man from Sweden smelled, you could smell. Everything a man from China tasted, your tongue knew. The machine was like another man—do you see what I was after? And by touching many of the buttons, each time you got into my machine, you could be a white man or a yellow man or a Negrito. You could be a child or a woman, even, if you wished to be very funny."

The husband and wife climbed from the car.

"Did you ever try to invent that machine?"

"It was so very long ago. I had forgotten until today. And today I was thinking, we could make use of it, we are in need of it. What a shame I never tried to put it all together. Someday some other man will do it."

"Some day," said John Webb.

"It has been a pleasure talking with you," said the old man. "God go with you."

"*Adiós, Señor* Garcia," they said.

The car drove slowly away, steaming. They stood watching it go, for a full minute. Then, without speaking, the husband reached over and took his wife's hand.

They entered the small town of Colonia on foot. They walked past the little shops—the butcher shop, the photographer's. People stopped and looked at them as they went by and did not stop looking at them as long as they were in sight. Every few seconds, as he walked, Webb put up his hand to touch the holster hidden under his coat, secretly, tentatively, like someone feeling for a tiny boil that is growing and growing every hour and every hour . . .

The patio of the Hotel Esposa was cool as a grotto under a blue waterfall. In it caged birds sang, and footsteps echoed like small rifle shots, clear and smooth.

"Remember? We stopped here years ago," said Webb, helping his wife up the steps. They stood in the cool grotto, glad of the blue shade.

"*Señor* Esposa," said John Webb, when a fat man came forward from the desk, squinting at them. "Do you remember me—John Webb? Five years ago—we played cards one night."

"Of course, of course." *Señor* Esposa bowed to the wife and shook hands briefly. There was an uncomfortable silence.

Webb cleared his throat. "We've had a bit of trouble, *señor*. Could we have a room for tonight only?"

"Your money is always good here."

"You mean you'll actually give us a room? We'll be glad to pay in advance. Lord, we need the rest. But, more than that, we need gas."

Leonora picked at her husband's arm. "Remember? We haven't a car any more."

"Oh. Yes." He fell silent for a moment and then sighed. "Well. Never mind the gas. Is there a bus out of here for the Capital soon?"

"All will be attended to, in time," said the manager nervously. "This way."

As they were climbing the stairs they heard a noise. Looking out they saw their car riding around and around the plaza, eight times, loaded with men who were shouting and singing and hanging on to the front fenders, laughing. Children and dogs ran after the car.

"I would like to own a car like that," said *Señor* Esposa.

He poured a little cool wine for the three of them, standing in the room on the third floor of the Esposa Hotel.

"To 'change,' " said *Señor* Esposa.

"I'll drink to that."

They drank. *Señor* Esposa licked his lips and wiped them on his coat sleeve. "We are always surprised and saddened to see the world change.

It is insane, they have run out on us, you say. It is unbelievable. And now, well—you are safe for the night. Shower and have a good supper. I won't be able to keep you more than one night, to repay you for your kindness to me five years ago."

"And tomorrow?"

"Tomorrow? Do not take any bus to the Capital, please. There are riots in the streets there. A few people from the North have been killed. It is nothing. It will pass in a few days. But you must be careful until those few days pass and the blood cools. There are many wicked people taking advantage of this day, *señor.* For forty-eight hours anyway, under the guise of a great resurgence of nationalism, these people will try to gain power. Selfishness and patriotism, *señor;* today I cannot tell one from the other. So—you must hide. That is a problem. The town will know you are here in another few hours. This might be dangerous to my hotel. I cannot say."

"We understand. It's good of you to help *this* much."

"If you need anything, call me." *Señor* Esposa drank the rest of the wine in his glass. "Finish the bottle," he said.

The fireworks began at nine that evening. First one skyrocket then another soared into the dark sky and burst out upon the winds, building architectures of flame. Each skyrocket, at the top of its ride, cracked open and let out a formation of streamers in red and white flame that made something like the dome of a beautiful cathedral.

Leonora and John Webb stood by the open window in their unlit room, watching and listening. As the hour latened, more people streamed into town from every road and path and began to roam, arm in arm, around the plaza, singing, barking like dogs, crowing like roosters, and then falling down on the tile sidewalks, sitting there, laughing, their heads thrown back, while the skyrockets burst explosive colors on the tilted faces. A brass band began to thump and wheeze.

"So here we are," said John Webb, "after a few hundred years of living high. So this is what's left of our white supremacy—you and I in a dark room in a hotel three hundred miles inside a celebrating country."

"You've got to see their side of it."

"Oh, I've seen it ever since I was that high. In a way, I'm glad they're happy. God knows they've waited long enough to be. But I wonder how long that happiness will last. Now that the scapegoat is gone, who will they blame for oppression, who will be as handy and as obvious and as guilty as you and I and the man who lived in this room before us?"

"I don't know."

"We were so convenient. The man who rented this room last month, he was convenient, he stood out. He made loud jokes about the natives' siestas. He refused to learn even a smattering of Spanish. Let them learn English, by God, and speak like men, he said. And he drank too much and whored too much with this country's women." He broke off and moved back from the window. He stared at the room.

The furniture, he thought. Where *he* put his dirty shoes upon the sofa, where *he* burnt holes in the carpet with cigarettes; the wet spot on the wall near the bed, God knows what or how he did *that*. The chairs scarred and kicked. It wasn't his hotel or his room; it was borrowed, it meant nothing. So this son-of-a-bitch went around the country for the past one hundred years, a traveling commercial, a Chamber of Commerce, and now here *we* are, enough like him to be his brother and sister, and there *they* are down there on the night of the Butlers' Ball. They don't know, or if they know they won't think of it, that tomorrow they'll be just as poor, just as oppressed as ever, that the whole machine will only have shifted into another gear.

Now the band had stopped playing below; a man had leaped up, shouting, on the bandstand. There was a flash of machetes in the air and the brown gleam of half-naked bodies.

The man on the bandstand faced the hotel and looked up at the dark room where John and Leonora Webb now stood back out of the intermittent flares.

The man shouted.

"What does he say?" asked Leonora.

John Webb translated: " 'It is now a free world,' he says."

The man yelled.

John Webb translated again. "He says, 'We are *free!*' "

The man lifted himself on his toes and made a motion of breaking manacles. "He says, 'No one owns us, no one in all the world.' "

The crowd roared and the band began to play, and while it was playing, the man on the grandstand stood glaring up at the room window, with all of the hatred of the universe in his eyes.

During the night there were fights and pummelings and voices lifted, arguments and shots fired. John Webb lay awake and heard the voice of *Señor* Esposa below, reasoning, talking quietly, firmly. And then the fading away of the tumult, the last rockets in the sky, the last breakings of bottles on the cobbles.

At five in the morning the air was warming into a new day. There was the softest of taps on the bedroom door.

"It is me, it is Esposa," said a voice.

John Webb hesitated, half-dressed, numbed on his feet from lack of sleep, then opened the door.

"What a night, what a night!" said *Señor* Esposa, coming in, shaking his head, laughing gently. "Did you hear that noise? Yes? They tried to come up here to your room. I prevented this."

"Thank you," said Leonora, still in bed, turned to the wall.

"They were all old friends. I made an agreement with them, anyway.

They were drunk enough and happy enough so they agreed to wait. I am to make a proposition to you two." Suddenly he seemed embarrassed. He moved to the window. "Everyone is sleeping late. A few are up. A few men. See them there on the far side of the plaza?"

John Webb looked out at the plaza. He saw the brown men talking quietly there about the weather, the world, the sun, this town, and perhaps the wine.

"*Señor,* have you ever been hungry in your life?"

"For a day, once."

"Only for a day. Have you always had a house to live in and a car to drive?"

"Until yesterday."

"Were you ever without a job?"

"Never."

"Did all of your brothers and sisters live to be twenty-one years old?"

"All of them."

"Even I," said *Señor* Esposa, "even *I* hate you a little bit now. For *I* have been without a home. *I* have been hungry. *I* have three brothers and one sister buried in that graveyard on the hill beyond the town, all dead of tuberculosis before they were nine years old."

Señor Esposa glanced at the men in the plaza. "Now, I am no longer hungry or poor, I have a car, I am alive. But I am one in a thousand. What can *you* say to them out there today?"

"I'll try to think of something."

"Long ago I stopped trying. *Señor,* we have *always* been a minority, we white people. I am Spanish, but I was born here. They tolerate me."

"We have never let ourselves think about our being a minority," said Webb, "and now it's hard to get used to the fact."

"You have behaved beautifully."

"Is that a virtue?"

"In the bull ring, yes; in war, yes; in anything like this, most assuredly yes. You do not complain, you do not make excuses. You do not run and make a spectacle of yourself. I think you are both very brave."

The hotel manager sat down, slowly, helplessly.

"I've come to offer you the chance to settle down," he said.

"We wanted to move on, if possible."

The manager shrugged. "Your car is stolen, I can do nothing to get it back. You cannot leave town. Remain then and accept my offer of a position in my hotel."

"You don't think there is any way for us to travel?"

"It might be twenty days, *señor,* or twenty years. You cannot exist without money, food, lodging. Consider my hotel and the work I can give you."

The manager arose and walked unhappily to the door and stood by the chair, touching Webb's coat, which was draped over it.

"What's the job?" asked Webb.

"In the kitchen," said the manager, and looked away.

John Webb sat on the bed and said nothing. His wife did not move.

Señor Esposa said, "It is the best I can do. What more can you ask of me? Last night, those others down in the plaza wanted both of you. Did you see the machetes? I bargained with them. You were lucky. I told them you would be employed in my hotel for the next twenty years, that you were my employees and deserve my protection!"

"You said *that!*"

"*Señor, señor,* be thankful! Consider! Where will you go? The jungle? You will be dead in two hours from the snakes. Then can you walk five hundred miles to a capital which will not welcome you? No—you must face the reality." *Señor* Esposa opened the door. "I offer you an honest job and you will be paid the standard wages of two pesos a day, plus meals. Would you rather be with me, or out in the plaza at noon with our friends? Consider."

The door was shut. *Señor* Esposa was gone.

Webb stood looking at the door for a long while.

Then he walked to the chair and fumbled with the holster under the draped white shirt. The holster was empty. He held it in his hands and blinked at its emptiness and looked again at the door through which *Señor* Esposa had just passed. He went over and sat down on the bed beside his wife. He stretched out beside her and took her in his arms and kissed her, and they lay there, watching the room get brighter with the new day.

At eleven o'clock in the morning, with the great doors on the windows of their room flung back, they began to dress. There were soap, towels, shaving equipment, even perfume in the bathroom, provided by Mr. Esposa.

John Webb shaved and dressed carefully.

At eleven-thirty he turned on the small radio near their bed. You could usually get New York or Cleveland or Houston on such a radio. But the air was silent. John Webb turned the radio off.

"There's nothing to go back to—nothing to go back for—nothing."

His wife sat on a chair near the door, looking at the wall.

"We could stay here and work," he said.

She stirred at last. "No. We couldn't do that, not really. Could we?"

"No, I guess not."

"There's no way we could do that. We're being consistent, anyway; spoiled, but consistent."

He thought a moment. "We could make for the jungle."

"I don't think we can move from the hotel without being seen. We don't want to try to escape and be caught. It would be far worse that way."

He nodded.

They both sat a moment.

"It might not be too bad, working here," he said.

"What would we be living for? Everyone's dead—your father, mine, your mother, mine, your brothers, mine, all our friends, everything gone, everything we understood."

He nodded.

"Or if we took the job, one day soon one of the men would touch me and you'd go after him, you know you would. Or someone would do something to you, and *I'd* do something."

He nodded again.

They sat for fifteen minutes, talking quietly. Then, at last, he picked up the telephone and ticked the cradle with his finger.

"*Bueno*," said a voice on the other end.

"*Señor* Esposa?"

"*Sí.*"

"*Señor* Esposa," he paused and licked his lips, "tell your friends we will be leaving the hotel at noon."

The phone did not immediately reply. Then with a sigh *Señor* Esposa said, "As you wish. You are sure——?"

The phone was silent for a full minute. Then it was picked up again and the manager said quietly, "My friends say they will be waiting for you on the far side of the plaza."

"We will meet them there," said John Webb.

"And *señor*——"

"Yes."

"Do not hate me, do not hate us."

"I don't hate anybody."

"It is a bad world, *señor*. None of us know how we got here or what we are doing. These men don't know what they are mad at, except they are mad. Forgive them and do not hate them."

"I don't hate them or you."

"Thank you, thank you." Perhaps the man on the far end of the telephone wire was crying. There was no way to tell. There were great lapses in his talking, in his breathing. After a while he said, "We don't know why we do anything. Men hit each other for no reason except they are unhappy. Remember that. I am your friend. I would help you if I could. But I cannot. It would be me against the town. Good-by, *señor*." He hung up.

John Webb sat in the chair with his hand on the silent phone. It was a moment before he glanced up. It was a moment before his eyes focused on an object immediately before him. When he saw it clearly, he still did not move, but sat regarding it, until a look of immensely tired irony appeared on his mouth. "Look here," he said at last.

Leonora followed his motion, his pointing.

They both sat looking at his cigarette which, neglected on the rim of the table while he telephoned, had burnt down so that now it had charred a black hole in the clean surface of the wood.

It was noon, with the sun directly over them, pinning their shadows under them as they started down the steps of the Hotel Esposa. Behind them, the birds fluted in their bamboo cages, and water ran in a little fountain bath. They were as neat as they could get, their faces and hands washed, their nails clean, their shoes polished.

Across the plaza two hundred yards away stood a small group of men, in the shade of a store-front overhang. Some of the men were natives from the jungle area, with machetes gleaming at their sides. They were all facing the plaza.

John Webb looked at them for a long while. That isn't everyone, he thought, that isn't the whole country. That's only the surface. That's only the thin skin over the flesh. It's not the body at all. Just the shell of an egg? Remember the crowds back home, the mobs, the riots? Always the same, there or here. A few mad faces up front, and the quiet ones far back, not taking part, letting things go, not wanting to be in it. The majority not moving. And so the few, the handful, take over and move for them.

His eyes did not blink. If we could break through that shell—God knows it's thin! he thought. If we could talk our way through that mob and get to the quiet people beyond . . . Can I do it? Can I say the right things? Can I keep my voice down?

He fumbled in his pockets and brought out a rumpled cigarette package and some matches.

I can try, he thought. How would the old man in the Ford have done it? I'll try to do it his way. When we get across the plaza, I'll start talking, I'll whisper if necessary. And if we move slowly through the mob, we might just possibly find our way to the other people and we'll be on high ground and we'll be safe.

Leonora moved beside him. She was so fresh, so well groomed in spite of everything, so new in all this oldness, so startling, that his mind flinched and jerked. He found himself staring at her as if she'd betrayed him by her salt-whiteness, her wonderfully brushed hair and her cleanly manicured nails and her bright-red mouth.

Standing on the bottom step, Webb lit a cigarette, took two or three long drags on it, tossed it down, stepped on it, kicked the flattened butt into the street, and said, "Here we go."

They stepped down and started around the far side of the plaza, past the few shops that were still open. They walked quietly.

"Perhaps they'll be decent to us."

"We can hope so."

They passed a photographic shop.

"It's another day. Anything can happen. I believe that. No—I don't really believe it. I'm only talking. I've got to talk or I wouldn't be able to walk," she said.

They passed a candy shop.

"Keep talking, then."

"I'm afraid," she said. "This can't be happening to us! Are we the last ones in the world?"

"Maybe next to the last."

They approached an open air *carnecería.*

God! he thought. How the horizons narrowed, how they came in. A year ago there weren't four directions, there were a million for us. Yesterday they got down to four; we could go to Juatala, Porto Bello, San Juan Clementas, or Brioconbria. We were satisfied to have our car. Then when we couldn't get gas, we were satisfied to have our clothes, then when they took our clothes, we were satisfied to have a place to sleep. Each pleasure they took away left us with one other creature comfort to hold on to. Did you see how we let go of one thing and clutched another so quickly? I guess that's human. So they took away everything. There's nothing left. Except us. It all boils down to just you and me walking along here, and thinking too goddamn much for my own good. And what counts in the end is whether they can take you away from me or me away from you, Lee, and I don't think they can do that. They've got everything else and I don't blame them. But they can't really do anything else to us now. When you strip all the clothes away and the doodads, you have two human beings who were either happy or unhappy together, and we have no complaints.

"Walk slowly," said John Webb.

"I am."

"Not too slowly, to look reluctant. Not too fast, to look as if you want to get it over with. Don't give them the satisfaction, Lee, don't give them a damn bit."

"I won't."

They walked. "Don't even touch me," he said, quietly. "Don't even hold my hand."

"Oh, please!"

"No, not even that."

He moved away a few inches and kept walking steadily. His eyes were straight ahead and their pace was regular.

"I'm beginning to cry, Jack."

"Goddamn it!" he said, measuredly, between his teeth, not looking aside. "Stop it! Do you want me to run? Is that what you want—do you want me to take you and run into the jungle, and let them hunt us, is that what you want, goddamn it, do you want me to fall down in the street here and grovel and scream, shut up, let's do this right, don't give them *anything*!"

"All right," she said, hands tight, her head coming up. "I'm not crying now. I won't cry."

"Good, damn it, that's good."

And still, strangely, they were not past the *carnecería.* The vision of red horror was on their left as they paced steadily forward on the hot tile sidewalk. The things that hung from hooks looked like brutalities and sins, like bad consciences, evil dreams, like gored flags and slaughtered promises. The redness, oh, the hanging, evil-smelling wetness and redness, the hooked and hung-high carcasses, unfamiliar, unfamiliar.

As he passed the shop, something made John Webb strike out a hand. He slapped it smartly against a strung-up side of beef. A mantle of blue buzzing flies lifted angrily and swirled in a bright cone over the meat.

Leonora said, looking ahead, walking, "They're all strangers! I don't know any of them. I wish I knew even *one* of them. I wish even *one* of them knew me!"

They walked on past the *carnecería.* The side of beef, red and irritable-looking, swung in the hot sunlight after they passed.

The flies came down in a feeding cloak to cover the meat, once it had stopped swinging.

QUESTIONS FOR DISCUSSION

1. "And the Rock Cried Out" is a story with an "unhappy ending." Most readers prefer stories with happy endings. Why would a happy ending to this story have been implausible?
2. Analyze the structure of "And the Rock Cried Out." (An analysis of the way a story progresses from an effective beginning to a plausible and effective ending involves a consideration of many things. Consider in your analysis these three at least: (1) The changes in our concept of both the protagonist(s) and the antagonist(s) in the story. (2) The employment of a kind of "movie technique" of "long shots," "medium shots" and "close-ups" in the telling of the story. (3) The use of a "frame," that is, the use of the same detail or "symbol" to open and end the story.)
3. What devices other than characterization and conflict does Bradbury use to help him achieve his purpose in this story?
4. Has "And the Rock Cried Out" a theme, an application to you, the reader? If so, define it.

CAROLINE GORDON
The Last Day in the Field

That was the fall when the leaves stayed green so long. We had a drouth in August and the ponds everywhere were dry and the watercourse shrunken. Then in September heavy rains came. Things greened up. It looked like winter was never coming.

"You aren't going to hunt this year, Aleck," Molly said. "Remember how you stayed awake nights last fall with that pain in your leg."

In October light frosts came. In the afternoons when I sat on the back porch going over my fishing tackle I marked their progress on the elderberry bushes that were left standing against the stable fence. The lower, spreading branches had turned yellow and were already sinking to the ground but the leaves in the top clusters still stood up stiff and straight.

"Ah-h, it'll get you yet!" I said, thinking how frost creeps higher and higher out of the ground each night of fall.

The dogs next door felt it and would thrust their noses through the wire fence scenting the wind from the north. When I walked in the back yard they would bound twice their height and whine, for meat scraps Molly said, but it was because they smelled blood on my old hunting coat.

They were almost matched liver-and-white pointers. The big dog had a beautiful, square muzzle and was deep-chested and rangy. The bitch, Judy, had a smaller head and not so good a muzzle but she was springy loined too and had one of the merriest tails I've ever watched.

When Joe Thomas, the boy that owned them, came home from the hardware store he would change his clothes and then come down the back way into the wired enclosure and we would stand there watching the dogs and wondering how they would work. Joe said they were keen as mustard. He was going to take them out the first good Saturday and wanted me to come along.

"I can't make it," I said, "my leg's worse this year than it was last."

The fifteenth of November was clear and so warm that we sat out on the porch till nine o'clock. It was still warm when we went to bed towards eleven. The change must have come in the middle of the night. I woke once, hearing the clock strike two, and felt the air cold on my face and thought before I went back to sleep that the weather had broken at last. When I woke again at dawn the cold air was slapping my face hard. I came wide awake, turned over in bed and looked out of the window.

There was a scaly-bark hickory tree growing on the east side of the house. You could see its upper branches from the bedroom window. The leaves had turned yellow a week ago. But yesterday evening when I walked out there in the yard they had still been flat with green streaks showing in them. Now they were curled up tight and a lot of leaves had fallen on to the ground.

I got out of bed quietly so as not to wake Molly, dressed and went down the back way over to the Thomas house. There was no one stirring but I knew which room Joe's was. The window was open and I could hear him snoring. I went up and stuck my head in.

"Hey," I said, "killing frost."

He opened his eyes and looked at me and then his eyes went shut. I reached my arm through the window and shook him. "Get up," I said, "we got to start right away."

He was awake now and out on the floor stretching. I told him to dress and be over at the house as quick as he could. I'd have breakfast ready for us both.

Aunt Martha had a way of leaving fire in the kitchen stove at night. There were red embers there now. I poked the ashes out and piled kindling on top of them. When the flames came up I put some heavier wood on, filled the coffee pot, and put some grease on in a skillet. By the time Joe got there I had coffee ready and some hoe cakes to go with our fried eggs. Joe had brought a thermos bottle. We put the rest of the coffee in it and I found a ham in the pantry and made some sandwiches.

While I was fixing the lunch Joe went down to the lot to hitch up. He was just driving Old Dick out of the stable when I came down the back steps. The dogs knew what was up, all right. They were whining and surging against the fence and Bob, the big dog, thrust his paw through and into the pocket of my hunting coat as I passed. While Joe was snapping on the leashes I got a few handfuls of straw from the rack and put it in the foot of the buggy. It was twelve miles where we were going; the dogs would need to ride warm coming back late.

Joe said he would drive. We got in the buggy and started out, up Seventh Street and on over to College and out through Scufftown. When we got into the nigger section we could see what a killing frost it had been. A light shimmer over all the ground still and the weeds around the cabins dark and matted the way they are when the frost hits them hard and twists them.

We drove on over the Red River bridge and up into the open country. At Jim Gill's place the cows had come up and were standing waiting to be milked but nobody was stirring yet from the house. I looked back from the top of the hill and saw that the frost mists still hung heavy in the bottom and thought it was a good sign. A day like this when the earth is warmer than the air currents is good for the hunter. Scent particles are borne on the warm air and birds will forage far on such a day.

It took us over an hour to get from Gloversville to Spring Creek. Joe wanted to get out as soon as we hit the big bottom there but I held him down and we drove on to the top of the ridge. We got out there, unhitched Old Dick and turned him into one of Rob Fayerlee's pastures —I thought how surprised Rob would be when he saw him grazing there—put our guns together, and started out, the dogs still on leash.

It was rough, broken ground, scrub oak, with a few gum trees and lots of buckberry bushes. One place a patch of corn ran clear up to the top of the ridge. As we passed along between the rows I could see the frost glistening on the north side of the stalks. I knew it was going to be a good day.

I walked over to the brow of the hill. From here you can see off over the whole valley—I've hunted every foot of it in my time—tobacco land, mostly. One or two patches of corn there on the side of the ridge. I thought we might start there and then I knew that wouldn't do. Quail will linger on the roost a cold day and feed in shelter during the morning. It is only in the afternoon that they will work out to the open.

The dogs were whining. Joe bent down and was about to slip their leashes. "Hey, boy," I said, "don't do that."

I turned around and looked down the other side of the ridge. It was better that way. The corn land of the bottoms ran high up on to the hill in several places there and where the corn stopped there were big patches of ironweed and buckberry. I knocked my pipe out on a stump.

"Let's go that way," I said.

Joe was looking at my old buckhorn whistle that I had slung around my neck. "I forgot to bring mine."

"All right," I said, "I'll handle 'em."

He unfastened their collars and cast off. They broke away, racing for the first hundred yards and barking, then suddenly swerved. The big dog took off to the right along the hillside. The bitch, Judy, skirted a belt of corn along the upper bottomlands. I kept my eye on the big dog. A dog that has bird sense will know cover when he sees it. This big Bob was an independent hunter, all right. I could see him moving fast through the scrub oaks, working his way down toward a patch of ironweed. He caught first scent just on the edge of the weed patch and froze with every indication of class, head up, nose stuck out, and tail straight in air. Judy, meanwhile, had been following the line of the corn field. A hundred yards away she caught sight of Bob's point and backed him.

We went up and flushed the birds. They got up in two bunches. I heard Joe's shot while I was in the act of raising my gun and I saw his bird fall not thirty paces from where I stood. I had covered the middle bird of the larger bunch—that's the one led by the boss cock—the way I usually do. He fell, whirling head over heels, driven a little forward by the impact. A well-centered shot. I could tell by the way the feathers fluffed as he tumbled.

The dogs were off through the grass. They had retrieved both birds. Joe stuck his in his pocket. He laughed. "I thought there for a minute you were going to let him get away."

I looked at him but I didn't say anything. It's a wonderful thing to be twenty years old.

The majority of the singles had flown straight ahead to settle in the rank grass that jutted out from the bottomland. Judy got down to work at once but the big dog broke off to the left, wanting to get footloose to find another covey. I thought of how Trecho, the best dog I ever had—the best dog any man ever had—used always to be wanting to do the same thing and I laughed.

"Naw, you don't," I said, "come back here, you scoundrel, and hunt these singles."

He stopped on the edge of a briar patch, looked at me and heeled up promptly. I clucked him out again. He gave me another look. I thought we were beginning to understand each other better. We got some nice points among those singles but we followed that valley along the creek bed and through two or three more corn fields without finding another covey. Joe was disappointed but I wasn't beginning to worry yet; you always make your bag in the afternoon.

It was twelve o'clock by this time, no sign of frost anywhere and the sun beating down steady on the curled-up leaves.

"Come on," I said, "let's go up to Buck's spring and eat."

We walked up the ravine whose bed was still moist with the fall rains and came out at the head of the hollow. They had cleared out some of the trees on the side of the ravine but the spring itself was the same: a deep pool welling up between the roots of an old sycamore. I unwrapped the sandwiches and the piece of cake and laid them on a stump. Joe got the thermos bottle out of his pocket. Something had gone wrong with it and the coffee was stone cold. We were about to drink it that way when Joe saw a good tin can flung down beside the spring. He made a trash fire and we put the coffee in the can and heated it to boiling.

It was warm in the ravine, sheltered from the wind, with the little fire burning. I turned my game leg so that the heat fell full on my knee. Joe had finished his last sandwich and was reaching for the cake.

"Good ham," he said.

"It's John Ferguson's," I told him.

He had got up and was standing over the spring. "Wonder how long this wood'll last, under water this way."

I looked at the sycamore root, green and slick where the thin stream of water poured over it, then my eyes went back to the dogs. They were tired, all right. Judy had gone off to lie down in a cool place at the side of the spring, but the big dog, Bob, lay there, his forepaws stretched out in front of him, never taking his eyes off our faces. I looked at him and thought how different he was from his mate and like some dogs I had known—and men too—who lived only for hunting and could never get enough no matter how long the day. There was something about his head and his markings that reminded one of another dog I used to hunt with a long time ago and I asked the boy who had trained him. He said the old fellow he bought the dogs from had been killed last spring, over in Trigg—Charley Morrison.

Charley Morrison! I remembered how he died, out hunting by himself and the gun had gone off, accidentally they said. Charley had called his dog to him, got blood over him and sent him home. The dog went, all right, but when they got there Charley was dead. Two years ago that was and now I was hunting the last dogs he'd ever trained. . . .

Joe lifted the thermos bottle. "Another cup?"

I held my cup out and he filled it. The coffee was still good and hot. I drank it, standing up, running my eye over the country in front of us. Afternoon is different from morning, more exciting. It isn't only as I say that you'll make your bag in the afternoon, but it takes more figuring. They're fed and rested and when they start out again they'll work in the open and over a wider range.

Joe was stamping out his cigarette: "Let's go."

The dogs were already out of sight but I could see the sedge grass ahead moving and I knew they'd be making for the same thing that took my eye: a spearhead of thicket that ran far out into this open field. We came up over a little rise. There they were, Bob on a point and Judy backing him not fifty feet from the thicket. I saw it was going to be tough shooting. No way to tell whether the birds were between the dog and the thicket or in the thicket itself. Then I saw that the cover was more open along the side of the thicket and I thought that that was the way they'd go if they were in the thicket. But Joe had already broken away to the left. He got too far to the side. The birds flushed to the right and left him standing, flat-footed, without a shot.

He looked sort of foolish and grinned.

I thought I wouldn't say anything and then I found myself speaking: "Trouble with you, you try to out-think the dog."

There was nothing to do about it, though. The chances were that the singles had pitched in the trees below. We went down there. It was hard hunting. The woods were open, the ground everywhere heavily carpeted with leaves. Dead leaves make a tremendous rustle when the dogs surge through them. It takes a good nose to cut scent keenly in such noisy cover. I kept my eye on Bob. He never faltered, getting over the ground in big, springy strides but combing every inch of it. We came to an open place in the woods. Nothing but hickory trees and bramble thickets overhung with trailing vines. Bob passed the first thicket and came to a beautiful point. We went up. He stood perfectly steady but the bird flushed out fifteen or twenty steps ahead of him. I saw it swing to the right, gaining altitude very quickly—woods birds will always cut back to known territory—and it came to me how it would be.

I called to Joe: "Don't shoot yet."

He nodded and raised his gun, following the bird with the barrel. It was directly over the treetops when I gave the word and he shot, scoring a clean kill.

He laughed excitedly as he stuck the bird in his pocket. "My God, man, I didn't know you could take that much time!"

We went on through the open woods. I was thinking about a day I'd had years ago in the woods at Grassdale, with my uncle, James Morris, and his son, Julian. Uncle James had given Julian and me hell for missing just such a shot. I can see him now standing up against a big pine tree, his face red from liquor and his gray hair ruffling in the wind: "*Let him alone! Let him alone!* And establish your lead as he climbs."

Joe was still talking about the shot he'd made. "Lord, I wish I could get another one like that."

"You won't," I said, "we're getting out of the woods now."

We struck a path that led due west and followed it for half a mile. My leg was stiff from the hip down now and every time I brought it over, the pain would start in my knee, Zing! and travel up and settle in the small of my back. I walked with my head down, watching the light catch on the ridges of Joe's brown corduroy trousers and then shift and catch again. Sometimes he would get on ahead and then there would be nothing but the black tree trunks coming up out of the dead leaves.

Joe was talking about some wild land up on the Cumberland. We could get up there on an early train. Have a good day. Might even spend the night. When I didn't answer he turned around: "Man, you're sweating."

I pulled my handkerchief out and wiped my face. "Hot work," I said.

He had stopped and was looking about him. "Used to be a spring somewhere around here."

He had found the path and was off. I sat down on a stump and mopped my face some more. The sun was halfway down through the trees now, the whole west woods ablaze with the light. I sat there and thought that in another hour it would be good and dark and I wished that the day could go on and not end so soon and yet I didn't see how I could make it much farther with my leg the way it was.

Joe was coming up the path with his folding cup full of water. I hadn't thought I was thirsty but the cold water tasted good. We sat there awhile and smoked, then Joe said that we ought to be starting back, that we must be a good piece from the rig by this time.

We set out, working north through the edge of the woods. It was rough going and I was thinking that it would be all I could do to make it back to the rig when we climbed a fence and came out at one end of a long field that sloped down to a wooded ravine. Broken ground, badly gullied and covered with sedge everywhere except where sumac thickets had sprung up—as birdy a place as ever I saw. I looked it over and knew I had to hunt it, leg or no leg, but it would be close work, for me and the dogs too.

I blew them in a bit and we stood there watching them cut up the cover. The sun was down now; there was just enough light left to see the dogs work. The big dog circled the far wall of the basin and came up wind just off the drain, then stiffened to a point. We walked down to it. The birds had obviously run a bit into the scraggly sumac stalks that bordered the ditch. My mind was so much on the dogs I forgot Joe. He took one step too many. The fullest blown bevy of the day roared up through the tangle. It had to be fast work. I raised my gun and scored with the only barrel I had time to peg. Joe shouted; I knew he had got one too.

We stood there trying to figure out which way the singles had gone but they had fanned out too quick for us, excited as we were, and after beating around awhile we gave up and went on.

We came to the rim of the swale, eased over it, crossed the dry creek bed that was drifted thick with leaves, and started up the other side. I had blown in the dogs, thinking there was no use for them to run their heads off now we'd started home, but they didn't come. I walked on a little farther, then I looked back and saw Bob's white shoulders through a tangle of cinnamon vine.

Joe had turned around too. "They've pinned a single out of that last covey," he said.

I looked over at him quick. "Your shot."

He shook his head. "No, you take it."

I limped back and flushed the bird. It went skimming along the buck-berry bushes that covered that side of the swale. In the fading light I could hardly make it out and I shot too quick. It swerved over the thicket and I let go with the second barrel. It staggered, then zoomed up. Up, up, up, over the rim of the hill and above the tallest hickories. It hung there for a second, its wings black against the gold light, before, wings still spread, it came whirling down, like an autumn leaf, like the leaves that were everywhere about us, all over the ground.

QUESTIONS FOR DISCUSSION

1. "The Last Day in the Field" may not seem, on first reading, to be a short story at all. It has, however, all of the required elements of fiction—conflict, character, and theme. Define and discuss each element. Then explain some of the reasons for the opening sentence in this question.
2. The conflict in this story is the problem that Aleck faces. Trace the various ways in which he tries to solve it. What is his final solution?
3. Structurally and thematically, time is an important device in this story. Explain why.
4. "The Last Day in the Field" also uses a great many kinds of contrast to accomplish its purpose. Discuss the use of contrast in the story, in particular the contrast between Aleck and Joe.
5. What is a tragedy? What is a tragic hero? Is "The Last Day in the Field" a tragedy? Does it have, among other things, the necessary "tragic effect" on a reader? If so, how does it accomplish that effect?

CARSON McCULLERS
A Tree, A Rock, A Cloud

It was raining that morning, and still very dark. When the boy reached the streetcar café he had almost finished his route and he went in for a cup of coffee. The place was an all-night café owned by a bitter and stingy man called Leo. After the raw, empty street, the café seemed friendly and bright: along the counter there were a couple of soldiers, three spinners from the cotton mill, and in a corner a man who sat hunched over with his nose and half his face down in a beer mug. The boy wore a helmet such as aviators wear. When he went into the café he unbuckled the chin strap and raised the right flap up over his pink little ear; often as he drank his coffee someone would speak to him in a friendly way. But this morning Leo did not look into his face and none of the men were talking. He paid and was leaving the café when a voice called out to him:

"Son! Hey Son!"

He turned back and the man in the corner was crooking his finger and nodding to him. He had brought his face out of the beer mug and he seemed suddenly very happy. The man was long and pale, with a big nose and faded orange hair.

"Hey Son!"

The boy went toward him. He was an undersized boy of about twelve, with one shoulder drawn higher than the other because of the weight of the paper sack. His face was shallow, freckled, and his eyes were round child eyes.

"Yeah Mister?"

The man laid one hand on the paper boy's shoulders, then grasped the boy's chin and turned his face slowly from one side to the other. The boy shrank back uneasily.

"Say! What's the big idea?"

The boy's voice was shrill; inside the café it was suddenly very quiet.

The man said slowly, "I love you."

All along the counter the men laughed. The boy, who had scowled and sidled away, did not know what to do. He looked over the counter at Leo, and Leo watched him with a weary, brittle jeer. The boy tried to laugh also. But the man was serious and sad.

"I did not mean to tease you, Son," he said. "Sit down and have a beer with me. There is something I have to explain."

Cautiously, out of the corner of his eye, the paper boy questioned the men along the counter to see what he should do. But they had gone back to their beer or their breakfast and did not notice him. Leo put a cup of coffee on the counter and a little jug of cream.

"He is a minor," Leo said.

The paper boy slid himself up onto the stool. His ear beneath the upturned flap of the helmet was very small and red. The man was nodding at him soberly. "It is important," he said. Then he reached in his hip pocket and brought out something which he held up in the palm of his hand for the boy to see.

"Look very carefully," he said.

The boy stared, but there was nothing to look at very carefully. The man held in his big, grimy palm a photograph. It was the face of a woman, but blurred, so that only the hat and the dress she was wearing stood out clearly.

"See?" the man asked.

The boy nodded and the man placed another picture in his palm. The woman was standing on a beach in a bathing suit. The suit made her stomach very big, and that was the main thing you noticed.

"Got a good look?" He leaned over closer and finally asked: "You ever seen her before?"

The boy sat motionless, staring slantwise at the man. "Not so I know of."

"Very well." The man blew on the photographs and put them back into his pocket. "That was my wife."

"Dead?" the boy asked.

Slowly the man shook his head. He pursed his lips as though about to whistle and answered in a long-drawn way: "Nuuu—" he said. "I will explain."

The beer on the counter before the man was in a large brown mug. He did not pick it up to drink. Instead he bent down and, putting his face over the rim, he rested there for a moment. Then with both hands he tilted the mug and sipped.

"Some night you'll go to sleep with your big nose in a mug and drown," said Leo. "Prominent transient drowns in beer. That would be a cute death."

The paper boy tried to signal to Leo. While the man was not looking he screwed up his face and worked his mouth to question soundlessly: "Drunk?" But Leo only raised his eyebrows and turned away to put some pink strips of bacon on the grill. The man pushed the mug away from him, straightened himself, and folded his loose crooked hands on the counter. His face was sad as he looked at the paper boy. He did not blink, but from time to time the lids closed down with delicate gravity over his pale green eyes. It was nearing dawn and the boy shifted the weight of the paper sack.

"I am talking about love," the man said. "With me it is a science."

The boy half slid down from the stool. But the man raised his forefinger, and there was something about him that held the boy and would not let him go away.

"Twelve years ago I married the woman in the photograph. She was my wife for one year, nine months, three days, and two nights. I loved her. Yes. . . ." He tightened his blurred, rambling voice and said again: "I loved her. I thought also that she loved me. I was a railroad engineer. She had all home comforts and luxuries. It never crept into my brain that she was not satisfied. But do you know what happened?"

"Mgneeow!" said Leo.

The man did not take his eyes from the boy's face. "She left me. I came in one night and the house was empty and she was gone. She left me."

"With a fellow?" the boy asked.

Gently the man placed his palm down on the counter. "Why naturally, Son. A woman does not run off like that alone."

The café was quiet, the soft rain black and endless in the street outside. Leo pressed down the frying bacon with the prongs of his long fork. "So you have been chasing the floozie for eleven years. You frazzled old rascal!"

For the first time the man glanced at Leo. "Please don't be vulgar. Besides, I was not speaking to you." He turned back to the boy and said in a trusting and secretive undertone, "Let's not pay any attention to him. O.K.?"

The paper boy nodded doubtfully.

"It was like this," the man continued. "I am a person who feels many things. All of my life one thing after another has impressed me. Moonlight. The leg of a pretty girl. One thing after another. But the point is that when I had enjoyed anything there was a peculiar sensation as though it was laying around loose in me. Nothing seemed to finish itself up or fit in with the other things. Women? I had my portion of them. The same. Afterwards laying around loose in me. I was a man who had never loved."

Very slowly he closed his eyelids, and the gesture was like a curtain drawn at the end of a scene in a play. When he spoke again his voice was excited and the words came fast—the lobes of his large, loose ears seemed to tremble.

"Then I met this woman. I was fifty-one years old and she always said she was thirty. I met her at a filling station and we were married within three days. And do you know what it was like? I just can't tell you. All I had ever felt was gathered together around this woman. Nothing lay around loose in me any more but was finished up by her."

The man stopped suddenly and stroked his long nose. His voice sank down to a steady and reproachful undertone: "I'm not explaining this right. What happened was this. There were these beautiful feelings and loose little pleasures inside me. And this woman was something like an assembly line for my soul. I run these little pieces of myself through her and I come out complete. Now do you follow me?"

"What was her name?" the boy asked.

"Oh," he said. "I called her Dodo. But that is immaterial."

"Did you try to make her come back?"

The man did not seem to hear. "Under the circumstances you can imagine how I felt when she left me."

Leo took the bacon from the grill and folded two strips of it between a bun. He had a gray face, with slitted eyes, and a pinched nose saddled by faint blue shadows. One of the mill workers signaled for more coffee and Leo poured it. He did not give refills on coffee free. The spinner ate breakfast there every morning, but the better Leo knew his customers the stingier he treated them. He nibbled his own bun as though he grudged it to himself.

"And you never got hold of her again?"

The boy did not know what to think of the man, and his child's face was uncertain with mingled curiosity and doubt. He was new on the paper route; it was still strange to him to be out in the town in the black, queer early morning.

"Yes," the man said. "I took a number of steps to get her back. I went around trying to locate her. I went to Tulsa where she had folks. And to Mobile. I went to every town she had ever mentioned to me, and I hunted down every man she had formerly been connected with. Tulsa, Atlanta, Chicago, Cheehaw, Memphis. . . . For the better part of two years I chased around the country trying to lay hold of her."

"But the pair of them had vanished from the face of the earth!" said Leo.

"Don't listen to him," the man said confidentially. "And also just forget those two years. They are not important. What matters is that around the third year a curious thing begun to happen to me."

"What?" the boy asked.

The man leaned down and tilted his mug to take a sip of beer. But as he hovered over the mug his nostrils fluttered slightly; he sniffed the stale-ness of the beer and did not drink. "Love is a curious thing to begin with. At first I thought only of getting her back. It was a kind of mania. But then as time went on I tried to remember her. But do you know what happened?"

"No," the boy said.

"When I laid myself down on a bed and tried to think about her my mind became a blank. I couldn't see her. I would take out her pictures and look. No good. Nothing doing. A blank. Can you imagine it?"

"Say Mac!" Leo called down the counter. "Can you imagine this bozo's mind a blank!"

Slowly, as though fanning away flies, the man waved his hand. His green eyes were concentrated and fixed on the shallow little face of the paper boy.

"But a sudden piece of glass on a sidewalk. Or a nickel tune in a music box. A shadow on a wall at night. And I would remember. It might happen in a street and I would cry or bang my head against a lamppost. You follow me?"

"A piece of glass . . ." the boy said.

"Anything. I would walk around and I had no power of how and when to remember her. You think you can put up a kind of shield. But remembering don't come to a man face forward—it corners around sideways. I was at the mercy of everything I saw and heard. Suddenly instead of me combing the countryside to find her she begun to chase me around in my very soul. *She* chasing *me*, mind you! and in my soul."

The boy asked finally: "What part of the country were you in then?"

"Ooh," the man groaned. "I was a sick mortal. It was like smallpox. I confess, Son, that I boozed. I fornicated. I committed any sin that suddenly appealed to me. I am loath to confess it but I will do so. When I recall that period it is all curdled in my mind, it was so terrible."

The man leaned his head down and tapped his forehead on the counter. For a few seconds he stayed bowed over in this position, the back of his stringy neck covered with orange furze, his hands with their long warped fingers held palm to palm in an attitude of prayer. Then the man straightened himself; he was smiling and suddenly his face was bright and tremulous and old.

"It was in the fifth year that it happened," he said. "And with it I started my science."

Leo's mouth jerked with a pale, quick grin. "Well none of we boys are getting any younger," he said. Then with sudden anger he balled up a dishcloth he was holding and threw it down hard on the floor. "You draggle-tailed old Romeo!"

"What happened?" the boy asked.

The old man's voice was high and clear: "Peace," he answered.

"Huh?"

"It is hard to explain scientifically, Son," he said. "I guess the logical explanation is that she and I had fleed around from each other for so long that finally we just got tangled up together and lay down and quit. Peace. A queer and beautiful blankness. It was spring in Portland and the rain came every afternoon. All evening I just stayed there on my bed in the dark. And that is how the science come to me."

The windows in the streetcar were pale blue with light. The two soldiers paid for their beers and opened the door—one of the soldiers combed his hair and wiped off his muddy puttees before they went outside. The three mill workers bent silently over their breakfasts. Leo's clock was ticking on the wall.

"It is this. And listen carefully. I meditated on love and reasoned it out. I realized what is wrong with us. Men fall in love for the first time. And what do they fall in love with?"

The boy's soft mouth was partly open and he did not answer.

"A woman," the old man said. "Without science, with nothing to go by, they undertake the most dangerous and sacred experience in God's earth. They fall in love with a woman. Is that correct, Son?"

"Yeah," the boy said faintly.

"They start at the wrong end of love. They begin at the climax. Can you wonder it is so miserable? Do you know how men should love?"

The old man reached over and grasped the boy by the collar of his leather jacket. He gave him a gentle little shake and his green eyes gazed down unblinking and grave.

"Son, do you know how love should be begun?"

The boy sat small and listening and still. Slowly he shook his head. The old man leaned closer and whispered:

"A tree. A rock. A cloud."

It was still raining outside in the street: a mild, gray, endless rain. The mill whistle blew for the six o'clock shift and the three spinners paid and went away. There was no one in the café but Leo, the old man, and the little paper boy.

"The weather was like this in Portland," he said. "At the time my science was begun. I meditated and I started very cautious. I would pick up something from the street and take it home with me. I bought a goldfish and I concentrated on the goldfish and I loved it. I graduated from one thing to another. Day by day I was getting this technique. On the road from Portland to San Diego——"

"Aw shut up!" screamed Leo suddenly. "Shut up! Shut up!"

The old man still held the collar of the boy's jacket; he was trembling and his face was earnest and bright and wild. "For six years now I have gone around by myself and built up my science. And now I am a master. Son, I can love anything. No longer do I have to think about it even. I see a street full of people and a beautiful light comes in me. I watch a bird in the sky. Or I meet a traveler on the road. Everything, Son. And anybody. All strangers and all loved? Do you realize what a science like mine can mean?"

The boy held himself stiffly, his hands curled tight around the counter edge. Finally he asked: "Did you ever really find that lady?"

"What? What say, Son?"

"I mean," the boy asked timidly. "Have you fallen in love with a woman again?"

The old man loosened his grasp on the boy's collar. He turned away and for the first time his green eyes had a vague and scattered look. He lifted the mug from the counter, drank down the yellow beer. His head was shaking slowly from side to side. Then finally he answered: "No, Son. You see that is the last step in my science. I go cautious. And I am not quite ready yet."

"Well!" said Leo. "Well well well!"

The old man stood in the open doorway. "Remember," he said. Framed there in the gray damp light of the early morning he looked shrunken and seedy and frail. But his smile was bright. "Remember I love you," he said with a last nod. And the door closed quietly behind him.

The boy did not speak for a long time. He pulled down the bangs on his forehead and slid his grimy little forefinger around the rim of his empty cup. Then without looking at Leo he finally asked:

"Was he drunk?"

"No," said Leo shortly.

The boy raised his clear voice higher. "Then was he a dope fiend?"

"No."

The boy looked up at Leo, and his flat little face was desperate, his voice urgent and shrill. "Was he crazy? Do you think he was a lunatic?" The paper boy's voice dropped suddenly with doubt. "Leo? Or not?"

But Leo would not answer him. Leo had run a night café for fourteen years, and he held himself to be a critic of craziness. There were the town characters and also the transients who roamed in from the night. He knew the manias of all of them. But he did not want to satisfy the questions of the waiting child. He tightened his pale face and was silent.

So the boy pulled down the right flap of his helmet and as he turned to leave he made the only comment that seemed safe to him, the only remark that could not be laughed down and despised:

"He sure has done a lot of traveling."

QUESTIONS FOR DISCUSSION

1. To what extent do the emotions that the story transmits depend upon characterization? Upon description? Upon contrast and irony?

Are the various moods throughout the story related to the final effect of the story? Why or why not?

2. The *topic* of "A Tree, A Rock, A Cloud" is love. What is the theme? Relate each character in the story to the theme. What devices other than character and situation does the author employ in order to define her theme?
3. Does the technique of having the transient narrate his story and philosophy detract in any way from the story's effectiveness in characterization? Its emotional effect? Its theme?
4. Why is it appropriate that the transient choose a small boy to narrate his story to? Why does it turn out to be ironical as well?
5. Paul Engle, distinguished American critic and poet, as editor of the annual O. Henry Awards anthology, *Prize Stories*, has said that he considers "A Tree, A Rock, A Cloud" "the most perfect short story in modern American literature." Can you explain, at least in part, why he might make such a statement?

2 Point of View

The basic methods of contemporary writers are still those of the first storytellers: the use of the five tools of action, dialogue, description, thoughts, and exposition put to the developing and resolving of a conflict, the portraying of characters, and the realizing of a theme. But in modern fiction another facet of fictional technique has come to assume such importance that it can be said to constitute a sixth tool. This facet is called *point of view.*

The term *point of view* as it applies to fiction is a severely technical one, and determining the point of view of any story involves answering these questions: Who tells the story? What is the relationship of that person to the story? What is the position from which the story gets told? Most analyses of fictional point of view attempt a division and subdivision by considering these questions simultaneously; further, most analyses employ different terminology for what is usually the same principle: what one critic, for example, will call the "neutral omniscient" point of view another will call the "objective" point of view. In trying to answer the above questions simultaneously, most analyses are, at best, complicated and, at worst, confusing. Hence, for purposes of simplification, the following discussion will treat these two aspects of point of view (*choice* of narrator and *position*) separately.

To begin with, a writer has two choices of narrator: he may employ first person ("I") or third person ("he"). Obviously, the story that is told in first person will differ radically—in style, vocabulary, even structure or content—from the story that is told in third person. We can illustrate this by reference to a possible story situation. Suppose that a writer chooses war as a story subject, and suppose that this writer hates war. He may, on the one hand, choose to allow his protagonist to tell his own story. Now suppose that his protagonist has a limited education, is provincial, and enjoys killing. Obviously, both the style of the story and the content will here be determined by the character of the protagonist; and whatever *negative* reaction toward war the writer wants from us must be accomplished by implication—by the use of irony, say. In other words, when a writer chooses to use the first-person narrator, he in effect secedes from his own story; he commits himself to the style, background, and character of his narrator. But suppose that this same writer chooses to tell this man's story in third person. Now, since the writer has interposed himself between his reader and his protagonist, the language and style will change; they will become the writer's language and style. Beyond that, even the content can change, for now the writer's attitude toward war can quite legitimately seep into his story.

Choice of narrator, then, has a great deal to do with the content, style, and effect of a story. The matter of position, of the relationship of the narrator to the story, plays an even more important part. Here we meet with the possibility of almost infinite variation, gradation, or combination. Narrative positions in stories can range from that extreme which Robert Penn Warren calls the *panoramic*, in which a story is viewed from constantly shifting positions, to that which he calls *strict focus*, a severely restricted position that is usually found only in the well-handled first-person narrative. If we allow for all these variations and gradations, we can say that basically there are four positions from which a story can be told: the omniscient point of view, the central point of view, the peripheral point of view, and the objective point of view.

The omniscient point of view might also be called the shifting or multiple or panoramic point of view. It is the oldest point of view in fiction, but for a number of reasons it is infrequently employed in modern stories. With this point of view, the writer assumes the freedom to move at will from one point in the story to another. He may, for example, tell one part of his story through the eyes and mind of one character, another through the eyes and mind of a second character. He may, at any point, shift from a character's position to his own, a shift known as author intrusion; or he may handle part of his material subjectively (that is, from the inside of someone's mind), another part objectively (that is, from the outside, as drama is handled). The omniscient point of view obviously offers a writer maximum scope and flexibility. But in the hands of an unskillful writer, no point of view is so subject to abuse: such a writer will shift his point of view needlessly and create confusions in pattern or direction or focus; or he will come between his reader and his story; or he will use this point of view as an excuse for not handling his theme or characterization indirectly. Thus, most writers prefer other points of view.

Of these, the central or limited omniscient point of view is the one used in most modern short stories. Here the story is told from the point of view of the central character; the writer allows himself access to the mind of this character but not the minds of any other characters in his story. It is the most popular of all fictional points of view because the purpose of most stories is centered in the experiences, reactions, or changes of the central character; what the protagonist comes to understand or experience is essentially what the author intends the reader to understand or experience (though, as we shall point out in a moment, this last generalization is subject to very careful modification).

In many stories, however, the author's purpose can best be accomplished by telling the story through the eyes of a minor character rather than the central one. We call this point of view *peripheral* because the story is told from the edge, so to speak, instead of from the center. For a certain kind of story, this point of view offers a writer a number of advantages. For example, the author may want to incorporate interpretations or attitudes which, if assigned to the main character, would destroy plausibility or consistency, and if assigned to himself (the writer) would constitute author intrusion. But if the writer chooses to approach his story from the position of a minor character, he can incorporate these comments without destroying other desired effects. In numerous other ways the peripheral point of view can achieve irony or thematic modification or depth of characterization or other effects that would be impossible were the story approached from any other position.

The most recent development in fiction is that of the objective point of view, which approaches a story completely from the outside. Perhaps the best way to describe it is to imagine that you are not *participating* in a story but are rather *watching* it from a seat in a theater. Indeed, the objective point of view is in part a result of the very strong influence of drama on modern fiction; and like drama, it does not permit us to enter, except indirectly by inference, into the minds or inner feelings of *any* character. Everything, in short, is viewed from the outside; the story accomplishes everything through the external actions, speech, or appearance of the characters, or through description of setting.

Where the omniscient point of view is at once the easiest point of view and the one most subject to abuse, the objective point of view is the most difficult to handle but the one least subject to abuse. However, it works best with only certain kinds of material. It is the point of view, for example, of the so-called slice-of-life story, which accomplishes its purpose best when it is allowed to speak completely for itself, without author or character comment. It is also found in stories that deal not with a single protagonist but with a relationship—in a story dealing with marriage, for example, where neither the husband nor the wife is the protagonist.

Now it is as important for us to be aware of a story's point of view as it is for us to follow the story's conflict, assess its characters, or interpret its theme. Indeed, we frequently cannot do any of these other things until we have considered the teller of the story—who he is, what his limitations are, what his involvement in or distance from the story is. In this regard, our first step is to identify the narrative point of view and to try to decide why the author chose one point of view over another. Definition, however, is only the first step and probably the simplest; it can, in fact, be done mechanically, simply by asking ourselves whose mind(s) we are allowed access to in the story.

The second step can be somewhat more delicate. In *The Rhetoric of Fiction*, Wayne Booth discusses what he calls the *authority* of a story's narrator, and this is as subject to variations as the possible positions from which a story can be approached. Every story is told by or through someone—an author, an "implied" author, a central character, a minor character, an anonymous and unidentified character, a number of characters—and what we make of the story is going to be determined in part by the reliability of that someone. Even the term *reliability* (or *authority*) has a special connotation; what we mean by it is how closely the *narrator's* attitudes toward, or feelings about, or interpretation of an experience approximates the *writer's* attitudes, feelings, or interpretation. As we have seen, behind every honest story is a writer who has certain views about life and who wants to communicate these to a reader. In doing so, he may choose any of a number of ways to get his "point" across. Ordinarily, if the story employs the omniscient point of view—that is, if the writer interprets his own story as he tells it—we can assume that the narrator is reliable. If the story is "objective," we can usually make the same assumption, though here an "implied" narrator may or may not represent the author. But as soon as a writer chooses to tell a story through the eyes of someone other than himself, we can no longer assume the reliability of the narrator. He *may* speak for the writer but much more frequently he does not. Marlow, for example, the narrator in some of Conrad's stories, *seems* to be reasonably reliable. At the other extreme, most narrators in

Ring Lardner's stories are clearly unreliable, and instead of accepting their interpretation we accept an opposite one. Between these two extremes, we can have an infinite number of variations and gradations. Thus, when we read a story told through a child's eyes, or through the eyes of a clearly stupid narrator, or through the eyes of a narrator who is presented sympathetically but whose understanding of the situation is incomplete, we must obviously make allowances for the narrator before we can hope to understand what the author wants to say to us.

D. H. LAWRENCE
The Blind Man

Isabel Pervin was listening for two sounds—for the sound of wheels on the drive outside and for the noise of her husband's footsteps in the hall. Her dearest and oldest friend, a man who seemed almost indispensable to her living, would drive up in the rainy dusk of the closing November day. The trap had gone to fetch him from the station. And her husband, who had been blinded in Flanders, and who had a disfiguring mark on his brow, would be coming in from the outhouses.

He had been home for a year now. He was totally blind. Yet they had been very happy. The Grange was Maurice's own place. The back was a farmstead, and the Wernhams, who occupied the rear premises, acted as farmers. Isabel lived with her husband in the handsome rooms in front. She and he had been almost entirely alone together since he was wounded. They talked and sang and read together in a wonderful and unspeakable intimacy. Then she reviewed books for a Scottish newspaper, carrying on her old interest, and he occupied himself a good deal with the farm. Sightless, he could still discuss everything with Wernham, and he could also do a good deal of work about the place—menial work, it is true, but it gave him satisfaction. He milked the cows, carried in the pails, turned the separator, attended to the pigs and horses. Life was still very full and strangely serene for the blind man, peaceful with the almost incomprehensible peace of immediate contact in darkness. With his wife he had a whole world, rich and real and invisible.

They were newly and remotely happy. He did not even regret the loss of his sight in these times of dark, palpable joy. A certain exultance swelled his soul.

But as time wore on, sometimes the rich glamour would leave them. Sometimes, after months of this intensity, a sense of burden overcame Isabel, a weariness, a terrible *ennui*, in that silent house approached between a colonnade of tall-shafted pines. Then she felt she would go mad, for she could not bear it. And sometimes he had devastating fits of depression, which seemed to lay waste his whole being. It was worse than depression—a black misery, when his own life was a torture to him, and when his presence was unbearable to his wife. The dread went down to the roots of her soul as these black days recurred. In a kind of panic she tried to wrap herself up still further in her husband. She forced the old spontaneous cheerfulness and joy to continue. But the effort it cost her was almost too much. She knew she could not keep it up. She felt she would scream with the strain, and would give anything, anything, to escape. She longed to possess her husband utterly; it gave her inordinate joy to have him entirely to herself. And yet, when again he was gone in a black and massive misery, she could not bear him, she could not bear herself; she wished she could be snatched away off the earth altogether, anything rather than live at this cost.

Dazed, she schemed for a way out. She invited friends, she tried to give him some further connection with the outer world. But it was no good. After all their joy and suffering, after their dark, great year of blindness and solitude and unspeakable nearness, other people seemed to them both shallow, rattling, rather impertinent. Shallow prattle seemed presumptuous. He became impatient and irritated, she was wearied. And so they lapsed into their solitude again. For they preferred it.

But now, in a few weeks' time, her second baby would be born. The first had died, an infant, when her husband first went out to France. She looked with joy and relief to the coming of the second. It would be her salvation. But also she felt some anxiety. She was thirty years old, her husband was a year younger. They both wanted the child very much. Yet she could not help feeling afraid. She had her husband on her hands, a terrible joy to her, and a terrifying burden. The child would occupy her love and attention. And then, what of Maurice? What would he do? If only she could feel that he, too, would be at peace and happy when the child came! She did so want to luxuriate in a rich, physical satisfaction of maternity. But the man, what would he do? How could she provide for him, how avert those shattering black moods of his, which destroyed them both?

She sighed with fear. But at this time Bertie Reid wrote to Isabel. He was her old friend, a second or third cousin, a Scotchman, as she was a Scotchwoman. They had been brought up near to one another, and all her life he had been her friend, like a brother, but better than her own brothers. She loved him—though not in the marrying sense. There was a sort of kinship between them, an affinity. They understood one another instinctively. But Isabel would never have thought of marrying Bertie. It would have seemed like marrying in her own family.

Bertie was a barrister and a man of letters, a Scotchman of the intellectual type, quick, ironical, sentimental, and on his knees before the woman he adored but did not want to marry. Maurice Pervin was different. He came of a good old country family—the Grange was not a very great distance from Oxford. He was passionate, sensitive, perhaps oversensitive, wincing—a big fellow with heavy limbs and a forehead that flushed painfully. For his mind was slow, as if drugged by the strong provincial blood that beat in his veins. He was very sensitive to his own mental slowness, his feelings being quick and acute. So that he was just the opposite to Bertie, whose mind was much quicker than his emotions, which were not so very fine.

From the first the two men did not like each other. Isabel felt that they *ought* to get on together. But they did not. She felt that if only each could have the clue to the other there would be such a rare understanding between them. It did not come off, however. Bertie adopted a slightly ironical attitude, very offensive to Maurice, who returned the Scotch irony with English resentment, a resentment which deepened sometimes into stupid hatred.

This was a little puzzling to Isabel. However, she accepted it in the course of things. Men were made freakish and unreasonable. Therefore, when Maurice was going out to France for the second time, she felt that, for her husband's sake, she must discontinue her friendship with Bertie. She wrote to the barrister to this effect. Bertram Reid simply replied that in this, as in all other matters, he must obey her wishes, if these were indeed her wishes.

For nearly two years nothing had passed between the two friends. Isabel rather gloried in the fact; she had no compunction. She had one great article of faith, which was, that husband and wife should be so important to one another, that the rest of the world simply did not count. She and Maurice were husband and wife. They loved one another. They would have children. Then let everybody and everything else fade into insignificance outside this connubial felicity. She professed herself quite happy and ready to receive Maurice's friends. She was happy and ready: the happy wife, the ready woman in possession. Without knowing why, the friends retired abashed, and came no more. Maurice, of course, took as much satisfaction in this connubial absorption as Isabel did.

He shared in Isabel's literary activities, she cultivated a real interest in agriculture and cattle-raising. For she, being at heart perhaps an emotional enthusiast, always cultivated the practical side of life and prided herself on her mastery of practical affairs. Thus the husband and wife had spent the five years of married life. The last had been one of blindness and unspeakable intimacy. And now Isabel felt a great indifference coming over her, a sort of lethargy. She wanted to be allowed to bear her child in peace, to nod by the fire and drift vaguely, physically, from day to day. Maurice was like an ominous thunder-cloud. She had to keep waking up to remember him.

When a little note came from Bertie, asking if he were to put up a tombstone to their dead friendship, and speaking of the real pain he felt on account of her husband's loss of sight, she felt a pang, a fluttering agitation of re-awakening. And she read the letter to Maurice.

"Ask him to come down," he said.

"Ask Bertie to come here!" she re-echoed.

"Yes—if he wants to."

Isabel paused for a few moments.

"I know he wants to—he'd only be too glad," she replied. "But what about you, Maurice? How would you like it?"

"I should like it."

"Well—in that case—— But I thought you didn't care for him——"

"Oh, I don't know. I might think differently of him now," the blind man replied. It was rather abstruse to Isabel.

"Well, dear," she said, "if you're quite sure——"

"I'm sure enough. Let him come," said Maurice.

So Bertie was coming, coming this evening, in the November rain and darkness. Isabel was agitated, racked with her old restlessness and indecision. She had always suffered from this pain of doubt, just an agonizing sense of uncertainty. It had begun to pass off, in the lethargy of maternity. Now it returned, and she resented it. She struggled as usual to maintain her calm, composed, friendly bearing, a sort of mask she wore over all her body.

A woman had lighted a tall lamp beside the table and spread the cloth. The long dining-room was dim, with its elegant but rather severe pieces of old furniture. Only the round table glowed softly under the light. It had a rich, beautiful effect. The white cloth glistened and dropped its heavy, pointed lace corners almost to the carpet, the china was old and handsome, creamy-yellow, with a blotched pattern of harsh red and deep blue, the cups large and bell-shaped, the teapot gallant. Isabel looked at it with superficial appreciation.

Her nerves were hurting her. She looked automatically again at the high, uncurtained windows. In the last dusk she could just perceive outside a huge fir-tree swaying its boughs: it was as if she thought it rather than saw it. The rain came flying on the window panes. Ah, why had she no peace? These two men, why did they tear at her? Why did they not come—why was there this suspense?

She sat in a lassitude that was really suspense and irritation. Maurice, at least, might come in—there was nothing to keep him out. She rose to her feet. Catching sight of her reflection in a mirror, she glanced at herself with a slight smile of recognition, as if she were an old friend to herself. Her face was oval and calm, her nose a little arched. Her neck made a beautiful line down to her shoulder. With hair knotted loosely behind, she had something of a warm, maternal look. Thinking this of herself, she arched her eyebrows and her rather heavy eyelids, with a little flicker of a smile, and for a moment her grey eyes looked amused and wicked, a little sardonic, out of her transfigured Madonna face.

Then, resuming her air of womanly patience—she was really fatally self-determined—she went with a little jerk towards the door. Her eyes were slightly reddened.

She passed down the wide hall and through a door at the end. Then she was in the farm premises. The scent of dairy, and of farm-kitchen, and of farm-yard and of leather almost overcame her: but particularly the scent of dairy. They had been scalding out the pans. The flagged passage in front of her was dark, puddled, and wet. Light came out from the open kitchen door. She went forward and stood in the doorway. The farm-people were at tea, seated at a little distance from her, round a long, narrow table, in the centre of which stood a white lamp. Ruddy faces, ruddy hands holding food, red mouths working, heads bent over the tea-cups: men, land-girls, boys: it was tea-time, feeding-time. Some faces caught sight of her. Mrs. Wernham, going round behind the chairs with a large black teapot, halting slightly in her walk, was not aware of her for a moment. Then she turned suddenly.

"Oh, is it Madam!" she exclaimed. "Come in, then, come in! We're at tea." And she dragged forward a chair.

"No, I won't come in," said Isabel. "I'm afraid I interrupt your meal."

"No—no—not likely, Madam, not likely."

"Hasn't Mr. Pervin come in, do you know?"

"I'm sure I couldn't say! Missed him, have you, Madam?"

"No, I only wanted him to come in," laughed Isabel, as if shyly.

"Wanted him, did ye? Get up, boy—get up, now——"

Mrs. Wernham knocked one of the boys on the shoulder. He began to scrape to his feet, chewing largely.

"I believe he's in top stable," said another face from the table.

"Ah! No, don't get up. I'm going myself," said Isabel.

"Don't you go out of a dirty night like this. Let the lad go. Get along wi' ye, boy," said Mrs. Wernham.

"No, no," said Isabel, with a decision that was always obeyed. "Go on with your tea, Tom. I'd like to go across to the stable, Mrs. Wernham."

"Did ever you hear tell!" exclaimed the woman.

"Isn't the trap late?" asked Isabel.

"Why, no," said Mrs. Wernham, peering into the distance at the tall, dim clock. "No, Madam—we can give it another quarter or twenty minutes yet, good—yes, every bit of a quarter."

"Ah! It seems late when darkness falls so early," said Isabel.

"It do, that it do. Bother the days, that they draw in so," answered Mrs. Wernham. "Proper miserable!"

"They are," said Isabel, withdrawing.

She pulled on her overshoes, wrapped a large tartan shawl around her, put on a man's felt hat, and ventured out along the causeways of the first yard. It was very dark. The wind was roaring in the great elms behind the outhouses. When she came to the second yard the darkness seemed deeper. She was unsure of her footing. She wished she had brought a lantern. Rain blew against her. Half she liked it, half she felt unwilling to battle.

She reached at last the just visible door of the stable. There was no sign of a light anywhere. Opening the upper half, she looked in: into a simple well of darkness. The smell of horses, and ammonia, and of warmth was startling to her, in that full night. She listened with all her ears but could hear nothing save the night, and the stirring of a horse.

"Maurice!" she called, softly and musically, though she was afraid. "Maurice—are you there?"

Nothing came from the darkness. She knew the rain and wind blew in upon the horses, the hot animal life. Feeling it wrong, she entered the stable and drew the lower half of the door shut, holding the upper part close. She did not stir, because she was aware of the presence of the dark hind-quarters of the horses, though she could not see them, and she was afraid. Something wild stirred in her heart.

She listened intensely. Then she heard a small noise in the distance—far away, it seemed—the chink of a pan, and a man's voice speaking a brief word. It would be Maurice, in the other part of the stable. She stood motionless, waiting for him to come through the partition door. The horses were so terrifyingly near to her, in the invisible.

The loud jarring of the inner door-latch made her start; the door was opened. She could hear and feel her husband entering and invisibly passing among the horses near to her, darkness as they were, actively intermingled. The rather low sound of his voice as he spoke to the horses came velvety to her nerves. How near he was, and how invisible! The darkness seemed to be in a strange swirl of violent life, just upon her. She turned giddy.

Her presence of mind made her call, quietly and musically:

"Maurice! Maurice—dea-ar!"

"Yes," he answered. "Isabel?"

She saw nothing, and the sound of his voice seemed to touch her.

"Hello!" she answered cheerfully, straining her eyes to see him. He was still busy, attending to the horses near her, but she saw only darkness. It made her almost desperate.

"Won't you come in, dear?" she said.

"Yes, I'm coming. Just half a minute. *Stand over—now!* Trap's not come, has it?"

"Not yet," said Isabel.

His voice was pleasant and ordinary, but it had a slight suggestion of the stable to her. She wished he would come away. Whilst he was so utterly invisible, she was afraid of him.

"How's the time?" he asked.

"Not yet six," she replied. She disliked to answer into the dark. Presently he came very near to her, and she retreated out of doors.

"The weather blows in here," he said, coming steadily forward, feeling for the doors. She shrank away. At last she could dimly see him.

"Bertie won't have much of a drive," he said, as he closed the doors.

"He won't indeed!" said Isabel calmly, watching the dark shape at the door.

"Give me your arm, dear," she said.

She pressed his arm close to her, as she went. But she longed to see him, to look at him. She was nervous. He walked erect, with face rather lifted, but with a curious tentative movement of his powerful, muscular legs. She could feel the clever, careful, strong contact of his feet with the earth, as she balanced against him. For a moment he was a tower of darkness to her, as if he rose out of the earth.

In the house-passage he wavered and went cautiously, with a curious look of silence about him as he felt for the bench. Then he sat down heavily. He was a man with rather sloping shoulders, but with heavy limbs, powerful legs that seemed to know the earth. His head was small, usually carried high and light. As he bent down to unfasten his gaiters and boots he did not look blind. His hair was brown and crisp, his hands were large, reddish, intelligent, the veins stood out in the wrists; and his thighs and knees seemed massive. When he stood up his face and neck were surcharged with blood, the veins stood out on his temples. She did not look at his blindness.

Isabel was always glad when they had passed through the dividing door into their own regions of repose and beauty. She was a little afraid of him, out there in the animal grossness of the back. His bearing also changed, as he smelt the familiar indefinable odour that pervaded his wife's surroundings, a delicate, refined scent, very faintly spicy. Perhaps it came from the potpourri bowls.

He stood at the foot of the stairs, arrested, listening. She watched him, and her heart sickened. He seemed to be listening to fate.

"He's not here yet," he said. "I'll go up and change."

"Maurice," she said, "you're not wishing he wouldn't come, are you?"

"I couldn't quite say," he answered. "I feel myself rather on the qui vive."

"I can see you are," she answered. And she reached up and kissed his cheek. She saw his mouth relax into a slow smile.

"What are you laughing at?" she said roguishly.

"You consoling me," he answered.

"Nay," she answered. "Why should I console you? You know we love each other—you know *how* married we are! What does anything else matter?"

"Nothing at all, my dear."

He felt for her face and touched it, smiling.

"*You're* all right, aren't you?" he asked anxiously.

"I'm wonderfully all right, love," she answered. "It's you I am a little troubled about, at times."

"Why me?" he said, touching her cheeks delicately with the tips of his fingers. The touch had an almost hypnotizing effect on her.

He went away upstairs. She saw him mount into the darkness, unseeing and unchanging. He did not know that the lamps on the upper corridor were unlighted. He went on into the darkness with unchanging step. She heard him in the bath-room.

Pervin moved about almost unconsciously in his familiar surroundings, dark though everything was. He seemed to know the presence of objects before he touched them. It was a pleasure to him to rock thus through a world of things, carried on the flood in a sort of blood-prescience. He did not think much or trouble much. So long as he kept this sheer immediacy of blood-contact with the substantial world he was happy, he wanted no intervention of visual consciousness. In this state there was a certain rich positivity, bordering sometimes on rapture. Life seemed to move in him like a tide lapping, lapping, and advancing, enveloping all things darkly. It was a pleasure to stretch forth the hand and meet the unseen object, clasp it, and possess it in pure contact. He did not try to remember, to visualize. He did not want to. The new way of consciousness substituted itself in him.

The rich suffusion of this state generally kept him happy, reaching its culmination in the consuming passion for his wife. But at times the flow would seem to be checked and thrown back. Then it would beat inside him like a tangled sea, and he was tortured in the shattered chaos of his own blood. He grew to dread this arrest, this throw-back, this chaos inside himself, when he seemed merely at the mercy of his own powerful and conflicting elements. How to get some measure of control or surety, this was the question. And when the question rose maddening in him, he would clench his fists as if he would *compel* the whole universe to submit to him. But it was in vain. He could not even compel himself.

Tonight, however, he was still serene, though little tremors of unreasonable exasperation ran through him. He had to handle the razor very carefully, as he shaved, for it was not at one with him, he was afraid of it. His hearing also was too much sharpened. He heard the woman lighting the lamps on the corridor, and attending to the fire in the visitors' room. And then, as he went to his room, he heard the trap arrive. Then came Isabel's voice, lifted and calling, like a bell ringing:

"Is it you, Bertie? Have you come?"

And a man's voice answered out of the wind:

"Hello, Isabel! There you are."

"Have you had a miserable drive? I'm so sorry we couldn't send a closed carriage. I can't see you at all, you know."

"I'm coming. No, I liked the drive—it was like Perthshire. Well, how are you? You're looking fit as ever, as far as I can see."

"Oh, yes," said Isabel. "I'm wonderfully well. How are you? Rather thin, I think——"

"Worked to death—everybody's old cry. But I'm all right, Ciss. How's Pervin?—isn't he here?"

"Oh, yes, he's upstairs changing. Yes, he's awfully well. Take off your wet things; I'll send them to be dried."

"And how are you both, in spirits? He doesn't fret?"

"No—no, not at all. No, on the contrary, really. We've been wonderfully happy, incredibly. It's more than I can understand—so wonderful: the nearness, and the peace——"

"Ah! Well, that's awfully good news——"

They moved away. Pervin heard no more. But a childish sense of desolation had come over him, as he heard their brisk voices. He seemed shut out—like a child that is left out. He was aimless and excluded, he did not know what to do with himself. The helpless desolation came over him. He fumbled nervously as he dressed himself, in a state almost of childishness. He disliked the Scotch accent in Bertie's speech, and the slight response it found on Isabel's tongue. He disliked the slight purr of complacency in the Scottish speech. He disliked intensely the glib way in which Isabel spoke of their happiness and nearness. It made him recoil. He was fretful and beside himself like a child, he had almost a childish nostalgia to be included in the life circle. And at the same time he was a man, dark and powerful and infuriated by his own weakness. By some fatal flaw, he could not be by himself, he had to depend on the support of another. And this very dependence enraged him. He hated Bertie Reid, and at the same time he knew the hatred was nonsense, he knew it was the outcome of his own weakness.

He went downstairs. Isabel was alone in the dining-room. She watched him enter, head erect, his feet tentative. He looked so strong-blooded and healthy and, at the same time, cancelled. Cancelled—that was the word that flew across her mind. Perhaps it was his scar suggested it.

"You heard Bertie come, Maurice?" she said.

"Yes—isn't he here?"

"He's in his room. He looks very thin and worn."

"I suppose he works himself to death."

A woman came in with a tray—and after a few minutes Bertie came down. He was a little dark man, with a very big forehead, thin, wispy hair, and sad, large eyes. His expression was inordinately sad—almost funny. He had odd, short legs.

Isabel watched him hesitate under the door, and glance nervously at her husband. Pervin heard him and turned.

"Here you are, now," said Isabel. "Come, let us eat."

Bertie went across to Maurice.

"How are you, Pervin?" he said, as he advanced.

The blind man stuck his hand out into space, and Bertie took it.

"Very fit. Glad you've come," said Maurice.

Isabel glanced at them, and glanced away, as if she could not bear to see them.

"Come," she said. "Come to table. Aren't you both awfully hungry? I am, tremendously."

"I'm afraid you waited for me," said Bertie, as they sat down.

Maurice had a curious monolithic way of sitting in a chair, erect and distant. Isabel's heart always beat when she caught sight of him thus.

"No," she replied to Bertie. "We're very little later than usual. We're having a sort of high tea, not dinner. Do you mind? It gives us such a nice long evening, uninterrupted."

"I like it," said Bertie.

Maurice was feeling, with curious little movements, almost like a cat kneading her bed, for his plate, his knife and fork, his napkin. He was getting the whole geography of his cover into his consciousness. He sat erect and inscrutable, remote-seeming. Bertie watched the static figure of the blind man, the delicate tactile discernment of the large, ruddy hands, and the curious mindless silence of the brow, above the scar. With difficulty he looked away, and without knowing what he did, picked up a little crystal bowl of violets from the table, and held them to his nose.

"They are sweet-scented," he said. "Where do they come from?"

"From the garden—under the windows," said Isabel.

"So late in the year—and so fragrant! Do you remember the violets under Aunt Bell's south wall?"

The two friends looked at each other and exchanged a smile, Isabel's eyes lighting up.

"Don't I?" she replied. "*Wasn't* she queer!"

"A curious old girl," laughed Bertie. "There's a streak of freakishness in the family, Isabel."

"Ah—but not in you and me, Bertie," said Isabel. "Give them to Maurice, will you?" she added, as Bertie was putting down the flowers. "Have you smelled the violets, dear? Do!—they are so scented."

Maurice held out his hand, and Bertie placed the tiny bowl against his large, warm-looking fingers. Maurices's hand closed over the thin white fingers of the barrister. Bertie carefully extricated himself. Then the two watched the blind man smelling the violets. He bent his head and seemed to be thinking. Isabel waited.

"Aren't they sweet, Maurice?" she said at last, anxiously.

"Very," he said. And he held out the bowl. Bertie took it. Both he and Isabel were a little afraid, and deeply disturbed.

The meal continued. Isabel and Bertie chatted spasmodically. The blind man was silent. He touched his food repeatedly, with quick, delicate touches of his knife-point, then cut irregular bits. He could not bear to be helped. Both Isabel and Bertie suffered: Isabel wondered why. She did not suffer when she was alone with Maurice. Bertie made her conscious of a strangeness.

After the meal the three drew their chairs to the fire, and sat down to talk. The decanters were put on a table near at hand. Isabel knocked the logs on the fire, and clouds of brilliant sparks went up the chimney. Bertie noticed a slight weariness in her bearing.

"You will be glad when your child comes now, Isabel?" he said.

She looked up to him with a quick wan smile.

"Yes, I shall be glad," she answered. "It begins to seem long. Yes, I shall be very glad. So will you, Maurice, won't you?" she added.

"Yes, I shall," replied her husband.

"We are both looking forward so much to having it," she said.

"Yes, of course," said Bertie.

He was a bachelor, three or four years older than Isabel. He lived in beautiful rooms overlooking the river, guarded by a faithful Scottish manservant. And he had his friends among the fair sex—not lovers, friends. So long as he could avoid any danger of courtship or marriage, he adored a few good women with constant and unfailing homage, and he was chivalrously fond of quite a number. But if they seemed to encroach on him, he withdrew and detested them.

Isabel knew him very well, knew his beautiful constancy, and kindness, also his incurable weakness, which made him unable ever to enter into close contact of any sort. He was ashamed of himself because he could not marry, could not approach women physically. He wanted to do so. But he could not. At the centre of him he was afraid, helplessly and even brutally afraid. He had given up hope, had ceased to expect any more that he could escape his own weakness. Hence he was a brilliant and successful barrister, also a *littérateur* of high repute, a rich man, and a great social success. At the centre he felt himself neuter, nothing.

Isabel knew him well. She despised him even while she admired him. She looked at his sad face, his little short legs, and felt contempt of him. She looked at his dark grey eyes, with their uncanny, almost childlike, intuition, and she loved him. He understood amazingly—but she had no fear of his understanding. As a man she patronized him.

And she turned to the impassive, silent figure of her husband. He sat leaning back, with folded arms, and face a little uptilted. His knees were straight and massive. She sighed, picked up the poker, and again began to prod the fire, to rouse the clouds of soft brilliant sparks.

"Isabel tells me," Bertie began suddenly, "that you have not suffered unbearably from the loss of sight."

Maurice straightened himself to attend but kept his arms folded.

"No," he said, "not unbearably. Now and again one struggles against it, you know. But there are compensations."

"They say it is much worse to be stone deaf," said Isabel.

"I believe it is," said Bertie. "Are there compensations?" he added, to Maurice.

"Yes. You cease to bother about a great many things." Again Maurice stretched his figure, stretched the strong muscles of his back, and leaned backwards, with uplifted face.

"And that is a relief," said Bertie. "But what is there in place of the bothering? What replaces the activity?"

There was a pause. At length the blind man replied, as out of a negligent, unattentive thinking:

"Oh, I don't know. There's a good deal when you're not active."

"Is there?" said Bertie. "What, exactly? It always seems to me that when there is no thought and no action, there is nothing."

Again Maurice was slow in replying.

"There is something," he replied. "I couldn't tell you what it is."

And the talk lapsed once more, Isabel and Bertie chatting gossip and reminiscence, the blind man silent.

At length Maurice rose restlessly, a big obtrusive figure. He felt tight and hampered. He wanted to go away.

"Do you mind," he said, "if I go and speak to Wernham?"

"No—go along, dear," said Isabel.

And he went out. A silence came over the two friends. At length Bertie said:

"Nevertheless, it is a great deprivation, Cissie."

"It is, Bertie. I know it is."

"Something lacking all the time," said Bertie.

"Yes, I know. And yet—and yet—Maurice is right. There is something else, something *there*, which you never knew was there, and which you can't express."

"What is there?" asked Bertie.

"I don't know—it's awfully hard to define it—but something strong and immediate. There's something strange in Maurice's presence—indefinable—but I couldn't do without it. I agree that it seems to put one's mind to sleep. But when we're alone I miss nothing; it seems awfully rich, almost splendid, you know."

"I'm afraid I don't follow," said Bertie.

They talked desultorily. The wind blew loudly outside, rain chattered on the window-panes, making a sharp drum-sound because of the closed, mellow-golden shutters inside. The logs burned slowly, with hot, almost invisible small flames. Bertie seemed uneasy, there were dark circles round his eyes. Isabel, rich with her approaching maternity, leaned looking into the fire. Her hair curled in odd, loose strands, very pleasing to the man. But she had a curious feeling of old woe in her heart, old, timeless night-woe.

"I suppose we're all deficient somewhere," said Bertie.

"I suppose so," said Isabel wearily.

"Damned, sooner or later."

"I don't know," she said, rousing herself. "I feel quite all right, you know. The child coming seems to make me indifferent to everything, just placid. I can't feel that there's anything to trouble about, you know."

"A good thing, I should say," he replied slowly.

"Well, there it is. I suppose it's just Nature. If only I felt I needn't trouble about Maurice, I should be perfectly content——"

"But you feel you must trouble about him?"

"Well—I don't know——" She even resented this much effort.

The night passed slowly. Isabel looked at the clock. "I say," she said. "It's nearly ten o'clock. Where can Maurice be? I'm sure they're all in bed at the back. Excuse me a moment."

She went out, returning almost immediately.

"It's all shut up and in darkness," she said. "I wonder where he is. He must have gone out to the farm——"

Bertie looked at her.

"I suppose he'll come in," he said.

"I suppose so," she said. "But it's unusual for him to be out now."

"Would you like me to go out and see?"

"Well—if you wouldn't mind. I'd go, but——" She did not want to make the physical effort.

Bertie put on an old overcoat and took a lantern. He went out from the side door. He shrank from the wet and roaring night. Such weather had a nervous effect on him: too much moisture everywhere made him feel almost imbecile. Unwilling, he went through it all. A dog barked violently at him. He peered in all the buildings. At last, as he opened the upper door of a sort of intermediate barn, he heard a grinding noise, and looking in, holding up his lantern, saw Maurice in his shirt-sleeves, standing listening, holding the handle of a turnip-pulper. He had been pulping sweet roots, a pile of which lay dimly heaped in a corner behind him.

"That you, Wernham?" said Maurice, listening.

"No, it's me," said Bertie.

A large, half-wild grey cat was rubbing at Maurice's leg. The blind man stooped to rub its sides. Bertie watched the scene, then unconsciously entered and shut the door behind him. He was in a high sort of barn-place, from which, right and left, ran off the corridors in front of the stalled cattle. He watched the slow, stooping motion of the other man, as he caressed the great cat.

Maurice straightened himself.

"You came to look for me?" he said.

"Isabel was a little uneasy," said Bertie.

"I'll come in. I like messing about doing these jobs."

The cat had reared her sinister, feline length against his leg, clawing at his thigh affectionately. He lifted her claws out of his flesh.

"I hope I'm not in your way at all at the Grange here," said Bertie, rather shy and stiff.

"My way? No, not a bit. I'm glad Isabel has somebody to talk to. I'm afraid it's I who am in the way. I know I'm not very lively company. Isabel's all right, don't you think? She's not unhappy, is she?"

"I don't think so."

"What does she say?"

"She says she's very content—only a little troubled about you."

"Why me?"

"Perhaps afraid that you might brood," said Bertie, cautiously.

"She needn't be afraid of that." He continued to caress the flattened grey head of the cat with his fingers. "What I am a bit afraid of," he resumed, "is that she'll find me a dead weight, always alone with me down here."

"I don't think you need think that," said Bertie, though this was what he feared himself.

"I don't know," said Maurice. "Sometimes I feel it isn't fair that she's saddled with me." Then he dropped his voice curiously. "I say," he asked secretly struggling, "is my face much disfigured? Do you mind telling me?"

"There is the scar," said Bertie, wondering. "Yes, it is a disfigurement. But more pitiable than shocking."

"A pretty bad scar, though," said Maurice.

"Oh, yes."

There was a pause.

"Sometimes I feel I am horrible," said Maurice, in a low voice, talking as if to himself. And Bertie actually felt a quiver of horror.

"That's nonsense," he said.

Maurice again straightened himself, leaving the cat.

"There's no telling," he said. Then again, in an odd tone, he added: "I don't really know you, do I?"

"Probably not," said Bertie.

"Do you mind if I touch you?"

The lawyer shrank away instinctively. And yet, out of very philanthropy, he said, in a small voice: "Not at all."

But he suffered as the blind man stretched out a strong, naked hand to him. Maurice accidentally knocked off Bertie's hat.

"I thought you were taller," he said, starting. Then he laid his hand on Bertie Reid's head, closing the dome of the skull in a soft, firm grasp, gathering it, as it were; then, shifting his grasp and softly closing again, with a fine, close pressure, till he had covered the skull and the face of the smaller man, tracing the brows, and touching the full, closed eyes, touching the small nose and the nostrils, the rough, short moustache, the mouth, the rather strong chin. The hand of the blind man grasped the shoulder, the arm, the hand of the other man. He seemed to take him, in the soft, travelling grasp.

"You seem young," he said quietly, at last.

The lawyer stood almost annihilated, unable to answer.

"Your head seems tender, as if you were young," Maurice repeated. "So do your hands. Touch my eyes, will you?—touch my scar."

Now Bertie quivered with revulsion. Yet he was under the power of the blind man, as if hypnotized. He lifted his hand, and laid the fingers to the scar, on the scarred eyes. Maurice suddenly covered them with his own hand, pressed the fingers of the other man upon his disfigured eye-sockets, trembling in every fibre, and rocking slightly, slowly, from side to side. He remained thus for a minute or more, whilst Bertie stood as if in a swoon, unconscious, imprisoned.

Then suddenly Maurice removed the hand of the other man from his brow, and stood holding it in his own.

"Oh, my God," he said, "we shall know each other now, shan't we? We shall know each other now."

Bertie could not answer. He gazed mute and terror-struck, overcome by his own weakness. He knew he could not answer. He had an unreasonable fear, lest the other man should suddenly destroy him. Whereas Maurice was actually filled with hot, poignant love, the passion of friendship. Perhaps it was this very passion of friendship which Bertie shrank from most.

"We're all right together now, aren't we?" said Maurice. "It's all right now, as long as we live, so far as we're concerned?"

"Yes," said Bertie, trying by any means to escape.

Maurice stood with head lifted, as if listening. The new delicate fulfillment of mortal friendship had come as revelation and surprise to him, something exquisite and unhoped-for. He seemed to be listening to hear if it were real.

Then he turned for his coat.

"Come," he said, "we'll go to Isabel."

Bertie took the lantern and opened the door. The cat disappeared. The two men went in silence along the causeways. Isabel, as they came, thought their footsteps sounded strange. She looked up pathetically and anxiously for their entrance. There seemed a curious elation about Maurice. Bertie was haggard, with sunken eyes.

"What is it?" she asked.

"We've become friends," said Maurice, standing with his feet apart, like a strange colossus.

"Friends!" re-echoed Isabel. And she looked again at Bertie. He met her eyes with a furtive, haggard look; his eyes were as if glazed with misery.

"I'm so glad," she said, in sheer perplexity.

"Yes," said Maurice.

He was indeed so glad. Isabel took his hand with both hers, and held it fast.

"You'll be happier now, dear," she said.

But she was watching Bertie. She knew that he had one desire—to escape from this intimacy, this friendship, which had been thrust upon him. He could not bear it that he had been touched by the blind man, his insane reserve broken in. He was like a mollusc whose shell is broken.

QUESTIONS FOR DISCUSSION

1. What is Isabel Pervin's function, structurally and thematically, in "The Blind Man"? What is the nature of her conflict? What is the thematic significance of her being pregnant?
2. What sides of human nature do Bertie Reid and Maurice Pervin represent?
3. The story can be divided into five sections. What is the point of view of each section? What structural or thematic principle is involved in Lawrence's shifting of his point of view? What is the symbolic and thematic focus of each section? How does Lawrence employ movement (from house to stable and back) in each section?
4. Discuss the "architecture" of the story—its use of contrast, its structural use of point of view, the "logic" of its progression.

JAMES JOYCE
A Little Cloud

Eight years before he had seen his friend off at the North Wall and wished him godspeed. Gallaher had got on. You could tell that at once by his travelled air, his well-cut tweed suit, and fearless accent. Few fellows had talents like his and fewer still could remain unspoiled by such success. Gallaher's heart was in the right place and he had deserved to win. It was something to have a friend like that.

Little Chandler's thoughts ever since lunchtime had been of his meeting with Gallaher, of Gallaher's invitation and of the great city London where Gallaher lived. He was called Little Chandler because though he was but slightly under the average stature, he gave one the idea of being a little man. His hands were white and small, his frame was fragile, his voice was quiet and his manners were refined. He took the greatest care of his fair silken hair and moustache and used perfume discreetly on his handkerchief. The half-moons of his nails were perfect and when he smiled you caught a glimpse of a row of childish white teeth.

As he sat at his desk in the King's Inns he thought what changes those eight years had brought. The friend whom he had known under a shabby and necessitous guise had become a brilliant figure on the London Press. He turned often from his tiresome writing to gaze out of the office window. The glow of a late autumn sunset covered the grass plots and walks. It cast a shower of kindly golden dust on the untidy nurses and decrepit old men who drowsed on the benches; it flickered upon all the moving figures—on the children who ran screaming along the gravel paths and on everyone who passed through the gardens. He watched the scene and thought of life; and (as always happened when he thought of life) he became sad. A gentle melancholy took possession of him. He felt how useless it was to struggle against fortune, this being the burden of wisdom which the ages had bequeathed to him.

He remembered the books of poetry upon his shelves at home. He had bought them in his bachelor days and many an evening, as he sat in the little room off the hall, he had been tempted to take one down from the bookshelf and read out something to his wife. But shyness had always held him back; and so the books had remained on their shelves. At times he repeated lines to himself and this consoled him.

When his hour had struck he stood up and took leave of his desk and of his fellow-clerks punctiliously. He emerged from under the feudal arch of the King's Inns, a neat modest figure, and walked swiftly down Henrietta Street. The golden sunset was waning and the air had grown sharp. A horde of grimy children populated the street. They stood or ran in the roadway or crawled up the steps before the gaping doors or squatted like mice upon the thresholds. Little Chandler gave them no thought. He picked his way deftly through all that minute vermin-like life and under the shadow of the gaunt spectral mansions in which the old nobility of Dublin had roystered. No memory of the past touched him, for his mind was full of a present joy.

He had never been in Corless's but he knew the value of the name. He knew that people went there after the theatre to eat oysters and drink liqueurs; and he had heard that the waiters there spoke French and German. Walking swiftly by at night he had seen cabs drawn up before the door and richly dressed ladies, escorted by cavaliers, alight and enter quickly. They wore noisy dresses and many wraps. Their faces were powdered and they caught up their dresses, when they touched earth, like alarmed Atalantas. He had always passed without turning his head to look. It was his habit to walk swiftly in the street even by day and whenever he found himself in the city late at night he hurried on his way apprehensively and excitedly. Sometimes, however, he courted the causes of his fear. He chose the darkest and narrowest streets and, as he walked boldly forward, the silence that was spread about his footsteps troubled him, the wandering, silent figures troubled him; and at times a sound of low fugitive laughter made him tremble like a leaf.

He turned to the right towards Capel Street. Ignatius Gallaher on the London Press! Who would have thought it possible eight years before. Still, now that he reviewed the past, Little Chandler could remember many signs of future greatness in his friend. People used to say that Ignatius Gallaher was wild. Of course, he did mix with a rakish set of fellows at that time, drank freely and borrowed money on all sides. In the end he had got mixed up in some shady affair, some money transaction: at least, that was one version of his flight. But nobody denied him talent. There was always a certain . . . something in Ignatius Gallaher that impressed you in spite of yourself. Even when he was out at elbows and at his wits' end for money he kept up a bold face. Little Chandler remembered (and the remembrance brought a slight flush of pride to his cheek) one of Ignatius Gallaher's sayings when he was in a tight corner:

"Half time now, boys," he used to say lightheartedly. "Where's my considering cap?"

That was Ignatius Gallaher all out; and, damn it, you couldn't but admire him for it.

Little Chandler quickened his pace. For the first time in his life he felt himself superior to the people he passed. For the first time his soul revolted against the dull inelegance of Capel Street. There was no doubt about it: if you wanted to succeed you had to go away. You could do nothing in Dublin. As he crossed Grattan Bridge he looked down the river towards the lower quays and pitied the poor stunted houses. They seemed to him a band of tramps, huddled together along the river-banks, their old coats covered with dust and soot, stupefied by the panorama of sunset and waiting for the first chill of night to bid them arise, shake themselves and begone. He wondered whether he could write a poem to express his idea. Perhaps Gallaher might be able to get it into some London paper for him. Could he write something original? He was not sure what idea he wished to express but the thought that a poetic moment had touched him took life within him like an infant hope. He stepped onward bravely.

Every step brought him nearer to London, farther from his own sober inartistic life. A light began to tremble on the horizon of his mind. He was not so old—thirty-two. His temperament might be said to be just at the point of maturity. There were so many different moods and impressions that he wished to express in verse. He felt them within him. He tried to weigh his soul to see if it was a poet's soul. Melancholy was the dominant note of his temperament, he thought, but it was a melancholy tempered by recurrences of faith and resignation and simple joy. If he could give expression to it in a book of poems perhaps men would listen. He would never be popular: he saw that. He could not sway the crowd but he might appeal to a little circle of kindred minds. The English critics, perhaps, would recognize him as one of the Celtic school by reason of the melancholy tone of his poems; besides that, he would put in allusions. He began to invent sentences and phrases from the notice which his book would get. *"Mr. Chandler has the gift of easy and graceful verse."* . . . *"A wistful sadness pervades these poems."* . . . *"The Celtic note."* It was a pity his name was not more Irish-looking. Perhaps it would be better to insert his mother's name before the surname: Thomas Malone Chandler, or better still: T. Malone Chandler. He would speak to Gallaher about it.

He pursued his revery so ardently that he passed his street and had to turn back. As he came near Corless's his former agitation began to overmaster him and he halted before the door in indecision. Finally he opened the door and entered.

The light and noise of the bar held him at the doorways for a few moments. He looked about him, but his sight was confused by the shining of many red and green wine-glasses. The bar seemed to him to be full of people and he felt that the people were observing him curiously. He glanced quickly to right and left (frowning slightly to make his errand appear serious), but when his sight cleared a little he saw that nobody had turned to look at him: and there, sure enough, was Ignatius Gallaher leaning with his back against the counter and his feet planted far apart.

"Hallo, Tommy, old hero, here you are! What is it to be? What will you have? I'm taking whisky: better stuff than we get across the water. Soda? Lithia? No mineral? I'm the same. Spoils the flavour. . . . Here, *garçon*, bring us two halves of malt whisky, like a good fellow. . . . Well, and how have you been pulling along since I saw you last? Dear God, how old we're getting! Do you see any signs of aging in me—eh, what? A little grey and thin on the top—what?"

Ignatius Gallaher took off his hat and displayed a large closely cropped head. His face was heavy, pale and clean-shaven. His eyes, which were of bluish slate-colour, relieved his unhealthy pallor and shone out plainly above the vivid orange tie he wore. Between these rival features the lips appeared very long and shapeless and colourless. He bent his head and felt with two sympathetic fingers the thin hair at the crown. Little Chandler shook his head as a denial. Ignatius Gallaher put on his hat again.

"It pulls you down," he said, "press life. Always hurry and scurry, looking for copy and sometimes not finding it: and then, always to have something new in your stuff. Damn proofs and printers, I say, for a few days. I'm deuced glad, I can tell you, to get back to the old country. Does a fellow good, a bit of a holiday. I feel a ton better since I landed again in dear dirty Dublin. . . . Here you are, Tommy. Water? Say when."

Little Chandler allowed his whisky to be very much diluted.

"You don't know what's good for you, my boy," said Ignatius Gallaher. "I drink mine neat."

"I drink very little as a rule," said Little Chandler modestly. "An odd half-one or so when I meet any of the old crowd: that's all."

"Ah, well," said Ignatius Gallaher, cheerfully, "here's to us and to old times and old acquaintance."

They clinked glasses and drank the toast.

"I met some of the old gang today," said Ignatius Gallaher. "O'Hara seems to be in a bad way. What's he doing?"

"Nothing," said Little Chandler. "He's gone to the dogs."

"But Hogan has a good sit, hasn't he?"

"Yes; he's in the Land Commission."

"I met him one night in London and he seemed to be very flush. . . Poor O'Hara! Boose, I suppose?"

"Other things, too," said Little Chandler shortly.

Ignatius Gallaher laughed.

"Tommy," he said, "I see you haven't changed an atom. You're the very same serious person that used to lecture me on Sunday mornings when I had a sore head and a fur on my tongue. You'd want to knock about a bit in the world. Have you never been anywhere even for a trip?"

"I've been to the Isle of Man," said Little Chandler.

Ignatius Gallaher laughed.

"The Isle of Man!" he said. "Go to London or Paris: Paris, for choice. That'd do you good."

"Have you seen Paris?"

"I should think I have! I've knocked about there a little."

"And is it really so beautiful as they say?" asked Little Chandler.

He sipped a little of his drink while Ignatius Gallaher finished his boldly.

"Beautiful?" said Ignatius Gallaher, pausing on the word and on the flavour of his drink. "It's not so beautiful, you know. Of course, it is beautiful. . . . But it's the life of Paris; that's the thing. Ah, there's no city like Paris for gaiety, movement, excitement. . . ."

Little Chandler finished his whisky and, after some trouble, succeeded in catching the barman's eye. He ordered the same again.

"I've been to the Moulin Rouge," Ignatius Gallaher continued when the barman had removed their glasses, "and I've been to all the Bohemian cafés. Hot stuff! Not for a pious chap like you, Tommy."

Little Chandler said nothing until the barman returned with two glasses: then he touched his friend's glass lightly and reciprocated the former toast. He was beginning to feel somewhat disillusioned. Gallaher's accent and way of expressing himself did not please him. There was something vulgar in his friend which he had not observed before. But perhaps it was only the result of living in London amid the bustle and competition of the Press. The old personal charm was still there under this new gaudy manner. And, after all, Gallaher had lived, he had seen the world. Little Chandler looked at his friend enviously.

"Everything in Paris is gay," said Ignatius Gallaher. "They believe in enjoying life—and don't you think they're right? If you want to enjoy yourself properly you must go to Paris. And, mind you, they've a great feeling for the Irish there. When they heard I was from Ireland they were ready to eat me, man."

Little Chandler took four or five sips from his glass.

"Tell me," he said, "is it true that Paris is so . . . immoral as they say?"

Ignatius Gallaher made a catholic gesture with his right arm.

"Every place is immoral," he said. "Of course you do find spicy bits in Paris. Go to one of the students' balls, for instance. That's lively, if you like, when the *cocottes* begin to let themselves loose. You know what they are, I suppose?"

"I've heard of them," said Little Chandler.

Ignatius Gallaher drank off his whisky and shook his head.

"Ah," he said, "you may say what you like. There's no woman like the Parisienne—for style, for go."

"Then it is an immoral city," said Little Chandler, with timid insistence—"I mean, compared with London or Dublin?"

"London!" said Ignatius Gallaher. "It's six of one and half-a-dozen of the other. You ask Hogan, my boy. I showed him a bit about London when he was over there. He'd open your eye. . . . I say, Tommy, don't make punch of that whisky: liquor up."

"No, really. . . ."

"O, come on, another one won't do you any harm. What is it? The same again, I suppose?"

"Well . . . all right."

"*François*, the same again. . . . Will you smoke, Tommy?"

Ignatius Gallaher produced his cigar-case. The two friends lit their cigars and puffed at them in silence until their drinks were served.

"I'll tell you my opinion," said Ignatius Gallaher, emerging after some time from the clouds of smoke in which he had taken refuge, "it's a rum world. Talk of immorality! I've heard of cases—what am I saying?—I've known them: cases of . . . immorality. . . ."

Ignatius Gallaher puffed thoughtfully at his cigar and then, in a calm historian's tone, he proceeded to sketch for his friend some pictures of the corruption which was rife abroad. He summarised the vices of many capitals and seemed inclined to award the palm to Berlin. Some things he could not vouch for (his friends had told him), but of others he had had personal experience. He spared neither rank nor caste. He revealed many of the secrets of religious houses on the Continent and described some of the practices which were fashionable in high society and ended by telling, with details, a story about an English duchess—a story which he knew to be true. Little Chandler was astonished.

"Ah, well," said Ignatius Gallaher, "here we are in old jog-along Dublin where nothing is known of such things."

"How dull you must find it," said Little Chandler, "after all the other places you've seen!"

"Well," said Ignatius Gallaher, "it's a relaxation to come over here, you know. And, after all, it's the old country, as they say, isn't it? You can't help having a certain feeling for it. That's human nature. . . . But tell me something about yourself. Hogan told me you had . . . tasted the joys of connubial bliss. Two years ago, wasn't it?"

Little Chandler blushed and smiled.

"Yes," he said. "I was married last May twelve months."

"I hope it's not too late in the day to offer my best wishes," said Ignatius Gallaher. "I didn't know your address or I'd have done so at the time."

He extended his hand, which Little Chandler took.

"Well, Tommy," he said, "I wish you and yours every joy in life, old chap, and tons of money, and may you never die till I shoot you. And that's the wish of a sincere friend, an old friend. You know that?"

"I know that," said Little Chandler.

"Any youngsters?" said Ignatius Gallaher.

Little Chandler blushed again.

"We have one child," he said.

"Son or daughter?"

"A little boy."

Ignatius Gallaher slapped his friend sonorously on the back.

"Bravo," he said, "I wouldn't doubt you, Tommy."

Little Chandler smiled, looked confusedly at his glass and bit his lower lip with three childishly white front teeth.

"I hope you'll spend an evening with us," he said, "before you go back. My wife will be delighted to meet you. We can have a little music and—"

"Thanks awfully, old chap," said Ignatius Gallaher, "I'm sorry we didn't meet earlier. But I must leave tomorrow night."

"Tonight, perhaps . . . ?"

"I'm awfully sorry, old man. You see I'm over here with another fellow, clever young chap he is too, and we arranged to go to a little card-party. Only for that. . . ."

"O, in that case. . . ."

"But who knows?" said Ignatius Gallaher considerately. "Next year I may take a little skip over here now that I've broken the ice. It's only a pleasure deferred."

"Very well," said Little Chandler, "the next time you come we must have an evening together. That's agreed now, isn't it?"

"Yes, that's agreed," said Ignatius Gallaher. "Next year if I come, *parole d'honneur*."

"And to clinch the bargain," said Little Chandler, "we'll just have one more now."

Ignatius Gallaher took out a large gold watch and looked at it.

"Is it to be the last?" he said. "Because you know, I have an a.p."

"O, yes, positively," said Little Chandler.

"Very well, then," said Ignatius Gallaher, "let us have another one as a *deoc an doruis*—that's good vernacular for a small whisky, I believe."

Little Chandler ordered the drinks. The blush which had risen to his face a few moments before was establishing itself. A trifle made him blush at any time: and now he felt warm and excited. Three small whiskies had gone to his head and Gallaher's strong cigar had confused his mind, for he was a delicate and abstinent person. The adventure of meeting Gallaher after eight years, of finding himself with Gallaher in Corless's surrounded by lights and noise, of listening to Gallaher's stories and of sharing for a brief space Gallaher's vagrant and triumphant life, upset the equipoise of his sensitive nature. He felt acutely the contrast between his own life and his friend's, and it seemed to him unjust. Gallaher was his inferior in birth and education. He was sure that he could do something better than his friend had ever done, or could ever do, something higher than mere tawdry journalism if he only got the chance. What was it that stood in his way? His unfortunate timidity! He wished to vindicate himself in some way, to assert his manhood. He saw behind Gallaher's refusal of his invitation. Gallaher was only patronising him by his friendliness just as he was patronising Ireland by his visit.

The barman brought their drinks. Little Chandler pushed one glass towards his friend and took up the other boldly.

"Who knows?" he said, as they lifted their glasses. "When you come next year I may have the pleasure of wishing long life and happiness to Mr. and Mrs. Ignatius Gallaher."

Ignatius Gallaher in the act of drinking closed one eye expressively over the rim of his glass. When he had drunk he smacked his lips decisively, set down his glass and said:

"No blooming fear of that, my boy. I'm going to have my fling first and see a bit of life and the world before I put my head in the sack—if I ever do."

"Some day you will," said Little Chandler calmly.

Ignatius Gallaher turned his orange tie and slate-blue eyes full upon his friend.

"You think so?" he said.

"You'll put your head in the sack," repeated Little Chandler stoutly, "like everyone else if you can find the girl."

He had slightly emphasised his tone and he was aware that he had betrayed himself; but, though the colour had heightened in his cheek, he did not flinch from his friend's gaze. Ignatius Gallaher watched him for a few moments and then said:

"If ever it occurs, you may bet your bottom dollar there'll be no mooning and spooning about it. I mean to marry money. She'll have a good fat account at the bank or she won't do for me."

Little Chandler shook his head.

"Why, man alive," said Ignatius Gallaher, vehemently, "do you know what it is? I've only to say the word and tomorrow I can have the woman and the cash. You don't believe it? Well, I know it. There are hundreds—what am I saying?—thousands of rich Germans and Jews, rotten with money, that'd only be too glad. . . . You wait a while, my boy. See if I don't play my cards properly. When I go about a thing I mean business, I tell you. You just wait."

He tossed his glass to his mouth, finished his drink and laughed loudly. Then he looked thoughtfully before him and said in a calmer tone:

"But I'm in no hurry. They can wait. I don't fancy tying myself up to one woman, you know."

He imitated with his mouth the act of tasting and made a wry face.

"Must get a bit stale, I should think," he said.

Little Chandler sat in the room off the hall, holding a child in his arms. To save money they kept no servant but Annie's young sister Monica came for an hour or so in the morning and an hour or so in the evening to help. But Monica had gone home long ago. It was a quarter to nine. Little Chandler had come home late for tea and, moreover, he had forgotten to bring Annie home the parcel of coffee from Bewley's. Of course she was in a bad humour and gave him short answers. She said she would do without any tea but when it came near the time at which the shop at the corner closed she decided to go out herself for a quarter of a pound of tea and two pounds of sugar. She put the sleeping child deftly in his arms and said:

"Here. Don't waken him."

A little lamp with a white china shade stood upon the table and its light fell over a photograph which was enclosed in a frame of crumpled horn. It was Annie's photograph. Little Chandler looked at it, pausing at the thin tight lips. She wore the pale blue summer blouse which he had brought her home as a present one Saturday. It had cost him ten and elevenpence; but what an agony of nervousness it had cost him! How he had suffered that day, waiting at the shop door until the shop was empty, standing at the counter and trying to appear at his ease while the girl piled ladies' blouses before him, paying at the desk and forgetting to take up the odd penny of his change, being called back by the cashier, and finally, striving to hide his blushes as he left the shop by examining the parcel to see if it was securely tied. When he brought the blouse home Annie kissed him and said it was very pretty and stylish; but when she heard the price she threw the blouse on the table and said it was a regular swindle to charge ten and elevenpence for it. At first she wanted to take it back but when she tried it on she was delighted with it, especially with the make of the sleeves, and kissed him and said he was very good to think of her.

Hm! . . .

He looked coldly into the eyes of the photograph and they answered coldly. Certainly they were pretty and the face itself was pretty. But he found something mean in it. Why was it so unconscious and ladylike? The composure of the eyes irritated him. They repelled him and defied him: there was no passion in them, no rapture. He thought of what Gallaher had said about rich Jewesses. Those dark Oriental eyes, he thought, how full they were of passion, of voluptuous longing! . . . Why had he married the eyes in the photograph?

He caught himself up at the question and glanced nervously round the room. He found something mean in the pretty furniture which he had bought for his house on the hire system. Annie had chosen it herself and it reminded him of her. It too was prim and pretty. A dull resentment against his life awoke within him. Could he not escape from his little house? Was it too late for him to try to live bravely like Gallaher? Could he go to London? There was the furniture still to be paid for. If he could only write a book and get it published, that might open the way for him.

A volume of Byron's poems lay before him on the table. He opened it cautiously with his left hand lest he should waken the child and began to read the first poem in the book:

> Hushed are the winds and still the evening gloom,
>   Not e'en a Zephyr wanders through the grove,
> Whilst I return to view my Margaret's tomb
>   And scatter flowers on the dust I love.

He paused. He felt the rhythm of the verse about him in the room. How melancholy it was! Could he, too, write like that, express the melancholy of his soul in verse? There were so many things he wanted to describe: his sensation of a few hours before on Grattan Bridge, for example. If he could get back again into that mood....

The child awoke and began to cry. He turned from the page and tried to hush it: but it would not be hushed. He began to rock it to and fro in his arms but its wailing cry grew keener. He rocked it faster while his eyes began to read the second stanza:

> Within this narrow cell reclines her clay,
>   That clay where once ...

It was useless. He couldn't read. He couldn't do anything. The wailing of the child pierced the drum of his ear. It was useless, useless! He was a prisoner for life. His arms trembled with anger and suddenly bending to the child's face he shouted:

"Stop!"

The child stopped for an instant, had a spasm of fright and began to scream. He jumped up from his chair and walked hastily up and down the room with the child in his arms. It began to sob piteously, losing its breath for four or five seconds, and then bursting out anew. The thin walls of the room echoed the sound. He tried to soothe it but it sobbed more convulsively. He looked at the contracted and quivering face of the child and began to be alarmed. He counted seven sobs without a break between them and caught the child to his breast in fright. If it died! ...

The door was burst open and a young woman ran in, panting.

"What is it? What is it?" she cried.

The child, hearing its mother's voice, broke out into a paroxysm of sobbing.

"It's nothing. Annie ... it's nothing.... He began to cry ..."

She flung her parcels on the floor and snatched the child from him.

"What have you done to him?" she cried, glaring into his face.

Little Chandler sustained for one moment the gaze of her eyes and his heart closed together as he met the hatred in them. He began to stammer:

"It's nothing. . . . He . . . he began to cry. . . . I couldn't . . . I didn't do anything. . . . What?"

Giving no heed to him she began to walk up and down the room, clasping the child tightly in her arms and murmuring:

"My little man! My little mannie! Was 'ou frightened, love? . . . There now, love! There now! . . . Lambabaun! Mamma's little lamb of the world! . . . There now!"

Little Chandler felt his cheeks suffused with shame and he stood back out of the lamplight. He listened while the paroxysm of the child's sobbing grew less and less; and tears of remorse started to his eyes.

QUESTIONS FOR DISCUSSION

1. Joyce conceived of his stories as *epiphanies,* a term that suggests a sudden insight or illumination. In what respects, both for Little Chandler and for the reader, is "A Little Cloud" an epiphany? The term, of course, is a religious one. How is the story like the religious experience suggested by Epiphany? How is the application of the term to this story ironical?
2. Little Chandler's basic character trait is suggested by his name. In what ways is he childish, immature? What are his hopes, dreams, aspirations? How are these further evidence of his immaturity?
3. Analyze the character of Gallaher. In what ways is Little Chandler's admiration for Gallaher the hero worship of a small boy for a bigger one?
4. "A Little Cloud" is divided into three sections. What does each contribute to the story? Each section is in itself a kind of miniature short story. Analyze each section as such.
5. What examples of irony can you find in the story? What examples of word play or other forms of wit can you find?
6. The point of view of "A Little Cloud" shifts from "central" to "objective," as for example in the second paragraph. Examine in particular the "objective" passages throughout the story. In what way do they change our interpretation of the "subjective" passages—those where we are in Little Chandler's mind? What effect do they have on our understanding of and attitude toward the story's characters, particularly Little Chandler and Gallaher? Would you say that these constitute "author intrusion"?

SHERWOOD ANDERSON
The Egg

My father was, I am sure, intended by nature to be a cheerful, kindly man. Until he was thirty-four years old he worked as a farmhand for a man named Thomas Butterworth whose place lay near the town of Bidwell, Ohio. He had then a horse of his own, and on Saturday evenings drove into town to spend a few hours in social intercourse with other farmhands. In town he drank several glasses of beer and stood about in Ben Head's saloon—crowded on Saturday evenings with visiting farmhands. Songs were sung and glasses thumped on the bar. At ten o'clock father drove home along a lonely country road, made his horse comfortable for the night, and himself went to bed, quite happy in his position in life. He had at that time no notion of trying to rise in the world.

It was in the spring of his thirty-fifth year that father married my mother, then a country school-teacher, and in the following spring I came wriggling and crying into the world. Something happened to the two people. They became ambitious. The American passion for getting up in the world took possession of them.

It may have been that mother was responsible. Being a school-teacher she had no doubt read books and magazines. She had, I presume, read of how Garfield, Lincoln, and other Americans rose from poverty to fame and greatness, and as I lay beside her—in the days of her lying-in—she may have dreamed that I would some day rule men and cities. At any rate she induced father to give up his place as a farmhand, sell his horse, and embark on an independent enterprise of his own. She was a tall silent woman with a long nose and troubled gray eyes. For herself she wanted nothing. For father and myself she was incurably ambitious.

The first venture into which the two people went turned out badly. They rented ten acres of poor stony land on Grigg's Road, eight miles from Bidwell, and launched into chicken-raising. I grew into boyhood on the place and got my first impressions of life there. From the beginning they were impressions of disaster, and if, in my turn, I am a gloomy man inclined to see the darker side of life, I attribute it to the fact that what should have been for me the happy joyous days of childhood were spent on a chicken farm.

One unversed in such matters can have no notion of the many and tragic things that can happen to a chicken. It is born out of an egg, lives for a few weeks as a tiny fluffy thing such as you will see pictured on Easter cards, then becomes hideously naked, eats quantities of corn and meal bought by the sweat of your father's brow, gets diseases called pip, cholera, and other names, stands looking with stupid eyes at the sun, becomes sick and dies. A few hens and now and then a rooster, intended to serve God's mysterious ends, struggle through to maturity. The hens lay eggs out of which come other chickens and the dreadful cycle is thus made complete. It is all unbelievably complex. Most philosophers must have been raised on chicken farms. One hopes for so much from a chicken and is so dreadfully disillusioned. Small chickens, just setting out on the journey of life, look so bright and alert and they are in fact so dreadfully stupid. They are so much like people they mix one up in one's judgments of life. If disease does not kill them, they wait until your expectations are thoroughly aroused and then walk under the wheels of a wagon—to go squashed and dead back to their maker. Vermin infest their youth, and fortunes must be spent for curative powders. In later life I have seen how a literature has been built up on the subject of fortunes to be made out of the raising of chickens. It is intended to be read by the gods who have just eaten of the tree of the knowledge of good and evil. It is a hopeful literature and declares that much may be done by simple ambitious people who own a few hens. Do not be led astray by it. It was not written for you. Go hunt for gold on the frozen hills of Alaska, put your faith in the honesty of a politician, believe if you will that the world is daily growing better and that good will triumph over evil, but do not read and believe the literature that is written concerning the hen. It was not written for you.

I, however, digress. My tale does not primarily concern itself with the hen. If correctly told it will center on the egg. For ten years my father and mother struggled to make our chicken farm pay and then they gave up that struggle and began another. They moved into the town of Bidwell, Ohio, and embarked in the restaurant business. After ten years of worry with incubators that did not hatch, and with tiny—and in their own way lovely—balls of fluff that passed on into semi-naked pullethood and from that into dead henhood, we threw all aside and, packing our belongings on a wagon, drove down Grigg's Road toward Bidwell, a tiny caravan of hope looking for a new place from which to start on our upward journey through life.

We must have been a sad-looking lot, not, I fancy, unlike refugees fleeing from a battlefield. Mother and I walked in the road. The wagon that contained our goods had been borrowed for the day from Mr. Albert

Griggs, a neighbor. Out of its sides stuck the legs of cheap chairs, and at the back of the pile of beds, tables, and boxes filled with kitchen utensils was a crate of live chickens, and on top of that the baby carriage in which I had been wheeled about in my infancy. Why we stuck to the baby carriage I don't know. It was unlikely other children would be born and the wheels were broken. People who have few possessions cling tightly to those they have. That is one of the facts that make life so discouraging.

Father rode on top of the wagon. He was then a bald-headed man of forty-five, a little fat, and from long association with mother and the chickens he had become habitually silent and discouraged. All during our ten years on the chicken farm he had worked as a laborer on neighboring farms and most of the money he had earned had been spent for remedies to cure chicken diseases, on Wilmer's White Wonder Cholera Cure or Professor Bidlow's Egg Producer or some other preparations that mother found advertised in the poultry papers. There were two little patches of hair on father's head just above his ear. I remember that as a child I used to sit looking at him when he had gone to sleep in a chair before the stove on Sunday afternoons in the winter. I had at that time already begun to read books and have notions of my own, and the bald path that led over the top of his head was, I fancied, something like a broad road, such a road as Caesar might have made on which to lead his legions out of Rome and into the wonders of an unknown world. The tufts of hair that grew above father's ears were, I thought, like forests. I fell into a half-sleeping, half-waking state and dreamed I was a tiny thing going along the road into a far beautiful place where there were no chicken farms and where life was a happy eggless affair.

One might write a book concerning our flight from the chicken farm into town. Mother and I walked the entire eight miles—she to be sure that nothing fell from the wagon and I to see the wonders of the world. On the seat of the wagon beside father was his greatest treasure. I will tell you of that.

On a chicken farm, where hundreds and even thousands of chickens come out of eggs, surprising things sometimes happen. Grotesques are born out of eggs as out of people. The accident does not often occur—perhaps once in a thousand births. A chicken is, you see, born that has four legs, two pairs of wings, two heads, or what not. The things do not live. They go quickly back to the hand of their maker that has for a moment trembled. The fact that the poor little things could not live was one of the tragedies of life to father. He had some sort of notion that if he could but bring into henhood or roosterhood a five-legged hen or a two-headed rooster his fortune would be made. He dreamed of taking the wonder about the county fairs and of growing rich by exhibiting it to other farmhands.

Pickled chickens in Pickleville

At any rate, he saved all the little monstrous things that had been born on our chicken farm. They were preserved in alcohol and put each in its own glass bottle. These he had carefully put into a box, and on our journey into town it was carried on the wagon seat beside him. He drove the horses with one hand and with the other clung to the box. When we got to our destination, the box was taken down at once and the bottles removed. All during our days as keepers of a restaurant in the town of Bidwell, Ohio, the grotesques in their little glass bottles sat on a shelf back of the counter. Mother sometimes protested, but father was a rock on the subject of his treasure. The grotesques were, he declared, valuable. People, he said, liked to look at strange and wonderful things.

Did I say that we embarked in the restaurant business in the town of Bidwell, Ohio? I exaggerated a little. The town itself lay at the foot of a low hill and on the shore of a small river. The railroad did not run through the town and the station was a mile away to the north at a place called Pickleville. There had been a cider mill and pickle factory at the station, but before the time of our coming they had both gone out of business. In the morning and in the evening busses came down to the station along a road called Turner's Pike from the hotel on the main street of Bidwell. Our going to the out-of-the-way place to embark in the restaurant business was mother's idea. She talked of it for a year and then one day went off and rented an empty store building opposite the railroad station. It was her idea that the restaurant would be profitable. Traveling men, she said, would be always waiting around to take trains out of town and town people would come to the station to await incoming trains. They would come to the restaurant to buy pieces of pie and drink coffee. Now that I am older I know that she had another motive in going. She was ambitious for me. She wanted me to rise in the world, to get into a town school and become a man of the towns.

At Pickleville father and mother worked hard, as they always had done. At first there was the necessity of putting our place into shape to be a restaurant. That took a month. Father built a shelf on which he put tins of vegetables. He painted a sign on which he put his name in large red letters. Below his name was the sharp command—"EAT HERE"—that was so seldom obeyed. A showcase was bought and filled with cigars and tobacco. Mother scrubbed the floor and the walls of the room. I went to school in the town and was glad to be away from the farm and from the presence of the discouraged, sad-looking chickens. Still I was not very joyous. In the evening I walked home from school along Turner's Pike and remembered the children I had seen playing in the town school yard. A troop of little girls had gone hopping about and singing. I tried that. Down along the frozen road I went hopping solemnly on one leg. "Hippity Hop To The Barber Shop," I sang shrilly. Then I stopped and looked doubtfully about. I was afraid of being seen in my gay mood. It must have seemed to me that I was doing a thing that should not be done by one who, like myself, had been raised on a chicken farm where death was a daily visitor.

Mother decided that our restaurant should remain open at night. At ten in the evening a passenger train went north past our door followed by a local freight. The freight crew had switching to do in Pickleville, and when the work was done they came to our restaurant for hot coffee and food. Sometimes one of them ordered a fried egg. In the morning at four they returned north-bound and again visited us. A little trade began to grow up. Mother slept at night and during the day tended the restaurant and fed our boarders while father slept. He slept in the same bed mother had occupied during the night and I went off to the town of Bidwell and to school. During the long nights, while mother and I slept, father cooked meats that were to go into sandwiches for the lunch baskets of our boarders. Then an idea in regard to getting up in the world came into his head. The American spirit took hold of him. He also became ambitious.

In the long nights when there was little to do, father had time to think. That was his undoing. He decided that he had in the past been an unsuccessful man because he had not been cheerful enough and that in the future he would adopt a cheerful outlook on life. In the early morning he came upstairs and got into bed with mother. She woke and the two talked. From my bed in the corner I listened.

It was father's idea that both he and mother should try to entertain the people who came to eat at our restaurant. I cannot now remember his words, but he gave the impression of one about to become in some obscure way a kind of public entertainer. When people, particularly young people from the town of Bidwell, came into our place, as on very rare occasions they did, bright entertaining conversation was to be made. From father's words I gathered that something of the jolly innkeeper effect was to be sought. Mother must have been doubtful from the first, but she said nothing discouraging. It was father's notion that a passion for the company of himself and mother would spring up in the breasts of the younger people of the town of Bidwell. In the evening bright happy groups would come singing down Turner's Pike. They would troop shouting with joy and laughter into our place. There would be song and festivity. I do not mean to give the impression that father spoke so elaborately of the matter. He was, as I have said, an uncommunicative man. "They want some place to go. I tell you they want some place to go," he said over and over. That was as far as he got. My own imagination has filled in the blanks.

For two or three weeks this notion of father's invaded our house. We did not talk much, but in our daily lives tried earnestly to make smiles take the place of glum looks. Mother smiled at the boarders and I, catching the infection, smiled at our cat. Father became a little feverish in his anxiety to please. There was, no doubt, lurking somewhere in him, a touch of the spirit of the showman. He did not waste much of his ammunition on the railroad men he served at night, but seemed to be waiting for a young man or woman from Bidwell to come in to show what he could do. On the counter in the restaurant there was a wire basket kept always filled with eggs, and it must have been before his eyes when the idea of being entertaining was born in his brain. There was something pre-natal about the way eggs kept themselves connected with the development of his idea. At any rate, an egg ruined his new impulse in life. Late one night I was awakened by a roar of anger coming from father's throat. Both mother and I sat upright in our beds. With trembling hands she lighted a lamp that stood on a table by her head. Downstairs the front door of our restaurant went shut with a bang and in a few minutes father tramped up the stairs. He held an egg in his hand and his hand trembled as though he were having a chill. There was a half-insane light in his eyes. As he stood glaring at us I was sure he intended throwing the egg at either mother or me. Then he laid it gently on the table beside the lamp and dropped on his knees beside mother's bed. He began to cry like a boy, and I, carried away by his grief, cried with him. The two of us filled the little upstairs room with our wailing voices. It is ridiculous, but of the picture we made I can remember only the fact that mother's hand continually stroked the bald path that ran across the top of his head. I have forgotten what mother said to him and how she induced him to tell her of what had happened downstairs. His explanation also has gone out of my mind. I remember only my own grief and fright and the shiny path over father's head glowing in the lamplight as he knelt by the bed.

As to what happened downstairs. For some unexplainable reason I know the story as well as though I had been a witness to my father's discomfiture. One in time gets to know many unexplainable things. On that evening young Joe Kane, son of a merchant of Bidwell, came to Pickleville to meet his father, who was expected on the ten-o'clock evening train from the South. The train was three hours late and Joe came into our place to loaf about and to wait for its arrival. The local freight train came in and the freight crew were fed. Joe was left alone in the restaurant with father.

From the moment he came into our place the Bidwell young man must have been puzzled by my father's actions. It was his notion that father was angry at him for hanging around. He noticed that the restaurant-keeper was apparently disturbed by his presence and he thought of going out. However, it began to rain and he did not fancy the long walk to town and back. He bought a five-cent cigar and ordered a cup of coffee. He had a newspaper in his pocket and took it out and began to read. "I'm waiting for the evening train. It's late," he said apologetically.

For a long time father, whom Joe Kane had never seen before, remained silently gazing at his visitor. He was no doubt suffering from an attack of stage fright. As so often happens in life he had thought so much and so often of the situation that now confronted him that he was somewhat nervous in its presence.

For one thing, he did not know what to do with his hands. He thrust one of them nervously over the counter and shook hands with Joe Kane. "How-de-do," he said. Joe Kane put his newspaper down and stared at him. Father's eyes lighted on the basket of eggs that sat on the counter and he began to talk. "Well," he began hesitatingly, "well, you have heard of Christopher Columbus, eh?" He seemed to be angry. "That Christopher Columbus was a cheat," he declared emphatically. "He talked of making an egg stand on its end. He talked, he did, and then he went and broke the end of the egg."

My father seemed to his visitor to be beside himself at the duplicity of Christopher Columbus. He muttered and swore. He declared it was wrong to teach children that Christopher Columbus was a great man when, after all, he cheated at the critical moment. He had declared he would make an egg stand on end and then, when his bluff had been called, he had done a trick. Still grumbling at Columbus, father took an egg from the basket on the counter and began to walk up and down. He rolled the egg between the palms of his hands. He smiled genially. He began to mumble words regarding the effect to be produced on an egg by the electricity that comes out of the human body. He declared that, without breaking its shell and by virtue of rolling it back and forth in his hands, he could stand the egg on its end. He explained that the warmth of his hands and the gentle rolling movement he gave the egg created a new center of gravity, and Joe Kane was mildly interested. "I have handled thousands of eggs," father said. "No one knows more about eggs than I do."

He stood the egg on the counter and it fell on its side. He tried the trick again and again, each time rolling the egg between the palms of his hands and saying the words regarding the wonders of electricity and the laws of gravity. When after a half-hour's effort he did succeed in making the egg stand for a moment, he looked up to find that his visitor was no longer watching. By the time he had succeeded in calling Joe Kane's attention to the success of his effort, the egg had again rolled over and lay on its side.

Afire with the showman's passion and at the same time a good deal disconcerted by the failure of his first effort, father now took the bottles containing the poultry monstrosities down from their place on the shelf and began to show them to his visitor. "How would you like to have seven legs and two heads like this fellow?" he asked, exhibiting the most remarkable of his treasures. A cheerful smile played over his face. He reached over the counter and tried to slap Joe Kane on the shoulder as he had seen men do in Ben Head's saloon when he was a young farmhand and drove to town on Saturday evenings. His visitor was made a little ill by the sight of the body of the terribly deformed bird floating in the alcohol in the bottle and got up to go. Coming from behind the counter, father took hold of the young man's arm and led him back to his seat. He grew a little angry and for a moment had to turn his face away and force himself to smile. Then he put the bottles back on the shelf. In an outburst of generosity he fairly compelled Joe Kane to have a fresh cup of coffee and another cigar at his expense. Then he took a pan and filling it with vinegar, taken from a jug that sat beneath the counter, he declared himself about to do a new trick. "I will heat this egg in this pan of vinegar," he said. "Then I will put it through the neck of a bottle without breaking the shell. When the egg is inside the bottle it will resume its normal shape and the shell will become hard again. Then I will give the bottle with the egg in it to you. You can take it about with you wherever you go. People will want to know how you got the egg in the bottle. Don't tell them. Keep them guessing. That is the way to have fun with this trick."

Father grinned and winked at his visitor. Joe Kane decided that the man who confronted him was mildly insane but harmless. He drank the cup of coffee that had been given him and began to read his paper again. When the egg had been heated in vinegar, father carried it on a spoon to the counter and going into a back room got an empty bottle. He was angry because his visitor did not watch him as he began to do his trick, but nevertheless went cheerfully to work. For a long time he struggled, trying to get the egg to go through the neck of the bottle. He put the pan of vinegar back on the stove, intending to reheat the egg, then picked it up and burned his fingers. After a second bath in the hot vinegar, the shell of the egg had been softened a little, but not enough for his purpose. He worked and worked and a spirit of desperate determination took possession of him. When he thought that at last the trick was about to be consummated, the delayed train came in at the station and Joe Kane started to go nonchalantly out at the door. Father made a last desperate effort to conquer the egg and make it do the thing that would establish his reputation as one who knew how to entertain guests who came into his restaurant. He worried the egg. He attempted to be somewhat rough with it. He swore and the sweat stood out on his forehead. The egg broke under his hand. When the contents spurted over his clothes, Joe Kane, who had stopped at the door, turned and laughed.

A roar of anger rose from my father's throat. He danced and shouted a string of inarticulate words. Grabbing another egg from the basket on the counter, he threw it, just missing the head of the young man as he dodged through the door and escaped.

Father came upstairs to mother and me with an egg in his hand. I do not know what he intended to do. I imagine he had some idea of destroying it, of destroying all eggs, and that he intended to let mother and me see him begin. When, however, he got into the presence of mother, something happened to him. He laid the egg gently on the table and dropped on his knees by the bed as I have already explained. He later decided to close the restaurant for the night and to come upstairs and get into bed. When he did so, he blew out the light and after much muttered conversation both he and mother went to sleep. I suppose I went to sleep also, but my sleep was troubled. I awoke at dawn and for a long time looked at the egg that lay on the table. I wondered why eggs had to be and why from the egg came the hen who again laid the egg. The question got into my blood. It has stayed there, I imagine, because I am the son of my father. At any rate, the problem remains unsolved in my mind. And that, I conclude, is but another evidence of the complete and final triumph of the egg—at least as far as my family is concerned.

QUESTIONS FOR DISCUSSION

1. This story is told in the first person. Analyze the character of the narrator. What are his feelings about his parents, what are his values, what is his "view" of the world he lives in? What does the style of the story—the diction, the choice of detail, the historical allusions, the syntax—reveal about him? Why *must* we have this kind of narrator for *this* story?
2. What is the stylistic *tone* of the story? Is the tone appropriate to the point of view and the theme?
3. Analyze the character of the father. What are the contradictory and conflicting aspects of his character? What methods does the author employ to suggest or reveal these traits? How would the story be affected had Anderson let *him* tell the story?
4. Analyze the character of the mother. Does she seem to be more "single-minded" than the father? Is there any suggested conflict between her character and "dreams" and the fathers'? If so, define it. How would the story be affected had Anderson let *her* tell the story?
5. The story *seems* to be essentially expository in nature; people seem to be characterized, action narrated, theme explored by *telling* rather than by *showing*. Is that really the case? If not, what devices does the writer use instead of dramatization to *suggest* both characterization and theme?
6. What is the function of the "essay" on the nature of chicken farming? Is it relevant to the basic concept of the story?
7. The story is "loaded" with symbols, or objects that, at least, can easily be given symbolic significance. What are some of them? Define what they symbolize.

W. SOMERSET MAUGHAM
Rain

It was nearly bed-time and when they awoke next morning land would be in sight. Dr. Macphail lit his pipe and, leaning over the rail, searched the heavens for the Southern Cross. After two years at the front and a wound that had taken longer to heal than it should, he was glad to settle down quietly at Apia for twelve months at least, and he felt already better for the journey. Since some of the passengers were leaving the ship next day at Pago-Pago they had had a little dance that evening and in his ears hammered still the harsh notes of the mechanical piano. But the deck was quiet at last. A little way off he saw his wife in a long chair talking with the Davidsons, and he strolled over to her. When he sat down under the light and took off his hat you saw that he had very red hair, with a bald patch on the crown, and the red, freckled skin which accompanies red hair; he was a man of forty, thin, with a pinched face, precise and rather pedantic; and he spoke with a Scots accent in a very low, quiet voice.

Between the Macphails and the Davidsons, who were missionaries, there had arisen the intimacy of shipboard, which is due to propinquity rather than to any community of taste. Their chief tie was the disapproval they shared of the men who spent their days and nights in the smoking-room playing poker or bridge and drinking. Mrs. Macphail was not a little flattered to think that she and her husband were the only people on board with whom the Davidsons were willing to associate, and even the doctor, shy but no fool, half unconsciously acknowledged the compliment. It was only because he was of an argumentative mind that in their cabin at night he permitted himself to carp.

"Mrs. Davidson was saying she didn't know how they'd have got through the journey if it hadn't been for us," said Mrs. Macphail, as she neatly brushed out her transformation. "She said we were really the only people on the ship they cared to know."

"I shouldn't have thought a missionary was such a big bug that he could afford to put on frills."

"It's not frills. I quite understand what she means. It wouldn't have been very nice for the Davidsons to have to mix with all that rough lot in the smoking-room."

"The founder of their religion wasn't so exclusive," said Dr. Macphail with a chuckle.

"I've asked you over and over again not to joke about religion," answered his wife. "I shouldn't like to have a nature like yours, Alec. You never look for the best in people."

He gave her a sidelong glance, with his pale, blue eyes, but did not reply. After many years of married life he had learned that it was more conducive to peace to leave his wife with the last word. He was undressed before she was, and climbing into the upper bunk he settled down to read himself to sleep.

When he came on deck next morning they were close to land. He looked at it with greedy eyes. There was a thin strip of silver beach rising quickly to hills covered to the top with luxuriant vegetation. The coconut trees, thick and green, came nearly to the water's edge, and among them you saw the grass houses of the Samoans; and here and there, gleaming white, a little church. Mrs. Davidson came and stood beside him. She was dressed in black and wore round her neck a gold chain, from which dangled a small cross. She was a little woman, with brown, dull hair very elaborately arranged, and she had prominent blue eyes behind invisible *pince-nez.* Her face was long, like a sheep's, but she gave no impression of foolishness, rather of extreme alertness; she had the quick movements of a bird. The most remarkable thing about her was her voice, high, metallic, and without inflection; it fell on the ear with a hard monotony, irritating to the nerves like the pitiless clamour of the pneumatic drill.

"This must seem like home to you," said Dr. Macphail, with his thin, difficult smile.

"Ours are low islands, you know, not like these. Coral. These are volcanic. We've got another ten days' journey to reach them."

"In these parts that's almost like being in the next street at home," said Dr. Macphail facetiously.

"Well, that's rather an exaggerated way of putting it, but one does look at distances differently in the South Seas. So far you're right."

Dr. Macphail sighed faintly.

"I'm glad we're not stationed here," she went on. "They say this is a terribly difficult place to work in. The steamers' touching makes the people unsettled; and then there's the naval station; that's bad for the natives. In our district we don't have difficulties like that to contend with. There are one or two traders, of course, but we take care to make them behave, and if they don't we make the place so hot for them they're glad to go."

Fixing the glasses on her nose she looked at the green island with a ruthless stare.

"It's almost a hopeless task for the missionaries here. I can never be sufficiently thankful to God that we are at least spared that."

Davidson's district consisted of a group of islands to the north of Samoa; they were widely separated and he had frequently to go long distances by canoe. At these times his wife remained at their headquarters and managed the mission. Dr. Macphail felt his heart sink when he considered the efficiency with which she certainly managed it. She spoke of the depravity of the natives in a voice which nothing could hush, but with a vehemently unctuous horror. Her sense of delicacy was singular. Early in their acquaintance she had said to him:

"You know, their marriage customs when we first settled in the islands were so shocking that I couldn't possibly describe them to you. But I'll tell Mrs. Macphail and she'll tell you."

Then he had seen his wife and Mrs. Davidson, their deck-chairs close together, in earnest conversation for about two hours. As he walked past them backwards and forwards for the sake of exercise, he had heard Mrs. Davidson's agitated whisper, like the distant flow of a mountain torrent, and he saw by his wife's open mouth and pale face that she was enjoying an alarming experience. At night in their cabin she repeated to him with bated breath all she had heard.

"Well, what did I say to you?" cried Mrs. Davidson, exultant, next morning. "Did you ever hear anything more dreadful? You don't wonder that I couldn't tell you myself, do you? Even though you are a doctor."

Mrs. Davidson scanned his face. She had a dramatic eagerness to see that she had achieved the desired effect.

"Can you wonder that when we first went there our hearts sank? You'll hardly believe me when I tell you it was impossible to find a single good girl in any of the villages."

She used the word *good* in a severely technical manner.

"Mr. Davidson and I talked it over, and we made up our minds the first thing to do was to put down the dancing. The natives were crazy about dancing."

"I was not averse to it myself when I was a young man," said Dr. Macphail.

"I guessed as much when I heard you ask Mrs. Macphail to have a turn with you last night. I don't think there's any real harm if a man dances with his wife, but I was relieved that she wouldn't. Under the circumstances I thought it better that we should keep ourselves to ourselves."

"Under what circumstances?"

Mrs. Davidson gave him a quick look through her *pince-nez,* but did not answer his question.

"But among white people it's not quite the same," she went on, "though I must say I agree with Mr. Davidson, who says he can't understand how a husband can stand by and see his wife in another man's arms, and as far as I'm concerned I've never danced a step since I married. But the native dancing is quite another matter. It's not only immoral in itself, but it distinctly leads to immorality. However, I'm thankful to God that we stamped it out, and I don't think I'm wrong in saying that no one has danced in our district for eight years."

But now they came to the mouth of the harbour and Mrs. Macphail joined them. The ship turned sharply and steamed slowly in. It was a great landlocked harbour big enough to hold a fleet of battleships; and all around it rose, high and steep, the green hills. Near the entrance, getting such breeze as blew from the sea, stood the governor's house in a garden. The Stars and Stripes dangled languidly from a flagstaff. They passed two or three trim bungalows, and a tennis court, and then they came to the quay with its warehouses. Mrs. Davidson pointed out the schooner, moored two or three hundred yards from the side, which was to take them to Apia. There was a crowd of eager, noisy, and good-humoured natives come from all parts of the island, some from curiosity, others to barter with the travellers on their way to Sydney; and they brought pineapples and huge bunches of bananas, *tapa* cloths, necklaces of shells or sharks' teeth, *kava*-bowls, and models of war canoes. American sailors, neat and trim, clean-shaven and frank of face, sauntered among them, and there was a little group of officials. While their luggage was being landed the Macphails and Mrs. Davidson watched the crowd. Dr. Macphail looked at the yaws from which most of the children and the young boys seemed to suffer, disfiguring sores like torpid ulcers, and his professional eyes glistened when he saw for the first time in his experience cases of elephantiasis, men going about with a huge, heavy arm or dragging along a grossly disfigured leg. Men and women wore the *lava-lava*.

"It's a very indecent costume," said Mrs. Davidson. "Mr. Davidson thinks it should be prohibited by law. How can you expect people to be moral when they wear nothing but a strip of red cotton round their loins?"

"It's suitable enough to the climate," said the doctor, wiping the sweat off his head.

Now that they were on land the heat, though it was so early in the morning, was already oppressive. Closed in by its hills, not a breath of air came in to Pago-Pago.

"In our islands," Mrs. Davidson went on in her high-pitched tones, "we've practically eradicated the *lava-lava*. A few old men still continue to wear it, but that's all. The women have all taken to the Mother Hubbard, and the men wear trousers and singlets. At the very beginning of our stay Mr. Davidson said in one of his reports: the inhabitants of these islands will never be thoroughly Christianized till every boy of more than ten years is made to wear a pair of trousers."

But Mrs. Davidson had given two or three of her bird-like glances at heavy grey clouds that came floating over the mouth of the harbour. A few drops began to fall.

"We'd better take shelter," she said.

They made their way with all the crowd to a great shed of corrugated iron, and the rain began to fall in torrents. They stood there for some time and then were joined by Mr. Davidson. He had been polite enough to the Macphails during the journey, but he had not his wife's sociability, and had spent much of his time reading. He was a silent, rather sullen man, and you felt that his affability was a duty that he imposed upon himself Christianly; he was by nature reserved and even morose. His appearance was singular. He was very tall and thin, with long limbs loosely jointed; hollow cheeks and curiously high cheek bones; he had so cadaverous an air that it surprised you to notice how full and sensual were his lips. He wore his hair very long. His dark eyes, set deep in their sockets, were large and tragic; and his hands with their big, long fingers, were finely shaped; they gave him a look of great strength. But the most striking thing about him was the feeling he gave you of suppressed fire. It was impressive and vaguely troubling. He was not a man with whom any intimacy was possible.

He brought now unwelcome news. There was an epidemic of measles, a serious and often fatal disease among the Kanakas, on the island, and a case had developed among the crew of the schooner which was to take them on their journey. The sick man had been brought ashore and put in hospital on the quarantine station, but telegraphic instructions had been sent from Apia to say that the schooner would not be allowed to enter the harbour till it was certain no other member of the crew was affected.

"It means we shall have to stay here for ten days at least."

"But I'm urgently needed at Apia," said Dr. Macphail.

"That can't be helped. If no more cases develop on board, the schooner will be allowed to sail with white passengers, but all native traffic is prohibited for three months."

"Is there a hotel here?" asked Mrs. Macphail.

Davidson gave a low chuckle.

"There's not."

"What shall we do then?"

"I've been talking to the governor. There's a trader along the front who has rooms that he rents, and my proposition is that as soon as the rain lets up we should go along there and see what we can do. Don't expect comfort. You've just got to be thankful if we get a bed to sleep on and a roof over our heads."

But the rain showed no sign of stopping, and at length with umbrellas and waterproofs they set out. There was no town, but merely a group of official buildings, a store or two, and at the back, among the coconut trees and plantains, a few native dwellings. The house they sought was about five minutes' walk from the wharf. It was a frame house of two storeys, with broad verandahs on both floors and a roof of corrugated iron. The owner was a half-caste named Horn, with a native wife surrounded by little brown children, and on the ground-floor he had a store where he sold canned goods and cottons. The rooms he showed them were almost bare of furniture. In the Macphails' there was nothing but a poor, worn bed with a ragged mosquito net, a rickety chair, and a washstand. They looked round with dismay. The rain poured down without ceasing.

"I'm not going to unpack more than we actually need," said Mrs. Macphail.

Mrs. Davidson came into the room as she was unlocking a portmanteau. She was very brisk and alert. The cheerless surroundings had no effect on her.

"If you'll take my advice you'll get a needle and cotton and start right in to mend the mosquito net," she said, "or you'll not be able to get a wink of sleep to-night."

"Will they be very bad?" asked Dr. Macphail.

"This is the season for them. When you're asked to a party at Government House at Apia you'll notice that all the ladies are given a pillow-slip to put their—their lower extremities in."

"I wish the rain would stop for a moment," said Mrs. Macphail. "I could try to make the place comfortable with more heart if the sun were shining."

"Oh, if you wait for that, you'll wait a long time. Pago-Pago is about the rainiest place in the Pacific. You see, the hills, and that bay, they attract the water, and one expects rain at this time of year anyway."

She looked from Macphail to his wife, standing helplessly in different parts of the room, like lost souls, and she pursed her lips. She saw that she must take them in hand. Feckless people like that made her impatient, but her hands itched to put everything in the order which came so naturally to her.

"Here, you give me a needle and cotton and I'll mend that net of yours, while you go on with your unpacking. Dinner's at one. Dr. Macphail, you'd better go down to the wharf and see that your heavy luggage has been put in a dry place. You know what these natives are, they're quite capable of storing it where the rain will beat in on it all the time."

The doctor put on his waterproof again and went downstairs. At the door Mr. Horn was standing in conversation with the quartermaster of the ship they had just arrived in and a second-class passenger whom Dr. Macphail had seen several times on board. The quartermaster, a little, shrivelled man, extremely dirty, nodded to him as he passed.

"This is a bad job about the measles, doc," he said. "I see you've fixed yourself up already."

Dr. Macphail thought he was rather familiar, but he was a timid man and he did not take offence easily.

"Yes, we've got a room upstairs."

"Miss Thompson was sailing with you to Apia, so I've brought her along here."

The quartermaster pointed with his thumb to the woman standing by his side. She was twenty-seven perhaps, plump, and in a coarse fashion pretty. She wore a white dress and a large white hat. Her fat calves in white cotton stockings bulged over the top of long white boots in glacé kid. She gave Macphail an ingratiating smile.

"The feller's tryin' to soak me a dollar and a half a day for the meanest sized room," she said in a hoarse voice.

"I tell you she's a friend of mine, Jo," said the quartermaster. "She can't pay more than a dollar, and you've sure got to take her for that."

The trader was fat and smooth and quietly smiling.

"Well, if you put it like that, Mr. Swan, I'll see what I can do about it. I'll talk to Mrs. Horn and if we think we can make a reduction we will."

"Don't try to pull that stuff with me," said Miss Thompson. "We'll settle this right now. You get a dollar a day for the room and not one bean more."

Dr. Macphail smiled. He admired the effrontery with which she bargained. He was the sort of man who always paid what he was asked. He preferred to be over-charged than to haggle. The trader sighed.

"Well, to oblige Mr. Swan I'll take it."

"That's the goods," said Miss Thompson. "Come right in and have a shot of hooch. I've got some real good rye in that grip if you'll bring it along, Mr. Swan. You come along too, doctor."

"Oh, I don't think I will, thank you," he answered. "I'm just going down to see that our luggage is all right."

He stepped out into the rain. It swept in from the opening of the harbour in sheets and the opposite shore was all blurred. He passed two or three natives clad in nothing but the *lava-lava,* with huge umbrellas over them. They walked finely, with leisurely movements, very upright; and they smiled and greeted him in a strange tongue as they went by.

It was nearly dinner-time when he got back, and their meal was laid in the trader's parlour. It was a room designed not to live in but for purposes of prestige, and it had a musty, melancholy air. A suite of stamped plush was arranged neatly round the walls, and from the middle of the ceiling, protected from the flies by yellow tissue paper, hung a gilt chandelier. Davidson did not come.

"I know he went to call on the governor," said Mrs. Davidson, "and I guess he's kept him to dinner."

A little native girl brought them a dish of Hamburger steak, and after a while the trader came up to see that they had everything they wanted.

"I see we have a fellow lodger, Mr. Horn," said Dr. Macphail.

"She's taken a room, that's all," answered the trader. "She's getting her own board."

He looked at the two ladies with an obsequious air.

"I put her downstairs so she shouldn't be in the way. She won't be any trouble to you."

"Is it someone who was on the boat?" asked Mrs. Macphail.

"Yes, ma'am, she was in the second cabin. She was going to Apia. She has a position as cashier waiting for her."

"Oh!"

When the trader was gone Macphail said:

"I shouldn't think she'd find it exactly cheerful having her meals in her room."

"If she was in the second cabin I guess she'd rather," answered Mrs. Davidson. "I don't exactly know who it can be."

"I happened to be there when the quartermaster brought her along. Her name's Thompson."

"It's not the woman who was dancing with the quartermaster last night?" asked Mrs. Davidson.

"That's who it must be," said Mrs. Macphail. "I wondered at the time what she was. She looked rather fast to me."

"Not good style at all," said Mrs. Davidson.

They began to talk of other things, and after dinner, tired with their early rise, they separated and slept. When they awoke, though the sky was still grey and the clouds hung low, it was not raining and they went for a walk on the high road which the Americans had built along the bay.

On their return they found that Davidson had just come in.

"We may be here for a fortnight," he said irritably. "I've argued it out with the governor, but he says there is nothing to be done."

"Mr. Davidson's just longing to get back to his work," said his wife, with an anxious glance at him.

"We've been away for a year," he said, walking up and down the verandah. "The mission has been in charge of native missionaries and I'm terribly nervous that they've let things slide. They're good men, I'm not saying a word against them, God-fearing, devout, and truly Christian men—their Christianity would put many so-called Christians at home to the blush—but they're pitifully lacking in energy. They can make a stand once, they can make a stand twice, but they can't make a stand all the time. If you leave a mission in charge of a native missionary, no matter how trustworthy he seems, in course of time you'll find he's let abuses creep in."

Mr. Davidson stood still. With his tall, spare form, and his great eyes flashing out of his pale face, he was an impressive figure. His sincerity was obvious in the fire of his gestures and in his deep, ringing voice.

"I expect to have my work cut out for me. I shall act and I shall act promptly. If the tree is rotten it shall be cut down and cast into the flames."

And in the evening after the high tea which was their last meal, while they sat in the stiff parlour, the ladies working and Dr. Macphail smoking his pipe, the missionary told them of his work in the islands.

"When we went there they had no sense of sin at all," he said. "They broke the commandments one after the other and never knew they were doing wrong. And I think that was the most difficult part of my work, to instil into the natives the sense of sin."

The Macphails knew already that Davidson had worked in the Solomons for five years before he met his wife. She had been a missionary in China, and they had become acquainted in Boston, where they were both spending part of their leave to attend a missionary congress. On their marriage they had been appointed to the islands in which they had laboured ever since.

In the course of all the conversations they had had with Mr. Davidson one thing had shone out clearly and that was the man's unflinching courage. He was a medical missionary, and he was liable to be called at any time to one or other of the islands in the group. Even the whaleboat is not so very safe a conveyance in the stormy Pacific of the wet season, but often he would be sent for in a canoe, and then the danger was great. In cases of illness or accident he never hesitated. A dozen times he had spent the whole night baling for his life, and more than once Mrs. Davidson had given him up for lost.

"I'd beg him not to go sometimes," she said, "or at least to wait till the weather was more settled, but he'd never listen. He's obstinate, and when he's once made up his mind, nothing can move him."

"How can I ask the natives to put their trust in the Lord if I am afraid to do so myself?" cried Davidson. "And I'm not, I'm not. They know that if they send for me in their trouble I'll come if it's humanly possible. And do you think the Lord is going to abandon me when I am on his business? The wind blows at his bidding and the waves toss and rage at his word."

Dr. Macphail was a timid man. He had never been able to get used to the hurtling of the shells over the trenches, and when he was operating in an advanced dressing-station the sweat poured from his brow and dimmed his spectacles in the effort he made to control his unsteady hand. He shuddered a little as he looked at the missionary.

"I wish I could say that I've never been afraid," he said.

"I wish you could say that you believed in God," retorted the other.

But for some reason, that evening the missionary's thoughts travelled back to the early days he and his wife had spent on the islands.

"Sometimes Mrs. Davidson and I would look at one another and the tears would stream down our cheeks. We worked without ceasing, day and night, and we seemed to make no progress. I don't know what I should have done without her then. When I felt my heart sink, when I was very near despair, she gave me courage and hope."

Mrs. Davidson looked down at her work, and a slight colour rose to her thin cheeks. Her hands trembled a little. She did not trust herself to speak.

"We had no one to help us. We were alone, thousands of miles from any of our own people, surrounded by darkness. When I was broken and weary she would put her work aside and take the Bible and read to me till peace came and settled upon me like sleep upon the eyelids of a child, and when at last she closed the book she'd say: 'We'll save them in spite of themselves.' And I felt strong again in the Lord, and I answered: 'Yes, with God's help I'll save them. I must save them.' "

He came over to the table and stood in front of it as though it were a lectern.

"You see, they were so naturally depraved that they couldn't be brought to see their wickedness. We had to make sins out of what they thought were natural actions. We had to make it a sin, not only to commit adultery and to lie and thieve, but to expose their bodies, and to dance and not to come to church. I made it a sin for a girl to show her bosom and a sin for a man not to wear trousers."

"How?" asked Dr. Macphail, not without surprise.

"I instituted fines. Obviously the only way to make people realise that an action is sinful is to punish them if they commit it. I fined them if they didn't come to church, and I fined them if they danced. I fined them if they were improperly dressed. I had a tariff, and every sin had to be paid for either in money or work. And at last I made them understand."

"But did they never refuse to pay?"

"How could they?" asked the missionary.

"It would be a brave man who tried to stand up against Mr. Davidson," said his wife, tightening her lips.

Dr. Macphail looked at Davidson with troubled eyes. What he heard shocked him, but he hesitated to express his disapproval.

"You must remember that in the last resort I could expel them from their church membership."

"Did they mind that?"

Davidson smiled a little and gently rubbed his hands.

"They couldn't sell their copra. When the men fished they got no share of the catch. It meant something very like starvation. Yes, they minded quite a lot."

"Tell him about Fred Ohlson," said Mrs. Davidson.

The missionary fixed his fiery eyes on Dr. Macphail.

"Fred Ohlson was a Danish trader who had been in the islands a good many years. He was a pretty rich man as traders go and he wasn't very pleased when we came. You see, he'd had things very much his own way. He paid the natives what he liked for their copra, and he paid in goods and whiskey. He had a native wife, but he was flagrantly unfaithful to her. He was a drunkard. I gave him a chance to mend his ways, but he wouldn't take it. He laughed at me."

Davidson's voice fell to a deep bass as he said the last words, and he was silent for a minute or two. The silence was heavy with menace.

"In two years he was a ruined man. He'd lost everything he'd saved in a quarter of a century. I broke him, and at last he was forced to come to me like a beggar and beseech me to give him a passage back to Sydney."

"I wish you could have seen him when he came to see Mr. Davidson," said the missionary's wife. "He had been a fine, powerful man, with a lot of fat on him, and he had a great big voice, but now he was half the size, and he was shaking all over. He'd suddenly become an old man."

With abstracted gaze Davidson looked out into the night. The rain was falling again.

Suddenly from below came a sound, and Davidson turned and looked questioningly at his wife. It was the sound of a gramophone, harsh and loud, wheezing out a syncopated tune.

"What's that?" he asked.

Mrs. Davidson fixed her *pince-nez* more firmly on her nose.

"One of the second-class passengers has a room in the house. I guess it comes from there."

They listened in silence, and presently they heard the sound of dancing. Then the music stopped, and they heard the popping of corks and voices raised in animated conversation.

"I daresay she's giving a farewell party to her friends on board," said Dr. Macphail. "The ship sails at twelve, doesn't it?"

Davidson made no remark, but he looked at his watch.

"Are you ready?" he asked his wife.

She got up and folded her work.

"Yes, I guess I am," she answered.

"It's early to go to bed yet, isn't it?" said the doctor.

"We have a good deal of reading to do," explained Mrs. Davidson. "Wherever we are, we read a chapter of the Bible before retiring for the night and we study it with the commentaries, you know, and discuss it thoroughly. It's a wonderful training for the mind."

The two couples bade one another good night. Dr. and Mrs. Macphail were left alone. For two or three minutes they did not speak.

"I think I'll go and fetch the cards," the doctor said at last.

Mrs. Macphail looked at him doubtfully. Her conversation with the Davidsons had left her a little uneasy, but she did not like to say that she thought they had better not play cards when the Davidsons might come in at any moment. Dr. Macphail brought them and she watched him, though with a vague sense of guilt, while he laid out his patience. Below the sound of revelry continued.

It was fine enough next day, and the Macphails, condemned to spend a fortnight of idleness at Pago-Pago, set about making the best of things. They went down to the quay and got out of their boxes a number of books. The doctor called on the chief surgeon of the naval hospital and went round the beds with him. They left cards on the governor. They passed Miss Thompson on the road. The doctor took off his hat, and she gave him a "Good morning, doc," in a loud, cheerful voice. She was dressed as on the day before, in a white frock, and her shiny white boots with their high heels, her fat legs bulging over the tops of them, were strange things on that exotic scene.

"I don't think she's very suitably dressed, I must say," said Mrs. Macphail. "She looks extremely common to me."

When they got back to their house, she was on the verandah playing with one of the trader's dark children.

"Say a word to her," Dr. Macphail whispered to his wife. "She's all alone here, and it seems rather unkind to ignore her."

Mrs. Macphail was shy, but she was in the habit of doing what her husband bade her.

"I think we're fellow lodgers here," she said, rather foolishly.

"Terrible, ain't it, bein' cooped up in a one-horse burg like this?" answered Miss Thompson. "And they tell me I'm lucky to have gotten a room. I don' see myself livin' in a native house, and that's what some have to do. I don't know why they don't have a hotel."

They exchanged a few more words. Miss Thompson, loud-voiced and garrulous, was evidently quite willing to gossip, but Mrs. Macphail had a poor stock of small talk and presently she said:

"Well, I think we must go upstairs."

In the evening when they sat down to their high-tea Davidson on coming in said:

"I see that woman downstairs has a couple of sailors sitting there. I wonder how she's gotten acquainted with them."

"She can't be very particular," said Mrs. Davidson.

They were all rather tired after the idle, aimless day.

"If there's going to be a fortnight of this I don't know what we shall feel like at the end of it," said Dr. Macphail.

"The only thing to do is to portion out the day to different activities," answered the missionary. "I shall set aside a certain number of hours to study and a certain number to exercise, rain or shine—in the wet season you can't afford to pay any attention to the rain—and a certain number to recreation."

Dr. Macphail looked at his companion with misgiving. Davidson's programme oppressed him. They were eating Hamburger steak again. It seemed the only dish the cook knew how to make. Then below the gramophone began. Davidson started nervously when he heard it, but said nothing. Men's voices floated up. Miss Thompson's guests were joining in a well-known song and presently they heard her voice too, hoarse and loud. There was a good deal of shouting and laughing. The four people upstairs, trying to make conversation, listened despite themselves to the clink of glasses and the scrape of chairs. More people had evidently come. Miss Thompson was giving a party.

"I wonder how she gets them all in," said Mrs. Macphail, suddenly breaking into a medical conversation between the missionary and her husband.

It showed whither her thoughts were wandering. The twitch of Davidson's face proved that, though he spoke of scientific things, his mind was busy in the same direction. Suddenly, while the doctor was giving some experience of practice on the Flanders front, rather prosily, he sprang to his feet with a cry.

"What's the matter, Alfred?" asked Mrs. Davidson.

"Of course! It never occurred to me. She's out of Iwelei."

"She can't be."

"She came on board at Honolulu. It's obvious. And she's carrying on her trade here. Here."

He uttered the last word with a passion of indignation.

"What's Iwelei?" asked Mrs. Macphail.

He turned his gloomy eyes on her and his voice trembled with horror.

"The plague stop of Honolulu. The Red Light district. It was a blot on our civilisation."

Iwelei was on the edge of the city. You went down side streets by the harbour, in the darkness, across a rickety bridge, till you came to a deserted road, all ruts and holes, and then suddenly you came out into the light. There was parking room for motors on each side of the road, and there were saloons, tawdry and bright, each one noisy with its mechanical piano, and there were barbers' shops and tobacconists. There was a stir in the air and a sense of expectant gaiety. You turned down a narrow alley, either to the right or to the left, for the road divided Iwelei into two parts, and you found yourself in the district. There were rows of little bungalows, trim and neatly painted in green, and the pathway between them was broad and straight. It was laid out like a garden-city. In its respectable regularity, its order and spruceness, it gave an impression of sardonic horror; for never can the search for love have been so systematised and ordered. The pathways were lit by a rare lamp, but they would have been dark except for the lights that came from the open windows of the bungalows. Men wandered about, looking at the women who sat at their windows, reading or sewing, for the most part taking no notice of the passersby; and like the women they were of all nationalities. There were Americans, sailors from the ships in port, enlisted men off the gunboats, sombrely drunk, and soldiers from the regiments, white and black, quartered on the island; there were Japanese, walking in twos and threes; Hawaiians, Chinese in long robes, and Filipinos in preposterous hats. They were silent and as it were oppressed. Desire is sad.

"It was the most crying scandal of the Pacific," exclaimed Davidson vehemently. "The missionaries had been agitating against it for years, and at last the local press took it up. The police refused to stir. You know their argument. They say that vice is inevitable and consequently the best thing is to localise and control it. The truth is, they were paid. Paid. They were paid by the saloon-keepers, paid by the bullies, paid by the women themselves. At last they were forced to move."

"I read about it in the papers that came on board in Honolulu," said Dr. Macphail.

"Iwelei, with its sin and shame, ceased to exist on the very day we arrived. The whole population was brought before the justices. I don't know why I didn't understand at once what that woman was."

"Now you come to speak of it," said Mrs. Macphail, "I remember seeing her come on board only a few minutes before the boat sailed. I remember thinking at the time she was cutting it rather fine."

"How dare she come here!" cried Davidson indignantly. "I'm not going to allow it."

He strode towards the door.

"What are you doing to do?" asked Macphail.

"What do you expect me to do? I'm going to stop it. I'm not going to have this house turned into—into . . ."

He sought for a word that should not offend the ladies' ears. His eyes were flashing and his pale face was paler still in his emotion.

"It sounds as though there were three or four men down there," said the doctor. "Don't you think it's rather rash to go in just now?"

The missionary gave him a contemptuous look and without a word flung out of the room.

"You know Mr. Davidson very little if you think the fear of personal danger can stop him in the performance of his duty," said his wife.

She sat with her hands nervously clasped, a spot of colour on her high cheek bones, listening to what was about to happen below. They all listened. They heard him clatter down the wooden stairs and throw open the door. The singing stopped suddenly, but the gramophone continued to bray out its vulgar tune. They heard Davidson's voice and then the noise of something heavy falling. The music stopped. He had hurled the gramophone on the floor. Then again they heard Davidson's voice, they could not make out the words, then Miss Thompson's, loud and shrill, then a confused clamour as though several people were shouting together at the top of their lungs. Mrs. Davidson gave a little gasp, and she clenched her hands more tightly. Dr. Macphail looked uncertainly from her to his wife. He did not want to go down, but he wondered if they expected him to. Then there was something that sounded like a scuffle.

The noise now was more distinct. It might be that Davidson was being thrown out of the room. The door was slammed. There was a moment's silence and they heard Davidson come up the stairs again. He went to his room.

"I think I'll go to him," said Mrs. Davidson.

She got up and went out.

"If you want me, just call," said Mrs. Macphail, and then when the other was gone: "I hope he isn't hurt."

"Why couldn't he mind his own business?" said Dr. Macphail.

They sat in silence for a minute or two and then they both started, for the gramophone began to play once more, defiantly, and mocking voices shouted hoarsely the words of an obscene song.

Next day Mrs. Davidson was pale and tired. She complained of headache, and she looked old and wizened. She told Mrs. Macphail that the missionary had not slept at all; he had passed the night in a state of frightful agitation and at five had got up and gone out. A glass of beer had been thrown over him and his clothes were stained and stinking. But a sombre fire glowed in Mrs. Davidson's eyes when she spoke of Miss Thompson.

"She'll bitterly rue the day when she flouted Mr. Davidson," she said. "Mr. Davidson has a wonderful heart and no one who is in trouble has ever gone to him without being comforted, but he has no mercy for sin, and when his righteous wrath is excited he's terrible."

"Why, what will he do?" asked Mrs. Macphail.

"I don't know, but I wouldn't stand in that creature's shoes for anything in the world."

Mrs. Macphail shuddered. There was something positively alarming in the triumphant assurance of the little woman's manner. They were going out together that morning, and they went down the stairs side by side. Miss Thompson's door was open, and they saw her in a bedraggled dressing-gown, cooking something in a chafing-dish.

"Good morning," she called. "Is Mr. Davidson better this morning?"

They passed her in silence, with their noses in the air, as if she did not exist. They flushed, however, when she burst into a shout of derisive laughter. Mrs. Davidson turned on her suddenly.

"Don't you dare to speak to me," she screamed. "If you insult me I shall have you turned out of here."

"Say, did I ask Mr. Davidson to visit with me?"

"Don't answer her," whispered Mrs. Macphail hurriedly.

They walked on till they were out of earshot.

"She's brazen, brazen," burst from Mrs. Davidson.

Her anger almost suffocated her.

And on their way home they met her strolling towards the quay. She had all her finery on. Her great white hat with its vulgar, showy flowers was an affront. She called out cheerily to them as she went by, and a couple of American sailors who were standing there grinned as the ladies set their faces to an icy stare. They got in just before the rain began to fall again.

"I guess she'll get her fine clothes spoilt," said Mrs. Davidson with a bitter sneer.

Davidson did not come in till they were half way through dinner. He was wet through, but he would not change. He sat, morose and silent, refusing to eat more than a mouthful, and he stared at the slanting rain. When Mrs. Davidson told him of their two encounters with Miss Thompson he did not answer. His deepening frown alone showed that he had heard.

"Don't you think we ought to make Mr. Horn turn her out of here?" asked Mrs. Davidson. "We can't allow her to insult us."

"There doesn't seem to be any other place for her to go," said Macphail.

"She can live with one of the natives."

"In weather like this a native hut must be a rather uncomfortable place to live in."

"I lived in one for years," said the missionary.

When the little native girl brought in the fried bananas which formed the sweet they had every day, Davidson turned to her.

"Ask Miss Thompson when it would be convenient for me to see her," he said.

The girl nodded shyly and went out.

"What do you want to see her for, Alfred?" asked his wife.

"It's my duty to see her. I won't act till I've given her every chance."

"You don't know what she is. She'll insult you."

"Let her insult me. Let her spit on me. She has an immortal soul, and I must do all that is in my power to save it."

Mrs. Davidson's ears rang still with the harlot's mocking laughter. "She's gone too far."

"Too far for the mercy of God?" His eyes lit up suddenly and his voice grew mellow and soft. "Never. The sinner may be deeper in sin than the depth of hell itself, but the love of the Lord Jesus can reach him still."

The girl came back with the message.

"Miss Thompson's compliments and as long as Rev. Davidson don't come in business hours she'll be glad to see him any time."

The party received it in stony silence, and Dr. Macphail quickly effaced from his lips the smile which had come upon them. He knew his wife would be vexed with him if he found Miss Thompson's effrontery amusing.

They finished the meal in silence. When it was over the two ladies got up and took their work. Mrs. Macphail was making another of the innumerable comforters which she had turned out since the beginning of the war, and the doctor lit his pipe. But Davidson remained in his chair and with abstracted eyes stared at the table. At last he got up and without a word went out of the room. They heard him go down and they heard Miss Thompson's defiant "Come in" when he knocked at the door. He remained with her for an hour. And Dr. Macphail watched the rain. It was beginning to get on his nerves. It was not like our soft English rain that drops gently on the earth; it was unmerciful and somehow terrible; you felt in it the malignancy of the primitive powers of nature. It did not pour, it flowed. It was like a deluge from heaven, and it rattled on the roof of corrugated iron with a steady persistence that was maddening. It seemed to have a fury of its own. And sometimes you felt that you must scream if it did not stop, and then suddenly you felt powerless, as though your bones had suddenly become soft; and you were miserable and hopeless.

Macphail turned his head when the missionary came back. The two women looked up.

"I've given her every chance. I have exhorted her to repent. She is an evil woman."

He paused, and Dr. Macphail saw his eyes darken and his pale face grown hard and stern.

"Now I shall take the whips with which the Lord Jesus drove the usurers and the money changers out of the Temple of the Most High."

He walked up and down the room. His mouth was close set, and his black brows were frowning.

"If she fled to the uttermost parts of the earth I should pursue her."

With a sudden movement he turned round and strode out of the room. They heard him go downstairs again.

"What is he going to do?" asked Mrs. Macphail.

"I don't know." Mrs. Davidson took off her *pince-nez* and wiped them. "When he is on the Lord's work I never ask him questions."

She sighed a little.

"What is the matter?"

"He'll wear himself out. He doesn't know what it is to spare himself."

Dr. Macphail learnt the first results of the missionary's activity from the half-caste trader in whose house they lodged. He stopped the doctor when he passed the store and came out to speak to him on the stoop. His fat face was worried.

"The Rev. Davidson has been at me for letting Miss Thompson have a room here," he said, "but I didn't know what she was when I rented it to her. When people come and ask if I can rent them a room all I want to know is if they've the money to pay for it. And she paid me for hers a week in advance."

Dr. Macphail did not want to commit himself.

"When all's said and done it's your house. We're very much obliged to you for taking us in at all."

Horn looked at him doubtfully. He was not certain yet how definitely Macphail stood on the missionary's side.

"The missionaries are in with one another," he said, hesitatingly. "If they get it in for a trader he may just as well shut up his store and quit."

"Did he want you to turn her out?"

"No, he said so long as she behaved herself he couldn't ask me to do that. He said he wanted to be just to me. I promised she shouldn't have no more visitors. I've just been and told her."

"How did she take it?"

"She gave me Hell."

The trader squirmed in his old ducks. He had found Miss Thompson a rough customer.

"Oh, well, I daresay she'll get out. I don't suppose she wants to stay here if she can't have anyone in."

"There's nowhere she can go, only a native house, and no native'll take her now, not now that the missionaries have got their knife in her."

Dr. Macphail looked at the falling rain.

"Well, I don't suppose it's any good waiting for it to clear up."

In the evening when they sat in the parlour Davidson talked to them of his early days at college. He had had no means and had worked his way through by doing odd jobs during the vacations. There was silence downstairs. Miss Thompson was sitting in her little room alone. But suddenly the gramophone began to play. She had set it on in defiance, to cheat her loneliness, but there was no one to sing, and it had a melancholy note. It was like a cry for help. Davidson took no notice. He was in the middle of a long anecdote and without change of expression went on. The gramophone continued. Miss Thompson put on one reel after another. It looked as though the silence of the night were getting on her nerves. It was breathless and sultry. When the Macphails went to bed they could not sleep. They lay side by side with their eyes wide open, listening to the cruel singing of the mosquitoes outside their curtain.

"What's that?" whispered Mrs. Macphail at last.

They heard a voice, Davidson's voice, through the wooden partition. It went on with a monotonous, earnest insistence. He was praying aloud. He was praying for the soul of Miss Thompson.

Two or three days went by. Now when they passed Miss Thompson on the road she did not greet them with ironic cordiality or smile; she passed with her nose in the air, a sulky look on her painted face, frowning, as though she did not see them. The trader told Macphail that she had tried to get lodging elsewhere, but had failed. In the evening she played through the various reels of her gramophone, but the pretence of mirth was obvious now. The ragtime had a cracked, heartbroken rhythm as though it were a onestep of despair. When she began to play on Sunday Davidson sent Horn to beg her to stop at once since it was the Lord's day. The reel was taken off and the house was silent except for the steady pattering of the rain on the iron roof.

"I think she's getting a bit worked up," said the trader next day to Macphail. "She don't know what Mr. Davidson's up to and it makes her scared."

Macphail had caught a glimpse of her that morning and it struck him that her arrogant expression had changed. There was in her face a hunted look. The half-caste gave him a side-long glance.

"I suppose you don't know what Mr. Davidson is doing about it?" he hazarded.

"No, I don't."

It was singular that Horn should ask him that question, for he also had the idea that the missionary was mysteriously at work. He had an impression that he was weaving a net around the woman, carefully, systematically, and suddenly, when everything was ready would pull the strings tight.

"He told me to tell her," said the trader, "that if at any time she wanted him she only had to send and he'd come."

"What did she say when you told her that?"

"She didn't say nothing. I didn't stop. I just said what he said I was to and then I beat it. I thought she might be going to start weepin'."

"I have no doubt the loneliness is getting on her nerves," said the doctor. "And the rain—that's enough to make anyone jumpy," he continued irritably. "Doesn't it ever stop in this confounded place?"

"It goes on pretty steady in the rainy season. We have three hundred inches in a year. You see, it's the shape of the bay. It seems to attract the rain from all over the Pacific."

"Damn the shape of the bay," said the doctor.

He scratched his mosquito bites. He felt very short-tempered. When the rain stopped and the sun shone, it was like a hothouse, seething, humid, sultry, breathless, and you had a strange feeling that everything was growing with a savage violence. The natives, blithe and childlike by reputation, seemed then, with their tattooing and their dyed hair, to have something sinister in their appearance; and when they pattered along at your heels with their naked feet you looked back instinctively. You felt they might at any moment come behind you swiftly and thrust a long knife between your shoulder blades. You could not tell what dark thoughts lurked behind their wide-set eyes. They had a little the look of ancient Egyptians painted on a temple wall, and there was about them the terror of what is immeasurably old.

The missionary came and went. He was busy, but the Macphails did not know what he was doing. Horn told the doctor that he saw the governor every day, and once Davidson mentioned him.

"He looks as if he had plenty of determination," he said, "but when you come down to brass tacks he has no backbone."

"I suppose that means he won't do exactly what you want," suggested the doctor facetiously.

The missionary did not smile.

"I want him to do what's right. It shouldn't be necessary to persuade a man to do that."

"But there may be differences of opinion about what is right."

"If a man had a gangrenous foot would you have patience with anyone who hesitated to amputate it?"

"Gangrene is a matter of fact."

"And Evil?"

What Davidson had done soon appeared. The four of them had just finished their midday meal, and they had not yet separated for the siesta which the heat imposed on the ladies and on the doctor. Davidson had little patience with the slothful habit. The door was suddenly flung open and Miss Thompson came in. She looked round the room and then went up to Davidson.

"You low-down skunk, what have you been saying about me to the governor?"

She was spluttering with rage. There was a moment's pause. Then the missionary drew forward a chair.

"Won't you be seated, Miss Thompson? I've been hoping to have another talk with you."

"You poor low-life bastard."

She burst into a torrent of insult, foul and insolent. Davidson kept his grave eyes on her.

"I'm indifferent to the abuse you think fit to heap on me, Miss Thompson," he said, "but I must beg you to remember that ladies are present."

Tears by now were struggling with her anger. Her face was red and swollen as though she were choking.

"What has happened?" asked Dr. Macphail.

"A feller's just been in here and he says I gotter beat it on the next boat."

Was there a gleam in the missionary's eyes? His face remained impassive.

"You could hardly expect the governor to let you stay here under the circumstances."

"You done it," she shrieked. "You can't kid me. You done it."

"I don't want to deceive you. I urged the governor to take the only possible step consistent with his obligations."

"Why couldn't you leave me be? I wasn't doin' you no harm."

"You may be sure that if you had I should be the last man to resent it."

"Do you think I want to stay on in this poor imitation of a burg? I don't look no busher, do I?"

"In that case I don't see what cause of complaint you have," he answered.

She gave an inarticulate cry of rage and flung out of the room. There was a short silence.

"It's a relief to know that the governor has acted at last," said Davidson finally. "He's a weak man and he shilly-shallied. He said she was only here for a fortnight anyway, and if she went on to Apia that was under British jurisdiction and had nothing to do with him."

The missionary sprang to his feet and strode across the room.

"It's terrible the way the men who are in authority seek to evade their responsibility. They speak as though evil that was out of sight ceased to be evil. The very existence of that woman is a scandal and it does not help matters to shift it to another of the islands. In the end I had to speak straight from the shoulder."

Davidson's brow lowered, and he protruded his firm chin. He looked fierce and determined.

"What do you mean by that?"

"Our mission is not entirely without influence at Washington. I pointed out to the governor that it wouldn't do him any good if there was a complaint about the way he managed things here."

"When has she got to go?" asked the doctor, after a pause.

"The San Francisco boat is due here from Sydney next Tuesday. She's to sail on that."

That was in five days' time. It was next day, when he was coming back from the hospital where for want of something better to do Macphail spent most of his mornings, that the half-caste stopped him as he was going upstairs.

"Excuse me, Dr. Macphail, Miss Thompson's sick. Will you have a look at her?"

"Certainly."

Horn led him to her room. She was sitting in a chair idly, neither reading nor sewing, staring in front of her. She wore her white dress and the large hat with the flowers on it. Macphail noticed that her skin was yellow and muddy under her powder, and her eyes were heavy.

"I'm sorry to hear you're not well," he said.

"Oh, I ain't sick really. I just said that, because I just had to see you. I've got to clear on a boat that's going to 'Frisco."

She looked at him and he saw that her eyes were suddenly startled. She opened and clenched her hands spasmodically. The trader stood at the door, listening.

"So I understand," said the doctor.

She gave a little gulp.

"I guess it ain't very convenient for me to go to 'Frisco just now. I went to see the governor yesterday afternoon, but I couldn't get to him. I saw the secretary, and he told me I'd got to take that boat and that was all there was to it. I just had to see the governor, so I waited outside his house this morning, and when he come out I spoke to him. He didn't want to speak to me, I'll say, but I wouldn't let him shake me off, and at last he said he hadn't no objection to my staying here till the next boat to Sydney if the Rev. Davidson will stand for it."

She stopped and looked at Dr. Macphail anxiously.

"I don't know exactly what I can do," he said.

"Well, I thought maybe you wouldn't mind asking him. I swear to God I won't start anything here if he'll just only let me stay. I won't go out of the house if that'll suit him. It's no more'n a fortnight."

"I'll ask him."

"He won't stand for it," said Horn. "He'll have you out on Tuesday, so you may as well make up your mind to it."

"Tell him I can get work in Sydney, straight stuff, I mean. 'Taint asking very much."

"I'll do what I can."

"And come and tell me right way, will you? I can't set down to a thing till I get the dope one way or the other."

It was not an errand that much pleased the doctor, and, characteristically perhaps, he went at it indirectly. He told his wife what Miss Thompson had said to him and asked her to speak to Mrs. Davidson. The missionary's attitude seemed rather arbitrary and it could do no harm if the girl were allowed to stay in Pago-Pago another fortnight. But he was not prepared for the result of his diplomacy. The missionary came to him straightway.

"Mrs. Davidson tells me that Thompson has been speaking to you."

Dr. Macphail, thus directly tackled, had the shy man's resentment at being forced out into the open. He felt his temper rising, and he flushed.

"I don't see that it can make any difference if she goes to Sydney rather than to San Francisco, and so long as she promises to behave while she's here it's dashed hard to persecute her."

The missionary fixed him with his stern eyes.

"Why is she unwilling to go back to San Francisco?"

"I didn't enquire," answered the doctor with some asperity. "And I think one does better to mind one's own business."

Perhaps it was not a very tactful answer.

"The governor has ordered her to be deported by the first boat that leaves the island. He's only done his duty and I will not interfere. Her presence is a peril here."

"I think you're very harsh and tyrannical."

The two ladies looked up at the doctor with some alarm, but they need not have feared a quarrel, for the missionary smiled gently.

"I'm terribly sorry you should think that of me, Dr. Macphail. Believe me, my heart bleeds for that unfortunate woman, but I'm only trying to do my duty."

The doctor made no answer. He looked out of the window sullenly. For once it was not raining and across the bay you saw nestling among the trees the huts of a native village.

"I think I'll take advantage of the rain stopping to go out," he said.

"Please don't bear me malice because I can't accede to your wish," said Davidson, with a melancholy smile. "I respect you very much, doctor, and I should be sorry if you thought ill of me."

"I have no doubt you have sufficiently good opinion of yourself to bear mine with equanimity," he retorted.

"That's one on me," chuckled Davidson.

When Dr. Macphail, vexed with himself because he had been uncivil to no purpose, went downstairs, Miss Thompson was waiting for him with her door ajar.

"Well," she said, "have you spoken to him?"

"Yes, I'm sorry, he won't do anything," he answered, not looking at her in his embarrassment.

But then he gave her a quick glance, for a sob broke from her. He saw that her face was white with fear. It gave him a shock of dismay. And suddenly he had an idea.

"But don't give up hope yet. I think it's a shame the way they're treating you and I'm going to see the governor myself."

"Now?"

He nodded. Her face brightened.

"Say, that's real good of you. I'm sure he'll let me stay if you speak for me. I just won't do a thing I didn't ought all the time I'm here."

Dr. Macphail hardly knew why he had made up his mind to appeal to the governor. He was perfectly indifferent to Miss Thompson's affairs, but the missionary had irritated him, and with him temper was a smouldering thing. He found the governor at home. He was a large, handsome man, a sailor, with a grey toothbrush moustache; and he wore a spotless uniform of white drill.

"I've come to see you about a woman who's lodging in the same house as we are," he said. "Her name's Thompson."

"I guess I've heard nearly enough about her, Dr. Macphail," said the governor, smiling. "I've given her the order to get out next Tuesday and that's all I can do."

"I wanted to ask you if you couldn't stretch a point and let her stay here till the boat comes in from San Francisco so that she can go to Sydney. I will guarantee her good behavior."

The governor continued to smile, but his eyes grew small and serious.

"I'd be very glad to oblige you, Dr. Macphail, but I've given the order and it must stand."

The doctor put the case as reasonably as he could, but now the governor ceased to smile at all. He listened sullenly, with averted gaze. Macphail saw that he was making no impression.

"I'm sorry to cause any lady inconvenience, but she'll have to sail on Tuesday and that's all there is to it."

"But what difference can it make?"

"Pardon me, doctor, but I don't feel called upon to explain my official actions except to the proper authorities."

Macphail looked at him shrewdly. He remembered Davidson's hint that he had used threats, and in the governor's attitude he read a singular embarrassment.

"Davidson's a damned busybody," he said hotly.

"Between ourselves, Dr. Macphail, I don't say that I have formed a very favorable opinion of Mr. Davidson, but I am bound to confess that he was within his rights in pointing out to me the danger that the presence of a woman of Miss Thompson's character was to a place like this where a number of enlisted men are stationed among a native population."

He got up and Dr. Macphail was obliged to do so too.

"I must ask you to excuse me. I have an engagement. Please give my respects to Mrs. Macphail."

The doctor left him crest-fallen. He knew that Miss Thompson would be waiting for him, and unwilling to tell her himself that he had failed, he went into the house by the back door and sneaked up the stairs as though he had something to hide.

At supper he was silent and ill-at-ease, but the missionary was jovial and animated. Dr. Macphail thought his eyes rested on him now and then with triumphant good-humour. It struck him suddenly that Davidson knew of his visit to the governor and of its ill success. But how on earth could he have heard of it? There was something sinister about the power of that man. After supper he saw Horn on the verandah and, as though to have a casual word with him, went out.

"She wants to know if you've seen the governor," the trader whispered.

"Yes. He wouldn't do anything. I'm awfully sorry. I can't do anything more."

"I knew he wouldn't. They daren't go against the missionaries."

"What are you talking about?" said Davidson affably, coming out to join them.

"I was just saying there was no chance of your getting over to Apia for at least another week," said the trader glibly.

He left them, and the two men returned into the parlour. Mr. Davidson devoted one hour after each meal to recreation. Presently a timid knock was heard at the door.

"Come in," said Mrs. Davidson, in her sharp voice.

The door was not opened. She got up and opened it. They saw Miss Thompson standing at the threshold. But the change in her appearance was extraordinary. This was no longer the flaunting hussy who had jeered at them in the road, but a broken, frightened woman. Her hair, as a rule so elaborately arranged, was tumbling untidily over her neck. She wore bedroom slippers and a skirt and blouse. They were unfresh and bedraggled. She stood at the door with the tears streaming down her face and did not dare to enter.

"What do you want?" said Mrs. Davidson harshly.

"May I speak to Mr. Davidson?" she said in a choking voice.

The missionary rose and went towards her.

"Come right in, Miss Thompson," he said in cordial tones. "What can I do for you?"

She entered the room.

"Say, I'm sorry for what I said to you the other day an' for—for everythin' else. I guess I was a bit lit up. I beg pardon."

"Oh, it was nothing. I guess my back's broad enough to bear a few hard words."

She stepped towards him with a movement that was horribly cringing.

"You've got me beat. I'm all in. You won't make me go back to 'Frisco?"

His genial manner vanished and his voice grew on a sudden hard and stern.

"Why don't you want to go back there?"

She cowered before him.

"I guess my people live there. I don't want them to see me like this. I'll go anywhere else you say."

"Why don't you want to go back to San Francisco?"

"I've told you."

He leaned forward, staring at her, and his great, shining eyes seemed to try to bore into her soul. He gave a sudden gasp.

"The penitentiary."

She screamed, and then she fell at his feet, clasping his legs.

"Don't send me back there. I swear to you before God I'll be a good woman. I'll give all this up."

She burst into a torrent of confused supplication and the tears coursed down her painted cheeks. He leaned over her and, lifting her face, forced her to look at him.

"Is that it, the penitentiary?"

"I beat it before they could get me," she gasped. "If the bulls grab me it's three years for mine."

He let go his hold of her and she fell in a heap on the floor, sobbing bitterly. Dr. Macphail stood up.

"This alters the whole thing," he said. "You can't make her go back when you know this. Give her another chance. She wants to turn over a new leaf."

"I'm going to give her the finest chance she's ever had. If she repents let her accept her punishment."

She misunderstood the words and looked up. There was a gleam of hope in her heavy eyes.

"You'll let me go?"

"No. You shall sail for San Francisco on Tuesday."

She gave a groan of horror and then burst into low, hoarse shrieks which sounded hardly human, and she beat her head passionately on the ground. Dr. Macphail sprang to her and lifted her up.

"Come on, you mustn't do that. You'd better go to your room and lie down. I'll get you something."

He raised her to her feet and partly dragging her, partly carrying her, got her downstairs. He was furious with Mrs. Davidson and with his wife because they made no effort to help. The half-caste was standing on the landing and with his assistance he managed to get her on the bed. She was moaning and crying. She was almost insensible. He gave her a hypodermic injection. He was hot and exhausted when he went upstairs again.

"I've got her to lie down."

The two women and Davidson were in the same positions as when he had left them. They could not have moved or spoken since he went.

"I was waiting for you," said Davidson, in a strange, distant voice. "I want you all to pray with me for the soul of our erring sister."

He took the Bible off a shelf, and sat down at the table at which they had supped. It had not been cleared, and he pushed the tea-pot out of the way. In a powerful voice, resonant and deep, he read to them the chapter in which is narrated the meeting of Jesus Christ with the woman taken in adultery.

"Now kneel with me and let us pray for the soul of our dear sister, Sadie Thompson."

He burst into a long, passionate prayer in which he implored God to have mercy on the sinful woman. Mrs. Macphail and Mrs. Davidson knelt with covered eyes. The doctor, taken by surprise, awkward and sheepish, knelt too. The missionary's prayer had a savage eloquence. He was extraordinarily moved, and as he spoke the tears ran down his cheeks. Outside, the pitiless rain fell, fell steadily, with a fierce malignity that was all too human.

At last he stopped. He paused for a moment and said:

"We will now repeat the Lord's prayer."

They said it and then, following him, they rose from their knees. Mrs. Davidson's face was pale and restful. She was comforted and at peace, but the Macphails felt suddenly bashful. They did not know which way to look.

"I'll just go down and see how she is," said Dr. Macphail.

When he knocked at her door it was opened for him by Horn. Miss Thompson was in a rocking-chair, sobbing quietly.

"What are you doing there?" exclaimed Macphail. "I told you to lie down."

"I can't lie down. I want to see Mr. Davidson."

"My poor child, what do you think is the good of it? You'll never move him."

"He said he'd come if I sent for him."

Macphail motioned to the trader.

"Go and fetch him."

He waited with her in silence while the trader went upstairs. Davidson came in.

"Excuse me for asking you to come here," she said, looking at him sombrely.

"I was expecting you to send for me. I knew the Lord would answer my prayer."

They stared at one another for a moment and then she looked away. She kept her eyes averted when she spoke.

"I've been a bad woman. I want to repent."

"Thank God! thank God! He has heard our prayers."

He turned to the two men.

"Leave me alone with her. Tell Mrs. Davidson that our prayers have been answered."

They went out and closed the door behind them.

"Gee whizz," said the trader.

That night Dr. Macphail could not get to sleep till late, and when he heard the missionary come upstairs he looked at his watch. It was two o'clock. But even then he did not go to bed at once, for through the wooden partition that separated their rooms he heard him praying aloud, till he himself, exhausted, feel asleep.

When he saw him next morning he was surprised at his appearance. He was paler than ever, tired, but his eyes shone with an inhuman fire. It looked as though he were filled with an overwhelming joy.

"I want you to go down presently and see Sadie," he said. "I can't hope that her body is better, but her soul—her soul is transformed."

The doctor was feeling wan and nervous.

"You were with her very late last night," he said.

"Yes, she couldn't bear to have me leave her."

"You look as pleased as Punch," the doctor said irritably.

Davidson's eyes shone with ecstasy.

"A great mercy has been vouchsafed me. Last night I was privileged to bring a lost soul to the loving arms of Jesus."

Miss Thompson was again in the rocking-chair. The bed had not been made. The room was in disorder. She had not troubled to dress herself, but wore a dirty dressing-gown, and her hair was tied in a sluttish knot. She had given her face a dab with a wet towel, but it was all swollen and creased with crying. She looked a drab.

She raised her eyes dully when the doctor came in. She was cowed and broken.

"Where's Mr. Davidson?" she asked.

"He'll come presently if you want him," answered Macphail acidly. "I came here to see how you were."

"Oh, I guess I'm O.K. You needn't worry about that."

"Have you had anything to eat?"

"Horn brought me some coffee."

She looked anxiously at the door.

"D'you think he'll come down soon? I feel as if it wasn't so terrible when he's with me."

"Are you still going on Tuesday?"

"Yes, he says I've got to go. Please tell him to come right along. You can't do me any good. He's the only one as can help me now."

"Very well," said Dr. Macphail.

During the next three days the missionary spent almost all his time with Sadie Thompson. He joined the others only to have his meals. Dr. Macphail noticed that he hardly ate.

"He's wearing himself out," said Mrs. Davidson pitifully. "He'll have a breakdown if he doesn't take care, but he won't spare himself."

She herself was white and pale. She told Mrs. Macphail that she had no sleep. When the missionary came upstairs from Miss Thompson he prayed till he was exhausted, but even then he did not sleep for long. After an hour or two he got up and dressed himself, and went for a tramp along the bay. He had strange dreams.

"This morning he told me that he'd been dreaming about the mountains of Nebraska," said Mrs. Davidson.

"That's curious," said Dr. Macphail.

He remembered seeing them from the windows of the train when he crossed America. They were like huge molehills, rounded and smooth, and they rose from the plain abruptly. Dr. Macphail remembered how it struck him that they were like a woman's breasts.

Davidson's restlessness was intolerable even to himself. But he was buoyed up by a wonderful exhilaration. He was tearing out by the roots the last vestiges of sin that lurked in the hidden corners of that poor woman's heart. He read with her and prayed with her.

"It's wonderful," he said to them one day at supper. "It's a true rebirth. Her soul, which was black as night, is now pure and white like the new-fallen snow. I am humble and afraid. Her remorse for all her sins is beautiful. I am not worthy to touch the hem of her garment."

"Have you the heart to send her back to San Francisco?" said the doctor. "Three years in an American prison. I should have thought you might have saved her from that?"

"Ah, but don't you see? It's necessary. Do you think my heart doesn't bleed for her? I love her as I love my wife and my sister. All the time that she is in prison I shall suffer all the pain that she suffers."

"Bunkum," cried the doctor impatiently.

"You don't understand because you're blind. She's sinned, and she must suffer. I know what she'll endure. She'll be starved and tortured and humiliated. I want her to accept the punishment of man as a sacrifice to God. I want her to accept it joyfully. She has an opportunity which is offered to very few of us. God is very good and very merciful."

Davidson's voice trembled with excitement. He could hardly articulate the words that tumbled passionately from his lips.

"All day I pray with her and when I leave her I pray again, I pray with all my might and main, so that Jesus may grant her this great mercy. I want to put in her heart the passionate desire to be punished so that at the end, even if I offered to let her go, she would refuse. I want her to feel that the bitter punishment of prison is the thank-offering that she places at the feet of our Blessed Lord, who gave his life for her."

The days passed slowly. The whole household, intent on the wretched, tortured woman downstairs, lived in a state of unnatural excitement. She was like a victim that was being prepared for the savage rites of a bloody idolatry. Her terror numbed her. She could not bear to let Davidson out of her sight; it was only when he was with her that she had courage, and she hung upon him with a slavish dependence. She cried a great deal, and she read the Bible, and prayed. Sometimes she was exhausted and apathetic. Then she did indeed look forward to her ordeal, for it seemed to offer an escape, direct and concrete, from the anguish she was enduring. She could not bear much longer the vague terrors which now assailed her. With her sins she had put aside all personal vanity, and she slopped about her room, unkempt and dishevelled, in her tawdry dressing-gown. She had not taken off her night-dress for four days, nor put on stockings. Her room was littered and untidy. Meanwhile the rain fell with a cruel persistence. You felt that the heavens must at last be empty of water, but still it poured down, straight and heavy, with a maddening iteration, on the iron roof. Everything was damp and clammy. There was mildew on the walls and on the boots that stood on the floor. Through the sleepless nights the mosquitoes droned their angry chant.

"If it would only stop raining for a single day it wouldn't be so bad," said Dr. Macphail.

They all looked forward to the Tuesday when the boat for San Francisco was to arrive from Sydney. The strain was intolerable. So far as Dr. Macphail was concerned, his pity and his resentment were alike extinguished by his desire to be rid of the unfortunate woman. The inevitable must be accepted. He felt he would breathe more freely when the ship had sailed. Sadie Thompson was to be escorted on board by a clerk in the governor's office. This person called on the Monday evening and told Miss Thompson to be prepared at eleven in the morning. Davidson was with her.

"I'll see that everything is ready. I mean to come on board with her myself."

Miss Thompson did not speak.

When Dr. Macphail blew out his candle and crawled cautiously under his mosquito curtains, he gave a sigh of relief.

"Well, thank God that's over. By this time to-morrow she'll be gone."

"Mrs. Davidson will be glad too. She says he's wearing himself to a shadow," said Mrs. Macphail. "She's a different woman."

"Who?"

"Sadie. I should never have thought it possible. It makes one humble."

Dr. Macphail did not answer, and presently he fell asleep. He was tired out, and he slept more soundly than usual.

He was awakened in the morning by a hand placed on his arm, and, starting up, saw Horn by the side of his bed. The trader put his finger on his mouth to prevent any exclamation from Dr. Macphail and beckoned to him to come. As a rule he wore shabby ducks, but now he was barefoot and wore only the *lava-lava* of the natives. He looked suddenly savage, and Dr. Macphail, getting out of bed, saw that he was heavily tattooed. Horn made him a sign to come on to the verandah. Dr. Macphail got out of bed and followed the trader out.

"Don't make a noise," he whispered. "You're wanted. Put on a coat and some shoes. Quick."

Dr. Macphail's first thought was that something had happened to Miss Thompson.

"What is it? Shall I bring my instruments?"

"Hurry, please, hurry."

Dr. Macphail crept back into the bedroom, put on a waterproof over his pajamas, and a pair of rubber-soled shoes. He rejoined the trader, and together they tiptoed down the stairs. The door leading out to the road was open and at it were standing half a dozen natives.

"What is it?" repeated the doctor.

"Come along with me," said Horn.

He walked out and the doctor followed him. The natives came after them in a little bunch. They crossed the road and came on to the beach. The doctor saw a group of natives standing round some object at the water's edge. They hurried along, a couple of dozen yards perhaps, and the natives opened out as the doctor came up. The trader pushed him forward. Then he saw, lying half in the water and half out, a dreadful object, the body of Davidson. Dr. Macphail bent down—he was not a man to lose his head in an emergency—and turned the body over. The throat was cut from ear to ear, and in the right hand was still the razor with which the deed was done.

"He's quite cold," said the doctor. "He must have been dead some time."

"One of the boys saw him lying there on his way to work just now and came and told me. Do you think he did it himself?"

"Yes. Someone ought to go for the police."

Horn said something in the native tongue, and two youths started off.

"We must leave him here till they come," said the doctor.

"They mustn't take him into my house. I won't have him in my house."

"You'll do what the authorities say," replied the doctor sharply. "In point of fact I expect they'll take him to the mortuary."

They stood waiting where they were. The trader took a cigarette from a fold in his *lava-lava* and gave one to Dr. Macphail. They smoked while they stared at the corpse. Dr. Macphail could not understand.

"Why do you think he did it?" asked Horn.

The doctor shrugged his shoulders. In a little while native police came along, under the charge of a marine, with a stretcher, and immediately afterwards a couple of naval officers and a naval doctor. They managed everything in a businesslike manner.

"What about the wife?" said one of the officers.

"Now that you've come I'll go back to the house and get some things on. I'll see that it's broken to her. She'd better not see him till he's been fixed up a little."

"I guess that's right," said the naval doctor.

When Dr. Macphail went back he found his wife nearly dressed.

"Mrs. Davidson's in a dreadful state about her husband," she said to him as soon as he appeared. "He hasn't been to bed all night. She heard him leave Miss Thompson's room at two, but he went out. If he's been walking about since then he'll be absolutely dead."

Dr. Macphail told her what had happened and asked her to break the news to Mrs. Davidson.

"But why did he do it?" she asked, horror-stricken.

"I don't know."

"But I can't. I can't."

"You must."

She gave him a frightened look and went out. He heard her go into Mrs. Davidson's room. He waited a minute to gather himself together and then began to shave and wash. When he was dressed he sat down on the bed and waited for his wife. At last she came.

"She wants to see him," she said.

"They've taken him to the mortuary. We'd better go down with her. How did she take it?"

"I think she's stunned. She didn't cry. But she's trembling like a leaf."

"We'd better go at once."

When they knocked at her door Mrs. Davidson came out. She was very pale, but dry-eyed. To the doctor she seemed unnaturally composed. No word was exchanged, and they set out in silence down the road. When they arrived at the mortuary Mrs. Davidson spoke.

"Let me go in and see him alone."

They stood aside. A native opened a door for her and closed it behind her. They sat down and waited. One or two white men came and talked to them in undertones. Dr. Macphail told them again what he knew of the tragedy. At last the door was quietly opened and Mrs. Davidson came out. Silence fell upon them.

"I'm ready to go back now," she said.

Her voice was hard and steady. Dr. Macphail could not understand the look in her eyes. Her pale face was very stern. They walked back slowly, never saying a word, and at last they came round the bend on the other side of which stood their house. Mrs. Davidson gave a gasp, and for a moment they stopped still. An incredible sound assaulted their ears. The gramophone which had been silent for so long was playing, playing ragtime loud and harsh.

"What's that?" cried Mrs. Macphail with horror.

"Let's go on," said Mrs. Davidson.

They walked up the steps and entered the hall. Miss Thompson was standing at her door, chatting with a sailor. A sudden change had taken place in her. She was no longer the cowed drudge of the last days. She was dressed in all her finery, in her white dress, with the high shiny boots over which her fat legs bulged in their cotton stockings; her hair was elaborately arranged; and she wore that enormous hat covered with gaudy flowers. Her face was painted, her eyebrows were boldly black, and her lips were scarlet. She held herself erect. She was the flaunting queen that they had known at first. As they came in she broke into a loud, jeering laugh; and then, when Mrs. Davidson involuntarily stopped, she collected the spittle in her mouth and spat. Mrs. Davidson cowered back, and two red spots rose suddenly to her cheeks. Then, covering her face with her hands, she broke away and ran quickly up the stairs. Dr. Macphail was outraged. He pushed past the woman into her room.

"What the devil are you doing?" he cried. "Stop that damned machine."

He went up to it and tore the record off. She turned on him.

"Say, doc, you can that stuff with me. What the hell are you doin' in my room?"

"What do you mean?" he cried. "What d'you mean?"

She gathered herself together. No one could describe the scorn of her expression or the contemptuous hatred she put into her answer.

"You men! You filthy, dirty pigs! You're all the same, all of you. Pigs! Pigs!"

Dr. Macphail gasped. He understood.

QUESTIONS FOR DISCUSSION

1. Explain the ending of the story: What did Macphail understand? What happened between Sadie and Davidson just before Davidson's suicide?
2. Why did Davidson commit suicide? Discuss his character traits, his psychological aberrations, and his religious and moral motivations for his final act. Is the motivation convincing?
3. "Rain" accomplishes its purpose through one central conflict (the conflict *within* Davidson) and four subordinate (external) conflicts. Define these and explain what each contributes to the story's conflict, characterization, and theme.
4. "Rain" can be considered a Freudian analysis of the results of religious fanaticism; it can also be considered a definition of healthy versus unhealthy morality. Define the following terms: Puritanism, Freudianism, pragmatism, Hebraism, and Christianity. Then explain the above statements.
5. Discuss the relationship of the environment to (a) the story, and (b) the theme of the story. What details of the environment are symbolic? What do they stand for? In what sense are the characters in "Rain" also symbols?
6. Define the ironies that are inherent in both Davidson's and Macphail's religious and moral positions.
7. What Biblical parallels can you find in "Rain"? (For example the story has many parallels to the book of Genesis.) What purpose do these parallels serve in the story?
8. The point of view of "Rain" is peripheral. Why has Maugham chosen this point of view? Could he have accomplished his theme by viewing the story from any other position? Why or why not? Maugham's choice of narrator is third person, though there is little question that Macphail is Maugham. Why, then, do you think that the author chose to tell the story in third person rather than first?

WILLIAM FAULKNER

That Evening Sun

I

Monday is no different from any other weekday in Jefferson now. The streets are paved now, and the telephone and electric companies are cutting down more and more of the shade trees—the water oaks, the maples and locusts and elms—to make room for iron poles bearing clusters of bloated and ghostly and bloodless grapes, and we have a city laundry which makes the rounds on Monday morning, gathering the bundles of clothes into bright-colored, specially made motorcars: the soiled wearing of a whole week now flees apparitionlike behind alert and irritable electric horns, with a long diminishing noise of rubber and asphalt like tearing silk, and even the Negro women who still take in white people's washing after the old custom, fetch and deliver it in automobiles.

But fifteen years ago, on Monday morning the quiet, dusty, shady streets would be full of Negro women with, balanced on their steady, turbaned heads, bundles of clothes tied up in sheets, almost as large as cotton bales, carried so without touch of hand between the kitchen door of the white house and the blackened washpot beside a cabin door in Negro Hollow.

Nancy would set her bundle on the top of her head, then upon the bundle in turn she would set the black straw sailor hat which she wore winter and summer. She was tall, with a high, sad face sunken a little where her teeth were missing. Sometimes we would go a part of the way down the lane and across the pasture with her, to watch the balanced bundle and the hat that never bobbed nor wavered, even when she walked down into the ditch and up the other side and stooped through the fence. She would go down on her hands and knees and crawl through the gap, her head rigid, uptilted, the bundle steady as a rock or a balloon, and rise to her feet again and go on.

Sometimes the husbands of the washing women would fetch and

deliver the clothes, but Jesus never did that for Nancy, even before Father told him to stay away from our house, even when Dilsey was sick and Nancy would come to cook for us.

And then about half the time we'd have to go down the lane to Nancy's cabin and tell her to come on and cook breakfast. We would stop at the ditch, because Father told us to not have anything to do with Jesus—he was a short black man, with a razor scar down his face—and we would throw rocks at Nancy's house until she came to the door, leaning her head around it without any clothes on.

"What yawl mean, chunking my house?" Nancy said. "What you little devils mean?"

"Father says for you to come on and get breakfast," Caddy said. "Father says it's over a half an hour now, and you've got to come this minute."

"I ain't studying no breakfast," Nancy said. "I going to get my sleep out."

"I bet you're drunk," Jason said. "Father says you're drunk. Are you drunk, Nancy?"

"Who says I is?" Nancy said. "I got to get my sleep out. I ain't studying no breakfast."

So after a while we quit chunking the cabin and went back home. When she finally came, it was too late for me to go to school. So we thought it was whiskey until that day they arrested her again and they were taking her to jail and they passed Mr. Stovall. He was the cashier in the bank and a deacon in the Baptist church, and Nancy began to say:

"When you going to pay me, white man? When you going to pay me, white man? It's been three times now since you paid me a cent—" Mr. Stovall knocked her down, but she kept on saying, "When you going to pay me, white man? It's been three times now since—" until Mr. Stovall kicked her in the mouth with his heel and the marshal caught Mr. Stovall back, and Nancy lying in the street, laughing. She turned her head and spat out some blood and teeth and said, "It's been three times now since he paid me a cent."

That was how she lost her teeth, and all that day they told about Nancy and Mr. Stovall, and all that night the ones that passed the jail could hear Nancy singing and yelling. They could see her hands holding to the window bars, and a lot of them stopped along the fence, listening to her and to the jailer trying to make her stop. She didn't shut up until almost daylight, when the jailer began to hear a bumping and scraping upstairs and he went up there and found Nancy hanging from the window bar. He said that it was cocaine and not whiskey, because no nigger would try to commit suicide unless he was full of cocaine, because a nigger full of cocaine wasn't a nigger any longer.

The jailer cut her down and revived her; then he beat her, whipped her. She had hung herself with her dress. She had fixed it all right, but when they arrested her she didn't have on anything except a dress and so she didn't have anything to tie her hands with and she couldn't make her hands let go of the window ledge. So the jailer heard the noise and ran up there and found Nancy hanging from the window, stark naked, her belly already swelling out a little, like a little balloon.

When Dilsey was sick in her cabin and Nancy was cooking for us, we could see her apron swelling out; that was before Father told Jesus to stay away from the house. Jesus was in the kitchen, sitting behind the stove, with his razor scar on his black face like a piece of dirty string. He said it was a watermelon that Nancy had under her dress.

"It never come off of your vine, though," Nancy said.

"Off of what vine?" Caddy said.

"I can cut down the vine it did come off of," Jesus said.

"What makes you want to talk like that before these chillen?" Nancy said. "Whyn't you go on to work? You done et. You want Mr. Jason to catch you hanging around his kitchen, talking that way before these chillen?"

"Talking what way?" Caddy said. "What vine?"

"I can't hang around white man's kitchen," Jesus said. "But white man can hang around mine. White man can come in my house, but I can't stop him. When white man want to come in my house, I ain't got no house. I can't stop him, but he can't kick me outen it. He can't do that."

Dilsey was still sick in her cabin. Father told Jesus to stay off our place, Dilsey was still sick. It was a long time. We were in the library after supper.

"Isn't Nancy through in the kitchen yet?" Mother said. "It seems to me that she has had plenty of time to have finished the dishes."

"Let Quentin go and see," Father said. "Go and see if Nancy is through, Quentin. Tell her she can go on home."

I went to the kitchen. Nancy was through. The dishes were put away and the fire was out. Nancy was sitting in a chair, close to the cold stove. She looked at me.

"Mother wants to know if you are through," I said.

"Yes," Nancy said. She looked at me. "I done finished." She looked at me.

"What is it?" I said. "What is it?"

"I ain't nothing but a nigger," Nancy said. "It ain't none of my fault."

She looked at me, sitting in the chair before the cold stove, the sailor hat on her head. I went back to the library. It was the cold stove and all, when you think of a kitchen being warm and busy and cheerful. And with a cold stove and the dishes all put away, and nobody wanting to eat at that hour.

"Is she through?" Mother said.

"Yessum," I said.

"What is she doing?" Mother said.

"She's not doing anything. She's through."

"I'll go and see," Father said.

"Maybe she's waiting for Jesus to come and take her home," Caddy said.

"Jesus is gone," I said. Nancy told us how one morning she woke up and Jesus was gone.

"He quit me," Nancy said. "Done gone to Memphis, I reckon. Dodging them city *po*-lice for a while, I reckon."

"And a good riddance," Father said. "I hope he stays there."

"Nancy's scaired of the dark," Jason said.

"So are you," Caddy said.

"I'm not," Jason said.

"Scairy cat," Caddy said.

"I'm not," Jason said.

"You, Candace!" Mother said. Father came back.

"I am going to walk down the lane with Nancy," he said. "She says that Jesus is back."

"Has she seen him?" Mother said.

"No. Some Negro sent her word that he was back in town. I won't be long."

"You'll leave me alone, to take Nancy home?" Mother said. "Is her safety more precious to you than mine?"

"I won't be long," Father said.

"You'll leave these children unprotected, with that Negro about?"

"I'm going too," Caddy said. "Let me go, Father."

"What would he do with them, if he were unfortunate enough to have them?" Father said.

"I want to go, too," Jason said.

"Jason!" Mother said. She was speaking to Father. You could tell that by the way she said the name. Like she believed that all day Father had been trying to think of doing the thing she wouldn't like the most, and that she knew all the time that after a while he would think of it. I stayed quiet, because Father and I both knew that Mother would want him to make me stay with her if she just thought of it in time. So Father didn't look at me. I was the oldest. I was nine and Caddy was seven and Jason was five.

"Nonsense," Father said. "We won't be long."

Nancy had her hat on. We came to the lane. "Jesus always been good to me," Nancy said. "Whenever he had two dollars, one of them was mine." We walked in the lane. "If I can just get through the lane," Nancy said, "I be all right then."

The lane was always dark. "This is where Jason got scaired on Hallowe'en," Caddy said.

"I didn't," Jason said.

"Can't Aunt Rachel do anything with him?" Father said. Aunt Rachel was old. She lived in a cabin beyond Nancy's, by herself. She had white hair and she smoked a pipe in the door, all day long; she didn't work any more. They said she was Jesus' mother. Sometimes she said she was and sometimes she said she wasn't any kin to Jesus.

"Yes you did," Caddy said. "You were scairder than Frony. You were scairder than T.P. even. Scairder than niggers."

"Can't nobody do nothing with him," Nancy said. "He say I done woke up the devil in him and ain't but one thing going to lay it down again."

"Well, he's gone now," Father said. "There's nothing for you to be afraid of now. And if you'd just let white men alone."

"Let what white men alone?" Caddy said. "How let them alone?"

"He ain't gone nowhere," Nancy said. "I can feel him. I can feel him now, in this lane. He hearing us talk, every word, hid somewhere, waiting. I ain't seen him, and I ain't going to see him again but once more, with that razor in his mouth. That razor on that string down his back, inside his shirt. And then I ain't going to be even surprised."

"I wasn't scaired," Jason said.

"If you'd behave yourself, you'd have kept out of this," Father said. "But it's all right now. He's probably in Saint Louis now. Probably got another wife by now and forgot all about you."

"If he has, I better not find out about it," Nancy said. "I'd stand there right over them, and every time he wropped her, I'd cut that arm off. I'd cut his head off and I'd slit her belly and I'd shove—"

"Hush," Father said.

"Slit whose belly, Nancy?" Caddy said.

"I wasn't scaired," Jason said. "I'd walk right down this lane by myself."

"Yah," Caddy said. "You wouldn't dare to put your foot down in it if we were not here too."

II

Dilsey was still sick, so we took Nancy home every night until Mother said, "How much longer is this going on? I to be left alone in this big house while you take home a frightened Negro?"

We fixed a pallet in the kitchen for Nancy. One night we waked up, hearing the sound. It was not singing and it was not crying, coming up the dark stairs. There was a light in Mother's room and we heard Father going down the hall, down the back stairs, and Caddy and I went into the hall. The floor was cold. Our toes curled away from it while we listened to the sound. It was like singing and it wasn't like singing, like the sound that Negroes make.

Then it stopped and we heard Father going down the back stairs, and we went to the head of the stairs. Then the sound began again, in the stairway, not loud, and we could see Nancy's eyes halfway up the stairs, against the wall. They looked like cat's eyes do, like a big cat against the wall, watching us. When we came down the steps to where she was, she quit making the sound again, and we stood there until Father came back up from the kitchen, with his pistol in his hand. He went back down with Nancy and they came back with Nancy's pallet.

We spread the pallet in our room. After the light in Mother's room went off, we could see Nancy's eyes again. "Nancy," Caddy whispered, "are you asleep, Nancy?"

Nancy whispered something. It was oh or no, I don't know which. Like nobody had made it, like it came from nowhere and went nowhere, until it was like Nancy was not there at all; that I had looked so hard at her eyes on the stairs that they had got printed on my eyeballs, like the sun does when you have closed your eyes and there is no sun. "Jesus," Nancy whispered. "Jesus."

"Was it Jesus?" Caddy said. "Did he try to come into the kitchen?"

"Jesus," Nancy said. Like this: Jeeeeeeeeeeeeeeeesus, until the sound went out, like a match or a candle does.

"It's the other Jesus she means," I said.

"Can you see us, Nancy?" Caddy whispered. "Can you see our eyes too?"

"I ain't nothing but a nigger," Nancy said. "God knows. God knows."

"What did you see down there in the kitchen?" Caddy whispered. "What tried to get in?"

"God knows," Nancy said. We could see her eyes. "God knows."

Dilsey got well. She cooked dinner. "You'd better stay in bed a day or two longer," Father said.

"What for?" Dilsey said. "If I had been a day later, this place would be to rack and ruin. Get on out of here now, and let me get my kitchen straight again."

Dilsey cooked supper too. And that night, just before dark, Nancy came into the kitchen.

"How do you know he's back?" Dilsey said. "You ain't seen him."

"Jesus is a nigger," Jason said.

"I can feel him," Nancy said. "I can feel him laying yonder in the ditch."

"Tonight?" Dilsey said. "Is he there tonight?"

"Dilsey's a nigger too," Jason said.

"You try to eat something," Dilsey said.

"I don't want nothing," Nancy said.

"I ain't a nigger," Jason said.

"Drink some coffee," Dilsey said. She poured a cup of coffee for Nancy. "Do you know he's out there tonight? How come you know it's tonight?"

"I know," Nancy said. "He's there, waiting. I know. I done lived with him too long. I know what he is fixing to do fore he know it himself."

"Drink some coffee," Dilsey said. Nancy held the cup to her mouth and blew into the cup. Her mouth pursed out like a spreading adder's, like a rubber mouth, like she had blown all the color out of her lips with blowing the coffee.

"I ain't a nigger," Jason said. "Are you a nigger, Nancy?"

"I hellborn, child," Nancy said. "I won't be nothing soon. I going back where I come from soon."

III

She began to drink the coffee. While she was drinking, holding the cup in both hands, she began to make the sound again. She made the sound into the cup and the coffee sploshed out onto her hands and her dress. Her eyes looked at us and she sat there, her elbows on her knees, holding the cup in both hands, looking at us across the wet cup, making the sound.

"Look at Nancy," Jason said. "Nancy can't cook for us now. Dilsey's got well now."

"You hush up," Dilsey said. Nancy held the cup in both hands, looking at us, making the sound, like there were two of them: one looking at us and the other making the sound. "Whyn't you let Mr. Jason telefoam the marshal?" Dilsey said. Nancy stopped then, holding the cup in her long brown hands. She tried to drink some coffee again, but it sploshed out of the cup, onto her hands and her dress, and she put the cup down. Jason watched her.

"I can't swallow it," Nancy said. "I swallows but it won't go down me."

"You go down to the cabin," Dilsey said. "Frony will fix you a pallet and I'll be there soon."

"Won't no nigger stop him," Nancy said.

"I ain't a nigger," Jason said. "Am I, Dilsey?"

"I reckon not," Dilsey said. She looked at Nancy. "I don't reckon so. What you going to do, then?"

Nancy looked at us. Her eyes went fast, like she was afraid there wasn't time to look, without hardly moving at all. She looked at us, at all three of us at one time. "You member that night I stayed in yawl's room?" she said. She told about how we waked up early the next morning, and played. We had to play quiet, on her pallet, until Father woke up and it was time to get breakfast. "Go and ask your maw to let me stay here tonight," Nancy said. "I won't need no pallet. We can play some more."

Caddy asked Mother. Jason went too. "I can't have Negroes sleeping in the bedrooms," Mother said. Jason cried. He cried until Mother said he couldn't have any dessert for three days if he didn't stop. Then Jason said he would stop if Dilsey would make a chocolate cake. Father was there.

"Why don't you do something about it?" Mother said. "What do we have officers for?"

"Why is Nancy afraid of Jesus?" Caddy said. "Are you afraid of Father, Mother?"

"What could the officers do?" Father said. "If Nancy hasn't seen him, how could the officers find him?"

"Then why is she afraid?" Mother said.

"She says he is there. She says she knows he is there tonight."

"Yet we pay taxes," Mother said. "I must wait here alone in this big house while you take a Negro woman home."

"You know that I am not lying outside with a razor," Father said.

"I'll stop if Dilsey will make a chocolate cake," Jason said. Mother told us to go out and Father said he didn't know if Jason would get a chocolate cake or not, but he knew what Jason was going to get in about a minute. We went back to the kitchen and told Nancy.

"Father said for you to go home and lock the door, and you'll be all right," Caddy said. "All right from what, Nancy? Is Jesus mad at you?" Nancy was holding the coffee cup in her hands again, her elbows on her knees and her hands holding the cup between her knees. She was looking into the cup. "What have you done that made Jesus mad?" Caddy said. Nancy let the cup go. It didn't break on the floor, but the coffee spilled out, and Nancy sat there with her hands still making the shape of the cup. She began to make the sound again, not loud. Not singing and not unsinging. We watched her.

"Here," Dilsey said. "You quit that, now. You get aholt of yourself. You wait here. I going to get Versh to walk home with you." Dilsey went out.

We looked at Nancy. Her shoulders kept shaking, but she quit making the sound. We stood and watched her.

"What's Jesus going to do to you?" Caddy said. "He went away."

Nancy looked at us. "We had fun that night I stayed in yawl's room, didn't we?"

"I didn't," Jason said. "I didn't have any fun."

"You were asleep in Mother's room," Caddy said. "You were not there."

"Let's go down to my house and have some more fun," Nancy said.

"Mother won't let us," I said. "It's too late now."

"Don't bother her," Nancy said. "We can tell her in the morning. She won't mind."

"She wouldn't let us," I said.

"Don't ask her now," Nancy said. "Don't bother her now."

"She didn't say we couldn't go," Caddy said.

"We didn't ask," I said.

"If you go, I'll tell," Jason said.

"We'll have fun," Nancy said. "They won't mind, just to my house. I been working for yawl a long time. They won't mind."

"I'm not afraid to go," Caddy said. "Jason is the one that's afraid. He'll tell."

"I'm not," Jason said.

"Yes, you are," Caddy said. "You'll tell."

"I won't tell," Jason said. "I'm not afraid."

"Jason ain't afraid to go with me," Nancy said. "Is you, Jason?"

"Jason is going to tell," Caddy said. The lane was dark. We passed the pasture gate. "I bet if something was to jump out from behind that gate, Jason would holler."

"I wouldn't," Jason said. We walked down the lane. Nancy was talking loud.

"What are you talking so loud for, Nancy?" Caddy said.

"Who; me?" Nancy said. "Listen at Quentin and Caddy and Jason saying I'm talking loud."

"You talk like there was five of us here," Caddy said. "You talk like Father was here too."

"Who; me talking loud, Mr. Jason?" Nancy said.

"Nancy called Jason 'Mister,' " Caddy said.

"Listen how Caddy and Quentin and Jason talk," Nancy said.

"We're not talking loud," Caddy said. "You're the one that's talking like Father—"

"Hush," Nancy said; "hush, Mr. Jason."

"Nancy called Jason 'Mister' aguh—"

"Hush," Nancy said. She was talking loud when we crossed the ditch and stooped through the fence where she used to stoop through with the clothes on her head. Then we came to her house. We were going fast then. She opened the door. The smell of the house was like the lamp and the smell of Nancy was like the wick, like they were waiting for one another to begin to smell. She lit the lamp and closed the door and put the bar up. Then she quit talking loud, looking at us.

"What're we going to do?" Caddy said.

"What do yawl want to do?" Nancy said.

"You said we would have some fun," Caddy said.

There was something about Nancy's house; something you could smell besides Nancy and the house. Jason smelled it, even. "I don't want to stay here," he said. "I want to go home."

"Go home, then," Caddy said.

"I don't want to go by myself," Jason said.

"We're going to have some fun," Nancy said.

"How?" Caddy said.

Nancy stood by the door. She was looking at us, only it was like she had emptied her eyes, like she had quit using them. "What do you want to do?" she said.

"Tell us a story," Caddy said. "Can you tell a story?"

"Yes," Nancy said.

"Tell it," Caddy said. We looked at Nancy. "You don't know any stories."

"Yes," Nancy said. "Yes I do."

She came and sat in a chair before the hearth. There was a little fire there. Nancy built it up, when it was already hot inside. She built a good blaze. She told a story. She talked like her eyes looked, like her eyes watching us and her voice talking to us did not belong to her. Like she was living somewhere else, waiting somewhere else. She was outside the cabin. Her voice was inside and the shape of her, the Nancy that could stoop under a barbed wire fence with a bundle of clothes balanced on her head as though without weight, like a balloon, was there. But that was all. "And so this here queen came walking up to the ditch, where that bad man was hiding. She was walking up to the ditch, and she say, 'If I can just get past this here ditch,' was what she say . . ."

"What ditch?" Caddy said. "A ditch like that one out there? Why did a queen want to go into a ditch?"

"To get to her house," Nancy said. She looked at us. "She had to cross the ditch to get into her house quick and bar the door."

"Why did she want to go home and bar the door?" Caddy said.

IV

Nancy looked at us. She quit talking. She looked at us. Jason's legs stuck straight out of his pants where he sat on Nancy's lap. "I don't think that's a good story," he said. "I want to go home."

"Maybe we had better," Caddy said. She got up from the floor. "I bet they are looking for us right now." She went toward the door.

"No," Nancy said. "Don't open it." She got up quick and passed Caddy. She didn't touch the door, the wooden bar.

"Why not?" Caddy said.

"Come back to the lamp," Nancy said. "We'll have fun. You don't have to go."

"We ought to go," Caddy said. "Unless we have a lot of fun." She and Nancy came back to the fire, the lamp.

"I want to go home," Jason said. "I'm going to tell."

"I know another story," Nancy said. She stood close to the lamp. She looked at Caddy, like when your eyes looked up at a stick balanced on your nose. She had to look down to see Caddy, but her eyes looked like that, like when you are balancing a stick.

"I won't listen to it," Jason said. "I'll bang on the floor."

"It's a good one," Nancy said. "It's better than the other one."

"What's it about?" Caddy said. Nancy was standing by the lamp. Her hand was on the lamp, against the light, long and brown.

"Your hand is on that hot globe," Caddy said. "Don't it feel hot to your hand?"

Nancy looked at her hand on the lamp chimney. She took her hand away, slow. She stood there, looking at Caddy, wringing her long hand as though it were tied to her wrist with a string.

"Let's do something else," Caddy said.

"I want to go home," Jason said.

"I got some popcorn," Nancy said. She looked at Caddy and then at Jason and then at me and then at Caddy again. "I got some popcorn."

"I don't like popcorn," Jason said. "I'd rather have candy."

Nancy looked at Jason. "You can hold the popper." She was still wringing her hand; it was long and limp and brown.

"All right," Jason said. "I'll stay a while if I can do that. Caddy can't hold it. I'll want to go home again if Caddy holds the popper."

Nancy built up the fire. "Look at Nancy putting her hands in the fire," Caddy said. "What's the matter with you, Nancy?"

"I got popcorn," Nancy said. "I got some." She took the popper from under the bed. It was broken. Jason began to cry.

"Now we can't have any popcorn," he said.

"We ought to go home, anyway," Caddy said. "Come on, Quentin."

"Wait," Nancy said; "wait. I can fix it. Don't you want to help me fix it?"

"I don't think I want any," Caddy said. "It's too late now."

"You help me, Jason," Nancy said. "Don't you want to help me?"

"No," Jason said. "I want to go home."

"Hush," Nancy said; "hush. Watch. Watch me. I can fix it so Jason can hold it and pop the corn." She got a piece of wire and fixed the popper.

"It won't hold good," Caddy said.

"Yes it will," Nancy said. "Yawl watch. Yawl help me shell some corn."

The popcorn was under the bed too. We shelled it into the popper and Nancy helped Jason hold the popper over the fire.

"It's not popping," Jason said. "I want to go home."

"You wait," Nancy said. "It'll begin to pop. We'll have fun then."

She was sitting close to the fire. The lamp was turned up so high it was beginning to smoke. "Why don't you turn it down some?" I said.

"It's all right," Nancy said. "I'll clean it. Yawl wait. The popcorn will start in a minute."

"I don't believe it's going to start," Caddy said. "We ought to start home, anyway. They'll be worried."

"No," Nancy said. "It's going to pop. Dilsey will tell um yawl with me. I been working for yawl long time. They won't mind if yawl at my house. You wait, now. It'll start popping any minute now."

Then Jason got some smoke in his eyes and he began to cry. He dropped the popper into the fire. Nancy got a wet rag and wiped Jason's face, but he didn't stop crying.

"Hush," she said. "Hush." But he didn't hush. Caddy took the popper out of the fire.

"It's burned up," she said. "You'll have to get some more popcorn, Nancy."

"Did you put all of it in?" Nancy said.

"Yes," Caddy said. Nancy looked at Caddy. Then she took the popper and opened it and poured the cinders into her apron and began to sort the grains, her hands long and brown, and we were watching her.

"Haven't you got any more?" Caddy said.

"Yes," Nancy said; "yes. Look. This here ain't burnt. All we need to do is—"

"I want to go home," Jason said. "I'm going to tell."

"Hush," Caddy said. We all listened. Nancy's head was already turned toward the barred door, her eyes filled with red lamplight. "Somebody is coming," Caddy said.

Then Nancy began to make that sound again, not loud, sitting there above the fire, her long hands dangling between her knees; all of a sudden water began to come out on her face in big drops, running down her face, carrying in each one a little turning ball of firelight like a spark until it dropped off her chin. "She's not crying," I said.

"I ain't crying," Nancy said. Her eyes were closed. "I ain't crying. Who is it?"

"I don't know," Caddy said. She went to the door and looked out. "We've got to go now," she said. "Here comes Father."

"I'm going to tell," Jason said. "Yawl made me come."

The water still ran down Nancy's face. She turned in her chair. "Listen. Tell him. Tell him we going to have fun. Tell him I take good care of yawl until in the morning. Tell him to let me come home with yawl and sleep on the floor. Tell him I won't need no pallet. We'll have fun. You member last time how we had so much fun?"

"I didn't have fun," Jason said. "You hurt me. You put smoke in my eyes. I'm going to tell."

V

Father came in. He looked at us. Nancy did not get up.

"Tell him," she said.

"Caddy made us come down here," Jason said. "I didn't want to."

Father came to the fire. Nancy looked up at him. "Can't you go to Aunt Rachel's and stay?" he said. Nancy looked up at Father, her hands between her knees. "He's not here," Father said. "I would have seen him. There's not a soul in sight."

"He in the ditch," Nancy said. "He waiting in the ditch yonder."

"Nonsense," Father said. He looked at Nancy. "Do you know he's there?"

"I got the sign," Nancy said.

"What sign?"

"I got it. It was on the table when I come in. It was a hog-bone, with blood meat still on it, laying by the lamp. He's out there. When yawl walk out that door, I gone."

"Gone where, Nancy?" Caddy said.

"I'm not a tattletale," Jason said.

"Nonsense," Father said.

"He out there," Nancy said. "He looking through that window this minute, waiting for yawl to go. Then I gone."

"Nonsense," Father said. "Lock up your house and we'll take you on to Aunt Rachel's."

"'Twon't do no good," Nancy said. She didn't look at Father now, but he looked down at her, at her long, limp, moving hands. "Putting it off won't do no good."

"Then what do you want to do?" Father said.

"I don't know," Nancy said. "I can't do nothing. Just put it off. And that don't do no good. I reckon it belong to me. I reckon what I going to get ain't no more than mine."

"Get what?" Caddy said. "What's yours?"

"Nothing," Father said. "You all must get to bed."

"Caddy made me come," Jason said.

"Go on to Aunt Rachel's," Father said.

"It won't do no good," Nancy said. She sat before the fire, her elbows on her knees, her long hands between her knees. "When even your own kitchen wouldn't do no good. When even if I was sleeping on the floor in the room with your chillen, and the next morning there I am, and blood—"

"Hush," Father said. "Lock the door and put out the lamp and go to bed."

"I scaired of the dark," Nancy said. "I scaired for it to happen in the dark."

"You mean you're going to sit right here with the lamp lighted?" Father said. Then Nancy began to make the sound again, sitting before the fire, her long hands between her knees. "Ah, damnation," Father said. "Come along, chillen. It's past bedtime."

"When yawl go home, I gone," Nancy said. She talked quieter now, and her face looked quiet, like her hands. "Anyway, I got my coffin money saved up with Mr. Lovelady." Mr. Lovelady was a short, dirty man who collected the Negro insurance, coming around to the cabins or the kitchens every Saturday morning, to collect fifteen cents. He and his wife lived at the hotel. One morning his wife committed suicide. They had a child, a little girl. He and the child went away. After a week or two he came back alone. We would see him going along the lanes and the back streets on Saturday mornings.

"Nonsense," Father said. "You'll be the first thing I'll see in the kitchen tomorrow morning."

"You'll see what you'll see, I reckon," Nancy said. "But it will take the Lord to say what that will be."

VI

We left her sitting before the fire.

"Come and put the bar up," Father said. But she didn't move. She didn't look at us again, sitting quietly there between the lamp and the fire. From some distance down the lane we could look back and see her through the open door.

"What, Father?" Caddy said. "What's going to happen?"

"Nothing," Father said. Jason was on Father's back so Jason was the tallest of all of us. We went down into the ditch. I looked at it, quiet. I couldn't see much where the moonlight and the shadows tangled.

"If Jesus *is* hid here, he can see us, can't he?" Caddy said.

"He's not there," Father said. "He went away a long time ago."

"You made me come," Jason said, high; against the sky it looked like Father had two heads, a little one and a big one. "I didn't want to."

We went up out of the ditch. We could still see Nancy's house and the open door, but we couldn't see Nancy now, sitting before the fire with the door open, because she was tired. "I just done got tired," she said. "I just a nigger. It ain't no fault of mine."

But we could hear her, because she began just after we came up out of the ditch, the sound that was not singing and not unsinging. "Who will do our washing now, Father?" I said.

"I'm not a nigger," Jason said, high and close above Father's head.

"You're worse," Caddy said, "you are a tattletale. If something was to jump out, you'd be scairder than a nigger."

"I wouldn't," Jason said.

"You'd cry," Caddy said.

"Caddy," Father said.

"I wouldn't!" Jason said.

"Scairy cat," Caddy said.

"Candace!" Father said.

QUESTIONS FOR DISCUSSION

1. "That Evening Sun" explores the relationship between two worlds—Negro and white. Discuss the relationship of each of the characters in the story to Nancy. Contrast the attitudes of the white children and the white adults toward Nancy. In what ways do these differ? In what ways are they alike?
2. Discuss the character of Nancy. Is she as childlike as the children in the story? If so, what implied bearing does this have on the story's theme? On the story's emotional effect?
3. What does the opening of the story contribute to the theme of the story?
4. The point of view of "That Evening Sun," like the point of view of "Rain," is peripheral. What, however, are the differences in *result* (in emotional effect, in characterization, in the definition of theme)?
5. Nancy is, in a plot sense, the protagonist of "That Evening Sun." In a thematic sense, however, can the narrator be considered the protagonist? What light might this throw on Faulkner's choice of his point of view?

3 Style: The Language of Fiction

Our responses to a story are controlled by language artfully arranged to achieve carefully prepared effects. "Style is conception," says Mark Schorer, fiction writer and critic. "It is style, and style primarily, that first conceives, then expresses, and finally tests subject matter and theme." Consider the testimony of some other writers on the importance of style (noting the style in which they express their observations):

"The knowledge everyone lacked was *analysis of style*, the understanding of how a phrase is constructed and articulated." (Gustave Flaubert)

"In 'Miss Brill,' I chose not only the length of every sentence, but even the sound of every paragraph to fit her, and to fit her on that day, at that very moment." (Katherine Mansfield)

"Often I ponder a quarter of an hour whether to place an adjective before or after its noun." (Henri Stendhal)

"Whatever you want to say, there is only one word to express it, one verb to set it in motion and only one adjective to describe it." (Guy de Maupassant)

"I want to use a minimum of words for a maximum effect. . . . Underwriting seems to be a species of underwater swimming. Is the pool empty? That is how it often looks." (Wright Morris)

"Reporting the extreme things as if they were the average things will start you on the art of fiction." (F. Scott Fitzgerald)

"If a writer of prose knows enough about what he is writing about he may omit things that he knows and the reader, if the writer is writing truly enough, will have a feeling of those things as strongly as though the writer had stated them. The dignity of movement of an iceberg is due to only one-eighth of it being above water." (Ernest Hemingway)

"A well-made phrase is a good action." (Emile Zola)

"A work that aspires, however humbly, to the condition of art should carry its justification in every line." (Joseph Conrad)

"One never tires of anything that is well written. Style is life! Indeed it is the life-blood of thought!" (Gustave Flaubert)

To detect ways in which a writer tries to affect his reader, analyze his style. The words a writer chooses to express feelings, thoughts, and actions will tell you a great deal about his relationship to his raw material and the way he wants his readers to respond to it. What are the dictates of style in a particular story? Is the style appropriate to the subject matter and to the point of view the author uses?

Together, style and point of view are the major technical considerations in analyzing a story. Variations on the writer's basic style are somewhat determined by the point of view he decides to employ. In a first-person story, stylistic questions revolve mainly around appropriateness in relation to the person telling the story and around ways the author manages his effects behind that limitation in style. The first paragraph of Hemingway's "In Another Country" is designed to do the work of a chapter in a novel: totally involve the reader, not with plot complications but with rhetorical intricacies submerged in a plain style. The third-person, central point of view Morris uses in "The Ram in the Thicket" allows him a freer use of language, but here style is still restricted by the nature of the protagonist through whose eyes we see the story. And if Fitzgerald's third-person omniscient point of view allows him maximum freedom of style, it also lays him open to the dangers of excess.

Despite its importance, style is one of the least discussed aspects of technique because descriptions of its effects are difficult and relatively dull. What, then, is style? Style is, narrowly speaking, the author's use of language: it is diction (choice of words) and syntax (arrangement of phrases) and the handling of sentence and paragraph units by varying patterns; it is the use of figurative language; it is, even, the deliberate, sometimes quirky, use of punctuation. And more. Few writers really arrive at a distinctive style of their own; it is easier to recognize most writers by their handling of other techniques. But it is distinctive style, among other things, that distinguishes most great writers from each other.

Generally, we may speak of simple, complex, and "middle-ground" styles; Hemingway uses the first, Fitzgerald the second, and Morris the third.

Economy, brevity, concreteness, clarity, and vividness are characteristics of the plain or simple style. Having deliberately limited himself to simple words and having banned most adjectives, Hemingway had to find a means of suggesting far more than he appears to state literally. To accomplish that, he arranged denotative words in patterns of sound and thought that resulted in evocations. It is his style in part that provides a Hemingway story with its sense of "depth," its "multi-levels of meaning."

Morris's style is, perhaps, more characteristic of the style most writers employ. The style of most fiction is a careful amalgam of words that denote and words that connote; some writers use denotative words more than others; some strive for connotative effects and thus move closer to poetry; some are too suggestive; some are not suggestive enough. The realistic writer chooses his details to create the illusion of actuality; the impressionistic writer chooses a different sort of detail for a different effect. But, like Morris, most writers try to evoke a sense of life rather than trying to render it literally and fully. In fiction, language more often connotes than denotes. Morris's style usually works by indirection, even when he seems to be making a literal statement; he underwrites his most important scenes, understates his major insights.

Of the complex, grand, or high style, Fitzgerald is one of our most magnificent practitioners. He strives for memorable phrases (even aphorisms and epigrams), for eloquence, for a controlled lyricism. He would have agreed with Zola: "We believe, quite wrongly, that the grand style is the product of some sublime terror always on the verge of pitching over into frenzy; the grand style is achieved through logic and clarity. . . . Genius is not to be found only in the feeling, in the *a priori* idea, but is also in the form and style." Except in *The Great Gatsby*, in which his style is almost perfectly controlled, Fitzgerald often lapsed into overstatement, overwriting. When a writer goes too far in his descriptive passages, becoming too lyrical, straining too grotesquely for wit, he presents us with a "purple passage," with "fine writing." His style becomes a baroque ornament on a Greek temple. A complex style often becomes pretentious, affected, overloaded with ornamental metaphors, exotic phrases, archaic words, formal phrases.

All fictional styles have certain elements in common. Here are some of the most important ones.

1. "Metaphorical language," says Mark Schorer, "gives any style its special quality, expresses, defines, evaluates theme, can be the basis of structure, as 'overthought' or 'underthought,' reveals to us the character of any imaginative work." That may be said as well of the careful avoidance of metaphorical language, as in Hemingway's best stories. But most writers suffer Flaubert's dilemma: "Comparisons consume me like flies." The problem is to include only those that relate to and enhance a master design. Even cliché expressions can be controlled to create transcendent effects. Wright Morris often transforms clichés in "The Ram in the Thicket," as in the scene in which Mr. Ormsby recalls the time he accidentally met his son in the darkness of the basement john.

2. Repetition is a characteristic of the style of most writers, but Hemingway employs it in an unusual way, within *sentences*, not just from sentence to sentence. Note, again, the opening of "In Another Country." Through the repetition of such words as *wind* and *cold*, and by positioning them as he does in his sentences, he conveys a tone and a rhythm of feeling that suggests the sort of person the narrator is and how he feels about the experiences he will relate. Every aspect of the story is prefigured in not only the elements but the style of that initial paragraph.

3. Prose, like poetry, has rhythm and cadence and texture, and texture can act upon a reader's mind almost sensually. Thus, a reader can *feel* the tightly woven texture of the Heminway style, the loose texture of the Fitzgerald style, the conversational, idiomatic texture of the Morris style. And texture will affect a reader's attitude toward what he is reading.

4. When a writer condenses his raw material, makes his style concise, and concentrates upon carefully selected elements, he creates a tension that translates language into physical and psychic events that *happen* to the reader. One of the techniques that keeps a reader moving from one psychic explosion (gentle or terrific) to another is pace; and even within sentences the master of style can keep a sense of movement going, thus making style an agent of action. To sustain a sense of movement even *within* the style, writers will try, within a single sentence, to cause one thing to impinge upon another. But stylistic lapses can impede this sensuous flow of language, as when the author stops to deliver an abstraction. There may be times—even in Hemingway's stories, certainly in Fitz-

gerald's—when an abstract statement is necessary, is "right." But more often it betrays somehow, somewhere, a stylistic failure on the part of the writer. "Go in fear of abstractions," Ezra Pound said, and he was only saying in different words what Chekhov said about the art of storytelling: the first principle, he said, was to *show*, not to *tell*.

ERNEST HEMINGWAY
In Another Country

In the fall the war was always there, but we did not go to it any more. It was cold in the fall in Milan and the dark came very early. Then the electric lights came on, and it was pleasant along the streets looking in the windows. There was much game hanging outside the shops, and the snow powdered in the fur of the foxes and the wind blew their tails. The deer hung stiff and heavy and empty, and small birds blew in the wind and the wind turned their feathers. It was a cold fall and the wind came down from the mountains.

We were all at the hospital every afternoon, and there were different ways of walking across the town through the dusk to the hospital. Two of the ways were alongside canals, but they were long. Always, though, you crossed a bridge across a canal to enter the hospital. There was a choice of three bridges. On one of them a woman sold roasted chestnuts. It was warm, standing in front of her charcoal fire, and the chestnuts were warm afterward in your pocket. The hospital was very old and very beautiful, and you entered through a gate and walked across a courtyard and out a gate on the other side. There were usually funerals starting from the courtyard. Beyond the old hospital were the new brick pavilions, and there we met every afternoon and were all very polite and interested in what was the matter, and sat in the machines that were to make so much difference.

The doctor came up to the machine where I was sitting and said: "What did you like best to do before the war? Did you practise a sport?"

I said: "Yes, football."

"Good," he said. "You will be able to play football again better than ever."

My knee did not bend and the leg dropped straight from the knee to the ankle without a calf, and the machine was to bend the knee and make it move as in riding a tricycle. But it did not bend yet, and instead the machine lurched when it came to the bending part. The doctor said: "That will all pass. You are a fortunate young man. You will play football again like a champion."

In the next machine was a major who had a little hand like a baby's. He winked at me when the doctor examined his hand, which was between two leather straps that bounced up and down and flapped the stiff fingers, and said: "And will I too play football, captain-doctor?" He had been a very great fencer, and before the war the greatest fencer in Italy.

The doctor went to his office in a back room and brought a photograph which showed a hand that had been withered almost as small as the major's, before it had taken a machine course, and after was a little larger. The major held the photograph with his good hand and looked at it very carefully. "A wound?" he asked.

"An industrial accident," the doctor said.

"Very interesting, very interesting," the major said, and handed it back to the doctor.

"You have confidence?"

"No," said the major.

There were three boys who came each day who were about the same age I was. They were all three from Milan, and one of them was to be a lawyer, and one was to be a painter, and one had intended to be a soldier, and after we were finished with the machines, sometimes we walked back together to the Café Cova, which was next door to the Scala. We walked the short way through the communist quarter because we were four together. The people hated us because we were officers, and from a wine-shop some one called out, "A basso gli ufficiali!" as we passed. Another boy who walked with us sometimes and made us five wore a black silk handkerchief across his face because he had no nose then and his face was to be rebuilt. He had gone out to the front from the military academy and been wounded within an hour after he had gone into the front line for the first time. They rebuilt his face, but he came from a very old family and they could never get the nose exactly right. He went to South America and worked in a bank. But this was a long time ago, and then we did not any of us know how it was going to be afterward. We only knew then that there was always the war, but that we were not going to it any more.

We all had the same medals, except the boy with the black silk bandage across his face, and he had not been at the front long enough to get any medals. The tall boy with a very pale face who was to be a lawyer had been a lieutenant of Arditi and had three medals of the sort we each had only one of. He had lived a very long time with death and was a little detached. We were all a little detached, and there was nothing that held us together except that we met every afternoon at the hospital.

Although, as we walked to the Cova through the tough part of town, walking in the dark, with light and singing coming out of the wine-shops, and sometimes having to walk into the street when the men and women would crowd together on the sidewalk so that we would have had to jostle them to get by, we felt held together by there being something that had happened that they, the people who disliked us, did not understand.

We ourselves all understood the Cova, where it was rich and warm and not too brightly lighted, and noisy and smoky at certain hours, and there were always girls at the tables and the illustrated papers on a rack on the wall. The girls at the Cova were very patriotic, and I found that the most patriotic people in Italy were the café girls—and I believe they are still patriotic.

The boys at first were very polite about my medals and asked me what I had done to get them. I showed them the papers, which were written in very beautiful language and full of *fratellanza* and *abnegazione*, but which really said, with the adjectives removed, that I had been given the medals because I was an American. After that their manner changed a little toward me, although I was their friend against outsiders. I was a friend, but I was never really one of them after they had read the citations, because it had been different with them and they had done very different things to get their medals. I had been wounded, it was true; but we all knew that being wounded, after all, was really an accident. I was never ashamed of the ribbons, though, and sometimes, after the cocktail hour, I would imagine myself having done all the things they had done to get their medals; but walking home at night through the empty streets with the cold wind and all the shops closed, trying to keep near the street lights, I knew that I would never have done such things, and I was very much afraid to die, and often lay in bed at night by myself, afraid to die and wondering how I would be when I went back to the front again.

The three with the medals were like hunting-hawks; and I was not a hawk, although I might seem a hawk to those who had never hunted; they, the three, knew better and so we drifted apart. But I stayed good friends with the boy who had been wounded his first day at the front, because he would never know now how he would have turned out; so he could never be accepted either, and I liked him because I thought perhaps he would not have turned out to be a hawk either.

The major, who had been the great fencer, did not believe in bravery, and spent much time while we sat in the machines correcting my grammar. He had complimented me on how I spoke Italian, and we talked together very easily. One day I had said that Italian seemed such an easy language to me that I could not take a great interest in it; everything was so easy to say. "Ah, yes," the major said. "Why, then, do you not take up the use of grammar?" So we took up the use of grammar, and soon Italian was such a difficult language that I was afraid to talk to him until I had the grammar straight in my mind.

The major came very regularly to the hospital. I do not think he ever missed a day, although I am sure he did not believe in the machines. There was a time when none of us believed in the machines, and one day the major said it was all nonsense. The machines were new then and it was we who were to prove them. It was an idiotic idea, he said, "a theory, like another." I had not learned my grammar, and he said I was a stupid impossible disgrace, and he was a fool to have bothered with me. He was a small man and he sat straight up in his chair with his right hand thrust into the machine and looked straight ahead at the wall while the straps thumped up and down with his fingers in them.

"What will you do when the war is over if it is over?" he asked me. "Speak grammatically!"

"I will go to the States."

"Are you married?"

"No, but I hope to be."

"The more of a fool you are," he said. He seemed very angry. "A man must not marry."

"Why, Signor Maggiore?"

"Don't call me 'Signor Maggiore.' "

"Why must not a man marry?"

"He cannot marry. He cannot marry," he said angrily. "If he is to lose everything, he should not place himself in a position to lose that. He should not place himself in a position to lose. He should find things he cannot lose."

He spoke very angrily and bitterly, and looked straight ahead while he talked.

"But why should he necessarily lose it?"

"He'll lose it," the major said. He was looking at the wall. Then he looked down at the machine and jerked his little hand out from between the straps and slapped it hard against his thigh. "He'll lose it," he almost shouted. "Don't argue with me!" Then he called to the attendant who ran the machines. "Come and turn this damned thing off."

He went back into the other room for the light treatment and the massage. Then I heard him ask the doctor if he might use his telephone and he shut the door. When he came back into the room, I was sitting in another machine. He was wearing his cape and had his cap on, and he came directly toward my machine and put his arm on my shoulder.

"I am so sorry," he said, and patted me on the shoulder with his good hand. "I would not be rude. My wife has just died. You must forgive me."

"Oh—" I said, feeling sick for him. "I am *so* sorry."

He stood there biting his lower lip. "It is very difficult," he said. "I cannot resign myself."

He looked straight past me and out through the window. Then he began to cry. "I am utterly unable to resign myself," he said and choked. And then crying, his head up looking at nothing, carrying himself straight and soldierly, with tears on both his cheeks and biting his lips, he walked past the machines and out the door.

The doctor told me that the major's wife, who was very young and whom he had not married until he was definitely invalided out of the war, had died of pneumonia. She had been sick only a few days. No one expected her to die. The major did not come to the hospital for three days. Then he came at the usual hour, wearing a black band on the sleeve of his uniform. When he came back, there were large framed photographs around the wall, of all sorts of wounds before and after they had been cured by the machines. In front of the machine the major used were three photographs of hands like his that were completely restored. I do not know where the doctor got them. I always understood we were the first to use the machines. The photographs did not make much difference to the major because he only looked out of the window.

QUESTIONS FOR DISCUSSION

1. In a Hemingway story, style and content are one: the style is appropriate to and reinforces every other element. In the first two paragraphs, Hemingway employs almost all the devices of his distinctive style. Analyze those paragraphs, discussing in particular Hemingway's syntax; his use of prepositions and pronouns; and the rhythm, cadence, and pace of his sentences.
2. Most writers try to repeat key words effectively from one sentence to another, but Hemingway is unusual in his deliberate repetition of the same word within the same sentence. What is the effect of that technique in the first two paragraphs? Analyze the use of repetition and variation of elements throughout the story. Analyze the effect of repetition in dialogue.
3. In *Death in the Afternoon,* Hemingway spoke of trying to achieve "a fourth and a fifth dimension" in his prose. In "In Another Country," how are style, extreme compression, severe implication, irony, and symbol and allusion used to achieve those added dimensions?
4. What is the emotional effect on the reader of Hemingway's style? In what ways is it appropriate to his subject matter, his theme?
5. Analyze Hemingway's use of adjectives. He deliberately avoids metaphors, similes, adjectives, and adverbs. How does he achieve effects usually created by those rhetorical elements?

6. What stylistic devices does Hemingway use to describe and characterize his characters?
7. How does the style itself express indirectly the essence of the narrator's mood and attitude toward the story he tells us? How is the style simultaneously descriptive and suggestive of the major's life as well?
8. One critic has defined the Hemingway theme as "Everything in life is a drug except reality, which is unbearable." Can you apply this general statement to "In Another Country"? What drugs can you find in the story? And what is "reality" in the story's context?

F. SCOTT FITZGERALD
Absolution

I

There was once a priest with cold, watery eyes, who, in the still of the night, wept cold tears. He wept because the afternoons were warm and long, and he was unable to attain a complete mystical union with our Lord. Sometimes, near four o'clock, there was a rustle of Swede girls along the path by his window, and in their shrill laughter he found a terrible dissonance that made him pray aloud for the twilight to come. At twilight the laughter and the voices were quieter, but several times he had walked past Romberg's Drug Store when it was dusk and the yellow lights shone inside and the nickel taps of the soda-fountain were gleaming, and he had found the scent of cheap toilet soap desperately sweet upon the air. He passed that way when he returned from hearing confessions on Saturday nights, and he grew careful to walk on the other side of the street so that the smell of the soap would float upward before it reached his nostrils as it drifted, rather like incense, toward the summer moon.

But there was no escape from the hot madness of four o'clock. From his window, as far as he could see, the Dakota wheat thronged the valley of the Red River. The wheat was terrible to look upon and the carpet pattern to which in agony he bent his eyes sent his thought brooding through grotesque labyrinths, open always to the unavoidable sun.

One afternoon when he had reached the point where the mind runs down like an old clock, his housekeeper brought into his study a beautiful, intense little boy of eleven named Rudolph Miller. The little boy sat down in a patch of sunshine, and the priest, at his walnut desk, pretended to be very busy. This was to conceal his relief that some one had come into his haunted room.

Presently he turned around and found himself staring into two enormous, staccato eyes, lit with gleaming points of cobalt light. For a moment their expression startled him—then he saw that his visitor was in a state of abject fear.

"Your mouth is trembling," said Father Schwartz, in a haggard voice.

The little boy covered his quivering mouth with his hand.

"Are you in trouble?" asked Father Schwartz, sharply. "Take your hand away from your mouth and tell me what's the matter."

The boy—Father Schwartz recognized him now as the son of a parishioner, Mr. Miller, the freight-agent—moved his hand reluctantly off his mouth and became articulate in a despairing whisper.

"Father Schwartz—I've committed a terrible sin."

"A sin against purity?"

"No, Father . . . worse."

Father Schwartz's body jerked sharply.

"Have you killed somebody?"

"No—but I'm afraid—" the voice rose to a shrill whimper.

"Do you want to go to confession?"

The little boy shook his head miserably. Father Schwartz cleared his throat so that he could make his voice soft and say some quiet, kind thing. In this moment he should forget his own agony, and try to act like God. He repeated to himself a devotional phrase, hoping that in return God would help him to act correctly.

"Tell me what you've done," said his new soft voice.

The little boy looked at him through his tears, and was reassured by the impression of moral resiliency which the distraught priest had created. Abandoning as much of himself as he was able to this man, Rudolph Miller began to tell his story.

"On Saturday, three days ago, my father he said I had to go to confession, because I hadn't been for a month, and the family they go every week, and I hadn't been. So I just as leave go, I didn't care. So I put it off till after supper because I was playing with a bunch of kids and father asked me if I went, and I said 'no,' and he took me by the neck and he said 'You go now,' so I said 'All right,' so I went over to church. And he yelled after me: 'Don't come back till you go.' . . ."

II

"On Saturday, Three Days Ago."

The plush curtain of the confessional rearranged its dismal creases, leaving exposed only the bottom of an old man's old shoe. Behind the curtain an immortal soul was alone with God and the Reverend Adolphus Schwartz, priest of the parish. Sound began, a labored whispering, sibilant and discreet, broken at intervals by the voice of the priest in audible question.

Rudolph Miller knelt in the pew beside the confessional and waited, straining nervously to hear, and yet not to hear what was being said within. The fact that the priest was audible alarmed him. His own turn came next, and the three or four others who waited might listen unscrupulously while he admitted his violations of the Sixth and Ninth Commandments.

Rudolph had never committed adultery, nor even coveted his neighbor's wife—but it was the confession of the associate sins that was particularly hard to contemplate. In comparison he relished the less shameful fallings away—they formed a grayish background which relieved the ebony mark of sexual offenses upon his soul.

He had been covering his ears with his hands, hoping that his refusal to hear would be noticed, and a like courtesy rendered to him in turn, when a sharp movement of the penitent in the confessional made him sink his face precipitately into the crook of his elbow. Fear assumed solid form, and pressed out a lodging between his heart and his lungs. He must try now with all his might to be sorry for his sins—not because he was afraid, but because he had offended God. He must convince God that he was sorry and to do so he must first convince himself. After a tense emotional struggle he achieved a tremulous self-pity, and decided that he was now ready. If, by allowing no other thought to enter his head, he could preserve this state of emotion unimpaired until he went into that large coffin set on end, he would have survived another crisis in his religious life.

For some time, however, a demoniac notion had partially possessed him. He could go home now, before his turn came, and tell his mother that he had arrived too late, and found the priest gone. This, unfortunately, involved the risk of being caught in a lie. As an alternative he could say that he *had* gone to confession, but this meant that he must avoid communion next day, for communion taken upon an uncleansed soul would turn to poison in his mouth, and he would crumple limp and damned from the altar-rail.

Again Father Schwartz's voice became audible.

"And for your———"

The words blurred to a husky mumble, and Rudolph got excitedly to his feet. He felt that it was impossible for him to go to confession this afternoon. He hesitated tensely. Then from the confessional came a tap, a creak, and a sustained rustle. The slide had fallen and the plush curtain trembled. Temptation had come to him too late....

"Bless me, Father, for I have sinned. . . . I confess to Almighty God and to you, Father, that I have sinned. . . . Since my last confession it has been one month and three days. . . . I accuse myself of—taking the Name of the Lord in vain...."

This was an easy sin. His curses had been but bravado—telling of them was little less than a brag.

". . . of being mean to an old lady."

The wan shadow moved a little on the latticed slat.

"How, my child?"

"Old lady Swenson," Rudolph's murmur soared jubilantly. "She got our baseball that we knocked in her window, and she wouldn't give it back, so we yelled 'Twenty-three, Skiddo,' at her all afternoon. Then about five o'clock she had a fit, and they had to have a doctor."

"Go on, my child."

"Of—of not believing I was the son of my parents."

"What?" The interrogation was distinctly startled.

"Of not believing that I was the son of my parents."

"Why not?"

"Oh, just pride," answered the penitent airily.

"You mean you thought you were too good to be the son of your parents?"

"Yes, Father." On a less jubilant note.

"Go on."

"Of being disobedient and calling my mother names. Of slandering people behind their back. Of smoking———"

Rudolph had now exhausted the minor offenses, and was approaching the sins it was agony to tell. He held his fingers against his face like bars as if to press out between them the shame in his heart.

"Of dirty words and immodest thoughts and desires," he whispered very low.

"How often?"

"I don't know."

"Once a week? Twice a week?"

"Twice a week."

"Did you yield to these desires?"

"No, Father."

"Were you alone when you had them?"

"No, Father. I was with two boys and a girl."

"Don't you know, my child, that you should avoid the occasions of sin as well as the sin itself? Evil companionship leads to evil desires and evil desires to evil actions. Where were you when this happened?"

"In a barn in back of———"

"I don't want to hear any names," interrupted the priest sharply.

"Well, it was up in the loft of this barn and this girl and—a fella, they were saying things—saying immodest things, and I stayed."

"You should have gone—you should have told the girl to go."

He should have gone! He could not tell Father Schwartz how his pulse had bumped in his wrist, how a strange, romantic excitement had possessed him when those curious things had been said. Perhaps in the houses of delinquency among the dull and hard-eyed incorrigible girls can be found those for whom has burned the whitest fire.

"Have you anything else to tell me?"

"I don't think so, Father."

Rudolph felt a great relief. Perspiration had broken out under his tight-pressed fingers.

"Have you told any lies?"

The question startled him. Like all those who habitually and instinctively lie, he had an enormous respect and awe for the truth. Something almost exterior to himself dictated a quick, hurt answer. "Oh, no, Father, I never tell lies."

For a moment, like the commoner in the king's chair, he tasted the pride of the situation. Then as the priest began to murmur conventional admonitions he realized that in heroically denying he had told lies, he had committed a terrible sin—he had told a lie in confession.

In automatic response to Father Schwartz's "Make an act of contrition," he began to repeat aloud meaninglessly:

"Oh, my God, I am heartily sorry for having offended Thee. . . ."

He must fix this now—it was a bad mistake—but as his teeth shut on the last words of his prayer there was a sharp sound, and the slat was closed.

A minute later when he emerged into the twilight the relief in coming from the muggy church into an open world of wheat and sky postponed the full realization of what he had done. Instead of worrying he took a deep breath of the crisp air and began to say over and over to himself the words "Blatchford Sarnemington, Blatchford Sarnemington!"

Blatchford Sarnemington was himself, and these words were in effect a lyric. When he became Blatchford Sarnemington a suave nobility flowed from him. Blatchford Sarnemington lived in great sweeping triumphs. When Rudolph half closed his eyes it meant that Blatchford had established dominance over him and, as he went by, there were envious mutters in the air: "Blatchford Sarnemington! There goes Blatchford Sarnemington."

He was Blatchford now for a while as he strutted homeward along the staggering road, but when the road braced itself in macadam in order to become the main street of Ludwig, Rudolph's exhilaration faded out and his mind cooled, and he felt the horror of his lie. God, of course, already knew of it—but Rudolph reserved a corner of his mind where he was safe from God, where he prepared the subterfuges with which he often tricked God. Hiding now in this corner he considered how he could best avoid the consequences of his misstatement.

At all costs he must avoid communion next day. The risk of angering God to such an extent was too great. He would have to drink water "by accident" in the morning, and thus, in accordance with a church law, render himself unfit to receive communion that day. In spite of its flimsiness this subterfuge was the most feasible that occurred to him. He accepted its risks and was concentrating on how best to put it into effect, as he turned the corner by Romberg's Drug Store and came in sight of his father's house.

III

Rudolph's father, the local freight-agent, had floated with the second wave of German and Irish stock to the Minnesota-Dakota country. Theoretically, great opportunities lay ahead of a young man of energy in that day and place, but Carl Miller had been incapable of establishing either with his superiors or his subordinates the reputation for approximate immutability which is essential to success in a hierarchic industry. Somewhat gross, he was, nevertheless, insufficiently hard-headed and unable to take fundamental relationships for granted, and this inability made him suspicious, unrestful, and continually dismayed.

His two bonds with the colorful life were his faith in the Roman Catholic Church and his mystical worship of the Empire Builder, James J. Hill. Hill was the apotheosis of that quality in which Miller himself was deficient—the sense of things, the feel of things, the hint of rain in the wind on the cheek. Miller's mind worked late on the old decisions of other men, and he had never in his life felt the balance of any single thing in his hands. His weary, sprightly, undersized body was growing old in Hill's gigantic shadow. For twenty years he had lived alone with Hill's name and God.

On Sunday morning, Carl Miller awoke in the dustless quiet of six o'clock. Kneeling by the side of the bed he bent his yellow-gray hair and the full dapple bangs of his mustache into the pillow, and prayed for several minutes. Then he drew off his night-shirt—like the rest of his generation he had never been able to endure pajamas—and clothed his thin, white, hairless body in woollen underwear.

He shaved. Silence in the other bedroom where his wife lay nervously asleep. Silence from the screened-off corner of the hall where his son's cot stood, and his son slept among his Alger books, his collection of cigar-bands, his mothy pennants—"Cornell," "Hamlin," and "Greetings from Pueblo, New Mexico"—and the other possessions of his private life. From outside Miller could hear the shrill birds and the whirring movement of the poultry, and, as an undertone, the low, swelling click-a-tick of the six-fifteen through-train for Montana and the green coast beyond. Then as the cold water dripped from the wash-rag in his hand he raised his head suddenly—he had heard a furtive sound from the kitchen below.

He dried his razor hastily, slipped his dangling suspenders to his shoulder, and listened. Some one was walking in the kitchen, and he knew by the light footfall that it was not his wife. With his mouth faintly ajar he ran quickly down the stairs and opened the kitchen door.

Standing by the sink, with one hand on the still dripping faucet and the other clutching a full glass of water, stood his son. The boy's eyes, still heavy with sleep, met his father's with a frightened, reproachful beauty. He was barefooted, and his pajamas were rolled up at the knees and sleeves.

For a moment they both remained motionless—Carl Miller's brow went down and his son's went up, as though they were striking a balance between the extremes of emotion which filled them. Then the bangs of the parent's mustache descended portentously until they obscured his mouth, and he gave a short glance around to see if anything had been disturbed.

The kitchen was garnished with sunlight which beat on the pans and made the smooth boards of the floor and table yellow and clean as wheat. It was the centre of the house where the fire burned and the tins fitted into tins like toys, and the steam whistled all day on a thin pastel note. Nothing was moved, nothing touched—except the faucet where beads of water still formed and dripped with a white flash into the sink below.

"What are you doing?"

"I got awful thirsty, so I thought I'd just come down and get———"

"I thought you were going to communion."

A look of vehement astonishment spread over his son's face.

"I forgot all about it."

"Have you drunk any water?"

"No———"

As the word left his mouth Rudolph knew it was the wrong answer, but the faded indignant eyes facing him had signalled up the truth before the boy's will could act. He realized, too, that he should never have come down-stairs; some vague necessity for verisimilitude had made him want to leave a wet glass as evidence by the sink; the honesty of his imagination had betrayed him.

"Pour it out," commanded his father, "that water!"

Rudolph despairingly inverted the tumbler.

"What's the matter with you, anyways?" demanded Miller angrily.

"Nothing."

"Did you go to confession yesterday?"

"Yes."

"Then why were you going to drink water?"

"I don't know—I forgot."

"Maybe you care more about being a little bit thirsty than you do about your religion."

"I forgot." Rudolph could feel the tears straining in his eyes.

"That's no answer."

"Well, I did."

"You better look out!" His father held to a high, persistent, inquisitory note: "If you're so forgetful that you can't remember your religion something better be done about it."

Rudolph filled a sharp pause with:

"I can remember it all right."

"First you begin to neglect your religion," cried his father, fanning his own fierceness, "the next thing you'll begin to lie and steal, and the *next* thing is the *reform* school!"

Not even this familiar threat could deepen the abyss that Rudolph saw before him. He must either tell all now, offering his body for what he knew would be a ferocious beating, or else tempt the thunderbolts by receiving the Body and Blood of Christ with sacrilege upon his soul. And of the two the former seemed more terrible—it was not so much the beating he dreaded as the savage ferocity, outlet of the ineffectual man, which would lie behind it.

"Put down that glass and go up-stairs and dress!" his father ordered, "and when we get to church, before you go to communion, you better kneel down and ask God to forgive you for your carelessness."

Some accidental emphasis in the phrasing of this command acted like a catalytic agent on the confusion and terror of Rudolph's mind. A wild, proud anger rose in him, and he dashed the tumbler passionately into the sink.

His father uttered a strained, husky sound, and sprang for him. Rudolph dodged to the side, tipped over a chair, and tried to get beyond the kitchen table. He cried out sharply when a hand grasped his pajama shoulder, then he felt the dull impact of a fist against the side of his head, and glancing blows on the upper part of his body. As he slipped here and there in his father's grasp, dragged or lifted when he clung instinctively to an arm, aware of sharp smarts and strains, he made no sound except that he laughed hysterically several times. Then in less than a minute the blows abruptly ceased. After a lull during which Rudolph was tightly held, and during which they both trembled violently and uttered strange, truncated words, Carl Miller half dragged, half threatened his son up-stairs.

"Put on your clothes!"

Rudolph was now both hysterical and cold. His head hurt him, and there was a long, shallow scratch on his neck from his father's fingernail, and he sobbed and trembled as he dressed. He was aware of his mother standing at the doorway in a wrapper, her wrinkled face compressing and squeezing and opening out into new series of wrinkles which floated and eddied from neck to brow. Despising her nervous ineffectuality and avoiding her rudely when she tried to touch his neck with witch-hazel, he made a hasty, choking toilet. Then he followed his father out of the house and along the road toward the Catholic church.

IV

They walked without speaking except when Carl Miller acknowledged automatically the existence of passers-by. Rudolph's uneven breathing alone ruffled the hot Sunday silence.

His father stopped decisively at the door of the church.

"I've decided you'd better go to confession again. Go in and tell Father Schwartz what you did and ask God's pardon."

"You lost your temper, too!" said Rudolph quickly.

Carl Miller took a step toward his son, who moved cautiously backward.

"All right, I'll go."

"Are you going to do what I say?" cried his father in a hoarse whisper.

"All right."

Rudolph walked into the church, and for the second time in two days entered the confessional and knelt down. The slat went up almost at once.

"I accuse myself of missing my morning prayers."

"Is that all?"

"That's all."

A maudlin exultation filled him. Not easily ever again would he be able to put an abstraction before the necessities of his ease and pride. An invisible line had been crossed, and he had become aware of his isolation—aware that it applied not only to those moments when he was Blatchford Sarnemington but that it applied to all his inner life. Hitherto such phenomena as "crazy" ambitions and petty shames and fears had been but private reservations, unacknowledged before the throne of his official soul. Now he realized unconsciously that his private reservations were himself—and all the rest a garnished front and a conventional flag. The pressure of his environment had driven him into the lonely secret road of adolescence.

He knelt in the pew beside his father. Mass began. Rudolph knelt up—when he was alone he slumped his posterior back against the seat—and tasted the consciousness of a sharp, subtle revenge. Beside him his father prayed that God would forgive Rudolph, and asked also that his own outbreak of temper would be pardoned. He glanced sidewise at this son, and was relieved to see that the strained, wild look had gone from his face and that he had ceased sobbing. The Grace of God, inherent in the Sacrament, would do the rest, and perhaps after Mass everything would be better. He was proud of Rudolph in his heart, and beginning to be truly as well as formally sorry for what he had done.

Usually, the passing of the collection box was a significant point for Rudolph in the services. If, as was often the case, he had no money to drop in he would be furiously ashamed and bow his head and pretend not to see the box, lest Jeanne Brady in the pew behind should take notice and suspect an acute family poverty. But today he glanced coldly into it as it skimmed under his eyes, noting with casual interest the large number of pennies it contained.

When the bell rang for communion, however, he quivered. There was no reason why God should not stop his heart. During the past twelve hours he had committed a series of mortal sins increasing in gravity, and he was now to crown them all with a blasphemous sacrilege.

"Domine, non sum dignus; ut intres sub tectum meum; sed tantum dic verbo, et sonabitur anima mea. . . ."

There was a rustle in the pews, and the communicants worked their ways into the aisle with downcast eyes and joined hands. Those of larger piety pressed together their fingertips to form steeples. Among these latter was Carl Miller. Rudolph followed him toward the altar-rail and knelt down, automatically taking up the napkin under his chin. The bell rang sharply, and the priest turned from the altar with the white Host held above the chalice:

"Corpus Domini nostri Jesu Christi custodiat animam tuam in vitam æternam."

A cold sweat broke out on Rudolph's forehead as the communion began. Along the line Father Schwartz moved, and with gathering nausea Rudolph felt his heart-valves weakening at the will of God. It seemed to him that the church was darker and that a great quiet had fallen, broken only by the inarticulate mumble which announced the approach of the Creator of Heaven and Earth. He dropped his head down between his shoulders and waited for the blow.

Then he felt a sharp nudge in his side. His father was poking him to sit up, not to slump against the rail; the priest was only two places away.

"Corpus Domini nostri Jesu Christi custodiat animam tuam in vitam æternam."

Rudolph opened his mouth. He felt the sticky wax taste of the wafer on his tongue. He remained motionless for what seemed an interminable period of time, his head still raised, the wafer undissolved in his mouth. Then again he started at the pressure of his father's elbow, and saw that the people were falling away from the altar like leaves and turning with blind downcast eyes to their pews, alone with God.

Rudolph was alone with himself, drenched with perspiration and deep in mortal sin. As he walked back to his pew the sharp taps of his cloven hoofs were loud upon the floor, and he knew that it was a dark poison he carried in his heart.

V

"Sagitta Volante in Die"

The beautiful little boy with eyes like blue stones, and lashes that sprayed open from them like flower-petals had finished telling his sin to Father Schwartz—and the square of sunshine in which he sat had moved forward half an hour into the room. Rudolph had become less frightened now; once eased of the story a reaction had set in. He knew that as long as he was in the room with this priest God would not stop his heart, so he sighed and sat quietly, waiting for the priest to speak.

Father Schwartz's cold watery eyes were fixed upon the carpet pattern on which the sun had brought out the swastikas and the flat bloomless vines and the pale echoes of flowers. The hall-clock ticked insistently toward sunset, and from the ugly room and from the afternoon outside the window arose a stiff monotony, shattered now and then by the reverberate clapping of a far-away hammer on the dry air. The priest's nerves were strung thin and the beads of his rosary were crawling and squirming like snakes upon the green felt of his table top. He could not remember now what it was he should say.

Of all the things in this lost Swede town he was most aware of this little boy's eyes—the beautiful eyes, with lashes that left them reluctantly and curved back as though to meet them once more.

For a moment longer the silence persisted while Rudolph waited, and the priest struggled to remember something that was slipping farther and farther away from him, and the clock ticked in the broken house. Then Father Schwartz stared hard at the little boy and remarked in a peculiar voice:

"When a lot of people get together in the best places things go glimmering."

Rudolph started and looked quickly at Father Schwartz's face.

"I said—" began the priest, and paused, listening. "Do you hear the hammer and the clock ticking and the bees? Well, that's no good. The thing is to have a lot of people in the centre of the world, wherever that happens to be. Then"—his watery eyes widened knowingly—"things go glimmering."

"Yes, Father," agreed Rudolph, feeling a little frightened.

"What are you going to be when you grow up?"

"Well, I was going to be a baseball-player for a while," answered Rudolph nervously, "but I don't think that's a very good ambition, so I think I'll be an actor or a Navy officer."

Again the priest stared at him.

"I see *exactly* what you mean," he said, with a fierce air.

Rudolph had not meant anything in particular, and at the implication that he had, he became more uneasy.

"This man is crazy," he thought, "and I'm scared of him. He wants me to help him out some way, and I don't want to."

"You look as if things went glimmering," cried Father Schwartz wildly. "Did you ever go to a party?"

"Yes, Father."

"And did you notice that everybody was properly dressed? That's what I mean. Just as you went into the party there was a moment when everybody was properly dressed. Maybe two little girls were standing by the door and some boys were leaning over the banisters, and there were bowls around full of flowers."

"I've been to a lot of parties," said Rudolph, rather relieved that the conversation had taken this turn.

"Of course," continued Father Schwartz triumphantly, "I knew you'd agree with me. But my theory is that when a whole lot of people get together in the best places things go glimmering all the time."

Rudolph found himself thinking of Blatchford Sarnemington.

'Please listen to me!" commanded the priest impatiently. "Stop worrying about last Saturday. Apostasy implies an absolute damnation only on the supposition of a previous perfect faith. Does that fix it?"

Rudolph had not the faintest idea what Father Schwartz was talking about, but he nodded and the priest nodded back at him and returned to his mysterious preoccupation.

"Why," he cried, "they have lights now as big as stars—do you realize that? I heard of one light they had in Paris or somewhere that was as big as a star. A lot of people had it—a lot of gay people. They have all sorts of things now that you never dreamed of."

"Look here—" He came nearer to Rudolph, but the boy drew away, so Father Schwatz went back and sat down in his chair, his eyes dried out and hot. "Did you ever see an amusement park?"

"No, Father."

"Well, go and see an amusement park." The priest waved his hand vaguely. "It's a thing like a fair, only much more glittering. Go to one at night and stand a little way off from it in a dark place—under dark trees. You'll see a big wheel made of lights turning in the air, and a long slide shooting boats down into the water. A band playing somewhere, and a smell of peanuts—and everything will twinkle. But it won't remind you of anything, you see. It will all just hang out here in the night like a colored balloon—like a big yellow lantern on a pole."

Father Schwartz frowned as he suddenly thought of something.

"But don't get up close," he warned Rudolph, "because if you do you'll only feel the heat and the sweat and the life."

All this talking seemed particularly strange and awful to Rudolph, because this man was a priest. He sat there, half terrified, his beautiful eyes open wide and staring at Father Schwartz. But underneath his terror he felt that his own inner convictions were confirmed. There was something ineffably gorgeous somewhere that had nothing to do with God. He no longer thought that God was angry at him about the original lie, because He must have understood that Rudolph had done it to make things finer in the confessional, brightening up the dinginess of his admissions by saying a thing radiant and proud. At the moment when he had affirmed immaculate honor a silver pennon had flapped out into the breeze somewhere and there had been the crunch of leather and the shine of silver spurs and a troop of horsemen waiting for dawn on a low green hill. The sun had made stars of light on their breastplates like the picture at home of the German cuirassiers at Sedan.

But now the priest was muttering inarticulate and heartbroken words, and the boy became wildly afraid. Horror entered suddenly in at the open window, and the atmosphere of the room changed. Father Schwartz collapsed precipitously down on his knees, and let his body settle back against a chair.

"Oh, my God!" he cried out, in a strange voice, and wilted to the floor.

Then a human oppression rose from the priest's worn clothes, and mingled with the faint smell of old food in the corners. Rudolph gave a sharp cry and ran in a panic from the house—while the collapsed man lay there quite still, filling his room, filling it with voices and faces until it was crowded with echolalia, and rang loud with a steady, shrill note of laughter.

Outside the window the blue sirocco trembled over the wheat, and girls with yellow hair walked sensuously along roads that bounded the fields, calling innocent, exciting things to the young men who were working in the lines between the grain. Legs were shaped under starchless gingham, and rims of the necks of dresses were warm and damp. For five hours now hot fertile life had burned in the afternoon. It would be night in three hours, and all along the land there would be these blonde Northern girls and the tall young men from the farms lying out beside the wheat, under the moon.

QUESTIONS FOR DISCUSSION

1. On the basis of style, compare the opening paragraph of "Absolution" with the opening of "In Another Country." What are some of the salient characteristics of Fitzgerald's style?
2. Fitzgerald uses some rather old-fashioned stylistic devices, such as personification. Analyze the first paragraph of Section III. Are such rich rhetorical flights, here and elsewhere in the story, evocative or do they exhaust the possibilities of emotion and meaning? Explain.
3. "The pressure of his environment had driven him into the lonely secret road of adolescence." Find other passages in which Fitzgerald's sometimes abstract style leads him into making overt thematic inter-

pretations of the story. Which are least effective? Which are most effective? Do Fitzgerald's intrusive commentaries exhaust the thematic implications of the story? Elaborate.

4. A writer's imagination works just as powerfully in creating style as it does in creating characters and plots. Fitzgerald had to *imagine* this unusual image of Rudolph's eyes: "enormous, staccato eyes, lit with gleaming points of cobalt light." Find at least five other passages in which Fitzgerald's imagination produces effective images through style.
5. Does Fitzgerald's style and its tone change when the point of view shifts from the priest to Rudolph, to Rudolph's father? What changes in the style occur in Sections IV and V as Rudolph himself changes?
6. Why is "Absolution" written from two points of view?
7. There are three "revelations" in the story—the priest's, the boy's, and the reader's. Define each.

WRIGHT MORRIS
The Ram in the Thicket

In this dream Mr. Ormsby stood in the yard—at the edge of the yard where the weeds began–and stared at a figure that appeared to be on a rise. This figure had the head of a bird with a crown of bright, exotic plumage—visible, somehow, in spite of the helmet he wore. Wisps of it appeared at the side, or shot through the top of it like a pillow leaking long sharp spears of yellow straw. Beneath the helmet was the face of a bird, a long face indescribably solemn, with eyes so pale they were like openings on the sky. The figure was clothed in a uniform, a fatigue suit that was dry at the top but wet and dripping about the waist and knees. Slung over the left arm, very casually, was a gun. The right arm was extended and above it hovered a procession of birds, an endless coming and going of all the birds he had ever seen. The figure did not speak—nor did the pale eyes turn to look at him—although it was for this, this alone, that Mr. Ormsby was there. The only sounds he heard were those his lips made for the birds, a wooing call of irresistible charm. As he stared Mr. Ormsby realized that he was pinned to something, a specimen pinned to a wall that had quietly moved up behind. His hands were fastened over his head and from the weight he felt in his wrists he knew he must be suspended there. He knew he had been brought there to be judged, sentenced, or whatever—and this would happen when the figure looked at him. He waited, but the sky-blue eyes seemed only to focus on the birds, and his lips continued to speak to them wooingly. They came and went, thousands of them, and there were so many, and all so friendly, that Mr. Ormsby, also, extended his hand. He did this although he knew that up to that moment his hands were tied—but strange to relate, in that gesture, he seemed to be free. Without effort he broke the bonds and his hand was free. No birds came—but in his palm he felt the dull drip of the alarm clock and he held it tenderly, like a living thing, until it ran down.

In the morning light the photograph at the foot of his bed was a little startling—for the boy stood alone on a rise, and he held, very casually, a

Reprinted by permission of the author.

gun. The face beneath the helmet had no features, but Mr. Ormsby would have known it just by the—well, just by the stance. He would have known it just by the way the boy held the gun. He held the gun like some women held their arms when their hands were idle, like parts of their body that for the moment were not much use. Without the gun it was as if some part of the boy had been amputated; the way he stood, even the way he walked was not quite right. But with the gun—what seemed out, fell into place.

He had given the boy a gun because he had never had a gun himself and not because he wanted him to kill anything. The boy didn't want to kill anything either—he couldn't very well with his first gun because of the awful racket the bee-bees made in the barrel. He had given him a thousand-shot gun—but the rattle the bee-bees made in the barrel made it impossible for the boy to get close to anything. And *that* was what had made a hunter out of him. He had to stalk everything in order to get close enough to hit it, and after you stalk it you naturally want to hit something. When he got a gun that would really shoot, and only made a racket after he shot it, it was only natural that he shot it better than anyone else. He said shoot, because the boy never seemed to realize that when he shot and hit something the something was dead. He simply didn't realize this side of things at all. But when he brought a rabbit home and fried it—by himself, for Mother wouldn't let *him* touch it—he never kidded them about the meat they ate themselves. He never really knew whether the boy did that out of kindness for Mother, or simply because he never thought about such things. He never seemed to feel like talking much about anything. He would sit and listen to Mother—he had never once been disrespectful—nor had he ever once heeded anything she said. He would listen, respectfully, and that was all. It was a known fact that Mother knew more about birds and bird migration than anyone in the state of Pennsylvania—except the boy. It was clear to him that the boy knew more, but for years it had been Mother's business and it meant more to her—the business did—than to the boy. But it was only natural that a woman who founded the League for Wild Life Conservation would be upset by a boy who lived with a gun. It was only natural–he was upset himself by the *idea* of it—but the boy and his gun somehow never bothered him. He had never seen a boy and a dog, or a boy and anything, any closer—and if the truth were known both the boy's dogs knew it, nearly died of it. Not that he wasn't friendly, or as nice to them as any boy, but they knew they simply didn't rate in a class with his gun. Without that gun the boy himself really looked funny, didn't know how to stand, and nearly fell over if you talked to him. It was only natural that he enlisted, and there was nothing he ever heard that surprised him less than their making a hero out of him. Nothing more natural than that they should name something after him. If the boy had had his choice it would have been a gun rather than a boat, a thousand-shot non-rattle bee-bee gun named Ormsby. But it would kill Mother if she knew—maybe it would kill nearly anybody—what he thought was the most natural thing of all. Let God strike him dead if he had known anything righter, anything more natural, than that the boy should be killed. That was something he could not explain, and would certainly never mention to Mother unless he slipped up some night and talked in his sleep.

He turned slowly on the bed, careful to keep the springs quiet, and as he lowered his feet he scooped his socks from the floor. As a precaution Mother had slept the first few months of their marriage in her corset—as a precaution and as an aid to self-control. In the fall they had ordered twin beds. Carrying his shoes—today, of all days, would be a trial for Mother—he tiptoed to the closet and picked up his shirt and pants. There was simply no reason, as he had explained to her twenty years ago, why she should get up when he could just as well get a bite for himself. He had made that suggestion when the boy was just a baby and she needed her strength. Even as it was she didn't come out of it any too well. The truth was, Mother was so thorough about everything she did that her breakfasts usually took an hour or more. When he did it himself he was out of the kitchen in ten, twelve minutes and without leaving any pile of dishes around. By himself he could quick-rinse them in a little hot water, but with Mother there was the dish pan and all of the suds. Mother had the idea that a meal simply wasn't a meal without setting the table and using half the dishes in the place. It was easier to do it himself, and except for Sunday, when they had brunch, he was out of the house an hour before she got up. He had a bite of lunch at the store and at four o'clock he did the day's shopping since he was right downtown anyway. There was a time he called her up and inquired as to what she thought she wanted, but since he did all the buying he knew that better himself. As secretary for the League of Women Voters she had enough on her mind in times like these without cluttering it up with food. Now that he left the store an hour early he usually got home in the midst of her nap or while she was taking her bath. As he had nothing else to do he prepared the vegetables, and dressed the meat, as Mother had never shown much of a flair for meat. There had been a year—when the boy was small and before he had taken up that gun—when she had made several marvelous lemon meringue pies. But feeling as she did about the gun—and she told them both how she felt about it—she didn't see why she should slave in the kitchen for people like that. She always spoke to them as *they*—or as *you* plural—from the time he had given the boy the gun. Whether this was because they were both men, both culprits, or both something else, they were never entirely separate things again. When she called *they* would both answer, and though the boy had been gone two years he still felt him *there,* right beside him, when Mother said *you.*

For some reason he could not understand—although the rest of the house was as neat as a pin, too neat—the room they *lived* in was always a mess. Mother refused to let the cleaning woman set her foot in it. Whenever she left the house she locked the door. Long, long ago, he had said something, and she had said something, and she had said she had wanted one room in the house where she could relax and just let her hair down. That had sounded so wonderfully human, so unusual for Mother, that he had been completely taken with it. As a matter of fact he still didn't know what to say. It was the only room in the house—except for the screened-in porch in the summer—where he could take off his shoes and open his shirt on his underwear. If the room was *clean*, it would be clean like all of the others, and that would leave him nothing but the basement and the porch. The way the boy took to the out-of-doors—he stopped looking for his cuff links, began to look for pins—was partially because he couldn't find a place in the house to sit down. They had just redecorated the house—the boy at that time was just a little shaver—and Mother had spread newspapers over everything. There hadn't been a chair in the place—except the straight-backed ones at the table—that hadn't been, that *wasn't* covered with a piece of newspaper. Anyone who had ever scrunched around on a paper knew what that was like. It was at that time that he had got the idea of having his pipe in the basement, reading in the bedroom, and the boy had taken to the out-of-doors. Because he had always wanted a gun himself, and because the boy was alone, with no kids around to play with, he had brought him home that damn gun. A thousand-shot gun by the name of Daisy—funny that he should remember the name—and five thousand bee-bees in a drawstring canvas bag.

That gun had been a mistake—he began to shave himself in tepid, lukewarm water rather than let it run hot, which would bang the pipes and wake Mother up. That gun had been a mistake—when the telegram came that the boy had been killed Mother hadn't said a word, but she made it clear whose fault it was. There was never any doubt, *any* doubt, as to just whose fault it was.

He stopped thinking while he shaved, attentive to the mole at the edge of his mustache, and leaned to the mirror to avoid dropping suds on the rug. There had been a time when he had wondered about an oriental throw rug in the bathroom, but over twenty years he had become accustomed to it. As a matter of fact he sort of missed it whenever they had guests with children and Mother remembered to take it up. Without the rug he always felt just a little uneasy, a little naked, in the bathroom, and this made him whistle or turn on the water and let it run. If it hadn't been for that he might not have noticed as soon as he did that Mother did the same thing whenever anybody was in the house. She turned on the water and let it run until she was through with the toilet, then she would flush it before she turned the water off. If you happen to have old-fashioned plumbing, and have lived with a person for twenty years, you can't help noticing little things like that. He had got to be a little like that himself: since the boy had gone he used the one in the basement or waited until he got down to the store. As a matter of fact it was more convenient, didn't wake Mother up, and he could have his pipe while he was sitting there.

With his pants on, but carrying his shirt—for he might get it soiled preparing breakfast—he left the bathroom and tiptoed down the stairs.

Although the boy had gone, was gone, that is, Mother still liked to preserve her slip covers and the kitchen linoleum. It was a good piece, well worth preserving, but unless there were guests in the house he never saw it—he nearly forgot that it was there. The truth was he had to look at it once a week, every time he put down the papers—but right now he couldn't tell you what color that linoleum was! He couldn't do it, and wondering what in the world color it was he bent over and peeked at it—blue. Blue and white, Mother's favorite colors of course.

Suddenly he felt the stirring in his bowels. Usually this occurred while he was rinsing the dishes after his second cup of coffee or after the first long draw on his pipe. He was not supposed to smoke in the morning, but it was more important to be regular that way than irregular with his pipe. Mother had been the first to realize this—not in so many words —but she would rather he did anything than not be able to do *that.*

He measured out a pint and a half of water, put it over a medium fire, and added just a pinch of salt. Then he walked to the top of the basement stairs, turned on the light, and at the bottom turned it off. He dipped his head to pass beneath a sagging line of wash, the sleeves dripping, and with his hands out, for the corner was dark, he entered the cell.

The basement toilet had been put in to accommodate the help, who had to use something, and Mother would not have them on her oriental rug. Until the day he dropped some money out of his pants and had to strike a match to look for it, he had never noticed what kind of a stool it was. Mother had picked it up secondhand—she had never told him where—because she couldn't see buying something new for a place always in the dark. It was very old, with a chain pull, and operated on a principle that invariably produced quite a splash. But in spite of that, he preferred it to the one at the store and very much more than the one upstairs. This was rather hard to explain since the seat was pretty cold in the winter and the water sometimes nearly froze. But it was private like no other room in the house. Considering that the house was as good as empty, that was a strange thing to say, but it was the only way to say how he felt. If he went off for a walk like the boy, Mother would miss him, somebody would see him, and he wouldn't feel right about it anyhow. All he wanted was a dark quiet place and the feeling that for five minutes, just five minutes, nobody would be looking for him. Who would ever believe five minutes like that were so hard to come by? The closest he had ever been to the boy—after he had given him the gun—was the morning he had found him here on the stool. It was then that the boy had said, *et tu, Brutus*, and they had both laughed so hard they had had to hold their sides. The boy had put his head in a basket of wash so Mother wouldn't hear. Like everything the boy said there were two or three ways to take it, and in the dark Mr. Ormsby could not see his face. When he stopped laughing the boy said, *Well, Pop, I suppose one flush ought to do,* but Mr. Ormsby had not been able to say anything. To be called Pop made him so weak that he had to sit right down on the stool, just like he was, and support his head in his hands. Just as he had never had a name for the boy, the boy had never had a name for him—none, that is, that Mother would permit him to use. Of all the names Mother couldn't stand, Pop was the worst, and he agreed with her, it was vulgar, common, and used by strangers to intimidate old men. He agreed with her, completely—until he heard the word in the boy's mouth. It was only natural that the boy would use it if he ever had the chance—but he never dreamed that any word, especially *that* word, could mean what it did. It made him weak, he had to sit down and pretend he was going about his business, and what a blessing it was that the place was dark. Nothing more was said, ever, but it remained their most important conversation—so important they were afraid to try and improve on it. Days later he remembered the rest of the boy's sentence, and how shocking it was but without any *sense* of shock. A blow so sharp that he had no sense of pain, only a knowing, as he had under gas, that he had been worked on. For two, maybe three minutes, there in the dark they had been what Mother called them, they were *they*—and they were there in the basement because they were so much alike. When the telegram came, and when he knew what he would find, he had brought it there, had struck a match, and read what it said. The match filled the cell with light and he saw—he couldn't help seeing—piles of tin goods in the space beneath the stairs. Several dozen cans of tuna fish and salmon, and since *he* was the one that had the points, bought the groceries, there was only one place Mother could have got such things. It had been a greater shock than the telegram—that was the honest-to-God's truth and anyone who knew Mother as well as he did would have felt the same. It was unthinkable, but there it was—and there were more on top of the water closet, where he peered while precariously balanced on the stool. Cans of pineapple, crabmeat, and tins of Argentine beef. He had been stunned, the match had burned down and actually scorched his fingers, and he nearly killed himself when he forgot and stepped off the seat. Only later in the morning—after he had sent the flowers to ease the blow for Mother—did he realize how such a thing *must* have occurred. Mother knew so many influential people, and before the war they gave her so much, that they had very likely given her all of this stuff as well. Rather than turn it down and needlessly alienate people, influential people, Mother had done the next best thing. While the war was on she refused to serve it, or profiteer in any way—and at the same time not alienate people foolishly. It had been an odd thing, certainly, that he should discover all of that by the same match that he read the telegram. Naturally, he never breathed a word of it to Mother, as something like that, even though she was not superstitious, would really upset her. It was one of those things that he and the boy would keep to themselves.

It would be like Mother to think of putting it in here, the very last place that the cleaning woman would look for it. The new cleaning woman would neither go upstairs nor down, and did whatever she did somewhere else. Mr. Ormsby lit a match to see if everything was all right—hastily blew it out when he saw that the can pile had increased. He stood up—then hurried up the stairs without buttoning his pants as he could hear the water boiling. He added half a cup, then measured three heaping tablespoons of coffee into the bottom of the double boiler, buttoned his pants. Looking at his watch he saw that it was seven-thirty-five. As it would be a hard day—sponsoring a boat was a man-size job—he would give Mother another ten minutes or so. He took two bowls from the cupboard, sat them on blue pottery saucers, and with the grapefruit knife in his hand walked to the icebox.

As he put his head in the icebox door—in order to see he had to—Mr. Ormsby stopped breathing and closed his eyes. What had been dying for some time was now dead. He leaned back, inhaled, leaned in again. The floor of the icebox was covered with a fine assortment of jars full of leftovers Mother simply could not throw away. Some of the jars were covered with little oilskin hoods, some with saucers, and some with paper snapped on with a rubber band. It was impossible to tell, from the outside, which one it was. Seating himself on the floor he removed them one at a time, starting at the front and working toward the back. As he had done this many times before, he got well into the problem, near the middle, before troubling to sniff anything. A jar which might have been carrots—it was hard to tell without probing—was now a furry marvel of green mold. It smelled only mildly, however, and Mr. Ormsby remembered that this was penicillin, the life-giver. A spoonful of cabbage—it had been three months since they had had cabbage—had a powerful stench but was still not the one he had in mind. There were two more jars of mold, the one screwed tight he left alone as it had a frosted look and the top of the lid bulged. The culprit, however, was not that at all, but in an open saucer on the next shelf—part of an egg—Mr. Ormsby had beaten the white himself. He placed the saucer on the sink and returned all but two of the jars to the icebox; the cabbage and the explosive looking one. If it smelled he took it out, otherwise Mother had to see for herself as she refused to take *their* word for these things.

When he was just a little shaver the boy had walked into the living room full of Mother's guests and showed them something in a jar. Mother had been horrified—but she naturally thought it a frog or something and not a bottle out of her own icebox. When one of the ladies asked the boy where in the world he had found it, he naturally said, *In the icebox*. Mother had never forgiven him. After that she forbade him to look in the box without permission, and the boy had not so much as peeked in it since. He would eat only what he found on the table, or ready to eat in the kitchen—or what he found at the end of those walks he took everywhere.

With the jar of cabbage and furry mold Mr. Ormsby made a trip to the garage, picked up the garden spade, walked around behind. At one time he had emptied the jars and merely buried the contents, but recently, since the war that is, he had buried it all. Part of it was a question of time—he had more work to do at the store—but the bigger part of it was to put an end to the jars. Not that it worked out that way—all Mother had to do was open a new one—but it gave him a real satisfaction to bury them. Now that the boy and his dogs were gone there was simply no one around the house to eat up all the food Mother saved.

There were worms in the fork of earth he had turned and he stood looking at them—*they* both had loved worms—when he remembered the water was boiling on the stove. He dropped everything and ran, ran right into Emil Ludlow, the milkman, before he noticed him. Still on the run he went up the steps and through the screen door into the kitchen—he was clear to the stove before he remembered the door would slam. He started back, but too late, and in the silence that followed the *bang* he stood with his eyes tightly closed, his fists clenched. Usually he remained in this condition until a sign from Mother—a thump on the floor or her voice at the top of the stairs. None came, however, only the sound of the milk bottles that Emil Ludlow was leaving on the porch. Mr. Ormsby gave him time to get away, waited until he heard the horse walking, then he went out and brought the milk in. At the icebox he remembered the water—why it was he had come running in the first place—and he left the door open and hurried to the stove. It was down to half a cup but not, thank heavens, dry. He added a full pint, then returned and put the milk in the icebox; took out the butter, four eggs, and a Flori-gold grapefruit. Before he cut the grapefruit he looked at his watch and seeing that it was ten minutes to eight, an hour before train time, he opened the stairway door.

"Ohhh Mother!" he called, and then returned to the grapefruit.

Ad astra per aspera, she said, and rose from the bed. In the darkness she felt about for her corset then let herself go completely for the thirty-five seconds it required to get it on. This done, she pulled the cord to the light that hung in the attic, and as it snapped on, in a firm voice she said, *Fiat lux.* Light having been made, Mother opened her eyes.

As the bulb hung in the attic, thirty feet away and out of sight, the closet remained in an afterglow, a twilight zone. It was not light, strictly speaking, but it was all Mother wanted to see. Seated on the attic stairs she trimmed her toenails with a pearl handled knife that Mr. Ormsby had been missing for several years. The blade was not so good any longer and using it too freely had resulted in ingrown nails on both of her big toes. But Mother preferred it to scissors which were proven, along with bathtubs, to be one of the most dangerous things in the home. *Even more than the battlefield, the most dangerous place in the world. Dry feet and hands before turning on lights, dry between toes.*

Without stooping she slipped into her sabots and left the closet, the light burning, and with her eyes dimmed, but not closed, went down the hall. Locking the bathroom door she stepped to the basin and turned on the cold water, then she removed several feet of paper from the toilet paper roll. This took time, as in order to keep the roller from squeaking, it had to be removed from its socket in the wall, then returned. One piece she put in the pocket of her kimono, the other she folded into a wad and used as a blotter to dab up spots on the floor. Turning up the water she sat down on the stool—then she got up to get a pencil and pad from the table near the window. On the first sheet she wrote—

Ars longa, vita brevis
Wildflower club, Sun. 4 pm.

She tore this off and filed it, tip showing, right at the front of her corset. On the next page—

ROGER—
Ivory Snow
Sani-Flush on Thurs.

As she placed this on top of the toilet paper roll she heard him call "First for breakfast." She waited until he closed the stairway door, then she stood up and turned on the shower. As it rained into the tub and splashed behind her in the basin, she lowered the lid, flushed the toilet. Until the water closet had filled, stopped gurgling, she stood at the window watching a squirrel cross the yard from tree to tree. Then she turned the shower off and noisily dragged the shower curtain, on its metal rings, back to the wall. She dampened her shower cap in the basin and hung it on the towel rack to dry, dropping the towel that was there down the laundry chute. This done, she returned to the basin and held her hands under the running water, now cold, until she was awake. With her index finger she massaged her gums—*there is no pyorrhea among the Indians*—and then, with the tips of her fingers, she dampened her eyes.

She drew the blind, and in the half light the room seemed to be full of lukewarm water, greenish in color. With a piece of Kleenex, she dried her eyes, then turned it to gently blow her nose, first the left side, then with a little more blow on the right. There was nothing to speak of, nothing, so she folded the tissue, slipped it into her pocket. Raising the blind, she faced the morning with her eyes softly closed, letting the light come in as prescribed—gradually. Eyes wide, she then stared for a full minute at the yard full of grackles, covered with grackles, before she *discovered* them. Running to the door, her head in the hall, her arm in the bathroom wildly pointing, she tried to whisper, loud-whisper to him, but her voice cracked.

"Roger," she called, a little hoarsely. "The window—run!"

She heard him turn from the stove and skid on the newspapers, bump into the sink, curse, then get up and on again.

"Blackbirds?" he whispered.

"Grackles!" she said, for the thousandth time she said *Grackles.*

"They're pretty!" he said.

"Family—" she said, ignoring him, "family *icteridae* American."

"Well—" he said.

"Roger!" she said, "something's burning."

She heard him leave the window and on his way back to the stove, on the same turn, skid on the papers again. She left him there and went down the hall to the bedroom, closed the door, and passed between the mirrors once more to the closet. From five dresses—*any woman with more than five dresses, at this time, should have the vote taken away from her*—she selected the navy blue sheer with pink lace yoke and kerchief, short bolero. At the back of the closet—but in order to see she had to return to the bathroom, look for the flashlight in the drawer full of rags and old tins of shoe polish—were three shelves, each supporting ten to twelve pairs of shoes, and a large selection of slippers were piled on the floor. On the second shelf were the navy blue pumps—*we all have one weakness, but between men and shoes you can give me shoes*—navy blue pumps with a cuban heel and a small bow. She hung the dress from the neck of the floor lamp, placed the shoes on the bed. From beneath the bed she pulled a hat box—the hat was new. Navy straw with shasta daisies, pink geraniums and a navy blue veil with pink and white fuzzy dots. She held it out where it could be seen in the mirror, front and side, without seeing herself—*it's not every day that one sponsors a boat.* Not every day, and she turned to the calendar on her night table, a bird calendar featuring the natural-color male goldfinch for the month of June. Under the date of June 23rd she printed the words, *family icteridae—yardful,* and beneath it—

Met Captain Sudcliffe and gave him U.S.S. *Ormsby*

When he heard Mother's feet on the stairs Mr. Ormsby cracked her soft-boiled eggs and spooned them carefully into her heated cup. He had spilled his own on the floor when he had run to look at the black—or whatever color they were—birds. As they were very, very soft he had merely wiped them up. As he buttered the toast—the four burned slices were on the back porch airing—Mother entered the kitchen and said, "Roger—*more* toast?"

"I was watching blackbirds," he said.

"Grack-les," she said. "Any bird is a *black*bird if the males are largely or entirely black."

Talk about male and female birds really bothered Mr. Ormsby. Although she was a girl of the old school Mother never hesitated, *anywhere*, to speak right out about male and female birds. A cow was a cow, a bull was a bull, but to Mr. Ormsby a bird was a bird.

"Among the birdfolk," said Mother, "the menfolk, so to speak, wear the feathers. The female has more serious work to do."

"How does that fit the blackbirds?" said Mr. Ormsby.

"Every rule," said Mother, "has an exception."

There was no denying the fact that the older Mother got the more distinguished she appeared. As for himself, what he saw in the mirror looked very much like the Roger Ormsby that had married Violet Ames twenty years ago. As the top of his head got hard the bottom tended to get a little soft, but otherwise there wasn't much change. But it was hard to believe that Mother was the pretty little pop-eyed girl—he had thought it was her corset that popped them—whose nipples had been like buttons on her dress. Any other girl would have looked like a you-know—but there wasn't a man in Media county, or anywhere else, who ever mentioned it. A man could think what he would think, but he was the only man who really knew what Mother was like. And how little she was like *that*.

"Three-seven-four east one-one-six," said Mother.

That was the way her mind worked, all over the place in one cup of coffee—birds one moment, Mrs. Dinardo the next.

He got up from the table and went after Mrs. Dinardo's letter—Mother seldom had time to read them unless he read them to her. Returning, he divided the rest of the coffee between them, unequally: three quarters for Mother, a swallow of grounds for himself. He waited a moment, wiping his glasses, while Mother looked through the window at another black bird. "Cowbird," she said, "*Molothrus ater.*"

"Dear Mrs. Ormsby," Mr. Ormsby began. Then he stopped to scan the page, as Mrs. Dinardo had a strange style and was not much given to writing letters. "Dear Mrs. Ormsby," he repeated, "I received your letter and I Sure was glad to know that you are both well and I know you often think of me I often think of you too—" He paused to get his breath—Mrs. Dinardo's style was not much for pauses—and to look at Mother. But Mother was still with the cowbird. "Well, Mrs. Ormsby," he continued, "I haven't a thing in a room that I know of the people that will be away from the room will be only a week next month. But come to See me I may have Something if you don't get Something." Mrs. Dinardo, for some reason, always capitalized the letter S which along with everything else didn't make it easier to read. "We are both well and he is Still in the Navy Yard. My I do wish the war was over it is So long. We are So tired of it do come and See us when you give them your boat. Wouldn't a Street be better than a boat? If you are going to name Something why not a Street? Here in my hand is news of a boat Sunk what is wrong with Ormsby on a Street? Well 116 is about the Same we have the river and its nice. If you don't find Something See me I may have Something. Best love, Mrs. Myrtle Dinardo."

It was quite a letter to get from a woman that Mother had known, known Mother, that is, for nearly eighteen years. Brought in to nurse the boy—he could never understand why a woman like Mother, with her figure—but anyhow, Mrs. Dinardo was brought in. Something in her milk, Dr. Paige said, when it was as plain as the nose on your face it was nothing in the milk, but something in the boy. He just refused, plain refused, to nurse with Mother. The way the little rascal would look at her, but not a sound out of him but gurgling when Mrs. Dinardo would scoop him up and go upstairs to their room—the only woman—other woman, that is, that Mother ever let step inside of it. She had answered an ad that Mother had run, on Dr. Paige's suggestion, and they had been like *that* from the first time he saw them.

"I'll telephone," said Mother.

On the slightest provocation Mother would call Mrs. Dinardo by long distance—she had to come down four flights of stairs to answer—and tell her she was going to broadcast over the radio or something. Although Mrs. Dinardo hardly knew one kind of bird from another, Mother sent her printed copies of every single one of her bird-lore lectures. She also sent her hand-pressed flowers from the garden.

"I'll telephone," repeated Mother.

"My own opinion—" began Mr. Ormsby, but stopped when Mother picked up her eggcup, made a pile of her plates, and started toward the sink. "I'll take care of that," he said. "Now you run along and telephone." But Mother walked right by him and took her stand at the sink. With one hand—with the other she held her kimono close about her—she let the water run into the large dish pan. Mr. Ormsby had hoped to avoid this; now he would have to first rinse, then dry, every piece of silver and every dish they had used. As Mother could only use one hand it would be even slower than usual.

"We don't want to miss our local," he said. "You better run along and let me do it."

"Cold water," she said, "for the eggs." He had long ago learned not to argue with Mother about the fine points of washing pots, pans, or dishes with bits of egg. He stood at the sink with the towel while she went about trying to make suds with a piece of stale soap in a little wire cage. As Mother refused to use a fresh piece of soap, nothing remotely like suds ever appeared. For this purpose, he kept a box of Gold Dust Twins concealed beneath the sink, and when Mother turned her back he slipped some in.

"There now," Mother said, and placed the rest of the dishes in the water, rinsed her fingers under the tap, paused to sniff at them.

"My own opinion—" Mr. Ormsby began, but stopped when Mother raised her finger, the index finger with the scar from the wart she once had. They stood quiet, and Mr. Ormsby listened to the water drip in the sink—the night before he had come down in his bare feet to shut it off. All of the taps dripped now and there was just nothing to do about it but put a rag or something beneath it to break the ping.

"Thrush!" said Mother. "Next to the nightingale the most popular of European songbirds."

"Very pretty," he said, although he simply couldn't hear a thing. Mother walked to the window, folding the collar of her kimono over her bosom and drawing the tails into a hammock beneath her behind. Mr. Ormsby modestly turned away. He quick-dipped one hand into the Gold Dust—drawing it out he slipped it into the dish pan and worked up a suds.

As he finished wiping the dishes she came in with a bouquet for Mrs. Dinardo and arranged it, for the moment, in a tall glass.

"According to her letter," Mr. Ormsby said, "she isn't too sure of having something—"

"Roger!" she said. "You're dripping."

Mr. Ormsby put his hands over the sink and said, "If we're going to be met right at the station I don't see where you're going to see Mrs. Dinardo. You're going to be met at the station and then you're going to sponsor the boat. My own opinion is that after the boat we come on home."

"I know that street of hers," said Mother. "There isn't a wildflower on it!"

On the wall above the icebox was a pad of paper and a blue pencil hanging by a string. As Mother started to write the point broke off, fell behind the icebox.

"Mother," he said, "you ever see my knife?"

"Milkman," said Mother. "If we're staying overnight we won't need milk in the morning."

In jovial tones Mr. Ormsby said, "I'll bet we're right back here before dark." That was all, that was *all* that he said. He had merely meant to call her attention to the fact that Mrs. Dinardo said—all but said—that she didn't have a room for them. But when Mother turned he saw that her mustache was showing, a sure sign that she was mad.

"Well—now," Mother said, and lifting the skirt of her kimono, swished around the cabinet and then he heard her on the stairs. From the landing at the top of the stairs she said, "In that case I'm sure there's no need for *my* going. I'm sure the Navy would just as soon have you. After all," she said, "it's *your* name on the boat!"

"Now, Mother," he said, just as she closed the door, *not* slammed it, just closed it as quiet and nice as you'd please. Although he had been through this a thousand times it seemed he was never ready for it, never knew when it would happen, never felt anything but nearly sick. He went into the front room and sat down on the chair near the piano—then got up to arrange the doily at the back of his head. Ordinarily he could leave the house and after three or four days it would blow over, but in all his life—their life—there had been nothing like this. The Government of the United States—he got up again and called, "OHHhhh Mother!"

No answer.

He could hear her moving around upstairs, but as she often went back to bed after a spat, just moving around didn't mean much of anything. He came back into the front room and sat down on the milk stool near the fireplace. It was the only seat in the room not protected with newspapers. The only thing the boy ever sat on when he had to sit on something. Somehow, thinking about that made him stand up. He could sit in the lawn swing, in the front yard, if Mother hadn't told everybody in town why it was that he, Roger Ormsby, would have to take the day off—not to sit in the lawn swing, not by a long shot. Everybody knew—Captain Sudcliffe's nice letter had appeared on the first page of the *Graphic*, under a picture of Mother leading a bird-lore hike in the Poconos. This picture bore the title LOCAL WOMAN HEADS DAWN BUSTERS, and marked Mother's appearance on the national bird-lore scene. But it was not one of her best pictures—it dated from way back in the twenties and those hipless dresses and round bucket hats were not Mother's type. Until they saw that picture, and the letter beneath it, some people had forgotten that Virgil was missing, and most of them seemed to think it was a good idea to swap him for a boat. The U.S.S. *Ormsby* was a permanent sort of thing. Although he was born and raised in the town hardly anybody knew very much about Virgil, but they all were pretty familiar with his boat. "How's that boat of yours coming along?" they would say, but in more than twenty years nobody had ever asked him about *his* boy. Whose boy? Well, that was just the point. Everyone agreed Ormsby was a fine name for a boat.

It would be impossible to explain to Mother, maybe to anybody for that matter, what this U.S.S. *Ormsby* business meant to him. "The" boy and "The" *Ormsby*—it was a pretty strange thing that they both had the definite article, and gave him the feeling he was facing a monument.

"Oh Rog-gerrr!" Mother called.

"Coming," he said, and made for the stairs.

From the bedroom Mother said, "However I might feel personally, I do have my *own* name to think of. I am not one of these people who can do as they please—Roger, are you listening?"

"Yes, Mother," he said.

"—with their life."

As he went around the corner he found a note pinned to the door.

Bathroom window up
Cellar door down
Is it blue or brown for Navy?

He stopped on the landing and looked up the stairs.

"Did you say something?" she said.

"No, Mother—" he said, then he added, "It's blue. For the Navy, Mother, it's blue."

QUESTIONS FOR DISCUSSION

1. In each of the three stories in this section, the point of view is different: first-person in Hemingway's story, third-person omniscient in Fitzgerald's, third-person central (with one brief shift to Mother's point of view) in Morris's. Given the point of view, what makes the style appropriate in each story? How does the point of view dictate the style in each story?
2. Analyze Morris's style to show how he achieves an effect of informality, a conversational tone. Discuss the effect of presenting Ormsby's long meditations and ruminations, then Mother's brief, crisp actions, meshed with her aphoristic thoughts and sayings, juxtaposed to more immediate dialogue scenes when they meet.
3. What relationship do you see between Morris's underwritten style, full of subtle references and implications, and the kind of characters delineated through that style?
4. Analyze those elements of Morris's style that create comic moments and effects.
5. One feature of Morris's style is his compulsion to play on words and to use clichés. Analyze the scene in which Ormsby encounters his son in the basement john. What does he do with clichés in that scene? With word play? With paradox?
6. Having eliminated conventional kinds of action, how does Morris invest his style itself with active qualities? Notice, for instance, that

he mixes many actions within a sentence, creating suspense with parenthetical delays: "Without stooping she slipped into her sabots and left the closet, the light burning, and with her eyes dimmed, but not closed, went down the hall." Find other devices that create a sense of movement within the style.

7. In rendering mental processes simultaneously with ordinary actions, Morris risks making his story too static. Impingement is one of the devices of style that he uses to combat the threat of a static quality. "When he heard Mother's feet on the stairs Mr. Ormsby cracked her soft-boiled eggs." The first action impinges upon the second, making the reader feel that something is happening immediately to him rather than being described statically to him; one also feels that two things are happening simultaneously. Find other instances of impingement and simultaneity in Morris's style.

4 Devices: Implication, Contrast and Irony, Symbol and Allusion

In earlier sections of this text, we have suggested that most stories gain their effects and meaning *primarily* through the interaction of character and situation. But in most stories, we also find other details, other passages, other juxtapositions that *add to* meaning or effect. The editors of this text call these "extra ingredients" *devices*, and we propose here to define and comment briefly on some of the most important and frequently used of these fictional devices.

Implication

The basic characteristic that differentiates fiction from nonfiction is its reliance upon implication. "Always show, never tell" was Chekhov's advice to fiction writers, and with minor exceptions writers have taken that as a general principle. But communication through implication or suggestion places certain burdens on the reader. Hence, some of the inevitable questions that arise when a student is asked to "interpret" a story are: Why do fiction writers handle characters and themes as they do? Why don't they just *say* what they mean?

We have already suggested one answer: The story that does not employ implication is less interesting than the one that does. Indeed, as you become an increasingly sophisticated reader, you will discover that a story's interest is in direct ratio to the extent to which it employs implication.

A second answer is to be discovered in the basic intent of fiction. Before it is anything else, a story is an attempt to communicate an experience. One ingredient of experience is emotion. And in the communication of emotion, the writer *must* use indirection; T. S. Eliot's generalization that one cannot transmit emotion directly is as valid for fiction as for poetry. To be more specific: a writer cannot *tell* you that a character is sad and produce sadness in you; you may *understand* his feelings, but you will not *feel* anything. The reason is that the writer has used an abstraction in order to try to transmit something that is concrete: sadness is a vague and general term for a countless number of specific feelings, each of them the product of a specific set of circumstances. Hence, if a writer is going to make you feel "sad," he must work indirectly. He must provide you with a convincing character with whom you can, in some degree, identify. He must place that character in a situation in which a specific emotional reaction is inherent. He may, in addition, employ other devices or techniques that help to evoke emotion—devices like imagery, rhythm, tone, irony, contrast. Meanwhile, you, the reader, must also do something. You are not the character in a given story nor are you in the character's position. But the writer assumes that you have been in similar situations and have experienced similar emotions, and if he can make you recall these, he can also evoke in you the emotions that attended them. And when he goes through this process, he is employing implication.

Or consider theme. Most generally, a writer handles theme indirectly because he distrusts the accuracy, the completeness, or the forcefulness of a generalization. A writer may quite humanly want to convince us that his interpretation of some aspect of the human condition is valid. To accomplish this, he can choose between two methods. On the one hand, he can appeal to his reader intellectually, through logic, reason, argument—that is, he can write an essay. On the other, he can appeal emotionally by subjecting his reader to an experience that seems to corroborate his thesis—that is, he can write a story. The first method will enable a reader to *understand* an abstract concept; the second can, with luck and skill, force the reader to *feel* the validity of that same concept.

The desire to transmit experience is the basic reason for the employment of implication in fiction. But there are others. One is a writer's desire for *accuracy*. It may seem paradoxical, but a writer often can say most accurately what he wants to say by *not* saying it. In all studies of the process of communication, it is a truism that the more one relies on abstractions or generalizations in order to transmit meaning, the less effectively one communicates; conversely, the more specific and concrete one is, the more clearly he conveys what he means. That basic principle has been known to storytellers from the beginning. Does one want to evoke a feeling of excitement in an audience? There are as many different feelings that we can call excitement as there are experiences that evoke the feeling. Hence, if we are to capture a specific and exact feeling that might be termed excitement, we must present the experience that evokes it.

Contrast and Irony

Any reader must soon become aware of the fact that *contrast* is one of the ever-present ingredients in fiction. It is to be found in every element of fiction and on every possible level of meaning or effect. It is the necessary a priori characteristic of all conflict, external or internal; the very concept of antagonist and protagonist presupposes conflict. Contrast is frequently one of the most important methods of defining and realizing character; the use of *foils* in stories is one of the least subtle ways by which writers "realize" people. And no reader can overlook for long the part that contrast plays in communicating emotional effect: the juxtaposition of two contrasting emotions, the use of understatement or exaggeration in such a way that style contrasts with content, the movement in a story from one emotion to an opposite emotion, all testify to the importance of contrast in making us feel an experience in fiction.

Because of its prevalence in fiction, one type of contrast demands particular attention. *Irony* may be defined as a contrast, a disparity between what actually is and what ought to be, or between what is and what seems to be, or between what is and what we could wish it to be. The heart of irony is incongruity, the linking together of opposites. So prevalent is it that one critic has gone so far as to insist that a story cannot exist without it; and it would indeed be difficult to find a story, modern or not, that does not contain at least one element of irony.

You will find irony assuming several forms. Easiest to recognize will be *verbal irony*; here a character (or a writer) will say one thing but mean the opposite. Other forms of irony are at once more important (to a story's theme or characterization or total effect) and more difficult to perceive. Irony, for example, may be inherent in a *situation*; a story in which a person spends a lifetime in the pursuit of money only to discover that the goal was not worth the struggle would be employing situational irony. Or a story can employ what one critic has called irony of *attitude*; a story might present us with a John Bircher who thinks of himself as democratic but whom the reader sees as the opposite of democratic. Or a story can employ the subtlest of all types of irony, *tonal irony*; by choice of word or phrase, by selection of detail, simply by shrewd juxtaposition, writers can suggest that what they seem to be saying should not be taken literally. The frequent use of *understatement* in fiction (stating the important as though it were trivial) and the use of *hyperbole* or *exaggeration* (stating the trivial as though it were important) are two examples of tonal irony.

Whatever form irony may assume, it is crucial that a reader be alert to it, for both a story's meaning and its effect may depend upon it. For as with other kinds of implication, irony is frequently a writer's main path to both accuracy and complexity. Through irony a writer can show awareness of the fact that life is made up of contradictions and paradoxes, that no truth is ever the whole and absolute truth, that black is never wholly black nor white wholly white, that the problems inherent in the human condition should not be taken either with the seriousness or the literalness with which most of us are inclined to take them. To put this in another way, irony helps to put life in its proper perspective. Thus, though it might be possible to create a story without it, it is probably true that no intelligent story exists that does not have in it some element of irony.

Symbol and Allusion

Two other devices used extensively by writers to help communicate effect or meaning are *symbol* and *allusion.*

In its simplest form a symbol is something (usually concrete) that stands for something else (usually abstract). Our world is full of such symbols: A skull and crossbones on a medicine bottle symbolize poison; a name on an office door symbolizes a person. If we have been taught the "correct" (that is, the agreed upon) meaning for these symbols, they present us with few problems, for in such objects as nameplates what we have is a concrete object that stands for a concrete object, a specific something that stands for a specific something. But most symbols are not precisely of this nature. The human mind works most comfortably on a concrete rather than an abstract level; hence one human impulse is to translate abstractions into concrete terms, to use concrete objects as substitutes for whole complexes of ideas or feelings. The American flag is one such symbol, the Cross is another; and because such substitutions are different in kind from those which have a specific one-for-one relationship, semanticists ordinarily call such symbols as nameplates *signs* and such symbols as flags *symbols*.

In the stories you have already read, you have doubtless been aware of the use of symbol. To cite only one example, you probably recognized that the hanging meat in "And the Rock Cried Out" did not stand *only* for a side of beef. If so, you have also been confronted with the two peculiar difficulties that symbols present to a reader. For one thing, you have not been taught the definition of this symbol or that one in a story. Indeed, you cannot be taught this, for fictional symbol derives its meaning largely from context, and that context differs from story to story. In other words, just as with character or theme, a reader must deduce the meaning of a symbol from the story in which it appears. As soon as you embark on such a deductive process, you will probably discover a second difficulty: because fictional symbols do stand for complex abstractions, they can seldom be defined with absolute and certain precision. In other words, there is no one "right" answer for what Bradbury's hanging meat stands for.

Nonetheless, we can make a number of generalizations about fictional symbols that can help us both to understand their function in stories and to define them with a reasonable degree of accuracy. To begin with, we can distinguish between two kinds of stories, those which are essentially *literal* and should be read thus, and those which are essentially *symbolic* and cannot be understood unless we understand their symbols. A literal story may have symbols in it, but we can understand it without recognizing their presence because the story's meaning or effect will depend primarily on its development of a situation. But in some stories, symbol is the primary method of communication, and without a translation of its symbols, the story will be without meaning.

Stories that operate primarily on a symbolic level can further be divided into *allegorical* and *symbolic* categories. The distinction between these has perhaps been put most shrewdly by Hollander and Lind in *The Art of the Story*. "The functional difference between allegory and symbolism," they point out, "is that whereas symbolism always means what it says and *also* something else, allegory primarily means something else."[1] Or, if we discuss this from the point of view of writing a story, rather than reading it, we can say that allegory begins with an idea, and the author then creates an object (frequently a character) that stands for that idea; symbol, in

[1] Robert Hollander and Sidney Lind, *The Art of the Story* (New York: American Book Company, 1968), p. 30.

contrast, begins with an object that then comes to suggest an idea. A story like *Pilgrim's Progress*, where Vanity Fair is chosen simply to represent an abstraction, not to be taken on a literal level as an actual place, is an allegory. A story like Flannery O'Connor's "Good Country People," where Hulga's wooden leg is at once a *real* wooden leg and suggestive of something else, is symbolic.

In symbolic stories, one may further distinguish between what we can call *established* symbols and what we can call *private* or *created* symbols. In some stories the symbols derive their meaning, at least in part, not from within the context of the story itself but from without it. If, for example, a writer uses a star in a story, and if it seems that the writer intends the star to be taken as a symbol, we can legitimately suspect that the star stands for hope or aspiration. We can assume this not because the story points us to this interpretation but because we have somewhere been taught to associate stars and hope. Many symbols in stories—water, or fire, or certain colors like black or white, or seasons of the year, or the time of day, or journeys, or symbols taken from myth or Freudian psychology—are of this established nature, though we must always be alert to the possibility that in a given story such symbols may have their meanings modified or even reversed. But other symbols can be private—that is, definable only within the context of the story in which they appear. If, for example, we were asked, without reference to any particular story, what a wooden leg might symbolize, we could not answer. But if we were asked what it symbolizes in "Good Country People," we could derive a definition from the story.

In contemporary fiction, the use of another device, that of the *literary allusion*, has become almost as common as the use of symbol. The allusion is a reference in one piece of literature to another piece of literature, and it is, of course, almost as old as literature itself. Nor has its usefulness as a device for both compression and enrichment greatly changed. If a Renaissance sonneteer, for example, quotes from an Horatian ode, he manages to add to his sonnet all of the implications, effects, or ideas of another poem. But in contemporary literature, the allusion can create problems that it did not create in the past, primarily the problem of recognition. In Shakespeare's day, readers tended to bring to a given play or poem a common reading background; hence, Shakespeare could assume that allusions to Horace or Virgil would be recognized by his audience. The contemporary writer can make no such assumption; even the most obvious allusion can pass by a reader unrecognized. But when allusions in a story are recognized, you will discover that as with symbol they enrich the meaning or effect of a story.

So much for definition. But definition fails to answer some persistent questions raised by students who are first introduced to the symbol or the allusion. Why, students ask, do writers use such devices? Why, apparently, do they go out of their way to make their meaning difficult or obscure? Does not the employment of the symbol or the allusion turn the reading of fiction into an intellectual game instead of the simple enjoyment of vicarious experience?

The most obvious reply to this is that writers use symbols (if not allusion) because the human mind works instinctively in terms of symbol. That can be substantiated in any number of ways—by the reliance of language upon simile and metaphor, for example, or by the persistence of symbol in proverbs and adages, or by the obvious abundance of symbol in our day-to-day lives. Beyond this, writers often use symbols because they cannot say what they want to say in any other way. What, for example, does the beer "stand for" in Graham Greene's "Brother" (in Section 6-A)? Within the context of the story, we *know*, but there is no abstract word that will define it precisely and completely.

Moreover, we must remember that a story is trying to do a great many things—create character, develop conflict, communicate emotion, suggest theme—and it is trying to do all these things simultaneously. Here symbol serves what is probably its most important function. For symbol in fiction will usually be found to be working double, triple, even quadruple duty. It is, as is allusion, a device that enables a writer to achieve *compression* and *complexity* at one and the same time.

Useful and effective as these devices can be, however, a reader should approach them with certain cautions in mind. In this century writers have used both symbol and allusion so extensively, and teachers have so emphasized them in their approach to literature, that a reader can emerge from a "study" of literature with some serious misconceptions. Hence, we conclude this discussion with a few warnings and admonitions.

1. Occasionally, we meet with a reader who insists on reading a story *only* on a literal level, who refuses to admit to the existence of symbol in fiction, and who either betrays this attitude with the question, "Do writers really think of these things when they write stories?" or who argues that to discuss a symbol is to "read into" a story what is not there. We have already noted that the strictly literal approach to story will make some stories incomprehensible. But even with those stories in which symbol is incidental rather than crucial, such a literal approach can seriously limit the meaning, implications, or effect of many stories.

2. At the opposite extreme is the reader who brings to his reading the assumption that all objects in all stories must be given symbolic value,

and that the art of reading is principally the art of "symbol hunting"; or, if there is any other legitimate subject for literary discussion, it is the identification of allusions or "sources" or "parallels" or "echoes." For such readers we must emphasize the fact that symbol and allusion are *devices*; like other fictional devices they are something the good writer never employs for their own sake, and the writer who incorporates symbols or allusions for this reason is guilty of bad writing just as the reader who finds symbols where none are intended is guilty of bad reading. We must also remember that symbol and allusion are only two of many fictional devices. The point of reading and discussing fiction is not to display one's ingenuity or to show off the breadth of one's reading background. Above all, we must remember that not all writers employ symbol or allusion; hence, we must resist the temptation to make every concrete object in every story stand for something other than what it is. Even in Hemingway, who probably used symbol as extensively as any writer in this century, we can find objects that can legitimately be taken only literally. As Saul Bellow has put it, a railway schedule in a story does not *always* suggest a leitmotif, a journey does not *always* symbolize a life, wood shavings do not *always* suggest the Cross.

3. From this it follows that objects in stories are to be treated as symbols only if there are clues that the author intended them to be so taken. And good stories will provide such clues. They will do so in a number of ways—by position, by repetition, by more than routine emphasis. If, before we leap to a symbolic interpretation of an object, we first ask ourselves how we know that the object is to be taken symbolically, and if secondly we ask ourselves how comfortably it fits as symbol into the total context of the story, we will avoid the temptation to turn every simile into a symbol.

4. Once we have determined that an object is to be given symbolic value, we must then be careful how we define it. Here we can take either one of two wrong turns. Among readers who have been newly introduced to symbol, the common fault is to think of definition as some kind of free association in which an object can mean anything one chooses to make it. For this reader we must emphasize that any definition is going to be limited in a number of ways by the context of the story in which the symbol appears. But an equally serious fault is to define a symbol not too broadly but too narrowly. This is a fault prevalent among modern professional critics; one literary critic, familiar with Freudian psychology, will somehow force sexual meaning on almost any fictional symbol; another, interested in myth, will give the same symbol a mythological definition. In both cases, the critic will have told the truth but not the whole truth.

WALTER VAN TILBURG CLARK
The Portable Phonograph

The red sunset, with narrow black cloud strips like threats across it, lay on the curved horizon of the prairie. The air was still and cold, and in it settled the mute darkness and greater cold of night. High in the air there was wind, for through the veil of the dusk the clouds could be seen gliding rapidly south and changing shapes. A queer sensation of torment, of two-sided, unpredictable nature, arose from the stillness of the earth air beneath the violence of the upper air. Out of the sunset, through the dead, matted grass and isolated weed stalks of the prairie, crept the narrow and deeply rutted remains of a road. In the road, in places, there were crusts of shallow, brittle ice. There were little islands of an old oiled pavement in the road too, but most of it was mud, now frozen rigid. The frozen mud still bore the toothed impress of great tanks, and a wanderer on the neighboring undulations might have stumbled, in this light, into large, partially filled-in and weed-grown cavities, their banks channeled and beginning to spread into badlands. These pits were such as might have been made by falling meteors, but they were not. They were the scars of gigantic bombs, their rawness already made a little natural by rain, seed, and time. Along the road there were rakish remnants of fence. There was also, just visible, one portion of tangled and multiple barbed wire still erect, behind which was a shelving ditch with small caves, now very quiet and empty, at intervals in its back wall. Otherwise there was no structure or remnant of a structure visible over the dome of the darkling earth, but only, in sheltered hollows, the darker shadows of young trees trying again.

Under the wuthering arch of the high wind a V of wild geese fled south. The rush of their pinions sounded briefly, and the faint, plaintive notes of their expeditionary talk. Then they left a still greater vacancy. There was the smell and expectation of snow, as there is likely to be when the wild geese fly south. From the remote distance, towards the red sky, came faintly the protracted howl and quick yap-yap of a prairie wolf.

North of the road, perhaps a hundred yards, lay the parallel and deeply intrenched course of a small creek, lined with leafless alders and willows. The creek was already silent under ice. Into the bank above it was dug a sort of cell, with a single opening, like the mouth of a mine tunnel. Within the cell there was a little red of fire, which showed dully through the opening, like a reflection or a deception of the imagination. The light came from the chary burning of four blocks of poorly aged peat, which gave off a petty warmth and much acrid smoke. But the precious remnants of wood, old fenceposts and timbers from the long-deserted dugouts, had to be saved for the real cold, for the time when a man's breath blew white, the moisture in his nostrils stiffened at once when he stepped out, and the expansive blizzards paraded for days over the vast open, swirling and settling and thickening, till the dawn of the cleared day when the sky was thin blue-green and the terrible cold, in which a man could not live for three hours unwarmed, lay over the uniformly drifted swell of the plain.

Around the smoldering peat four men were seated cross-legged. Behind them, traversed by their shadows, was the earth bench, with two old and dirty army blankets, where the owner of the cell slept. In a niche in the opposite wall were a few tin utensils which caught the glint of the coals. The host was rewrapping in a piece of daubed burlap four fine, leather-bound books. He worked slowly and very carefully and at last tied the bundle securely with a piece of grass-woven cord. The other three looked intently upon the process, as if a great significance lay in it. As the host tied the cord he spoke. He was an old man, his long, matted beard and hair gray to nearly white. The shadows made his brows and cheekbones appear gnarled, his eyes and cheeks deeply sunken. His big hands, rough with frost and swollen by rheumatism, were awkward but gentle at their task. He was like a prehistoric priest performing a fateful ceremonial rite. Also his voice had in it a suitable quality of deep, reverent despair, yet perhaps at the moment a sharpness of selfish satisfaction.

"When I perceived what was happening," he said, "I told myself, 'It is the end. I cannot take much; I will take these.' "

"Perhaps I was impractical," he continued. "But for myself, I do not regret, and what do we know of those who will come after us? We are the doddering remnant of a race of mechanical fools. I have saved what I love; the soul of what was good in us is here; perhaps the new ones will make a strong enough beginning not to fall behind when they become clever."

He rose with slow pain and placed the wrapped volumes in the niche with his utensils. The others watched him with the same ritualistic gaze.

"Shakespeare, the Bible, *Moby Dick*, the *Divine Comedy*," one of them said softly. "You might have done worse, much worse."

"You will have a little soul left until you die," said another harshly. "That is more than is true of us. My brain becomes thick, like my hands." He held the big, battered hands, with their black nails, in the glow to be seen.

"I want paper to write on," he said. "And there is none."

The fourth man said nothing. He sat in the shadow farthest from the fire, and sometimes his body jerked in its rags from the cold. Although he was still young, he was sick and coughed often. Writing implied a greater future than he now felt able to consider.

The old man seated himself laboriously and reached out, groaning at the movement, to put another block of peat on the fire. With bowed heads and averted eyes his three guests acknowledged his magnanimity.

"We thank you, Dr. Jenkins, for the reading," said the man who had named the books.

They seemed then to be waiting for something. Dr. Jenkins understood but was loath to comply. In an ordinary moment he would have said nothing. But the words of *The Tempest,* which he had been reading, and the religious attention of the three made this an unusual occasion.

"You wish to hear the phonograph," he said grudgingly.

The two middle-aged men stared into the fire, unable to formulate and expose the enormity of their desire.

The young man, however, said anxiously, between suppressed coughs, "Oh, please," like an excited child.

The old man rose again in his difficult way and went to the back of the cell. He returned and placed tenderly upon the packed floor, where the firelight might fall upon it, an old portable phonograph in a black case. He smoothed the top with his hand and then opened it. The lovely green-felt-covered disk became visible.

"I have been using thorns as needles," he said. "But tonight, because we have a musician among us"—he bent his head to the young man, almost invisible in the shadow—"I will use a steel needle. There are only three left."

The two middle-aged men stared at him in speechless adoration. The one with the big hands, who wanted to write, moved his lips, but the whisper was not audible.

"Oh, don't!" cried the young man, as if he were hurt. "The thorns will do beautifully."

"No," the old man said. "I have become accustomed to the thorns, but they are not really good. For you, my young friend, we will have good music tonight."

"After all," he added generously, and beginning to wind the phonograph, which creaked, "they can't last forever."

"No, nor we," the man who needed to write said harshly. "The needle, by all means."

"Oh, thanks," said the young man. "Thanks," he said again in a low, excited voice, and then stifled his coughing with a bowed head.

"The records, though," said the old man when he had finished winding, "are a different matter. Already they are very worn. I do not play them more than once a week. One, once a week, that is what I allow myself.

"More than a week I cannot stand it; not to hear them," he apologized.

"No, how could you?" cried the young man. "And with them here like this."

"A man can stand anything," said the man who wanted to write, in his harsh, antagonistic voice.

"Please, the music," said the young man.

"Only the one," said the old man. "In the long run, we will remember more that way."

He had a dozen records with luxuriant gold and red seals. Even in that light the others could see that the threads of the records were becoming worn. Slowly he read out the titles and the tremendous, dead names of the composers and the artists and the orchestras. The three worked upon the names in their minds, carefully. It was difficult to select from such a wealth what they would at once most like to remember. Finally the man who wanted to write named Gershwin's "New York."

"Oh, no!" cried the sick young man, and then could say nothing more because he had to cough. The others understood him, and the harsh man withdrew his selection and waited for the musician to choose.

The musician begged Dr. Jenkins to read the titles again, very slowly, so that he could remember the sounds. While they were read he lay back against the wall, his eyes closed, his thin, horny hand pulling at his light beard, and listened to the voices and the orchestras and the single instruments in his mind.

When the reading was done he spoke despairingly. "I have forgotten," he complained. "I cannot hear them clearly.

"There are things missing," he explained.

"I know," said Dr. Jenkins. "I thought that I knew all of Shelley by heart. I should have brought Shelley."

"That's more soul than we can use," said the harsh man. "*Moby Dick* is better.

"By God, we can understand that," he emphasized.

The Doctor nodded.

"Still," said the man who had admired the books, "we need the absolute if we are to keep a grasp on anything.

"Anything but these sticks and peat clods and rabbit snares," he said bitterly.

"Shelley desired an ultimate absolute," said the harsh man. "It's too much," he said. "It's no good; no earthly good."

The musician selected a Debussy nocturne. The other considered and approved. They rose to their knees to watch the Doctor prepare for the playing, so that they appeared to be actually in an attitude of worship. The peat glow showed the thinness of their bearded faces, and the deep lines in them, and revealed the condition of their garments. The other two continued to kneel as the old man carefully lowered the needle onto the spinning disk, but the musician suddenly drew back against the wall again, with his knees up, and buried his face in his hands.

At the first notes of the piano the listeners were startled. They stared at each other. Even the musician lifted his head in amazement but then quickly bowed it again, strainingly, as if he were suffering from a pain he might not be able to endure. They were all listening deeply, without movement. The wet, blue-green notes tinkled forth from the old machine and were individual, delectable presences in the cell. The individual, delectable presences swept into a sudden tide of unbearably beautiful dissonance and then continued fully the swelling and ebbing of that tide, the dissonant inpourings, and the resolutions, and the diminishments, and the little, quiet wavelets of interlude lapping between. Every sound was piercing and singularly sweet. In all the men except the musician there occurred rapid sequences of tragically heightened recollection. He heard nothing but what was there. At the final, whispering disappearance, but moving quietly so that the others would not hear him and look at him, he let his head fall back in agony, as if it were drawn there by the hair, and clenched the fingers of one hand over his teeth. He sat that way while the others were silent and until they began to breathe again normally. His drawn-up legs were trembling violently.

Quickly Dr. Jenkins lifted the needle off, to save it and not to spoil the recollection with scraping. When he had stopped the whirling of the sacred disk he courteously left the phonograph open and by the fire, in sight.

The others, however, understood. The musician rose last, but then abruptly, and went quickly out at the door without saying anything. The others stopped at the door and gave their thanks in low voices. The Doctor nodded magnificently.

"Come again," he invited, "in a week. We will have the 'New York.'"

When the two had gone together, out towards the rimed road, he stood in the entrance, peering and listening. At first there was only the resonant boom of the wind overhead, and then far over the dome of the dead, dark plain the wolf cry lamenting. In the rifts of clouds the Doctor saw four stars flying. It impressed the Doctor that one of them had just been obscured by the beginning of a flying cloud at the very moment he heard what he had been listening for, a sound of suppressed coughing. It was not near by, however. He believed that down against the pale alders he could see the moving shadow.

With nervous hands he lowered the piece of canvas which served as his door and pegged it at the bottom. Then quickly and quietly, looking at the piece of canvas frequently, he slipped the records into the case, snapped the lid shut, and carried the phonograph to his couch. There, pausing often to stare at the canvas and listen, he dug earth from the wall and disclosed a piece of board. Behind this there was a deep hole in the wall, into which he put the phonograph. After a moment's consideration he went over and reached down his bundle of books and inserted it also. Then, guardedly, he once more sealed up the hole with the board and the earth. He also changed his blankets and the grass-stuffed sack which served as a pillow, so that he could lie facing the entrance. After carefully placing two more blocks of peat upon the fire he stood for a long time watching the stretched canvas, but it seemed to billow naturally with the first gusts of a lowering wind. At last he prayed, and got in under his blankets, and closed his smoke-smarting eyes. On the inside of the bed, next the wall, he could feel with his hand the comfortable piece of lead pipe.

QUESTIONS FOR DISCUSSION

1. What emotional effect does Clark want from this story? Why? What basic methods does he employ in order to achieve it?
2. Define and discuss the basic irony on which the theme of "The Portable Phonograph" rests.
3. The characterization in "The Portable Phonograph" is flat; we can even call it shadowy. Is this a weakness in the story? Is there any relationship between Clark's shadowy characterization—his failure to provide sharp character differentiation—and his theme? Does the shadowy characterization subtract anything from the emotional effect of the story? Why or why not?
4. Most of the symbols in "The Portable Phonograph" fall into three categories: nature symbols, symbols from civilization (like the books), and symbols of destruction. List and define as many of the symbols as you can find in the story. Then define what they *contribute* to the story. Do they, for example, illuminate theme? Contribute irony? Contribute in any way to the emotional effect of the story (as in the opening)? How many can you find that do many things simultaneously?

FLANNERY O'CONNOR
Good Country People

Besides the neutral expression that she wore when she was alone, Mrs. Freeman had two others, forward and reverse, that she used for all her human dealings. Her forward expression was steady and driving like the advance of a heavy truck. Her eyes never swerved to left or right but turned as the story turned as if they followed a yellow line down the center of it. She seldom used the other expression because it was not often necessary for her to retract a statement, but when she did, her face came to a complete stop, there was an almost imperceptible movement of her black eyes, during which they seemed to be receding, and then the observer would see that Mrs. Freeman, though she might stand there as real as several grain sacks thrown on top of each other, was no longer there in spirit. As for getting anything across to her when this was the case, Mrs. Hopewell had given it up. She might talk her head off. Mrs. Freeman could never be brought to admit herself wrong on any point. She would stand there and if she could be brought to say anything, it was something like, "Well, I wouldn't of said it was and I wouldn't of said it wasn't," or letting her gaze range over the top kitchen shelf where there was an assortment of dusty bottles, she might remark, "I see you ain't ate many of them figs you put up last summer."

They carried on their most important business in the kitchen at breakfast. Every morning Mrs. Hopewell got up at seven o'clock and lit her gas heater and Joy's. Joy was her daughter, a large blonde girl who had an artificial leg. Mrs. Hopewell thought of her as a child though she was thirty-two years old and highly educated. Joy would get up while her mother was eating and lumber into the bathroom and slam the door, and before long, Mrs. Freeman would arrive at the back door. Joy would hear her mother call, "Come on in," and then they would talk for a while in low voices that were indistinguishable in the bathroom. By the time Joy came in, they had usually finished the weather report and were on one or the other of Mrs. Freeman's daughters, Glynese or Carramae. Joy called them Glycerin and Caramel. Glynese, a redhead, was eighteen and had many admirers; Carramae, a blonde, was only fifteen but already married and pregnant. She could not keep anything on her stomach. Every morning Mrs. Freeman told Mrs. Hopewell how many times she had vomited since the last report.

Mrs. Hopewell liked to tell people that Glynese and Carramae were two of the finest girls she knew and that Mrs. Freeman was a *lady* and that she was never ashamed to take her anywhere or introduce her to anybody they might meet. Then she would tell how she had happened to hire the Freemans in the first place and how they were a godsend to her and how she had had them four years. The reason for her keeping them so long was that they were not trash. They were good country people. She had telephoned the man whose name they had given as a reference and he had told her that Mr. Freeman was a good farmer but that his wife was the nosiest woman ever to walk the earth. "She's got to be into everything," the man said. "If she don't get there before the dust settles, you can bet she's dead, that's all. She'll want to know all your business. I can stand him real good," he had said, "but me nor my wife neither could have stood that woman one more minute on this place." That had put Mrs. Hopewell off for a few days.

She had hired them in the end because there were no other applicants but she had made up her mind beforehand exactly how she would handle the woman. Since she was the type who had to be into everything, then, Mrs. Hopewell had decided, she would not only let her be into everything, she would *see to it* that she was into everything—she would give her the responsibility of everything, she would put her in charge. Mrs. Hopewell had no bad qualities of her own but she was able to use other people's in such a constructive way that she never felt the lack. She had hired the Freemans and she had kept them four years.

Nothing is perfect. This was one of Mrs. Hopewell's favorite sayings. Another was: that is life! And still another, the most important, was: well, other people have their opinions too. She would make these statements, usually at the table, in a tone of gentle insistence as if no one held them but her, and the large hulking Joy, whose constant outrage had obliterated every expression from her face, would stare just a little to the side of her, her eyes icy blue, with the look of someone who has achieved blindness by an act of will and means to keep it.

When Mrs. Hopewell said to Mrs. Freeman that life was like that, Mrs. Freeman would say, "I always said so myself." Nothing had been arrived at by anyone that had not first been arrived at by her. She was quicker than Mr. Freeman. When Mrs. Hopewell said to her after they had been on the place a while, "You know, you're the wheel behind the wheel," and winked, Mrs. Freeman had said, "I know it. I've always been quick. It's some that are quicker than others."

"Everybody is different," Mrs. Hopewell said.

"Yes, most people is," Mrs. Freeman said.

"It takes all kinds to make the world."

"I always said it did myself."

The girl was used to this kind of dialogue for breakfast and more of it for dinner; sometimes they had it for supper too. When they had no guests they ate in the kitchen because that was easier. Mrs. Freeman always managed to arrive at some point during the meal and to watch them finish it. She would stand in the doorway if it were summer but in the winter she would stand with one elbow on top of the refrigerator and look down on them, or she would stand by the gas heater, lifting the back of her skirt slightly. Occasionally she would stand against the wall and roll her head from side to side. At no time was she in any hurry to leave. All this was very trying on Mrs. Hopewell but she was a woman of great patience. She realized that nothing is perfect and that in the Freemans she had good country people and that if, in this day and age, you get good country people, you had better hang onto them.

She had had plenty of experience with trash. Before the Freemans she had averaged one tenant family a year. The wives of these farmers were not the kind you would want to be around you for very long. Mrs. Hopewell, who had divorced her husband long ago, needed someone to walk over the fields with her; and when Joy had to be impressed for these services, her remarks were usually so ugly and her face so glum that Mrs. Hopewell would say, "If you can't come pleasantly, I don't want you at all," to which the girl, standing square and rigid-shouldered with her neck thrust slightly forward, would reply, "If you want me, here I am—LIKE I AM."

Mrs. Hopewell excused this attitude because of the leg (which had been shot off in a hunting accident when Joy was ten). It was hard for Mrs. Hopewell to realize that her child was thirty-two now and that for more than twenty years she had had only one leg. She thought of her still as a child because it tore her heart to think instead of the poor stout girl in her thirties who had never danced a step or had any *normal* good times. Her name was really Joy but as soon as she was twenty-one and away from home, she had had it legally changed. Mrs. Hopewell was certain that she had thought and thought until she had hit upon the ugliest name in any language. Then she had gone and had the beautiful name, Joy, changed without telling her mother until after she had done it. Her legal name was Hulga.

When Mrs. Hopewell thought the name, Hulga, she thought of the broad blank hull of a battleship. She would not use it. She continued to call her Joy to which the girl responded but in a purely mechanical way.

Hulga had learned to tolerate Mrs. Freeman who saved her from taking walks with her mother. Even Glynese and Carramae were useful when they occupied attention that might otherwise have been directed at her. At first she had thought she could not stand Mrs. Freeman for she had found that it was not possible to be rude to her. Mrs. Freeman would take on strange resentments and for days together she would be sullen but the source of her displeasure was always obscure; a direct attack, a positive leer, blatant ugliness to her face—these never touched her. And without warning one day, she began calling her Hulga.

She did not call her that in front of Mrs. Hopewell who would have been incensed but when she and the girl happened to be out of the house together, she would say something and add the name Hulga to the end of it, and the big spectacled Joy-Hulga would scowl and redden as if her privacy had been intruded upon. She considered the name her personal affair. She had arrived at it first purely on the basis of its ugly sound and then the full genius of its fitness had struck her. She had a vision of the name working like the ugly sweating Vulcan who stayed in the furnace and to whom, presumably, the goddess had to come when called. She saw it as the name of her highest creative act. One of her major triumphs was that her mother had not been able to turn her dust into Joy, but the greater one was that she had been able to turn it herself into Hulga. However, Mrs. Freeman's relish for using the name only irritated her. It was as if Mrs. Freeman's beady steel-pointed eyes had penetrated far enough behind her face to reach some secret fact. Something about her seemed to fascinate Mrs. Freeman and then one day Hulga realized that it was the artificial leg. Mrs. Freeman had a special fondness for the details of secret infections, hidden deformities, assaults upon children. Of diseases, she preferred the lingering or incurable. Hulga had heard Mrs. Hopewell give her the details of the hunting accident, how the leg had been literally blasted off, how she had never lost consciousness. Mrs. Freeman could listen to it any time as if it had happened an hour ago.

When Hulga stumped into the kitchen in the morning (she could walk without making the awful noise but she made it—Mrs. Hopewell was certain—because it was ugly-sounding), she glanced at them and did not speak. Mrs. Hopewell would be in her red kimono with her hair tied around her head in rags. She would be sitting at the table, finishing her breakfast and Mrs. Freeman would be hanging by her elbow outward from the refrigerator, looking down at the table. Hulga always put her eggs on the stove to boil and then stood over them with her arms folded, and Mrs. Hopewell would look at her—a kind of indirect gaze divided between her and Mrs. Freeman—and would think that if she would only keep herself up a little, she wouldn't be so bad looking. There was nothing wrong with her face that a pleasant expression wouldn't help. Mrs. Hopewell said that people who looked on the bright side of things would be beautiful even if they were not.

Whenever she looked at Joy this way, she could not help but feel that it would have been better if the child had not taken the Ph.D. It had certainly not brought her out any and now that she had it, there was no more excuse for her to go to school again. Mrs. Hopewell thought it was nice for girls to go to school to have a good time but Joy had "gone through." Anyhow, she would not have been strong enough to go again. The doctors had told Mrs. Hopewell that with the best of care, Joy might see forty-five. She had a weak heart. Joy had made it plain that if it had not been for this condition, she would be far from these red hills and good country people. She would be in a university lecturing to people who knew what she was talking about. And Mrs. Hopewell could very well picture her there, looking like a scarecrow and lecturing to more of the same. Here she went about all day in a six-year-old skirt and a yellow sweat shirt with a faded cowboy on a horse embossed on it. She thought this was funny; Mrs. Hopewell thought it was idiotic and showed simply that she was still a child. She was brilliant but she didn't have a grain of sense. It seemed to Mrs. Hopewell that every year she grew less like other people and more like herself—bloated, rude, and squint-eyed. And she said such strange things! To her own mother she had said—without warning, without excuse, standing up in the middle of a meal with her face purple and her mouth half full—"Women! do you ever look inside? Do you ever look inside and see what you are *not?* God!" she had cried sinking down again and staring at her plate, "Malebranche was right: we are not our own light. We are not our own light!" Mrs. Hopewell had no idea to this day what brought that on. She had only made the remark, hoping Joy would take it in, that a smile never hurt anyone.

The girl had taken the Ph.D. in philosophy and this left Mrs. Hopewell at a complete loss. You could say, "My daughter is a nurse," or "My daughter is a school teacher," or even, "My daughter is a chemical engineer." You could not say, "My daughter is a philosopher." That was something that had ended with the Greeks and Romans. All day Joy sat on her neck in a deep chair, reading. Sometimes she went for walks but she didn't like dogs or cats or birds or flowers or nature or nice young men. She looked at nice young men as if she could smell their stupidity.

One day Mrs. Hopewell had picked up one of the books the girl had just put down and opening it at random, she read, "Science, on the other hand, has to assert its soberness and seriousness afresh and declare that it is concerned solely with what-is. Nothing—how can it be for science anything but a horror and a phantasm? If science is right, then one thing stands firm: science wishes to know nothing of nothing. Such is after all the strictly scientific approach to Nothing. We know it by wishing to know nothing of Nothing." These words had been underlined with a blue pencil and they worked on Mrs. Hopewell like some evil incantation in gibberish. She shut the book quickly and went out of the room as if she were having a chill.

This morning when the girl came in, Mrs. Freeman was on Carramae. "She thrown up four times after supper," she said, "and was up twict in the night after three o'clock. Yesterday she didn't do nothing but ramble in the bureau drawer. All she did. Stand up there and see what she could run up on."

"She's got to eat," Mrs. Hopewell muttered, sipping her coffee, while she watched Joy's back at the stove. She was wondering what the child had said to the Bible salesman. She could not imagine what kind of a conversation she could possibly have had with him.

He was a tall gaunt hatless youth who had called yesterday to sell them a Bible. He had appeared at the door, carrying a large black suitcase that weighted him so heavily on one side that he had to brace himself against the door facing. He seemed on the point of collapse but he said in a cheerful voice, "Good morning, Mrs. Cedars!" and set the suitcase down on the mat. He was not a bad-looking young man though he had on a bright blue suit and yellow socks that were not pulled up far enough. He had prominent face bones and a streak of sticky-looking brown hair falling across his forehead.

"I'm Mrs. Hopewell," she said.

"Oh!" he said, pretending to look puzzled but with his eyes sparkling, "I saw it said 'The Cedars,' on the mailbox so I thought you was Mrs. Cedars!" and he burst out in a pleasant laugh. He picked up the satchel and under cover of a pant, he fell forward into her hall. It was rather as if the suitcase had moved first, jerking him after it. "Mrs. Hopewell!" he said and grabbed her hand. "I hope you are well!" and he laughed again and then all at once his face sobered completely. He paused and gave her a straight earnest look and said, "Lady, I've come to speak of serious things."

"Well, come in," she muttered, none too pleased because her dinner was almost ready. He came into the parlor and sat down on the edge of a straight chair and put the suitcase between his feet and glanced around the room as if he were sizing her up by it. Her silver gleamed on the two sideboards; she decided he had never been in a room as elegant as this.

"Mrs. Hopewell," he began, using her name in a way that sounded almost intimate, "I know you believe in Chrustian service."

"Well yes," she murmured.

"I know," he said and paused, looking very wise with his head cocked on one side, "that you're a good woman. Friends have told me."

Mrs. Hopewell never liked to be taken for a fool. "What are you selling?" she asked.

"Bibles," the young man said and his eye raced around the room before he added, "I see you have no family Bible in your parlor, I see that is the one lack you got!"

Mrs. Hopewell could not say, "My daughter is an atheist and won't let me keep the Bible in the parlor." She said, stiffening slightly, "I keep my Bible by my bedside." This was not the truth. It was in the attic somewhere.

"Lady," he said, "the word of God ought to be in the parlor."

"Well, I think that's a matter of taste," she began. "I think . . ."

"Lady," he said, "for a Chrustian, the word of God ought to be in every room in the house besides in his heart. I know you're a Chrustian because I can see it in every line of your face."

She stood up and said, "Well, young man, I don't want to buy a Bible and I smell my dinner burning."

He didn't get up. He began to twist his hands and looking down at them, he said softly, "Well lady, I'll tell you the truth—not many people want to buy one nowadays and besides, I know I'm real simple. I don't know how to say a thing but to say it. I'm just a country boy." He glanced up into her unfriendly face. "People like you don't like to fool with country people like me!"

"Why!" she cried, "good country people are the salt of the earth! Besides, we all have different ways of doing, it takes all kinds to make the world go 'round. That's life!"

"You said a mouthful," he said.

"Why, I think there aren't enough good country people in the world!" she said, stirred. "I think that's what's wrong with it!"

His face had brightened. "I didn't intraduce myself," he said. "I'm Manley Pointer from out in the country around Willohobie, not even from a place, just from near a place."

"You wait a minute," she said. "I have to see about my dinner." She went out to the kitchen and found Joy standing near the door where she had been listening.

"Get rid of the salt of the earth," she said, "and let's eat."

Mrs. Hopewell gave her a pained look and turned the heat down under the vegetables. "*I* can't be rude to anybody," she murmured and went back into the parlor.

He had opened the suitcase and was sitting with a Bible on each knee.

"You might as well put those up," she told him. "I don't want one."

"I appreciate your honesty," he said. "You don't see any more real honest people unless you go way out in the country."

"I know," she said, "real genuine folks!" Through the crack in the door she heard a groan.

"I guess a lot of boys come telling you they're working their way through college," he said, "but I'm not going to tell you that. Somehow," he said, "I don't want to go to college. I want to devote my life to Chrustian service. See," he said, lowering his voice, "I got this heart condition. I may not live long. When you know it's something wrong with you and you may not live long, well then, lady . . ." He paused, with his mouth open, and stared at her.

He and Joy had the same condition! She knew that her eyes were filling with tears but she collected herself quickly and murmured, "Won't you stay for dinner? We'd love to have you!" and was sorry the instant she heard herself say it.

"Yes mam," he said in an abashed voice, "I would sher love to do that!"

Joy had given him one look on being introduced to him and then throughout the meal had not glanced at him again. He had addressed several remarks to her, which she had pretended not to hear. Mrs. Hopewell could not understand deliberate rudeness, although she lived with it, and she felt she had always to overflow with hospitality to make up for Joy's lack of courtesy. She urged him to talk about himself and he did. He said he was the seventh child of twelve and that his father had been crushed under a tree when he himself was eight years old. He had been crushed very badly, in fact, almost cut in two and was practically not recognizable. His mother had got along the best she could by hard working and she had always seen that her children went to Sunday School and that they read the Bible every evening. He was now nineteen years old and he had been selling Bibles for four months. In that time he had sold seventy-seven Bibles and had the promise of two more sales. He wanted to become a missionary because he thought that was the way you could do most for people. "He who losest his life shall find it," he said simply and he was so sincere, so genuine and earnest that Mrs. Hopewell would not for the world have smiled. He prevented his peas from sliding onto the table by blocking them with a piece of bread which he later cleaned his plate with. She could see Joy observing sidewise how he handled his knife and fork and she saw too that every few minutes, the boy would dart a keen appraising glance at the girl as if he were trying to attract her attention.

After dinner Joy cleared the dishes off the table and disappeared and Mrs. Hopewell was left to talk with him. He told her again about his childhood and his father's accident and about various things that had happened to him. Every five minutes or so she would stifle a yawn. He sat for two hours until finally she told him she must go because she had an appointment in town. He packed his Bibles and thanked her and prepared to leave, but in the doorway he stopped and wrung her hand and said that not on any of his trips had he met a lady as nice as her and he asked if he could come again. She had said she would always be happy to see him.

Joy had been standing in the road, apparently looking at something in the distance, when he came down the steps toward her, bent to the side with his heavy valise. He stopped where she was standing and confronted her directly. Mrs. Hopewell could not hear what he said but she trembled to think what Joy would say to him. She could see that after a minute Joy said something and that then the boy began to speak again, making an excited gesture with his free hand. After a minute Joy said something else at which the boy began to speak once more. Then to her amazement, Mrs. Hopewell saw the two of them walk off together, toward the gate. Joy had walked all the way to the gate with him and Mrs. Hopewell could not imagine what they had said to each other, and she had not yet dared to ask.

Mrs. Freeman was insisting upon her attention. She had moved from the refrigerator to the heater so that Mrs. Hopewell had to turn and face her in order to seem to be listening. "Glynese gone out with Harvey Hill again last night," she said. "She had this sty."

"Hill," Mrs. Hopewell said absently, "is that the one who works in the garage?"

"Nome, he's the one that goes to chiropractor school," Mrs. Freeman said. "She had this sty. Been had it two days. So she says when he brought her in the other night he says, 'Lemme get rid of that sty for you,' and she says, 'How?' and he says, 'You just lay yourself down acrost the seat of that car and I'll show you.' So she done it and he popped her neck. Kept on a-popping it several times until she made him quit. This morning," Mrs. Freeman said, "she ain't got no sty. She ain't got no traces of a sty."

"I never heard of that before," Mrs. Hopewell said.

"He ast her to marry him before the Ordinary," Mrs. Freeman went on, "and she told him she wasn't going to be married in no *office*."

"Well, Glynese is a fine girl," Mrs. Hopewell said. "Glynese and Carramae are both fine girls."

"Carramae said when her and Lyman was married Lyman said it sure felt sacred to him. She said he said he wouldn't take five hundred dollars for being married by a preacher."

"How much would he take?" the girl asked from the stove.

"He said he wouldn't take five hundred dollars," Mrs. Freeman repeated.

"Well we all have work to do," Mrs. Hopewell said.

"Lyman said it just felt more sacred to him," Mrs. Freeman said. "The doctor wants Carramae to eat prunes. Says instead of medicine. Says them cramps is coming from pressure. You know where I think it is?"

"She'll be better in a few weeks," Mrs. Hopewell said.

"In the tube," Mrs. Freeman said. "Else she wouldn't be as sick as she is."

Hulga had cracked her two eggs into a saucer and was bringing them to the table along with a cup of coffee that she had filled too full. She sat down carefully and began to eat, meaning to keep Mrs. Freeman there by questions if for any reason she showed an inclination to leave. She could perceive her mother's eye on her. The first roundabout question would be about the Bible salesman and she did not wish to bring it on. "How did he pop her neck?" she asked.

Mrs. Freeman went into a description of how he had popped her neck. She said he owned a '55 Mercury but that Glynese said she would rather marry a man with only a '36 Plymouth who would be married by a preacher. The girl asked what if he had a '32 Plymouth and Mrs. Freeman said what Glynese had said was a '36 Plymouth.

Mrs. Hopewell said there were not many girls with Glynese's common sense. She said what she admired in those girls was their common sense. She said that reminded her that they had had a nice visitor yesterday, a young man selling Bibles. "Lord," she said, "he bored me to death but he was so sincere and genuine I couldn't be rude to him. He was just good country people, you know," she said, "—just the salt of the earth."

"I seen him walk up," Mrs. Freeman said, "and then later—I seen him walk off," and Hulga could feel the slight shift in her voice, the slight insinuation, that he had not walked off alone, had he? Her face remained expressionless but the color rose into her neck and she seemed to swallow it down with the next spoonful of egg. Mrs. Freeman was looking at her as if they had a secret together.

"Well, it takes all kinds of people to make the world go 'round," Mrs. Hopewell said. "It's very good we aren't all alike."

"Some people are more alike than others," Mrs. Freeman said.

Hulga got up and stumped, with about twice the noise that was necessary, into her room and locked the door. She was to meet the Bible salesman at ten o'clock at the gate. She had thought about it half the night. She had started thinking of it as a great joke and then she had begun to see profound implications in it. She had lain in bed imagining dialogues for them that were insane on the surface but that reached below to depths that no Bible salesman would be aware of. Their conversation yesterday had been of this kind.

He had stopped in front of her and had simply stood there. His face was bony and sweaty and bright, with a little pointed nose in the center of it, and his look was different from what it had been at the dinner table. He was gazing at her with open curiosity, with fascination, like a child watching a new fantastic animal at the zoo, and he was breathing as if he had run a great distance to reach her. His gaze seemed somehow familiar but she could not think where she had been regarded with it before. For almost a minute he didn't say anything. Then on what seemed an insuck of breath, he whispered, "You ever ate a chicken that was two days old?"

The girl looked at him stonily. He might have just put this question up for consideration at the meeting of a philosophical association. "Yes," she presently replied as if she had considered it from all angles.

"It must have been mighty small!" he said triumphantly and shook all over with little nervous giggles, getting very red in the face, and subsiding finally into his gaze of complete admiration, while the girl's expression remained exactly the same.

"How old are you?" he asked softly.

She waited some time before she answered. Then in a flat voice she said, "Seventeen."

His smiles came in succession like waves breaking on the surface of a little lake. "I see you got a wooden leg," he said. "I think you're real brave. I think you're real sweet."

The girl stood blank and solid and silent.

"Walk to the gate with me," he said. "You're a brave sweet little thing and I liked you the minute I seen you walk in the door."

Hulga began to move forward.

"What's your name?" he asked, smiling down on the top of her head.

"Hulga," she said.

"Hulga," he murmured, "Hulga. Hulga. I never heard of anybody name Hulga before. You're shy, aren't you, Hulga?" he asked.

She nodded, watching his large red hand on the handle of the giant valise.

"I like girls that wear glasses," he said. "I think a lot. I'm not like these people that a serious thought don't ever enter their heads. It's because I may die."

"I may die too," she said suddenly and looked up at him. His eyes were very small and brown, glittering feverishly.

"Listen," he said, "don't you think some people was meant to meet on account of what all they got in common and all? Like they both think serious thoughts and all?" He shifted the valise to his other hand so that the hand nearest her was free. He caught hold of her elbow and shook it a little. "I don't work on Saturday," he said. "I like to walk in the woods and see what Mother Nature is wearing. O'er the hills and far away. Pic-nics and things. Couldn't we go on a pic-nic tomorrow? Say yes, Hulga," he said and gave her a dying look as if he felt his insides about to drop out of him. He had even seemed to sway slightly toward her.

During the night she had imagined that she seduced him. She imagined that the two of them walked on the place until they came to the storage barn beyond the two back fields and there, she imagined, that things came to such a pass that she very easily seduced him and that then, of course, she had to reckon with his remorse. True genius can get an idea across even to an inferior mind. She imagined that she took his remorse in hand and changed it into a deeper understanding of life. She took all his shame away and turned it into something useful.

She set off for the gate at exactly ten o'clock, escaping without drawing Mrs. Hopewell's attention. She didn't take anything to eat, forgetting that food is usually taken on a picnic. She wore a pair of slacks and a dirty white shirt, and as an afterthought, she had put some Vapex on the collar of it since she did not own any perfume. When she reached the gate no one was there.

She looked up and down the empty highway and had the furious feeling that she had been tricked, that he had only meant to make her walk to the gate after the idea of him. Then suddenly he stood up, very tall, from behind a bush on the opposite embankment. Smiling, he lifted his hat which was new and wide-brimmed. He had not worn it yesterday and she wondered if he had bought it for the occasion. It was toast-colored with a red and white band around it and was slightly too large for him. He stepped from behind the bush still carrying the black valise. He had on the same suit and the same yellow socks sucked down in his shoes from walking. He crossed the highway and said, "I knew you'd come!"

The girl wondered acidly how he had known this. She pointed to the valise and asked, "Why did you bring your Bibles?"

He took her elbow, smiling down on her as if he could not stop. "You can never tell when you'll need the word of God, Hulga," he said. She had a moment in which she doubted that this was actually happening and then they began to climb the embankment. They went down into the pasture toward the woods. The boy walked lightly by her side, bouncing on his toes. The valise did not seem to be heavy today; he even swung it. They crossed half the pasture without saying anything and then, putting his hand easily on the small of her back, he asked softly, "Where does your wooden leg join on?"

She turned an ugly red and glared at him and for an instant the boy looked abashed. "I didn't mean you no harm," he said. "I only meant you're so brave and all. I guess God takes care of you."

"No," she said, looking forward and walking fast, "I don't even believe in God."

At this he stopped and whistled. "No!" he exclaimed as if he were too astonished to say anything else.

She walked on and in a second he was bouncing at her side, fanning with his hat. "That's very unusual for a girl," he remarked, watching her out of the corner of his eye. When they reached the edge of the wood, he put his hand on her back again and drew her against him without a word and kissed her heavily.

The kiss, which had more pressure than feeling behind it, produced that extra surge of adrenalin in the girl that enables one to carry a packed trunk out of a burning house, but in her, the power went at once to the brain. Even before he released her, her mind, clear and detached and ironic anyway, was regarding him from a great distance, with amusement but with pity. She had never been kissed before and she was pleased to discover that it was an unexceptional experience and all a matter of the mind's control. Some people might enjoy drain water if they were told it was vodka. When the boy, looking expectant but uncertain, pushed her gently away, she turned and walked on, saying nothing as if such business, for her, were common enough.

He came along panting at her side, trying to help her when he saw a root that she might trip over. He caught and held back the long swaying blades of thorn vine until she had passed beyond them. She led the way and he came breathing heavily behind her. Then they came out on a sunlit hillside, sloping softly into another one a little smaller. Beyond, they could see the rusted top of the old barn where the extra hay was stored.

The hill was sprinkled with small pink weeds. "Then you ain't saved?" he asked suddenly, stopping.

The girl smiled. It was the first time she had smiled at him at all. "In my economy," she said, "I'm saved and you are damned but I told you I didn't believe in God."

Nothing seemed to destroy the boy's look of admiration. He gazed at her now as if the fantastic animal at the zoo had put its paw through the bars and given him a loving poke. She thought he looked as if he wanted to kiss her again and she walked on before he had the chance.

"Ain't there somewheres we can sit down sometime?" he murmured, his voice softening toward the end of the sentence.

"In that barn," she said.

They made for it rapidly as if it might slide away like a train. It was a large two-story barn, cool and dark inside. The boy pointed up the ladder that led into the loft and said, "It's too bad we can't go up there."

"Why can't we?" she asked.

"Yer leg," he said reverently.

The girl gave him a contemptuous look and putting both hands on the ladder, she climbed it while he stood below, apparently awestruck. She pulled herself expertly through the opening and then looked down at him and said, "Well, come on if you're coming," and he began to climb the ladder, awkwardly bringing the suitcase with him.

"We won't need the Bible," she observed.

"You never can tell," he said, panting. After he had got into the loft, he was a few seconds catching his breath. She had sat down in a pile of straw. A wide sheath of sunlight, filled with dust particles, slanted over her. She lay back against a bale, her face turned away, looking out the front opening of the barn where hay was thrown from a wagon into the loft. The two pink-speckled hillsides lay back against a dark ridge of woods. The sky was cloudless and cold blue. The boy dropped down by her side and put one arm under her and the other over her and began methodically kissing her face, making little noises like a fish. He did not remove his hat but it was pushed far enough back not to interfere. When her glasses got in his way, he took them off of her and slipped them into his pocket.

The girl at first did not return any of the kisses but presently she began to and after she had put several on his cheek, she reached his lips and remained there, kissing him again and again as if she were trying to draw all the breath out of him. His breath was clear and sweet like a child's and the kisses were sticky like a child's. He mumbled about loving her and about knowing when he first seen her that he loved her, but the mumbling was like the sleepy fretting of a child being put to sleep by his mother. Her mind, throughout this, never stopped or lost itself for a second to her feelings. "You ain't said you loved me none," he whispered finally, pulling back from her. "You got to say that."

She looked away from him off into the hollow sky and then down at a black ridge and then down farther into what appeared to be two green swelling lakes. She didn't realize he had taken her glasses but this landscape could not seem exceptional to her for she seldom paid any close attention to her surroundings.

"You got to say it," he repeated. "You got to say you love me."

She was always careful how she committed herself. "In a sense," she began, "if you use the word loosely, you might say that. But it's not a word I use. I don't have illusions. I'm one of those people who see *through* to nothing."

The boy was frowning. "You got to say it. I said it and you got to say it," he said.

The girl looked at him almost tenderly. "You poor baby," she murmured. "It's just as well you don't understand," and she pulled him by the neck, face-down, against her. "We are all damned," she said, "but some of us have taken off our blindfolds and see that there's nothing to see. It's a kind of salvation."

The boy's astonished eyes looked blankly through the ends of her hair. "Okay," he almost whined, "but do you love me or don'tcher?"

"Yes," she said and added, "in a sense. But I must tell you something. There mustn't be anything dishonest between us." She lifted his head and looked him in the eye. "I am thirty years old," she said. "I have a number of degrees."

The boy's look was irritated but dogged. "I don't care," he said. "I don't care a thing about what all you done. I just want to know if you love me or don'tcher?" and he caught her to him and wildly planted her face with kisses until she said, "Yes, yes."

"Okay then," he said, letting her go. "Prove it."

She smiled, looking dreamily out on the shifty landscape. She had seduced him without even making up her mind to try. "How?" she asked, feeling that he should be delayed a little.

He leaned over and put his lips to her ear. "Show me where your wooden leg joins on," he whispered.

The girl uttered a sharp little cry and her face instantly drained of color. The obscenity of the suggestion was not what shocked her. As a child she had sometimes been subject to feelings of shame but education had removed the last traces of that as a good surgeon scrapes for cancer; she would no more have felt it over what he was asking than she would have believed in his Bible. But she was as sensitive about the artificial leg as a peacock about his tail. No one ever touched it but her. She took care of it as someone else would his soul, in private and almost with her own eyes turned away. "No," she said.

"I known it," he muttered, sitting up. "You're just playing me for a sucker."

"Oh no no!" she cried. "It joins on at the knee. Only at the knee. Why do you want to see it?"

The boy gave her a long penetrating look. "Because," he said, "it's what makes you different. You ain't like anybody else."

She sat staring at him. There was nothing about her face or her round freezing-blue eyes to indicate that this had moved her; but she felt as if her heart had stopped and left her mind to pump her blood. She decided that for the first time in her life she was face to face with real innocence. This boy, with an instinct that came from beyond wisdom, had touched the truth about her. When after a minute, she said in a hoarse high voice, "All right," it was like surrendering to him completely. It was like losing her own life and finding it again, miraculously, in his.

Very gently he began to roll the slack leg up. The artificial limb, in a white sock and brown flat shoe, was bound in a heavy material like canvas and ended in an ugly jointure where it was attached to the stump. The boy's face and his voice were entirely reverent as he uncovered it and said, "Now show me how to take it off and on."

She took it off for him and put it back on again and then he took it off himself, handling it as tenderly as if it were a real one. "See!" he said with a delighted child's face. "Now I can do it myself!"

"Put it back on," she said. She was thinking that she would run away with him and that every night he would take the leg off and every morning put it back on again. "Put it back on," she said.

"Not yet," he murmured, setting it on its foot out of her reach. "Leave it off for a while. You got me instead."

She gave a little cry of alarm but he pushed her down and began to kiss her again. Without the leg she felt entirely dependent on him. Her brain seemed to have stopped thinking altogether and to be about some other function that it was not very good at. Different expressions raced back and forth over her face. Every now and then the boy, his eyes like two steel spikes, would glance behind him where the leg stood. Finally she pushed him off and said, "Put it back on me now."

"Wait," he said. He leaned the other way and pulled the valise toward him and opened it. It had a pale blue spotted lining and there were only two Bibles in it. He took one of these out and opened the cover of it. It was hollow and contained a pocket flask of whiskey, a pack of cards, and a small blue box with printing on it. He laid these out in front of her one at a time in an evenly-spaced row, like one presenting offerings at the shrine of a goddess. He put the blue box in her hand. THIS PRODUCT TO BE USED ONLY FOR THE PREVENTION OF DISEASE, she read, and dropped it. The boy was unscrewing the top of the flask. He stopped and pointed, with a smile, to the deck of cards. It was not an ordinary deck but one with an obscene picture on the back of each card. "Take a swig," he said, offering her the bottle first. He held it in front of her, but like one mesmerized, she did not move.

Her voice when she spoke had an almost pleading sound. "Aren't you," she murmured, "aren't you just good country people?"

The boy cocked his head. He looked as if he were just beginning to understand that she might be trying to insult him. "Yeah," he said, curling his lip slightly, "but it ain't held me back none. I'm as good as you any day in the week."

"Give me my leg," she said.

He pushed it farther away with his foot. "Come on now, let's begin to have us a good time," he said coaxingly. "We ain't got to know one another good yet."

"Give me my leg!" she screamed and tried to lunge for it but he pushed her down easily.

"What's the matter with you all of a sudden?" he asked, frowning as he screwed the top on the flask and put it quickly back inside the Bible. "You just a while ago said you didn't believe in nothing. I thought you was some girl!"

Her face was almost purple. "You're a Christian!" she hissed. "You're a fine Christian! You're just like them all—say one thing and do another. You're a perfect Christian, you're . . ."

The boy's mouth was set angrily. "I hope you don't think," he said in a lofty indignant tone, "that I believe in that crap! I may sell Bibles but I know which end is up and I wasn't born yesterday and I know where I'm going!"

"Give me my leg!" she screeched. He jumped up so quickly that she barely saw him sweep the cards and the blue box back into the Bible and throw the Bible into the valise. She saw him grab the leg and then she saw it for an instant slanted forlornly across the inside of the suitcase with a Bible at either side of its opposite ends. He slammed the lid shut and snatched up the valise and swung it down the hole and then stepped through himself.

When all of him had passed but his head, he turned and regarded her with a look that no longer had any admiration in it. "I've gotten a lot of interesting things," he said. "One time I got a woman's glass eye this way. And you needn't to think you'll catch me because Pointer ain't really my name. I use a different name at every house I call at and don't stay nowhere long. And I'll tell you another thing, Hulga," he said, using the name as if he didn't think much of it, "you ain't so smart. I been believing in nothing ever since I was born!" and then the toast-colored hat disappeared down the hole and the girl was left, sitting on the straw in the dusty sunlight. When she turned her churning face toward the opening, she saw his blue figure struggling successfully over the green speckled lake.

Mrs. Hopewell and Mrs. Freeman, who were in the back pasture, digging up onions, saw him emerge a little later from the woods and head across the meadow toward the highway. "Why, that looks like that nice dull young man that tried to sell me a Bible yesterday," Mrs. Hopewell said, squinting. "He must have been selling them to the Negroes back in there. He was so simple," she said, "but I guess the world would be better off if we were all that simple."

Mrs. Freeman's gaze drove forward and just touched him before he disappeared under the hill. Then she returned her attention to the evil-smelling onion shoot she was lifting from the ground. "Some can't be that simple," she said. "I know I never could."

QUESTIONS FOR DISCUSSION

1. On first reading, "Good Country People" may strike you as antireligious. The author, however, is a Roman Catholic. Can you reconcile the story and the author's beliefs—that is, *is* the story sacrilegious?
2. If "Good Country People" is, centrally, the story of Hulga and the Bible salesman, the lengthy characterizations of Mrs. Hopewell and Mrs. Freeman, as well as several long passages in the story, seem to be digressions. Can you show that they are not? Are they functional in terms of the story or the theme or both?
3. We have defined effective fiction as that fiction that interprets honestly and intelligently a genuine human problem, of the kind that happens to 99 percent of the people 99 percent of the time. Considered as narrative, does "Good Country People" satisfy this requirment? Does it satisfy it thematically?
4. Allen Tate has called this story "the most powerful story of maimed souls by a contemporary writer." What do you think he meant?

KATHERINE ANNE PORTER
Flowering Judas

Braggioni sits heaped upon the edge of a straight-backed chair much too small for him, and sings to Laura in a furry, mournful voice. Laura has begun to find reasons for avoiding her own house until the latest possible moment, for Braggioni is there almost every night. No matter how late she is, he will be sitting there with a surly, waiting expression, pulling at his kinky yellow hair, thumbing the strings of his guitar, snarling a tune under his breath. Lupe the Indian maid meets Laura at the door, and says with a flicker of a glance towards the upper room, "He waits."

Laura wishes to lie down, she is tired of her hairpins and the feel of her long tight sleeves, but she says to him, "Have you a new song for me this evening?" If he says yes, she asks him to sing it. If he says no, she remembers his favorite one, and asks him to sing it again. Lupe brings her a cup of chocolate and a plate of rice, and Laura eats at the small table under the lamp, first inviting Braggioni, whose answer is always the same: "I have eaten, and besides, chocolate thickens the voice."

Laura says, "Sing, then," and Braggioni heaves himself into song. He scratches the guitar familiarly as though it were a pet animal, and sings passionately off key, taking the high notes in a prolonged painful squeal. Laura, who haunts the markets listening to the ballad singers, and stops every day to hear the blind boy playing his reed-flute in Sixteenth of September Street, listens to Braggioni with pitiless courtesy, because she dares not smile at his miserable performance. Nobody dares to smile at him. Braggioni is cruel to everyone, with a kind of specialized insolence, but he is so vain of his talents, and so sensitive to slights, it would require a cruelty and vanity greater than his own to lay a finger on the vast cureless wound of his self-esteem. It would require courage, too, for it is dangerous to offend him, and nobody has this courage.

Braggioni loves himself with such tenderness and amplitude and eternal charity that his followers—for he is a leader of men, a skilled revolutionist, and his skin has been punctured in honorable warfare—warm themselves in the reflected glow, and say to each other: "He has a real nobility, a love of humanity raised above mere personal affections." The excess of this self-love has flowed out, inconveniently for her, over Laura, who, with so many others, owes her comfortable situation and her salary to him. When he is in a very good humor, he tells her, "I am tempted to forgive you for being a *gringa. Gringita!*" and Laura, burning, imagines herself leaning forward suddenly, and with a sound backhanded slap wiping the suety smile from his face. If he notices her eyes at these moments he gives no sign.

She knows what Braggioni would offer her, and she must resist tenaciously without appearing to resist, and if she could avoid it she would not admit even to herself the slow drift of his intention. During these long evenings which have spoiled a long month for her, she sits in her deep chair with an open book on her knees, resting her eyes on the consoling rigidity of the printed page when the sight and sound of Braggioni singing threaten to identify themselves with all her remembered afflictions and to add their weight to her uneasy premonitions of the future. The gluttonous bulk of Braggioni has become a symbol of her many disillusions, for a revolutionist should be lean, animated by heroic faith, a vessel of abstract virtues. This is nonsense, she knows it now and is ashamed of it. Revolution must have leaders, and leadership is a career for energetic men. She is, her comrades tell her, full of romantic error, for what she defines as cynicism in them is merely "a developed sense of reality." She is almost too willing to say, "I am wrong, I suppose I don't really understand the principles," and afterward she makes a secret truce with herself, determined not to surrender her will to such expedient logic. But she cannot help feeling that she had been betrayed irreparably by the disunion between her way of living and her feeling of what life should be, and at times she is almost contented to rest in this sense of grievance as a private store of consolation. Sometimes she wishes to run away, but she stays. Now she longs to fly out of this room, down the narrow stairs, and into the street where the houses lean together like conspirators under a single mottled lamp, and leave Braggioni singing to himself.

Instead she looks at Braggioni, frankly and clearly, like a good child who understands the rules of behavior. Her knees cling together under sound blue serge, and her round white collar is not purposely nun-like. She wears the uniform of an idea, and has renounced vanities. She was born Roman Catholic, and in spite of her fear of being seen by someone who might make a scandal of it, she slips now and again into some crumbling little church, kneels on the chilly stone, and says a Hail Mary on the gold rosary she bought in Tehuantepec. It is no good and she ends by examining the altar with its tinsel flowers and ragged brocades, and feels tender about the battered doll-shape of some male saint whose white, lace-trimmed drawers hang limply around his ankles below the hieratic dignity of his velvet robe. She has encased herself in a set of principles derived from her early training, leaving no detail of gesture or of personal taste untouched, and for this reason she will not wear lace made on machines. This is her private heresy, for in her special group the machine is sacred, and will be the salvation of the workers. She loves fine lace, and there is a tiny edge of fluted cobweb on this collar, which is one of twenty precisely alike, folded in blue tissue paper in the upper drawer of her clothes chest.

Braggioni catches her glance solidly as if he had been waiting for it, leans forward, balancing his paunch between his spread knees, and sings with tremendous emphasis, weighing his words. He has, the song relates, no father and no mother, nor even a friend to console him; lonely as a wave of the sea he comes and goes, lonely as a wave. His mouth opens round and yearns sideways, his balloon cheeks grow oily with the labor of song. He bulges marvelously in his expensive garments. Over his lavender collar, crushed upon a purple necktie, held by a diamond hoop: over his ammunition belt of tooled leather worked in silver, buckled cruelly around his gasping middle: over the tops of his glossy yellow shoes Braggioni swells with ominous ripeness, his mauve silk hose stretched taut, his ankles bound with the stout leather thongs of his shoes.

When he stretches his eyelids at Laura she notes again that his eyes are the true tawny yellow cat's eyes. He is rich, not in money, he tells her, but in power, and this power brings with it the blameless ownership of things, and the right to indulge his love of small luxuries. "I have a taste for the elegant refinements," he said once, flourishing a yellow silk handkerchief before her nose. "Smell that? It is Jockey Club, imported from New York." Nonetheless he is wounded by life. He will say so presently. "It is true everything turns to dust in the hand, to gall on the tongue." He sighs and his leather belt creaks like a saddle girth. "I am disappointed in everything as it comes. Everything." He shakes his head. "You, poor thing, you will be disappointed too. You are born for it. We are more alike than you realize in some things. Wait and see. Some day you will remember what I have told you, you will know that Braggioni was your friend."

Laura feels a slow chill, a purely physical sense of danger, a warning in her blood that violence, mutilation, a shocking death, wait for her with lessening patience. She has translated this fear into something homely, immediate, and sometimes hesitates before crossing the street. "My personal fate is nothing, except as the testimony of a mental attitude," she reminds herself, quoting from some forgotten philosophic primer, and is sensible enough to add, "Anyhow, I shall not be killed by an automobile if I can help it."

"It may be true I am as corrupt, in another way, as Braggioni," she thinks in spite of herself, "as callous, as incomplete," and if this is so, any kind of death seems preferable. Still she sits quietly, she does not run. Where could she go? Uninvited she has promised herself to this place; she can no longer imagine herself as living in another country, and there is no pleasure in remembering her life before she came here.

Precisely what is the nature of this devotion, its true motives, and what are its obligations? Laura cannot say. She spends part of her days in Xochimilco, near by, teaching Indian children to say in English, "The cat is on the mat." When she appears in the classroom they crowd about her with smiles on their wise, innocent, clay-colored faces, crying, "Good morning, my titcher!" in immaculate voices, and they make of her desk a fresh garden of flowers every day.

During her leisure she goes to union meetings and listens to busy important voices quarreling over tactics, methods, internal politics. She visits the prisoners of her own political faith in their cells, where they entertain themselves with counting cockroaches, repenting of their indiscretions, composing their memoirs, writing out manifestoes and plans for their comrades who are still walking about free, hands in pockets, sniffing fresh air. Laura brings them food and cigarettes and a little money, and she brings messages disguised in equivocal phrases from the men outside who dare not set foot in the prison for fear of disappearing into the cells kept empty for them. If the prisoners confuse night and day, and complain, "Dear little Laura, time doesn't pass in this infernal hole, and I won't know when it is time to sleep unless I have a reminder," she brings them their favorite narcotics, and says in a tone that does not wound them with pity, "Tonight will really be night for you," and though her Spanish amuses them, they find her comforting, useful. If they lose patience and all faith, and curse the slowness of their friends in coming to their rescue with money and influence, they trust her not to repeat everything, and if she inquires, "Where do you think we can find money, or influence?" they are certain to answer, "Well, there is Braggioni, why doesn't he do something?"

She smuggles letters from headquarters to men hiding from firing squads in back streets in mildewed houses, where they sit in tumbled beds and talk bitterly as if all Mexico were at their heels, when Laura knows positively they might appear at the band concert in the Alameda on Sunday morning, and no one would notice them. But Braggioni says, "Let them sweat a little. The next time they may be careful. It is very restful to have them out of the way for a while." She is not afraid to knock on any door in any street after midnight, and enter in the darkness, and say to one of these men who is really in danger: "They will be looking for you—seriously—tomorrow morning after six. Here is some money from Vicente. Go to Vera Cruz and wait."

She borrows money from the Roumanian agitator to give to his bitter enemy the Polish agitator. The favor of Braggioni is their disputed territory, and Braggioni holds the balance nicely, for he can use them both. The Polish agitator talks love to her over café tables, hoping to exploit what he believes is her secret sentimental preference for him, and he gives her misinformation which he begs her to repeat as the solemn truth to certain persons. The Roumanian is more adroit. He is generous with his money in all good causes, and lies to her with an air of ingenuous candor, as if he were her good friend and confidant. She never repeats anything they may say. Braggioni never asks questions. He has other ways to discover all that he wishes to know about them.

Nobody touches her, but all praise her gray eyes, and the soft, round under lip which promises gayety, yet is always grave, nearly always firmly closed: and they cannot understand why she is in Mexico. She walks back and forth on her errands, with puzzled eyebrows, carrying her little folder of drawings and music and school papers. No dancer dances more beautifully than Laura walks, and she inspires some amusing, unexpected ardors, which cause little gossip, because nothing comes of them. A young captain who had been a soldier in Zapata's army attempted, during a horseback ride near Cuernavaca, to express his desire for her with the noble simplicity befitting a rude folk-hero: but gently, because he was gentle. This gentleness was his defeat, for when he alighted, and removed her foot from the stirrup, and essayed to draw her down into his arms, her horse, ordinarily a tame one, shied fiercely, reared and plunged away. The young hero's horse careered blindly after his stablemate, and the hero did not return to the hotel until rather late that evening. At breakfast he came to her table in full charro dress, gray buckskin jacket and trousers with strings of silver buttons down the leg, and he was in a humorous, careless mood. "May I sit with you?" and "You are a wonderful rider. I was terrified that you might be thrown and dragged. I should never have forgiven myself. But I cannot admire you enough for your riding!"

"I learned to ride in Arizona," said Laura.

"If you will ride with me again this morning, I promise you a horse that will not shy with you," he said. But Laura remembered that she must return to Mexico City at noon.

Next morning the children made a celebration and spent their playtime writing on the blackboard, "We lov ar ticher," and with tinted chalks they drew wreaths of flowers around the words. The young hero wrote her a letter: "I am a very foolish, wasteful, impulsive man. I should have first said I love you, and then you would not have run away. But you shall see me again." Laura thought, "I must send him a box of colored crayons," but she was trying to forgive herself for having spurred her horse at the wrong moment.

A brown, shock-haired youth came and stood in her patio one night and sang like a lost soul for two hours, but Laura could think of nothing to do about it. The moonlight spread a wash of gauzy silver over the clear spaces of the garden, and the shadows were cobalt blue. The scarlet blossoms of the Judas tree were dull purple, and the names of the colors repeated themselves automatically in her mind, while she watched not the boy, but his shadow, fallen like a dark garment across the fountain rim, trailing in the water. Lupe came silently and whispered expert counsel in her ear: "If you will throw him one little flower, he will sing another song or two and go away." Laura threw the flower, and he sang a last song and went away with the flower tucked in the band of his hat. Lupe said, "He is one of the organizers of the Typographers Union, and before that he sold corridos in the Merced market, and before that, he came from Guanajuato, where I was born. I would not trust any man, but I trust least those from Guanajuato."

She did not tell Laura that he would be back again the next night, and the next, nor that he would follow her at a certain fixed distance around the Merced market, through Zócola, up Francisco I. Madero Avenue, and so along the Paseo de la Reforma to Chapultepec Park, and into the Philosopher's Footpath, still with that flower withering in his hat, and an indivisible attention in his eyes.

Now Laura is accustomed to him, it means nothing except that he is nineteen years old and is observing a convention with all propriety, as though it were founded on a law of nature, which in the end it might well prove to be. He is beginning to write poems which he prints on a wooden press, and he leaves them stuck like handbills in her door. She is pleasantly disturbed by the abstract, unhurried watchfulness of his black eyes which will in time turn easily towards another object. She tells herself that throwing the flower was a mistake, for she is twenty-two years old and knows better; but she refuses to regret it, and persuades herself that her negation of all external events as they occur is a sign that she is gradually perfecting herself in the stoicism she strives to cultivate against that disaster she fears, though she cannot name it.

She is not at home in the world. Every day she teaches children who remain strangers to her, though she loves their tender round hands and their charming opportunist savagery. She knocks at unfamiliar doors not knowing whether a friend or a stranger shall answer, and even if a known face emerges from the sour gloom of that unknown interior, still it is the face of a stranger. No matter what this stranger says to her, nor what her message to him, the very cells of her flesh reject knowledge and kinship in one monotonous word. No. No. No. She draws her strength from this one holy talismanic word which does not suffer her to be led into evil. Denying everything, she may walk anywhere in safety, she looks at everything without amazement.

No, repeats this firm unchanging voice of her blood; and she looks at Braggioni without amazement. He is a great man, he wishes to impress this simple girl who covers her great round breasts with thick dark cloth, and who hides long, invaluably beautiful legs under a heavy skirt. She is almost thin except for the incomprehensible fullness of her breasts, like a nursing mother's, and Braggioni, who considers himself a judge of women, speculates again on the puzzle of her notorious virginity, and takes the liberty of speech which she permits without a sign of modesty, indeed, without any sort of sign, which is disconcerting.

"You think you are so cold, *gringita!* Wait and see. You will surprise yourself some day! May I be there to advise you!" He stretches his eyelids at her, and his ill-humored cat's eyes waver in a separate glance for the two points of light marking the opposite ends of a smoothly drawn path between the swollen curve of her breasts. He is not put off by that blue serge, nor by her resolutely fixed gaze. There is all the time in the world. His cheeks are bellying with the wind of song. "O girl with the dark eyes," he sings, and reconsiders. "But yours are not dark. I can change all that. O girl with the green eyes, you have stolen my heart away!" then his mind wanders to the song, and Laura feels the weight of his attention being shifted elsewhere. Singing thus, he seems harmless, he is quite harmless, there is nothing to do but sit patiently and say "No," when the moment comes. She draws a full breath, and her mind wanders also, but not far. She dares not wander too far.

Not for nothing has Braggioni taken pains to be a good revolutionist and a professional lover of humanity. He will never die of it. He has the malice, the cleverness, the wickedness, the sharpness of wit, the hardness of heart, stipulated for loving the world profitably. *He will never die of it.* He will live to see himself kicked out from his feeding trough by other hungry world-saviors. Traditionally he must sing in spite of his life which drives him to bloodshed, he tells Laura, for his father was a Tuscany peasant who drifted to Yucatan and married a Maya woman: a woman of race, an aristocrat. They gave him the love and knowledge of music, thus: and under the rip of his thumbnail, the strings of the instrument complain like exposed nerves.

Once he was called Delgadito by all the girls and married women who ran after him; he was so scrawny all his bones showed under his thin cotton clothing, and he could squeeze his emptiness to the very backbone with his two hands. He was a poet and the revolution was only a dream then; too many women loved him and sapped away his youth, and he could never find enough to eat anywhere, anywhere! Now he is a leader of men, crafty men who whisper in his ear, hungry men who wait for hours outside his office for a word with him, emaciated men with wild faces who waylay him at the street gate with a timid, "Comrade, let me tell you . . ." and they blow the foul breath from their empty stomachs in his face.

He is always sympathetic. He gives them handfuls of small coins from his own pocket, he promises them work, there will be demonstrations, they must join the unions and attend the meetings, above all they must be on the watch for spies. They are closer to him than his own brothers, without them he can do nothing—until tomorrow, comrade!

Until tomorrow. "They are stupid, they are lazy, they are treacherous, they would cut my throat for nothing," he says to Laura. He has good food and abundant drink, he hires an automobile and drives in the Paseo on Sunday morning, and enjoys plenty of sleep in a soft bed beside a wife who dares not disturb him; and he sits pampering his bones in easy billows of fat, singing to Laura, who knows and thinks these things about him. When he was fifteen, he tried to drown himself because he loved a girl, his first love, and she laughed at him. "A thousand women have paid for that," and his tight little mouth turns down at the corners. Now he perfumes his hair with Jockey Club, and confides to Laura: "One woman is really as good as another for me, in the dark. I prefer them all."

His wife organizes unions among the girls in the cigarette factories, and walks in picket lines, and even speaks at meetings in the evening. But she cannot be brought to acknowledge the benefits of true liberty. "I tell her I must have my freedom, net. She does not understand my point of view." Laura has heard this many times. Braggioni scratches the guitar and meditates. "She is an instinctively virtuous woman, pure gold, no doubt of that. If she were not, I should lock her up, and she knows it."

His wife, who works so hard for the good of the factory girls, employs part of her leisure lying on the floor weeping because there are so many women in the world, and only one husband for her, and she never knows where nor when to look for him. He told her: "Unless you can learn to cry when I am not here, I must go away for good." That day he went away and took a room at the Hotel Madrid.

It is this month of separation for the sake of higher principles that has been spoiled not only for Mrs. Braggioni, whose sense of reality is beyond criticism, but for Laura, who feels herself bogged in a nightmare. Tonight Laura envies Mrs. Braggioni, who is alone, and free to weep as much as she pleases about a concrete wrong. Laura has just come from a visit to the prison, and she is waiting for tomorrow with a bitter anxiety as if tomorrow may not come, but time may be caught immovably in this hour, with herself transfixed, Braggioni singing on forever, and Eugenio's body not yet discovered by the guard.

Braggioni says: "Are you going to sleep?" Almost before she can shake her head, he begins telling her about the May-day disturbances coming on in Morelia, for the Catholics hold a festival in honor of the Blessed Virgin, and the Socialists celebrate their martyrs on that day. "There will be two independent processions, starting from either end of town, and they will march until they meet, and the rest depends . . ." He asks her to oil and load his pistols. Standing up, he unbuckles his ammunition belt, and spreads it laden across her knees. Laura sits with the shells slipping through the cleaning cloth dipped in oil, and he says again he cannot understand why she works so hard for the revolutionary idea unless she loves some man who is in it. "Are you not in love with someone?" "No," says Laura. "And no one is in love with you?" "No." "Then it is your own fault. No woman need go begging. Why, what is the matter with you? The legless beggar woman in the Alameda has a perfectly faithful lover. Did you know that?"

Laura peers down the pistol barrel and says nothing, but a long, slow faintness rises and subsides in her; Braggioni curves his swollen fingers around the throat of the guitar and softly smothers the music out of it, and when she hears him again he seems to have forgotten her, and is speaking in the hypnotic voice he uses when talking in small rooms to a listening, close-gathered crowd. Some day this world, now seemingly so composed and eternal, to the edges of every sea shall be merely a tangle of gaping trenches, of crashing walls and broken bodies. Everything must be torn from its accustomed place where it has rotted for centuries, hurled skyward and distributed, cast down again clean as rain, without separate identity. Nothing shall survive that the stiffened hands of poverty have created for the rich and no one shall be left alive except the elect spirits destined to procreate a new world cleansed of cruelty and injustice, ruled by benevolent anarchy: "Pistols are good, I love them, cannon are even better, but in the end I pin my faith to good dynamite," he concludes, and strokes the pistol lying in her hands. "Once I dreamed of destroying this city, in case it offered resistance to General Ortíz, but it fell into his hands like an overripe pear."

He is made restless by his own words, rises and stands waiting. Laura holds up the belt to him: "Put that on, and go kill somebody in Morelia, and you will be happier," she says softly. The presence of death in the room makes her bold. "Today, I found Eugenio going into a stupor. He refused to allow me to call the prison doctor. He had taken all the tablets I brought him yesterday. He said he took them because he was bored."

"He is a fool, and his death is his own business," says Braggioni, fastening his belt carefully.

"I told him if he had waited only a little while longer, you would have got him set free," says Laura. "He said he did not want to wait."

"He is a fool and we are well rid of him," says Braggioni, reaching for his hat.

He goes away. Laura knows his mood has changed, she will not see him any more for a while. He will send word when he needs her to go on errands into strange streets, to speak to the strange faces that will appear, like clay masks with the power of human speech, to mutter their thanks to Braggioni for his help. Now she is free, and she thinks, I must run while there is time. But she does not go.

Braggioni enters his own house where for a month his wife has spent many hours every night weeping and tangling her hair upon her pillow. She is weeping now, and she weeps more at the sight of him, the cause of all her sorrows. He looks about the room. Nothing is changed, the smells are good and familiar, he is well acquainted with the woman who comes toward him with no reproach except grief on her face. He says to her tenderly: "You are so good, please don't cry any more, you dear good creature." She says, "Are you tired, my angel? Sit here and I will wash your feet." She brings a bowl of water, and kneeling, unlaces his shoes, and when from her knees she raises her sad eyes under her blackened lids, he is sorry for everything, and bursts into tears. "Ah, yes, I am hungry, I am tired, let us eat something together," he says, between sobs. His wife leans her head on his arm and says, "Forgive me!" and this time he is refreshed by the solemn, endless rain of her tears.

Laura takes off her serge dress and puts on a white linen nightgown and goes to bed. She turns her head a little to one side, and lying still, reminds herself that it is time to sleep. Numbers tick in her brain like little clocks, soundless doors close of themselves around her. If you would sleep, you must not remember anything, the children will say tomorrow, good morning, my teacher, the poor prisoners who come every day bringing flowers to their jailor. 1-2-3-4-5—it is monstrous to confuse love with revolution, night with day, life with death—ah, Eugenio!

The tolling of the midnight bell is a signal, but what does it mean? Get up, Laura, and follow me: come out of your sleep, out of your bed, out of this strange house. What are you doing in this house? Without a word, without fear she rose and reached for Eugenio's hand, but he eluded her with a sharp, sly smile and drifted away. This is not all, you shall see—Murderer, he said, follow me, I will show you a new country, but it is far away and we must hurry. No, said Laura, not unless you take my hand, no; and she clung first to the stair rail, and then to the topmost branch of the Judas tree that bent down slowly and set her upon the earth, and then to the rocky ledge of a cliff, and then to the jagged wave of a sea that was not water but a desert of crumbling stone. Where are you taking me, she asked in wonder but without fear. To death, and it is a long way off, and we must hurry, said Eugenio. No, said Laura, not unless you take my hand. Then eat these flowers, poor prisoner, said Eugenio in a voice of pity, take and eat: and from the Judas tree he stripped the warm bleeding flowers, and held them to her lips. She saw that his hand was fleshless, a cluster of small white petrified branches, and his eye sockets were without light, but she ate the flowers greedily for they satisfied both hunger and thirst. Murderer! said Eugenio, and Cannibal! This is my body and my blood. Laura cried No! and at the sound of her own voice, she awoke trembling, and was afraid to sleep again.

QUESTIONS FOR DISCUSSION

1. Define precisely the conflict within Laura. Then, on the basis of this definition, define the topic and theme of "Flowering Judas."
2. One very central group of symbols in "Flowering Judas" are drawn from orthodox religion. Find as many of these as you can, and define

their function and meaning *in the story*. Are these religious symbols, allusions, and parallels appropriate to the theme and purpose of the story? Are they dramatically effective?

3. What symbols other than religious (clothing, for example, or settings) are used in the story? How do they contribute to the story's theme?
4. Discuss the function in the story of the following characters: Braggioni's wife; the young man who serenades Laura; Eugenio.
5. Discuss the relationship between the style of this story and its purpose. (For example, Miss Porter uses paradox freely and frequently; the story is full of such phrases as "ominous ripeness" or "this sense of grievance as a private store of consolation." Why?)
6. "Flowering Judas" employs exposition (that is, direct statement as opposed to dramatization and implication) much more freely than any story you have yet read. Does the story suffer from this?

5 Genres: Humor, Satire, and Fantasy

To this point our emphasis in this text has been on the techniques of fiction, on the methods by which writers achieve their various purposes and effects. And for the most part, the stories we have thus far examined have been both serious and realistic. There are, however, three kinds of stories —humorous stories, satirical stories, and fantasies—which we have not yet considered.

There have been numerous attempts, none of them completely successful, to define and analyze humor; to attempt to do either here, particularly within two or three pages, would therefore be both impudent and foolish. For one thing, what one time or place or person will find amusing, another will not. For another, humorus fiction covers a considerable stretch of mountain and plain; farce is humor, and so is satire; slapstick comedy is humor, and so is a subtle and essentially realistic portrayal of some comic aspect of human nature. But if we can neither define nor analyze the term, we can point out a few of the characteristics found in most humorous or satirical stories.

There is, to begin with, the matter of *surprise* in humor, of the *unexpected.* Surprise can assume innumerable forms, of course; it may appear in a minor and incidental detail, an unexpected line of dialogue, a surprising action; it may, as well, take the form of a major reversal in a story's direction or outcome. In the stories in this section, you will find that much of the humor relies on some kind of surprise. In "First

Confession," for example, much of the story's humor hinges on the sudden reversal in direction from the confession as anticipated to the confession as realized. It is, of course, this same kind of surprise, unexpected twist, or reversal that makes jokes funny. Second, there is the matter of *contrast.* Contrast is universal in both humor and satire, and, like surprise, it may assume many forms. Some stories derive humor from understating the important or from exaggerating the trivial. Other stories derive the same effect from a contrast between tone and subject matter; a facetious treatment of the subject of murder would be an example. Still others will employ incongruity or irony. But perhaps the most important kind of contrast in either humor or satire is this: Like other kinds of stories, both humor and satire present to us incident and people and idea; but unlike most "serious" fiction, the actions or traits of these people, or the ideas or ideals or attitudes that they hold, or the things that they do, are held up against a contrasting and *implied* standard of behavior or attitude or idea or action. What we have, therefore, is one form of irony, since the implied (and nonexistent) standard usually makes sense where the existing one does not; what we have is a contrast between what is and what ought to be. Thus, in order to get the point of such a story, we must recognize what this contrast is and what it involves. To reduce this to the concrete, in order to get the point of "The Forks," we must recognize that the values and attitudes of the Monsignor are by implication held up against, and contrasted with, the values and attitudes of the priesthood as they ought to be. We must understand, for example, that the Roman priest takes the vows of poverty, chastity, and obedience in order to get the humor of the references to the Monsignor's car as "her." Part of the difficulty, therefore, of appreciating the satire in "The Forks" lies in the fact that the values of the Monsignor are contrasted to a set of *implied* values. Contrast, in fact, is always implied in humor and satire, because humor in fiction is precisely like humor in anecdote or joke; in order for fiction to provoke amusement, it must speak for itself, its point must remain unexplained.

Surprise, contrast, implication—these are basic elements in both humor and satire. But thus far we have treated the two as one. Is there any difference between humor and satire?

If there is (and sometimes the line is fine), it lies not in method but in intent and purpose; that is, the two can be differentiated on the basis of the attitudes of the authors toward the subject matter of the story. Humor is, in general, congenial, good-natured, tolerant; satire is intolerant. We may, it is true, laugh *at* someone in a humorous story, frequently because the author handles his material in such a way as to make us feel superior; but the laughter will not be malicious. The laughter in satire, however, *is* malicious. The intent of humor is always to provoke amusement; the intent of satire is to provoke reform. For this reason, a great deal of satire is not even funny; such satires as Swift's *A Modest Proposal* or Orwell's *1984* are not funny at all. In short, behind satire lies seriousness; behind humor lies amusement. This is not to say that humorous fiction is to be taken lightly; humor can accomplish things that satire cannot. It can, for example, make us more tolerant of the faults and foibles of our fellow human beings; even more important, it can provide us with a needed perspective on our own traits, values, or attitudes.

Our grouping of fantasy with humor and satire is a grouping of convenience only; unless a fantasy is humorous, the two genres have little in common. A fantasy is a story in which the common, familiar experiences of human life are ignored, in which the generally accepted principles of life are disregarded, in which we are introduced to an unfamiliar world or to human experiences that follow no familiar pattern.

There are two types of fantasy. The first we can call *escape* fantasy; much of contemporary science fiction is of this kind. We have already observed that the reader of escape fiction wants to retreat from this world into another, more congenial one; and escape fantasy provides this opportunity by transferring the reader to a different world or a different time or place.

Because some fantasy is escape literature, the instinctive reaction of the reader to a story that transfers him to an unfamiliar world or presents him with strange experiences—experiences that apparently contradict known "laws"—is to assume that because the story is *fantastic*, it can have nothing important to say about the real world in which we live. But a great many fantasies are written for quite another purpose than to provide escape. This kind of fantasy is analogous to non-Euclidian geometry, which is based on the assumption that the sum of the angles of a triangle do *not* equal 180°; this seems to be nonsense, but then non-Euclidian geometry was partly responsible for the discovery of radar. In the same way, a writer's assumption that the real world is a world other than the one we are familiar with may lead to a statement of theme that can have a very real bearing on our concept of nature or our understanding of the human condition.

The intelligent reader, therefore, does not dismiss fantasy because it fails to coincide with his conception of the world. Rather, he approaches fantasy by granting the writer his terms and then examining the story on those terms. And having done this, he then tries to discover the *reasons* that lie behind the writer's particular approach to his story material.

This first step is similar to our basic approach to a realistic story. In the realistic story we grant the writer an initial concession; we then test the story for plausibility of conflict and character and for significance. In fantasy we employ the same approach; the only difference is in the nature of the concession that we make to the writer. Where in the realistic story we allow the writer a single coincidence, in the fantasy we allow him to "repeal" a natural law. But from this point we expect the writer to adhere to the principles of storytelling just as strictly as if he were writing a story about the world with which we are familiar. Our first approach to fantasy, then, is to test the validity of the story *as story.*

Our second approach also parallels our approach to the realistic story. We have seen that serious writers choose incidents and characters with a theme in mind, and that from the relationship of action, character, and emotion in a story we derive a meaning. This is as true of fantasy as of realistic fiction. Thus, our second step should be to look for the meaning behind the story and to examine the relationship between the story and the theme.

When we do this, we will probably discover why the writer chose fantasy rather than realism. Like other writers, the writer of fantasy intends, among other things, to interpret his world and ours. If he chooses fantasy as his medium, he apparently assumes that fantasy will say what he has to say more clearly and effectively than would any other approach. And part of the job of analyzing and critically evaluating a fantasy will involve a consideration of whether the writer's assumption seems to be a sound one.

JOHN COLLIER
Bottle Party

Franklin Fletcher dreamed of luxury in the form of tiger-skins and beautiful women. He was prepared, at a pinch, to forgo the tiger-skins. Unfortunately the beautiful women seemed equally rare and inaccessible. At his office and at his boarding-house the girls were mere mice, or cattish, or kittenish, or had insufficiently read the advertisements. He met no others. At thirty-five he gave up, and decided he must console himself with a hobby, which is a very miserable second-best.

He prowled about in odd corners of the town, looking in at the windows of antique dealers and junk-shops, wondering what on earth he might collect. He came upon a poor shop, in a poor alley, in whose dusty window stood a single object: it was a full-rigged ship in a bottle. Feeling rather like that himself, he decided to go in and ask the price.

The shop was small and bare. Some shabby racks were ranged about the walls, and these racks bore a large number of bottles, of every shape and size, containing a variety of objects which were interesting only because they were in bottles. While Franklin still looked about, a little door opened, and out shuffled the proprietor, a wizened old man in a smoking-cap, who seemed mildly surprised and mildly pleased to have a customer.

He showed Franklin bouquets, and birds of paradise, and the Battle of Gettysburg, and miniature Japanese gardens, and even a shrunken human head, all stoppered up in bottles. "And what," said Frank, "are those, down there on the bottom shelf?"

"They are not much to look at," said the old man. "A lot of people think they are all nonsense. Personally, I like them."

He lugged out a few specimens from their dusty obscurity. One seemed to have nothing but a little dried-up fly in it, others contained what might have been horse-hairs or straws, or mere wisps of heaven knows what; some appeared to be filled with grey or opalescent smoke. "They are," said the old man, "various sorts of genii, jinns, sibyls, demons, and such things. Some of them, I believe, are much harder, even than a full-rigged ship, to get into a bottle."

"Oh, but come! This is New York," said Frank.

"All the more reason," said the old man, "to expect the most extraordinary jinns in bottles. I'll show you. Wait a moment. The stopper is a little stiff."

"You mean there's one in there?" said Frank. "And you're going to let it out?"

"Why not?" replied the old man, desisting in his efforts, and holding the bottle up to the light. "This one—Good heavens! *Why not,* indeed! My eyes are getting weak. I very nearly undid the wrong bottle. A very ugly customer, that one! Dear me! It's just as well I didn't get that stopper undone. I'd better put him right back in the rack. I must remember he's in the lower right-hand corner. I'll stick a label on him one of these days. Here's something more harmless."

"What's in that?" said Frank.

"Supposed to be the most beautiful girl in the world," said the old man. "All right, if you like that sort of thing. Myself, I've never troubled to undo her. I'll find something more interesting."

"Well, from a scientific point of view," said Frank, "I—"

"Science isn't everything," said the old man. "Look at this." He held up one which contained a tiny, mummified, insect-looking object, just visible through the grime. "Put your ear to it," he said.

Frank did so. He heard, in a sort of whistling nothing of a voice, the words, "Louisiana Lad, Saratoga, four-fifteen. Louisiana Lad, Saratoga, four-fifteen," repeated over and over again.

"What on earth is that?" said he.

"That," said the old man, "is the original Cumaean Sibyl. Very interesting. She's taken up racing."

"Very interesting," said Frank. "All the same, I'd just like to see that other. I adore beauty."

"A bit of an artist, eh?" said the old man. "Believe me, what you really want is a good, all-round, serviceable type. Here's one, for example. I recommend this little fellow from personal experience. He's practical. He can fix you anything."

"Well, if that's so," said Frank, "why haven't you got a palace, tiger-skins, and all that?"

"I had all that," said the old man. "And he fixed it. Yes, this was my first bottle. All the rest came from him. First of all I had a palace, pictures, marbles, slaves. And, as you say, tiger-skins. I had him put Cleopatra on one of them."

"What was she like?" cried Frank.

"All right," said the old man, "if you like that sort of thing. I got bored with it. I thought to myself, 'What I'd like, really, is a little shop, with all sorts of things in bottles.' So I had him fix it. He got me the sibyl. He got me the ferocious fellow there. In fact, he got me all of them."

"And now he's in there?" said Frank.

"Yes, he's in there," said the old man. "Listen to him."

Frank put his ear to the bottle. He heard, uttered in the most plaintive tones, "Let me out. Do let me out. Please let me out. I'll do anything. Let me out. I'm harmless. Please let me out. Just for a little while. Do let me out. I'll do anything. Please—"

Frank looked at the old man. "He's there all right," he said. "He's there."

"Of course he's there," said the old man. "I wouldn't sell you an empty bottle. What do you take me for? In fact, I wouldn't sell this one at all, for sentimental reasons, only I've had the shop a good many years now, and you're my first customer."

Frank put his ear to the bottle again. "Let me out. Let me out. Oh, please let me out. I'll—"

"My God!" said Frank uneasily. "Does he go on like that *all* the time?"

"Very probably," said the old man. "I can't say I listen. I prefer the radio."

"It seems rather tough on him," said Frank sympathetically.

"Maybe," said the old man. "They don't seem to like bottles. Personally, I do. They fascinate me. For example, I—"

"Tell me," said Frank. "Is he really harmless?"

"Oh, yes," said the old man. "Bless you, yes. Some say they're tricky—eastern blood and all that—I never found him so. I used to let him out; he'd do his stuff, then back he'd go again. I must say, he's very efficient."

"He could get me anything?"

"Absolutely anything."

"And how much do you want for him?" said Frank.

"Oh, I don't know," said the old man. "Ten million dollars, perhaps."

"I say! I haven't got that. Still, if he's as good as you say, maybe I could work it off on the hire purchase system."

"Don't worry. We'll say five dollars instead. I've got all I want, really. Shall I wrap him up for you?"

Frank paid over his five dollars, and hurried home with the precious bottle, terrified of breaking it. As soon as he was in his room he pulled out the stopper. Out flowed a prodigious quantity of greasy smoke, which immediately solidified into the figure of a gross and fleshy Oriental, six feet in height, with rolls of fat, a hook nose, a wicked white to his eye, vast double chins, altogether like a film-producer, only larger. Frank, striving desperately for something to say, ordered shashlik, kebabs, and Turkish delight. These were immediately forthcoming.

Frank, having recovered his balance, noted that these modest offerings were of surpassing quality, and set upon dishes of solid gold, superbly engraved, and polished to a dazzling brightness. It is by little details of this description that one may recognize a really first-rate servant. Frank was delighted, but restrained his enthusiasm. "Gold plates," said he, "are all very well. Let us, however, get down to brass tacks. I should like a palace."

"To hear," said his dusky henchman, "is to obey."

"It should," said Frank, "be of suitable size, suitably situated, suitably furnished, suitable pictures, suitable marbles, hangings, and all that. I should like there to be a large number of tiger-skins. I am very fond of tiger-skins."

"They shall be there," said his slave.

"I am," said Frank, "a bit of an artist, as your late owner remarked. My art, so to speak, demands the presence, upon these tiger-skins, of a number of young women, some blonde, some brunette, some *petite*, some Junoesque, some languorous, some vivacious, all beautiful, and they need not be over-dressed. I hate over-dressing. It is vulgar. Have you got that?"

"I have," said the jinn.

"Then," said Frank, "let *me* have it."

"Condescend only," said his servant, "to close your eyes for the space of a single minute, and opening them you shall find yourself surrounded by the agreeable objects you have described."

"O.K.," said Frank. "But no tricks, mind!"

He closed his eyes as requested. A low, musical humming, whooshing sound rose and fell about him. At the end of the minute he looked around. There were the arches, pillars, marbles, hangings, etc. of the most exquisite palace imaginable, and wherever he looked he saw a tiger-skin, and on every tiger-skin there reclined a young woman of surpassing beauty, who was certainly not vulgarly over-dressed.

Our good Frank was, to put it mildly, in an ecstasy. He darted to and fro like a honey-bee in a florist's shop. He was received everywhere with smiles sweet beyond description, and with glances of an open or a veiled responsiveness. Here was a shoulder turned, but by no means a cold shoulder. Here were open arms, and such arms! Here was love dissembled, but vainly dissembled. Here was love triumphant. "I must say," said Frank at a later hour, "I have spent a really delightful afternoon. I have enjoyed it thoroughly."

"Then may I crave," said the jinn, who was at the moment serving him his supper, "may I crave the boon of being allowed to act as your butler, and as general minister to your pleasures, instead of being returned to that abominable bottle?"

"I don't see why not," said Frank. "It certainly seems rather tough that, after having fixed all this up, you should be crammed back into the bottle again. Very well, act as my butler, but understand, whatever the convention may be, I wish you never to enter a room without knocking. And above all—no tricks."

The jinn, with a soapy smile of gratitude, withdrew, and Frank shortly retired to his harem, where he passed the evening as pleasantly as he had passed the afternoon.

Some weeks went by, entirely filled with these agreeable pastimes, till Frank, in obedience to a law which not even the most efficient jinns can set aside, found himself growing a little over-particular, a little blasé, a little inclined to criticize and find fault.

"These," said he to his jinn, "are very pretty young creatures, if you like that sort of thing, but I imagine they can hardly be first-rate, or I should feel more interest in them. I am, after all, a connoisseur; nothing can please me but the very best. Take them away. Roll up all the tiger-skins but one."

"It shall be done," said the jinn. "Behold, it is accomplished."

"And on that remaining tiger-skin," said Frank, "put me Cleopatra herself."

The next moment, Cleopatra was there, looking, it must be admitted, absolutely superb. "Hullo!" she said. "Here I am, on a tiger-skin again!"

"*Again?*" cried Frank, suddenly reminded of the old man in the shop. "Here! Take her back. Bring me Helen of Troy."

Next moment, Helen of Troy was there. "Hullo!" she said. "Here I am, on a tiger-skin again!"

"Again?" cried Frank. "Damn that old man! Take her away. Bring me Queen Guinevere."

Guinevere said exactly the same thing; so did Madame la Pompadour, Lady Hamilton, and every other famous beauty that Frank could think of. "No wonder," said he, "that that old man was such an extremely wizened old man! The old fiend! The old devil! He has properly taken the gilt off all the gingerbread. Call me jealous if you like; I will not play second fiddle to that ugly old rascal. Where shall I find a perfect creature, worthy of the embraces of such a connoisseur as I am?"

"If you are deigning to address that question to me," said the jinn, "let me remind you that there was, in that shop, a little bottle which my late master had never unstoppered, because I supplied him with it after he had lost interest in matters of this sort. Nevertheless it has the reputation of containing the most beautiful girl in the whole world."

"You are right," cried Frank. "Get me that bottle without delay."

In a few seconds the bottle lay before him. "You may have the afternoon off," said Frank to the jinn.

"Thank you," said the jinn. "I will go and see my family in Arabia. I have not seen them for a long time." With that he bowed and withdrew. Frank turned his attention to the bottle, which he was not long in unstoppering.

Out came the most beautiful girl you can possibly imagine. Cleopatra and all that lot were hags and frumps compared with her. "Where am I?" said she. "What is this beautiful palace? What am I doing on a tiger-skin? Who is this handsome young prince?"

"It's me!" cried Frank, in a rapture. "It's me!"

The afternoon passed like a moment in Paradise. Before Frank knew it the jinn was back, ready to serve up supper. Frank must sup with his charmer, for this time it was love, the real thing. The jinn, entering with the viands, rolled up his wicked eyes at the sight of so much beauty.

It happened that Frank, all love and restlessness, darted out into the garden between two mouthfuls, to pluck his beloved a rose. The jinn, on the pretence of serving her wine, edged up very closely. "I don't know if you remember me," said he in a whisper. "I used to be in the next bottle to you. I have often admired you through the glass."

"Oh, yes," said she. "I remember you quite well."

At that moment Frank returned. The jinn could say no more, but he stood about the room, inflating his monstrous chest, and showing off his plump and dusky muscles. "You need not be afraid of him," said Frank. "He is only a jinn. Pay no attention to him. Tell me if you really love me."

"Of course I do," said she.

"Well, say so," said he. "Why don't you say so?"

"I have said so," said she. "Of course I do. Isn't that saying so?"

This vague, evasive reply dimmed all Frank's happiness, as if a cloud had come over the sun. Doubt sprang up in his mind, and entirely ruined moments of exquisite bliss.

"What are you thinking of?" he would say.

"I don't know," she would reply.

"Well, you ought to know," he would say, and then a quarrel would begin.

Once or twice he even ordered her back into her bottle. She obeyed with a malicious and secretive smile.

"Why should she give that sort of smile?" said Frank to the jinn, to whom he confided his distress.

"I cannot tell," replied the jinn. "Unless she has a lover concealed in there."

"Is it possible?" cried Frank in consternation.

"It is surprising," said the jinn, "how much room there is in one of these bottles."

"Come out!" cried Frank. "Come out at once!"

His charmer obediently emerged. "Is there anyone else in that bottle?" cried Frank.

"How could there be?" she asked, with a look of rather overdone innocence.

"Give me a straight answer," said he. "Answer me yes or no."

"Yes or no," she replied maddeningly.

"You double-talking, two-timing little bitch!" cried Frank. "I'll go in and find out for myself. If I find anybody, God help him and you!"

With that, and with an intense effort of the will, he flowed himself into the bottle. He looked all around: there was no one. Suddenly he heard a sound above him. He looked up, and there was the stopper being thrust in.

"What are you doing?" cried he.

"We are putting in the stopper," said the jinn.

Frank cursed, begged, prayed, and implored. "Let me out!" he cried. "Let me out. Please let me out. Do let me out. I'll do anything. Let me out, do."

The jinn, however, had other matters to attend to. Frank had the infinite mortification of beholding these other matters through the glassy walls of his prison. Next day he was picked up, whisked through the air, and deposited in the dirty little shop, among the other bottles, from which this one had never been missed.

There he remained for an interminable period, covered all over with dust, and frantic with rage at the thought of what was going on in his exquisite palace, between his jinn and his faithless charmer. In the end, some sailors happened to drift into the shop, and, hearing this bottle contained the most beautiful girl in the world, they bought it up by general subscription of the fo'c'sle. When they unstoppered him at sea, and found it was only poor Frank, their disappointment knew no bounds, and they used him with the utmost barbarity.

QUESTIONS FOR DISCUSSION

1. "Bottle Party" is, of course, fantasy. Would you also classify it as humor or satire? Why?
2. Characterization in "Bottle Party" is thin—Franklin Fletcher is, actually, reduced to a single character trait, that of lechery. Would fuller characterization improve the story or defeat the story's purpose?
3. In the opening of the story, the shopkeeper explains at some length the "various sorts of genii, jinns, sibyls, demons" that he has for sale. Is this opening "padded" or necessary to the story's purpose, effect, and theme?
4. The late George Baker divided humor into three categories: farce, in which improbable people did improbable things; low comedy, in which probable people did probable things that were yet funny; and high comedy, where humor obtains not from people and their actions but from idea—where humor is primarily intellectual. In which category would you put "Bottle Party"?
5. Has "Bottle Party" a theme? If so, define it. Do you believe this theme as you would believe the theme of a "serious" or "realistic" story? If so, why?
6. Do you find the ending of "Bottle Party" appropriate to the story's purpose and theme, or is it merely "gimmicky"?

FRANK O'CONNOR
First Confession

All the trouble began when my grandfather died and my grandmother—my father's mother—came to live with us. Relations in the one house are a strain at the best of times, but, to make matters worse, my grandmother was a real old countrywoman and quite unsuited to the life in town. She had a fat, wrinkled old face, and, to Mother's great indignation, went round the house in bare feet—the boots had her crippled, she said. For dinner she had a jug of porter and a pot of potatoes with—sometimes—a bit of salt fish, and she poured out the potatoes on the table and ate them slowly, with great relish, using her fingers by way of a fork.

Now, girls are supposed to be fastidious, but I was the one who suffered most from this. Nora, my sister, just sucked up to the old woman for the penny she got every Friday out of the old-age pension, a thing I could not do. I was too honest, that was my trouble; and when I was playing with Bill Connell, the sergeant-major's son, and saw my grandmother steering up the path with the jug of porter sticking out from beneath her shawl I was mortified. I made excuses not to let him come into the house, because I could never be sure what she would be up to when we went in.

When Mother was at work and my grandmother made the dinner I wouldn't touch it. Nora once tried to make me, but I hid under the table from her and took the bread-knife with me for protection. Nora let on to be very indignant (she wasn't, of course, but she knew Mother saw through her, so she sided with Gran) and came after me. I lashed out at her with the bread-knife, and after that she left me alone. I stayed there till Mother came in from work and made my dinner, but when Father came in later Nora said in a shocked voice: "Oh, Dadda, do you know what Jackie did at dinnertime?" Then, of course, it all came out; Father gave me a flaking; Mother interfered, and for days after that he didn't speak to me and Mother barely spoke to Nora. And all because of that old woman! God knows, I was heart-scalded.

Then, to crown my misfortunes, I had to make my first confession and communion. It was an old woman called Ryan who prepared us for these. She was about the one age with Gran; she was well-to-do, lived in a big house on Montenotte, wore a black cloak and bonnet, and came every day to school at three o'clock when we should have been going home, and talked to us of hell. She may have mentioned the other place as well, but that could only have been by accident, for hell had the first place in her heart.

She lit a candle, took out a new half-crown, and offered it to the first boy who would hold one finger—only one finger!—in the flame for five minutes by the school clock. Being always very ambitious I was tempted to volunteer, but I thought it might look greedy. Then she asked were we afraid of holding one finger—only one finger!—in a little candle flame for five minutes and not afraid of burning all over in roasting hot furnaces for all eternity. "All eternity! Just think of that! A whole lifetime goes by and it's nothing, not even a drop in the ocean of your sufferings." The woman was really interesting about hell, but my attention was all fixed on the half-crown. At the end of the lesson she put it back in her purse. It was a great disappointment; a religious woman like that, you wouldn't think she'd bother about a thing like a half-crown.

Another day she said she knew a priest who woke one night to find a fellow he didn't recognize leaning over the end of his bed. The priest was a bit frightened—naturally enough—but he asked the fellow what he wanted, and the fellow said in a deep, husky voice that he wanted to go to confession. The priest said it was an awkward time and wouldn't it do in the morning, but the fellow said that last time he went to confession, there was one sin he kept back, being ashamed to mention it, and now it was always on his mind. Then the priest knew it was a bad case, because the fellow was after making a bad confession and committing a mortal sin. He got up to dress, and just then the cock crew in the yard outside, and—lo and behold!—when the priest looked around there was no sign of the fellow, only a smell of burning timber, and when the priest looked at his bed didn't he see the print of two hands burned in it? That was because the fellow had made a bad confession. This story made a shocking impression on me.

But the worst of all was when she showed us how to examine our conscience. Did we take the name of the Lord, our God, in vain? Did we honour our father and our mother? (I asked her did this include grandmothers and she said it did.) Did we love our neighbors as ourselves? Did we covet our neighbour's goods? (I thought of the way I felt about the penny that Nora got every Friday.) I decided that, between one thing and another, I must have broken the whole ten commandments, all on account of that old woman, and so far as I could see, so long as she remained in the house I had no hope of ever doing anything else.

I was scared to death of confession. The day the whole class went I let on to have a toothache, hoping my absence wouldn't be noticed; but at three o'clock, just as I was feeling safe, along comes a chap with a message from Mrs. Ryan that I was to go to confession myself on Saturday and be at the chapel for communion with the rest. To make it worse, Mother couldn't come with me and sent Nora instead.

Now, that girl had ways of tormenting me that Mother never knew of. She held my hand as we went down the hill, smiling sadly and saying how sorry she was for me, as if she were bringing me to the hospital for an operation.

"Oh, God help us!" she moaned. "Isn't it a terrible pity you weren't a good boy? Oh, Jackie, my heart bleeds for you! How will you ever think of all your sins? Don't forget you have to tell him about the time you kicked Gran on the shin."

"Lemme go!" I said, trying to drag myself free of her. "I don't want to go to confession at all."

"But sure, you'll have to go to confession, Jackie," she replied in the same regretful tone. "Sure, if you didn't, the parish priest would be up to the house, looking for you. 'Tisn't, God knows, that I'm not sorry for you. Do you remember the time you tried to kill me with the bread-knife under the table? And the language you used to me? I don't know what he'll do with you at all, Jackie. He might have to send you up to the bishop."

I remember thinking bitterly that she didn't know the half of what I had to tell—if I told it. I knew I couldn't tell it, and understood perfectly why the fellow in Mrs. Ryan's story made a bad confession; it seemed to me a great shame that people wouldn't stop criticizing him. I remember that steep hill down to the church, and the sunlit hillsides beyond the valley of the river, which I saw in the gaps between the houses like Adam's last glimpse of Paradise.

Then, when she had manœuvred me down the long flight of steps to the chapel yard, Nora suddenly changed her tone. She became the raging malicious devil she really was.

"There you are!" she said with a yelp of triumph, hurling me through the church door. "And I hope he'll give you the penitential psalms, you dirty little caffler."

I knew then I was lost, given up to eternal justice. The door with the coloured-glass panels swung shut behind me, the sunlight went out and gave place to deep shadow, and the wind whistled outside so that the silence within seemed to crackle like ice under my feet. Nora sat in front of me by the confession box. There were a couple of old women ahead of her, and then a miserable-looking poor devil came and wedged me in at the other side, so that I couldn't escape even if I had the courage. He joined his hands and rolled his eyes in the direction of the roof, muttering aspirations in an anguished tone, and I wondered had he a grandmother too. Only a grandmother could account for a fellow behaving in that heartbroken way, but he was better off than I, for he at least could go and confess his sins; while I would make a bad confession and then die in the night and be continually coming back and burning people's furniture.

Nora's turn came, and I heard the sound of something slamming, and then her voice as if butter wouldn't melt in her mouth, and then another slam, and out she came. God, the hypocrisy of women! Her eyes were lowered, her head was bowed, and her hands were joined very low down on her stomach, and she walked up the aisle to the side altar looking like a saint. You never saw such an exhibition of devotion; and I remembered the devilish malice with which she had tormented me all the way from our door, and wondered were all religious people like that, really. It was my turn now. With the fear of damnation in my soul I went in, and the confessional door closed of itself behind me.

It was pitch-dark and I couldn't see priest or anything else. Then I really began to be frightened. In the darkness it was a matter between God and me, and He had all the odds. He knew what my intentions were before I even started; I had no chance. All I had ever been told about confession got mixed up in my mind, and I knelt to one wall and said: "Bless me, father, for I have sinned; this is my first confession." I waited for a few minutes, but nothing happened, so I tried it on the other wall. Nothing happened there either. He had me spotted all right.

It must have been then that I noticed the shelf at about one height with my head. It was really a place for grown-up people to rest their elbows, but in my distracted state I thought it was probably the place you were supposed to kneel. Of course, it was on the high side and not very deep, but I was always good at climbing and managed to get up all right. Staying up was the trouble. There was room only for my knees, and nothing you could get a grip on but a sort of wooden moulding a bit above it. I held on to the moulding and repeated the words a little louder, and this time something happened all right. A slide was slammed back; a little light entered the box, and a man's voice said: "Who's there?"

"'Tis me, father," I said for fear he mightn't see me and go away again. I couldn't see him at all. The place the voice came from was under the moulding, about level with my knees, so I took a good grip on the moulding and swung myself down till I saw the astonished face of a young priest looking at me. He had to put his head on one side to see me, and I had to put mine on one side to see him, so we were more or less talking to one another upside-down. It struck me as a queer way of hearing confessions, but I didn't feel it my place to criticize.

"Bless me, father, for I have sinned; this is my first confession," I rattled off in all one breath, and swung myself down the least shade more to make it easier for him.

"What are you doing up there?" he shouted in an angry voice, and the strain the politeness was putting on my hold of the moulding, and the shock of being addressed in such an uncivil tone, were too much for me. I lost my grip, tumbled, and hit the door an unmerciful wallop before I found myself flat on my back in the middle of the aisle. The people who had been waiting stood up with their mouths open. The priest opened the door of the middle box and came out, pushing his biretta back from his forehead; he looked something terrible. Then Nora came scampering down the aisle.

"Oh, you dirty little caffler!" she said. "I might have known you'd do it. I might have known you'd disgrace me. I can't leave you out of my sight for one minute."

Before I could even get to my feet to defend myself she bent down and gave me a clip across the ear. This reminded me that I was so stunned I had even forgotten to cry, so that people might think I wasn't hurt at all, when in fact I was probably maimed for life. I gave a roar out of me.

"What's all this about?" the priest hissed, getting angrier than ever and pushing Nora off me. "How dare you hit the child like that, you little vixen?"

"But I can't do my penance with him, father," Nora cried, cocking an outraged eye up at him.

"Well, go and do it, or I'll give you some more to do," he said, giving me a hand up. "Was it coming to confession you were, my poor man?" he asked me.

" 'Twas, father," said I with a sob.

"Oh," he said respectfully, "a big hefty fellow like you must have terrible sins. Is this your first?"

" 'Tis, father," said I.

"Worse and worse," he said gloomily. "The crimes of a lifetime. I don't know will I get rid of you at all today. You'd better wait now till I'm finished with these old ones. You can see by the looks of them they haven't much to tell."

"I will, father," I said with something approaching joy.

The relief of it was really enormous. Nora stuck out her tongue at me from behind his back, but I couldn't even be bothered retorting. I knew from the very moment that man opened his mouth that he was intelligent above the ordinary. When I had time to think, I saw how right I was. It only stood to reason that a fellow confessing after seven years would have more to tell than people that went every week. The crimes of a lifetime, exactly as he said. It was only what he expected, and the rest was the cackle of old women and girls with their talk of hell, the bishop, and the penitential psalms. That was all they knew. I started to make my examination of conscience, and barring the one bad business of my grandmother it didn't seem so bad.

The next time, the priest steered me into the confession box himself and left the shutter back the way I could see him get in and sit down at the further side of the grille from me.

"Well, now," he said, "what do they call you?"

"Jackie, father," said I.

"And what's a-trouble to you, Jackie?"

"Father," I said, feeling I might as well get it over while I had him in good humour, "I had it all arranged to kill my grandmother."

He seemed a bit shaken by that, all right, because he said nothing for quite a while.

"My goodness," he said at last, "that'd be a shocking thing to do. What put that into your head?"

"Father," I said, feeling very sorry for myself, "she's an awful woman."

"Is she?" he asked. "What way is she awful?"

"She takes porter, father," I said, knowing well from the way Mother talked of it that this was a mortal sin, and hoping it would make the priest take a more favourable view of my case.

"Oh, my!" he said, and I could see he was impressed.

"And snuff, father," said I.

"That's a bad case, sure enough, Jackie," he said.

"And she goes round in her bare feet, father," I went on in a rush of self-pity, "and she knows I don't like her, and she gives pennies to Nora and none to me, and my da sides with her and flakes me, and one night I was so heart-scalded I made up my mind I'd have to kill her."

"And what would you do with the body?" he asked with great interest.

"I was thinking I could chop that up and carry it away in a barrow I have," I said.

"Begor, Jackie," he said, "do you know you're a terrible child?"

"I know, father," I said, for I was just thinking the same thing myself. "I tried to kill Nora too with a bread-knife under the table, only I missed her."

"Is that the little girl that was beating you just now?" he asked.

"'Tis, father."

"Someone will go for her with a bread-knife one day, and he won't miss her," he said rather cryptically. "You must have great courage. Between ourselves, there's a lot of people I'd like to do the same to but I'd never have the nerve. Hanging is an awful death."

"Is it, father?" I asked with the deeper interest—I was always very keen on hanging. "Did you ever see a fellow hanged?"

"Dozens of them," he said solemnly. "And they all died roaring."

"Jay!" I said.

"Oh, a horrible death!" he said with great satisfaction. "Lots of the fellows I saw killed their grandmothers too, but they all said 'twas never worth it."

He had me there for a full ten minutes talking, and then walked out the chapel yard with me. I was genuinely sorry to part with him, because he was the most entertaining character I'd ever met in the religious line. Outside, after the shadow of the church, the sunlight was like the roaring of waves on a beach; it dazzled me; and when the frozen silence melted and I heard the screech of trams on the road my heart soared. I knew now I wouldn't die in the night and come back, leaving marks on my mother's furniture. It would be a great worry to her, and the poor soul had enough.

Nora was sitting on the railing, waiting for me, and she put on a very sour puss when she saw the priest with me. She was mad jealous because a priest had never come out of the church with her.

"Well," she asked coldly, after he left me, "what did he give you?"

"Three Hail Marys," I said.

"Three Hail Marys," she repeated incredulously. "You mustn't have told him anything."

"I told him everything," I said confidently.

"About Gran and all?"

"About Gran and all."

(All she wanted was to be able to go home and say I'd made a bad confession.)

"Did you tell him you went for me with the bread-knife?" she asked with a frown.

"I did to be sure."

"And he only gave you three Hail Marys?"

"That's all."

She slowly got down from the railing with a baffled air. Clearly, this was beyond her. As we mounted the steps back to the main road she looked at me suspiciously.

"What are you sucking?" she asked.

"Bullseyes."

"Was it the priest gave them to you?"

"'Twas."

"Lord God," she wailed bitterly, "some people have all the luck! 'Tis no advantage to anybody trying to be good. I might just as well be a sinner like you."

QUESTIONS FOR DISCUSSION

1. Compare the devices (contrast, irony, surprise, reversal) used by Collier to achieve a humorous effect and tone to those used by O'Connor. In what respects are the two stories *technically* similar? In what respects do they differ?
2. Compare the handling of character in "First Confession" to that in "Bottle Party." Would you say that O'Connor's characters are more plausible? If so, does this detract in any way from the humorous effect? If O'Connor's characterization is fuller, would you say that

"First Confession" is a "better" story than "Bottle Party"? Why or why not?

3. "First Confession" deals with a very serious topic—the matter of human sin and guilt (as well as some definition, perhaps, of "sin"). Does the humorous treatment add to or detract from the thematic significance of the story? Defend your position.

J. F. POWERS
The Forks

That summer when Father Eudex got back from saying Mass at the orphanage in the morning, he would park Monsignor's car, which was long and black and new like a politician's, and sit down in the cool of the porch to read his office. If Monsignor was not already standing in the door, he would immediately appear there, seeing that his car had safely returned, and inquire:

"Did you have any trouble with her?"

Father Eudex knew too well the question meant, Did you mistreat my car?

"No trouble, Monsignor."

"Good," Monsignor said, with imperfect faith in his curate, who was not a car owner. For a moment Monsignor stood framed in the screen door, fumbling his watch fob as for a full-length portrait, and then he was suddenly not there.

"Monsignor," Father Eudex said, rising nervously, "I've got a chance to pick up a car."

At the door Monsignor slid into his frame again. His face expressed what was for him intense interest.

"Yes? Go on."

"I don't want to have to use yours every morning."

"It's all right."

"And there are other times." Father Eudex decided not to be maudlin and mention sick calls, nor be entirely honest and admit he was tired of busses and bumming rides from parishioners. "And now I've got a chance to get one—cheap."

Monsignor, smiling, came alert at *cheap*.

"New?"

"No, I wouldn't say it's new."

Monsignor was openly suspicious now. "What kind?"

"It's a Ford."

"And not new?"

"Not new, Monsignor—but in good condition. It was owned by a retired farmer and had good care."

Monsignor sniffed. He *knew* cars. "V-Eight, Father?"

"No," Father Eudex confessed. "It's a Model A."

Monsignor chuckled as though this were indeed the damnedest thing he had ever heard.

"But in very good condition, Monsignor."

"You said that."

"Yes. And I could take it apart if anything went wrong. My uncle had one."

"No doubt." Monsignor uttered a laugh at Father Eudex's rural origins. Then he delivered the final word, long delayed out of amusement. "It wouldn't be prudent, Father. After all, this isn't a country parish. You know the class of people we get here."

Monsignor put on his Panama hat. Then, apparently mistaking the obstinacy in his curate's face for plain ignorance, he shed a little more light. "People watch a priest, Father. *Damnant quod non intelligunt.* It would never do. You'll have to watch your tendencies."

Monsignor's eyes tripped and fell hard on the morning paper lying on the swing where he had finished it.

"Another flattering piece about that crazy fellow. . . . There's a man who might have gone places if it weren't for his mouth! A bishop doesn't have to get mixed up in all that stuff!"

Monsignor, as Father Eudex knew, meant unions, strikes, race riots—all that stuff.

"A parishioner was saying to me only yesterday it's getting so you can't tell the Catholics from the Communists, with the priests as bad as any. Yes, and this fellow is the worst. He reminds me of that bishop a few years back—at least he called himself a bishop, a Protestant—that was advocating companionate marriages. It's not that bad, maybe, but if you listened to some of them you'd think that Catholicity and capitalism were incompatible!"

"The Holy Father—"

"The Holy Father's in Europe, Father. Mr. Memmers lives in this parish. I'm his priest. What can I tell him?"

"Is it Mr. Memmers of the First National, Monsignor?"

"It is, Father. And there's damned little cheer I can give a man like Memmers. Catholics, priests, and laity alike—yes, and princes of the Church, all talking atheistic communism!"

This was the substance of their conversation, always, the deadly routine in which Father Eudex played straight man. Each time it happened he seemed to participate, and though he should have known better he justified his participation by hoping that it would not happen again, or in quite the same way. But it did, it always did, the same way, and Monsignor, for all his alarums, had nothing to say really and meant one thing only, the thing he never said—that he dearly wanted to be, and was not, a bishop.

Father Eudex could imagine just what kind of bishop Monsignor would be. His reign would be a wise one, excessively so. His mind was made up on everything, excessively so. He would know how to avoid the snares set in the path of the just man, avoid them, too, in good taste and good conscience. He would not be trapped as so many good shepherds before him had been trapped, poor souls—caught in fair-seeming dilemmas of justice that were best left alone, like the first apple. It grieved him, he said, to think of those great hearts broken in silence and solitude. It was the worst kind of exile, alas! But just give him the chance and he would know what to do, what to say, and, more important, what not to do, not to say—neither yea nor nay for him. He had not gone to Rome for nothing. For him the dark forest of decisions would not exist; for him, thanks to hours spent in prayer and meditation, the forest would vanish as dry grass before fire, his fire. He knew the mask of evil already—birth control, indecent movies, salacious books—and would call these things by their right names and dare to deal with them for what they were, these new occasions for the old sins of the cities of the plains.

But in the meantime—oh, to have a particle of the faith that God had in humanity! Dear, trusting God forever trying them beyond their feeble powers, ordering terrible tests, fatal trials by nonsense (the crazy bishop). And keeping Monsignor steadily warming up on the side lines, ready to rush in, primed for the day that would perhaps never dawn.

At one time, so the talk went, there had been reason to think that Monsignor was headed for a bishopric. Now it was too late; Monsignor's intercessors were all dead; the cupboard was bare; he knew it at heart, and it galled him to see another man, this *crazy* man, given the opportunity, and making such a mess of it.

Father Eudex searched for and found a little salt for Monsignor's wound. "The word's going around he'll be the next archbishop," he said.

"I won't believe it," Monsignor countered hoarsely. He glanced at the newspaper on the swing and renewed his horror. "If that fellow's right, Father, I'm"—his voice cracked at the idea—"*wrong!*"

Father Eudex waited until Monsignor had started down the steps to the car before he said, "It could be."

"I'll be back for lunch, Father. I'm taking her for a little spin."

Monsignor stopped in admiration a few feet from the car—her. He was as helpless before her beauty as a boy with a birthday bicycle. He could not leave her alone. He had her out every morning and afternoon and evening. He was indiscriminate about picking people up for a ride in her. He kept her on a special diet—only the best of gas and oil and grease, with daily rubdowns. He would run her only on the smoothest roads and at so many miles an hour. That was to have stopped at the first five hundred, but only now, nearing the thousand mark, was he able to bring himself to increase her speed, and it seemed to hurt him more than it did her.

Now he was walking around behind her to inspect the tires. Apparently O.K. He gave the left rear fender an amorous chuck and eased into the front seat. Then they drove off, the car and he, to see the world, to explore each other further on the honeymoon.

Father Eudex watched the car slide into the traffic, and waited, on edge. The corner cop, fulfilling Father Eudex's fears, blew his whistle and waved his arms up in all four directions, bringing traffic to a standstill. Monsignor pulled expertly out of line and drove down Clover Boulevard in a one-car parade; all others stalled respectfully. The cop, as Monsignor passed, tipped his cap, showing a bald head. Monsignor, in the circumstances, could not acknowledge him, though he knew the man well—a parishioner. He was occupied with keeping his countenance kindly, grim, and exalted, that the cop's faith remain whole, for it was evidently inconceivable to him that Monsignor should ever venture abroad unless to bear the Holy Viaticum, always racing with death.

Father Eudex, eyes baleful but following the progress of the big, black car, saw a hand dart out of the driver's window in a wave. Monsignor would combine a lot of business with pleasure that morning, creating what he called "good will for the Church"—all morning in the driver's seat toasting passersby with a wave that was better than a blessing. How he loved waving to people!

Father Eudex overcame his inclination to sit and stew about things by going down the steps to meet the mailman. He got the usual handful for the Monsignor—advertisements and amazing offers, the unfailing crop of chaff from dealers in church goods, organs, collection schemes, insurance, and sacramental wines. There were two envelopes addressed to Father Eudex, one a mimeographed plea from a missionary society which he might or might not acknowledge with a contribution, depending upon what he thought of the cause—if it was really lost enough to justify a levy on his poverty—and the other a cheque for a hundred dollars.

The cheque came in an eggshell envelope with no explanation except a tiny card, "Compliments of the Rival Tractor Company," but even that was needless. All over town clergymen had known for days that the cheques were on the way again. Some, rejoicing, could hardly wait. Father Eudex, however, was one of those who could.

With the passing of hard times and the coming of the fruitful war years, the Rival Company, which was a great one for public relations, had found the best solution to the excess-profits problem to be giving. Ministers and even rabbis shared in the annual jack pot, but Rival employees were largely Catholic and it was the cheques to the priests that paid off. Again, some thought it was a wonderful idea, and others thought that Rival, plagued by strikes and justly so, had put their alms to work.

There was another eggshell envelope, Father Eudex saw, among the letters for Monsignor, and knew his cheque would be for two hundred, the premium for pastors.

Father Eudex left Monsignor's mail on the porch table by his cigars. His own he stuck in his back pocket, wanting to forget it, and went down the steps into the yard. Walking back and forth on the shady side of the rectory where the lilies of the valley grew and reading his office, he gradually drifted into the back yard, lured by a noise. He came upon Whalen, the janitor, pounding pegs into the ground.

Father Eudex closed the breviary on a finger. "What's it all about, Joe?"

Joe Whalen snatched a piece of paper from his shirt and handed it to Father Eudex. "He gave it to me this morning."

He—it was the word for Monsignor among them. A docile pronoun only, and yet when it meant the Monsignor it said, and concealed, nameless things.

The paper was a plan for a garden drawn up by the Monsignor in his fine hand. It called for a huge fleur-de-lis bounded by smaller crosses—and these Maltese—a fountain, a sundial, and a cloister walk running from the rectory to the garage. Later there would be birdhouses and a ten-foot wall of thick grey stones, acting as a moat against the eyes of the world. The whole scheme struck Father Eudex as expensive and, in this country, Presbyterian.

When Monsignor drew the plan, however, he must have been in his medieval mood. A spouting whale jostled with Neptune in the choppy waters of the fountain. North was indicated in the legend by a winged cherub huffing and puffing.

Father Eudex held the plan up against the sun to see the watermark. The stationery was new to him, heavy, simulated parchment, with the Church of the Holy Redeemer and Monsignor's name embossed, three initials, W. F. X., William Francis Xavier. With all those initials the man could pass for a radio station, a chancery wit had observed, or if his last name had not been Sweeney, Father Eudex added now, for high Anglican.

Father Eudex returned the plan to Whalen, feeling sorry for him and to an extent guilty before him—if only because he was a priest like Monsignor (now turned architect) whose dream of a monastery garden included the overworked janitor under the head of "labour."

Father Eudex asked Whalen to bring another shovel. Together, almost without words, they worked all morning spading up crosses, leaving the big fleur-de-lis to the last. Father Eudex removed his coat first, then his collar, and finally was down to his undershirt.

Toward noon Monsignor rolled into the driveway.

He stayed in the car, getting red in the face, recovering from the pleasure of seeing so much accomplished as he slowly recognized his curate in Whalen's helper. In a still, appalled voice he called across the lawn,

"Father," and waited as for a beast that might or might not have sense enough to come.

Father Eudex dropped his shovel and went over to the car, shirtless.

Monsignor waited a moment before he spoke, as though annoyed by the everlasting necessity, where this person was concerned, to explain. "Father," he said quietly at last, "I wouldn't do any more of that—if I were you. Rather, in any event, I wouldn't."

"All right, Monsignor."

"To say the least, it's not prudent. If necessary"—he paused as Whalen came over to dig a cross within earshot—"I'll explain later. It's time for lunch now."

The car, black, beautiful, fierce with chromium, was quiet as Monsignor dismounted, knowing her master. Monsignor went around to the rear, felt a tire, and probed a nasty cinder in the tread.

"Look at that," he said, removing the cinder.

Father Eudex thought he saw the car lift a hoof, gaze around, and thank Monsignor with her headlights.

Monsignor proceeded at a precise pace to the back door of the rectory. There he held the screen open momentarily, as if remembering something or reluctant to enter before himself—such was his humility—but then called to Whalen with an intimacy that could never exist between them.

"Better knock off now, Joe."

Whalen turned in on himself. "*Joe*—is it!"

Father Eudex removed his clothes from the grass. His hands were all blisters, but in them he found a little absolution. He apologized to Joe for having to take the afternoon off. "I can't make it, Joe. Something turned up."

"Sure, Father."

Father Eudex could hear Joe telling his wife about it that night—yeah, the young one got in wrong with the old one again. Yeah, the old one, he don't believe in it, work, for them.

Father Eudex paused in the kitchen to remember he knew not what. It was in his head, asking to be let in, but he did not place it until he heard Monsignor in the next room complaining about the salad to the housekeeper. It was the voice of dear, dead Aunt Hazel, coming from the summer he was ten. He translated the past into the present: I can't come out and play this afternoon, Joe, on account of my monsignor won't let me.

In the dining room Father Eudex sat down at the table and said grace. He helped himself to a chop, creamed new potatoes, pickled beets, jelly, and bread. He liked jelly. Monsignor passed the butter.

"That's supposed to be a tutti-frutti salad," Monsignor said, grimacing at his. "But she used green olives."

Father Eudex said nothing.

"I said she used green olives."

"I like green olives all right."

"*I* like green olives, but *not* in tutti-frutti salad."

Father Eudex replied by eating a green olive, but he knew it could not end there.

"Father," Monsignor said in a new tone. "How would you like to go away and study for a year?"

"Don't think I'd care for it, Monsignor. I'm not the type."

"You're no canonist, you mean?"

"That's one thing."

"Yes. Well, there are other things it might not hurt you to know. To be quite frank with you, Father, I think you need broadening."

"I guess so," Father Eudex said thickly.

"And still, with your tendencies . . . and with the universities honeycombed with Communists. No, that would never do. I think I meant seasoning, not broadening."

"Oh."

"No offense?"

"No offense."

Who would have thought a little thing like an olive could lead to all this, Father Eudex mused—who but himself, that is, for his association with Monsignor had shown him that anything could lead to everything. Monsignor was a master at making points. Nothing had changed since the day Father Eudex walked into the rectory saying he was the new assistant. Monsignor had evaded Father Eudex's hand in greeting, and a few days later, after he began to get the range, he delivered a lecture on the whole subject of handshaking. It was Middle West to shake hands, or South West, or West in any case, and it was not done where he came from, and—why had he ever come from where he came from? Not to be reduced to shaking hands, you could bet! Handshaking was worse than footwashing and unlike that pious practice there was nothing to support it. And from handshaking Monsignor might go into a general discussion of Father Eudex's failings. He used the open forum method, but he was the only speaker and there was never time enough for questions from the audience. Monsignor seized his examples at random from life. He saw Father Eudex coming out of his bedroom in pyjama bottoms only and so told him about the dressing gown, its purpose, something of its history. He advised Father Eudex to barber his armpits, for it was being done all over now. He let Father Eudex see his bottle of cologne, "Steeple," special for clergymen, and said he should not be afraid of it. He suggested that Father Eudex shave his face oftener, too. He loaned him his Rogers Peet catalogue, which had sketches of clerical blades togged out in the latest, and prayed that he would stop going around looking like a rabbinical student.

He found Father Eudex reading *The Catholic Worker* one day and had not trusted him since. Father Eudex's conception of the priesthood was evangelical in the worst sense, barbaric, gross, foreign to the mind of the Church, which was one of two terms he used as sticks to beat him with. The other was taste. The air of the rectory was often heavy with The Mind of the Church and Taste.

Another thing. Father Eudex could not conduct a civil conversation. Monsignor doubted that Father Eudex could even think to himself with anything like agreement. Certainly any discussion with Father Eudex ended inevitably in argument or sighing. Sighing! Why didn't people talk up if they had anything to say? No, they'd rather sigh! Father, don't ever, ever sigh at me again!

Finally, Monsignor did not like Father Eudex's table manners. This came to a head one night when Monsignor, seeing his curate's plate empty and all the silverware at his place unused except for a single knife, fork, and spoon, exploded altogether, saying it had been on his mind for weeks, and then descending into the vernacular he declared that Father Eudex did not know the forks—now perhaps he could understand that! Meals, unless Monsignor had guests or other things to struggle with, were always occasions of instruction for Father Eudex, and sometimes of chastisement.

And now he knew the worst—if Monsignor was thinking of recommending him for a year of study, in a Sulpician seminary probably, to learn the forks. So this was what it meant to be a priest. *Come, follow me. Going forth, teach ye all nations. Heal the sick, raise the dead, cleanse the lepers, cast out devils.* Teach the class of people we get here? Teach Mr. Memmers? Teach Communists? Teach Monsignors? And where were the poor? The lepers of old? The lepers were in their colonies with nuns to nurse them. The poor were in their holes and would not come out. Mr. Memmers was in his bank, without cheer. The Communists were in their universities, awaiting a sign. And he was at table with Monsignor, and it was enough for the disciple to be as his master, but the housekeeper had used green olives.

Monsignor inquired, "Did you get your cheque today?"

Father Eudex looked up, considered. "I got *a* cheque," he said.

"From the Rival people, I mean?"

"Yes."

"Good. Well, I think you might apply it on the car you're wanting. A decent car. That's a worthy cause." Monsignor noticed that he was not taking it well. "Not that I mean to dictate what you shall do with your little windfall, Father. It's just that I don't like to see you mortifying yourself with a Model A—and disgracing the Church."

"Yes," Father Eudex said, suffering.

"Yes. I dare say you don't see the danger, just as you didn't a while ago when I found you making a spectacle of yourself with Whalen. You just don't see the danger because you just don't think. Not to dwell on it, but I seem to remember some overshoes."

The overshoes! Monsignor referred to them as to the Fall. Last winter Father Eudex had given his overshoes to a freezing picket. It had got back to Monsignor and—good Lord, a man could have his sympathies, but he had no right clad in the cloth to endanger the prestige of the Church by siding in these wretched squabbles. Monsignor said he hated to think of all the evil done by people doing good! Had Father Eudex ever heard of the Albigensian heresy, or didn't the seminary teach that any more?

Father Eudex declined dessert. It was strawberry mousse.

"Delicious," Monsignor said. "I think I'll let her stay."

At that moment Father Eudex decided that he had nothing to lose. He placed his knife next to his fork on the plate, adjusted them this way and that until they seemed to work a combination in his mind, to spring a lock which in turn enabled him to speak out.

"Monsignor," he said. "I think I ought to tell you I don't intend to make use of that money. In fact—to show you how my mind works—I have even considered endorsing the cheque to the strikers' relief fund."

"So," Monsignor said calmly—years in the confessional had prepared him for anything.

"I'll admit I don't know whether I can in justice. And even if I could I don't know that I would. I don't know why . . . I guess hush money, no matter what you do with it, is lousy."

Monsignor regarded him with piercing baby blue eyes. "You'd find it pretty hard to prove, Father, that *any* money *in se* is . . . what you say it is. I would quarrel further with the definition 'hush money.' It seems to me nothing if not rash that you would presume to impugn the motive of the Rival Company in sending out those cheques. You would seem to challenge the whole concept of good works—not that I am ignorant of the misuses to which money can be put." Monsignor, changing tack, tucked it all into a sigh. "Perhaps I'm just a simple soul, and it's enough for me to know personally some of the people in the Rival Company and to know them good people. Many of them Catholic . . ." A throb had crept into Monsignor's voice. He shut it off.

"I don't mean anything that subtle, Monsignor," Father Eudex said. "I'm just telling you, as my pastor, what I'm going to do with the cheque. Or what I'm not going to do with it. I don't know what I'm going to do with it. Maybe send it back."

Monsignor rose from the table, slightly smiling. "Very well, Father. But there's always the poor."

Monsignor took leave of Father Eudex with a laugh. Father Eudex felt it was supposed to fool him into thinking that nothing he had said would be used against him. It showed, rather, that Monsignor was not winded, that he had broken wild curates before, plenty of them, and that he would ride again.

Father Eudex sought the shade of the porch. He tried to read his office, but was drowsy. He got up for a glass of water. The saints in Ireland used to stand up to their necks in cold water, but not for drowsiness. When he came back to the porch a woman was ringing the doorbell. She looked like a customer for rosary beads.

"Hello," he said.

"I'm Mrs. Klein, Father, and I was wondering if you could help me out."

Father Eudex straightened a porch chair for her. "Please sit down."

"It's a German name, Father. Klein was German descent," she said, and added with a silly grin, "It ain't what you think, Father."

"I beg your pardon."

"Klein. Some think it's a Jew name. But they stole it from Klein."

Father Eudex decided to come back to that later. "You were wondering if I could help you?"

"Yes, Father. It's personal."

"Is it matter for confession?"

"Oh no, Father." He had made her blush.

"Then go ahead."

Mrs. Klein peered into the honeysuckle vines on either side of the porch for alien ears.

"No one can hear you, Mrs. Klein."

"Father—I'm just a poor widow," she said, and continued as though Father Eudex had just slandered the man. "Klein was awful good to me, Father."

"I'm sure he was."

"So good . . . and he went and left me all he had." She had begun to cry a little.

Father Eudex nodded gently. She was after something, probably not money, always the best bet—either that or a drunk in the family—but this one was not Irish. Perhaps just sympathy.

"I come to get your advice, Father. Klein always said, 'If you got a problem, Freda, see the priest.'"

"Do you need money?"

"I got more than I can use from the bakery."

"You have a bakery?"

Mrs. Klein nodded down the street. "That's my bakery. It was Klein's. The Purity."

"I go by there all the time," Father Eudex said, abandoning himself to her. He must stop trying to shape the conversation and let her work it out.

"Will you give me your advice, Father?" He felt that she sensed his indifference and interpreted it as his way of rejecting her. She either had no idea how little sense she made or else supreme faith in him, as a priest, to see into her heart.

"Just what is it you're after, Mrs. Klein?"

"He left me all he had, Father, but it's just laying in the bank."

"And you want me to tell you what to do with it?"

"Yes, Father."

Father Eudex thought this might be interesting, certainly a change. He went back in his mind to the seminary and the class in which they had considered the problem of inheritances. Do we have any unfulfilled obligations? Are we sure? . . . Are there any impedimenta?

"Do you have any dependents, Mrs. Klein—any children?"

"One boy, Father. I got him running the bakery. I pay him good—too much, Father."

"Is 'too much' a living wage?"

"Yes, Father. He ain't got a family."

"A living wage is not too much," Father Eudex handed down, sailing into the encyclical style without knowing it.

Mrs. Klein was smiling over having done something good without knowing precisely what it was.

"How old is your son?"

"He's thirty-six, Father."

"Not married?"

"No, Father, but he's got him a girl." She giggled, and Father Eudex, embarrassed, retied his shoe.

"But you don't care to make a will and leave this money to your son in the usual way?"

"I guess I'll have to . . . if I die." Mrs. Klein was suddenly crushed and haunted, but whether by death or charity, Father Eudex did not know.

"You don't have to, Mrs. Klein. There are many worthy causes. And the worthiest is the cause of the poor. My advice to you, if I understand your problem, is to give what you have to someone who needs it."

Mrs. Klein just stared at him.

"You could even leave it to the archdiocese," he said, completing the sentence to himself: but I don't recommend it in your case . . . with your tendencies. You look like an Indian giver to me.

But Mrs. Klein had got enough. "Huh!" she said, rising. "Well! You *are* a funny one!"

And then Father Eudex realized that she had come to him for a broker's tip. It was in the eyes. The hat. The dress. The shoes. "If you'd like to speak to the pastor," he said, "come back in the evening."

"You're a nice young man," Mrs. Klein said, rather bitter now and bent on getting away from him. "But I got to say this—you ain't much of a priest. And Klein said if I got a problem, see the priest—huh! You ain't much of a priest! What time's your boss come in?"

"In the evening," Father Eudex said. "Come any time in the evening."

Mrs. Klein was already down the steps and making for the street.

"You might try Mr. Memmers at the First National," Father Eudex called, actually trying to help her, but she must have thought it was just some more of his nonsense and did not reply.

After Mrs. Klein had disappeared Father Eudex went to his room. In the hallway upstairs Monsignor's voice, coming from the depths of the clerical nap, halted him.

"Who was it?"

"A woman," Father Eudex said. "A woman seeking good counsel."

He waited a moment to be questioned, but Monsignor was not awake enough to see anything wrong with that, and there came only a sigh and a shifting of weight that told Father Eudex he was simply turning over in bed.

Father Eudex walked into the bathroom. He took the Rival cheque from his pocket. He tore it into little squares. He let them flutter into the toilet. He pulled the chain—hard.

He went to his room and stood looking out the window at nothing. He could hear the others already giving an account of their stewardship, but could not judge them. I bought baseball uniforms for the school. I bought the nuns a new washing machine. I purchased a Mass kit for a Chinese missionary. I bought a set of matched irons. Mine helped pay for keeping my mother in a rest home upstate. I gave mine to the poor.

And you, Father?

QUESTIONS FOR DISCUSSION

1. "The Forks" is satirical rather than humorous. Discuss the differences between it and "First Confession" in method, attitude, tone, effect, and purpose.
2. Define and discuss what is implied in "The Forks" as against what is stated, what *is* in contrast to what *ought to be.* Then define the theme or purpose of the story.
3. Discuss the relationship between Powers' style (especially his metaphors and slang) and his characterization; his emotional effect; his theme.
4. Relate each section of the story to the ending. Is the ending motivated? What does the ending add to Powers' theme? How does it modify or change his emotional effect? In what way is it ironical? In what way could the final pathos effect reform, which we have defined as the purpose of satire?

DONALD BARTHELME
Report

Our group is against the war. But the war goes on. I was sent to Cleveland to talk to the engineers. The engineers were meeting in Cleveland. I was supposed to persuade them not to do what they are going to do. I took United's 4:45 from LaGuardia arriving in Cleveland at 6:13. Cleveland is dark blue at that hour. I went directly to the motel, where the engineers were meeting. Hundreds of engineers attended the Cleveland meeting. I noticed many fractures among the engineers, bandages, traction. I noticed what appeared to be fracture of the carpal scraphoid in six examples. I noticed numerous fractures of the humeral shaft, of the os calcis, of the pelvic girdle. I noticed a high incidence of clay-shoveller's fracture. I could not account for these fractures. The engineers were making calculations, taking measurements, sketching on the blackboard, drinking beer, throwing bread, buttonholing employers, hurling glasses into the fireplace. They were friendly.

They were friendly. They were full of love and information. The chief engineer wore shades. Patella in Monk's traction, clamshell fracture by the look of it. He was standing in a slum of beer bottles and microphone cable. "Have some of this chicken à la Isambard Kingdom Brunel the Great Ingineer," he said. "And declare who you are and what we can do for you. What is your line, distinguished guest?"

"Software," I said. "In every sense. I am here representing a small group of interested parties. We are interested in your thing, which seems to be functioning. In the midst of so much dysfunction, function is interesting. Other people's things don't seem to be working. The State Department's thing doesn't seem to be working. The U.N.'s thing doesn't seem to be working. The democratic left's thing doesn't seem to be working. Buddha's thing—"

"Ask us anything about our thing, which seems to be working," the chief engineer said. "We will open our hearts and heads to you, Software Man, because we want to be understood and loved by the great lay public, and have our marvels appreciated by that public, for which we daily unsung produce tons of new marvels each more life-enhancing than the last. Ask us anything. Do you want to know about evaporated thin-film metallurgy? Monolithic and hybrid integrated-circuit processes? The algebra of inequalities? Optimization theory? Complex high-speed micro-miniature closed and open loop systems? Fixed variable mathematical cost searches? Epitaxial deposition of semi-conductor materials? Gross interfaced space gropes? We also have specialists in the cuckooflower, the doctorfish, and the dumdum bullet as these relate to aspects of today's expanding technology, and they do in the damnedest ways."

I spoke to him then about the war. I said the same things people always say when they speak against the war. I said that the war was wrong. I said that large countries should not burn down small countries. I said that the government had made a series of errors. I said that these errors once small and forgivable were now immense and unforgivable. I said that the government was attempting to conceal its original errors under layers of new errors. I said that the government was sick with error, giddy with it. I said that ten thousand of our soldiers had already been killed in pursuit of the government's errors. I said that tens of thousands of the enemy's soldiers and civilians had been killed because of various errors, ours and theirs. I said that we are responsible for errors made in our name. I said that the government should not be allowed to make additional errors.

"Yes, yes," the chief engineer said, "there is doubtless much truth in what you say, but we can't possibly *lose* the war, can we? And stopping is losing, isn't it? The war regarded as a process, stopping regarded as an abort? We don't know *how* to lose a war. That skill is not among our skills. Our array smashes their array, that is what we know. That is the process. That is what is.

"But let's not have any more of this dispiriting downbeat counter-productive talk. I have a few new marvels here I'd like to discuss with you just briefly. A few new marvels that are just about ready to be gaped at by the admiring layman. Consider for instance the area of real-time online computer-controlled wish evaporation. Wish evaporation is going to be crucial in meeting the rising expectations of the world's peoples, which are as you know rising entirely too fast."

I noticed then distributed about the room a great many transverse fractures of the ulna. "The development of the pseudo-ruminant stomach for underdeveloped peoples," he went on, "is one of our interesting things you should be interested in. With the pseudo-ruminant stomach they can chew cuds, that is to say, eat grass. Blue is the most popular color worldwide and for that reason we are working with certain strains of your native Kentucky *Poa pratensis*, or bluegrass, as the staple input for the p/r stomach cycle, which would also give a shot in the arm to our balance-of-payments thing don't you know. . . ." I noticed about me then a great number of metatarsal fractures in banjo splints. "The kangaroo initiative . . . eight hundred thousand harvested last year . . . highest percentage of edible protein of any herbivore yet studied . . ."

"Have new kangaroos been planted?"

The engineer looked at me.

"I intuit your hatred and jealousy of our thing," he said. "The ineffectual always hate our thing and speak of it as anti-human, which is not at all a meaningful way to speak of our thing. Nothing mechanical is alien to me," he said (amber spots making bursts of light in his shades), "because I am human, in a sense, and if I think it up, then 'it' is human too, whatever 'it' may be. Let me tell you, Software Man, we have been damned forbearing in the matter of this little war you declare yourself to be interested in. Function is the cry, and our thing is functioning like crazy. There are things we could do that we have not done. Steps we could take that we have not taken. These steps are, regarded in a certain light, the light of our enlightened self-interest, quite justifiable steps. We could, of course, get irritated. We could, of course, *lose patience.*

"We could, of course, release thousands upon thousands of self-powered crawling-along-the-ground lengths of titanium wire eighteen inches long with a diameter of .0005 centimetres (that is to say, invisible) which, scenting an enemy, climb up his trouser leg and wrap themselves around his neck. We have developed those. They are within our capabilities. We could, of course, release in the arena of the upper air our new improved pufferfish toxin which precipitates an identity crisis. No special technical problems there. That is almost laughably easy. We could, of course, place up to two million maggots in their rice within twenty-four hours. The maggots are ready, massed in secret staging areas in Alabama. We have hypodermic darts capable of piebalding the enemy's pigmentation. We have rots, blights, and rusts capable of attacking his alphabet. Those are dandies. We have a hut-shrinking chemical which penetrates the fibres of the bamboo, causing it, the hut, to strangle its occupants. This operates only after 10 P.M., when people are sleeping. Their mathematics are at the mercy of a suppurating surd we have invented. We have a family of fishes trained to attack their fishes. We have the deadly testicle-destroying telegram. The cable-companies are coöperating. We have a green substance that, well, I'd rather not talk about. We have a secret word that, if pronounced, produces multiple fractures in all living things in an area the size of four football fields."

"That's why—"

"Yes. Some damned fool couldn't keep his mouth shut. The point is that the whole structure of enemy life is within our power to *rend, vitiate, devour,* and *crush.* But that's not the interesting thing."

"You recount these possibilities with uncommon relish."

"Yes I realize that there is too much relish here. But *you* must realize that these capabilities represent in and of themselves highly technical and complex and interesting problems and hurdles on which our boys have expended many thousands of hours of hard work and brilliance. And that the effects are often grossly exaggerated by irresponsible victims. And that the whole thing represents a fantastic series of triumphs for the multi-disciplined problem-solving team concept."

"I appreciate that."

"We *could* unleash all this technology at once. You can imagine what would happen then. But that's not the interesting thing."

"What is the interesting thing?"

"The interesting thing is that we have a *moral sense*. It is on punched cards, perhaps the most advanced and sensitive moral sense the world has ever known."

"Because it is on punched cards?"

"It considers all considerations in endless and subtle detail," he said. "It even quibbles. With this great new moral tool, how can we go wrong? I confidently predict that, although we *could* employ all this splendid new weaponry I've been telling you about, *we're not going to do it.*"

"We're not going to do it?"

I took United's 5:44 from Cleveland arriving at Newark at 7:19. New Jersey is bright pink at that hour. Living things move about the surface of New Jersey at that hour molesting each other only in traditional ways. I made my report to the group. I stressed the friendliness of the engineers. I said, It's all right. I said, We have a moral sense. I said, *We're not going to do it.* They didn't believe me.

QUESTIONS FOR DISCUSSION

1. What elements of humor, satire, fantasy does Barthelme employ? Which term most accurately applies to this story? Why?
2. There is very little development of either character or situation in "Report." How does Barthelme use the devices of humor, satire, and fantasy in his style? Cite examples of his use of contrast, exaggeration, surprise, reversal, and especially implication. Look for puns, double meanings, allusions, and repetitions.
3. "Report" is as compact as a poem, as brief as a joke or a bumper sticker. Barthelme fires one-line jokes at us so rapidly we feel as if we are on a roller coaster. Analyze the rhetorical devices Barthelme uses to create this sense of comic exhilaration. Consider in particular the effect of his proliferation of scientific terms. How is the satirical point served by your inability to understand most of those terms?
4. Many of Barthelme's points and effects are achieved by ironic juxtapositions throughout the story—such juxtapositions as horribly

destructive inventions and a "moral sense." Find and discuss as many of these as you can.

5. Bathelme quite obviously makes the engineer and his colleagues ridiculously inhuman. But what about the narrator and *his* group? What is the implied profession of the "Software Man"? How exactly does he *react* to the things the engineer says to him? What does this reaction contribute to the total meaning and effect of the story?

A. E. COPPARD

Adam and Eve and Pinch Me

. . . and in the whole of his days, vividly at the end of the afternoon—he repeated it again and again to himself—the kind country spaces had *never* absorbed *quite* so rich a glamour of light, so miraculous a bloom of clarity. He could feel streaming in his own mind, in his bones, the same crystalline brightness that lay upon the land. Thoughts and images went flowing through him as easily and amiably as fish swim in their pools; and as idly, too, for one of his speculations took up the theme of his family name. There was such an agreeable oddness about it, just as there was about all the luminous sky today, that it touched him as just a little remarkable. What *did* such a name connote, signify, or symbolize? It was a rann of a name, but it had euphony! Then again, like the fish, his ambulating fancy flashed into other shallows, and he giggled as he paused, peering at the buds in the brake. Turning back towards his house again he could see, beyond its roofs, the spire of the Church tinctured richly as the vane: all round him was a new grandeur upon the grass of the fields, and the spare trees had shadows below that seemed to support them in the manner of a plinth, more real than themselves, and the dykes and any chance heave of the level fields were underlined, as if for special emphasis, with long shades of mysterious blackness.

With a little drift of emotion that had at other times assailed him in the wonder and ecstasy of pure light, Jaffa Codling pushed through the slit in the back hedge and stood within his own garden. The gardener was at work. He could hear the voices of the children about the lawn at the other side of the house. He was very happy, and the place was beautiful, a fine white many-windowed house rising from a lawn bowered with plots of mould, turreted with shrubs, and overset with a vast walnut tree. This house had deep clean eaves, a roof of faint coloured slates that, after rain, glowed dully, like onyx or jade, under the red chimneys, and half-way up at one end was a balcony set with black balusters. He went to a French window that stood open and stepped into the dining room. There was no one within, and, on that lonely instant, a strange feeling of emptiness dropped upon him. The clock ticked almost as if it had been caught in some indecent act; the air was dim and troubled after that glory outside. Well, now, he would go up at once to his study and write down for his new book the ideas and images he had accumulated—beautiful rich thoughts they were—during that wonderful afternoon. He went to mount the stairs and he was passed by one of the maids; humming a silly song she brushed past him rudely, but he was an easy-going man—maids were unteachably tiresome—and reaching the landing he sauntered towards his room. The door stood slightly open and he could hear voices within. He put his hand upon the door . . . it would not open any further. What the devil . . . he pushed—like the bear in the tale—and he pushed, and he pushed—was there something against it on the other side? He put his shoulder to it . . . some wedge must be there, and *that* was extraordinary. Then his whole apprehension was swept up and whirled as by an avalanche—Mildred, his wife, was in there; he could hear her speaking to a man in fair soft tones and the rich phrases that could be used only by a woman yielding a deep affection to him. Codling kept still. Her words burned on his mind and thrilled him as if spoken to himself. There was a movement in the room, then utter silence. He again thrust savagely at the partly open door, but he could not stir it. The silence within continued. He beat upon the door with his fists, crying: "Mildred, Mildred!" There was no response, but he could hear the rocking arm-chair commence to swing to and fro. Pushing his hand round the edge of the door he tried to thrust his head between the opening. There was not space for this, but he could just peer into the corner of a mirror hung near, and this is what he saw: the chair at one end of its swing, a man sitting in it, and upon one arm of it Mildred, the beloved woman, with her lips upon the man's face, caressing him with her hands. Codling made another effort to get into the room —as vain as it was violent. "Do you hear me, Mildred?" he shouted. Apparently neither of them heard him; they rocked to and fro while he gazed stupefied. What, in the name of God, . . . What's this . . . was she bewitched . . . were there such things after all as magic, devilry!

He drew back and held himself quite steadily. The chair stopped swaying, and the room grew awfully still. The sharp ticking of the clock in the hall rose upon the house like the tongue of some perfunctory mocker. Couldn't they hear the clock? . . . Couldn't they hear his heart? He had to put his hand upon his heart, for, surely, in that great silence inside there, they would hear its beat, growing so loud now that it seemed almost to stun him! Then in a queer way he found himself reflecting, observing, analysing his own actions and intentions. He found some of them to be just a little spurious, counterfeit. He felt it would be easy, so perfectly easy to flash in one blast of anger and annihilate the two. He would do nothing of the kind. There was no occasion for it. People didn't really do that sort of thing, or, at least, not with a genuine passion. There was no need for anger. His curiosity was satisfied, quite satisfied, he was certain, he had not the remotest interest in the man. A welter of unexpected thoughts swept upon his mind as he stood there. As a writer of books he was often stimulated by the emotions and impulses of other people, and now his own surprise was beginning to intrigue him, leaving him, O, quite unstirred emotionally, but interesting him profoundly.

He heard the maid come stepping up the stairway again, humming her silly song. He did not want a scene, or to be caught eavesdropping, and so turned quickly to another door. It was locked. He sprang to one beyond it; the handle would not turn. "Bah! what's *up* with 'em?" But the girl was now upon him, carrying a tray of coffee things. "O, Mary!" he exclaimed casually, "I . . ." To his astonishment the girl stepped past him as if she did not hear or see him, tapped upon the door of his study, entered, and closed the door behind her. Jaffa Codling then got really angry. "Hell! were the blasted servants in it!" He dashed to the door again and tore at the handle. It would not even turn, and, though he wrenched with fury at it, the room was utterly sealed against him. He went away for a chair with which to smash the effrontery of that door. No, he wasn't angry, either with his wife or this fellow—Gilbert, she had called him—who had a strangely familiar aspect as far as he had been able to take it in; but when one's servants . . . faugh!

The door opened and Mary came forth smiling demurely He was a few yards further along the corridor at that moment. "Mary!" he shouted, "leave the door open!" Mary carefully closed it and turned her back on him. He sprang after her with bad words bursting from him as she went towards the stairs and flitted lightly down, humming all the way as if in derision. He leaped downwards after her three steps at a time, but she trotted with amazing swiftness into the kitchen and slammed the door in his face. Codling stood, but kept his hands carefully away from the door, kept them behind him. "No, no," he whispered cunningly, "there's something fiendish about door handles today, I'll go and get a bar, or a butt of timber," and, jumping out into the garden for some such thing, the miracle happened to him. For it was nothing else than a miracle, the unbelievable, the impossible, simple and laughable if you will, but having as much validity as any miracle can ever invoke. It was simple and laughable because by all the known physical laws he should have collided with his gardener, who happened to pass the window with his wheelbarrow as Codling jumped out on to the path. And it was unbelievable that they should not, and impossible that they *did* not collide; and it was miraculous, because Codling stood for a brief moment in the garden path and the wheelbarrow of Bond, its contents, and Bond himself passed apparently through the figure of Codling as if he were so much air, as if he were not a living breathing man but just a common ghost. There was no impact, just a momentary breathlessness. Codling stood and looked at the retreating figure going on utterly unaware of him. It is interesting to record that Codling's first feelings were mirthful. He giggled. He was jocular. He ran along in front of the gardener, and let him pass through him once more; then after him again; he scrambled into the man's barrow, and was wheeled about by this incomprehensible thick-headed gardener who was dead to all his master's efforts to engage his attention. Presently he dropped the wheelbarrow and went away, leaving Codling to cogitate upon the occurrence. There was no room for doubt, some essential part of him had become detached from the obviously not less vital part. He felt he was essential because he was responding to the experience, he was reacting in the normal way to normal stimuli, although he happened for the time being to be invisible to his fellows and unable to communicate with them. How had it come about—this queer thing? How could he discover what part of him had cut loose, as it were? There was no question of this being death; death wasn't funny, it wasn't a joke; he had still all his human instincts. You didn't get angry with a faithless wife or joke with a fool of a gardener if you were dead, certainly not! He had realized enough of himself to know he was the usual man of instincts, desires, and prohibitions, complex and contradictory; his family history for a million or two years would have denoted that, not explicitly—obviously impossible—but suggestively. He had found himself doing things he had no desire to do, doing things he had a desire *not* to do, thinking thoughts that had no contiguous meanings, no meanings that could be related to his general experience. At odd times he had been chilled—aye, and even agreeably surprised—at the immense potential evil in himself. But still, this was no mere Jekyll and Hyde affair, that a man and his own ghost should separately inhabit the same world was a horse of quite another colour. The other part of him was alive and active somewhere . . . as alive . . . as alive . . . yes, as *he* was, but dashed if he knew where! What a lark when they got back to each other and compared notes! In his tales he had brooded over so many imagined personalities, followed in the track of so many psychological enigmas that he *had* felt at times a stranger to himself. What if, after all, that brooding had given him the faculty of projecting this figment of himself into the world of men. Or was he some unrealized latent element of being without its natural integument, doomed now to drift over the ridge of the world for ever. Was it his personality, his spirit? Then how was the dashed thing working? Here was he with the most wonderful happening in human experience, and he couldn't differentiate or disinter things. He was like a new Adam flung into some old Eden.

There was Bond tinkering about with some plants a dozen yards in front of him. Suddenly his three children came round from the other side of the house, the youngest boy leading them, carrying in his hand a small sword which was made, not of steel, but of some more brightly shining material; indeed it seemed at one moment to be of gold, and then again of flame, transmuting everything in its neighbourhood into the likeness of flame, the hair of the little girl Eve, a part of Adam's tunic; and the fingers of the boy Gabriel as he held the sword were like pale tongues of fire. Gabriel, the youngest boy, went up to the gardener and gave the sword into his hands, saying: "Bond, is this sword any good?" Codling saw the gardener take the weapon and examine it with a careful sort of smile; his great gnarled hands became immediately transparent, the blood could be seen moving diligently about the veins. Codling was so interested in the sight that he did not gather in the gardener's reply. The little boy was dissatisfied and repeated his question, "No, but Bond, *is* this sword any good?" Codling rose, and stood by invisible. The three beautiful children were grouped about the great angular figure of the gardener in his soiled clothes, looking up now into his face, and now at the sword, with anxiety in all their puckered eyes. "Well, Marse Gabriel," Codling could hear him reply, "as far as a sword goes, it may be a good un, or it may be a bad un, but, good as it is, it can never be anything but a bad thing." He then gave it back to them; the boy Adam held the haft of it, and the girl Eve rubbed the blade with curious fingers. The younger boy stood looking up at the gardener with unsatisfied gaze. "But, Bond, *can't* you say if this sword's any *good?*" Bond turned to his spade and trowels. "Mebbe the shape of it's wrong, Marse Gabriel, though it seems a pretty handy size." Saying this he moved off across the lawn. Gabriel turned to his brother and sister and took the sword from them; they all followed after the gardener and once more Gabriel made inquiry: "Bond, is this sword any *good?*" The gardener again took it and made a few passes in the air like a valiant soldier at exercise. Turning then, he lifted a bright curl from the head of Eve and cut it off with a sweep of the weapon. He held it up to look at it critically and then let it fall to the ground. Codling sneaked behind him and, picking it up, stood stupidly looking at it. "Mebbe, Marse Gabriel," the gardener was saying, "it ud be better made of steel, but it has a smartish edge on it." He went to pick up the barrow but Gabriel seized it with a spasm of anger, and cried out: "No, no, Bond, will you say, just yes or no, Bond, is this sword any *good?*" The gardener stood still, and looked down at the little boy, who repeated his question—"just yes or no, Bond!" "No, Marse Gabriel!" "Thank you, Bond," replied the child with dignity, "that's all we wanted to know," and, calling to his mates to follow him, he ran away to the other side of the house.

Codling stared again at the beautiful lock of hair in his hand, and felt himself grow so angry that he picked up a strange looking flowerpot at his feet and hurled it at the retreating gardener. It struck Bond in the middle of the back and, passing clean through him, broke on the wheel of his barrow, but Bond seemed to be quite unaware of this catastrophe. Codling rushed after, and, taking the gardener by the throat, he yelled, "Damn you, will you tell me what all this means?" But Bond proceeded calmly about his work unnoticing, carrying his master about as if he were a clinging vapour, or a scarf hung upon his neck. In a few moments, Codling dropped exhausted to the ground. "What . . . O Hell . . . what, what am I to do?" he groaned. "What has happened to me? What shall I *do?* What *can* I do?" He looked at the broken flowerpot. "Did I invent that?" he pulled out his watch. "That's a real watch, I hear it ticking, and it's six o'clock." Was he dead or disembodied or mad? What was this infernal lapse of identity? And who the devil, yes, who was it upstairs with Mildred? He jumped to his feet and hurried to the window; it was shut; to the door, it was fastened; he was powerless to open either. Well! well! this was experimental psychology with a vengeance, and he began to chuckle again. He'd have to write to McDougall about it. Then he turned and saw Bond wheeling across the lawn towards him again. "*Why* is that fellow always shoving that infernal green barrow around?" he asked, and, the fit of fury seizing him again, he rushed towards Bond, but, before he reached him, the three children danced into the garden again, crying, with great excitement, "Bond, O, Bond!" The gardener stopped and set down the terrifying barrow; the children crowded about him, and Gabriel held out another shining thing, asking: "Bond, is this box any good?" The gardener took the box and at once his eyes lit up with interest and delight. "O, Marse Gabriel, where'd ye get it?" "Bond," said the boy impatiently, "is the box any *good?*" "Any good?" echoed the man. "Why, Marse Gabriel, Marse Adam, Miss Eve, look yere!" Holding it down in front of them, he lifted the lid from the box and a bright coloured bird flashed out and flew round and round above their heads. "O," screamed Gabriel with delight, "it's a kingfisher!" "That's what it is," said Bond, "a kingfisher!" "Where?" asked Adam. "Where?" asked Eve. "There it flies—round the fountain—see it? see it?" "No," said Adam. "No," said Eve.

"O, do, do, see it," cried Gabriel, "here it comes, it's coming!" and, holding his hands on high, and standing on his toes, the child cried out as happy as the bird which Codling saw flying above them.

"I can't see it," said Adam.

"Where is it, Gaby?" asked Eve.

"O, you stupids," cried the boy. "*There* it goes. There it goes . . . there . . . it's gone!"

He stood looking brightly at Bond, who replaced the lid.

"What shall we do now?" he exclaimed eagerly. For reply, the gardener gave the box into his hand, and walked off with the barrow. Gabriel took the box over to the fountain. Codling, unseen, went after him, almost as excited as the boy; Eve and her brother followed. They sat upon the stone tank that held the falling water. It was difficult for the child to unfasten the lid; Codling attempted to help him, but he was powerless. Gabriel looked up into his father's face and smiled. Then he stood up and said to the others:

"Now, *do* watch it this time."

They all knelt carefully beside the water. He lifted the lid and, behold, a fish like a gold carp, but made wholly of fire, leaped from the box into the fountain. The man saw it dart down into the water, he saw the water bubble up behind it, he heard the hiss that the junction of fire and water produces, and saw a little track of steam follow the bubbles about the tank until the figure of the fish was consumed and disappeared. Gabriel, in ecstasies, turned to his sister with blazing happy eyes, exclaiming:

"There! Evey!"

"What was it?" asked Eve, nonchalantly, "I didn't see anything."

"More didn't I," said Adam.

"Didn't you see that lovely fish?"

"No," said Adam.

"No," said Eve.

"O, stupids," cried Gabriel, "it went right past the bottom of the water."

"Let's get a fishin' hook," said Adam.

"No, no, no," said Gabriel, replacing the lid of the box. "O no."

Jaffa Codling had remained on his knees staring at the water so long that, when he looked around him again, the children had gone away. He got up and went to the door, and that was closed; the windows, fastened. He went moodily to a garden bench and sat on it with folded arms. Dusk had begun to fall into the shrubs and trees, the grass to grow dull, the air chill, the sky to muster its gloom. Bond had overturned his barrow, stalled his tools in the lodge, and gone to his home in the village. A curious cat came round the house and surveyed the man who sat chained to his seven-horned dilemma. It grew dark and fearfully silent. Was the world empty now? Some small thing, a snail perhaps, crept among the dead leaves in the hedge, with a sharp, irritating noise. A strange flood of mixed thoughts poured through his mind until at last one idea disentangled itself, and he began thinking with tremendous fixity of little Gabriel. He wondered if he could brood or meditate, or "will" with sufficient power to bring him into the garden again. The child had just vaguely recognized him for a moment at the waterside. He'd try that dodge, telepathy was a mild kind of a trick after so much of the miraculous. If he'd lost his blessed body, at least the part that ate and smoked and talked to Mildred. . . . He stopped as his mind stumbled on a strange recognition. . . . What a joke, of course . . . idiot . . . not to have seen *that.* He stood up in the garden with joy . . . of course, *he* was upstairs with Mildred, it was himself, the other bit of him, that Mildred had been talking to. What a howling fool he'd been.

He found himself concentrating his mind on the purpose of getting the child Gabriel into the garden once more, but it was with a curious mood that he endeavoured to establish this relationship. He could not fix his will into any calm intensity of power, or fixity of purpose, or pleasurable mental ecstasy. The utmost force seemed to come with a malicious threatening splenetic "entreaty." That damned snail in the hedge broke the thread of his meditation; a dog began to bark sturdily from a distant farm; the faculties of his mind became joggled up like a child's picture puzzle, and he brooded unintelligibly upon such things as skating and steam engines, and Elizabethan drama so lapped about with themes like jealousy and chastity. Really now, Shakespeare's Isabella was the most consummate snob in. . . . He looked up quickly to his wife's room and saw Gabriel step from the window to the balcony as if he were fearful of being seen. The boy lifted up his hands and placed the bright box on the rail of the balcony. He looked up at the faint stars for a moment or two, and then carefully released the lid of the box. What came out of it and rose into the air appeared to Codling to be just a piece of floating light, but as it soared above the roof he saw it grow to be a little ancient ship, with its hull and fully set sails and its three masts all of faint primrose flame colour. It cleaved through the air, rolling slightly as a ship through the wave, in widening circles above the house, making a curving ascent until it lost the shape of a vessel and became only a moving light hurrying to some sidereal shrine. Codling glanced at the boy on the balcony, but in that brief instant something had happened, the ship had burst like a rocket and released three coloured drops of fire which came falling slowly, leaving beautiful grey furrows of smoke in their track. Gabriel leaned over the rail with outstretched palms, and, catching the green star and the blue one as they drifted down to him, he ran with a rill of laughter back into the house. Codling sprang forward just in time to catch the red star; it lay vividly blasting his own palm for a monstrous second, and then, slipping through, was gone. He stared at the ground, at the balcony, the sky, and then heard an exclamation . . . his wife stood at his side.

"Gilbert! How you frightened me!" she cried. "I thought you were in your room; come along in to dinner." She took his arm and they walked up the steps into the dining room together. "Just a moment," said her husband, turning to the door of the room. His hand was upon the handle, which turned easily in his grasp, and he ran upstairs to his own room. He opened the door. The light was on, the fire was burning brightly, a smell of cigarette smoke about, pen and paper upon his desk, the Japanese book-knife, the gilt matchbox, everything all right, no one there. He picked up a book from his desk. . . . *Monna Vanna.* His bookplate was in it—*Ex Libris—Gilbert Cannister.* He put it down beside the green dish; two yellow oranges were in the green dish, and two most deliberately green Canadian apples rested by their side. He went to the door and swung it backwards and forwards quite easily. He sat on his desk trying to piece the thing together, glaring at the print and the book-knife and the smart matchbox, until his wife came up behind him exclaiming: "Come along, Gilbert!"

"Where are the kids, old man?" he asked her, and, before she replied, he had gone along to the nursery. He saw the two cots, his boy in one, his girl in the other. He turned whimsically to Mildred, saying, "There *are* only two, *are* there?" Such a question did not call for reply, but he confronted her as if expecting some assuring answer. She was staring at him with her bright beautiful eyes.

"Are there?" he repeated.

"How strange you should ask me that now!" she said. . . . "If you're a very good man . . . perhaps. . . ."

"Mildred!"

She nodded brightly.

He sat down in the rocking chair, but got up again saying to her gently—"We'll call him Gabriel."

"But, suppose—"

"No, no," he said, stopping her lovely lips, "I know all about him." And he told her a pleasant little tale.

QUESTIONS FOR DISCUSSION

1. Your first problem in understanding "Adam and Eve and Pinch Me" is to follow exactly *what happens* in the story. It is a story in which one part of a man apparently gets separated from another part. Read the ending very carefully. Read, as well, those portions of the story in which Jaffa Codling speculates on the experience he is undergoing—as for example when he determines that he is "a new Adam flung into some old Eden." Can you now define what part of the man has become separated from what other part? Exactly what happens to each part?
2. Thematically, "Adam and Eve and Pinch Me" can be described as a story that attempts some definition of the nature of man. The following questions are for the purpose of leading you to the discovery of that definition.

   A. What do you make of the names of the characters in the story?

   B. Almost all of the physical objects in the story are, on one level, symbols. List as many of these as you can. Which ones are established Biblical or mythical symbols (the names of the children or the sword or the box are examples)? Which ones are Freudian (the closed door, for example)? Which ones (like the star) are simply common established symbols?
3. Having defined (through an analysis of what happens in the story as well as through a definition of the key symbols) the theme of "Adam and Eve and Pinch Me," can you now explain why the author decided that he could realize his purpose more effectively by writing a fantasy rather than a realistic story?

6 Some Differences between Popular and Serious Fiction

A. Entertainment and Beyond

Originally, most of the stories in *Studies in the Short Story* appeared in magazines or even newspapers—perishable, transient media of mass communication. Each magazine creates its own environment which we approach with certain attitudes, enter with rather clear expectations, and in which we experience various effects, before, during, and after we read a story. Usually we move on, leaving that issue of the magazine, and the story, behind. But sometimes the story's lingering effect may haunt us. Some people remember the first story they ever read by John Updike or Ray Bradbury or Donald Barthelme and the magazine in which they discovered it. An anthology is a different kind of environment; each story affects the reader within an academic context, an atmosphere, usually, of high seriousness.

We've tried to offer in this and in the following section a contrasting experience—between the reflective mood of a literature anthology and the immediacy of a popular culture magazine environment. Our assumption is that you may see the elements, techniques, and effects of fiction more clearly when they are presented in stories that are relatively straightforward. The first two stories in this section were chosen from recent issues of popular mass-circulation magazines of two distinct types. Both are decidedly commercial—conceived to appeal to the tastes of the so-called general reader. We've tried to be representative: "Just Saying You Love Me Doesn't Make It So" by Meg Campbell is from *Redbook*, a magazine for women; "The Harry Hastings Method" by Warner Law is from *Playboy*, a magazine for men; we offer then, a story by a woman, and one by a man. Last, we offer a story by Graham Greene because he has made a living from his writing for over four decades with stories that range from commercial to literary, and has consciously categorized his fiction on the title pages as "entertainments" or serious "novels."

The terms *commercial* and *serious* run the risk all labels do of distorting. We mean to be descriptive not evaluative in our use of them. For purposes of study, it is best, perhaps, to think of serious fiction as being *different* from commercial fiction rather than better. If in our evaluation of both types we consider what each sets out to achieve, we may see that the master craftsman of the commercial story and the fine serious writer meet in the neutral realm of excellence. "Title" by Barth (in Section 7), a serious experimental story, and "The Harry Hastings Method" by Law, a commercial story, are comparable: the first overtly discusses the storytelling process, the second illustrates it; but Barth's ideal reader will respond to a subtle kind of suspense (having said *that*, what can he possibly say next?) and Law's ideal reader will enjoy Hasting's lectures to the narrator on the art of writing effectively. For the student of fiction, the primary question is not, "Which story is best?" but "How does each story *do* what it does to the reader?" Obviously, some stories, commercial or serious, are better than others, and we expect that your comparisons of the three in this section will reveal variations of quality. The analytical problem is: How do you account for those variations? Did we include "Brother" by Graham Greene because it lies midway between commercial and serious on a spectrum of quality? You decide. This question may be relevant: What characteristics of each of the two types does Greene's story have?

So far, this anthology has provided you with a vocabulary and concepts for analyzing *what happens* in fiction and *how*: you have contemplated the elements of fiction with critical deliberateness. But for these three stories, we ask that you simply focus sharply on your own responses to the techniques the writer employs. Give full reign to your taste, your normal, natural responses and reactions (sympathetic or not). Then go one step further than you usually do when reading fiction in magazines by examining aspects of the experiences you had while reading these stories. Imagine reading them in the magazines you know best. Reread the stories, trying to become aware of the methods the authors used to achieve their effects on you. Looking back, ask, "How did he do that to me?"

We want to emphasize here that all readers *experience* a story first, before they become aware of the components of its quality: effectiveness of characterization, development of conflict, brilliance of style. Even scholars, critics, and other serious readers, including writers, seldom subject a story to critical analysis during a first reading, and many good stories never get a second reading. As you have already discovered, a story does become richer the more you reread it; at the same time, we must remember that most stories are read in the normal course of daily life—as magazine stories are read—once, on the move.

It is extremely important to remember something else you have by now discovered: Critical analysis is a conscious, deliberate act of secondary importance; the most important aspects of the experience of reading a story are mysterious and incommunicable. Just as a writer (both of your editors are primarily fiction writers) is not aware of *all* the effects he has achieved, no teacher, no general reader can describe with subjective lyricism nor delineate with critical acumen what is most important in a fictional experience. But the kind of conscious discussion we have been conducting about those secondary elements can develop a receptivity to almost everything a writer consciously or unconsciously has achieved. As the avant-garde section will illustrate, your experiences in reading a story parallel the author's involvement in the creative process, and "The Harry Hastings Method" is a further, though different, demonstration of that parallel process. Just as earlier conscious analysis of his art somehow stimulates elements in the writer's story that he is unaware of as he writes, your conscious scrutiny of the way fiction works will enable you to respond more readily, less deliberately, to a writer's many intentions and effects the first time you read a story. And just as a writer may never fully realize what he has created, you may have experiences in reading a story that you can never quite describe or analyze. So it is important to remember this: Analyzing a story is never meant to be the same as, nor a substitute for, reading it in the more usual way; *but* once having spent a period of time consciously examining your responses to the author's artistry, you will be more receptive to the stories—whether commercial or serious—you choose to read after this course ends.

The first two stories in this section are included not only to entertain you, but to provide you with demonstrations of fictional elements, techniques, and effects that are perhaps more visible than those in the more complexly conceived stories you have already studied. We are not assuming that every member of your class reads only commercial stories. Some have been reading Hemingway, Baldwin, and Faulkner since early high school; some have studied fiction before. Understanding each story for its own sake is less important than seeing how some aspect of the creative process is employed in it; so, whether you think a story is good or mediocre, whether it bores you or changes your life, is not the issue. Even the reader with a well-developed critical mind and discriminating tastes can benefit from a study of commercial fiction, just as writers themselves do. Albert Camus, a great philosophical writer, has said he used *The Postman Always Rings Twice* by James M. Cain, a master craftsman of best-seller fiction, as a basis for his masterpiece *The Stranger*, both of which open with "narrative hooks" (a device associated with commercial fiction): "They threw me off the hay truck about noon" (*Postman*); "Mother died today. Or, maybe, yesterday; I can't be sure" (*The Stranger*).

By temperament or by conscious strategy, the commercial writer strives for immediate effects, knowing most of his readers are looking for a "good story" that will provide instant gratification of an already passing desire for diversion, entertainment, or escape. He has fixed assumptions about his likely readers and manipulates as immediately and effectively as he can their attitudes and expectations. Despite their dissimilarity in content, note the use of similar techniques in the opening paragraphs of the first two stories. Both attempt to accost the reader with a tug at his sleeve as he passes. But in identifying commercial fiction, it is not enough simply to cite isolated technical devices. You may consider the opening line of Greene's "Brother" a more blatant narrative hook: "The Communists were the first to appear."

While the serious writer may think less consciously of *who* his readers may be, he does take great care to create effects (as in his use of symbolism) to which he expects attentive readers to respond. He assumes that his reader is an intelligent, sensitive, imaginative collaborator in the creative process, who expects, even insists, that the author make demands; and who expects to derive, perhaps through several readings, a lasting intellectual, spiritual, and esthetic pleasure from every aspect of the experience the author has created.

In a sense every writer is a "con man" who calculates an effect upon his "mark," the reader; but unlike the con man, he knows he must "pay off" in the end. "The Harry Hastings Method" may be read as a parable, a demonstration of the relationship between the commercial writer and his reader. But, with more complex ramifications, that relationship exists also between the serious writer and his reader.

David Madden

MEG CAMPBELL
Just Saying You Love Me Doesn't Make It So

I sat waiting in the deepening November twilight for Jack's return. Embarrasingly enough, it was the high spot of my day. Today the wait seemed longer than usual, and I shifted impatiently on the car seat, trying to push my mind ahead to Jack's arrival. But it kept slithering relentlessly back to Mother's letter.

I was standing in the kitchen this afternoon, skimming through the mail, two bags of groceries still to put away, when a phrase in my mother's letter stopped me. "Remember Lewis Russell?" she wrote. "Well, he and his wife are moving to your area . . ." I stood paralyzed. Being Mother, she rattled on. "I always rather hoped that one day you and Lewis . . ."

Yes, Ma, I know. Some old tune. Haven't been many requests for that one lately, have there? And since Jack and I have been married for almost three years now, don't you think we really might just drop it from the repertoire?

Lewis. Married. Well, of course he's married, dummy; so are you, aren't you? What did you think—that he lighted one white candle for you every cocktail hour?

Maybe not a *white* candle.

Oh, please.

But the truth was, it did surprise me. I visualized Lewis often—too often for any kind of successful resignation—but always as he was during our happy times. For me, he was suspended permanently against the old-gold autumn backdrop of my senior year at college. Behind my eyes I could see him, tall and thin and loose-jointed, scuffing through drifting leaves—his sweater ragged, his head at an arrogant angle, his eyes the same intense blue as the southern sky. It was a time of unbearable riches, a time when I lived so near the surface that the blazing beauty that was a quiet college town in Indian summer kept my eyes stinging with tears.

I had kept that memory cherished behind a pane, but now the pane was shattered. Framed in its shards I saw Lewis' white face and heard his strained voice saying, "You can't do it! You can't! This isn't your decision to make alone!"

And my own voice, brittle and distant: "Well, I have decided. I can't do it your way, Lewis. My God, I hate this too—don't you see that? I just can't do anything else, that's all."

There were quick tears in his eyes; his cheek muscles knotted under the skin. The look of pride and sureness I so loved was gone, leaving a pale and pleading boy, a stranger—and thus easy to withstand when he whispered, not looking at me, "Please, Nan. Please."

"Lewis, *no*! Now, look, let's not—" Voice of sweet reason.

But suddenly the arrogant look was back and he wheeled on me. "You little bitch!"

He did not touch me, but the force of his anger sent me reeling back, stunned, and I stumbled. He put out a quick hand; then he jerked it back and turned on his heel and walked away through the spinning leaves. I called weakly after him, "Lewis, wait! Lewis?"

He must have heard. I swore to myself later that he must have heard. But he did not turn. Would anything be different if he had? I never knew the answer.

I stood in my tiny, littered kitchen, holding a head of lettuce, turning it in my hands, and suddenly I dug both thumbnails viciously into the crisp green leaves.

"Oh, Lewis," I whispered. "Oh, Lewis."

Jack was striding across the platform, coming toward me. I marveled as always that he could be so like the others—a drab, overcoated figure with a briefcase—and yet as soon as I recognized him, so different. He had such a sturdy, individual walk. He tilted his head to one side and smiled the instant he caught sight of me.

"Hi." I lifted my face for his kiss. It came. On such eternal verities is my security founded.

"Hi, sweets. Slide over."

"Oh, Jack, listen—I'm sorry; I didn't pick up your suit at the cleaners."

"No big deal."

"Well, I meant to. I just . . ."

"No points for good intentions!" Seeing my stricken expression, he laughed and said, "I'm just *kidding*, honey!"

"Sorry," I mumbled. "Did you have a good day?"

"Fairly awful. Gloria . . . the new girl? She's leaving."

"But you spent all that time breaking her in!"

"Well, but now she's getting married. All starry-eyed, and stuff. I told her she could keep her job—I harbor no prejudices against the married—but her attitude is, she has to move to the suburbs, fire off a few kids, do the thing right." He laughed.

"Oh." I thought of Gloria, a girl who knew where her duty lay.

Dinner was late, and nothing to shout about when it came. Jack polished his off with every appearance of sincere relish and asked for more.

"Oh, darling, I *am* sorry; there's not any left," I said. "This is all I fixed. I thought it would be enough. I really—"

"That's okay. It doesn't matter."

I stood at the sink with my head down, near tears. Jack came and put his arms around me. "Anne," he said gently, "why do you let these things bug you so much? You know they aren't all that important."

"I know, but—"

"I've been thinking," he went on, smoothing my hair and rocking me a little back and forth. "Sometime we really are going to have to get on with it."

"With what?"

"Oh, young 'uns, suburbia, barbecue grill, PTA. You know—real life." He grinned.

I turned away and began to scatter cleanser on the drainboard. "Like Gloria? Probably. One of these days."

"I just thought you might have been thinking along those lines yourself."

"No, not really. I sort of like us the way we are."

"We do have a good time, don't we?" He kissed my ear and went back to the evening paper.

I scrubbed relentlessly at the drainboard, my mind, like my hand, moving in tight, mechanical circles.

But I did think about it later, lying in bed with Jack breathing peacefully beside me, and I could not account for the feeling of terror that gripped me—a half-dreaming feeling, like coils of rope looping themselves silently around my legs and arms and body until I was rendered entirely immobile. Having children seemed to me to be the most permanent thing in this life, and maybe . . . maybe even more irrevocable than a marriage vow.

It was a disloyal thought. I kissed Jack's closed eyes. I do love you, Jack. I do. I swear.

But I lay awake for a long time, staring through the window at the street light, which was diffuse and glowing in an aureole of mist, and thinking, Maybe one of these days . . .

I won't run into Lewis, I assured myself. This is too big a town. Still, it was inevitable that I would see him sometime. And in the three weeks after Mother's letter came I had not left the apartment once without applying my eye make-up. I would stare at my face in the mirror and want to jeer, but I put on the eye make-up anyway.

It was a Thursday afternoon, and I was downtown doing errands. I had just dashed into the branch bank to cash a check. Lewis was standing near the elevator, talking to two men.

I knew it was he before I saw his face: the long, taut line of his body; the lift of his head. As though he felt my gaze, he turned his head abruptly and looked straight at me.

I sat down in the nearest chair. I just sat there, not thinking, looking ahead, until I felt him cross the room and stand beside me.

"I'll be damned. It *is* you."

"Hello, Lewis."

"I just can't believe this."

"I live here now."

"Do you? I do too. Just moved here, actually. Come and have lunch or a drink, or something."

"I've had lunch, thanks."

"Then you can watch me bolt a sandwich. I'm starving. Come on." He held the door for me.

Alice, I thought dazedly, going through the looking glass.

He looked only a little different. Better kept, better cared for, scrubbed and brushed. His face in repose still had a rather proud, shut-away look; but his smile was open and unexpected.

This isn't real, I thought. It doesn't matter what I say, because this isn't really happening; this is an episode in some soap opera.

"This is no soap opera, honey," an inner voice said snidely; "this is your life."

Oh, *stop* it.

"Club sandwich," said Lewis to the waitress. "And . . . what? Whisky sour?"

I nodded.

"One whisky sour and one bourbon and water. Thank you."

We smiled tentatively at each other.

"You look great," he said.

At least, I thought, I had eye make-up on.

He began eating crackers, ripping them loose from a little cellophane packet, and soon the table was scattered with crumbs.

"So you're married," he said.

"Yes, and you too, huh?"

"Mm-hmm. Aren't you going to eat any of these? You make me look like a glutton. Any children?"

"No. You?"

Brief pause. "No." He hesitated. "It's not—"

"No," I said hurriedly. "Nothing to do with that."

The waitress brought his club sandwich. He picked up one section by its cellophane-swathed toothpick and set it on a napkin in front of me.

"Just one. Be good for you, Nan."

I had to look away. In some history class Lewis had gleaned the fact that Anne Boleyn's nickname had been Nan, and since then he had never called me anything else.

"Sadie, Sadie, married lady." He shook his head, watching me. "So. Are you happy?"

"Yes."

"You like it here in the North?"

"Oh, well . . ."

"It's not home, is it?"

"No."

"Are you working, or anything?"

"I have a part-time job at a real-estate office three days a week."

"What about your art? Aren't you doing anything with your art?" His tone was so indignant, I had to smile.

"I was never that good, Lewis. Run of the mill, that's all."

"Bull," he said firmly. "You were lazy, *that's* all."

I said apologetically, "I keep meaning to get my stuff out again. I'll get around to it sometime."

He made a skeptical face. "You are *worthless*—you know that, girl?"

I leaned back against the padded wall of the booth as he attacked his sandwich, thinking of the energy with which he bent life to fit him and reflecting that I had about as much of that quality myself as a piece of dough.

"What about you?" I said curiously. "Are you happy?"

"Yep," he said easily. "I sure am."

"Your wife—what's she like?"

"Oh, blond, little . . ." He smiled. "Determined type—you know?"

I could aim nothing but uncharitable thoughts in her direction.

"It's good to see you again," I said, watching him.

"Been a long time, hasn't it?" His face was suddenly serious. "I wondered about you a lot."

"Did you?" I was touched.

He wasn't looking at me. "Wondered what the little kid would have been like, too, sometimes."

"Lewis, my God." My stomach clenched in pain. "Don't!"

"Sorry." He looked up in faint surprise and smiled. "I didn't mean to be maudlin at lunch. Okay?"

He seemed so incredibly relaxed, at ease. I gave the barest of nods and said almost inaudibly, "Lewis—I'm really sorry about—about . . ."

"You ought to be," he said calmly. "You little idiot."

"You're so *casual*."

"I was upset enough about it at the time, I promise you. It happened. And it hurt. But now"—he gave the ghost of a shrug—"it's over." He made an involuntary gesture of pushing something away. "Life goes on. Now, there's a profundity." He looked at me. "I've never understood, really, why you did it."

"I was such a *child*," I said desperately. "And scared. Scared of everything—of having the baby, of my family's knowing, of what people would say if I dropped out of school and had to get married. . . . I was scared of the alternative too, but sheer panic carried me through it, I guess."

"You didn't love me."

"Lewis, I—that wasn't it. Believe me."

"Well, you didn't love me enough, then, to take the responsibility for . . . The thing is, Nan, we knew the score and we took the risk. But then you tried to back out, run away, erase what happened."

"Maybe I did," I said, thinking that it was true. "But it doesn't mean I didn't *love* you. You talk as if love and responsibility were the same thing. They aren't at all!"

"We're talking about different kinds of love, I guess."

"Love is love," I said sullenly. "Don't get all semantic about it."

"And then too," he went on inexorably, "you weren't exactly the parental type, somehow."

"And you were, of course!"

"Well, strangely enough, I think I am, you know. I've always rather wanted to have children."

"And give up your own life? Your freedom?" I thought of my dark dream, the coils of rope tightening around me.

"Well, okay—look," he said impatiently. "You kept your precious freedom. You've still got it. What are you doing with it? You haven't so much as picked up a paintbrush!"

I stared at him, unable to muster any defense for this new line of attack.

And then abruptly his tone changed. "Oh, Nan, hell, I'm sorry. I didn't mean to rant and rave. I guess the truth is, I've probably nursed a small grudge since it happened. But it's out of my system now."

"But, Lewis . . ." It trailed off.

"Have you finished chewing up that orange slice? I've got to get back. New boy has to work hard, you know."

He stood up and shrugged carelessly into his tweed coat. I wondered fleetingly if his wife had helped choose it.

He tucked my arm through his as we walked back down the sidewalk. The dead leaves swirled around us, as dry as ashes. It was getting colder.

"Guess what!" said Lewis confidingly. "Kay says she thinks she might be pregnant. Isn't that fantastic?"

"That's wonderful," I murmured.

"You know," he went on in the same soft, hesitant voice, "this might sound dumb, but for a while I was scared she couldn't have any. I thought it was some kind of Biblical retribution, or something."

I stared at him. "But you can't really think . . . Anyway it was me, not you."

"Well, but I let you. And maybe I could have changed your mind." He looked at me and I knew he was hearing my voice calling him back.

"You couldn't have," I said urgently.

"Well. Anyway . . ."

I could see he was thinking that it no longer mattered.

We stood outside the bank, buffeted by the cutting wind. He looked down at me, and there was affection in his eyes as well as sadness, and an indefinable something else, but no regret. He hugged me, and I felt the coat that his wife had probably chosen scrape briefly against my cheek.

Then he was gone.

I ran, shivering violently with cold and tension, feeling that the chill had sliced into my bones.

As I drove to the station I kept thinking about Lewis, seeing him more clearly than I ever had before. He grappled with life, met it head on; he was no drifter. And the things he'd said to me—little truths that nicked and stung. He called them the way he saw them, that was all.

But what Lewis had not said—hadn't said but must have guessed—was that now I was doing the same thing to Jack that I once had done to him.

I thought of the sterility of what I had given Jack, and I wanted desperately to tell him how sorry I was. But what good would that do? Only in time . . .

Maybe, I thought wearily—maybe love and responsibility are the same thing after all. Now, there's a profundity, as Lewis says.

I sat waiting for Jack. I always seemed to be waiting, hedging, postponing life. I saw Jack coming down the platform. He looked tired; his face was drawn and his shoulders were hunched against the wind. He spotted the car and waved. And he looked a little surprised, but pleased, as I got out and went to meet him.

QUESTIONS FOR DISCUSSION

1. How well does the author handle the device of the flashback (there are even flashbacks within flashbacks)? Do they enhance the story's effects or confuse the reader? Are the juxtapositions of present and past dramatic, suggestive, and meaningful? Explain.

2. How does coincidence operate in this story? Does it contribute to the story's specific effects or does it rather give the story an air of contrivance?
3. Cite instances where the author tries to give you a sense of Nan's everyday life, juxtaposing such domestic details against moments of emotional intensity. Note how the author ends the first flashback in the kitchen. Is the head of lettuce an apt detail? How well does the author handle that moment, especially in relation to the line, "Oh, Lewis!"
4. Examine the author's use of dialogue. Does it sound authentic? Study the lines for unintentional puns, as in the scene when Jack steps off the train. In which scene is dialogue most important? At which moments in that scene is dialogue most effective? Least effective?
5. Analyze the author's use of similes and metaphors and lyrical passages. Are they well chosen? Are images repeated, with variations, throughout the story?
6. " 'Hi.' I lifted my face for his kiss. It came. On such eternal verities is my security founded." Discuss this passage as setting the narrator's tone, attitude, and style. Find other such passages and analyze them. See, for instance, the passage in which she lies in bed that night.
7. Evaluate the author's strategy in her handling of theme in the last conversation between Nan and Lewis and in the final five paragraphs.

WARNER LAW

The Harry Hastings Method

Susie Plimson says I should keep on practicing my writing. She's been my teacher at Hollywood High Adult Education in the Professional Writing course and says I am still having trouble with my syntaxes and my tenses and very kindly gave me private lessons at her place, and she is dark-haired and very pretty and about my age (which is 25) and, in addition, she has great big boobs.

Susie says if I really want to be a professional writer, I should write about what I really know about—if it is interesting—and while I did do a hitch in the Navy some time back, I was on a destroyer tender and never heard a shot fired except in practice, which I don't think is a highly interesting matter to describe.

But one thing I know a lot about is working the houses in the Hollywood hills. The people who live up there are not particularly stinking rich, but then, I've never been interested in valuable paintings or diamond necklaces, anyway, because what do you do with them?

But there are usually portable radios and TV sets and auto tape decks and now and then there is some cash lying around, or a fur, or a few pieces of fairly good jewelry, or maybe a new leather jacket—all things easy to dispose of.

This is an area of winding streets and a lot of trees and bushes, and the houses are mostly set back from the street and are some distance from their neighbors, and so it is an easy vicinity to work. There's no bus service up there at all, so everybody needs a car or two, and if there is no auto in the carport, you can be pretty sure that no one is home.

There are rural-type mailboxes on the street and people are always stuffing them with business cards and circulars, like ads for house cleaning and landscaping and such, so I had a lot of cards printed for various things, like for a house-painting firm, and some for the "Bulldog Burglar Protection Agency," which say we will install all kinds of silent burglar alarms, and bells will ring in our office and we will have radio cars there in a few minutes. I also have some Pest Control and House Repair cards. None of these firms exists, of course, but neither do the phone numbers on my cards.

But while I drive slowly around the hills in my little VW bus and put my cards in the boxes, I can get a pretty good idea of who is home and who isn't, and who is gone all day, and so forth.

By the way, my truck is lettered with: H. STUSSMAN INC. GENERAL HOUSE REPAIRS on one side and FERGUSON PEST CONTROL. EVERYBODY LOVES US BUT YOUR PESTS! on the other side. I make these up myself. My theory is that nobody can ever see both sides of my truck at the same time, which will really confuse witnesses, if there are any. Of course I change the truck signs every week, and every month I paint the truck a different color.

When I decide that a certain house is ripe for hitting, I go and ring the doorbell. If I am wrong and someone is home—this is seldom—I ask them if their house happens to be swarming with disease-infested rats. Since there are no rats at all in these hills, they always say no and I leave.

If nobody answers the doorbell, it is, of course, another matter. Most of these houses have locks that could be opened by blindfolded monkeys. Not one of them has any kind of burglar alarm. There are watchdogs in some houses, but these I avoid, because you never know a friendly dog from a vicious one until you've been chewed up. And, of course, I would not hurt any dog if you paid me.

What I am getting to is about one particular house up there. It's a fairly new one-story modern style, up a driveway, but you can see the carport from the street below. In casing the place for some time, I figured that a man probably lived there alone. There was only one car, a great big new Mercedes, and this man drove off every weekday morning at nine. I saw him a few times and he was a nice-looking gentleman of about 45. He was always gone all day, so I guessed he had an office job.

So one day, I drove my truck up the driveway and got out and saw a sign: BEWARE OF THE DOG—and, at the same time, this little pooch comes out of a dog door and up to me, and he is a black bundle of hair and the wiggliest, happiest little puppy you ever saw. I picked him up and let him lick my face and saw that he had a tag on his collar that read: CUDDLES. MY OWNER IS HARRY HASTINGS. There was also a phone number.

I rang the doorbell, but nobody came. The front-door lock was so stupid that I opened it with a plastic card.

Inside—well, you have never seen such a sloppy-kept house. Not dirty—just sloppy. There was five days' worth of dishes in the sink. I found out later that this Harry Hastings has a maid who comes and cleans once a week, but meantime, this character just throws his dirty shirts and socks on the floor. What a slob.

I turned out to be right about his living alone. There was only one single bed in use—which, of course, was not made, and I doubt if he makes it from one year to the next. There was no sign of any female presence, which I don't wonder, the way this Hastings lives.

One of his rooms is an office, and this was *really* a mess. Papers all over the desk and also all over the floor. This room stank of old cigarette butts, of which smell I am very conscious since I gave up smoking.

From what I found on his desk, I learned that this Harry Hastings is a TV writer. He writes kind of spooky stuff, like this Rodney Serling. I took one of his scripts, to study. From his income-tax returns, which were lying around for all the world to see, I saw he made nearly $23,000 gross the year before.

But most of the furniture in the house is pretty grubby and the drapes need replacing, which made me wonder what this character spent all his money on, besides the Mercedes. He had a new electric typewriter and a great big color-TV set, which would take four men to move, and a hi-fi, but no art objects or decent silver or gold cuff links or things like that.

It wasn't till I went through his clothes closet that I found out that most of his bread went into his wardrobe. There was about $5000 worth of new apparel in there, most of it hand-tailored and from places like where Sinatra and Dean Martin get their outfits. Very Mod and up to date. I tried on a couple of jackets and it turns out that this Hastings and me are exactly the same size! I mean *exactly*. These clothes looked like they had been tailored for me alone, after six fittings. Only his shoes didn't fit me, sad to say.

I was very pleased, indeed, I can tell you, as I have always had trouble getting fitted off the rack. Also, I like to dress in the latest fashion when I take Susie to nice places.

So I took the entire wardrobe, including shirts and ties. I decided to take the typewriter, which I needed for my writing-class homework. The machine I had kept skipping.

But I wanted to try out the typewriter before I took it, and also, I thought I would leave a note for this Hastings, so he wouldn't think I was some kind of crude thug. So I typed:

> Dear Mr. Hastings: I am typing this to see if your typewriter works OK. I see that it does. I am not taking it to sell it, but I need it because I am trying to become a professional writer like you, which I know because I saw your scripts on your desk, and I am taking one to help me with my work, for studying.
>
> I wish to make you a compliment anent your fine wardrobe of clothes. As it happened, they are like they have been made for me only. I am not taking them to sell them but because I need some good clothes to wear. Your shoes do not fit me, so I am leaving them.
>
> I am also not taking your hi-fi, because there is a terrible screech in the treble. I like your dog and I will give him a biskit.
>
> *A Friend*

Well, some three months or so now passed, because there was no sense in hitting Hastings' house again until he had time to get a new bunch of clothes together.

But when I thought the time was ripe, I drove by there again and saw a little VW in the carport, and also, there was a big blonde woman shaking rugs.

I drove up and asked her if her house was swarming with disease-infested rats, and she said she didn't think so but that she was only the once-a-week cleaning lady. She sounded Scandinavian. I took note that this was a Wednesday.

I went back the next Monday. No car in the carport. But on the way to the house, there was a new sign, hand-lettered on a board, and it read: BEWARE! VICIOUS WATCHDOG ON DUTY! THIS DOG HAS BEEN TRAINED TO GO FOR THE TESTICLES! YOU HAVE BEEN WARNED! PROCEED NO FARTHER!

Well, this gives me pause, as you can well imagine. But then I remember that this Hastings is a writer with an ingenious and inventive mind, and I do not believe this sign for one moment. Cuddles is my friend. So I start for the house and suddenly, this enormous Alsatian jumps through the dog door and runs straight at me, growling and snarling, and then he leaps and knocks me down and, sure enough, starts chewing around my crotch. But then out comes Cuddles, and I am sure there is a dog language, for he woofed at this monster dog as if in reproach, as if to say, "Knock it off. This is a friend. Leave him alone." So pretty soon, both dogs are licking me.

But when I get to the front door, I find that this Hastings has installed a new, burglarproof lock. I walk around the house and find that there are new locks on both the kitchen door and the laundry-room door. They must have set Hastings back about 75 bucks.

There are also a lot of sliding-glass doors around the house, but I don't like to break plate glass, because I know how expensive it is to replace. But I finally locate a little louvered window by the laundry-room door and I find that by breaking only one louver and cutting the screen, I can reach through and around and open the door.

Inside, I find that the house is just as messy as before. This guy will *die* a slob.

But when I get to his bedroom, here is this note, Scotch-taped to his closet door. It is dusty and looks like it has been there for months. It says:

> Dear Burglar: Just in *case* you are the same young man who was in here a few months ago, I think I must tell you that you have a long way to go before you will be a professional writer.
>
> "Anent" is archaic and should be avoided. A "wardrobe of clothes" is redundant. It is "biscuit," not "biskit." Use your dictionary!
>
> I know you are a young man, because both my cleaning woman and a 19-year-old neighbor have seen you and your truck. If you have gotten

this far into my house, you cannot be stupid. Have you ever thought of devoting your talents to something a little higher than burgling people such as me?

Harry Hastings

Inside his closet are two fabulous new suits, plus a really great red-and-blue-plaid cashmere sports coat. I take these and am about to leave when I remember there is something I want to tell Hastings.

In his office, there is a new electric typewriter, on which I type:

> Dear Mr. Hastings: Thank you for your help. In return, I want to tell you that I read the script of yours I took and I think it is pretty good, except that I don't believe that the man should go back to his wife. I mean, after she tried to poison him three times. This is just my opinion, of course.
>
> I do not have a dictionary, so I am taking yours. Thank you.
>
> *A Friend*

I, of course, do not take this new typewriter, partly because I already have one and also because I figure he will need it to make money with so he can replace his wardrobe again.

Four months go by before I figure it is time to hit his house again. By this time, my clothes are getting kind of tired, and also the styles have changed, some.

This time, when I drive up to the house one afternoon, there is a new hand-lettered sign:

> THIS HOUSE IS PROTECTED BY THE BULLDOG BURGLAR PROTECTION AGENCY! THERE ARE SILENT ALARMS EVERYWHERE! IF THEY ARE TRIPPED, RADIO CARS WILL CONVERGE AT ONCE! PROCEED NO FARTHER! YOU HAVE BEEN WARNED!

Come *on*, now! I and I alone am the *nonexistent* Bulldog Burglar Protection Agency! I'd put my card in his mailbox! This is really one cheap-skate smart-ass bastard, this Harry Hastings.

When I get near the house, the dogs come out and I give them a little loving, and then I see a note on the front door:

> Dear Jack: Welcome! Hope you had a nice trip. The key is hidden where it always has been. I didn't have to go to work today. I've run down the hill to get some Scotch and some steaks. Be back in a few minutes. The gals are coming at six.
>
> *Harry*

Well, this gives me pause. I finally decide that this is not the right day to hit the house. This could, of course, be another of Hastings' tricks, but I can't be sure. So I leave.

But a few days later, I come back and this same goddamn note to Jack is still on the door, only now it is all yellowed. You would think that this lame-brain would at least write a new note every day, welcoming Bert or Sam or Harriet or Hazel or whoever. The truth is that this Hastings is so damn smart, when you think about it, that he is actually stupid.

The broken louver and the screen have by now been replaced, but when I break the glass and cut the screen and reach around to open the laundry door, I find that this bastard has installed chains and bolts on the inside.

Well, as any idiot knows, you can't bolt all your doors from the inside when you go out, so one door has to be openable, and I figure it has to be the front door; but the only way I can get in is to break a big frosted-plate-glass window to the left of it and reach through and open the door. As I said, I'm not happy to break plate glass, but this Hastings has left me no choice, so I knock out a hole just big enough for me to reach through and open the door and go in.

This time, there is *another* note on his closet door:

Dear Burglar: Are you incapable of pity? By now, you must be the best-dressed burglar in Hollywood. But how many clothes can you *wear*? You might like to know that my burglary insurance has been canceled. My new watchdog cost me $100 and I have spent a small fortune on new locks and bolts and chains. Now I fear you are going to start smashing my plate-glass windows, which can cost as much as $90 to replace. There is only one new suit in this closet. All my other clothes I keep now either in my car or at my office. Take the suit, if you must, but never return, for, by God, you will be sorry, indeed, if you do. I have a terrible revenge in mind.

Harry Hastings

P.S. You still have time to reform yourself.

P.P.S. I don't like his going back to his poisoning wife, either. But the network insisted on a "Happy Ending."

H. H.

Well, I am not about to fall for all this noise about pity. Any man who has a dog trained to go for my testicles and who uses my own Bulldog Agency against me is not, in my mind, deserving of too much sympathy.

So I take the suit, which is a just-beautiful Edwardian eight-button, in gray sharkskin.

Now quite a few months pass and I begin to feel a little sorry for this character, and I decide to let him alone, forever.

But then, one day, when I am out working, some bastard breaks into my own pad, which is three rooms over a private garage in Hollywood. This son of a bitch takes every stitch of clothing I own.

By this time, I am heavily dating Susie Plimson, and she likes good dressers. So, while I am not too happy about it, I decide I have to pay Hastings another visit.

No dogs come out this time when I walk to the front door. But on it is a typed note, which says:

> HELGA! DO NOT OPEN THIS DOOR! Since you were here last week, I bought a PUMA, for burglar protection. This is a huge cat, a cougar or a mountain lion, about four feet long, not including the tail. The man I bought it from told me it was fairly tame, but it is NOT! It has tried to attack both dogs, who are OK and are locked in the guest room. I myself have just gone down to my doctor's to have stitches taken in my face and neck and arms. This ferocious puma is wandering loose inside the house. The S.P.C.A. people are coming soon to capture it and take it away. I tried to call you and tell you not to come today, but you had already left. Whatever you do, if the S.P.C.A. has not come before you, DO NOT UNDER ANY CIRCUMSTANCES OPEN THIS DOOR!!

Well, naturally, this gave me considerable pause. Helga was obviously the blonde cleaning woman. But this was a Tuesday and she came on Wednesdays. Or she used to. But she could have changed her days.

I stroll around the outside of the house. But all of the curtains and drapes are drawn and I can't see in. As I pass the guest-room windows, the two dogs bark inside. So this much of the note on the door is true.

So I wander back to the front door and I think and I ponder. Is there really a puma in there or is this just another one of Hastings' big fat dirty lies?

After all, it is one hell of a lot of trouble to buy and keep a puma just to protect a few clothes. And it is also expensive, and this Hastings I know by now is a cheap skate. It costs him not one thin dime to put this stupid note to Helga on his front door and, God knows, it would terrify most anybody who wanted to walk in.

Susie told us in class that in every story, there is like a moment of decision. I figured this was mine.

After about five minutes of solid thought, I finally make my decision. There *is* no puma in there. It's just that this smart-ass bastard wants me to think that there is a puma in there.

So I decide to enter the house, by breaking another hole in the now-replaced frosted-plate-glass window to the left of the front door. So I break out a small portion of this glass.

And I peer through this little hole I've made and I see nothing. No puma. I listen. I don't hear any snarling cat or anything. No puma. Just the same, there *could* be a puma in there and it could be crouching silently just inside the door, waiting to pounce and bite my hand off when I put it in. Very carefully, I put some fingers in and wiggle them. No puma. And so I put my arm in and reach and turn the doorknob from the inside and open the door a crack. No snarl from a puma —whatever pumas snarl like. I open the door a little wider and I call, "Here, pussy-pussy! Here, puma-puma! *Nice* puma!" No response.

I creep in very cautiously, looking around, ready to jump back and out and slam the door on this beast, if necessary. But there is no puma.

And then I realize that my decision was, of course, right and there is no goddamn puma in this goddamn house. But still, I am sweating like a pig and breathing heavily, and I suddenly figure out what Susie means when she talks about "the power of the written word." With just a piece of writing, this bastard Hastings transferred an idea from his crazy imagination into my mind, and I was willing to believe it.

So I walk down the hall to his bedroom door, which is shut, and there is *another* typed note on it:

> Dear Burglar: OK. So there is no puma. Did you really think I'd let a huge cat mess up my nice neat house?
>
> However, I am now going to give you a *serious* warning. DO NOT OPEN THIS DOOR! One of the engineers at our studio has invented a highly sophisticated security device and I've borrowed one of his models. It's hidden in the bedroom and it works by means of ultrasonic waves. They are soundless and they have a fantastically destructive and permanent effect on brain tissue. It takes less than a minute of exposure. You will not notice any brain-numbing effects at once, but in a few days, your memory will start to go, and then your reasoning powers, and so, for your *own* sake, DO NOT ENTER THIS ROOM!
>
> *Harry Hastings*

Well, I really had to hand it to this loony character. No wonder he made a lot of money as a writer. I, of course, do not believe *one word* of this, *at all*, therefore, I go into the bedroom and hurry around to see if there is any hidden electronic device, but, of course, there is not. Naturally.

Then I see another note, on the closet door, and it says:

> Dear Burglar: I don't suppose I should have expected you to believe that one, with your limited imagination and your one-track mind. By the way, where do you *go* in all my clothes? You must be quite a swinger.
>
> There are only a few new things in the closet. But before you take them, I suggest you sniff them. You will notice a kind of cologne smell, but this is only to disguise another odor. I have a pal who was in Chemical Warfare and he has given me a liquid that can be sprayed inside clothing. No amount of dry cleaning can ever entirely remove it. When the clothes are worn, the heat of the body converts this substance into a heavy gas that attacks the skin and produces the most frightful

and agonizingly painful blisters, from the ankles to the neck. Never forget that you have been *warned.*

Harry Hastings

Well, I don't believe this for one moment, and so I open the closet door. All there is is one pair of slacks and a sports coat. But this coat looks like the very same *plaid cashmere* I took before and the son of a bitch stole from *me*! But then I realize this could not be so, but it was just that Hastings liked this coat so much he went out and bought another just like it.

Anyway, I find myself sniffing these. They smell of cologne, all right, but nothing else, and I know, of course, that this kind of gas stuff does not exist at all except in Hastings' wild imagination, which I am coming to admire by now.

As I drive back to my pad, I start to laugh when I think of all the stupid and fantastic things that Hastings has tried to put into my mind today by the power of suggestion, and I realize that he almost succeeded. *Almost,* but not quite.

When I get home and climb the outside stairs to my front door, there are three envelopes taped to it, one above another. There are no names on them, but they are numbered, 1, 2, 3. I do not know what in hell all this could be about, but I open 1 and I read:

Dear Burglar: The plaid cashmere coat you have over your arm right now is *not* a replacement for the one you stole. It is the *same identical coat. Think* about this before you open envelope 2.

Harry Hastings

Well, of *course* I think about this as I stand there with my mouth sort of hanging open. All of a sudden, it *hits* me! *Harry Hastings* was the son of a bitch who stole all his clothes back! But how did he know where I *live*? How could he know I was going to hit his house *today*? My hands are all fumbles as I open 2. Inside, it says:

Dear Burglar: To answer your questions: On your *third* visit to my house, my young neighbor saw you and followed you home in his car, and so found out just where you live. Later, in my own good time, I easily entered this place with a bent paper clip and retrieved my own clothes. Today, my neighbor called me at my office and said you were inside my house again. Later, I phoned him and he said you had come out, with my coat. So I've had time to come here and write and leave these notes. I also have had time to do something else, which you will read about in 3.

Harry Hastings

I open this third envelope very fast, indeed, because I figure that if Hastings knows all this, the fuzz will be along any minute. In it, I read:

Dear Burglar: I got the puma idea from a friend out in the Valley who has one in a large cage in his yard. Long ago, I asked him if I might borrow this huge cat for a day sometime, and he said yes and that he didn't like burglars, either. He has a large carrying cage for the puma. I called him this morning the moment I heard you were inside my house and he drove the puma right over *here* and we released the huge cat inside your place. She is now in there, wandering around loose. I have done this partly because I am vengeful and vindictive by nature and partly because I've made my living for years as a verisimilitudinous (look it up later) writer, and I deeply resent anyone I cannot fool. The puma that is now inside is my childish way of getting even. This is no *trick* this time! If you have any brains at *all*, DO NOT OPEN THIS DOOR! Just get out of town before the police arrive, which will be in about half an hour. Goodbye.

Harry Hastings

P.S. The puma's name is Carrie—as if that would help you any.

Well, I read in a story once where somebody was called a "quivering mass of indecisive jelly," and that is what I was right then. I simply did not know *what* to think or believe. If this was any door but mine, I could walk away. But all my *cash* was hidden inside and I *had* to get it before I could leave town.

So I stand there and I sweat and I think and I think and after a long time, it comes to me that *this* time, this bastard Hastings is finally telling the *truth*. Besides, I can hear little noises from inside. There *is* a puma in there! I know it! But I have to get *in* there, just the same!

I finally figure that if I open the door fast and step back, Carrie might just scoot past me and away. But maybe she will attack me. But then I figure if I wrap the sports coat around one arm and the slacks around the other, maybe I can fend off Carrie long enough to grab a chair and then force her into my bathroom, the way lion tamers do, and then slam the door on her, and then grab my cash and run out of there, and the police can worry about her when they come.

So this is what I decide to do, only it is some time before I can get up the nerve to unlock the door and push it open. I unlock the door and I stand there. But finally, I think, "Oh, hell, you *got* to do it, sooner or later," and so I push my door open and stand back.

No puma jumps at me. Nothing happens at all. But then I look around the corner of my door and *Harry Hastings* is sitting inside. Not with a gun or anything. He is sitting very calmly behind the old card table I use as a desk, with a cigarette in his mouth and a pencil in his hand, and I see one of my stories in front of him.

I walk in and just stand there with my face on and cannot think of any clever remark to make, when he says: "Tell me one thing. *Did* you or did you *not* really believe there was a puma in here?"

If I remember right—I was pretty shook up then—I nodded and I said, "Yes, sir. Yes. I really did."

Then he smiled a big smile and said, "Well, thank heaven for *that.* I was beginning to think I was losing my grip. I feel a little better now. Sit down. I want to talk to you. By the way, your syntax is terrible and your grammar is worse. I've been making some corrections while waiting for you. However, that's not what I want to talk to you about. Sit down. Stop trembling, will you, and sit down!"

I sat.

As I write now, I am the co-owner and manager of the Puma Burglar Protection Agency. Harry Hastings is my silent partner and he put up $2000 for financing. Susie helps me with my accounts. I have 130 clients now, at five dollars a month each. The reason it's so cheap is that we use the Harry Hastings Method. That is, we don't bother with burglar alarms or things like that. I just patrol around and keep putting up and changing signs and notices and notes on front doors. Already, the burglary rate in my area has been cut by two thirds.

This very morning, I got a little letter from Harry Hastings with two new ideas for front-door notes. One is: CLARA! I HAVE ALREADY CALLED THE POLICE AND THEY WILL BE HERE IN MINUTES! DO NOT CALL THEM AGAIN! GEORGE IS LOCKED IN THE BATHROOM AND CAN'T GET OUT, SO WE WILL BE SAFE TILL THEY GET HERE!

The second one is: NOTICE! BECAUSE OF A FRIGHTFULLY CONTAGIOUS DISEASE, THIS HOUSE HAS BEEN EVACUATED AND QUARANTINED. IT MUST ABSOLUTELY NOT BE ENTERED UNTIL IT HAS BEEN FUMIGATED!

Harry Hastings says that I should be sure to warn the householder to remove this notice before any large parties.

QUESTIONS FOR DISCUSSION

1. Compare "The Harry Hastings Method" and "Just Saying You Love Me Doesn't Make It So" on the basis of plot, structure, and pace.
2. In retrospect, the Campbell story may seem to you more "realistic" than the Law story. But as you read each *for the first time,* which one "worked best" for you?
3. Analyze the wit and humor in the narrator's style. Discuss also the development of witty situations as well as witty language. Do some of the "gag lines" misfire? Which ones? Why?
4. "Bulldog Burglar Protection Agency" is introduced into the story, then brought back in later with a twist. What other elements in the story are introduced, then developed? Does the repetition of such elements delight you? Try to determine why.
5. Discuss the parallels between the unnamed narrator and Harry. Why are these crucial to the effect of the story?

6. What can you learn about the elements, techniques, and effects of fiction writing by reading this story as a parable or demonstration of the way writers try to affect readers? Note, for example, Harry's letters to the burglar. How does the writer maneuver the reader's responses in ways similar to Harry's maneuvering of the burglar in his notes?
7. This story is about a contest between a professional writer and an amateur writer. Discuss it as a contest as well between the reader and the writer.

GRAHAM GREENE
Brother

The Communists were the first to appear. They walked quickly, a group of about a dozen, up the boulevard which runs from Combat to Ménilmontant; a young man and a girl lagged a little way behind because the man's leg was hurt and the girl was helping him along. They looked impatient, harassed, hopeless, as if they were trying to catch a train which they knew already in their hearts they were too late to catch.

The proprietor of the café saw them coming when they were still a long way off; the lamps at that time were still alight (it was later that the bullets broke the bulbs and dropped darkness all over that quarter of Paris), and the group showed up plainly in the wide barren boulevard. Since sunset only one customer had entered the café, and very soon after sunset firing could be heard from the direction of Combat; the Métro station had closed hours ago. And yet something obstinate and undefeatable in the proprietor's character prevented him from putting up the shutters; it might have been avarice; he could not himself have told what it was as he pressed his broad yellow forehead against the glass and stared this way and that, up the boulevard and down the boulevard.

But when he saw the group and their air of hurry he began immediately to close his café. First he went and warned his only customer, who was practising billiard shots, walking round and round the table, frowning and stroking a thin moustache between shots, a little green in the face under the low diffused lights.

"The Reds are coming," the proprietor said, "you'd better be off. I'm putting up the shutters."

"Don't interrupt. They won't harm me," the customer said. "This is a tricky shot. Reds in baulk. Off the cushion. Screw on spot." He shot his ball straight into a pocket.

"I knew you couldn't do anything with that," the proprietor said, nodding his bald head. "You might just as well go home. Give me a hand with the shutters first. I've sent my wife away." The customer turned on him maliciously, rattling the cue between his fingers. "It was your talking that spoilt the shot. You've cause to be frightened, I dare say. But I'm a poor man. I'm safe. I'm not going to stir." He went across to his coat and took out a dry cigar. "Bring me a bock." He walked round the table on his toes and the balls clicked and the proprietor padded back into the bar, elderly and irritated. He did not fetch the beer but began to close the shutters; every move he made was slow and clumsy. Long before he had finished the group of Communists was outside.

He stopped what he was doing and watched them with furtive dislike. He was afraid that the rattle of the shutters would attract their attention. If I am very quiet and still, he thought, they may go on, and he remembered with malicious pleasure the police barricade across the Place de la République. That will finish them. In the meanwhile I must be very quiet, very still, and he felt a kind of warm satisfaction at the idea that worldly wisdom dictated the very attitude most suited to his nature. So he stared through the edge of a shutter, yellow, plump, cautious, hearing the billiard balls crackle in the other room, seeing the young man come limping up the pavement on the girl's arm, watching them stand and stare with dubious faces up the boulevard towards Combat.

But when they came into the café he was already behind the bar, smiling and bowing and missing nothing, noticing how they had divided forces, how six of them had begun to run back the way they had come.

The young man sat down in a dark corner above the cellar stairs and the others stood round the door waiting for something to happen. It gave the proprietor an odd feeling that they should stand there in his café not asking for a drink, knowing what to expect, when he, the owner, knew nothing, understood nothing. At last the girl said "Cognac," leaving the others and coming to the bar, but when he had poured it out for her, very careful to give a fair and not a generous measure, she simply took it to the man sitting in the dark and held it to his mouth.

"Three francs," the proprietor said. She took the glass and sipped a little and turned it so that the man's lips might touch the same spot. Then she knelt down and rested her forehead against the man's forehead and so they stayed.

"Three francs," the proprietor said, but he could not make his voice bold. The man was no longer visible in his corner, only the girl's back, thin and shabby in a black cotton frock, as she knelt, leaning forward to find the man's face. The proprietor was daunted by the four men at the door, by the knowledge that they were Reds who had no respect for private property, who would drink his wine and go away without paying, who would rape his women (but there was only his wife, and she was not there), who would rob his bank, who would murder him as soon as look at him. So with fear in his heart he gave up the three francs as lost rather than attract any more attention.

Then the worst that he contemplated happened.

One of the men at the door came up to the bar and told him to pour out four glasses of cognac. "Yes, yes," the proprietor said, fumbling with the cork, praying secretly to the Virgin to send an angel, to send the police, to send the Gardes Mobiles, now, immediately, before the cork came out, "that will be twelve francs."

"Oh, no," the man said, "we are all comrades here. Share and share alike. Listen," he said, with earnest mockery, leaning across the bar, "all we have is yours just as much as it's ours, comrade," and stepping back a pace he presented himself to the proprietor, so that he might take his choice of stringy tie, of threadbare trousers, of starved features. "And it follows from that, comrade, that all you have is ours. So four cognacs. Share and share alike."

"Of course," the proprietor said, "I was only joking." Then he stood with bottle poised, and the four glasses tingled upon the counter. "A machine-gun," he said, "up by Combat," and smiled to see how for the moment the men forgot their brandy as they fidgeted near the door. Very soon now, he thought, and I shall be quit of them.

"A machine-gun," the Red said incredulously, "they're using machine-guns?"

"Well," the proprietor said, encouraged by this sign that the Gardes Mobiles were not very far away, "you can't pretend that you aren't armed yourselves." He leant across the bar in a way that was almost paternal. "After all, you know, your ideas—they wouldn't do in France. Free love."

"Who's talking of free love?" the Red said.

The proprietor shrugged and smiled and nodded at the corner. The girl knelt with her head on the man's shoulder, her back to the room. They were quite silent and the glass of brandy stood on the floor beside them. The girl's beret was pushed back on her head and one stocking was laddered and darned from knee to ankle.

"What, those two? They aren't lovers."

"I," the proprietor said, "with my bourgeois notions would have thought . . ."

"He's her brother," the Red said.

The men came clustering round the bar and laughed at him, but softly as if a sleeper or a sick person were in the house. All the time they were listening for something. Between their shoulders the proprietor could look out across the boulevard; he could see the corner of the Faubourg du Temple.

"What are you waiting for?"

"For friends," the Red said. He made a gesture with open palm as if to say, You see, we share and share alike. We have no secrets.

Something moved at the corner of the Faubourg du Temple.

"Four more cognacs," the Red said.

"What about those two?" the proprietor asked.

"Leave them alone. They'll look after themselves. They're tired."

How tired they were. No walk up the boulevard from Ménilmontant could explain the tiredness. They seemed to have come farther and fared a great deal worse than their companions. They were more starved; they were infinitely more hopeless, sitting in their dark corner away from the friendly gossip, the amicable desperate voices which now confused the proprietor's brain, until for a moment he believed himself to be a host entertaining friends.

He laughed and made a broad joke directed at the two of them; but they made no sign of understanding. Perhaps they were to be pitied, cut off from the camaraderie round the counter; perhaps they were to be envied for their deeper comradeship. The proprietor thought for no reason at all of the bare grey trees of the Tuileries like a series of exclamation marks drawn against the winter sky. Puzzled, disintegrated, with all his bearings lost, he stared out through the door towards the Faubourg.

It was as if they had not seen each other for a long while and would soon again be saying good-bye. Hardly aware of what he was doing he filled the four glasses with brandy. They stretched out worn blunted fingers for them.

"Wait," he said. "I've got something better than this"; then paused, conscious of what was happening across the boulevard. The lamplight splashed down on blue steel helmets; the Gardes Mobiles were lining out across the entrance to the Faubourg, and a machine-gun pointed directly at the café windows.

So, the proprietor thought, my prayers are answered. Now I must do my part, not look, not warn them, save myself. Have they covered the side door? I will get the other bottle. Real Napoleon brandy. Share and share alike.

He felt a curious lack of triumph as he opened the trap of the bar and came out. He tried not to walk quickly back towards the billiard room. Nothing that he did must warn these men; he tried to spur himself with the thought that every slow casual step he took was a blow for France, for his café, for his savings. He had to step over the girl's feet to pass her; she was asleep. He noted the sharp shoulder blades thrusting through the cotton, and raised his eyes and met her brother's, filled with pain and despair.

He stopped. He found he could not pass without a word. It was as if he needed to explain something, as if he belonged to the wrong party. With false bonhomie he waved the corkscrew he carried in the other's face. "Another cognac, eh?"

"It's no good talking to them," the Red said. "They're German. They don't understand a word."

"German?"

"That's what's wrong with his leg. A concentration camp."

The proprietor told himself that he must be quick, that he must put a door between him and them, that the end was very close, but he was bewildered by the hopelessness in the man's gaze. "What's he doing here?" Nobody answered him. It was as if his question were too foolish to need a reply. With his head sunk upon his breast the proprietor went past, and the girl slept on. He was like a stranger leaving a room where all the rest are friends. A German. They don't understand a word; and up, up through the heavy darkness of his mind, through the avarice and the dubious triumph, a few German words remembered from very old days climbed like spies into the light: a line from the *Lorelei* learnt at school, *Kamerad* with its war-time suggestion of fear and surrender, and oddly from nowhere the phrase *mein Bruder.* He opened the door of the billiard room and closed it behind him and softly turned the key.

"Spot in baulk," the customer explained and leant across the great green table, but while he took aim, wrinkling his narrow peevish eyes, the firing started. It came in two bursts with a rip of glass between. The girl cried out something, but it was not one of the words he knew. Then feet ran across the floor, the trap of the bar slammed. The proprietor sat back against the table and listened and listened for any further sound; but silence came in under the door and silence through the keyhole.

"The cloth. My God, the cloth," the customer said, and the proprietor looked down at his own hand which was working the corkscrew into the table.

"Will this absurdity ever end?" the customer said. "I shall go home."

"Wait," the proprietor said. "Wait." He was listening to voices and footsteps in the other room. These were voices he did not recognize. Then a car drove up and presently drove away again. Somebody rattled the handle of the door.

"Who is it?" the proprietor called.

"Who are you? Open that door."

"Ah," the customer said with relief, "the police. Where was I now? Spot in baulk." He began to chalk his cue. The proprietor opened the door. Yes, the Gardes Mobiles had arrived; he was safe again, though his windows were smashed. The Reds had vanished as if they had never been. He looked at the raised trap, at the smashed electric bulbs, at the broken bottle which dripped behind the bar. The café was full of men, and he remembered with odd relief that he had not had time to lock the side door.

"Are you the owner?" the officer asked. "A bock for each of these men and a cognac for myself. Be quick about it."

The proprietor calculated: "Nine francs fifty," and watched closely with bent head the coins rattle down upon the counter.

"You see," the officer said with significance, "we pay." He nodded towards the side door. "Those others: did they pay?"

No, the proprietor admitted, they had not paid, but as he counted the coins and slipped them into the till, he caught himself silently repeating the officer's order—"A bock for each of these men." Those others, he thought, one's got to say that for them, they weren't mean about the drink. It was four cognacs with them. But, of course, they did not pay. "And my windows," he complained aloud with sudden asperity, "what about my windows?"

"Never you mind," the officer said, "the government will pay. You have only to send in your bill. Hurry up now with my cognac. I have no time for gossip."

"You can see for yourself," the proprietor said, "how the bottles have been broken. Who will pay for that?"

"Everything will be paid for," the officer said.

"And now I must go to the cellar to fetch more."

He was angry at the reiteration of the word pay. They enter my café, he thought, they smash my windows, they order me about and think that all is well if they pay, pay, pay. It occurred to him that these men were intruders.

"Step to it," the officer said and turned and rebuked one of the men who had leant his rifle against the bar.

At the top of the cellar stairs the proprietor stopped. They were in darkness, but by the light from the bar he could just make out a body half-way down. He began to tremble violently, and it was some seconds before he could strike a match. The young German lay head downwards, and the blood from his head had dropped on to the step below. His eyes were open and stared back at the proprietor with the old despairing expression of life. The proprietor would not believe that he was dead. "Kamerad," he said bending down, while the match singed his fingers and went out, trying to recall some phrase in German, but he could only remember, as he bent lower still, "mein Bruder." Then suddenly he turned and ran up the steps, waved the match-box in the officer's face, and called out in a low hysterical voice to him and his men and to the customer stooping under the low green shade, "Cochons. Cochons."

"What was that? What was that?" the officer exclaimed. "Did you say that he was your brother? It's impossible," and he frowned incredulously at the proprietor and rattled the coins in his pocket.

QUESTIONS FOR DISCUSSION

1. How apt and effective, comparatively, are the titles of these three stories? Which is most enticing? Least? Why? Headnotes written by the magazine editors accompanied the first two stories. "Just Saying You Love Me Doesn't Make Is So": "We've all done things in the past that we regret. But not all of us grow up, marry—and keep right on making the same kind of mistake." "The Harry Hastings Method": "When a smart burglar matches wits with a smarter television writer, the contest is bound to be bizarre." How do you suppose these headnotes would have affected your approach to the two stories if you had read them in *Redbook* and *Playboy*? Would a headnote enhance "Brother"? Explain.
2. Compare the first paragraphs of these three stories for relative effectiveness. How do the writers attract your interest (or fail to)? What specific elements do they introduce that are developed throughout? In what ways do their final paragraphs reiterate minor or major elements introduced in the initial paragraphs?
3. Define the function of the couple in "Brother"; of the billiard player. If they, together with the proprietor, represent certain "segments" of humanity, what segments are they? How does the term *brother* apply to each?
4. Discuss the implications of the story's images, especially darkness and light, shutters and doors, the café itself and the street outside, trees, brandy and bock beer, clothing, money.
5. Discuss the irony of the ending—both the proprietor's final words to the capitalists and the officer's reply.
6. Discuss pro and con this assertion: Considered as a serious story, "Brother" is too neat, contrived, sentimental, and theme-ridden, and the symbolism and irony are too obvious, inept, and artificial. Cite specific instances.
7. Compare the Campbell, Law, and Greene stories on the basis of (a) effective storytelling (suspense, surprise, "delight"); (b) effective characterization; (c) significance of theme; (d) ultimate effect on the reader. Which story did you like best on first reading? On rereading? Why? Which might be termed commercial stories? Why?

B. Honesty and Dishonesty in Fiction

The reader of this text-anthology has, to this point, read a number of stories that, to most critics of the genre, would be considered exceptional, a few that would be considered superior, and only one or two that would be written off as run-of-the-mill or inferior. This is to be expected, for most anthologists try to select the best stories of the best writers, the story that gets written perhaps once in five thousand times.

And to this point, the implication of this text has been that bad stories, like accidents, are unplanned, that they occur because of a lack of skill or talent on the part of the writer. Such is not always the case. For some stories that seem, to the uncritical reader, to work are, to the demanding reader, ineffective. Many of these stories are written by very skillful writers, and they work for the uncritical reader because these writers have learned a number of devices for disguising the central weaknesses of their stories. Professional writers call these devices "gimmicks," and they are usually resorted to because the magazines that buy these stories make certain editorial demands that can only be satisfied by such tricks as "planting" or stock response or manipulation. We call this kind of story "dishonest" to distinguish it from the story that is ineffective simply because a writer lacked the skill to bring it off.

Readers may object to our use of this terminology. If the test of fiction, they will ask, is that it work, what difference does the author's method make? The answer is that to the critical reader, these stories do not work. For the naïve reader, a "slick" story like "Just Saying You Love Me" or a clever but contrived story like "The Jewelry" may *seem* to manage a genuine emotional effect or a significant theme or, simply, a plausible and interesting story. But if you compare stories like these to stories that are genuinely skillful and honest, you will perhaps discover that what once appeared to be significant is either false or shallow, and that what once seemed to be a genuine emotional effect is in reality shallow, contrived, diluted.

Here, however, permit us a brief aside. There was a time when our remarks here would have applied to most of the stories appearing in large-circulation, slick magazines or in those specialized magazines that we call "pulp." Such is no longer the case, for the market for such stories has, in the past three decades, steadily shrunk; the few large-circulation magazines that have survived have had to adjust editorial policy to a smaller and more sophisticated audience, and honest and skillful stories are now as likely to appear in *Cosmospolitan* or *Playboy* as in *The Virginia Quarterly Review* or *Harper's*. Moreover, where one market has almost disappeared, another has replaced it. In theory, the "little magazine" was founded to provide serious writers with a market that would not impose taboos or other editorial restrictions, that would publish any story which was good. But there is as much dishonesty to be found in the little magazine story as there once was in the slick or pulp story; the only distinction is that the dishonesty is of a different kind. Where the editors of mass-circulation magazines may have insisted on innocuous, noncontroversial themes, on surprise or happy endings, on sentimentality, the editors of the little magazines may distrust any story that *is* a story, or that is not obscure enough to test the ingenuity of an "elite" reader, or that is not loaded with symbolism for its own sake or with allusions put there to display the writer's erudition. The remarks that follow will be concerned with dishonesty in commercial or popular fiction—in those stories that appear regularly in magazines ranging from *Argosy* through *Redbook* to *Playboy* or the science fiction magazines (some of which no writer needs to be defensive about) or, even more particularly, in more than half of the paperback novels now on newsstands. But the reader should bear two things in mind. First, if the editors of this text had to choose between the "dishonest" commercial story and the "dishonest" little-magazine story, they would prefer the former. Second, both inferior and superior fiction can be found in almost any publication; we need only point out, for example, that "Just Saying You Love Me" and Ann Petry's "The Witness" (Section 8) appeared in *Redbook*.

Dishonesty in Conflict

The most common kind of dishonesty in the handling of conflict is one form or another of *plot manipulation.* Plot manipulation involves wrenching out of an established direction the external action of a story without regard to the other elements in that story; the writer usually does this by violating the principles of character plausibility, consistency, or motivation. Let us consider here two common reasons for plot manipulation and three devices by which writers can disguise this weakness in a story.

The most frequent reason is that the writer wants to force a happy ending on a story. Now there is nothing wrong with a happy ending so long as it is also logical and convincing; when the protagonist in a story is stronger than the antagonist, it is logical that he should triumph. But in many story situations the antagonist is the stronger; and though we may *want* the protagonist to win, logic tells us that the antagonist *should* win. Many writers, however, know that the average reader dislikes unhappy endings, and these writers will try to give that reader what he wants. Moreover, the writer of commercial stories knows that, in order to sell his story, he must subscribe to the principle of poetic justice, which means that good, no matter how weak, always triumphs over evil, no matter how strong. Since the antagonist in a commercial story usually symbolizes evil and the protagonist good, the outcome of many stories, in terms of this principle, is predetermined.

But the commercial writer cannot count too heavily on a reader's naïveté; he must somehow make his resolution *seem* convincing whether it is or not. To accomplish this, he may resort to a gimmick; in commercial fiction the most common of these gimmicks is called a "plant." Planting is, quite simply, the use of disguised coincidence in the resolution of a conflict; the coincidence is disguised by planting it somewhere in the opening of the story and then keeping it alive throughout the story until it is needed for the ending. More frequently than not, this use of coincidence is combined with the overbalancing of the forces in a story in favor of the antagonist (a common technique for increasing suspense). The result is that the ending of such a story will, for the critical reader, be unconvincing.

A second way by which writers disguise basic weaknesses in the handling of conflict is by resorting to *melodrama.* The dictionary defines melodrama as "literature which emphasizes the sensational in situation or action," and in modern fiction the emphasis takes the form of action for the sake of action, violence for the sake of violence, sex for the sake of sex. The modern-formula spy novel and the costume historical novel are two cases in point; here a writer, by introducing ravishing nymphomaniacs or repeated violence or a great deal of external action, can take a reader's mind off such things as adequate character motivation or plausibility of story line.

Still another device is the *surprise ending.* This we find employed in two ways.

The story with the sudden, unexpected plot reversal that O. Henry popularized over half a century ago is still occasionally found in commercial fiction. If it follows the O. Henry formula, we find that the entire *raison d'être* of the story is the surprise. Such a story is easily recognized. For one thing, it cannot be re-read with any pleasure or profit simply because the reader knows the ending. For another, such a story, read today, usually is forgotten tomorrow. For a third, close examination of this kind of story will more than likely reveal that the surprise has been effected by such things as plot manipulation or inadequately motivated character change.

But writers may employ the surprise ending not for its own sake but for the purpose of disguising other inherent weaknesses in a story. Fiction employs many kinds of surprise; indeed, if stories did not perpetually surprise us—by revelation of character, by twists and turns in conflict development, by just the "right" detail in the "right" place, by the witty turn of phrase or the startling metaphor—they would lose much of the interest they hold for us. Surprise, in short, is one of the legitimate tools of a writer. But knives are tools, too, and they can be used to peel apples or to murder wives. And one type of surprise, the unexpected plot reversal, can be used primarily to distract us, to jerk our minds away from basic story weaknesses that would otherwise disturb us.

Which is not to say that all stories with surprise endings are to be written off. Good stories with happy endings do get written; so do good stories with surprise endings. But such an ending must be managed without sacrificing more central and crucial requirements; such an ending must be both logical and functional. If logical, it will violate none of the other principles of effective storytelling. If functional, it will also provide us with a final flash of illumination that will make clear—will capture, so to speak—the meaning, purpose, direction, and effect of the *whole* story. The story that manages this is a comparative rarity, but among the three stories in this section, the readers will find one such. They will also find one that does not. And they will find a third that, employing the identical "plot," does not attempt surprise at all. A comparison of the three will, we think, prove illuminating.

Dishonesty in Characterization

Dishonest or ineffective characterization in a story usually stems from one of two causes. The first is that ineffective characterization is easier than effective characterization, both for the writer and for the reader. The second is that such characterization offers the commercial writer certain advantages that honest characterization does not. What are those advantages?

In popular fiction the most common kind of dishonest character is the *stock* character; again and again we meet in commercial fiction the handsome and athletic hero, the hard-working but unexciting middle-aged husband, the "typical" suburban housewife. We call these characters *stock* because they are borrowed rather than created; they are kept in a kind of community warehouse from whence a member of the writing fraternity can check them out whenever they will fit into a story idea. A stock character enormously simplifies the writers' job, first because it relieves them of the necessity of observing and analyzing, of examining the drives, motives, traits of their people; second, because it relieves them of the necessity of viewing every story as a special and difficult problem. Such a character also simplifies the job of reading, for to the reader it is already familiar, predictable, uncomplicated, and therefore comfortable.

Almost inevitably, the stock character is also an oversimplified or *flat* character. In one sense, of course, all fictional characters are oversimplified; even the longest novel could not present us with a character as complex as the simplest human being. But honest writers will at least give us the *effect* of complexity; they will try, to the limits of their skill and understanding, to explore all those pertinent aspects of character that relate to the story situation; they will, if nothing else, avoid working in blacks and whites. Commercial writers, however, will not, sometimes because they are unwilling to make the effort, more often because they know that their readers do not want complex characterization. For simple characterization is at once less demanding and more comfortable. Average readers may *know* that people in life are not simply black and white or one-dimensional, that instead they are rather complex and paradoxical mixtures of selfishness and altruism, idealism and opportunism, good and evil, just as they also know that most problems in life are not easily solvable. But average readers do not want their fiction to force them to wrestle with these truths. In life, most of us, if we could, would have the people we know easily predictable and understandable, just as we would have life's problems easily resolvable, and if life cannot grant us the wish, fiction can.

Most oversimplified characters appear in fiction because readers prefer them; most *shadowy* characters appear because writers find them convenient. A shadowy character is one whose traits are only vaguely presented, and writers find this character convenient because it makes the outcome of many plot stories more convincing. We can illustrate this with one example. A common formula in commercial fiction assumes that there is more good than bad in people and illustrates this theme by regenerating a "bad" character. But it is difficult for writers to present convincingly the reform of a genuinely bad person, because reform requires very strong, very credible motivation. But writers can employ various tricks in order to *seem* to effect this reform. They can, for example, present the bad side of a character vaguely (usually by telling rather than showing) and present the potentially good side of the character more forcefully (usually by dramatizing). The result is that we never really believe in the bad side of the character and hence find it easy to accept his reform.

Food without caloric content will ultimately prove dissatisfying no matter what the sugar content. Similarly, for the critical and demanding reader, commercial fiction will prove dissatisfying, and if it does, its characterization may be largely responsible. Characterization is the heart of fiction; it is also the element that places the most severe demands upon both writer and reader; and critical readers will ask more of the characters who people fiction than many commercial writers are prepared to give them. Mature readers do not resent, but welcome, demands made upon them. They do not want easy or comfortable or reassuring reading, but insight. Since they know that in life human beings are individuals and not copies stamped out in some factory, they will not believe in the stock character. Since they also know that human beings are complex, they will distrust the story that buys its heroes and villains too cheaply. And because the material that the commercial writer uses to create the shadowy character seems like cardboard to them, they will be unable to believe in what happens to that character simply because they will be unable to believe in the character itself. The mature reader demands from fiction the effect of life; the characters in fiction are the foundation of that effect, and the story without adequate or convincing characterization is a house built on sand which no trick, no disguise, can transform into rock.

Dishonesty in Emotional Effect

A genuine emotional effect in fiction rests upon our understanding of, identification with, and sympathy for a given character in a given situation. It therefore follows that if, by disregarding the principles that make for convincing conflict and characterization, a writer strains our credulity, he will also sacrifice any emotional effect that might otherwise have been gained.

But why, we may ask, do some readers insist that they derive emotion from a superficial or manipulated story? Again the answer lies in the fact that writers often resort to tricks in order to cover up the basic lack of emotion in a story. Most of these devices come under the heading of what we call *sentimentality.* Sentimentality is frequently confused with pathos, which is a perfectly legitimate and genuine emotional response; but what we mean by sentimentality is *any* emotional response that is in excess of the occasion. For example, we feel pathos at the ending of "And the Rock Cried Out"; Bradbury has *earned* that emotion by drawing characters *who are worth feeling sorry for* and by placing them in a situation that elicits sympathy.

Sentimentality, then, is any emotion that is not earned by the writer through honest, convincing characterization and skillfully handled conflict. And in order to see why many stories are basically sentimental, let us consider a possible story situation. Suppose a writer sees a small boy helping an old lady across a busy street. Now this writer can arouse in a reader a superficial emotion by simply presenting the incident. But the honest writer, knowing that there is potential emotion in this incident, realizes that he must answer some crucial questions before it can be made real to the reader. Who is the old lady, and is she worth helping across a street? Who is the boy, and why is he doing this—altruism or hope for a reward? Until the writer answers questions like those, this incident will remain material for sentimentality but not for honest emotional reaction.

But many writers, disregarding such questions, prefer to resort instead to tricks that they hope will achieve the *effect* more easily. One such trick is the *stock response,* which may be defined as the use of any character, situation, or concept whose emotional meaning has been established outside the specific piece of fiction in which it occurs. For example, most Americans have a certain emotional reaction when they come upon the word *mother*; they get a synthetic feeling when they see or hear the word, a feeling we may mistake for tenderness or love. Thus, a writer who wants this feeling can try to get it simply by making a character in a story a mother.

But why, if we *do* feel something, is the method dishonest? Simply because the emotion so derived will be shallow and superficial. Consider what happens when we attach to the noun *mother* the adjective *drunken.* Any emotional effect that can be destroyed so easily is shallow.

Writers employ other devices that result in sentimentality. They may, for example, *editorialize*—that is, they may resort to telling us how we *should* feel or how they *want* us to feel. Or they may overwrite, poetize, use heightened style to try to capture an emotion that is not there to begin with, and this use of what has been called the "purple passage" is an indication that something basic to genuine emotion is lacking in the story itself. For the honest writer, knowing that only his characters and situation can do his work for him, will, if he wants a strong emotional effect, probably underwrite rather than overwrite. Consider, for example, the style in the last scene of Hemingway's "In Another Country."

Dishonesty in Theme

Most types of dishonesty in fiction stem from either falsification or oversimplification. The manipulated conflict is a falsification of what ordinarily happens in life. The stock or shadowy or flat character is an oversimplication. Sentimentality is falsification of emotion. Similarly, the same oversimplification or falsification is the basic characteristic of the dishonest theme.

The dishonest theme is almost always stereotyped; it is the product not of a writer's observations of and thoughts about life, but of mass opinion and prejudice. Generally it is a lie, for it is a statement not of what we really believe but of what we want to believe. You will find the stereotyped theme in all those stories that tell you that true love always overcomes all obstacles, or that honesty is the best policy, or that good always overcomes evil. You will also find it in the story that suggests that all parents are jerks and all teen-agers the fount of all wisdom and morality; or in the story that suggests that the total meaning of existence is easy and promiscuous sex; or in the story that portrays all police as fascist pigs, or all southerners as potential lynchers, or all blacks as unjustly persecuted. The stock theme, in other words, is a borrowed theme. It represents a refusal on the part of the writer to challenge an axiom. Good writers practice skepticism, practice clear and intelligent observation of themselves and their world; they work hard at what Hemingway called "writing truly"; and they put into their stories what they have observed and concluded to be the truth, not what society has told them is the truth or what most of us wish were the truth.

The dishonest theme is also oversimplified because the writer fails or refuses to take into account all the ramifications or implications of a given theme. For example, it is possible that the principle of poetic justice is operative in this world. But to the naïve writer, poetic justice merely means that the black hat gets put in prison and the white hat gets the girl and the ranch. We all know, however, that in life a good many good people never get any of life's breaks and that a good many bastards never seem to get anything else. Yet there may be compensations for the good but unlucky person, and reckonings for the other. The point is, honest writers will really examine all this before writing about it; they will first determine whether they believe in poetic justice, and then they will determine exactly why and to what extent. Honest writers will not accept a theme that they have not thought about, tested against their observations of life, and come to believe in.

Virgil Scott

GUY DE MAUPASSANT
The Jewelry

Having met the girl one evening, at the house of the office superintendent, M. Lantin became enveloped in love as in a net.

She was the daughter of a provincial tax collector, who had been dead for several years. Afterward she had come to Paris with her mother, who made regular visits to several *bourgeois* families of the neighborhood, in hopes of being able to get her daughter married. They were poor and respectable, quiet and gentle. The young girl seemed to be the very ideal of that pure good woman to whom every young man dreams of entrusting his future. Her modest beauty had a charm of angelic shyness; and the slight smile that always dwelt about her lips seemed a reflection of her heart. plant

Everybody sang her praises; all who knew her kept saying: "The man who gets her will be lucky. No one could find a nicer girl than that."

M. Lantin, who was then chief clerk in the office of the Minister of the Interior, with a salary of 3,500 francs a year, asked for her hand, and married her.

He was unutterably happy with her. She ruled his home with an economy so adroit that they really seemed to live in luxury. It would be impossible to conceive of any attentions, tendernesses, playful caresses which she did not lavish upon her husband; and such was the charm of her person that, six years after he married her, he loved her even more than he did the first day.

There were only two points upon which he ever found fault with her —her love of the theatre, and her passion for false jewelry.

Her lady friends (she was acquainted with the wives of several small officeholders) were always bringing her tickets for the theatres; whenever there was a performance that made a sensation, she always had her loge secured, even for first performances; and she would drag her husband with her to all these entertainments, which used to tire him horribly after his day's work. So at last he begged her to go to the theatre with some lady acquaintances who would consent to see her home afterward. She refused for quite a while—thinking it would not look very well to go out thus unaccompanied by her husband. But finally she yielded, just to please him; and he felt infinitely grateful to her for it.

Now this passion for the theatre at last evoked in her the desire of dress. It was true that her *toilette* remained simple, always in good taste, but modest; and her sweet grace, her irresistible grace, ever smiling and shy, seemed to take fresh charm from the simplicity of her dresses. But she got into the habit of suspending in her pretty ears two big cut pebbles, fashioned in imitation of diamonds; and she wore necklaces of false pearls, bracelets of false gold, and haircombs studded with paste imitations of precious stones.

Her husband, who felt shocked by this love of tinsel and show, would often say: "My dear, when one has not the means to afford real jewelry, one should appear adorned with one's natural beauty and grace only—and these gifts are the rarest of jewels."

But she would smile sweetly and answer: "What does it matter? I like those things—that is my little whim. I know you are right; but one can't make oneself over again. I've always loved jewelry so much!"

And then she would roll the pearls of the necklaces between her fingers, and make the facets of the cut crystals flash in the light, repeating: "Now look at them—see how well the work is done. You would swear it was real jewelry."

He would then smile in his turn, and declare to her: "You have the tastes of a regular gypsy."

Sometimes, in the evening, when they were having a chat by the fire, she would rise and fetch the morocco box in which she kept her "stock" (as M. Lantin called it)—would put it on the tea table, and begin to examine the false jewelry with passionate delight, as if she experienced some secret and mysterious sensations of pleasure in their contemplation; and she would insist on putting one of the necklaces round her husband's neck, and laugh till she couldn't laugh any more, crying out: "Oh! how funny you look!" Then she would rush into his arms, and kiss him furiously.

One winter's night, after she had been to the Opera, she came home chilled through, and trembling. Next day she had a bad cough. Eight days after that, she died of pneumonia.

Lantin came close to following her into the tomb. His despair was so frightful that in one single month his hair turned white. He wept from morning till night, feeling his heart torn by inexpressible suffering, ever haunted by the memory of her, by the smile, by the voice, by all the charm of the dead woman.

Time did not assuage his grief. Often during office hours his fellow-clerks went off to a corner to chat about this or that topic of the day—his cheeks might have been seen to swell up all of a sudden, his nose wrinkle, his eyes fill with water; he would pull a frightful face, and begin to sob.

He had kept his dead companion's room just in the order she had left it, and he used to lock himself up in it every evening to think about her. All the furniture, and even all her dresses, remained in the same place they had been on the last day of her life.

But life became hard for him. His salary, which, in his wife's hands, had amply sufficed for all household needs, now proved scarcely sufficient to supply his own few wants. And he asked himself in astonishment how she had managed always to furnish him with excellent wines and with delicate eating which he could not now afford at all with his scanty means.

He got a little into debt, like men obliged to live by their wits. At last one morning when he happened to find himself without a cent in his pocket, and a whole week to wait before he could draw his monthly salary, he thought of selling something; and almost immediately it occurred to him to sell his wife's "stock"—for he had always borne a secret grudge against the flash-jewelry that used to annoy him so much in former days. The mere sight of it, day after day, somewhat spoiled the sad pleasure of thinking of his darling.

He tried a long time to make a choice among the heap of trinkets she had left behind her; for up to the very last day of her life she had kept obstinately buying them, bringing home some new thing almost every night. And finally he resolved to take the big pearl necklace which she used to like the best of all, and which he thought ought certainly to be worth six or eight francs, as it was really very nicely mounted for an imitation necklace.

He put it in his pocket, and walked toward the office, following the boulevards, and looking for some jewelry store on the way, where he could enter with confidence.

Finally he saw a place and went in; feeling a little ashamed of thus exposing his misery, and of trying to sell such a trifling object.

"Sir," he said to the jeweler, "please tell me what this is worth."

The jeweler took the necklace, examined it, weighed it, took up a magnifying glass, called his clerk, talked to him in whispers, put down the necklace on the counter, and drew back a little bit to judge of its effect at a distance.

M. Lantin, feeling very much embarrassed by all these ceremonies, opened his mouth and began to declare: "Oh? I know it can't be worth much" . . . when the jeweler interrupted him by saying:

"Well, sir, that is worth between twelve and fifteen thousand francs; but I cannot buy it unless you can let me know exactly how you came by it."

The widower's eyes opened enormously, and he stood gaping, unable to understand. Then after a while he stammered out: "You said? . . . Are you sure?" The jeweler, misconstruing the cause of this astonishment, replied in a dry tone: "Go elsewhere if you like, and see if you can get any more for it. The very most I would give for it is fifteen thousand. Come back and see me again, if you can't do better."

M. Lantin, feeling perfectly idiotic, took his necklace and departed; obeying a confused desire to find himself alone and to get a chance to think.

But the moment he found himself in the street again, he began to laugh, and he muttered to himself: "The fool! Oh! what a fool! If I had only taken him at his word. Well, well! A jeweler who can't tell paste from real jewelry!"

And he entered another jewelry store, at the corner of the Rue de la Paix. The moment the jeweler set eyes on the necklace, he exclaimed: "Hello! I know that necklace well—it was sold here!"

M. Lantin, very nervous, asked:

"What's it worth?"

"Sir, I sold it for twenty-five thousand francs. I am willing to buy it back again for eighteen thousand, if you can prove to me satisfactorily, according to legal prescriptions, how you came into possession of it." This time, M. Lantin was simply paralyzed with astonishment. He said: "Well . . . but please look at it again, sir. I always thought until now that it was . . . was false."

The jeweler said: "Will you give me your name, sir?"

"Certainly. My name is Lantin; I am employed at the office of the Minister of the Interior. I live at No. 16, Rue des Martyrs." symbol

The merchant opened the register, looked, and said: "Yes; this necklace was sent to the address of Madame Lantin, 16 Rue des Martyrs, on July 20, 1876."

And the two men looked into each other's eyes—the clerk wild with surprise; the jeweler suspecting he had a thief before him.

The jeweler resumed:

"Will you be kind enough to leave this article here for twenty-four hours only—I'll give you a receipt."

M. Lantin stuttered: "Yes—ah! certainly." And he went out, folding up the receipt, which he put in his pocket.

Then he crossed the street, went the wrong way, found out his mistake, returned by way of the Tuileries, crossed the Seine, found out he had taken the wrong road again, and went back to the Champs-Elysées without being able to get one clear idea into his head. He tried to reason, to understand. His wife could never have bought so valuable an object as that. Certainly not. But then, it must have been a present! . . . A present from whom? What for?

He stopped and stood stock-still in the middle of the avenue.

A horrible suspicion swept across his mind. . . . She? . . . But then all those other pieces of jewelry must have been presents also! . . . Then it seemed to him that the ground was heaving under his feet; that a tree, right in front of him, was falling toward him; he thrust out his arms instinctively, and fell senseless.

He recovered his consciousness again in a drug store to which some bystanders had carried him. He had them lead him home, and he locked himself into his room.

Until nightfall he cried without stopping, biting his handkerchief to keep himself from screaming out. Then, completely worn out with grief and fatigue, he went to bed, and slept a leaden sleep.

A ray of sunshine awakened him, and he rose and dressed himself slowly to go to the office. It was hard to have to work after such a shock. Then he reflected that he might be able to excuse himself to the superintendent, and he wrote to him. Then he remembered he would have to go back to the jeweler's; and shame made his face purple. He remained thinking a long time. Still he could not leave the necklace there; he put on his coat and went out.

It was a fine day; the sky extended all blue over the city, and seemed to make it smile. Strollers were walking aimlessly about, with their hands in their pockets.

Lantin thought as he watched them passing: "How lucky the men are who have fortunes! With money a man can even shake off grief. You can go where you please, travel, amuse yourself! Oh! if I were only rich!"

He suddenly discovered he was hungry, not having eaten anything since the evening before. But his pockets were empty; and he remembered the necklace. Eighteen thousand francs! Eighteen thousand francs! That was a sum—that was!

He made his way to the Rue de la Paix and began to walk backward and forward on the sidewalk in front of the store. Eighteen thousand francs! Twenty times he started to go in; but shame always kept him back.

Still he was hungry—very hungry—and had not a cent. He made one brusque resolve, and crossed the street almost at a run, so as not to let himself have time to think over the matter; and he rushed into the jeweler's.

As soon as he saw him, the merchant hurried forward, and offered him a chair with smiling politeness. Even the clerks came forward to stare at Lantin, with gaiety in their eyes and smiles about their lips.

The jeweler said: "Sir, I made inquiries; and if you are still so disposed, I am ready to pay you down the price I offered you."

The clerk stammered: "Why, yes—sir, certainly."

The jeweler took from a drawer eighteen big bills, counted them, and held them out to Lantin, who signed a little receipt, and thrust the money feverishly into his pocket.

Then, as he was on the point of leaving, he turned to the ever-smiling merchant, and said, lowering his eyes: "I have some—I have some other jewelry, which came to me in the same—from the same inheritance. Would you purchase them also from me?"

The merchant bowed, and answered: "Why, certainly, sir—certainly. . . ." One of the clerks rushed out to laugh at his ease; another kept blowing his nose as hard as he could.

Lantin, impassive, flushed and serious, said: "I will bring them to you."

And he hired a cab to get the jewelry.

When he returned to the store, an hour later, he had not yet lunched. They examined the jewelry, piece by piece, putting a value on each. Nearly all had been purchased from that very house.

Lantin, now, disputed estimates made, got angry, insisted on seeing the books, and talked louder and louder the higher the estimates grew.

The big diamond earrings were worth 20,000 francs; the bracelets, 35,000; the brooches, rings, and medallions, 16,000; a set of emeralds and sapphires, 14,000; a solitaire, suspended from a gold neckchain, 40,000; the total value being estimated at 196,000 francs.

The merchant observed with mischievous good nature: "The person who owned these must have put all her savings into jewelry."

Lantin answered with gravity: "Perhaps that is as good a way of saving money as any other." And he went off, after having agreed with the merchant that an expert should make a counter-estimate for him the next day.

When he found himself in the street again, he looked at the Vendôme Column with the desire to climb it, as if it were a May pole. He felt jolly enough to play leapfrog over the Emperor's head, up there in the blue sky.

He lunched at Voisin's restaurant, and ordered wine at 20 francs a bottle.

Then he hired a cab and drove out to the Bois. He looked at the carriages passing with a sort of contempt, and a wild desire to yell out to the passers-by: "I am rich, too—I am! I have 200,000 francs!"

The recollection of the office suddenly came back to him. He drove there, walked right into the superintendent's private room, and said: "Sir, I come to give you my resignation. I have just come into a fortune of *three* hundred thousand francs." Then he shook hands all round with his fellow-clerks; and told them all about his plans for a new career. Then he went to dinner at the Café Anglais.

Finding himself seated at the same table with a man who seemed to him quite genteel, he could not resist the itching desire to tell him, with a certain air of coquetry, that he had just inherited a fortune of *four* hundred thousand francs.

For the first time in his life he went to the theatre without feeling bored by the performance; and he spent the night in revelry and debauch.

Six months after he married again. His second wife was the most upright of spouses, but had a terrible temper. She made his life very miserable.

a twist - he was happy w/a tart who was able to fool him -

QUESTIONS FOR DISCUSSION

1. This story involves several radical changes in M. Lantin, beginning with his falling in love, ending with his euphoria over discovering himself rich. How are each of these changes handled? What devices or methods of presentation does De Maupassant employ in order to make them credible? Which ones do you find easiest to believe? Which ones most difficult? Why?
2. For what reasons can the ending of this story be called "dishonest"?
3. What parts of M. Lantin's story are dramatized? What parts are presented by exposition? Why do you think De Maupassant chose the method of presentation he did at each point in the story?
4. Define the theme of "The Jewelry." Then explain what relationship, if any, the ending of the story has to do with this theme. (You will later be asked to compare the ending of "The Jewelry" with that of "The Necklace.")

Hard for me to believe his change toward the money. He was horrified that his wife wasn't really what he thought she was -

GUY DE MAUPASSANT
The Necklace

She was one of those pretty and charming girls who are sometimes, as if by a mistake of destiny, born in a family of clerks. She had no dowry, no expectations, no means of being known, understood, loved, wedded by any rich and distinguished man; and she let herself be married to a little clerk at the Ministry of Public Instruction.

She dressed plainly because she could not dress well, but she was as unhappy as though she had really fallen from her proper station, since with women there is neither caste nor rank; and beauty, grace, and charm act instead of family and birth. Natural fineness, instinct for what is elegant, suppleness of wit, are the sole hierarchy, and make from women of the people the equals of the very greatest ladies.

She suffered ceaselessly, feeling herself born for all the delicacies and all the luxuries. She suffered from the poverty of her dwelling, from the wretched look of the walls, from the worn-out chairs, from the ugliness of the curtains. All those things, of which another woman of her rank would never even have been conscious, tortured her and made her angry. The sight of the little Breton peasant who did her humble housework aroused in her regrets which were despairing, and distracted dreams. She thought of the silent antechambers hung with Oriental tapestry, lit by tall bronze candelabra, and of the two great footmen in knee breeches who sleep in the big armchairs, made drowsy by the heavy warmth of the hot-air stove. She thought of the long *salons* fitted up with ancient silk, of the delicate furniture carrying priceless curiosities, and of the coquettish perfumed boudoirs made for talks at five o'clock with intimate friends, with men famous and sought after, whom all women envy and whose attention they all desire.

insight into character

When she sat down to dinner, before the round table covered with a tablecloth three days old, opposite her husband, who uncovered the soup tureen and declared with an enchanted air, "Ah, the good *pot-au-feu!* I don't know anything better than that," she thought of dainty dinners, of shining silverware, of tapestry which peopled the walls with ancient personages and with strange birds flying in the midst of a fairy forest; and she thought of delicious dishes served on marvelous plates, and of the whispered gallantries which you listen to with a sphinxlike smile, while you are eating the pink flesh of a trout or the wings of a quail.

She had no dresses, no jewels, nothing. And she loved nothing but that; she felt made for that. She would so have liked to please, to be envied, to be charming, to be sought after.

She had a friend, a former schoolmate at the convent, who was rich, and whom she did not like to go and see any more, because she suffered so much when she came back.

But one evening, her husband returned home with a triumphant air, and holding a large envelope in his hand.

"There," said he. "Here is something for you."

She tore the paper sharply, and drew out a printed card which bore these words:

"The Minister of Public Instruction and Mme. Georges Ramponneau request the honor of M. and Mme. Loisel's company at the palace of the Ministry on Monday evening, January eighteenth."

Instead of being delighted, as her husband hoped, she threw the invitation on the table with disdain, murmuring:

"What do you want me to do with that?"

"But, my dear, I thought you would be glad. You never go out, and this is such a fine opportunity. I had awful trouble to get it. Everyone wants to go; it is very select, and they are not giving many invitations to clerks. The whole official world will be there."

She looked at him with an irritated eye, and she said, impatiently:

"And what do you want me to put on my back?"

He had not thought of that; he stammered:

"Why, the dress you go to the theater in. It looks very well, to me."

He stopped, distracted, seeing that his wife was crying. Two great tears descended slowly from the corners of her eyes toward the corners of her mouth. He stuttered:

"What's the matter? What's the matter?"

But, by violent effort, she had conquered her grief, and she replied, with a calm voice, while she wiped her wet cheeks:

"Nothing. Only I have no dress and therefore I can't go to this ball. Give your card to some colleague whose wife is better equipped than I."

He was in despair. He resumed:

"Come, let us see, Mathilde. How much would it cost, a suitable dress, which you could use on other occasions, something very simple?"

She reflected several seconds, making her calculations and wondering also what sum she could ask without drawing on herself an immediate refusal and a frightened exclamation from the economical clerk.

Finally, she replied, hesitatingly:

"I don't know exactly, but I think I could manage it with four hundred francs."

He had grown a little pale, because he was laying aside just that

her reaction is believable

amount to buy a gun and treat himself to a little shooting next summer on the plain of Nanterre, with several friends who went to shoot larks down there, of a Sunday.

But he said:

"All right. I will give you four hundred francs. And try to have a pretty dress."

The day of the ball drew near, and Mme. Loisel seemed sad, uneasy, anxious. Her dress was ready, however. Her husband said to her one evening:

"What is the matter? Come, you've been so queer these last three days."

And she answered:

"It annoys me not to have a single jewel, not a single stone, nothing to put on. I shall look like distress. I should almost rather not go at all."

He resumed:

"You might wear natural flowers. It's very stylish at this time of the year. For ten francs you can get two or three magnificent roses."

She was not convinced.

"No; there's nothing more humiliating than to look poor among other women who are rich." Key to her character shallow

But her husband cried:

"How stupid you are! Go look up your friend Mme. Forestier, and ask her to lend you some jewels. You're quite thick enough with her to do that."

She uttered a cry of joy:

"It's true. I never thought of it."

The next day she went to her friend and told of her distress.

Mme. Forestier went to a wardrobe with a glass door, took out a large jewel-box, brought it back, opened it, and said to Mme. Loisel:

"Choose, my dear."

She saw first of all some bracelets, then a pearl necklace, then a Venetian cross, gold and precious stones of admirable workmanship. She tried on the ornaments before the glass, hesitated, could not make up her mind to part with them, to give them back. She kept asking:

"Haven't you any more?" never satisfied

"Why, yes. Look. I don't know what you like."

All of a sudden she discovered, in a black satin box, a superb necklace of diamonds, and her heart began to beat with an immoderate desire. Her hands trembled as she took it. She fastened it around her throat, outside her high-necked dress, and remained lost in ecstasy at the sight of herself.

Then she asked, hesitating, filled with anguish:

"Can you lend me that, only that?"

"Why, yes, certainly."

She sprang upon the neck of her friend, kissed her passionately, then fled with her treasure.

The day of the ball arrived. Mme. Loisel made a great success. She was prettier than them all, elegant, gracious, smiling, and crazy with joy. All the men looked at her, asked her name, endeavored to be introduced. All the attachés of the Cabinet wanted to waltz with her. She was remarked by the minister himself.

She danced with intoxication, with passion, made drunk by pleasure, forgetting all, in the triumph of her beauty, in the glory of her success, in a sort of cloud of happiness composed of all this homage, of all this admiration, of all these awakened desires, and of that sense of complete victory which is so sweet to a woman's heart.

She went away about four o'clock in the morning. Her husband had been sleeping since midnight, in a little deserted anteroom, with three other gentlemen whose wives were having a very good time. He threw over her shoulders the wraps which he had brought, modest wraps of common life, whose poverty contrasted with the elegance of the ball dress. She felt this, and wanted to escape so as not to be remarked by the other women, who were enveloping themselves in costly furs.

Loisel held her back.

"Wait a bit. You will catch cold outside. I will go and call a cab."

But she did not listen to him, and rapidly descended the stairs. When they were in the street they did not find a carriage; and they began to look for one, shouting after the cabmen whom they saw passing by at a distance.

They went down toward the Seine, in despair, shivering with cold. At last they found on the quay one of those ancient noctambulant coupés which, exactly as if they were ashamed to show their misery during the day, are never seen round Paris until after nightfall.

It took them to their door in the Rue des Martyrs, and once more, sadly, they climbed up homeward. All was ended, for her. And as to him, he reflected that he must be at the Ministry at ten o'clock.

She removed the wraps, which covered her shoulders, before the glass, so as once more to see herself in all her glory. But suddenly she uttered a cry. She had no longer the necklace around her neck!

Her husband, already half undressed, demanded:

"What is the matter with you?"

She turned madly towards him:

"I have—I have—I've lost Mme. Forestier's necklace."

He stood up, distracted.

"What!—how?—impossible!"

And they looked in the folds of her dress, in the folds of her cloak, in her pockets, everywhere. They did not find it.

He asked:

"You're sure you had it on when you left the ball?"

"Yes, I felt it in the vestibule of the palace."

"But if you had lost it in the street we should have heard it fall. It must be in the cab."

"Yes. Probably. Did you take his number?"

"No. And you, didn't you notice it?"

"No."

They looked, thunderstruck, at one another. At last Loisel put on his clothes.

"I shall go back on foot," said he, "over the whole route which we have taken to see if I can find it."

And he went out. She sat waiting on a chair in her ball dress, without strength to go to bed, overwhelmed, without fire, without a thought.

Her husband came back about seven o'clock. He had found nothing.

He went to Police Headquarters, to the newspaper offices, to offer a reward; he went to the cab companies—everywhere, in fact, whither he was urged by the least suspicion of hope.

She waited all day, in the same condition of mad fear before this terrible calamity.

Loisel returned at night with a hollow, pale face; he had discovered nothing.

"You must write to your friend," said he, "that you have broken the clasp of her necklace and that you are having it mended. That will give us time to turn round."

She wrote at his dictation.

At the end of a week they had lost all hope.

And Loisel, who had aged five years, declared:

"We must consider how to replace that ornament."

The next day they took the box which had contained it, and they went to the jeweler whose name was found within. He consulted his books.

"It was not I, madame, who sold that necklace; I must simply have furnished the case."

Then they went from jeweler to jeweler, searching for a necklace like the other, consulting their memories, sick both of them with chagrin and anguish.

They found, in a shop at the Palais Royal, a string of diamonds which seemed to them exactly like the one they looked for. It was worth forty thousand francs. They could have it for thirty-six.

So they begged the jeweler not to sell it for three days yet. And they made a bargain that he should buy it back for thirty-four thousand francs, in case they found the other one before the end of February.

Loisel possessed eighteen thousand francs which his father had left him. He would borrow the rest.

He did borrow, asking a thousand francs of one, five hundred of another, five louis here, three louis there. He gave notes, took up ruinous obligations, dealt with usurers and all the race of lenders. He compromised all the rest of his life, risked his signature without even knowing if he could meet it, and, frightened by the pains yet to come, by the black misery which was about to fall upon him, by the prospect of all the physical privations and of all the moral tortures which he was to suffer, he went to get the new necklace, putting down upon the merchant's counter thirty-six thousand francs.

When Mme. Loisel took back the necklace, Mme. Forestier said to her, with a chilly manner:

"You should have returned it sooner; I might have needed it."

She did not open the case, as her friend had so much feared. If she had detected the substitution, what would she have thought, what would she had said? Would she not have taken Mme. Loisel for a thief?

Mme. Loisel now knew the horrible existence of the needy. She took her part, moreover, all of a sudden, with heroism. That dreadful debt must be paid. She would pay it. They dismissed their servant; they changed their lodgings; they rented a garret under the roof.

She came to know what heavy housework meant and the odious cares of the kitchen. She washed the dishes, using her rosy nails on the greasy pots and pans. She washed the dirty linen, the shirts, and the dishcloths, which she dried upon a line; she carried the slops down to the street every morning, and carried up the water, stopping for breath at every landing. And, dressed like a woman of the people, she went to the fruiterer, the grocer, the butcher, her basket on her arm, bargaining, insulted, defending her miserable money sou by sou.

Each month they had to meet some notes, renew others, obtain more time.

Her husband worked in the evening making a fair copy of some tradesman's accounts, and late at night he often copied manuscript for five sous a page.

And this life lasted for ten years.

At the end of ten years, they had paid everything, everything, with the rates of usury, and the accumulations of the compound interest.

Mme. Loisel looked old now. She had become the woman of impoverished households—strong and hard and rough. With frowsy hair, skirts askew, and red hands, she talked loud while washing the floor with great swishes of water. But sometimes, when her husband was at the office, she sat down near the window, and she thought of that gay evening of long ago, of that ball where she had been so beautiful and so fêted.

What would have happened if she had not lost that necklace? Who knows? Who knows? How life is strange and changeful! How little a thing is needed for us to be lost or to be saved!

But, one Sunday, having gone to take a walk in the Champs Elysées to refresh herself from the labor of the week, she suddenly perceived a woman who was leading a child. It was Mme. Forestier, still young, still beautiful, still charming.

Mme. Loisel felt moved. Was she going to speak to her? Yes, certainly. And now that she had paid, she was going to tell her all about it. Why not?

She went up.

"Good-day, Jeanne."

The other, astonished to be familiarly addressed by this plain goodwife, did not recognize her at all, and stammered:

"But—madam!—I do not know—You must be mistaken."

"No. I am Mathilde Loisel."

Her friend uttered a cry.

"Oh, my poor Mathilde! How you are changed!"

"Yes, I have had days hard enough, since I have seen you, days wretched enough—and that because of you!"

"Of me! How so?"

"Do you remember that diamond necklace which you lent me to wear at the ministerial ball?"

"Yes. Well?"

"Well, I lost it."

"What do you mean? You brought it back."

"I brought you back another just like it. And for this we have been ten years paying. You can understand that it was not easy for us, us who had nothing. At last it is ended, and I am very glad."

Mme. Forestier had stopped.

"You say that you bought a necklace of diamonds to replace mine?"

"Yes. You never noticed it, then! They were very like."

And she smiled with a joy which was proud and naïve at once.

Mme. Forestier, strongly moved, took her two hands.

"Oh, my poor Mathilde! Why, my necklace was paste. It was worth at most five hundred francs!"

QUESTIONS FOR DISCUSSION

1. "The Necklace" *seems* to be built on a number of coincidences. List *all* of the turning points in the story. Then discuss Mme. Loisel's motivation at each of these points. Are these turning points coincidental (manipulated) or not? Consider particularly at each point Mme. Loisel's alternatives, her choices of action.
2. What is Mme. Loisel's dominant character trait? What are her values? What change does she undergo after the loss of the necklace? Is this a change in trait or not? Now compare the *way* in which Mme. Loisel is presented to us with the way either M. Lantin or his wife are presented to us in "The Jewelry." What are the differences in terms of plausibility, complexity, and so on?
3. Compare very carefully the opening and ending of the story, noting

in particular Mme. Loisel's "mood," her "frame of mind" in each section. Then comment on whether the story has a happy or an unhappy ending.

4. Compare the surprise ending of "The Jewelry" to that of "The Necklace." What is the relationship of each *to the rest of the story*? Does either ending "distract," "jerk your mind away from" the rest of the story? Does either ending force you instead to think harder about the rest of the story?
5. Define the point of view of "The Necklace." In terms of the point of view, could the disclosure at the end of the story have *plausibly* occurred at any other point in the story—that is, does the author "cheat" by withholding information for the sake of his surprise ending? Now define the point of view of "The Jewelry." Can you find any differences between the two stories in this respect?
6. What is the theme of "The Necklace"? What has the ending (including the necklace, used as symbol) to do with this theme? In other words, does this ending "illuminate" the theme of the story? Can the same be said for the ending of "The Jewelry"?

Turn of the Screw

HENRY JAMES
Paste

"I've found a lot more things," her cousin said to her the day after the second funeral; "they're up in her room—but they're things I wish *you'd* look at."

The pair of mourners, sufficiently stricken, were in the garden of the vicarage together, before luncheon, waiting to be summoned to that meal, and Arthur Prime had still in his face the intention, she was moved to call it rather than the expression, of feeling something or other. Some such appearance was in itself of course natural within a week of his step-mother's death, within three of his father's; but what was most present to the girl, herself sensitive and shrewd, was that he seemed somehow to brood without sorrow, to suffer without what she in her own case would have called pain. He turned away from her after this last speech—it was a good deal his habit to drop an observation and leave her to pick it up without assistance. If the vicar's widow, now in her turn finally translated, had not really belonged to him it was not for want of her giving herself, so far as he ever would take her; and she had lain for three days all alone at the end of the passage, in the great cold chamber of hospitality, the dampish greenish room where visitors slept and where several of the ladies of the parish had, without effect, offered, in pairs and successions, piously to watch with her. His personal connexion with the parish was now slighter than ever, and he had really not waited for this opportunity to show the ladies what he thought of them. She felt that she herself had, during her doleful month's leave from Bleet, where she was governess, rather taken her place in the same snubbed order; but it was presently, none the less, with a better little hope of coming in for some remembrance, some relic, that she went up to look at the things he had spoken of, the identity of which, as a confused cluster of bright objects on a table in the darkened room, shimmered at her as soon as she had opened the door.

They met her eyes for the first time, but in a moment, before touching them, she knew them as things of the theatre, as very much too fine to have been with any verisimilitude things of the vicarage. They were too dreadfully good to be true, for her aunt had had no jewels to speak of, and these were coronets and girdles, diamonds, rubies and sapphires. Flagrant tinsel and glass, they looked strangely vulgar, but if after the first queer shock of them she found herself taking them up it was for the very proof, never yet so distinct to her, of a far-off faded story. An honest widowed cleric with a small son and a large sense of Shakespeare had, on a brave latitude of habit as well as of taste—since it implied his having in very fact dropped deep into the "pit"—conceived for an obscure actress several years older than himself an admiration of which the prompt offer of his reverend name and hortatory hand was the sufficiently candid sign. The response had perhaps in those dim years, so far as eccentricity was concerned, even bettered the proposal, and Charlotte, turning the tale over, had long since drawn from it a measure of the career renounced by the undistinguished comédienne—doubtless also tragic, or perhaps pantomimic, at a pinch—of her late uncle's dreams. This career could n't have been eminent and must much more probably have been comfortless.

"You see what it is—old stuff of the time she never liked to mention."

Our young woman gave a start; her companion had after all rejoined her and had apparently watched a moment her slightly scared recognition. "So I said to myself," she replied. Then to show intelligence, yet keep clear of twaddle: "How peculiar they look!"

"They look awful," said Arthur Prime. "Cheap gilt, diamonds as big as potatoes. These are trappings of a ruder age than ours. Actors do themselves better now."

"Oh now," said Charlotte, not to be less knowing, "actresses have real diamonds."

"Some of them." Arthur spoke dryly.

"I mean the bad ones—the nobodies too."

"Oh some of the nobodies have the biggest. But mamma was n't of that sort."

"A nobody?" Charlotte risked.

"Not a nobody to whom somebody—well, not a nobody with diamonds. It is n't all worth, this trash, five pounds."

There was something in the old gewgaws that spoke to her, and she continued to turn them over. "They're relics. I think they have their melancholy and even their dignity."

Arthur observed another pause. "Do you care for them?" he then asked. "I mean," he promptly added, "as a souvenir."

"Of you?" Charlotte threw off.

"Of me? What have I to do with it? Of your poor dead aunt who was so kind to you," he said with virtuous sternness.

"Well, I'd rather have them than nothing."

"Then please take them," he returned in a tone of relief which expressed somehow more of the eager than of the gracious.

"Thank you." Charlotte lifted two or three objects up and set them down again. Though they were lighter than the materials they imitated they were so much more extravagant that they struck her in truth as rather an awkward heritage, to which she might have preferred even a matchbox or a penwiper. They were indeed shameless pinchbeck. "Had you any idea she had kept them?"

"I don't at all believe she *had* kept them or knew they were there, and I'm very sure my father did n't. They had quite equally worked off any tenderness for the connexion. These odds and ends, which she thought had been given away or destroyed, had simply got thrust into a dark corner and been forgotten."

Charlotte wondered. "Where then did you find them?"

"In that old tin box"—and the young man pointed to the receptacle from which he had dislodged them and which stood on a neighbouring chair. "It's rather a good box still, but I'm afraid I can't give you *that*."

The girl took no heed of the box; she continued only to look at the trinkets. "What corner had she found?"

"She had n't 'found' it," her companion sharply insisted; "she had simply lost it. The whole thing had passed from her mind. The box was on the top shelf of the old school-room closet, which, until one put one's head into it from a step-ladder, looked, from below, quite cleared out. The door's narrow and the part of the closet to the left goes well into the wall. The box had stuck there for years."

Charlotte was conscious of a mind divided and a vision vaguely troubled, and once more she took up two or three of the subjects of this revelation; a big bracelet in the form of a gilt serpent with many twists and beady eyes, a brazen belt studded with emeralds and rubies, a chain, of flamboyant architecture, to which, at the Theatre Royal Little Peddlington, Hamlet's mother must have been concerned to attach the portrait of the successor to Hamlet's father. "Are you very sure they're not really worth something? Their mere weight alone—!" she vaguely observed, balancing a moment a royal diadem that might have crowned one of the creations of the famous Mrs. Jarley.

But Arthur Prime, it was clear, had already thought the question over and found the answer easy. "If they had been worth anything to speak of she would long ago have sold them. My father and she had unfortunately never been in a position to keep any considerable value locked up." And while his companion took in the obvious force of this he went on with a flourish just marked enough not to escape her: "If they're worth anything at all—why you're only the more welcome to them."

Charlotte had now in her hand a small bag of faded figured silk—one of those antique conveniences that speak to us, in terms of evaporated camphor and lavender, of the part they have played in some personal history; but though she had for the first time drawn the string she looked much more at the young man than at the questionable treasure it appeared to contain. "I shall like them. They're all I have."

"All you have—?"

"That belonged to her."

He swelled a little, then looked about him as if to appeal—as against her avidity—to the whole poor place. "Well, what else do you want?"

"Nothing. Thank you very much." With which she bent her eyes on the article wrapped, and now only exposed, in her superannuated satchel—a string of large pearls, such a shining circle as might once have graced the neck of a provincial Ophelia and borne company to a flaxen wig. "This perhaps *is* worth something. Feel it." And she passed him the necklace, the weight of which she had gathered for a moment into her hand.

He measured it in the same way with his own, but remained quite detached. "Worth at most thirty shillings."

"Not more?"

"Surely not if it's paste?"

"But *is* it paste?"

He gave a small sniff of impatience. "Pearls nearly as big as filberts?"

"But they're heavy," Charlotte declared.

"No heavier than anything else." And he gave them back with an allowance for her simplicity. "Do you imagine for a moment they're real?"

She studied them a little, feeling them, turning them round. "Might n't they possibly be?"

"Of that size—stuck away with that trash?"

"I admit it is n't likely," Charlotte presently said. "And pearls are so easily imitated."

"That's just what—to a person who knows—they're not. These have no lustre, no play."

"No—they *are* dull. They're opaque."

"Besides," he lucidly enquired, "how could she ever have come by them?"

"Might n't they have been a present?"

Arthur stared at the question as if it were almost improper. "Because actresses are exposed—?" He pulled up, however, not saying to what, and before she could supply the deficiency had, with the sharp ejaculation of "No, they might n't!" turned his back on her and walked away. His manner made her feel she had probably been wanting in tact, and before he returned to the subject, the last thing that evening, she had satisfied herself of the ground of his resentment. They had been talking of her departure the next morning, the hour of her train and the fly that would come for her, and it was precisely these things that gave him his effective chance. "I really can't allow you to leave the house under the impression that my stepmother was at *any* time of her life the sort of person to allow herself to be approached—"

"With pearl necklaces and that sort of thing?" Arthur had made for her somehow the difficulty that she could n't show him she understood him without seeming pert.

It at any rate only added to his own gravity. "That sort of thing, exactly."

"I didn't think when I spoke this morning—but I see what you mean."

"I mean that she was beyond reproach," said Arthur Prime.

"A hundred times yes."

"Therefore if she could n't, out of her slender gains, ever have paid for a row of pearls—"

"She could n't, in that atmosphere, ever properly have had one? Of course she could n't. I've seen perfectly since our talk," Charlotte went on, "that that string of beads is n't even as an imitation very good. The little clasp itself does n't seem even gold. With false pearls, I suppose," the girl mused, "it naturally would n't be."

"The whole thing's rotten paste," her companion returned as if to have done with it. "If it were *not*, and she had kept it all these years hidden—"

"Yes?" Charlotte sounded as he paused.

"Why I should n't know what to think!"

"Oh I see." She had met him with a certain blankness, but adequately enough, it seemed, for him to regard the subject as dismissed; and there was no reversion to it between them before, on the morrow, when she had with difficulty made a place for them in her trunk, she carried off these florid survivals.

At Bleet she found small occasion to revert to them and, in an air charged with such quite other references, even felt, after she had laid them away, much enshrouded, beneath various piles of clothing, that they formed a collection not wholly without its note of the ridiculous. Yet she was never, for the joke, tempted to show them to her pupils, though Gwendolen and Blanche in particular always wanted, on her return, to know what she had brought back; so that without an accident by which the case was quite changed they might have appeared to enter on a new phase of interment. The essence of the accident was the sudden illness, at the last moment, of Lady Bobby, whose advent had been so much counted on to spice the five days' feast laid out for the coming of age of the eldest son of the house; and its equally marked effect was the dispatch of a pressing message, in quite another direction, to Mrs. Guy, who, could she by a miracle be secured—she was always engaged ten parties deep—might be trusted to supply, it was believed, an element of exuberance scarcely less potent. Mrs. Guy was already known to several of the visitors already on the scene, but she was n't yet known to our young lady, who found her, after many wires and counterwires had at last determined the triumph of her arrival, a strange charming little red-haired black-dressed woman, a person with the face of a baby and the authority of a commodore. She took on the spot the discreet, the exceptional young governess into the confidence of her designs and, still more, of her doubts; intimating that it was a policy she almost always promptly pursued.

"To-morrow and Thursday are all right," she said frankly to Charlotte on the second day, "but I'm not half-satisfied with Friday."

"What improvement then do you suggest?"

"Well, my strong point, you know, is *tableaux vivants*."

"Charming. And what is your favourite character?"

"Boss!" said Mrs. Guy with decision; and it was very markedly under that ensign that she had, within a few hours, completely planned her campaign and recruited her troop. Every word she uttered was to the point, but none more so than, after a general survey of their equipment, her final enquiry of Charlotte. She had been looking about, but half-appeased, at the muster of decoration and drapery. "We shall be dull. We shall want more colour. You've nothing else?"

Charlotte had a thought. "No—I've *some* things."

"Then why don't you bring them?"

The girl weighed it. "Would you come to my room?"

"No," said Mrs. Guy—"bring them to-night to mine."

So Charlotte, at the evening's end, after candlesticks had flickered through brown old passages bedward, arrived at her friend's door with the burden of her aunt's relics. But she promptly expressed a fear. "Are they too garish?"

When she had poured them out on the sofa Mrs. Guy was but a minute, before the glass, in clapping on the diadem. "Awfully jolly—we can do Ivanhoe!"

"But they're only glass and tin."

"Larger than life they are, *rather!*—which is exactly what's wanted for tableaux. *Our* jewels, for historic scenes, don't tell—the real thing falls short. Rowena must have rubies as big as eggs. Leave them with me," Mrs. Guy continued—"they'll inspire me. Good-night."

The next morning she was in fact—yet very strangely—inspired. "Yes, *I'll* do Rowena. But I don't, my dear, understand."

"Understand what?"

Mrs. Guy gave a very lighted stare. "How you come to have such things."

Poor Charlotte smiled. "By inheritance."

"Family jewels?"

"They belonged to my aunt, who died some months ago. She was on the stage a few years in early life, and these are a part of her trappings."

"She left them to you?"

"No; my cousin, her stepson, who naturally has no use for them, gave them to me for remembrance of her. She was a dear kind thing, always so nice to me, and I was fond of her."

Mrs. Guy had listened with frank interest. "But it's *he* who must be a dear kind thing!"

Charlotte wondered. "You think so?"

"Is *he*," her friend went on, "also 'always so nice' to you?"

The girl, at this, face to face there with the brilliant visitor in the deserted breakfast-room, took a deeper sounding. "What is it?"

"Don't you know?"

Something came over her. "The pearls—?" But the question fainted on her lips.

"Does n't *he* know?"

Charlotte found herself flushing. "They're *not* paste?"

"Haven't you looked at them?"

She was conscious of two kinds of embarrassment. "*You* have?"

"Very carefully."

"And they're real?"

Mrs. Guy became slightly mystifying and returned for all answer: "Come again, when you've done with the children, to my room."

Our young woman found she had done with the children that morning so promptly as to reveal to them a new joy, and when she reappeared before Mrs. Guy this lady had already encircled a plump white throat with the only ornament, surely, in all the late Mrs. Prime's—the effaced Miss Bradshaw's—collection, in the least qualified to raise a question. If Charlotte had never yet once, before the glass, tied the string of pearls about her own neck, this was because she had been capable of no such stoop to approved "imitation"; but she had now only to look at Mrs. Guy to see that, so disposed, the ambiguous objects might have passed for frank originals. "What in the world have you done to them?"

"Only handled them, understood them, admired them and put them on. That's what pearls want; they want to be worn—it wakes them up. They're alive, don't you see? How *have* these been treated? They must have been buried, ignored, despised. They were half-dead. Don't you *know* about pearls?" Mrs. Guy threw off as she fondly fingered the necklace.

"How *should* I? Do *you?*"

"Everything. These were simply asleep, and from the moment I really touched them—well," said their wearer lovingly, "it only took one's eye!"

"It took more than mine—though I did just wonder; and than Arthur's," Charlotte brooded. She found herself almost panting. "Then their value—?"

"Oh their value's excellent."

The girl, for a deep contemplative moment, took another plunge into the wonder, the beauty and the mystery. "Are you *sure?*"

Her companion wheeled round for impatience. "Sure? For what kind of an idiot, my dear, do you take me?"

It was beyond Charlotte Prime to say. "For the same kind as Arthur —and as myself," she could only suggest. "But my cousin did n't know. He thinks they're worthless."

"Because of the rest of the lot? Then your cousin's an ass. But what— if, as I understood you, he gave them to you—has he to do with it?"

"Why if he gave them to me as worthless and they turn out precious—!"

"You must give them back? I don't see that—if he was such a noodle. He took the risk."

Charlotte fed, in fancy, on the pearls, which decidedly were exquisite, but which at the present moment somehow presented themselves much more as Mrs. Guy's than either as Arthur's or as her own. "Yes—he did take it; even after I had distinctly hinted to him that they looked to me different from the other pieces."

"Well then!" said Mrs. Guy with something more than triumph—with a positive odd relief.

But it had the effect of making our young woman think with more intensity. "Ah you see he thought they could n't be different, because—so peculiarly—they should n't be."

"Should n't? I don't understand."

"Why how would she have got them?"—so Charlotte candidly put it.

"She? Who?" There was a capacity in Mrs. Guy's tone for a sinking of persons—!

"Why the person I told you of: his stepmother, my uncle's wife— among whose poor old things, extraordinarily thrust away and out of sight, he happened to find them."

Mrs. Guy came a step nearer to the effaced Miss Bradshaw. "Do you mean she may have stolen them?"

"No. But she had been an actress."

"Oh well then," cried Mrs. Guy, "would n't that be just how?"

"Yes, except that she wasn't at all a brillant one, nor in receipt of large pay." The girl even threw off a nervous joke. "I'm afraid she could n't have been our Rowena."

Mrs. Guy took it up. "Was she very ugly?"

"No. She may very well, when young, have looked rather nice."

"Well then!" was Mrs. Guy's sharp comment and fresh triumph.

"You mean it was a present? That's just what he so dislikes the idea of her having received—a present from an admirer capable of going such lengths."

"Because she would n't have taken it for nothing? *Speriamo*—that she wasn't a brute. The 'length' her admirer went was the length of the whole row. Let us hope she was just a little kind!"

"Well," Charlotte went on, "that she was 'kind' might seem to be shown by the fact that neither her husband, nor his son, nor I, his niece, knew or dreamed of her possessing anything so precious; by her having kept the gift all the rest of her life beyond discovery—out of sight and protected from suspicion."

"As if you mean"—Mrs. Guy was quick—"she had been wedded to it and yet was ashamed of it? Fancy," she laughed while she manipulated the rare beads, "being ashamed of *these!*"

"But you see she had married a clergyman."

"Yes, she must have been 'rum.' But at any rate he had married *her*. What did he suppose?"

"Why that she had never been of the sort by whom such offerings are encouraged."

"Ah my dear, the sort by whom they're *not*—!" But Mrs. Guy caught herself up. "And her stepson thought the same?"

"Overwhelmingly."

"Was he then, if only her stepson—"

"So fond of her as that comes to? Yes; he had never known, consciously, his real mother, and, without children of her own, she was very patient and nice with him. And *I* liked her so," the girl pursued, "that at the end of ten years, in so strange a manner, to 'give her away'—"

"Is impossible to you? Then don't!" said Mrs. Guy with decision.

"Ah but if they're real I can't keep them!" Charlotte, with her eyes on them, moaned in her impatience. "It's too difficult."

"Where's the difficulty, if he has such sentiments that he'd rather sacrifice the necklace than admit it, with the presumption it carries with it, to be genuine? You've only to be silent."

"And keep it? How can *I* ever wear it?"

"You'd have to hide it, like your aunt?" Mrs. Guy was amused. "You can easily sell it."

Her companion walked round her for a look at the affair from behind. The clasp was certainly, doubtless intentionally, misleading, but everything else was indeed lovely. "Well, I must think. Why did n't *she* sell them?" Charlotte broke out in her trouble.

Mrs. Guy had an instant answer. "Does n't that prove what they secretly recalled to her? You've only to be silent!" she ardently repeated.

"I must think—I must think!"

Mrs. Guy stood with her hands attached but motionless. "Then you want them back?"

As if with the dread of touching them Charlotte retreated to the door. "I'll tell you to-night."

"But may I wear them?"

"Meanwhile?"

"This evening—at dinner."

It was the sharp selfish pressure of this that really, on the spot, determined the girl; but for the moment, before closing the door on the question, she only said: "As you like!"

They were busy much of the day with preparation and rehearsal, and at dinner that evening the concourse of guests was such that a place among them for Miss Prime failed to find itself marked. At the time the company rose she was therefore alone in the school-room, where, towards eleven o'clock, she received a visit from Mrs. Guy. This lady's white shoulders heaved, under the pearls, with an emotion that the very red lips which formed, as if for the full effect, the happiest opposition of colour, were not slow to translate. "My dear, you should have seen the sensation—they've had a success!"

Charlotte, dumb a moment, took it all in. "It *is* as if they knew it—they're more and more alive. But so much the worse for both of us! I can't," she brought out with an effort, "be silent."

"You mean to return them?"

"If I don't I'm a thief."

Mrs. Guy gave her a long hard look: what was decidedly not of the baby in Mrs. Guy's face was a certain air of established habit in the eyes. Then, with a sharp little jerk of her head and a backward reach of her bare beautiful arms, she undid the clasp and, taking off the necklace, laid it on the table. "If you do you're a goose."

"Well, of the two—!" said our young lady, gathering it up with a sigh. And as if to get it, for the pang it gave, out of sight as soon as possible, she shut it up, clicking the lock, in the drawer of her own little table; after which, when she turned again, her companion looked naked and plain without it. "But what will you say?" it then occurred to her to demand.

"Downstairs—to explain?" Mrs. Guy was after all trying at least to keep her temper. "Oh I'll put on something else and say the clasp's broken. And you won't of course name *me* to him," she added.

"As having undeceived me? No—I'll say that, looking at the thing more carefully, it's my own private idea."

"And does he know how little you really know?"

"As an expert—surely. And he has always much the conceit of his own opinion."

"Then he won't believe you—as he so hates to. He'll stick to his judgement and maintain his gift, and we shall have the darlings back!" With which reviving assurance Mrs. Guy kissed her young friend for good-night.

She was not, however, to be gratified or justified by any prompt event, for, whether or no paste entered into the composition of the ornament in question, Charlotte shrank from the temerity of dispatching it to town by post. Mrs. Guy was thus disappointed of the hope of seeing the business settled—"by return," she had seemed to expect—before the end of the revels. The revels, moreover, rising to a frantic pitch, pressed for all her attention, and it was at last only in the general confusion of leave-taking that she made, parenthetically, a dash at the person in the whole company with whom her contact had been most interesting.

"Come, what will you take for them?"

"The pearls? Ah, you'll have to treat with my cousin."

Mrs. Guy, with quick intensity, lent herself. "Where then does he live?"

"In chambers in the Temple. You can find him."

"But what's the use, if *you* do neither one thing nor the other?"

"Oh I *shall* do the 'other,'" Charlotte said: "I'm only waiting till I go up. You want them so awfully?" She curiously, solemnly again, sounded her.

"I'm dying for them. There's a special charm in them—I don't know what it is: they tell so their history."

"But what do you know of that?"

"Just what they themselves say. It's all *in* them—and it comes out. They breathe a tenderness—they have the white glow of it. My dear," hissed Mrs. Guy in supreme confidence and as she buttoned her glove —"they're things of love!"

"Oh!" our young woman vaguely exclaimed.

"They're things of passion!"

"Mercy!" she gasped, turning short off. But these words remained, though indeed their help was scarce needed, Charlotte being in private face to face with a new light, as she by this time felt she must call it, on the dear dead kind colourless lady whose career had turned so sharp a corner in the middle. The pearls had quite taken their place as a revelation. She might have received them for nothing—admit that; but she could n't have kept them so long and so unprofitably hidden, could n't have enjoyed them only in secret, for nothing; and she had mixed them in her reliquary with false things in order to put curiosity and detection off the scent. Over this strange fact poor Charlotte interminably mused: it became more touching, more attaching for her than she could now confide to any ear. How bad or how happy—in the sophisticated sense of Mrs. Guy and the young man at the Temple—the effaced Miss Bradshaw must have been to have had to be so mute! The little governess at Bleet put on the necklace now in secret sessions; she wore it sometimes under her dress; she came to feel verily a haunting passion for it. Yet in her penniless state she would have parted with it for money; she gave herself also to dreams of what in this direction it would do for her. The sophistry of her so often saying to herself that Arthur had after all definitely pronounced her welcome to any gain from his gift that might accrue—this trick remained innocent, as she perfectly knew it for what it was. Then there was always the possibility of his—as she could only picture it—rising to the occasion. Might n't he have a grand magnanimous moment?—might n't he just say "Oh I could n't of course have afforded to let you have it if I had known; but since you *have* got it, and have made out the truth by your own wit, I really can't screw myself down to the shabbiness of taking it back"?

She had, as it proved, to wait a long time—to wait till, at the end of several months, the great house of Bleet had, with due deliberation, for the season, transferred itself to town; after which, however, she fairly snatched at her first freedom to knock, dressed in her best and armed with her disclosure, at the door of her doubting kinsman. It was still with doubt and not quite with the face she had hoped that he listened to her story. He had turned pale, she thought, as she produced the necklace, and he appeared above all disagreeably affected. Well, perhaps there was reason, she more than ever remembered; but what on earth was one, in close touch with the fact, to do? She had laid the pearls on his table, where, without his having at first put so much as a finger to them, they met his hard cold stare.

"I don't believe in them," he simply said at last.

"That's exactly then," she returned with some spirit, "what I wanted to hear!"

She fancied that at this his colour changed; it was indeed vivid to her afterwards—for she was to have a long recall of the scene—that she had made him quite angrily flush. "It's a beastly unpleasant imputation, you know!"—and he walked away from her as he had always walked at the vicarage.

"It's none of *my* making, I'm sure," said Charlotte Prime. "If you're afraid to believe they're real—"

"Well?"—and he turned, across the room, sharp round at her.

"Why it's not my fault."

He said nothing more, for a moment, on this; he only came back to the table. "They're what I originally said they were. They're rotten paste."

"Then I may keep them?"

"No. I want a better opinion."

"Than your own?"

"Than *your* own." He dropped on the pearls another queer stare; then, after a moment, bringing himself to touch them, did exactly what she had herself done in the presence of Mrs. Guy at Bleet—gathered them together, marched off with them to a drawer, put them in and clicked the key. "You say I'm afraid," he went on as he again met her; "but I shan't be afraid to take them to Bond Street."

"And if the people say they're real—"

He had a pause and then his strangest manner. "They won't say it! They shan't!"

There was something in the way he brought it out that deprived poor Charlotte, as she was perfectly aware, of any manner at all. "Oh!" she simply sounded, as she had sounded for her last word to Mrs. Guy; and within a minute, without more conversation, she had taken her departure.

A fortnight later she received a communication from him, and toward the end of the season one of the entertainments in Eaton Square was graced by the presence of Mrs. Guy. Charlotte was not at dinner, but she came down afterwards, and this guest, on seeing her, abandoned a very beautiful young man on purpose to cross and speak to her. The guest displayed a lovely necklace and had apparently not lost her habit of overflowing with the pride of such ornaments.

"Do you see?" She was in high joy.

They were indeed splendid pearls—so far as poor Charlotte could feel that she knew, after what had come and gone, about such mysteries. The poor girl had a sickly smile. "They're almost as fine as Arthur's."

"Almost? Where, my dear, are your eyes? They *are* 'Arthur's'!" After which, to meet the flood of crimson that accompanied her young friend's start: "I tracked them—after your folly, and, by miraculous luck, recognised them in the Bond Street window to which he had disposed of them."

"*Disposed* of them?" Charlotte gasped. "He wrote me that I had insulted his mother and that the people had shown him he was right—had pronounced them utter paste."

Mrs. Guy gave a stare. "Ah I told you he would n't bear it! No. But I had, I assure you," she wound up, "to drive my bargain!"

Charlotte scarce heard or saw; she was full of her private wrong. "He wrote me," she panted, "that he had smashed them."

Mrs. Guy could only wonder and pity. "He's really morbid!" But it was n't quite clear which of the pair she pitied; though the young person employed in Eaton Square felt really morbid too after they had separated and she found herself full of thought. She even went the length of asking herself what sort of a bargain Mrs. Guy had driven and whether the marvel of the recognition in Bond Street had been a veracious account of the matter. Hadn't she perhaps in truth dealt with Arthur directly? It came back to Charlotte almost luridly that she had had his address.

QUESTIONS FOR DISCUSSION

1. What are the most obvious differences—especially in purpose and intent and effect—between "Paste" and either "The Jewelry" or "The Necklace"? Why do you think James chose *not* to "surprise" us with the revelation that the necklace is genuine?
2. Why does James choose to make *only* the necklace genuine? Is he

using it and the "vulgar trash" symbolically, as De Maupassant does in "The Necklace"?

3. Compare the characterization in this story to that in "The Necklace." In "Paste." Why is this characterization (of both M. Lantin and the wife) flat and shadowy? Why would the story have been very difficult to write had the author characterized more effectively?
4. Why do you think James made his motivation more difficult by making the actress Arthur's stepmother rather than his mother (or even his wife) and by having Arthur's father die *before* the stepmother? In other words, exactly why is Arthur reluctant to believe in a "past" for his stepmother?
5. Explain the function in the story of the allusions or references to Hamlet's mother, to Ophelia, and to Rowena in Sir Walter Scott's *Ivanhoe.*
6. Define clearly the "moral positions" of the three basic characters in the story. With which position—Arthur Prime's, Charlotte's, or Mrs. Guy's—do you, in *this* story, sympathize and why?
7. The story does end with a "surprise"; Arthur sells the necklace, an admission on his part that his stepmother has had a "past." The ending is, however, ambiguous. Did Arthur sell the necklace on Bond Street, or did he "deal directly" with Mrs. Guy? What difference does this make in our interpretation of Arthur's motivations? And what are the implications of his lie to Charlotte?
8. Style is of the very first importance in this story; it helps to characterize, it is constantly both witty and ironical, and most important of all, it keeps us "straight" on the direction, the emphasis, the intent of the story. Define the story's point of view. Then find as many examples as you can of irony through style, of *double-entendre,* of descriptive words or phrases (like "vulgar," "flamboyant," "shameless," "questionable," "brazen," or like the opening ". . . the intention . . . of feeling something or other") that "control" the story in any of these ways.

7 Avant-Garde and Experimental Fiction

You have now learned a number of techniques for analyzing and interpreting some of the ways fiction works. But you have also learned that to some degree every story, even the simplest, defies definite interpretation, and that is especially true of the three in this section. These stories are so far outside recognizable contexts that they cannot be judged good or poor—they simply *are.* Avant-garde stories seem immune to literary analysis. No literary criteria can be applied to the question, "Are the writers in control of their materials?" Some critics labor to explain and describe what innovative fiction strives to achieve; but there is an inherent contradiction in trying to explain a story that was originally conceived to defy analysis. All we can expect to do here, then, is suggest a *few* ways of approaching and perhaps getting into stories (or "fictions") by avant-garde, experimental, or innovative writers ("fictionists" is the name most prefer).

Arguments Defending Avant-Garde Fiction's Effects

Experimental writers reject traditional techniques because those techniques fail to depict facets of our contemporary experience. Glibly, sympathetic commentators continue to cite conditions that by now have become clichés: Bureaucracy and technology have dehumanized civilized man; overwhelming social dislocations have fragmented individual identity; even group identity has proven inadequate; scientific and psychological models for living have failed; life since the end of World War II has become boring, insipid, banal, dull, conformist.

Racial, social, and economic inequality, the threat of the bomb, insane wars, and political treachery inspire in many innovative fictionists a pessimistic view of man as a degraded creature. Nothing is sacred; nothing is absolute; no patterns in life, society, or art are valid. These writers strive to destroy all art forms and show through their own methods the madness of all human existence. They argue that as mankind experiences rapid social and psychological changes, fiction should simultaneously reflect and contribute to the process of change. But traditional fiction has failed to do that, they charge, because the possibilities of its forms have been exhausted. Experimental writers often point out that while other art media reflect a changing world, short fiction remains the most "conservative art of midcentury," the "most self-imitative," the most predictable and formulaic. Fictionists are inspired by innovations in other media more than by those in their own: abstract expressionist painting, free-form sculpture, method acting, modern dance, the improvisations of jazz, the music of chance.

In "Title," John Barth's writer-narrator recognizes the fictionists' special problem: "I believe literature's not likely ever to manage abstraction successfully, like sculpture for example. . . . Well, because wood and iron have a native appeal and first-order reality, whereas words are artificial to begin with, invented specifically to represent" something else. In "The Birds," Ronald Sukenick's writer-narrator, like Barth's, wants to do what sculpture, theater, even music are doing, what prose fiction hasn't done, isn't doing, won't, perhaps can't, do: "Destroy this as you read. It is printed in a soluble ink which you can lick off the page sentence by sentence. The ink has various flavors depending on the parts of speech to make this easier to understand and swallow." The conditions of his medium allow him only to pretend to offer the reader such an experience.

As Borges', Barth's, and Sukenick's fictions illustrate, innovative writing often derives as much from pop as from high-culture models. Experimental writers often use popular fiction elements as their material and distort it to their own purposes, to explode, they tell us, conventional forms and to outrage the bourgeoisie. In "The Birds," the narrator holds up a "folk-art" project as a model for fiction—Simone Rodia's Watts Towers. " 'Built entirely without design precedent or orderly planning, created bit by bit on sheer impulse, a natural artist's instinct, and the fantasy of the moment.' "

When a work is created in that manner, "Connections proliferate, meanings drop away."

Innovative writers are trying to add their own contributions to those of other art media in the effort to break out of traditional forms. In several introductions to collections of avant-garde writing, commentators offer the following characteristics of the new fiction: It makes use of aspects of past innovations; of the symbolist, dada, surrealist, impressionistic, expressionistic, imagist movements in various media. It reflects elements of bohemian, beatnik, hippie, and other subcultures. Its techniques are those of the con man and the magician. It has an aggressively comic spirit that revels in nonsense as an end in itself, that employs elements of satire, parody, burlesque, lampoon, invective, and black humor. Not afraid to take uncalculated risks, this new fiction strives to be vital, exuberant, and audacious.

Innovative writers attempt, their defenders tell us, to experience phenomena purely, innocently: The naked "I" sees with a naked eye. They use techniques that "fracture" the "purely personal flow of perception," producing a "non-narrative succession of fragmented impressions" and "revelatory moments." The focus is "on the experiencing mind" of the author (and/or character) and the reader. Some innovative fiction focuses upon dreams and the subconscious as manifestations of mankind's true nature; it explodes the barriers between the conscious and the unconscious life; using the stream of consciousness method, these writers discover in free association relationships among objects and events that rational means cannot uncover. It is no wonder, then, that much avant-garde writing has an air of being under the influence of mysterious, mythic forces. It is incantatory, visionary, and prophetic. To achieve those effects, each experimental writer reaches for a unique style, using techniques that "shatter syntax" to recycle, revive, or resurrect what such writers consider to be a used-up or dead language; they labor to forge a pure language, free of empty rhetoric.

Innovative writers attempt, we are told, a "calculated demolition of the conventions" of fiction to break down "the applicability of traditional categories both of judgment and description," categories such as "perceptiveness, good taste, intelligence, the ability to create credible characters, the satisfactory resolution of themes." They are against chronological structure and plot (against the elements of conflict, exposition, complication, revelation, resolution). Refusing to create illusions of real life, they are attracted to bizarre subject matter and depict "implausible people doing incredible things." They are against such messages and themes as "the discovery of love, the loss of innocence, reconciliation to the fact of death, the renunciation of self-interest, the recognition of evil."

Anti-story (1971) is an anthology of fiction that reveals what is happening in the experimental realm. Philip Stevick, the editor, provides us with some very suggestive titles and subtitles of sections: The new fiction is "against mimesis" (imitation of life); it is fiction about fiction, he says. It is against "reality," preferring to explore the uses of fantasy. It is against depicting "events," asserting instead the primacy of the author's creative voice. Against "subject," it is "fiction in search of something to be about." It is against "the middle range of experience," reaching for "new forms of extremity." It is against intellectual "analysis," trying to make us experience "the phenomenal world" directly. It is against "meaning," exploring instead "forms of the absurd." It is against "scale," insisting that a novel can be as short as one paragraph.

Commentators on innovative fiction argue that willful obscurity may enable the imagination to explore possibilities and to push into far-out realms where transformations may occur. In the innovative approach, they point out, there is an infinite range of structural possibilities. A common method is juxtaposition (or "montage," a term from the movies, or "collage," a term from art); episodes or images are forced together that have no logical relation. Many innovative works reach beyond the limitations of the normal printed page. Each page becomes a visual unit; the reader encounters the fiction first through the naked eye; words are mixed with photos and other page-exploding graphics, causing impingements of words upon images. Each fiction extends the possibilities of life and art.

Innovative fiction breaks up the surface appearances of everyday life and remains unresolved on levels of action, theme, and character. Refusing to impose order upon disorder, innovators force their readers to ride the wild horses of chaos. To force us to experience the relativity of all things, they distort chronology, thwart continuity. They offer us experiences in disintegration, for their fictions do not progressively cohere; they self-destruct, line by line. Unlike traditional stories, the commentators warn, innovative fictions offer not patterns to live by, but freedom from patterns. Everything in the fiction is pure invention; and what we experience is the imagination at play. The fiction does not reflect the real world; it is its own world, and we must accept it as an alternative world. Each fiction is atypical, idiosyncratic, an act of pure creation; the world the author creates exists nowhere beyond the page; it exists only in a language continuum. It does not report on already made and finished things and events; it is in itself a new thing, a new event. Each fiction is *about* the process of its own creation. A world created by imagination and intuition, it is an esthetic object, a "self-contained, artificial universe."

André Gide's personal credo may stand for the innovative fictionist: My function is to disturb." Innovative writers and critics assume or claim that the new fiction, using "techniques that perpetually astonish," has certain effects on the reader (even those that sound negative are, in these writers' frame of reference, positive). Innovative fiction does violence to the reader; it startles, provokes, disorients, disturbs, frightens, alienates him—blows his mind. Its impact is almost physical; it rapes the reader's senses and sensibility. It violates his preconceptions and expectations about life and art; it shatters ethical and spiritual certainties. Inviting the reader's subjective responses, it "foments radically unusual states of mind." It can inspire the reader's own experimentations in perception and behavior that may change his life. Ronald Sukenick has said in an interview that innovative "fiction is one of the ways we have of creating ourselves." For the reader, experimental fictions offer "experiences to respond to, not problems to figure out." We should "improvise our art as we improvise our lives. No hysterical impositions of meaning."

Arguments Attacking Avant-Garde Fiction's Effects

Readers who resist innovative writing cite many of the characteristics described so far as reasons for their rejection of it. In a culture that has few norms to which the majority conforms, few techniques are shocking, hostile critics point out. The majority's most powerful resistance to these experiments is neglect or indifference. But some readers react with overt hostility, charging that innovative writers are arrogantly subjective, willfully perverse, self-indulgent, self-conscious and, in their leftist views, self-righteous. They produce claustrophobic, irrational, deranged, and paranoid works that reek of futility. They write out of destructive, antisocial impulses. Dark, decadent, amoral, subversive, anarchistic, offensively violent, often pornographic, and blasphemous, their abstract, abstruse, arbitrary, ambiguous, bizarre, obscure works lack form, unity, coherence, and control. Because these writers assume too much of the reader, their fictions are to some readers too complex, difficult, exasperating, depressing; to others they are simply too cute, shallow, and boring; and they are often in bad taste. The anti-heroes of these unrealistic concoctions fail to achieve insights, to learn from their experiences. Innovative works, these readers insist, are of only passing interest or relevance; and some are fraudulent put-ons.

These unsympathetic readers further argue that a major limitation of avant-garde writing lies in its very nature: Because the innovative writer can choose only to be free, his freedom is a self-contradiction. On the other hand, the eclectic writer is much freer to choose; he can skillfully use both traditional and innovative techniques. The innovative writer often simply exaggerates a single device or technique that most writers use as one among many in the creative process; he becomes captive in story after story of his one exaggeration. The anti-story's basic problem, the unsympathetic reader insists, lies in its negative impulse: It thrives by virtue of being what something else is not, and thus narrows rather than expands possibilities.

Since their visions differ radically from the majority view, innovative writers often feel they are outlaws in society; as outsiders, they pride themselves on the labels their critics paste on them; they turn every hostile objection into a possible description of their experimental intent; thus when a critic shows how an innovative work violates the rules of traditional fiction, he succeeds only in describing the work's achievement.

Hostile critics charge that innovative writers make pretentious, sometimes hysterical claims to originality in vision and technique, seemingly ignorant of a fact of literary history: that innovation always runs parallel to tradition, that the one never does nor should replace the other. Scholars are fond of citing one of the very earliest novels—*The Life and Opinions of Tristram Shandy, Gentleman* (1760)—which contains numerous innovative devices, techniques, and ways of rendering human perception. "The machinery of my work is a species by itself," says the author, Laurence Sterne, through Shandy. "Two contrary motions are introduced into it, and reconciled, which were thought to be at variance with each other. In a word, my work is digressive, and it is progressive, too, and at the same time." Many graphic devices, such as blank or black pages, and drawings or signs and symbols, were introduced in *Tristram Shandy*. A recent young French novelist offered a novel in a box; readers were invited to reassemble the loose pages any way they wished; few readers did. Steve Katz in *The Exaggerations of Peter Prince* (1968), an odd-sized book, employs photographs, rejected or revised pages of the novel, different sizes and styles of print, drawings, blank spaces, marginalia, as though Sterne had never lived. You can blow up the same monument only once, these scholars observe, and Sterne lit the first fuse.

Three Avant-Garde Fictionists Speak for Themselves

Experimental writing may prove less difficult if you keep the foregoing pro and con observations in mind, and if you realize that every story offers the reader hints about ways it should be read. "A shapeless mass of contradictory rough drafts" is what the novel *The Garden of Fork-*

ing Paths once seemed to its fictional author's great-grandson, Yu Tsun, who narrates Borges' own story called "The Garden of Forking Paths." All three stories in this section may appear that way to you at first. " 'What *is* all this nonsense about?' " Barth's narrator in "Title" asks himself, and then answers himself, " 'It may not be nonsense.' "

All art is in a primary sense about *itself*; every story is *about* the process of storytelling, about the relationship between the writer and the reader. That is more obvious in experimental than in traditional stories. One way to gather clues to understanding the work of innovators is to look at passages from the fictions themselves. Certainly Borges, Barth, and Sukenick are deliberately self-conscious fictionists.

"In the Garden of Forking Paths," we may take Stephen Albert's description of his problems as a reader of Ts'ui Pên's novel to be Borges' explanation to his readers of the way his own story may be read: "Re-reading the whole work confirmed this theory. In all fiction, when a man is faced with alternatives he chooses one at the expense of the others." That is true for the writer, the main character, and the reader of traditional fiction, but in experimental fiction, "In the almost unfathomable Ts'ui Pên, he chooses—simultaneously—all of them. He thus *creates* various futures, various times which start others that will in their turn branch out and bifurcate in other times. This is the cause of the contradictions in the novel. . . . In Ts'ui Pên's work, all the possible solutions occur, each one being the point of departure for other bifurcations. Sometimes the pathways of this labyrinth converge." Those passages suggest a way of approaching most experimental fictions, especially the three in this section.

The reader of a story always goes through a creative process that parallels the writer's; that, too, is especially clear in experimental fictions, particularly in "Title," in which the narrator obviously and deliberately confronts and analyzes problems the writer faces. The narrator states a premise on which most innovative fictions are created: "Everything's finished. Name eight. Story, novel, literature, art, humanism, humanity, the self itself." He reviews the writer's and the reader's old-fashioned attitudes toward a story: "Once upon a time you were satisfied with incidental felicities and niceties of technique: the unexpected image, the refreshingly accurate word-choice, the memorable simile that yields deeper and subtler significances upon reflection . . ." He envisions the fictionists' future task: "The final possibility is to turn ultimacy, exhaustion, paralyzing self-consciousness and the . . . weight of accumulated history. . . . Go on. Go on. To turn ultimacy against itself to make something new and valid, the essence whereof would be the impossibility of making something new."

To Sukenick, traditional fiction is "for the birds"—innovative fiction is pure flight. The narrator of Sukenick's fiction wants "to write a story that does a lot of . . . majestic infolding and outfolding. No petty invective and venom. No comic bits, no noodgy satire. . . . Calm, slow exfoliations. The life cycle of Whistling Swans." With his readers, he wants to cruise "among fantastic shapes, formations piling shifting flowing, distortions of distortions of distortions at all altitudes," on an "ocean of streaming transformations." Frustrated with traditional techniques, he creates out of the conviction that "What matters is to hurl the words at the silence of the page like grenades. With feeling. Look out!" Having offered the reader two very different versions of bird talk, he asks, "But then again, what does it matter what they say? What matters is that they carve shapes from nothingness, decorate the silence, make melodious distinctions to distinguish one moment finely from the next." Having finally perceived the meaning of "ear-tree" (an enigma repeated often in the fiction), he "drops off into a profound slumber," because what really matters is not to decipher the carrier pigeon's message, but to behold its flight.

These three stories will seem much less difficult to you on second or third reading. To respond most fully, even readers who crave innovative writing must re-read a fiction several times. Just let each fiction happen to you the first time you read it. Many innovators remind us that "in the beginning was the word . . . and the word was made flesh." They try to expose us to the pure, bracing potency of the word. The best way to get into innovative fiction's sometimes murky waters, then, is to plunge from the highest diving board.

JORGE LUIS BORGES
The Garden of Forking Paths

To Victoria Ocampo

In his *A History of the World War* (page 212), Captain Liddell Hart reports that a planned offensive by thirteen British divisions, supported by fourteen hundred artillery pieces, against the German line at Serre-Montauban, scheduled for July 24, 1916, had to be postponed until the morning of the 29th. He comments that torrential rain caused this delay—which lacked any special significance. The following deposition, dictated by, read over, and then signed by Dr. Yu Tsun, former teacher of English at the Tsingtao *Hochschule,* casts unsuspected light upon this event. The first two pages are missing.

* * * * * * * * * * *

. . . and I hung up the phone. Immediately I recollected the voice that had spoken in German. It was that of Captain Richard Madden. Madden, in Viktor Runeberg's office, meant the end of all our work and—though this seemed a secondary matter, *or should have seemed so to me*—of our lives also. His being there meant that Runeberg had been arrested or murdered.* Before the sun set on this same day, I ran the same risk. Madden was implacable. Rather, to be more accurate, he was obliged to be implacable. An Irishman in the service of England, a man suspected of equivocal feelings if not of actual treachery, how could he fail to welcome and seize upon this extraordinary piece of luck: the discovery, capture and perhaps the deaths of two agents of Imperial Germany?

*** A malicious and outlandish statement. In point of fact, Captain Richard Madden had been attacked by the Prussian spy Hans Rabener, alias Viktor Runeberg, who drew an automatic pistol when Madden appeared with orders for the spy's arrest. Madden, in self defense, had inflicted wounds of which the spy later died.—*Note by the manuscript editor.***

I went up to my bedroom. Absurd though the gesture was, I closed and locked the door. I threw myself down on my narrow iron bed, and waited on my back. The never changing rooftops filled the window, and the hazy six o'clock sun hung in the sky. It seemed incredible that this day, a day without warnings or omens, might be that of my implacable death. In despite of my dead father, in despite of having been a child in one of the symmetrical gardens of Hai Feng, was I to die now?

Then I reflected that all things happen, happen to one, precisely *now*. Century follows century, and things happen only in the present. There are countless men in the air, on land and at sea, and all that really happens happens to me. . . . The almost unbearable memory of Madden's long horseface put an end to these wandering thoughts.

In the midst of my hatred and terror (now that it no longer matters to me to speak of terror, now that I have outwitted Richard Madden, now that my neck hankers for the hangman's noose), I knew that the fast-moving and doubtless happy soldier did not suspect that I possessed the Secret—the name of the exact site of the new British artillery park on the Ancre. A bird streaked across the misty sky and, absently, I turned it into an airplane and then that airplane into many in the skies of France, shattering the artillery park under a rain of bombs. If only my mouth, before it should be silenced by a bullet, could shout this name in such a way that it could be heard in Germany. . . . My voice, my human voice, was weak. How could it reach the ear of the Chief? The ear of that sick and hateful man who knew nothing of Runeberg or of me except that we were in Staffordshire. A man who, sitting in his arid Berlin office, leafed infinitely through newspapers, looking in vain for news from us. I said aloud, "I must flee."

I sat up on the bed, in senseless and perfect silence, as if Madden was already peering at me. Something—perhaps merely a desire to prove my total penury to myself—made me empty out my pockets. I found just what I knew I was going to find. The American watch, the nickel-plated chain and the square coin, the key ring with the useless but compromising keys to Runeberg's office, the notebook, a letter which I decided to destroy at once (and which I did not destroy), a five shilling piece, two single shillings and some pennies, a red and blue pencil, a handkerchief —and a revolver with a single bullet. Absurdly I held it and weighed it in my hand, to give myself courage. Vaguely I thought that a pistol shot can be heard for a great distance.

In ten minutes I had developed my plan. The telephone directory gave me the name of the one person capable of passing on the information. He lived in a suburb of Fenton, less than half an hour away by train.

I am a timorous man. I can say it now, now that I have brought my incredibly risky plan to an end. It was not easy to bring about, and I know that its execution was terrible. I did not do it for Germany—no!

Such a barbarous country is of no importance to me, particularly since it had degraded me by making me become a spy. Furthermore, I knew an Englishman—a modest man—who, for me, is as great as Goethe. I did not speak with him for more than an hour, but during that time, he *was* Goethe.

I carried out my plan because I felt the Chief had some fear of those of my race, of those uncountable forebears whose culmination lies in me. I wished to prove to him that a yellow man could save his armies. Besides, I had to escape the Captain. His hands and voice could, at any moment, knock and beckon at my door.

Silently, I dressed, took leave of myself in the mirror, went down the stairs, sneaked a look at the quiet street, and went out. The station was not far from my house, but I thought it more prudent to take a cab. I told myself that I thus ran less chance of being recognized. The truth is that, in the deserted street, I felt infinitely visible and vulnerable. I recall that I told the driver to stop short of the main entrance. I got out with a painful and deliberate slowness.

I was going to the village of Ashgrove, but took a ticket for a station further on. The train would leave in a few minutes, at eight-fifty. I hurried, for the next would not go until half past nine. There was almost no one on the platform. I walked through the carriages. I remember some farmers, a woman dressed in mourning, a youth deep in Tacitus' *Annals* and a wounded, happy soldier.

At last the train pulled out. A man I recognized ran furiously, but vainly, the length of the platform. It was Captain Richard Madden. Shattered, trembling, I huddled in the distant corner of the seat, as far as possible from the fearful window.

From utter terror I passed into a state of almost abject happiness. I told myself that the duel had already started and that I had won the first encounter by besting my adversary in his first attack—even if it was only for forty minutes—by an accident of fate. I argued that so small a victory prefigured a total victory. I argued that it was not so trivial, that were it not for the precious accident of the train schedule, I would be in prison or dead. I argued, with no less sophism, that my timorous happiness was proof that I was man enough to bring this adventure to a successful conclusion. From my weakness I drew strength that never left me.

I foresee that man will resign himself each day to new abominations, that soon only soldiers and bandits will be left. To them I offer this advice: *Whosoever would undertake some atrocious enterprise should act as if it were already accomplished, should impose upon himself a future as irrevocable as the past.*

Thus I proceeded, while with the eyes of a man already dead, I contemplated the fluctuations of the day which would probably be my last, and watched the diffuse coming of night.

The train crept along gently, amid ash trees. It slowed down and stopped, almost in the middle of a field. No one called the name of a station. "Ashgrove?" I asked some children on the platform. "Ashgrove," they replied. I got out.

A lamp lit the platform, but the children's faces remained in a shadow. One of them asked me: "Are you going to Dr. Stephen Albert's house?" Without waiting for my answer, another said: "The house is a good distance away but you won't get lost if you take the road to the left and bear to the left at every crossroad." I threw them a coin (my last), went down some stone steps and started along a deserted road. At a slight incline, the road ran downhill. It was a plain dirt way, and overhead the branches of trees intermingled, while a round moon hung low in the sky as if to keep me company.

For a moment I thought that Richard Madden might in some way have divined my desperate intent. At once I realized that this would be impossible. The advice about turning always to the left reminded me that such was the common formula for finding the central courtyard of certain labyrinths. I know something about labyrinths. Not for nothing am I the great-grandson of Ts'ui Pên. He was Governor of Yunnan and gave up temporal power to write a novel with more characters than there are in the *Hung Lou Mêng*, and to create a maze in which all men would lose themselves. He spent thirteen years on these oddly assorted tasks before he was assassinated by a stranger. His novel had no sense to it and nobody ever found his labyrinth.

Under the trees of England I meditated on this lost and perhaps mythical labyrinth. I imagined it untouched and perfect on the secret summit of some mountain; I imagined it drowned under rice paddies or beneath the sea; I imagined it infinite, made not only of eight-sided pavilions and of twisting paths but also of rivers, provinces and kingdoms. . . . I thought of a maze of mazes, of a sinuous, ever growing maze which would take in both past and future and would somehow involve the stars.

Lost in these imaginary illusions I forgot my destiny—that of the hunted. For an undetermined period of time I felt myself cut off from the world, an abstract spectator. The hazy and murmuring countryside, the moon, the decline of the evening, stirred within me. Going down the gentle sloping road I could not feel fatigue. The evening was at once intimate and infinite.

The road kept descending and branching off, through meadows misty in the twilight. A high-pitched and almost syllabic music kept coming and going, moving with the breeze, blurred by the leaves and by distance.

I thought that a man might be an enemy of other men, of the differing moments of other men, but never an enemy of a country: not of fireflies, words, gardens, streams, or the West wind.

Meditating thus I arrived at a high, rusty iron gate. Through the railings I could see an avenue bordered with poplar trees and also a kind of summer house or pavilion. Two things dawned on me at once, the first trivial and the second almost incredible: the music came from the pavilion and that music was Chinese. That was why I had accepted it fully, without paying it any attention. I do not remember whether there was a bell, a push-button, or whether I attracted attention by clapping my hands. The stuttering sparks of the music kept on.

But from the end of the avenue, from the main house, a lantern approached; a lantern which alternately, from moment to moment, was crisscrossed or put out by the trunks of the trees; a paper lantern shaped like a drum and colored like the moon. A tall man carried it. I could not see his face for the light blinded me.

He opened the gate and spoke slowly in my language.

"I see that the worthy Hsi P'eng has troubled himself to see to relieving my solitude. No doubt you want to see the garden?"

Recognizing the name of one of our consuls, I replied, somewhat taken aback.

"The garden?"

"The garden of forking paths."

Something stirred in my memory and I said, with incomprehensible assurance:

"The garden of my ancestor, Ts'ui Pên."

"Your ancestor? Your illustrious ancestor? Come in."

The damp path zigzagged like those of my childhood. When we reached the house, we went into a library filled with books from both East and West. I recognized some large volumes bound in yellow silk—manuscripts of the Lost Encyclopedia which was edited by the Third Emperor of the Luminous Dynasty. They had never been printed. A phonograph record was spinning near a bronze phoenix. I remember also a rose-glazed jar and yet another, older by many centuries, of that blue color which our potters copied from the Persians. . . .

Stephen Albert was watching me with a smile on his face. He was, as I have said, remarkably tall. His face was deeply lined and he had gray eyes and a gray beard. There was about him something of the priest, and something of the sailor. Later, he told me he had been a missionary in Tientsin before he "had aspired to become a Sinologist."

We sat down, I upon a large, low divan, he with his back to the window and to a large circular clock. I calculated that my pursuer, Richard Madden, could not arrive in less than an hour. My irrevocable decision could wait.

"A strange destiny," said Stephen Albert, "that of Ts'ui Pên—Governor of his native province, learned in astronomy, in astrology and tireless in the interpretation of the canonical books, a chess player, a famous poet and a calligrapher. Yet he abandoned all to make a book and a labyrinth. He gave up all the pleasures of oppression, justice, of a well-stocked bed, of banquets, and even of erudition, and shut himself up in the Pavilion of the Limpid Sun for thirteen years. At his death, his heirs found only a mess of manuscripts. The family, as you doubtless know, wished to consign them to the fire, but the executor of the estate—a Taoist or a Buddhist monk—insisted on their publication."

"Those of the blood of Ts'ui Pên," I replied, "still curse the memory of that monk. Such a publication was madness. The book is a shapeless mass of contradictory rough drafts. I examined it once upon a time: the hero dies in the third chapter, while in the fourth he is alive. As for that other enterprise of Ts'ui Pên . . . his Labyrinth. . . ."

"Here is the Labyrinth?" Albert said, pointing to a tall, laquered writing cabinet.

"An ivory labyrinth?" I exclaimed. "A tiny labyrinth indeed . . . !"

"A symbolic labyrinth," he corrected me. "An invisible labyrinth of time. I, a barbarous Englishman, have been given the key to this transparent mystery. After more than a hundred years most of the details are irrecoverable, lost beyond all recall, but it isn't hard to image what must have happened. At one time, Ts'ui Pên must have said; 'I am going into seclusion to write a book,' and at another, 'I am retiring to construct a maze.' Everyone assumed these were separate activities. No one realized that the book and the labyrinth were one and the same. The Pavilion of the Limpid Sun was set in the middle of an intricate garden. This may have suggested the idea of a physical maze.

"Ts'ui Pên died. In all the vast lands which once belonged to your family, no one could find the labyrinth. The novel's confusion suggested that *it* was the labyrinth. Two circumstances showed me the direct solution to the problem. First, the curious legend that Ts'ui Pên had proposed to create an infinite maze, second, a fragment of a letter which I discovered."

Albert rose. For a few moments he turned his back to me. He opened the top drawer in the high black and gilded writing cabinet. He returned holding in his hand a piece of paper which had once been crimson but which had faded with the passage of time: it was rose colored, tenuous, quadrangular. Ts'ui Pên's calligraphy was justly famous. Eagerly, but without understanding, I read the words which a man of my own blood had written with a small brush: "I leave to various future times, but not to all, my garden of forking paths."

I handed back the sheet of paper in silence. Albert went on:

"Before I discovered this letter, I kept asking myself how a book could be infinite. I could not imagine any other than a cyclic volume, circular. A volume whose last page would be the same as the first and so have the possibility of continuing indefinitely. I recalled, too, the night in the middle of *The Thousand and One Nights* when Queen Scheherezade, through a magical mistake on the part of her copyist, started to tell the story of *The Thousand and One Nights,* with the risk of again arriving at the night upon which she will relate it, and thus on to infinity. I also imagined a Platonic hereditary work, passed on from father to son, to which each individual would add a new chapter or correct, with pious care, the work of his elders.

"These conjectures gave me amusement, but none seemed to have the remotest application to the contradictory chapters of Ts'ui Pên. At this point, I was sent from Oxford the manuscript you have just seen.

"Naturally, my attention was caught by the sentence, 'I leave to various future times, but not to all, my garden of forking paths.' I had no sooner read this, than I understood. *The Garden of Forking Paths* was the chaotic novel itself. The phrase 'to various future times, but not to all' suggested the image of bifurcating in time, not in space. Rereading the whole work confirmed this theory. In all fiction, when a man is faced with alternatives he chooses one at the expense of the others. In the almost unfathomable Ts'ui Pên, he chooses—simultaneously—all of them. He thus *creates* various futures, various times which start others that will in their turn branch out and bifurcate in other times. This is the cause of the contradictions in the novel.

"Fang, let us say, has a secret. A stranger knocks at his door. Fang makes up his mind to kill him. Naturally there are various possible outcomes. Fang can kill the intruder, the intruder can kill Fang, both can be saved, both can die and so on and so on. In Ts'ui Pên's work, all the possible solutions occur, each one being the point of departure for other bifurcations. Sometimes the pathways of this labyrinth converge. For example, you come to this house; but in other possible pasts you are my enemy; in others my friend.

"If you will put up with my atrocious pronunciation, I would like to read you a few pages of your ancestor's work."

His countenance, in the bright circle of lamplight, was certainly that of an ancient, but it shone with something unyielding, even immortal.

With slow precision, he read two versions of the same epic chapter. In the first, an army marches into battle over a desolate mountain pass. The bleak and somber aspect of the rocky landscape made the soldiers feel that life itself was of little value, and so they won the battle easily. In the second, the same army passes through a palace where a banquet is in progress. The splendor of the feast remained a memory throughout the glorious battle, and so victory followed.

With proper veneration I listened to these old tales, although perhaps with less admiration for them in themselves than for the fact that they had been thought out by one of my own blood, and that a man of a distant empire had given them back to me, in the last stage of a desperate adventure, on a Western island. I remember the final words, repeated at the end of each version like a secret command: "Thus the heroes fought, with tranquil heart and bloody sword. They were resigned to killing and to dying."

At that moment I felt within me and around me something invisible and intangible pullulating. It was not the pullulation of two divergent, parallel, and finally converging armies, but an agitation more inaccessible, more intimate, prefigured by them in some way. Stephen Albert continued:

"I do not think that your illustrious ancestor toyed idly with variations. I do not find it believable that he would waste thirteen years laboring over a never ending experiment in rhetoric. In your country the novel is an inferior genre; in Ts'ui Pên's period, it was a despised one. Ts'ui Pên was a fine novelist but he was also a man of letters who, doubtless, considered himself more than a mere novelist. The testimony of his contemporaries attests to this, and certainly the known facts of his life confirm his leanings toward the metaphysical and the mystical. Philosophical conjectures take up the greater part of his novel. I know that of all problems, none disquieted him more, and none concerned him more than the profound one of time. Now then, this is the *only* problem that does not figure in the pages of *The Garden*. He does not even use the word which means *time*. How can these voluntary omissions be explained?"

I proposed various solutions, all of them inadequate. We discussed them. Finally Stephen Albert said: "In a guessing game to which the answer is chess, which word is the only one prohibited?" I thought for a moment and then replied:

"The word is *chess*."

"Precisely," said Albert. "*The Garden of Forking Paths* is an enormous guessing game, or parable, in which the subject is time. The rules of the game forbid the use of the word itself. To eliminate a word completely, to refer to it by means of inept phrases and obvious paraphrases, is perhaps the best way of drawing attention to it. This, then, is the tortuous method of approach preferred by the oblique Ts'ui Pên in every meandering of his interminable novel. I have gone over hundreds of manuscripts, I have corrected errors introduced by careless copyists, I have worked out the plan from this chaos, I have restored, or believe I have restored, the original. I have translated the whole work. I can state categorically that not once has the word *time* been used in the whole book.

"The explanation is obvious. *The Garden of Forking Paths* is a picture, incomplete yet not false, of the universe such as Ts'ui Pên conceived it to be. Differing from Newton and Schopenhauer, your ancestor did not think of time as absolute and uniform. He believed in an infinite series of times, in a dizzily growing, ever spreading network of diverging, converging and parallel times. This web of time—the strands of which approach one another, bifurcate, intersect or ignore each other through the centuries—embraces *every* possibility. We do not exist in most of them. In some you exist and not I, while in others I do, and you do not, and in yet others both of us exist. In this one, in which chance has favored me, you have come to my gate. In another, you, crossing the garden, have found me dead. In yet another, I say these very same words, but am an error, a phantom."

"In all of them," I enunciated, with a tremor in my voice. "I deeply appreciate and am grateful to you for the restoration of Ts'ui Pên's garden."

"Not in *all*," he murmured with a smile. "Time is forever dividing itself toward innumerable futures and in one of them I am your enemy."

Once again I sensed the pullulation of which I have already spoken. It seemed to me that the dew-damp garden surrounding the house was infinitely saturated with invisible people. All were Albert and myself, secretive, busy and multiform in other dimensions of time. I lifted my eyes and the short nightmare disappeared. In the black and yellow garden there was only a single man, but this man was as strong as a statue and this man was walking up the path and he was Captain Richard Madden.

"The future exists now," I replied. "But I am your friend. Can I take another look at the letter?"

Albert rose from his seat. He stood up tall as he opened the top drawer of the high writing cabinet. For a moment his back was again turned to me. I had the revolver ready. I fired with the utmost care: Albert fell without a murmur, at once. I swear that his death was instantaneous, as if he had been struck by lightning.

What remains is unreal and unimportant. Madden broke in and arrested me. I have been condemned to hang. Abominably, I have yet triumphed! The secret name of the city to be attacked got through to Berlin. Yesterday it was bombed. I read the news in the same English newspapers which were trying to solve the riddle of the murder of the learned Sinologist Stephen Albert by the unknown Yu Tsun. The Chief, however, had already solved this mystery. He knew that my problem was to shout, with my feeble voice, above the tumult of war, the name of the city called Albert, and that I had no other course open to me than to kill someone of that name. He does not know, for no one can, of my infinite penitence and sickness of the heart.

—Translated by *Helen Temple* and *Ruthven Todd*

QUESTIONS FOR DISCUSSION

1. Find and discuss passages that suggest the way the fictionist may want you to approach his fiction. Consider, for instance, the passage on p. 358 that begins: "*The Garden of Forking Paths* is an enormous guessing game, or parable . . ." and ends, ". . . not once has the word *time* been used in the whole book."
2. What questions and implications are raised by the first two missing pages of Yu Tsun's deposition, and by the footnote?
3. Why does Borges make his narrator tell the reader very early that he has "outwitted" Madden, thus apparently undercutting the element of suspense? How does that strategy, used more than once, affect the reader's response to the story from segment to segment?
4. Borges, speaking metaphorically, has called this a detective story. Who is the detective and what is his mode of operation?
5. Specifically, how do the narrator's ways of perceiving, his imaginings, his meditations on space and time and other matters, anticipate and parallel particular aspects of his visit with Stephen Albert?
6. What are some of the thematic implications of Yu Tsun's killing of the man to whom he was grateful?
7. What questions remain unanswered, and why?

JOHN BARTH
Title

Beginning: in the middle, past the middle, nearer three-quarters done, waiting for the end. Consider how dreadful so far: passionlessness, abstraction, pro, dis. And it will get worse. Can we possibly continue?

Plot and theme: notions vitiated by this hour of the world but as yet not successfully succeeded. Conflict, complication, no climax. The worst is to come. Everything leads to nothing: future tense; past tense; present tense. Perfect. The final question is, Can nothing be made meaningful? Isn't that the final question? If not, the end is at hand. Literally, as it were. Can't stand any more of this.

I think she comes. The story of our life. This is the final test. Try to fill the blank. Only hope is to fill the blank. Efface what can't be faced or else fill the blank. With words or more words, otherwise I'll fill the blank with this noun here in my prepositional object. Yes, she already said that. And I think. What now. Everything's been said already, over and over; I'm as sick of this as you are; there's nothing to say. Say nothing.

What's new? Nothing.

Conventional startling opener. Sorry if I'm interrupting the Progress of Literature, she said, in a tone that adjective clause suggesting good-humored irony but in fact defensively and imperfectly masking a taunt. The conflict is established though as yet unclear in detail. Standard conflict. Let's skip particulars. What do you want from me? What'll the story be this time? Same old story. Just thought I'd see if you were still around. Before. What? Quit right here. Too late. Can't we start over? What's past is past. On the contrary, what's forever past is eternally present. The future? Blank. All this is just fill in. Hang on.

Still around. In what sense? Among the gerundive. What is that supposed to mean? Did you think I meant to fill in the blank? Why should I? On the other hand, why not? What makes you think I wouldn't fill in the blank instead? Some conversation this is. Do you want to go on, or shall we end it right now? Suspense. I don't care for this either. It'll be over soon enough in any case. But it gets worse and worse. Whatever happens, the ending will be deadly. At least let's have just one real conversation. Dialogue or monologue? What has it been from the first? Don't ask me. What is there to say at this late date? Let me think; I'm trying to think. Same old story. Or. Or? Silence.

This isn't so bad. Silence. There are worse things. Name three. This, that, the other. Some choices. Who said there was a choice?

Let's try again. That's what I've been doing; I've been thinking while you've been blank. Story of Our Life. However, this may be the final complication. The ending may be violent. That's been said before. Who cares? Let the end be blank; anything's better than this.

It didn't used to be so bad. It used to be less difficult. Even enjoyable. For whom? Both of us. To do what? Complicate the conflict. I am weary of this. What, then? To complete this sentence, if I may bring up a sore subject. That never used to be a problem. Now it's impossible; we just can't manage it. You can't fill in the blank; I can't fill in the blank. Or won't. Is this what we're going to talk about, our obscene verbal problem? It'll be our last conversation. Why talk at all? Are you paying attention? I dare you to quit now! Never dare a desperate person. On with it, calmly, one sentence after another, like a recidivist. A what? A common noun. Or another common noun. Hold tight. Or a chronic forger, let's say; committed to the pen for life. Which is to say, death. The point, for pity's sake! Not yet. Forge on.

We're more than halfway through, as I remarked at the outset: youthful vigor, innocent exposition, positive rising action—all that is behind us. How sophisticated we are today. I'll ignore her, he vowed, and went on. In this dehuman, exhausted, ultimate adjective hour, when every humane value has become untenable, and not only love, decency, and beauty but even compassion and intelligibility are no more than one or two subjective complements to complete the sentence. . . .

This is a story? It's a story, he replied equably, or will be if the author can finish it. Without interruption I suppose you mean? she broke in. I can't finish anything; that is my final word. Yet it's these interruptions that make it a story. Escalate the conflict further. Please let me start over.

Once upon a time you were satisfied with incidental felicities and niceties of technique: the unexpected image, the refreshingly accurate word-choice, the memorable simile that yields deeper and subtler significances upon reflection, like a memorable simile. Somebody please stop me. Or arresting dialogue, so to speak. For example?

Why do you suppose it is, she asked, long participial phrase of the breathless variety characteristic of dialogue attributions in nineteenth-century fiction, that literate people such as we talk like characters in a story? Even supplying the dialogue-tags, she added with wry disgust. Don't put words in her mouth. The same old story, an old-fashioned one at that. Even if I should fill in the blank with my idle pen? Nothing new about that, to make a fact out of a figure. At least it's good for something. Every story is penned in red ink, to make a figure out of a fact. This whole idea is insane.

And might therefore be got away with.

No turning back now, we've gone too far. Everything's finished. Name eight. Story, novel, literature, art, humanism, humanity, the self itself. Wait: the story's not finished. And you and I, Howard? whispered Martha, her sarcasm belied by a hesitant alarm in her glance, flickering as it were despite herself to the blank instrument in his hand. Belied indeed; put that thing away! And what does flickering modify? A person who can't verb adverb ought at least to speak correctly.

A tense moment in the evolution of the story. Do you know, declared the narrator, one has no idea, especially nowadays, how close the end may be, nor will one necessarily be aware of it when it occurs. Who can say how near this universe has come to mere cessation? Or take two people, in a story of the sort it once was possible to tell. Love affairs, literary genres, third item in exemplary series, fourth—everything blossoms and decays, does it not, from the primitive and classical through the mannered and baroque to the abstract, stylized, dehumanized, unintelligible, blank. And you and I, Rosemary? Edward. Snapped! Patience. The narrator gathers that his audience no longer cherishes him. And conversely. But little does he know of the common noun concealed for months in her you name it, under her eyelet chemise. This is a slip. The point is the same. And she fetches it out nightly as I dream, I think. That's no slip. And she regards it and sighs, a quantum grimlier each night it may be. Is this supposed to be amusing? The world might end before this sentence, or merely someone's life. And/or someone else's. I speak metaphorically. Is the sentence ended? Very nearly. No telling how long a sentence will be until one reaches the stop. It sounds as if somebody intends to fill in the blank. What *is* all this nonsense about?

It may not be nonsense. Anyhow it will presently be over. As the narrator was saying, things have been kaput for some time, and while we may be pardoned our great reluctance to acknowledge it, the fact is that the bloody century for example is nearing the three-quarter mark, and the characters in this little tale, for example, are similarly past their prime, as is the drama. About played out. Then God damn it let's ring the curtain. Wait wait. We're left with the following three possibilities, at least in theory. Horseshit. Hold onto yourself, it's too soon to fill in the blank. I hope this will be a short story.

Shorter than it seems. It seems endless. Be thankful it's not a novel. The novel is predicate adjective, as is the innocent anecdote of bygone days when life made a degree of sense and subject joined to complement by copula. No longer are these things the case, as you have doubtless remarked. There was I believe some mention of possibilities, three in number. The first is rejuvenation: having become an exhausted parody of itself, perhaps a form—Of what? Of anything—may rise neoprimitively from its own ashes. A tiresome prospect. The second, more appealing I'm sure but scarcely likely at this advanced date, is that moribund what-have-yous will be supplanted by vigorous new: the demise of the novel and short story, he went on to declare, needn't be the end of narrative art, nor need the dissolution of a used-up blank fill in the blank. The end of one road might be the beginning of another. Much good that'll do me. And you may not find the revolution as bloodless as you think, either. Shall we try it? Never dare a person who is fed up to the ears.

The final possibility is a temporary expedient, to be sure, the self-styled narrator of this so-called story went on to admit, ignoring the hostile impatience of his audience, but what is not, and every sentence completed is a step closer to the end. That is to say, every day gained is a day gone. Matter of viewpoint, I suppose. Go on. I am. Whether anyone's paying attention or not. The final possibility is to turn ultimacy, exhaustion, paralyzing self-consciousness and the adjective weight of accumulated history. . . . Go on. Go on. To turn ultimacy against itself to make something new and valid, the essence whereof would be the impossibility of making something new. What a nauseating notion. And pray how does it bear upon the analogy uppermost in everyone's mind? We've gotten this far, haven't we? Look how far we've come together. Can't we keep on to the end? I think not. Even another sentence is too many. Only if one believes the end to be a long way off; actually it might come at any moment; I'm surprised it hasn't before now. Nothing does when it's expected to.

Silence. There's a fourth possibility, I suppose. Silence. General anesthesia. Self-extinction. Silence.

Historicity and self-awareness, he asseverated, while ineluctable and even greatly to be prized, are always fatal to innocence and spontaneity. Perhaps adjective period. Whether in a people, an art, a love affair, on a fourth term added not impossibly to make the third less than ultimate. In the name of suffering humanity cease this harangue. It's over. And the story? Is there a plot here? What's all this leading up to?

No climax. There's the story. Finished? Not quite. Story of our lives. The last word in fiction, in fact. I chose the first-person narrative viewpoint in order to reflect interest from the peculiarities of the technique (such as the normally unbearable self-consciousness, the abstraction, and the blank) to the nature and situation of the narrator and his companion, despite the obvious possibility that the narrator and his companion might be mistaken for the narrator and his companion. Occupational hazard. The technique is advanced, as you see, but the situation of the characters is conventionally dramatic. That being the case, may one of them, or one who may be taken foı one of them, make a longish speech in the old-fashioned manner, charged with obsolete emotion? Of course.

I begin calmly, though my voice may rise as I go along. Sometimes it seems as if things could instantly be altogether different and more admirable. The times be damned, one still wants a man vigorous, confident, bold, resourceful, adjective, and adjective. One still wants a woman spirited, spacious of heart, loyal, gentle, adjective, adjective. That man and that woman are as possible as the ones in this miserable story, and a good deal realer. It's as if they live in some room of our house that we can't find the door to, though it's so close we can hear echoes of their voices. Experience has made them wise instead of bitter; knowledge has mellowed instead of souring them; in their forties and fifties, even in their sixties, they're gayer and stronger and more authentic than they were in their twenties; for the twenty-year-olds they have only affectionate sympathy. So? Why aren't the couple in this story that man and woman, so easy to imagine? God, but I am surfeited with clever irony! Ill of sickness! Parallel phrase to wrap up series! This last-resort idea, it's dead in the womb, excuse the figure. A false pregnancy, excuse the figure. God damn me though if that's entirely my fault. Acknowledge your complicity. As you see, I'm trying to do something about the present mess; hence this story. Adjective in the noun! Don't lose your composure. You tell me it's self-defeating to talk about it instead of just up and doing it; but to acknowledge what I'm doing while I'm doing it is exactly the point. Self-defeat implies a victor, and who do you suppose it is, if not blank? That's the only victory left. Right? Forward! Eyes open.

No. The only way to get out of a mirror-maze is to close your eyes and hold out your hands. And be carried away by a valiant metaphor, I suppose, like a simile.

There's only one direction to go in. Ugh. We must make something out of nothing. Impossible. Mystics do. Not only turn contradiction into paradox, but *employ* it, to go on living and working. Don't bet on it. I'm betting my cliché on it, yours too. What is that supposed to mean? On with the refutation; every denial is another breath, every word brings us closer to the end.

Very well: to write this allegedly ultimate story is a form of artistic fill in the blank, or an artistic form of same, if you like. I don't. What I mean is, same idea in other terms. The storyteller's alternatives, as far as I can see, are a series of last words, like an aging actress making one farewell appearance after another, or actual blank. And I mean literally fill in the blank. Is this a test? But the former is contemptible in itself, and the latter will certainly become so when the rest of the world shrugs its shoulders and goes on about its business. Just as people would do if adverbial clause of obvious analogical nature. The fact is, the narrator has narrated himself into a corner, a state of affairs more tsk-tsk than boo-hoo, and because his position is absurd he calls the world absurd. That some writers lack lead in their pencils does not make writing obsolete. At this point they were both smiling despite themselves. At this point they were both flashing hatred despite themselves. Every woman has a blade concealed in the neighborhood of her garters. So disarm her, so to speak, don't geld yourself. At this point they were both despite themselves. Have we come to the point at last? Not quite. Where there's life there's hope.

There's no hope. This isn't working. But the alternative is to supply an alternative. That's no alternative. Unless I make it one. Just try; quit talking about it, quit talking, quit! Never dare a desperate man. Or woman. That's the one thing that can drive even the first part of a conventional metaphor to the second part of same. Talk, talk, talk. Yes yes, go on, I believe literature's not likely ever to manage abstraction successfully, like sculpture for example, is that a fact, what a time to bring up that subject, anticlimax, that's the point, do set forth the exquisite reason. Well, because wood and iron have a native appeal and first-order reality, whereas words are artificial to begin with, invented specifically to represent. Go on, please go on. I'm going. Don't you dare. Well, well, weld iron rods into abstract patterns, say, and you've still got real iron, but arrange words into abstract patterns and you've got nonsense. Nonsense is right. For example. On, God damn it; take linear plot, take resolution of conflict, take third direct object, all that business, they may very well be obsolete notions, indeed they are, no doubt untenable at this late date, no doubt at all, but in fact we still lead our lives by clock and calendar, for example, and though the seasons recur our mortal human time does not; we grow old and tired, we think of how things used to be or might have been and how they are now, and in fact, and in fact we get exasperated and desperate and out of expedients and out of words.

Go on. Impossible. I'm going, too late now, one more step and we're done, you and I. Suspense. The fact is, you're driving me to it, the fact is that people still lead lives, mean and bleak and brief as they are, briefer than you think, and people have characters and motives that we divine more or less inaccurately from their appearance, speech, behavior, and the rest, you aren't listening, go on then, what do you think I'm doing, people still fall in love, and out, yes, in and out, and out and in, and they please each other, and hurt each other, isn't that the truth, and they do these things in more or less conventionally dramatic fashion, unfashionable or not, go on, I'm going, and what goes on between them is still not only the most interesting but the most important thing in the bloody murderous world, pardon the adjectives. And that my dear is what writers have got to find ways to write about in this adjective adjective hour of the ditto ditto same noun as above, or their, that is to say our, accursed self-consciousness will lead them, what is to say us, to here it comes, say it straight out, I'm going to, say it in plain English for once, that's what I'm leading up to, me and my bloody anticlimactic noun, we're pushing each other to fill in the blank.

Goodbye. Is it over? Can't you read between the lines? One more step. Goodbye suspense goodbye.

Blank.

Oh God comma I abhor self-consciousness. I despise what we have come to; I loathe our loathesome loathing, our place our time our situation, our loathsome art, this ditto necessary story. The blank of our lives. It's about over. Let the *dénouement* be soon and unexpected, painless if possible, quick at least, above all soon. Now now! How in the world will it ever

QUESTIONS FOR DISCUSSION

1. Find and discuss passages that suggest the way the fictionist may want you to approach his fiction. Consider, for instance, those passages concerning the relationship between the fabricator of fiction and his reader.
2. Who is the narrator? Is he Barth himself? To whom is the narrator speaking? Who is "she" and what is her function in this fiction?
3. What is the narrator's predicament? Discuss the various aspects of that predicament and the ways those aspects relate to and affect each other?
4. What is the author's strategy? Consider, for instance, the effect of juxtaposing questions about the creative process with brief attempts to create characters and a story. What other strategies does Barth employ?
5. Analyze Barth's style to determine the wellsprings of his wit.
6. Examine the following words and phrases as ways of making the story more accessible to you: "fill in the blank," "story of our lives," "nothing." Discuss the implications throughout this fiction of those and other such often-repeated phrases and words.
7. Discuss the relevance to "Title" of this assertion: Paradoxically, to deny the existence of something in fiction is to enhance its actuality as a product of the author's and the reader's imaginations.

RONALD SUKENICK
The Birds

The the the

Nuthatch walks up the tree a Prussian soldier pivots walks back down

birds

the

Nuthatch slick arctic acrobat seal bullets through blank air silence of page the stream carries mainly on its glassy surface rippled clouds inventing themselves from minute to minute toss in a stone

The the I want to tell you the story about "ear-tree." It was on Icelandic that eighteen-hour flight from Luxemburg where your feet swell up. We cruised among fantastic shapes, formations piling shifting flowing, distortions of distortions of distortions at all altitudes. The plane skimmed across a kind of ocean of streaming transformations, the wings clipped white tumuli, and on the actual ocean waves were ripples were wrinkles, viscid metal crawling across the earth, the land itself a slower lava, somewhat thicker, especially that of Iceland, where that was what it was. I was looking out over the wing as I watched a wisp of white blew back from the engine, then another, another, and after a pause, a band of grey I looked up the aisle for the stewardess when I looked back the smoke was roiling from the engine a greasy black plume with suddenly red at its root . . .

Wings pulled in it allowed itself to fall, a stroke of scarlet from green to green.

It began in '62 a Chinese restaurant naturally midtown I remember very well because that was the phase when I had a thing with fortune cookies I am always interested in any overt confrontation

with chance though if you stop to think about it every moment is such a confrontation for each of us as likely to provide the cue for something tasty an

adventure something other than sex a coincidence in any case one was tired of sex I mean of thinking about it preferably a

coincidence such things renew my faith in the unknown however the fortune merely said, "You will soon plan another oriental meal" but that wasn't the interesting thing.

Corrosive chatter. Starlings are a bore, despite iridescences. They're too precocious, and have no intelligence. "We put the snake live into the freezer it was at least two feet long and when we took it out it was frozen into this really interesting shape stiff as a board but then we hung it up and it began to smell. What ever happened to Phillip Morris? And mockies? There always used to be a lot of mockies. I had an aunt who always used to smoke Phillip Morris. She got lung cancer though. She was a mockie. She's dead now. I guess that's what happens to them."

The Yellow-shafted Flicker appears around April. The male has a black "mustache." Its strange laugh haunts the woods but seems to be a courtship cry. Lovemaking involves reciprocal undulations of the long necks like oriental dancers. The underwing is an astonishing pink-gold. Note the pure white rump in flight.

The dress was made of clinging white nylon jersey of a thinness that in certain angles of light would outline the thighs or reveal the curve of a breast and which, when taut against the skin, assumed something of the warm flesh tone. The loose ankle-length curtain of skirt was slit at the side to the top of the thigh. The backless halter scooped down to the point at which the swell and division of the buttocks become apparent, and was slashed to the waist in front, baring both the inner and outer curves of the breasts, leaving the nipples free to poke and bob through the material.

"A pattern was seen in the use of females to bite and kick the policemen" *New York Times* 5/7/68.

Its drumming, distinct from other peckers, resembles the sound of a muffled machine gun, a soft, hollow automatic weapon.

He came stumbling up in Tompkins Square with his red scabby face and clapped a hand on my shoulder: "Say buddy I'm a junkie no I mean not a junkie a wino." That was how I met Sparrow. Oh nobody knew what his name really was we called him Sparrow. After the saying, "Hot as a Sparrow."

He used to say things to me like, "The salient fact about American culture is that we all have to get back to nipples and start over again. Whole cockamanie country." He's also the one who said, "I wuz-a fuck 'is-a wife." When he talked like that we used to call him "the Cardinal" because he seemed so intellectual. Like a Cardinal I mean, if you really look at one.

With one stroke rose half an arc then wings pulled in allowed itself to fall like diving over a wave.

I want to write a story that does a lot of infolding and outfolding. Majestic infolding and outfolding. No petty invective and venom. No comic bits, no noodgy satire like Shawanga Lodge casino. Calm, slow exfoliations. The life cycle of Whistling Swans. Inexorable curves of passion. Rise and fall of continents. Concrete. Innocent. Beautiful. No meaning.

30 million Americans living in poverty
it says in I. F. Stone
in the richest country in the world
people eat clay to still the pains of an empty belly
children come to school too hungry to learn
and the infants of the poor suffer
irreversible brain damage from protein deprivation
the 42.7% of our farmers
with incomes of less than $2,500 a year
received only 4.5% of total farm subsidies
while the top 10%
many of them farm corporations or vertical trusts
received 64.5%
with a budget allocated 80% to the Pentagon
and 10% to health education and welfare

This is what I call pure poetry. This is the New American Poetry, the poetry of pure fact. This is the purity that has been missing from our poems.

Red-winged Blackbirds floating in like Piper Cubs, suns on shoulders. Phoebe brooding on her egg. Towhee, Picasso camouflage, comic butler in tails. Catbird chat. Brown Thrasher variations. Oriole riff. Pheasants waltz across the road. In the field a Crow barks. A Hawk hangs in the air, absolutely still. Grouse explode in the underbrush. Doves at their vespers. Invisible, huge in the night sky, a train of Canada Geese goes honking and gabbling full five minutes from engine to caboose.

There was an item on the menu and the Chinese was translated as "Ear-tree." It was right between Shar Ding Op (chickens, Chinese frankfurter, water chestnut) and Hong Hong Duk (lobster nails, pig flesh, Chinese vegetable). Myself I was all for getting the "Ten Ingredient." I felt expansive and experimental. But Phoebe, who was a big girl, tended toward "Mile High Rice," with maybe an order of "Stopped Duck," or "Blistered Beef," whatever that was. So then we asked ourselves, well, what would "the Sparrow" do? Our eyes met for an instant. There was no doubt about it: "Ear-tree." We didn't even have to speak.

"Seen as how I'm a nice guy, I'll give you a tip. We like to stop guys with long hair, especially in old cars. They look like students. You're a teacher. Teach and be taught."

I put the ticket in my pocket. "Yeah. Well I didn't know driving with studded snow tires was illegal in this state after May first as of ten days ago." I opened my car door.

"Hey. Come 'ere."

I walked back to the patrol car.

"It's not illegal."

"No?"

"No. It's unlawful."

"Oh."

I walked back to my car and opened the door.

"Hey. Come 'ere."

I walked back to the patrol car.

"Ya know what illegal is?"

"No, what?"

"It's a sick bird. Hah hah hah."

Q. When does a bird break the law?

A. When it's a Robin.

Q. What characteristic distinguishes the Bald Eagle?

A. Its balls.

Q. When is a bird not a bird?

A. When it's a horse.

poor Americans are four times as likely to die
before the age of 35 as the average citizen
Negro women in Mississippi die
six times as often in childbirth as white women
in some urban ghettos of the North
one child in ten dies in infancy
the health gap between rich and poor is growing
in 1940 the infant mortality rate for non-whites
was 70% higher than that for whites
in 1962 the rate was 90% greater
the life expectancy of an American Negro is 61 years
that of a white American
is 68
it says
in the *Sunday*
Times

The Downy Woodpecker, in his prison outfit, is easily confused with the Hairy, which in fact is almost identical. However the Downy is smaller than the Hairy, and its call, *pik,* is softer than Hairy's. The Black-capped Chickadee is the friendliest of acrobats. The Bobwhite is a gallinaceous bird, very henny in other words, and acts it. But let us ascend from the ridiculous to the majestic. The Whistling Swan is common. It has a wingspan of over seven feet. Like other swans, it has a "deep, ponderous flight," neck extended. When swimming neck is stiff and straight; secondaries are not raised.

Q. What bird would you be glad to see if you were out of gas?
A. The Petrel.
Q. What birds can't fly straight?
A. Terns.
Q. What birds are often run over by trains?
A. Rails.
Q. What bird's ass would you not want to sit on?
A. The Pintail's.
Q. Which-a bird is not-a yours-a?
A. Myna.
Q. When does a bird make a sacrifice?
A. When it's a Bunting.
Q. What bird blows his whistle?
A. Old Dickcissel, old Dickcissel.

birds

the

what do they say

through the empty air

keep-back keep-back

peter-peter-peter

tea-cher tea-cher

o-say mari-a

hurry worry flurry blurry

drink-your-tea drink-your-tea

old sam peabodypeabodypeabody

ticket-ticket-ticket-ticket

wide-a-wake

rounde-lay rounde-lay

trees trees if you please

witchery-witchery-witchery

whip-three-beers

chicky-tucky-tuck

chicky-tucky-tuck

We are all, of course, familiar with that kind of anthropomorphic slop. What do the birds really say when you listen hard and understand what they are saying? They say k-a-a-a. They say kwrrk. They say

kow-kow-kow

keeur kleep

kzrrt

prrrp bzee

plick

rronk tlu-tlu

krr-oww

zrurrr wheet

peent

tsweep cuh-cuh

churree

che-bunk kraaa

che-bek

jeet hooah

tschizzik

kirrik ssllick

karr-reek

kwuririp kek-kek-kek

kee-oo

auw churweeoo

ooah-ooo-oo-oo

pchip ee pcheewee breep

But then again, what does it matter what they say? What matters is that they carve shapes from nothingness, decorate the silence, make melodious distinctions to distinguish one moment finely from the next.

I

call waiter. What thisee here, I say. He say, That is "ear-tree," a delicious Oriental specialty. But Phoebe no likee. What is? she ask. She little girl, no muchee eatee. "Ear-tree" is a popular and delicious Cantonese dish, say waiter. He Chinee fella. It is highly recommended, he say. But what is? I say. Waiter shrug and stare to other sidee room with inscrutable Chinee face. No likee, Phoebe say. You got Chicken Chow Mein. Waiter nod. I order Chop Suey. Then other customer come. They order "ear-tree." Waiter go in kitchen, we hear yellee to cook: Two spaghettis! I callee waiter. What this "ear-tree," I say. I pointee at menu. You say is Canton dish. Then waiter answer: It doesn't matter what you say. What matters is to hurl the words at the silence of the page like hand grenades. With feeling. Look out! someone screamed. He's got a gun!

"But why 'ear-tree'?" asked Phoebe, wide-eyed. She was a slim, light-haired pale face on summer vacation from Bryn Mawr College, but with very big boobs.

"Ah, these ees the ow-you-say question my young chérie," answered Sparrow. She was at the same time flattered and offended by his insistence that she use his first name, for it implied both a compliment and an impropriety. Why, she wondered, as she stared out the porthole and watched the clouds transform themselves from moment to moment, feeling the touch of his sharkskin on her bare microskirted thigh, did her parents allow a trip to Europe in the company of this strange, dark, manly business acquaintance of her father's, with his profile, his greying sideburns, and his carriage and skin texture that reminded her so much of an erect cock? She quivered a bit in her seat, and fastened her safety belt. He was mainly Latin in descent, from a Franco-Italian Spanish family with an intermixture of Greco-Moorish blood, that settled on the island of Malta some centuries ago in the wake of the conquest of Jerusalem. Sparrow. Spiro? Ero? She wondered if it was his real name. He was the kind of person that might be incognito. The jetliner shuddered through a cumulonimbus. She pulled a lever easing her seat into a reclining position that thrust her long full firm young thighs up and forward from the pelvis where the thin stuff of her microgarb caught and bunched under her seatbelt.

"But why 'ear-tree'?" asked Phoebe.

"My charming eediot," rejoined his vibrant basso, "if we knew these . . ." His middle and index fingers grazed her thigh confidentially, and came to rest near the hem of her skirt. She pretended not to notice, since she didn't know what else to do, and turned to look through the porthole where she saw a sheep running across the wing, no not a sheep a puff of smoke, another, another then after a pause a band of grey a plume of roiling black with suddenly red at its root . . .

"Built entirely without design precedent or orderly planning, created bit by bit on sheer impulse, a natural artist's instinct, and the fantasy of the moment": Simone Rodia's Watts Towers. Connections proliferate, meanings drop away.

Sparrow left England traveling as a young Greek sailor named George and Nick. I found him easily before the ship had cleared harbor leaning against the starboard rail in tight white pants and striped blue shirt. The day was blue with white clouds, whitecaps, gulls dove and hung above the churning stern. The gulls of Dover scream like Harpies and fly on wings of rusty iron. Sparrow was traveling as a young Greek sailor named George and Nick, but he spoke with a thick Italian accent. "'owza da boy?" he greeted me. His theory was that from his Italian accent he would be taken for a notorious Neapolitan intellectual known as "the Cardinal" who was inclined to proletarian dress and argot as a disguise. If however he were recognized as the Greek sailor boy George and Nick masquerading as the Cardinal in proletdrag, he would still be ahead of the game. This was the evasive measure known as bifurcation. While the authorities are interrogating George and Nick, Sparrow slips out between the two of them. Or if they settle on George, Nick sidles off and meantime George subdivides into Sparrow-Spiro-Ero. The principle here is progressive fission as in certain microorganisms. They never catch up with you, whoever you are. But this, ironically, is the hang-up of the method, since some agents have been left stranded in a maze of sloughed identities nursing a king-size identity problem. Often you will see an old hand slap a green agent on the back, wink, and growl avuncularly, "Say kid, what you say we go fission?" This is the process referred to, so beware.

Sparrow pointed toward a couple standing on the bridge next to the skipper, and slipped a homing pigeon out of his attaché case. The man was tall and slender, suntanned, and of a distinguished allure in the French sense. The woman was tall and slender, suntanned, and also of a distinguished allure, etc. At this distance it was a little difficult to tell them apart, though they were both quite distinct from the skipper, who was pale and squat and emanated banality. The bird ruffled and fluttered, happy to escape its confinement. Sparrow set it on his wrist, raised it high in the air, and whispered "Dai! Dai!" The pigeon flapped off while Sparrow began reciting the Paolo and Francesca episode from the fifth canto of the *Commedia.* We watched as the bird hovered over the woman's head for a moment, then perched on her shoulder. We watched as she reached up and removed the message from the bird's leg, still looking straight ahead. We watched as she swallowed the note, took the pigeon, twisted its neck, and let it flop to the deck. Then the suntanned man was standing alone on the bridge, near the squat skipper, still looking straight ahead. Sparrow pointed to the man and shrugged. "I wuz-a fuck 'iz-a wife," he said in explanation. Just then said lady appeared at the rail near us and stood there looking straight ahead. "Beh!" said Sparrow. Was he as surprised as I was to recognize Phoebe? There was probably no telling. She looked straight ahead, her eyes on the horizon. The gulls dipped and hung in our wake. Sparrow cleared his throat. "Ear-tree," he said. Phoebe turned to him, her charcoal eyes smouldering in her olive face: "Millions of people are starving. A sixth of the population lives in poverty. In the richest nation in the world, in the history of the world. Abroad we practice mass murder, at home slow genocide. How long can we continue to regard as democratic a nation run like a company town for corporate profit, built-in poverty, endemic racism? Starving children suffer irreversible brain damage while Senators get rich.

Soldiers die while profits soar. Democracy by tear gas, Mace, and political assassination. What are we going to do?"

"We like to stop guys with long hair and old cars," he said. "First of all old cars are a drug on the market like. I mean seen as how you got an old car it means you ain't got a new car right. And if all you was to pay is a few bucks on an old car you ain't puttin much back into the system are yiz? And that breaks the law of the market which is free enterprise.

"Now we ain't got nothin against long hair see. But what about all these guys that set up shop as barbers, they gotta make their profit, right? That breaks the law of supply and demand.

"Now another thing is long hair ain't neat like. And if it ain't neat it's unruly. And if it's unruly it's unlawful in this state according to a law on the books as of ten days ago by which appearance can be considered an extension of overt behavior during periods of national emergency such as for example now.

"Now seen as how guys with long hair and old cars don't fit in a system for guys with old hair and long cars, what that means is you're a troublemaker which is an offense by the new law that considers mental attitude an extension of overt behavior during times of national emergency 063589 state penal code and authorizes the arresting officer to put certain questions to the accused according to the mental stop-and-search provision on grounds of reasonable suspicion like long hair and old cars. Wrong answers are considered grounds for perjury.

Part I *Short Answer* (10 points)

1. How would you define "illegal"?
2. What characteristic distinguishes the Bald Eagle?
3. When does a bird break the law?
4. What birds can't fly straight?
5. What bird's ass would you not want to sit on?

Part II *Essay* (90 points)

Choose *one* of the following:

a) This story is "entirely without design precedent or orderly planning, created bit by bit on sheer impulse, a natural artist's instinct, and the fantasy of the moment." Why do you think the police don't like that? Discuss.

b) What is "ear-tree"? Give examples.

In Part II, I answered b). This was my answer: "Connections proliferate, meanings disperse. The painter studies his nude, his landscape."

IN A SPIRIT OF JOY AND REVOLUTIONARY EXULTATION, THOUSANDS OF STUDENTS OCCUPIED THE SORBONNE TODAY.

THE STUDENTS STARTED MOVING INTO THE UNIVERSITY LATE LAST NIGHT, AFTER COMPLETING THEIR JOINT PROTEST MARCH WITH THE WORKERS OF PARIS AND SPENDING THE EVENING DANCING ON THE COBBLED STREETS OF THE LATIN QUARTER.

IN THE GRANDIOSE COBBLED COURTYARD OF THE MAIN BUILDING A SMALL JAZZ BAND PLAYED ALL THROUGH THE NIGHT.

AFTER 10 DAYS OF BLOODY CLASHES WITH THE POLICE, NOT A SINGLE POLICEMAN WAS IN SIGHT. STUDENTS IN WHITE HELMETS DIRECTED TRAFFIC. THE GOVERNMENT HAD SURRENDERED THIS PART OF THE CITY TO THE STUDENTS.

HUNDREDS OF THOUSANDS OF STUDENTS TOOK TO THE STREETS NOT ONLY IN PARIS BUT IN MOST PROVINCIAL CITIES.

MANY HAD A FEAR THAT GOVERNMENTAL POWER HAD BROKEN DOWN.

THE STUDENTS THEMSELVES DELIBERATELY HARKED BACK TO THE BATTLE CRIES THAT HAD SERVED EARLIER FRENCH REVOLUTIONARIES.

TWO THOUSAND WORKERS, IMITATING THE REBELLIOUS STUDENTS OF THE SORBONNE, HAVE OCCUPIED THE AIRCRAFT CONSTRUCTION PLANT OF SUD-AVIATION AT NANTES, ON THE ATLANTIC COAST, AND ARE HOLDING THE PLANT MANAGER AND HIS PRINCIPAL AIDES PRISONERS.

THE WORKERS, WHO WERE ALREADY ON STRIKE, MOVED INTO THE PLANT EARLY LAST NIGHT AND WELDED THE MAIN GATE CLOSED. THEY THREW UP BARRICADES ON THE ROADS LEADING TO THE PLANT. THEY CLOSED DOWN THE NANTES AIRPORT, WHICH IS ADJACENT TO THE FACTORY.

FRANCE'S SOCIAL REVOLT SPREAD AND CHANGED IN NATURE TODAY AS AN ESTIMATED 100,000 STRIKERS OCCUPIED DOZENS OF FACTORIES IN ALL PARTS OF THE COUNTRY.

THE STRIKE MOVEMENT SPREAD SO SWIFTLY THAT, WITHIN HALF AN HOUR EARLY THIS EVENING, REPORTS REACHED PARIS THAT SEVEN MAJOR INDUSTRIAL PLANTS AND SHIPYARDS HAD BEEN TAKEN OVER IN LE HAVRE ALONE.

PRODUCERS AND DIRECTORS OF THE GOVERNMENT'S TELEVISION AND RADIO SYSTEM WENT ON STRIKE AND THE SYSTEM'S NEWSMEN VOTED TO REFUSE TO ACCEPT

ANY FURTHER DIRECTIVES FROM THE INFORMATION MINISTRY OR OTHER GOVERNMENT AGENCIES ON THEIR NEWS REPORTS.

WORKERS SEIZED THE GOLD-DOMED OPERA AND THE OPERA COMIQUE.

THE SPEECHES AT THE NATIONAL ASSEMBLY SEEMED STRANGELY IRRELEVANT. FRANCOIS MITTERAND, THE OPPOSITION LEADER, AND WALDECK ROCHET, THE HEAD OF THE COMMUNIST PARTY, WERE AS HOPELESSLY OUT OF TOUCH AS PREMIER GEORGES POMPIDOU. THEY WERE ALL PART OF THE "ESTABLISHMENT."

ONE OF THE STUDENT LEADERS, DANIEL COIN-BENDIT, CALLED THE COMMUNISTS "STALLINIST CREEPS." MR. COHN-BENDIT, CALLED DANNY THE RED, APPEARS TO HOLD VIEWS CLOSE TO ANARCHISM.

THE BLACK FLAG OF THE ANARCHISTS MADE ITS APPEARANCE DURING THE MASSIVE PARADE OF STUDENTS AND WORERS YEKSTERDAY.

THE RED FLAG WAS HOISTED OVER SEVERAL PLANTS.

THE RED AND THE BLACK FLAGS APPEARED TOGETHER, AN ABNORMAL SITUATION BECAUSE THE COMMUNISTS AND ANARCHISTS HAVE LONG BEEN ENEMIES. THE JOINT APPEARANCE WAS ONE OF THE MANY SIGNS THAT SOMETHING NEW HAD HAPPENED.

IF THE MOVEMENT IS AN UNCONTROLLED REVOLUTIONARY UPSURGE, THE COUNTRY MAY BE PLUNGED INTO ANARCHY.

THE DECISION OF THE WORKERS APPEARS TO HAVE BEEN A SPONTANEOUS MOVE BY THE RANK-AND-FILE STRIKERS, WHO ACTED WITHOUT ORDERS FROM POLITICAL PARTIES OR LABOR UNIONS.

THE STUDENT REVOLT WAS SIMILARLY UNOFFICIAL IN ITS ORIGIN.

IT IS THIS POPULAR AND REVOLUTIONARY CHARACTER OF THE MOVEMENT THAT LEADS MANY OBSERVERS TO FEEL THAT THE STUDENTS MAY HAVE UNLEASHED FORCES THAT CANNOT BE HARNESSED OR TAMED BY CONVENTIONAL MEANS, EITHER BY THE GOVERNMENT OR THE TRADITIONAL OPPOSITION PARTIES, INCLUDING THE COMMUNISTS.

JUST WHAT CAUSED THE STUDENTS' AND WORKERS' REVOLT TO ASSUME SUCH EXPLOSIVE DIMENSIONS IS STILL A MYSTERY TO MOT OBSERVER HERE.

MANY HAVE LINKED THE DISILLUSION OF THE FRENCH STUDENT TO A GLOBAL STUDENT MALAISE.

THE GAULLIST ADMINISTRATION, LIKE MANY PRIVATE CITIZENS, IS CONVINCED THAT A TRULY REVOLUTIONARY SITUATION EXISTS AND THAT THE DEMOCRATIC INSTITUTIONS OF FRANCE ARE THREATENED.

THE PRINCIPAL THREAT LIES IN THE SPONTANEOUS, POPULAR AND UTTERLY UNCONTROLLED NATURE OF THE MOVEMENT.

THE REVOLT, BY ITS SPONTANEOUS, TOTALLY UNCONTROLLED AND UNCONTROLLABLE NATURE HAD BECOME A TRULY REVOLUTIONARY EVENT.

IF THE COMMUNIST PARTY HAS MANAGED TO TAKE OVER THE MOVEMENT, THEN, IRONICALLY, THE INSTITUTIONS ARE SAFE AND THE POLITICAL CONTEST IS LIKELY TO MOVE BACK INTO THE NATIONAL ASSEMBLY, WITH VOTES OF CONFIDENCE AND VOTES OF CENSURE AND TRADITIONAL SPEECHES—AND SOONER OR LATER A NEW ELECTION.

SOMETHING HAS BEEN CREATED THAT IS IRREVERSIBLE. THERE WILL BE NO GOING BACK TO THE STATUS QUO.

The police want an end to this disorder and that depends on one question and one question only: What is "ear-tree"? This in turn leads us to the matter of the identity of the man called "Ero." Destroy this as you read. It is printed in a soluble ink which you can lick off the page sentence by sentence. The ink has various flavors depending on the parts of speech to make this easier to understand and swallow.

To get to the point, the police suspect a plot, yet all they see is disorder. They suspect that disorder is part of the plot, if not the point of it. They imagine that they merely have to figure out the plot to put an end to the disorder. But they don't understand the plot and believe the explanation lies with the meaning of the word "ear-tree." In turn they believe that this meaning will lead them to a man called Ero. In real life Ero is an eminent ornithologist, but the police believe that he is the leader of an international liberation conspiracy, and that only in his mind are all the connections coherently held together, the whole matter fully understood. To make matters worse, they aren't even sure whether Ero is dead or alive, or for that matter whether that is his right name.

I first met Ero in Tompkins Square Park. He was disguised as a bum. Although he was given to a kind of banal chattering—he sometimes compared himself to a Starling—I soon realized that this was a mere verbal subterfuge, so to speak, which could not prevent the escape of sudden flashes of the profoundest insight. For example he once remarked, almost as a non sequitur, that the whole country had to get back to nipples. It was not long before I was captivated by his brilliance and charisma. At about that point I met another of his admirers, an English "bird" named Phoebe. Though she attended an American college, she was married; however, she had an ambiguous relation with her husband, and while she traveled with him a good deal, she spent much of the time in the protection of her parents. Ero once indicated to me quite clearly that there had been something between them, but then, she was beautiful and he—he was Ero.

To continue, at that time Phoebe and I used to frequent Chinese restaurants. That was because it used to be Ero's way to plant his messages in fortune cookies and leave strictly to chance whether you received them or not—Ero favored chance because he said we must remain open to the unknown. They say that he still does this, and that you might for all you know receive a message from him yourself in your very next fortune cookie—a message that might change your life. Anyway we were sitting in this Cantonese place in midtown, speaking Pigeon English to put the natives at ease and to confuse the police. The waiter recommended "ear-tree"—could he have been Ero?—but when he ordered it for someone else called it "spaghetti."

At first I thought that "ear-tree" had something to do with birds—a kind of tree that birds liked to sing in, or to. Ero was of course filled with bird lore. Birds were something special for him. He said that bird songs constituted a kind of code which, when correctly deciphered, turned out to have absolutely no meaning. On the other hand he had a whole system of private symbolism worked out on the basis of what the various species meant to him, and would often express himself in its terms. This was a code the police never cracked, though God knows they tried. For example, he once sent me a message composed completely of bird images. These involved the Red-winged Blackbird, the Phoebe, the Rufous-sided Towhee, the Catbird, the Brown Thrasher, the Oriole (Orchard), the Pheasant, the Crow, the Hawk, the Grouse, the Dove, the Canada Goose, in that order. Knowing his system based on his emotional response to different birds, I worked the symbols out as follows:

Red-winged Blackbird = calm dash
Phoebe = domestic
Rufous-sided Towhee = human comedy
Catbird = eccentric relativism
Brown Thrasher = rich
Oriole (Orchard) = hot butter
Pheasant = beautiful fortune, pathetic sacrifice
Crow = wisdom floats intensely
Hawk = kill with grace
Grouse = explosion
Dove = dumb animals
Canada Goose = away, away

Decoded and allowing for variation in the given images in which the birds appeared, this means, roughly: "The *calm dash* of our once *domestic* culture has faded along with our old *human comedy*. In its place we have an *eccentric relativism* that is as *rich* as experience itself, yet as slippery as *hot butter*. Today's tragic hero is a man of *beautiful fortune, pathetic sacrifice*—his role as rich as the flux itself, and his denouement as meaningless. But in this streaming chaos *wisdom floats intensely* could one but be deadly enough with the fine net of intelligence. For wisdom and art mean precisely to kill the quick of our experience as it races past, but to *kill with grace* so that the victim may be preserved, as if alive, from oblivion. The universe is a long, an infinite *explosion* in which we are driven for an instant like *dumb animals* as it rushes *away, away*."

Unfortunately, when I showed this interpretation to Ero, he got very angry and tore it up. When I asked what his system of bird symbolism meant to him he replied: "Nothing. A feather here and there, a color, a squawk, disconnected, opaque, totally self-contained, ending in a triumph of birdness, song and soar, itself opaque and without equivalent, but the feeling ordered and defined—like that of a bird's song, or of its flight."

That was my last encounter with Ero, as such. Immediately after that he assumed the guise of Spiro the spy, then of the Cardinal, then of George and Nick, and then literally disappeared in a welter of dividing and subdividing identities—Orson, Chet Nexus, the Beach Boy, Madame Lafayette, the Light-fingered Trio—to name just a few. Originally intended as an evasive measure against an assassination plot, this frenzy of transformations, some believe, may have made him a victim of terminal identity fission, a malignant psychological disorder which progressively rarefies the ego so that it ultimately loses consciousness of itself and in effect ceases to exist. Some say that he was seized and murdered in one of his ephemeral metamorphoses—thrown overboard by the squat skipper and the pimply homosexual second mate as George and Nick, on board a plane that crashed in mysterious circumstances off Iceland, shot dead in a Chinese restaurant by a Cuban exile who ordered "ear-tree" and got spaghetti. No one really knows.

What we do now know definitely, or at least what I know and you will in thirty seconds, is the meaning of "ear-tree." Shhh. It was on Icelandic that eighteen-hour flight from Luxemburg where your feet swell up when the insight came to me. Three A.M. and I couldn't sleep. We had been traveling maybe nine, ten hours. Nothing could have been further from my mind than that old riddle. I leaned back against my pillow and thought *oreiller*, French for pillow. I had been in France. Then I thought *pommier*, apple tree, *cerisier*, cherry tree, *pêcher*, peach tree, *oranger*, orange tree. Then I thought *oreille*, ear. Then I thought viola! *oreiller*, "ear-tree." But why "ear-tree" on a Chinese menu? Of course!

Spaghetti. In Chinese restaurants in France, *lo-mein,* which as we know was brought from China to Italy as *spaghetti,* is often called *pilaf* or *pilaw,* from the Arabic, because it is used as a pillow for some kind of ragout or sauce. So some Chinese who knew neither French nor English nor Arabic very well, translated *lo-mein* to *pilaw, pilaw* to *oreiller,* and *oreiller* from French to English as "ear-tree." I immediately dropped off into a profound slumber from which I awoke next morning completely refreshed.

When I arrived in New York, I went back to that same Chinese restaurant and ordered a large "ear-tree." It was of excellent quality, at least three stars, and I polished it off with tremendous satisfaction. The message in my fortune cookie read: "Connections proliferate, meanings are dispelled. The traveler studies out his map."

"Je suis réellement désolé I'm really sorry to have waited so long before answering you but I am totally caught up in the events that have taken place in May and in June in France. You've undoubtedly had some echoes but it's difficult to imagine the extraordinary enthusiasm that sustained the young people during the month of May."

"To form a perfect conception of the beauty and elegance of these Swans, you must observe them when they are not aware of your proximity . . . the neck, which at other times is held stiffly upright, moves in graceful curves . . . with a sudden effort a flood of water is thrown over the back and wings, when it is seen rolling off in sparkling globules, like so many large pearls. The bird then shakes its wings, beats the water, and as if giddy with delight shoots away, gliding . . . with surprising agility and grace. Imagine, reader, that a flock of fifty Swans are thus sporting before you, as they have more than once in my sight, and you will feel, as I have felt, more happy and void of care than I can describe."

The dress was made of clinging white nylon jersey of a thinness that in certain angles of light would outline the thighs or reveal the curve of a breast and which, when taut against the skin, assumed something of the warm flesh tone. Slashed to the waist, it left the nipples free to poke and bob through the material.

in the richest country in the world/ people eat clay to still the pains of an empty belly/ children come to school too hungry to learn/ and the infants of the poor suffer/ irreversible brain damage from protein deprivation

JUST WHAT CAUSED THE STUDENTS' AND WORKERS' REVOLT TO ASSUME SUCH EXPLOSIVE DIMENSIONS IS STILL A MYSTERY TO MOT OBSERVER HERE MANY HAVE LINKED THE DISILLUSION OF THE FRENCH STUDENT TO A GLOBAL STUDENT MALAISE

Ero is an eminent ornithologist,

but the police believe that he is the leader of an international liberation conspiracy, and that only in his mind are all the connections coherently held together

"A pattern was seen in the use of females to bite and kick the policemen" *New York Times* 5/7/68. Its drumming, distinct from other peckers, resembles the sound of a muffled machine gun, a soft, hollow automatic weapon.

"Les manifestations sur les barricades the demonstrations on the barricades were only one aspect, perhaps secondary, of this surprising movement, much more astonishing was the climate in the streets. We organized every day and during the month of May all-day meetings each of which gathered up to a hundred people sometimes until two in the morning."

THE REVOLT BY ITS SPONTANEOUS TOTALLY UNCONTROLLED AND UNCONTROLLABLE NATURE HAD BECOME A TRULY REVOLUTIONARY EVENT

"Spontanément spontaneously, the people raised the real problems, confusedly felt and it was this, exactly that was extraordinary—it was not a question of the usual political theories struggling but of notions as vague as human dignity, the responsibility of each man, the infinite resources of the emotion of enthusiasm facing efficiency, the power of technology—"

IF THE MOVEMENT IS AN UNCONTROLLED REVOLUTIONARY UPSURGE THE COUNTRY MAY BE PLUNGED INTO ANARCHY

"entirely without design precedent or orderly planning, created bit by bit on sheer impulse"

coincidence such things renew my faith in the unknown I am always interested in any overt confrontation with chance though if you stop to think about it every moment is such a confrontation for each of us Ero favored chance because he said we must remain open to the unknown

the stream carries mainly on its glassy surface rippled clouds inventing themselves from minute to minute, fantastic shapes, formations piling shifting flowing, distortions of distortions of distortions

"Nous attendons we await November, December but also the movements that cannot fail to appear in Italy, Germany perhaps the United States . . ."

in the richest country in the world

an international liberation conspiracy

the children of the poor

caused the revolt to assume such explosive
spontaneous
totally uncontrolled and uncontrollable
a soft hollow automatic
weapon
left the nipples free to poke and bob
much more astonishing was the climate in the streets
a small jazz band played all
through the night
the infinite resources of the motion of enthusiasm
created bit by bit on sheer impulse
we await November December
formations piling shifting flowing
we must remain open
to the unknown
the bird then shakes its wings beats the water and shoots away gliding like other Swans it has a deep ponderous flight the underwing is an astonishing pink-gold stroke of scarlet from green to green Nuthatch bullets through blank air Red-winged Blackbirds floating in in the field a Crow barks

Pheasants waltz across the road
Grouse explode in the underbrush
a Hawk

hangs
in the air

birds

the

QUESTIONS FOR DISCUSSION

1. Find and discuss passages that suggest the way the fictionist may want you to approach his fiction. Consider, for instance, passages in which Sukenick ridicules theme or message-mongering and symbol hunting.
2. What relationships does Sukenick suggest between descriptions of birds and descriptions of other actions (human and mechanical)?

3. Discuss the effect of Sukenick's use of the technique of juxtaposition: birds/ planes/ actual world events/ fictive events in a spy story framework/ comments on the process of making fictions. Major and trivial ideas and events are juxtaposed, sometimes in the same line; what does that scale of importance imply?
4. Why does the narrator repeat several passages subtly throughout the fiction and numerous passages obviously at the end?
5. Discuss the relevance to "Title" and "The Birds" of this assertion: These fictionists simultaneously burlesque reality and literature and ponder their natures in dead earnest.
6. Would a reshuffling of the order, time scheme, and scale of importance of events in the three fictions in this section violate their intentions?
7. Discuss similarities and contrasts among these three pieces regarding their comments on the process of making fictions.
8. Examine and compare the styles of these three fictions, the fictionists' use of abstract statements, repetitions and variations, their careful use of words and the way they position words in a sentence. Do some words resonate as words do in lines of poetry? Find instances of word play (puns and the like). Why do these fictionists use clichés at times, with stereotyped characters and trite situations, especially in "Title" and "The Birds"?
9. Discuss the relevance to all three fictions of the following statement made by the narrator of "The Death of the Novel," Sukenick's novella: "I hate chronology, that's what kills me. . . . This story works on the principle of simultaneous multiplicity, or the knack of keeping several things on your mind at once. That is the central fact of our mental atmosphere."

8 More Stories

EDGAR ALLAN POE

The Man That Was Used Up

A Tale of the Late Bugaboo and Kickapoo Campaign

Pleurez, pleurez, mes yeux, et fondez vous en eau!
La moitié de ma vie a mis l'autre au tombeau.
CORNEILLE

I cannot just now remember when or where I first made the acquaintance of that truly fine-looking fellow, Brevet Brigadier General John A. B. C. Smith. Some one *did* introduce me to the gentleman, I am sure—at some public meeting, I know very well—held about something of great importance, no doubt—at some place or other, I feel convinced, —whose name I have unaccountably forgotten. The truth is—that the introduction was attended, upon my part, with a degree of anxious embarrassment which operated to prevent any definite impressions of either time or place. I am constitutionally nervous—this, with me, is a family failing, and I can't help it. In especial, the slightest appearance of mystery—of any point I cannot exactly comprehend—puts me at once into a pitiable state of agitation.

There was something, as it were, remarkable—yes, *remarkable*, although this is but a feeble term to express my full meaning—about the entire individuality of the personage in question. He was, perhaps, six feet in height, and of a presence singularly commanding. There was an *air distingué* pervading the whole man, which spoke of high breeding, and hinted at high birth. Upon this topic—the topic of Smith's personal appearance—I have a kind of melancholy satisfaction in being minute. His head of hair would have done honor to a Brutus;—nothing could be more richly flowing, or possess a brighter gloss. It was of a jetty black; —which was also the color, or more properly the no-color of his unimaginable whiskers. You perceive I cannot speak of these latter without enthusiasm; it is not too much to say that they were the handsomest pair of whiskers under the sun. At all events, they encircled, and at times partially overshadowed, a mouth utterly unequalled. Here were the most entirely even, and the most brilliantly white of all conceivable teeth.

From between them, upon every proper occasion, issued a voice of surpassing clearness, melody, and strength. In the matter of eyes, also, my acquaintance was pre-eminently endowed. Either one of such a pair was worth a couple of the ordinary ocular organs. They were of a deep hazel exceedingly large and lustrous; and there was perceptible about them, ever and anon, just that amount of interesting obliquity which gives pregnancy to expression.

The bust of the General was unquestionably the finest bust I ever saw. For your life you could not have found a fault with its wonderful proportion. This rare peculiarity set off to great advantage a pair of shoulders which would have called up a blush of conscious inferiority into the countenance of the marble Apollo. I have a passion for fine shoulders, and may say that I never beheld them in perfection before. The arms altogether were admirably modelled. Nor were the lower limbs less superb. These were, indeed, the *ne plus ultra* of good legs. Every connoisseur in such matters admitted the legs to be good. There was neither too much flesh nor too little,—neither rudeness nor fragility. I could not imagine a more graceful curve than that of the *os femoris,* and there was just that due gentle prominence in the rear of the *fibula* which goes to the conformation of a properly proportioned calf. I wish to God my young and talented friend Chiponchipino, the sculptor, had but seen the legs of Brevet Brigadier General John A. B. C. Smith.

But although men so absolutely fine-looking are neither as plenty as reasons or blackberries, still I could not bring myself to believe that *the remarkable* something to which I alluded just now,—that the odd air of *je ne sais quoi* which hung about my new acquaintance,—lay altogether, or indeed at all, in the supreme excellence of his bodily endowments. Perhaps it might be traced to the *manner;*—yet here again I could not pretend to be positive. There *was* a primness, not to say stiffness, in his carriage—a degree of measured and, if I may so express it, of rectangular precision attending his every movement, which, observed in a more diminutive figure, would have had the least little savor in the world of affectation, pomposity, or constraint, but which, noticed in a gentleman of his undoubted dimensions, was readily placed to the account of reserve, *hauteur*—of a commendable sense, in short, of what is due to the dignity of colossal proportion.

The kind friend who presented me to General Smith whispered in my ear some few words of comment upon the man. He was a *remarkable* man—a *very* remarkable man—indeed one of the *most* remarkable men of the age. He was an especial favorite, too, with the ladies—chiefly on account of his high reputation for courage.

"In *that* point he is unrivalled—indeed he is a perfect desperado—a downright fire-eater, and no mistake," said my friend, here dropping his voice excessively low, and thrilling me with the mystery of his tone.

"A downright fire-eater, and *no* mistake. Showed *that,* I should say, to some purpose, in the late tremendous swamp-fight, away down South, with the Bugaboo and Kickapoo Indians." [Here my friend opened his eyes to some extent.] "Bless my soul!—blood and thunder, and all that! —*prodigie*s of valor!—heard of him of course?—you know he's the man——"

"Man alive, how *do* you do? why, how *are* ye? *very* glad to see ye, indeed!" here interrupted the General himself, seizing my companion by the hand as he drew near, and bowing stiffly but profoundly, as I was presented. I then thought (and I think so still) that I never heard a clearer nor a stronger voice, nor beheld a finer set of teeth: but I *must* say that I was sorry for the interruption just at that moment, as, owing to the whispers and insinuations aforesaid, my interest had been greatly excited in the hero of the Bugaboo and Kickapoo campaign.

However, the delightfully luminous conversation of Brevet Brigadier General John A. B. C. Smith soon completely dissipated this chagrin. My friend leaving us immediately, we had quite a long *tête-à-tête,* and I was not only pleased but *really*—instructed. I never heard a more fluent talker, or a man of greater general information. With becoming modesty, he forebore, nevertheless, to touch upon the theme I had just then most at heart—I mean the mysterious circumstances attending the Bugaboo war—and, on my own part, what I conceive to be a proper sense of delicacy forbade me to broach the subject; although, in truth, I was exceedingly tempted to do so. I perceived, too, that the gallant soldier preferred topics of philosophical interest, and that he delighted, especially, in commenting upon the rapid march of mechanical invention. Indeed, lead him where I would, this was a point to which he invariably came back.

"There is nothing at all like it," he would say; "we are a wonderful people, and live in a wonderful age. Parachutes and rail-roads—man-traps and spring-guns! Our steam-boats are upon every sea, and the Nassau balloon packet is about to run regular trips (fare either way only twenty pounds sterling) between London and Timbuctoo. And who shall calculate the immense influence upon social life—upon arts—upon commerce—upon literature—which will be the immediate result of the great principles of electro-magnetics! Nor, is this all, let me assure you! There is really no end to the march of invention. The most wonderful—the most ingenious—and let me add, Mr.—Mr.—Thompson, I believe, is your name—let me add, I say the most *useful*—the most truly *useful*—mechanical contrivances are daily springing up like mushrooms, if I may so express myself, or, more figuratively, like—ah—grasshoppers—like grasshoppers, Mr. Thompson—about us and ah—ah—ah—around us!"

Thompson, to be sure, is not my name; but it is needless to say that I left General Smith with a heightened interest in the man, with an exalted opinion of his conversational powers, and a deep sense of the valuable privileges we enjoy in living in this age of mechanical invention. My curiosity, however, had not been altogether satisfied, and I resolved to prosecute immediate inquiry among my acquaintances, touching the Brevet Brigadier General himself, and particularly respecting the tremendous events *quorum pars magna fuit,* during the Bugaboo and Kickapoo campaign.

The first opportunity which presented itself, and which (*horresco referens*) I did not in the least scruple to seize, occurred at the Church of the Reverend Doctor Drummummupp, where I found myself established, one Sunday, just at sermon time, not only in the pew, but by the side of that worthy and communicative little friend of mine, Miss Tabitha T. Thus seated, I congratulated myself, and with much reason, upon the very flattering state of affairs. If any person knew any thing about Brevet Brigadier General John A. B. C. Smith, that person, it was clear to me, was Miss Tabitha T. We telegraphed a few signals and then commenced, *sotto voce,* a brisk *tête-à-tête.*

"Smith!" said she in reply to my every earnest inquiry: "Smith!—why, not General John A. B. C.? Bless me, I thought you *knew* all about *him!* This is a wonderfully inventive age! Horrid affair that!—a bloody set of wretches, those Kickapoos!—fought like a hero—prodigies of valor—immortal renown. Smith!—Brevet Brigadier General John A. B. C.!—why, you know he's the man——"

"Man," here broke in Doctor Drummummupp, at the top of his voice, and with a thump that came near knocking the pulpit about our ears; "man that is born of a woman hath but a short time to live; he cometh up and is cut down like a flower!" I started to the extremity of the pew, and perceived by the animated looks of the divine, that the wrath which had nearly proved fatal to the pulpit had been excited by the whispers of the lady and myself. There was no help for it; so I submitted with a good grace, and listened, in all the martyrdom of dignified silence, to the balance of that very capital discourse.

Next evening found me a somewhat late visitor at the Rantipole Theatre, where I felt sure of satisfying my curiosity at once, by merely stepping into the box of those exquisite specimens of affability and omniscience, the Misses Arabella and Miranda Cognoscenti. That fine tragedian, Climax, was doing Iago to a very crowded house, and I experienced some little difficulty in making my wishes understood; especially as our box was next the slips, and completely overlooked the stage.

"Smith!" said Miss Arabella, as she at length comprehended the purport of my query; "Smith?—why, not General John A. B. C.?"

"Smith!" inquired Miranda, musingly. "God bless me, did you ever behold a finer figure?"

"Never, madam, but *do* tell me——"

"Or so inimitable grace?"

"Never, upon my word!—But pray, inform me——"

"Or so just an appreciation of stage effect?"

"Madam!"

"Or a more delicate sense of the true beauties of Shakespeare? Be so good as to look at that leg!"

"The devil!" and I turned again to her sister.

"Smith!" said she, "why, not General John A. B. C.? Horrid affair that, wasn't it?—great wretches, those Bugaboos—savage and so on—but we live in a wonderfully inventive age!—Smith!—O yes! great man!—perfect desperado—immortal renown—prodigies of valor! *Never heard!*" [This was given in a scream.] "Bless my soul! why, he's the man——"

"—mandragora
Nor all the drowsy syrups of the world
Shall ever medicine thee to that sweet sleep
Which thou ow'dst yesterday!"

here roared our Climax just in my ear, and shaking his fist in my face all the time, in a way that I *couldn't* stand, and I *wouldn't.* I left the Misses Cognoscenti immediately, went behind the scenes forthwith, and gave the beggarly scoundrel such a thrashing as I trust he will remember till the day of his death.

At the *soirée* of the lovely widow, Mrs. Kathleen O'Trump, I was confident that I should meet with no similar disappointment. Accordingly, I was no sooner seated at the card-table, with my pretty hostess for a *vis-a-vis,* than I propounded those questions the solution of which had become a matter so essential to my peace.

"Smith!" said my partner, "why, not General John A. B. C.? Horrid affair that, wasn't it?—diamonds did you say?—terrible wretches those Kickapoos!—we are playing *whist,* if you please, Mr. Tattle—however, this is the age of invention, most certainly *the* age, one may say—*the* age *par excellence*—speak French?—oh, quite a hero—perfect desperado! —*no hearts,* Mr. Tattle? I don't believe it!—Immortal renown and all that!—prodigies of valor! *Never heard!!*—why, bless me, he's the man——"

"Mann?—*Captain* Mann!" here screamed some little feminine interloper from the farthest corner of the room. "Are you talking about Captain Mann and the duel?—oh, I *must* hear—do tell—go on, Mrs. O'Trump!—do now go on!" And go on Mrs. O'Trump did—all about a certain Captain Mann, who was either shot or hung, or should have been both shot and hung. Yes! Mrs. O'Trump, she went on, and I—I went off. There was no chance of hearing any thing farther that evening in regard to Brevet Brigadier General John A. B. C. Smith.

Still I consoled myself with the reflection that the tide of ill-luck would not run against me forever, and so determined to make a bold push for information at the rout of that bewitching little angel, the graceful Mrs. Pirouette.

"Smith!" said Mrs. P., as we twirled about together in a *pas de zephyr,*

"Smith?—why, not General John A. B. C.? Dreadful business that of the Bugaboos, wasn't it?—dreadful creatures, those Indians!—*do* turn out your toes! I really am ashamed of you—man of great courage, poor fellow!—but this is a wonderful age for invention—O dear me, I'm out of breath—quite a desperado—prodigies of valor—*never heard!!*—can't believe it—I shall have to sit down and enlighten you—Smith! why, he's the man——"

"Man-*Fred,* I tell you!" here bawled out Miss Bas-Bleu, as I led Mrs. Pirouette to a seat. "Did ever anybody hear the like? It's Man-*Fred,* I say, and not at all by any means Man-*Friday.*" Here Miss Bas-Bleu beckoned to me in a very peremptory manner; and I was obliged, will I nill I, to leave Mrs. P. for the purpose of deciding a dispute touching the title of a certain poetical drama of Lord Byron's. Although I pronounced, with great promptness, that the true title was Man-*Friday,* and not by any means Man-*Fred* yet when I returned to seek Mrs. Pirouette she was not to be discovered, and I made my retreat from the house in a very bitter spirit of animosity against the whole race of the Bas-Bleus.

Matters had now assumed a really serious aspect, and I resolved to call at once upon my particular friend, Mr. Theodore Sinivate; for I knew that here at least I should get something like definite information.

"Smith!" said he, in his well known peculiar way of drawling out his syllables; "Smith!—why, not General John A. B. C.? Savage affair that with the Kickapo-o-o-os, wasn't it? Say, don't you think so?—perfect despera-a-ado—great pity, 'pon my honor!—wonderfully inventive age! —pro-o-odigies of valor! By the by, did you ever hear about Captain Ma-a-a-a-n?"

"Captain Mann be d—d!" said I; "please to go on with your story."

"Hem!—oh well!—quite *la même cho-o-ose,* as we say in France. Smith, eh? Brigadier-General John A. B. C.? I say"—[here Mr. S. thought proper to put his finger to the side of his nose]—"I say, you don't mean to insinuate now, really and truly, and conscientiously, that you don't know all about that affair of Smith's, as well as I do, eh? Smith? John A—B—C.? Why, bless me, he's the ma-a-an——"

"*Mr.* Sinivate," said I, imploringly, "*is* he the man in the mask?"

"No-o-o!" said he, looking wise, "nor the man in the mo-o-on."

This reply I considered a pointed and positive insult, and so left the house at once in high dudgeon, with a firm resolve to call my friend, Mr. Sinivate, to a speedy account for his ungentlemanly conduct and ill breeding.

In the meantime, however, I had no notion of being thwarted touching the information I desired. There was one resource left me yet. I would go to the fountain head. I would call forthwith upon the General himself, and demand, in explicit terms, a solution of this abominable piece of mystery. Here, at least, there should be no chance for equivocation. I would be plain, positive, peremptory—as short as pie-crust—as concise as Tacitus or Montesquieu.

It was early when I called, and the General was dressing, but I pleaded urgent business, and was shown at once into his bedroom by an old negro valet, who remained in attendance during my visit. As I entered the chamber, I looked about, of course, for the occupant, but did not immediately perceive him. There was a large and exceedingly odd looking bundle of something which lay close by my feet on the floor, and, as I was not in the best humor in the world, I gave it a kick out of the way.

"Hem! ahem! rather civil that, I should say!" said the bundle, in one of the smallest, and altogether the funniest little voices, between a squeak and a whistle, that I ever heard in all the days of my existence.

"Ahem! rather civil that, I should observe."

I fairly shouted with terror, and made off, at a tangent, into the farthest extremity of the room.

"God bless me, my dear fellow!" here again whistled the bundle, "what—what—what—why, what *is* the matter? I really believe you don't know me at all."

What *could* I say to all this—what *could* I? I staggered into an armchair, and, with staring eyes and open mouth, awaited the solution of the wonder.

"Strange you shouldn't know me though, isn't it?" presently re-squeaked the nondescript, which I now perceived was performing upon the floor some inexplicable evolution, very analogous to the drawing on of a stocking. There was only a single leg, however, apparent.

"Strange you shouldn't know me though, isn't it? Pompey, bring me that leg!" Here Pompey handed the bundle a very capital cork leg, already dressed, which it screwed on in a trice; and then it stood upright before my eyes.

"And a bloody action it *was*," continued the thing, as if in a soliloquy; "but then one mustn't fight with the Bugaboos and Kickapoos, and think of coming off with a mere scratch. Pompey, I'll thank you now for that arm. Thomas" [turning to me] "is decidedly the best hand at a cork leg; but if you should ever want an arm, my dear fellow, you must really let me recommend you to Bishop." Here Pompey screwed on an arm.

"We had rather hot work of it, that you may say. Now, you dog, slip on my shoulders and bosom. Pettit makes the best shoulders, but for a bosom you will have to go to Ducrow."

"Bosom!" said I.

"Pompey, will you *never* be ready with that wig? Scalping is a rough process, after all; but then you can procure such a capital scratch at De L'Orme's."

"Scratch!"

"Now, you nigger, my teeth! For a *good* set of these you had better go to Parmly's at once; high prices, but excellent work. I swallowed some very capital articles, though, when the big Bugaboo rammed me down with the butt end of his rifle."

"Butt end! ram down!! my eye!!!"

"O yes, by the way, my eye—here, Pompey, you scamp, screw it in! Those Kickapoos are not so very slow at a gouge; but he's a belied man, that Dr. Williams, after all; you can't imagine how well I see with the eyes of his make."

I now began very clearly to perceive that the object before me was nothing more nor less than my new acquaintance, Brevet Brigadier General John A. B. C. Smith. The manipulations of Pompey had made, I must confess, a very striking difference in the appearance of the personal man. The voice, however, still puzzled me no little; but even this apparent mystery was speedily cleared up.

"Pompey, you black rascal," squeaked the General, "I really do believe you would let me go out without my palate."

Hereupon, the negro, grumbling out an apology, went up to his master, opened his mouth with the knowing air of a horse-jockey, and adjusted therein a somewhat singular-looking machine, in a very dexterous manner, that I could not altogether comprehend. The alteration, however, in the entire expression of the General's countenance was instantaneous and surprising. When he again spoke, his voice had resumed all that rich melody and strength which I had noticed upon our original introduction.

"D—n the vagabonds—!" said he, in so clear a tone that I positively started at the change, "D—n the vagabonds! they not only knocked in the roof of my mouth, but took the trouble to cut off at least seven-eighths of my tongue. There isn't Bonfanti's equal, however, in America, for really good articles of this description. I can recommend you to him with confidence," [here the General bowed,] "and assure you that I have the greatest pleasure in so doing."

I acknowledged his kindness in my best manner, and took leave of him at once, with a perfect understanding of the true state of affairs—with a full comprehension of the mystery which had troubled me so long. It was evident. It was a clear case. Brevet Brigadier General John A. B. C. Smith was the man—was *the man that was used up*.

NATHANIEL HAWTHORNE

My Kinsman, Major Molineux

After the kings of Great Britain had assumed the right of appointing the colonial governors, the measures of the latter seldom met with the ready and general approbation which had been paid to those of their predecessors, under the original charters. The people looked with most jealous scrutiny to the exercise of power which did not emanate from themselves, and they usually rewarded their rulers with slender gratitude for the compliances by which, in softening their instructions from beyond the sea, they had incurred the reprehension of those who gave them. The annals of Massachusetts Bay will inform us, that of six governors in the space of about forty years from the surrender of the old charter, under James II., two were imprisoned by a popular insurrection; a third, as Hutchinson inclines to believe, was driven from the province by the whizzing of a musket-ball; a fourth, in the opinion of the same historian, was hastened to his grave by continual bickerings with the House of Representatives; and the remaining two, as well as their successors, till the Revolution, were favored with few and brief intervals of peaceful sway. The inferior members of the court party, in times of high political excitement, led scarcely a more desirable life. These remarks may serve as a preface to the following adventures, which chanced upon a summer night, not far from a hundred years ago. The reader, in order to avoid a long and dry detail of colonial affairs, is requested to dispense with an account of the train of circumstances that had caused much temporary inflammation of the popular mind.

It was near nine o'clock of a moonlight evening, when a boat crossed the ferry with a single passenger, who had obtained his conveyance at that unusual hour by the promise of an extra fare. While he stood on the landing-place, searching in either pocket for the means of fulfilling his agreement, the ferryman lifted a lantern, by the aid of which, and the newly risen moon, he took a very accurate survey of the stranger's figure. He was a youth of barely eighteen years, evidently country-bred, and now, as it should seem, upon his first visit to town. He was clad in a coarse gray coat, well worn, but in excellent repair; his under garments were durably constructed of leather, and fitted tight to a pair of serviceable and well-shaped limbs; his stockings of blue yarn were the incontrovertible work of a mother or a sister; and on his head was a three-cornered hat, which in its better days had perhaps sheltered the graver brow of the lad's father. Under his left arm was a heavy cudgel formed of an oak sapling, and retaining a part of the hardened root; and his equipment was completed by a wallet, not so abundantly stocked as to incommode the vigorous shoulders on which it hung. Brown, curly hair, well-shaped features, and bright, cheerful eyes were nature's gifts, and worth all that art could have done for his adornment.

The youth, one of whose names was Robin, finally drew from his pocket the half of a little province bill of five shillings, which, in the depreciation in that sort of currency, did but satisfy the ferryman's demand, with the surplus of a sexangular piece of parchment, valued at three pence. He then walked forward into the town, with as light a step as if his day's journey had not already exceeded thirty miles, and with as eager an eye as if he were entering London city, instead of the little metropolis of a New England colony. Before Robin had proceeded far, however, it occurred to him that he knew not whither to direct his steps; so he paused, and looked up and down the narrow street, scrutinizing the small and mean wooden buildings that were scattered on either side.

"This low hovel cannot be my kinsman's dwelling," thought he, "nor yonder old house, where the moonlight enters at the broken casement; and truly I see none hereabouts that might be worthy of him. It would have been wise to inquire my way of the ferryman, and doubtless he would have gone with me, and earned a shilling from the Major for his pains. But the next man I meet will do as well."

He resumed his walk, and was glad to perceive that the street now became wider, and the houses more respectable in their appearance. He soon discerned a figure moving on moderately in advance, and hastened his steps to overtake it. As Robin drew nigh, he saw that the passenger was a man in years, with a full periwig of gray hair, a wide-skirted coat of dark cloth, and silk stockings rolled above his knees. He carried a long and polished cane, which he struck down perpendicularly before him at every step; and at regular intervals he uttered two successive hems, of a peculiarly solemn and sepulchral intonation. Having made these observations, Robin laid hold of the skirt of the old man's coat, just when the light from the open door and windows of a barber's shop fell upon both their figures.

"Good evening to you, honored sir," said he, making a low bow, and still retaining his hold of the skirt. "I pray you tell me whereabouts is the dwelling of my kinsman, Major Molineux."

The youth's question was uttered very loudly; and one of the barbers, whose razor was descending on a well-soaped chin, and another who was dressing a Ramillies wig, left their occupations, and came to the door.

The citizen, in the mean time, turned a long-favored countenance upon Robin, and answered him in a tone of excessive anger and annoyance. His two sepulchral hems, however, broke into the very centre of his rebuke, with most singular effect, like a thought of the cold grave obtruding among wrathful passions.

"Let go my garment, fellow! I tell you, I know not the man you speak of. What! I have authority, I have—hem, hem—authority; and if this be the respect you show for your betters, your feet shall be brought acquainted with the stocks by daylight, tomorrow morning!"

Robin released the old man's skirt, and hastened away, pursued by an ill-mannered roar of laughter from the barber's shop. He was at first considerably surprised by the result of his question, but, being a shrewd youth, soon thought himself able to account for the mystery.

"This is some country representative," was his conclusion, "who has never seen the inside of my kinsman's door, and lacks the breeding to answer a stranger civilly. The man is old, or verily—I might be tempted to turn back and smite him on the nose. Ah, Robin, Robin! even the barber's boys laugh at you for choosing such a guide! You will be wiser in time, friend Robin."

He now became entangled in a succession of crooked and narrow streets, which crossed each other, and meandered at no great distance from the water-side. The smell of tar was obvious to his nostrils, the masts of vessels pierced the moonlight above the tops of the buildings, and the numerous signs, which Robin paused to read, informed him that he was near the centre of business. But the streets were empty, the shops were closed, and lights were visible only in the second stories of a few dwelling-houses. At length, on the corner of a narrow lane, through which he was passing, he beheld the broad countenance of a British hero swinging before the door of an inn, whence proceeded the voices of many guests. The casement of one of the lower windows was thrown back, and a very thin curtain permitted Robin to distinguish a party at supper, round a well-furnished table. The fragrance of the good cheer steamed forth into the outer air, and the youth could not fail to recollect that the last remnant of his traveling stock of provision had yielded to his morning appetite, and that noon had found and left him dinnerless.

"Oh, that a parchment three-penny might give me a right to sit down at yonder table!" said Robin, with a sigh. "But the Major will make me welcome to the best of his victuals; so I will even step boldly in, and inquire my way to his dwelling."

He entered the tavern, and was guided by the murmur of voices and the fumes of tobacco to the public-room. It was a long and low apartment, with oaken walls, grown dark in the continual smoke, and a floor which was thickly sanded, but of no immaculate purity. A number of persons—the larger part of whom appeared to be mariners, or in some way connected with the sea—occupied the wooden benches, or leather-bottomed chairs, conversing on various matters, and occasionally lending their attention to some topic of general interest. Three or four little groups were draining as many bowls of punch, which the West India trade had long since made a familiar drink in the colony. Others, who had the appearance of men who lived by regular and laborious handicraft, preferred the insulated bliss of an unshared potation, and became more taciturn under its influence. Nearly all, in short, evinced a predilection for the Good Creature in some of its various shapes, for this is a vice to which, as Fast Day sermons of a hundred years ago will testify, we have a long hereditary claim. The only guests to whom Robin's sympathies inclined him were two or three sheepish countrymen, who were using the inn somewhat after the fashion of a Turkish caravansary; they had gotten themselves into the darkest corner of the room, and heedless of the Nicotian atmosphere, were supping on the bread of their own ovens, and the bacon cured in their own chimney-smoke. But though Robin felt a sort of brotherhood with these strangers, his eyes were attracted from them to a person who stood near the door, holding whispered conversation with a group of ill-dressed associates. His features were separately striking almost to grotesqueness, and the whole face left a deep impression on the memory. The forehead bulged out into a double prominence, with a vale between; the nose came boldly forth in an irregular curve, and its bridge was of more than a finger's breadth; the eyebrows were deep and shaggy, and the eyes glowed beneath them like fire in a cave.

While Robin deliberated of whom to inquire respecting his kinsman's dwelling, he was accosted by the innkeeper, a little man in a stained white apron, who had come to pay his professional welcome to the stranger. Being in the second generation from a French Protestant, he seemed to have inherited the courtesy of his parent nation; but no variety of circumstances was ever known to change his voice from the one shrill note in which he now addressed Robin.

"From the country, I presume, sir?" said he, with a profound bow. "Beg leave to congratulate you on your arrival, and trust you intend a long stay with us. Fine town here, sir, beautiful buildings, and much that may interest a stranger. May I hope for the honor of your commands in respect to supper?"

"The man sees a family likeness! The Rogue has guessed that I am related to the Major!" thought Robin, who had hitherto experienced little superfluous civility.

All eyes were now turned on the country lad, standing at the door, in his worn three-cornered hat, gray coat, leather breeches, and glue yarn stockings, leaning on an oaken cudgel, and bearing a wallet on his back.

Robin replied to the courteous innkeeper, with such an assumption of confidence as befitted the Major's relative. "My honest friend," he said, "I shall make it a point to patronize your house on some occasion, when"—here he could not help lowering his voice—"when I may have more than a parchment three-pence in my pocket. My present business," continued he, speaking with lofty confidence, "is merely to inquire my way to the dwelling of my kinsman, Major Molineux."

There was a sudden and general movement in the room, which Robin interpreted as expressing the eagerness of each individual to become his guide. But the innkeeper turned his eyes to a written paper on the wall, which he read, or seemed to read, with occasional recurrences to the young man's figure.

"What have we here?" said he, breaking his speech into little dry fragments. "'Left the house of the subscriber, bounden servant, Hezekiah Mudge,—had on, when he went away, gray coat, leather breeches, master's third-best hat. One pound currency reward to whosoever shall lodge him in any jail of the province.' Better trudge, boy; better trudge!"

Robin had begun to draw his hand towards the lighter end of the oak cudgel, but a strange hostility in every countenance induced him to relinquish his purpose of breaking the courteous innkeeper's head. As he turned to leave the room, he encountered a sneering glance from the bold-featured personage whom he had before noticed; and no sooner was he beyond the door, than he heard a general laugh, in which the innkeeper's voice might be distinguished, like the dropping of small stones into a kettle.

"Now, is it not strange," thought Robin, with his usual shrewdness,—"is it not strange that the confession of an empty pocket should outweigh the name of my kinsman, Major Molineux? Oh, if I had one of those grinning rascals in the woods, where I and my oak sapling grew up together, I would teach him that my arm is heavy though my purse be light!"

On turning the corner of the narrow lane, Robin found himself in a spacious street, with an unbroken line of lofty houses on each side, and a steepled building at the upper end, whence the ringing of a bell announced the hour of nine. The light of the moon, and the lamps from the numerous shop-windows, discovered people promenading on the pavement, and amongst them Robin hoped to recognize his hitherto inscrutable relative. The result of his former inquiries made him unwilling to hazard another, in a scene of such publicity, and he determined to walk slowly and silently up the street, thrusting his face close to that of every elderly gentleman, in search of the Major's lineaments. In his progress, Robin encountered many gay and gallant figures. Embroidered garments of showy colors, enormous periwigs, gold-laced hats, and silver-hilted swords glided past him and dazzled his optics. Travelled youths, imitators of the European fine gentlemen of the period, trod jauntily along, half dancing to the fashionable tunes which they hummed, and making poor Robin ashamed of his quiet and natural gait. At length, after many pauses to examine the gorgeous display of goods in the shop-windows, and after suffering some rebukes for the impertinence of his scrutiny into people's faces, the Major's kinsman found himself near the steepled building, still unsuccessful in his search. As yet, however, he had seen only one side of the thronged street; so Robin crossed, and continued the same sort of inquisition down the opposite pavement, with stronger hopes than the philosopher seeking an honest man, but with no better fortune. He had arrived about midway towards the lower end, from which his course began, when he overheard the approach of some one who struck down a cane on the flag-stones at every step, uttering, at regular intervals, two sepulchral hems.

"Mercy on us!" quoth Robin, recognizing the sound.

Turning a corner, which chanced to be close at his right hand, he hastened to pursue his researches in some other part of the town. His patience now was wearing low, and he seemed to feel more fatigue from his rambles since he crossed the ferry, than from his journey of several days on the other side. Hunger also pleaded loudly within him, and Robin began to balance the propriety of demanding, violently, and with lifted cudgel, the necessary guidance from the first solitary passenger whom he should meet. While a resolution to this effect was gaining strength, he entered a street of mean appearance, on either side of which a row of ill-built houses was straggling towards the harbor. The moonlight fell upon no passenger along the whole extent, but in the third domicile which Robin passed there was a half-opened door, and his keen glance detected a woman's garment within.

"My luck may be better here," said he to himself.

Accordingly, he approached the door, and beheld it shut closer as he did so; yet an open space remained, sufficing for the fair occupant to observe the stranger, without a corresponding display on her part. All that Robin could discern was a strip of scarlet petticoat, and the occasional sparkle of an eye, as if the moonbeams were trembling on some bright thing.

"Pretty mistress," for I may call her so with a good conscience, thought the shrewd youth, since I know nothing to the contrary,—"my sweet pretty mistress, will you be kind enough to tell me whereabouts I must seek the dwelling of my kinsman, Major Molineux?"

Robin's voice was plaintive and winning, and the female, seeing nothing to be shunned in the handsome country youth, thrust open the door, and came forth into the moonlight. She was a dainty little figure, with a white neck, round arms, and a slender waist, at the extremity of which her scarlet petticoat jutted out over a hoop, as if she were standing in a balloon. Moreover, her face was oval and pretty, her hair dark beneath the little cap, and her bright eyes possessed a sly freedom, which triumphed over those of Robin.

"Major Molineux dwells here," said this fair woman.

Now, her voice was the sweetest Robin had heard that night, the airy counterpart of a stream of melted silver; yet he could not help doubting whether that sweet voice spoke Gospel truth. He looked up and down the mean street, and then surveyed the house before which they stood. It was a small, dark edifice of two stories, the second of which projected over the lower floor, and the front apartment had the aspect of a shop for petty commodities.

"Now, truly, I am in luck," replied Robin, cunningly, "and so indeed is my kinsman, the Major, in having so pretty a housekeeper But I prithee trouble him to step to the door; I will deliver him a message from his friends in the country, and then go back to my lodgings at the inn."

"Nay, the Major has been abed this hour or more," said the lady of the scarlet petticoat; "and it would be to little purpose to disturb him to-night, seeing his evening draught was of the strongest. But he is a kind-hearted man, and it would be as much as my life's worth to let a kinsman of his turn away from the door. You are the good old gentleman's very picture, and I could swear that was his rainy-weather hat. Also he has garments very much resembling those leather small-clothes. But come in, I pray, for I bid you hearty welcome in his name."

So saying, the fair and hospitable dame took our hero by the hand; and the touch was light, and the force was gentleness, and though Robin read in her eyes what he did not hear in her words, yet the slender-waisted woman in the scarlet petticoat proved stronger than the athletic country youth. She had drawn his half-willing footsteps nearly to the threshold, when the opening of a door in the neighborhood startled the Major's housekeeper, and, leaving the Major's kinsman, she vanished speedily into her own domicile. A heavy yawn preceded the appearance of a man, who, like the Moonshine of Pyramus and Thisbe, carried a lantern, needlessly aiding his sister luminary in the heavens. As he walked sleepily up the street, he turned his broad, dull face on Robin, and displayed a long staff, spiked at the end.

"Home, vagabond, home!" said the watchman, in accents that seemed to fall asleep as soon as they were uttered. "Home, or we'll set you in the stock by peep of day!"

"This is the second hint of the kind," thought Robin. "I wish they would end my difficulties, by setting me there to-night."

Nevertheless, the youth felt an instinctive antipathy towards the guardian of midnight order, which at first prevented him from asking his usual question. But just when the man was about to vanish behind the corner, Robin resolved not to lose the opportunity, and shouted lustily after him,—

"I say, friend! will you guide me to the house of my kinsman, Major Molineux?"

The watchman made no reply, but turned the corner and was gone; yet Robin seemed to hear the sound of drowsy laughter stealing along the solitary street. At that moment, also, a pleasant titter saluted him from the open window above his head; he looked up, and caught the sparkle of a saucy eye; a round arm beckoned to him, and next he heard light footsteps descending the staircase within. But Robin, being of the household of a New England clergyman, was a good youth, as well as a shrewd one; so he resisted temptation, and fled away.

He now roamed desperately, and at random, through the town, almost ready to believe that a spell was on him, like that by which a wizard of his country had once kept three pursuers wandering, a whole winter night, within twenty paces of the cottage which they sought. The streets lay before him, strange and desolate, and the lights were extinguished in almost every house. Twice, however, little parties of men, among whom Robin distinguished individuals in outlandish attire, came hurrying along; but, though on both occasions they paused to address him, such intercourse did not at all enlighten his perplexity. They did but utter a few words in some language of which Robin knew nothing, and perceiving his inability to answer, bestowed a curse upon him in plain English and hastened away. Finally, the lad determined to knock at the door of every mansion that might appear worthy to be occupied by his kinsman, trusting that perseverance would overcome the fatality that had hitherto thwarted him. Firm in this resolve, he was passing beneath the walls of a church, which formed the corner of two streets, when, as he turned into the shade of its steeple, he encountered a bulky stranger, muffled in a cloak. The man was proceeding with the speed of earnest business, but Robin planted himself full before him, holding the oak cudgel with both hands across his body as a bar to further passage.

"Halt, honest man, and answer me a question," said he, very resolutely. "Tell me, this instant, whereabouts is the dwelling of my kinsman, Major Molineux!"

"Keep your tongue between your teeth, fool, and let me pass!" said a deep, gruff voice, which Robin partly remembered. "Let me pass, I say, or I'll strike you to the earth!"

"No, no, neighbor!" cried Robin, flourishing his cudgel, and then thrusting its larger end close to the man's muffled face. "No, no, I'm not the fool you take me for, nor do you pass till I have an answer to my question. Whereabouts is the dwelling of my kinsman, Major Molineux?"

The stranger, instead of attempting to force his passage, stepped back into the moonlight, unmuffled his face, and stared full into that of Robin.

"Watch here an hour, and Major Molineux will pass by," said he.

Robin gazed with dismay and astonishment on the unprecedented physiognomy of the speaker. The forehead with its double prominence, the broad hooked nose, the shaggy eyebrows, and fiery eyes were those which he had noticed at the inn, but the man's complexion had undergone a singular, or, more properly, a twofold change. One side of the face blazed an intense red, while the other was black as midnight, the division line being in the broad bridge of the nose; and a mouth which seemed to extend from ear to ear was black or red, in contrast to the color of the cheek. The effect was as if two individual devils, a fiend of fire and a fiend of darkness, had united themselves to form this infernal visage. The stranger grinned in Robin's face, muffled his parti-colored features, and was out of sight in a moment.

"Strange things we travellers see!" ejaculated Robin.

He seated himself, however, upon the steps of the church-door, resolving to wait the appointed time for his kinsman. A few moments were consumed in philosophical speculations upon the species of man who had just left him; but having settled this point shrewdly, rationally, and satisfactorily, he was compelled to look elsewhere for his amusement. And first he threw his eyes along the street. It was of more respectable appearance than most of those into which he had wandered, and the moon, creating, like the imaginative power, a beautiful strangeness in familiar objects, gave something of romance to a scene that might not have possessed it in the light of day. The irregular and often quaint architecture of the houses, some of whose roofs were broken into numerous little peaks, while others ascended, steep and narrow, into a single point, and others again were square; the pure snow-white of some of their complexions, the aged darkness of others, and the thousand sparklings, reflected from bright substances in the walls of many; these matters engaged Robin's attention for a while, and then began to grow wearisome. Next he endeavored to define the forms of distant objects, starting away, with almost ghostly indistinctness, just as his eye appeared to grasp them; and finally he took a minute survey of an edifice which stood on the opposite side of the street, directly in front of the church-door, where he was stationed. It was a large, square mansion, distinguished from its neighbors by a balcony, which rested on tall pillars, and by an elaborate Gothic window, communicating therewith.

"Perhaps this is the very house I have been seeking," thought Robin.

Then he strove to speed away the time, by listening to a murmur which swept continually along the street, yet was scarcely audible, except to an unaccustomed ear like his; it was a low, dull, dreamy sound, compounded of many noises, each of which was at too great a distance to be separately heard. Robin marvelled at this snore of a sleeping town, and marvelled more whenever its continuity was broken by now and then a distant shout, apparently loud where it originated. But altogether it was a sleep-inspiring sound, and, to shake off its drowsy influence, Robin arose, and climbed a window-frame, that he might view the interior of the church. There the moonbeams came trembling in, and fell down upon the deserted pews, and extended along the quiet aisles. A fainter yet more awful radiance was hovering around the pulpit, and one solitary ray had dared to rest upon the open page of the great Bible. Had nature, in that deep hour, become a worshipper in the house which man had builded? Or was that heavenly light the visible sanctity of the place,—visible because no earthly and impure feet were within the walls? The scene made Robin's heart shiver with a sensation of loneliness stronger than he had ever felt in the remotest depths of his native woods; so he turned away and sat down again before the door. There were graves around the church, and now an uneasy thought obtruded into Robin's breast. What if the object of his search, which had been so often and so strangely thwarted, were all the time mouldering in his shroud? What if his kinsman should glide through yonder gate, and nod and smile to him in dimly passing by?

"Oh that any breathing thing were here with me!" said Robin.

Recalling his thoughts from this uncomfortable track, he sent them over forest, hill, and stream, and attempted to imagine how that evening of ambiguity and weariness had been spent by his father's household. He pictured them assembled at the door, beneath the tree, the great old tree, which had been spared for its huge twisted trunk and venerable shade, when a thousand leafy brethren fell. There, at the going down of the summer sun, it was his father's custom to perform domestic worship, that the neighbors might come and join with him like brothers of the family, and that the wayfaring man might pause to drink at that fountain, and keep his heart pure by freshening the memory of home. Robin distinguished the seat of every individual of the little audience; he saw the good man in the midst, holding the Scriptures in the golden light that fell from the western clouds; he beheld him close the book and all rise up to pray. He heard the old thanksgivings for daily mercies, the old supplications for their continuance, to which he had so often listened in weariness, but which were now among his dear remembrances. He perceived the slight inequality of his father's voice when he came to speak of the absent one; he noted how his mother turned her face to the broad and knotted trunk; how his elder brother scorned, because the beard was rough upon his upper lip, to permit his features to be moved; how the younger sister drew down a low hanging branch before her eyes; and how the little one of all, whose sports had hitherto broken the decorum of the scene, understood the prayer for her playmate, and burst into clamorous grief. Then he saw them go in at the door; and when Robin would have entered also, the latch tinkled into its place, and he was excluded from his home.

"Am I here, or there?" cried Robin, starting; for all at once, when his thoughts had become visible and audible in a dream, the long, wide solitary street shone out before him.

He aroused himself, and endeavored to fix his attention steadily upon the large edifice which he had surveyed before. But still his mind kept vibrating between fancy and reality; by turns, the pillars of the balcony lengthened into the tall, bare stems of pines, dwindled down to human figures, settled again into their true shape and size, and then commenced a new succession of changes. For a single moment, when he deemed himself awake, he could have sworn that a visage—one which he seemed to remember, yet could not absolutely name as his kinsman's—was looking towards him from the Gothic window. A deeper sleep wrestled with and nearly overcame him, but fled at the sound of footsteps along the opposite pavement. Robin rubbed his eyes, discerned a man passing at the foot of the balcony, and addressed him in a loud, peevish, and lamentable cry.

"Hallo, friend! must I wait here all night for my kinsman, Major Molineux?"

The sleeping echoes awoke, and answered the voice; and the passenger, barely able to discern a figure sitting in the oblique shade of the steeple, traversed the street to obtain a nearer view. He was himself a gentleman in his prime, of open, intelligent, cheerful, and altogether prepossessing countenance. Perceiving a country youth, apparently homeless and without friends, he accosted him in a tone of real kindness, which had become strange to Robin's ears.

"Well, my good lad, why are you sitting here?" inquired he. "Can I be of service to you in any way?"

"I'm afraid not, sir," replied Robin, despondingly; "yet I shall take it kindly, if you'll answer me a single question. I've been searching, half the night, for one Major Molineux; now, sir, is there really such a person in these parts, or am I dreaming?"

"Major Molineux! The name is not altogether strange to me," said the gentleman, smiling. "Have you any objection to telling me the nature of your business with him?"

Then Robin briefly related that his father was a clergyman, settled on a small salary, at a long distance back in the country, and that he and Major Molineux were brothers' children. The Major, having inherited riches, and acquired civil and military rank, had visited his cousin, in great pomp, a year or two before; had manifested much interest in Robin and an elder brother, and, being childless himself, had thrown out hints respecting the future establishment of one of them in life. The elder brother was destined to succeed to the farm which his father cultivated in the interval of sacred duties; it was therefore determined that Robin should profit by his kinsman's generous intentions, especially as he seemed to be rather the favorite, and was thought to possess other necessary endowments.

"For I have the name of being a shrewd youth," observed Robin, in this part of his story.

"I doubt not you deserve it," replied his new friend, good-naturedly; "but pray proceed."

"Well, sir, being nearly eighteen years old, and well grown, as you see," continued Robin, drawing himself up to his full height, "I thought it high time to begin the world. So my mother and sister put me in handsome trim, and my father gave me half the remnant of his last year's salary, and five days ago I started for this place, to pay the Major a visit. But, would you believe it, sir! I crossed the ferry a little after dark, and have yet found nobody that would show me the way to his dwelling; only, an hour or two since, I was told to wait here, and Major Molineux would pass by."

"Can you describe the man who told you this?" inquired the gentleman.

"Oh, he was a very ill-favored fellow, sir," replied Robin, "with two great bumps on his forehead, a hook nose, fiery eyes; and, what struck me as the strangest, his face was of two different colors. Do you happen to know such a man, sir?"

"Not intimately," answered the stranger, "but I chanced to meet him a little time previous to your stopping me. I believe you may trust his word, and that the Major will very shortly pass through this street. In the mean time, as I have a singular curiosity to witness your meeting, I will sit down here upon the steps and bear you company."

He seated himself accordingly, and soon engaged his companion in animated discourse. It was but a brief continuance, however, for a noise of shouting, which had long been remotely audible, drew so much nearer that Robin inquired its cause.

"What may be the meaning of this uproar?" asked he. "Truly, if your town be always as noisy, I shall find little sleep while I am an inhabitant."

"Why, indeed, friend Robin, there do appear to be three or four riotous fellows abroad to-night," replied the gentleman. "You must not expect all the stillness of your native woods here in our streets. But the watch will shortly be at the heels of these lads and—"

"Ay, and set them in the stocks by peep of day," interrupted Robin, recollecting his own encounter with the drowsy lantern-bearer. "But, dear sir, if I may trust my ears, an army of watchmen would never make head against such a multitude of rioters. There were at least a thousand voices went up to make that one shout."

"May not a man have several voices, Robin, as well as two complexions?" said his friend.

"Perhaps a man may; but Heaven forbid that a woman should!" responded the shrewd youth, thinking of the seductive tones of the Major's housekeeper.

The sounds of a trumpet in some neighboring street now became so evident and continual, that Robin's curiosity was strongly excited. In addition to the shouts, he heard frequent bursts from many instruments of discord, and a wild and confused laughter filled up the intervals. Robin rose from the steps, and looked wistfully towards a point whither people seemed to be hastening.

"Surely some prodigious merry-making is going on," exclaimed he. "I have laughed very little since I left home, sir, and should be sorry to lose an opportunity. Shall we step round the corner by that darkish house, and take our share of the fun?"

"Sit down again, sit down, good Robin," replied the gentleman, laying his hand on the skirt of the gray coat. "You forget that we must wait here for your kinsman; and there is reason to believe that he will pass by, in the course of a very few moments."

The near approach of the uproar had now disturbed the neighborhood; windows flew open on all sides; and many heads in the attire of the pillow, and confused by sleep suddenly broken, were protruded to the gaze of whoever had leisure to observe them. Eager voices hailed each other from house to house, all demanding the explanation, which not a soul could give. Half-dressed men hurried towards the unknown commotion, stumbling as they went over the stone steps that thrust themselves into the narrow foot-walk. The shouts, the laughter, and the tuneless bray, the antipodes of music, came onwards with increasing din, till scattered individuals, and then denser bodies, began to appear round a corner at the distance of a hundred yards.

"Will you recognize your kinsman, if he passes in this crowd?" inquired the gentleman.

"Indeed, I can't warrant it, sir; but I'll take my stand here, and keep a bright lookout," answered Robin, descending to the outer edge of the pavement.

A mighty stream of people now emptied into the street, and came rolling slowly towards the church. A single horseman wheeled the corner in the midst of them, and close behind him came a band of fearful wind-instruments, sending forth a fresher discord now that no intervening buildings kept it from the ear. Then a redder light disturbed the moonbeams, and a dense multitude of torches shone along the street, concealing, by their glare, whatever object they illuminated. The single horseman, clad in a military dress, and bearing a drawn sword, rode onward as the leader, and, by his fierce and variegated countenance, appeared like war personified; the red of one cheek was an emblem of fire and sword; the blackness of the other betokened the mourning that attends them. In his train were wild figures in the Indian dress, and many fantastic shapes without a model, giving the whole march a visionary air, as if a dream had broken forth from some feverish brain, and were sweeping visibly through the midnight streets. A mass of people, inactive, except as applauding spectators, hemmed the procession in; and several women ran along the sidewalk, piercing the confusion of heavier sounds with their shrill voices of mirth or terror.

"The double-faced fellow has his eye upon me," muttered Robin, with an indefinite but an uncomfortable idea that he was himself to bear a part in the pageantry.

The leader turned himself in the saddle, and fixed his glance full upon the country youth, as the steed went slowly by. When Robin had freed his eyes from those fiery ones, the musicians were passing before him, and the torches were close at hand; but the unsteady brightness of the latter formed a veil which he could not penetrate. The rattling of wheels over the stones sometimes found its way to his ear, and confused traces of a human form appeared at intervals, and then melted into the vivid light. A moment more, and the leader thundered a command to halt: the trumpets vomited a horrid breath, and then held their peace; the shouts and laughter of the people died away, and there remained only a universal hum, allied to silence. Right before Robin's eyes was an uncovered cart. There the torches blazed the brightest, there the moon shone out like day, and there, in tar-and-feathery dignity, sat his kinsman, Major Molineux!

He was an elderly man, of large and majestic person, and strong, square features, betokening a steady soul; but steady as it was, his enemies had found means to shake it. His face was pale as death, and far more ghastly; the broad forehead was contracted in his agony, so that his eyebrows formed one grizzled line; his eyes were red and wild, and the foam hung white upon his quivering lip. His whole frame was agitated by a quick and continual tremor, which his pride strove to quell, even in those circumstances of overwhelming humiliation. But perhaps the bitterest pang of all was when his eyes met those of Robin; for he evidently knew him on the instant, as the youth stood witnessing the foul disgrace of a head grown gray in honor. They stared at each other in silence, and Robin's knees shook, and his hair bristled, with a mixture of pity and terror. Soon, however, a bewildering excitement began to seize upon his mind; the preceding adventures of the night, the unexpected appearance of the crowd, the torches, the confused din and the hush that followed, the spectre of his kinsman reviled by that great multitude,—all this, and, more than all, a perception of tremendous ridicule in the whole scene, affected him with a sort of mental inebriety. At that moment a voice of sluggish merriment saluted Robin's ears; he turned instinctively, and just behind the corner of the church stood the lantern-bearer, rubbing his eyes, and drowsily enjoying the lad's amazement. Then he heard a peal of laughter like the ringing of silvery bells; a woman twitched his arm, a saucy eye met his, and he saw the lady of the scarlet petticoat. A sharp, dry cachinnation appealed to his memory, and, standing on tiptoe in the crowd, with his white apron over his head, he beheld the courteous little innkeeper. And lastly, there sailed over the heads of the multitude a great, broad laugh, broken in the midst by two sepulchral hems; thus, "Haw, haw, haw,—hem, hem,—haw, haw, haw, haw!"

The sound proceeded from the balcony of the opposite edifice, and thither Robin turned his eyes. In front of the Gothic window stood the old citizen, wrapped in a wide gown, his gray periwig exchanged for a night-cap, which was thrust back from his forehead, and his silk stockings hanging about his legs. He supported himself on his polished cane in a fit of convulsive merriment, which manifested itself on his solemn old features like a funny inscription on a tombstone. Then Robin seemed to hear the voices of the barbers, of the guests of the inn, and of all who had made sport of him that night. The contagion was spreading among the multitude, when all at once, it seized upon Robin, and he set forth a shout of laughter that echoed through the street,—every man shook his sides, every man emptied his lungs, but Robin's shout was the loudest there. The cloud-spirits peeped from their silvery islands, as the congregated mirth went roaring up the sky! The Man in the Moon heard the far bellow. "Oho," quoth he, "the old earth is frolicsome to-night!"

When there was a momentary calm in that tempestuous sea of sound, the leader gave the sign, the procession resumed its march. On they went, like fiends that throng in mockery around some dead potentate, mighty no more, but majestic still in his agony. On they went, in counterfeited pomp, in senseless uproar, in frenzied merriment, trampling all on an old man's heart. On swept the tumult, and left a silent street behind.

"Well, Robin, are you dreaming?" inquired the gentleman, laying his hand on the youth's shoulder.

Robin started, and withdrew his arm from the stone post to which he had instinctively clung, as the living stream rolled by him. His cheek was somewhat pale, and his eye not quite as lively as in the earlier part of the evening.

"Will you be kind enough to show me the way to the ferry?" said he, after a moment's pause.

"You have, then, adopted a new subject of inquiry?" observed his companion, with a smile.

"Why, yes, sir," replied Robin, rather dryly. "Thanks to you, and to my other friends, I have at last met my kinsman, and he will scarce desire to see my face again. I begin to grow weary of a town life, sir. Will you show me the way to the ferry?"

"No, my good friend Robin,—not to-night, at least," said the gentleman. "Some few days hence, if you wish it, I will speed you on your journey. Or, if you prefer to remain with us, perhaps, as you are a shrewd youth, you may rise in the world without the help of your kinsman, Major Molineux."

ANTON CHEKHOV
The Lament

It is twilight. A thick wet snow is slowly twirling around the newly lighted street lamps, and lying in soft thin layers on roofs, on horses' backs, on people's shoulders and hats. The cab-driver Iona Potapov is quite white, and looks like a phantom; he is bent double as far as a human body can bend double; he is seated on his box; he never makes a move. If a whole snowdrift fell on him, it seems as if he would not find it necessary to shake it off. His little horse is also quite white, and remains motionless; its immobility, its angularity, and its straight wooden-looking legs, even close by, give it the appearance of a gingerbread horse worth a *kopek*. It is, no doubt, plunged in deep thought. If you were snatched from the plow, from your usual gray surroundings, and were thrown into this slough full of monstrous lights, unceasing noise, and hurrying people, you too would find it difficult not to think.

Iona and his little horse have not moved from their place for a long while. They left their yard before dinner, and up to now, not a fare. The evening mist is descending over the town, the white lights of the lamps replacing brighter rays, and the hubbub of the street getting louder. "Cabby for Viborg way!" suddenly hears Iona. "Cabby!"

Iona jumps, and through his snow-covered eyelashes sees an officer in a greatcoat, with his hood over his head.

"Viborg way!" the officer repeats. "Are you asleep, eh? Viborg way!"

With a nod of assent Iona picks up the reins, in consequence of which layers of snow slip off the horse's back and neck. The officer seats himself in the sleigh, the cabdriver smacks his lips to encourage his horse, stretches out his neck like a swan, sits up, and, more from habit than necessity, brandishes his whip. The little horse also stretches its neck, bends its wooden-looking legs, and makes a move undecidedly.

"What are you doing, werewolf!" is the exclamation Iona hears from the dark mass moving to and fro, as soon as they have started.

"Where the devil are you going? To the r-r-right!"

"You do not know how to drive. Keep to the right!" calls the officer angrily.

A coachman from a private carriage swears at him; a passerby, who has run across the road and rubbed his shoulder against the horse's nose, looks at him furiously as he sweeps the snow from his sleeve. Iona shifts about on his seat as if he were on needles, moves his elbows as if he were trying to keep his equilibrium, and gapes about like someone suffocating, who does not understand why and wherefore he is there.

"What scoundrels they all are!" jokes the officer; "one would think they had all entered into an agreement to jostle you or fall under your horse."

Iona looks round at the officer, and moves his lips. He evidently wants to say something, but the only sound that issues is a snuffle.

"What?" asks the officer.

Iona twists his mouth into a smile, and with an effort says hoarsely:

"My son, *barin*, died this week."

"Hm! What did he die of?"

Iona turns with his whole body toward his fare, and says:

"And who knows! They say high fever. He was three days in the hospital, and then died. . . . God's will be done."

"Turn round! The devil!" sounds from the darkness. "Have you popped off, old doggie, eh? Use your eyes!"

"Go on, go on," says the officer, "otherwise we shall not get there by tomorrow. Hurry up a bit!"

The cabdriver again stretches his neck, sits up, and, with a bad grace, brandishes his whip. Several times again he turns to look at his fare, but the latter has closed his eyes, and apparently is not disposed to listen. Having deposited the officer in the Viborg, he stops by the tavern, doubles himself up on his seat, and again remains motionless, while the snow once more begins to cover him and his horse. An hour, and another. . . . Then, along the footpath, with a squeak of galoshes, and quarreling, come three young men, two of them tall and lanky, the third one short and humpbacked.

"Cabby, to the Police Bridge!" in a cracked voice calls the humpback. "The three of us for two *griveniks!*"

Iona picks up his reins, and smacks his lips. Two *griveniks* is not a fair price, but he does not mind whether it is a *rouble* or five *kopeks*—to him it is all the same now, so long as they are fares. The young men, jostling each other and using bad language, approach the sleigh, and all three at once try to get onto the seat; then begins a discussion as to which two shall sit and who shall be the one to stand. After wrangling, abusing each other, and much petulance, it is at last decided that the humpback shall stand, as he is the smallest.

"Now then, hurry up!" says the humpback in a twanging voice, as he takes his place and breathes in Iona's neck. "Old furry! Here, mate, what a cap you have! There is not a worse one to be found in all Petersburg! . . ."

"He-he!—he-he!" giggles Iona. "Such a . . ."

"Now you, 'such a,' hurry up, are you going the whole way at this pace? Are you? . . . Do you want it in the neck?"

"My head feels like bursting," says one of the lanky ones. "Last night at the Donkmasovs, Vaska and I drank the whole of four bottles of cognac."

"I don't understand what you lie for," says the other lanky one angrily; "you lie like a brute."

"God strike me, it's the truth!"

"It's as much the truth as that a louse coughs!"

"He, he," grins Iona, "what gay young gentlemen!"

"Pshaw, go to the devil!" says the humpback indignantly.

"Are you going to get on or not, you old pest? Is that the way to drive? Use the whip a bit! Go on, devil, go on, give it to him well!"

Iona feels at his back the little man wriggling, and the tremble in his voice. He listens to the insults hurled at him, sees the people, and little by little the feeling of loneliness leaves him. The humpback goes on swearing until he gets mixed up in some elaborate six-foot oath, or chokes with coughing. The lankies begin to talk about a certain Nadejda Petrovna. Iona looks round at them several times; he waits for a temporary silence, then, turning round again, he murmurs:

"My son . . . died this week."

"We must all die," sighs the humpback, wiping his lips after an attack of coughing. "Now, hurry up, hurry up! Gentlemen, I really cannot go any farther like this! When will he get us there?"

"Well, just you stimulate him a little in the neck!"

"You old pest, do you hear, I'll bone your neck for you! If one treated the like of you with ceremony one would have to go on foot! Do you hear, old serpent Gorinytch! Or do you not care a spit?"

Iona hears rather than feels the blows they deal him.

"He, he," he laughs. "They are gay young gentlemen, God bless em!"

"Cabby, are you married?" asks a lanky one.

"I? He, he, gay young gentlemen! Now I have only a wife and the moist ground. . . . He, ho, ho . . . that is to say, the grave. My son has died, and I am alive. . . . A wonderful thing, death mistook the door . . . instead of coming to me, it went to my son. . . ."

Iona turns round to tell them how his son died, but at this moment, the humpback, giving a little sigh, announces, "Thank God, we have at last reached our destination," and Iona watches them disappear through the dark entrance. Once more he is alone, and again surrounded by silence. . . . His grief, which has abated for a short while, returns and rends his heart with greater force. With an anxious and hurried look, he searches among the crowds passing on either side of the street to find whether there may be just one person who will listen to him. But the crowds hurry by without noticing him or his trouble. Yet it is such an immense, illimitable grief. Should his heart break and the grief pour out, it would flow over the whole earth, so it seems, and yet no one sees it. It has managed to conceal itself in such an insignificant shell that no one can see it even by day and with a light.

Iona sees a hall porter with some sacking, and decides to talk to him.

"Friend, what sort of time is it?" he asks.

"Past nine. What are you standing here for? Move on."

Iona moves on a few steps, doubles himself up, and abandons himself to his grief. He sees it is useless to turn to people for help. In less than five minutes he straightens himself, holds up his head as if he felt some sharp pain, and gives a tug at the reins; he can bear it no longer. "The stables," he thinks, and the little horse, as if it understood, starts off at a trot.

About an hour and a half later Iona is seated by a large dirty stove. Around the stove, on the floor, on the benches, people are snoring; the air is thick and suffocatingly hot. Iona looks at the sleepers, scratches himself, and regrets having returned so early.

"I have not even earned my fodder," he thinks. "That's what's my trouble. A man who knows his job, who has had enough to eat, and his horse too, can always sleep peacefully."

A young cabdriver in one of the corners half gets up, grunts sleepily, and stretches towards a bucket of water.

"Do you want a drink?" Iona asks him.

"Don't I want a drink!"

"That's so? Your good health! But listen, mate—you know, my son is dead. . . . Did you hear? This week, in the hospital. . . . It's a long story."

Iona looks to see what effect his words have, but sees none—the young man has hidden his face and is fast asleep again. The old man sighs, and scratches his head. Just as much as the young one wants to drink, the old man wants to talk. It will soon be a week since his son died, and he has not been able to speak about it properly to anyone. One must tell it slowly and carefully; how his son fell ill, how he suffered, what he said before he died, how he died. One must describe every detail of the funeral, and the journey to the hospital to fetch the dead son's clothes. His daughter Anissia has remained in the village—one must talk about her too. Is it nothing he has to tell? Surely the listener would gasp and sigh, and sympathize with him? It is better, too, to talk to women; although they are stupid, two words are enough to make them sob.

"I'll go and look after my horse," thinks Iona; "there's always time to sleep. No fear of that!"

He puts on his coat, and goes to the stables to his horse; he thinks of the corn, the hay, the weather. When he is alone, he dares not think of his son; he can speak about him to anyone, but to think of him, and picture him to himself, is unbearably painful.

"Are you tucking in?" Iona asks his horse, looking at its bright eyes; "go on, tuck in, though we've not earned our corn, we can eat hay. Yes!

I am too old to drive—my son could have, not I. He was a first-rate cabdriver. If only he had lived!"

Iona is silent for a moment, then continues:

"That's how it is, my old horse. There's no more Kuzma Ionitch. He has left us to live, and he went off pop. Now let's say, you had a foal, you were the foal's mother, and suddenly, let's say, that foal went and left you to live after him. It would be sad, wouldn't it?"

The little horse munches, listens, and breathes over its master's hand....

Iona's feelings are too much for him, and he tells the little horse the whole story.

STEPHEN CRANE
The Open Boat

[A Tale Intended to Be after the Fact. Being the Experience of Four Men from the Sunk Steamer "Commodore."]

I

None of them knew the color of the sky. Their eyes glanced level, and were fastened upon the waves that swept toward them. These waves were of the hue of slate, save for the tops, which were of foaming white, and all of the men knew the colors of the sea. The horizon narrowed and widened, and dipped and rose, and at all times its edge was jagged with waves that seemed thrust up in points like rocks. Many a man ought to have a bath-tub larger than the boat which here rode upon the sea. These waves were most wrongfully and barbarously abrupt and tall, and each froth-top was a problem in small-boat navigation.

The cook squatted in the bottom and looked with both eyes at the six inches of gunwale which separated him from the ocean. His sleeves were rolled over his fat forearms, and the two flaps of his unbuttoned vest dangled as he bent to bail out the boat. Often he said: "Gawd! That was a narrow clip." As he remarked it he invariably gazed eastward over the broken sea.

The oiler, steering with one of the two oars in the boat, sometimes raised himself suddenly to keep clear of water that swirled in over the stern. It was a thin little oar and it seemed often ready to snap.

The correspondent, pulling at the other oar, watched the waves and wondered why he was there.

The injured captain, lying in the bow, was at this time buried in that profound dejection and indifference which comes, temporarily at least, to even the bravest and most enduring when, willy nilly, the firm fails, the army loses, the ship goes down. The mind of the master of a vessel is rooted deep in the timbers of her, though he commands for a day or a decade, and this captain had on him the stern impression of a scene in the greys of dawn of seven turned faces, and later a stump of a top-mast with a white ball on it that slashed to and fro at the waves, went low and lower, and down. Thereafter there was something strange in his voice. Although steady, it was deep with mourning, and of a quality beyond oration or tears.

"Keep 'er a little more south, Billie," said he.

" 'A little more south,' sir," said the oiler in the stern.

A seat in this boat was not unlike a seat upon a bucking broncho, and by the same token, a broncho is not much smaller. The craft pranced and reared, and plunged like an animal. As each wave came, and she rose for it, she seemed like a horse making at a fence outrageously high. The manner of her scramble over these walls of water is a mystic thing, and, moreover, at the top of them were ordinarily these problems in white water, the foam racing down from the summit of each wave, requiring a new leap, and a leap from the air. Then, after scornfully bumping a crest, she would slide, and race, and splash down a long incline, and arrive bobbing and nodding in front of the next menace.

A singular disadvantage of the sea lies in the fact that after successfully surmounting one wave you discover that there is another behind it just as important and just as nervously anxious to do something effective in the way of swamping boats. In a ten-foot dingey one can get an idea of the resources of the sea in the line of waves that is not probable to the average experience which is never at sea in a dingey. As each slatey wall of water approached, it shut all else from the view of the men in the boat, and it was not difficult to imagine that this particular wave was the final outburst of the ocean, the last effort of the grim water. There was a terrible grace in the move of the waves, and they came in silence, save for the snarling of the crests.

In the wan light, the faces of the men must have been grey. Their eyes must have glinted in strange ways as they gazed steadily astern. Viewed from a balcony, the whole thing would doubtless have been weirdly picturesque. But the men in the boat had no time to see it, and if they had had leisure there were other things to occupy their minds. The sun swung steadily up the sky, and they knew it was broad day because the color of the sea changed from slate to emerald-green, streaked with amber lights, and the foam was like tumbling snow. The process of the breaking day was unknown to them. They were aware only of this effect upon the color of the waves that rolled toward them.

In disjointed sentences the cook and the correspondent argued as to the difference between a life-saving station and a house of refuge. The cook had said: "There's a house of refuge just north of the Mosquito Inlet Light, and as soon as they see us, they'll come off in their boat and pick us up."

"As soon as who see us?" said the correspondent.

"The crew," said the cook.

"Houses of refuge don't have crews," said the correspondent. "As I understand them, they are only places where clothes and grub are stored for the benefit of shipwrecked people. They don't carry crews."

"Oh, yes, they do," said the cook.

"No, they don't," said the correspondent.

"Well, we're not there yet, anyhow," said the oiler, in the stern.

"Well," said the cook, "perhaps it's not a house of refuge that I'm thinking of as being near Mosquito Inlet Light. Perhaps it's a life-saving station."

"We're not there yet," said the oiler, in the stern.

II

As the boat bounced from the top of each wave, the wind tore through the hair of the hatless men, and as the craft plopped her stern down again the spray splashed past them. The crest of each of these waves was a hill, from the top of which the men surveyed, for a moment, a broad tumultuous expanse, shining and wind-riven. It was probably splendid. It was probably glorious, this play of the free sea, wild with lights of emerald and white and amber.

"Bully good thing it's an on-shore wind," said the cook. "If not, where would we be? Wouldn't have a show."

"That's right," said the correspondent.

The busy oiler nodded his assent.

Then the captain, in the bow, chuckled in a way that expressed humor, contempt, tragedy, all in one. "Do you think we've got much of a show now, boys?" said he.

Whereupon the three were silent, save for a trifle of hemming and hawing. To express any particular optimism at this time they felt to be childish and stupid, but they all doubtless possessed this sense of the situation in their mind. A young man thinks doggedly at such times. On the other hand, the ethics of their condition was decidedly against any open suggestion of hopelessness. So they were silent.

"Oh, well," said the captain, soothing his children, "we'll get ashore all right."

But there was that in his tone which made them think, so the oiler quoth: "Yes! If this wind holds!"

The cook was bailing: "Yes! If we don't catch hell in the surf."

Canton flannel gulls flew near and far. Sometimes they sat down on the sea, near patches of brown seaweed that rolled on the waves with a movement like carpets on a line in a gale. The birds sat comfortably in groups, and they were envied by some in the dingey, for the wrath of the sea was no more to them than it was to a covey of prairie chickens a thousand miles inland. Often they came very close and stared at the men with black bead-like eyes. At these times they were uncanny and sinister in their unblinking scrutiny, and the men hooted angrily at them, telling them to be gone. One came, and evidently decided to alight on the top of the captain's head. The bird flew parallel to the boat and did not circle, but made short sidelong jumps in the air in chicken-fashion. His black eyes were wistfully fixed upon the captain's head. "Ugly brute," said the oiler to the bird. "You look as if you were made with a jack-knife." The cook and the correspondent swore darkly at the creature. The captain naturally wished to knock it away with the end of the heavy painter; but he did not dare do it, because anything resembling an emphatic gesture would have capsized this freighted boat, and so with his open hand, the captain gently and carefully waved the gull away. After it had been discouraged from the pursuit the captain breathed easier on account of his hair, and others breathed easier because the bird struck their minds at this time as being somehow gruesome and ominous.

In the meantime the oiler and the correspondent rowed. And also they rowed.

They sat together in the same seat, and each rowed an oar. Then the oiler took both oars; then the correspondent took both oars; then the oiler; then the correspondent. They rowed and they rowed. The very ticklish part of the business was when the time came for the reclining one in the stern to take his turn at the oars. By the very last star of truth, it is easier to steal eggs from under a hen than it was to change seats in the dingey. First the man in the stern slid his hand along the thwart and moved with care, as if he were of Sèvres. Then the man in the rowing seat slid his hand along the other thwart. It was all done with the most extraordinary care. As the two sidled past each other, the whole party kept watchful eyes on the coming wave, and the captain cried: "Look out now! Steady there!"

The brown mats of seaweed that appeared from time to time were like islands, bits of earth. They were traveling, apparently, neither one way nor the other. They were, to all intents, stationary. They informed the men in the boat that it was making progress slowly toward the land.

The captain, rearing cautiously in the bow, after the dingey soared on a great swell, said that he had seen the lighthouse at Mosquito Inlet. Presently the cook remarked that he had seen it. The correspondent was at the oars then, and for some reason he too wished to look at the lighthouse, but his back was toward the far shore and the waves were important, and for some time he could not seize an opportunity to turn his head. But at last there came a wave more gentle than the others, and when at the crest of it he swiftly scoured the western horizon.

"See it?" said the captain.

"No," said the correspondent slowly, "I didn't see anything."

"Look again," said the captain. He pointed. "It's exactly in that direction."

At the top of another wave, the correspondent did as he was bid, and this time his eyes chanced on a small still thing on the edge of the swaying horizon. It was precisely like the point of a pin. It took an anxious eye to find a lighthouse so tiny.

"Think we'll make it, captain?"

"If this wind holds and the boat don't swamp, we can't do much else," said the captain.

The little boat, lifted by each towering sea, and splashed viciously by the crests, made progress that in the absence of seaweed was not apparent to those in her. She seemed just a wee thing wallowing, miraculously top-up, at the mercy of five oceans. Occasionally, a great spread of water, like white flames, swarmed into her.

"Bail her, cook," said the captain serenely.

"All right, captain," said the cheerful cook.

III

It would be difficult to describe the subtle brotherhood of men that was here established on the seas. No one said that it was so. No one mentioned it. But it dwelt in the boat, and each man felt it warm him. They were a captain, an oiler, a cook, and a correspondent, and they were friends, friends in a more curiously iron-bound degree than may be common. The hurt captain, lying against the water-jar in the bow, spoke always in a low voice and calmly, but he could never command a more ready and swiftly obedient crew than the motley three of the dingey. It was more than a mere recognition of what was best for the common safety. There was surely in it a quality that was personal and heartfelt. And after this devotion to the commander of the boat there was this comradeship that the correspondent, for instance, who had been taught to be cynical of men, knew even at the time was the best experience of his life. But no one said that it was so. No one mentioned it.

"I wish we had a sail," remarked the captain. "We might try my overcoat on the end of an oar and give you two boys a chance to rest." So the cook and the correspondent held the mast and spread wide the overcoat. The oiler steered, and the little boat made good way with her new rig. Sometimes the oiler had to scull sharply to keep a sea from breaking into the boat, but otherwise sailing was a success.

Meanwhile the lighthouse had been growing slowly larger. It had now almost assumed color, and appeared like a little grey shadow on the sky. The man at the oars could not be prevented from turning his head rather often to try for a glimpse of this little grey shadow.

At last, from the top of each wave the men in the tossing boat could see land. Even as the lighthouse was an upright shadow on the sky, this land seemed but a long black shadow on the sea. It certainly was thinner than paper. "We must be about opposite New Smyrna," said the cook, who had coasted this shore often in schooners. "Captain, by the way, I believe they abandoned that life-saving station there about a year ago."

"Did they?" said the captain.

The wind slowly died away. The cook and the correspondent were not now obliged to slave in order to hold high the oar. But the waves continued their old impetuous swooping at the dingey, and the little craft, no longer under way, struggled woundily over them. The oiler or the correspondent took the oars again.

Shipwrecks are *à propos* of nothing. If men could only train for them and have them occur when the men had reached pink condition, there would be less drowning at sea. Of the four in the dingey none had slept any time worth mentioning for two days and two nights previous to embarking in the dingey, and in the excitement of clambering about the deck of a foundering ship they had also forgotten to eat heartily.

For these reasons, and for others, neither the oiler nor the correspondent was fond of rowing at this time. The correspondent wondered ingenuously how in the name of all that was sane could there be people who thought it amusing to row a boat. It was not an amusement; it was a diabolical punishment, and even a genius of mental aberrations could never conclude that it was anything but a horror to the muscles and a crime against the back. He mentioned to the boat in general how the amusement of rowing struck him, and the weary-faced oiler smiled in full sympathy. Previously to the foundering, by the way, the oiler had worked double-watch in the engine-room of the ship.

"Take her easy, now, boys," said the captain. "Don't spend yourselves. If we have to run a surf you'll need all your strength, because we'll sure have to swim for it. Take your time."

Slowly the land arose from the sea. From a black line it became a line of black and a line of white, trees and sand. Finally, the captain said that he could make out a house on the shore. "That's the house of refuge, sure," said the cook. "They'll see us before long, and come out after us."

The distant lighthouse reared high. "The keeper ought to be able to make us out now, if he's looking through a glass," said the captain. "He'll notify the life-saving people."

"None of those other boats could have got ashore to give word of the wreck," said the oiler, in a low voice. "Else the lifeboat would be out hunting us."

Slowly and beautifully the land loomed out of the sea. The wind came again. It had veered from the north-east to the south-east. Finally, a new sound struck the ears of the men in the boat. It was the low thunder of the surf on the shore. "We'll never be able to make the lighthouse now," said the captain. "Swing her head a little more north, Billie," said he.

" 'A little more north,' sir," said the oiler.

Whereupon the little boat turned her nose once more down the wind, and all but the oarsman watched the shore grow. Under the influence of this expansion doubt and direful apprehension was leaving the minds of the men. The management of the boat was still most absorbing, but it could not prevent a quiet cheerfulness. In an hour, perhaps, they would be ashore.

Their backbones had become thoroughly used to balancing in the boat, and they now rode this wild colt of a dingey like circus men. The correspondent thought that he had been drenched to the skin, but happening to feel in the top pocket of his coat, he found therein eight cigars. Four of them were soaked with sea-water; four were perfectly scathless. After a search, somebody produced three dry matches, and thereupon the four waifs rode impudently in their little boat, and with an assurance of an impending rescue shining in their eyes, puffed at the big cigars and judged well and ill of all men. Everybody took a drink of water.

IV

"Cook," remarked the captain, "there don't seem to be any signs of life about your house of refuge."

"No," replied the cook. "Funny they don't see us!"

A broad stretch of lowly coast lay before the eyes of the men. It was of dunes topped with dark vegetation. The roar of the surf was plain, and sometimes they could see the white lip of a wave as it spun up the beach. A tiny house was blocked out black upon the sky. Southward, the slim lighthouse lifted its little grey length.

Tide, wind, and waves were swinging the dingey northward. "Funny they don't see us," said the men.

The surf's roar was here dulled, but its tone was, nevertheless, thunderous and mighty. As the boat swam over the great rollers, the men sat listening to this roar. "We'll swamp sure," said everybody.

It is fair to say here that there was not a life-saving station within twenty miles in either direction, but the men did not know this fact, and in consequence they made dark and opprobrious remarks concerning the eyesight of the nation's life-savers. Four scowling men sat in the dingey and surpassed records in the invention of epithets.

"Funny they don't see us."

The lightheartedness of a former time had completely faded. To their sharpened minds it was easy to conjure pictures of all kinds of incompetency and blindness and, indeed, cowardice. There was the shore of the populous land, and it was bitter and bitter to them that from it came no sign.

"Well," said the captain, ultimately, "I suppose we'll have to make a try for ourselves. If we stay out here too long, we'll none of us have strength left to swim after the boat swamps."

And so the oiler, who was at the oars, turned the boat straight for the shore. There was a sudden tightening of muscle. There was some thinking.

"If we don't all get ashore—" said the captain. "If we don't all get ashore, I suppose you fellows know where to send news of my finish?"

They then briefly exchanged some addresses and admonitions. As for the reflections of the men, there was a great deal of rage in them. Perchance they might be formulated thus: "If I am going to be drowned—if I am going to be drowned—if I am going to be drowned, why in the name of the seven mad gods who rule the sea, was I allowed to come thus far and contemplate sand and trees? Was I brought here merely to have my nose dragged away as I was about to nibble the sacred cheese of life? It is preposterous. If this old ninny-woman, Fate, can not do better than this, she should be deprived of the management of men's fortunes. She is an old hen who knows not her intention. If she has decided to drown me, why did she not do it in the beginning and save me all this trouble? The whole affair is absurd. . . . But no, she cannot mean to drown me. She dare not drown me. She cannot drown me. Not after all this work." Afterward the man might have had an impulse to shake his fist at the clouds: "Just you drown me, now, and then hear what I call you!"

The billows that came at this time were more formidable. They seemed always just about to break and roll over the little boat in a turmoil of foam. There was a preparatory and long growl in the speech of them. No mind unused to the sea would have concluded that the dingey could ascend these sheer heights in time. The shore was still afar. The oiler was a wily surfman. "Boys," he said swiftly, "she won't live three minutes more, and we're too far out to swim. Shall I take her to sea again, captain?"

"Yes! Go ahead!" said the captain.

This oiler, by a series of quick miracles, and fast and steady oarsmanship, turned the boat in the middle of the surf and took her safely to sea again.

There was a considerable silence as the boat bumped over the furrowed sea to deeper water. Then somebody in gloom spoke. "Well, anyhow, they must have seen us from the shore by now."

The gulls went in slanting flight up the wind toward the grey desolate east. A squall, marked by dingy clouds, and clouds brick-red, like smoke from a burning building, appeared from the south-east.

"What do you think of those life-saving people? Ain't they peaches?"

"Funny they haven't seen us."

"Maybe they think we're out here for sport! Maybe they think we're fishin'. Maybe they think we're damned fools."

It was a long afternoon. A changed tide tried to force them southward, but the wind and wave said northward. Far ahead, where coastline, sea, and sky formed their mighty angle, there were little dots which seemed to indicate a city on the shore.

"St. Augustine?"

The captain shook his head. "Too near Mosquito Inlet."

And the oiler rowed, and then the correspondent rowed. Then the oiler rowed. It was a weary business. The human back can become the seat of more aches and pains than are registered in books for the composite anatomy of a regiment. It is a limited area, but it can become the theatre of innumerable muscular conflicts, tangles, wrenches, knots, and other comforts.

"Did you ever like to row, Billie?" asked the correspondent.

"No," said the oiler. "Hang it!"

When one exchanged the rowing-seat for a place in the bottom of the boat, he suffered a bodily depression that caused him to be careless of everything save an obligation to wiggle one finger. There was cold seawater swashing to and fro in the boat, and he lay in it. His head, pillowed on a thwart, was within an inch of the swirl of a wave crest, and sometimes a particularly obstreperous sea came in-board and drenched him once more. But these matters did not annoy him. It is almost certain that if the boat had capsized he would have tumbled comfortably out upon the ocean as if he felt sure that it was a great soft mattress.

"Look! There's a man on the shore!"

"Where?"

"There! See 'im? See 'im?"

"Yes, sure! He's walking along."

"Now he's stopped. Look! He's facing us!"

"He's waving at us!"

"So he is! By thunder!"

"Ah, now we're all right! Now we're all right! There'll be a boat out here for us in half-an-hour."

"He's going on. He's running. He's going up to that house there."

The remote beach seemed lower than the sea, and it required a searching glance to discern the little black figure. The captain saw a floating stick and they rowed to it. A bath-towel was by some weird chance in the boat, and tying this on the stick, the captain waved it. The oarsman did not dare turn his head, so he was obliged to ask questions.

"What's he doing now?"

"He's standing still again. He's looking, I think. . . . There he goes again. Toward the house. . . . Now he's stopped again."

"Is he waving at us?"

"No, not now! He was, though."

"Look! There comes another man!"

"He's running."

"Look at him go, would you."

"Why, he's on a bicycle. Now he's met the other man. They're both waving at us. Look!"

"There comes something up the beach."

"What the devil is that thing?"

"Why it looks like a boat."

"Why, certainly it's a boat."

"No, it's on wheels."

"Yes, so it is. Well, that must be the life-boat. They drag them along shore on a wagon."

"That's the life-boat, sure."

"No, by———, it's—it's an omnibus."

"I tell you it's a life-boat."

"It is not! It's an omnibus. I can see it plain. See? One of these big hotel omnibuses."

"By thunder, you're right. It's an omnibus, sure as fate. What do you suppose they are doing with an omnibus? Maybe they are going around collecting the life-crew, hey?"

"That's it, likely. Look! There's a fellow waving a little black flag. He's standing on the steps of the omnibus. There come those other two fellows. Now they're all talking together. Look at the fellow with the flag. Maybe he ain't waving it."

"That ain't a flag, is it? That's his coat. Why, certainly, that's his coat."

"So it is. It's his coat. He's taken it off and is waving it around his head. But would you look at him swing it."

"Oh, say, there isn't any life-saving station there. That's just a winter resort hotel omnibus that has brought over some of the boarders to see us drown."

"What's that idiot with the coat mean? What's he signaling, anyhow?"

"It looks as if he were trying to tell us to go north. There must be a life-saving station up there."

"No! He thinks we're fishing. Just giving us a merry hand. See? Ah, there, Willie!"

"Well, I wish I could make something out of those signals. What do you suppose he means?"

"He don't mean anything. He's just playing."

"Well, if he'd just signal us to try the surf again, or to go to sea and wait, or go north, or go south, or go to hell—there would be some reason in it. But look at him. He just stands there and keeps his coat revolving like a wheel. The ass!"

"There come more people."

"Now there's quite a mob. Look! Isn't that a boat?"

"Where? Oh, I see where you mean. No, that's no boat."

"That fellow is still waving his coat."

"He must think we like to see him do that. Why don't he quit it? It don't mean anything."

"I don't know. I think he is trying to make us go north. It must be that there's a life-saving station there somewhere."

"Say, he ain't tired yet. Look at 'im wave."

"Wonder how long he can keep that up. He's been revolving his coat ever since he caught sight of us. He's an idiot. Why aren't they getting men to bring a boat out? A fishing boat—one of those big yawls—could come out here all right. Why don't he do something?"

"Oh, it's all right, now."

"They'll have a boat out here for us in less than no time, now that they've seen us."

A faint yellow tone came into the sky over the low land. The shadows on the sea slowly deepened. The wind bore coldness with it, and the men began to shiver.

"Holy smoke!" said one, allowing his voice to express his impious mood, "if we keep on monkeying out here! If we've got to flounder out here all night!"

"Oh, we'll never have to stay here all night! Don't you worry. They've seen us now, and it won't be long before they'll come chasing out after us."

The shore grew dusky. The man waving a coat blended gradually into this gloom, and it swallowed in the same manner the omnibus and the group of people. The spray, when it dashed uproariously over the side, made the voyagers shrink and swear like men who were being branded.

"I'd like to catch the chump who waved the coat. I feel like soaking him one, just for luck."

"Why? What did he do?"

"Oh, nothing, but then he seemed so damned cheerful."

In the meantime the oiler rowed, and then the correspondent rowed, and then the oiler rowed. Grey-faced and bowed forward, they mechanically, turn by turn, plied the leader oars. The form of the lighthouse had vanished from the southern horizon, but finally a pale star appeared, just lifting from the sea. The streaked saffron in the west passed before the all-merging darkness, and the sea to the east was black. The land had vanished, and was expressed only by the low and drear thunder of the surf.

"If I am going to be drowned—if I am going to be drowned—if I am going to be drowned, why, in the name of the seven mad gods who rule the sea, was I allowed to come thus far and contemplate sand and trees? Was I brought here merely to have my nose dragged away as I was about to nibble the sacred cheese of life?"

The patient captain, drooped over the water-jar, was sometimes obliged to speak to the oarsman.

"Keep her head up! Keep her head up!"

"'Keep her head up,' sir." The voices were weary and low.

This was surely a quiet evening. All save the oarsman lay heavily and listlessly in the boat's bottom. As for him, his eyes were just capable of noting the tall black waves that swept forward in a most sinister silence, save for an occasional subdued growl of a crest.

The cook's head was on a thwart, and he looked without interest at the water under his nose. He was deep in other scenes. Finally he spoke. "Billie," he murmured, dreamfully, "what kind of pie do you like best?"

V

"Pie," said the oiler and the correspondent, agitatedly. "Don't talk about those things, blast you!"

"Well," said the cook, "I was just thinking about ham sandwiches and—"

A night on the sea in an open boat is a long night. As darkness settled finally, the shine of the light, lifting from the sea in the south, changed to full gold. On the northern horizon a new light appeared, a small bluish gleam on the edge of the waters. These two lights were the furniture of the world. Otherwise there was nothing but waves.

Two men huddled in the stern, and distances were so magnificent in the dingey that the rower was enabled to keep his feet partly warmed by thrusting them under his companions. Their legs indeed extended far under the rowing-seat until they touched the feet of the captain forward. Sometimes, despite the efforts of the tired oarsman, a wave came piling into the boat, an icy wave of the night, and the chilling water soaked them anew. They would twist their bodies for a moment and groan, and sleep the dead sleep once more, while the water in the boat gurgled about them as the craft rocked.

The plan of the oiler and the correspondent was for one to row until he lost the ability, and then arouse the other from his sea-water couch in the bottom of the boat.

The oiler plied the oars until his head drooped forward, and the overpowering sleep blinded him. And he rowed yet afterward. Then he touched a man in the bottom of the boat, and called his name. "Will you spell me for a little while?" he said, meekly.

"Sure, Billie," said the correspondent, awakening and dragging himself to a sitting position. They exchanged places carefully, and the oiler, cuddling down in the sea-water at the cook's side, seemed to go to sleep instantly.

The particular violence of the sea had ceased. The waves came without snarling. The obligation of the man at the oars was to keep the boat headed so that the tilt of the rollers would not capsize her, and to preserve her from filling when the crests rushed past. The black waves were silent and hard to be seen in the darkness. Often one was almost upon the boat before the oarsman was aware.

In a low voice the correspondent addressed the captain. He was not sure that the Captain was awake, although this iron man seemed to be always awake. "Captain, shall I keep her making for that light north, sir?"

The same steady voice answered him. "Yes. Keep it about two points off the port bow."

The cook had tied a life-belt around himself in order to get even the warmth which this clumsy cork contrivance could donate, and he seemed almost stove-like when a rower, whose teeth invariably chattered wildly as soon as he ceased his labor, dropped down to sleep.

The correspondent, as he rowed, looked down at the two men sleeping under-foot. The cook's arm was around the oiler's shoulders, and, with their fragmentary clothing and haggard faces, they were the babes of the sea, a grotesque rendering of the old babes in the wood.

Later he must have grown stupid at his work, for suddenly there was a growling of water, and a crest came with a roar and a swash into the boat, and it was a wonder that it did not set the cook afloat in his life-belt. The cook continued to sleep, but the oiler sat up, blinking his eyes and shaking with the new cold.

"Oh, I'm awful sorry, Billie," said the correspondent contritely.

"That's all right, old boy," said the oiler, and lay down again and was asleep.

Presently it seemed that even the captain dozed, and the correspondent thought that he was the one man afloat on all the oceans. The wind had a voice as it came over the waves, and it was sadder than the end.

There was a long, loud swishing astern of the boat, and a gleaming trail of phosphorescence, like blue flame, was furrowed on the black waters. It might have been made by a monstrous knife.

Then there came a stillness, while the correspondent breathed with the open mouth and looked at the sea.

Suddenly there was another swish and another long flash of bluish light, and this time it was alongside the boat, and might almost have been reached with an oar. The correspondent saw an enormous fin speed like a shadow through the water, hurling the crystalline spray and leaving the long glowing trail.

The correspondent looked over his shoulder at the captain. His face was hidden, and he seemed to be asleep. He looked at the babes of the sea. They certainly were asleep. So, being bereft of sympathy, he leaned a little way to one side and swore softly into the sea.

But the thing did not then leave the vicinity of the boat. Ahead or astern, on one side or the other, at intervals long or short, fled the long sparkling streak, and there was to be heard the whirroo of the dark fin. The speed and power of the thing was greatly to be admired. It cut the water like a gigantic and keen projectile.

The presence of this biding thing did not affect the man with the same horror that it would if he had been a picnicker. He simply looked at the sea dully and swore in an undertone.

Nevertheless, it is true that he did not wish to be alone. He wished one of his companions to awaken by chance and keep him company with it. But the captain hung motionless over the water-jar, and the oiler and the cook in the bottom of the boat were plunged in slumber.

VI

"If I am going to be drowned—if I am going to be drowned—if I am going to be drowned, why, in the name of the seven mad gods who rule the sea, was I allowed to come thus far and contemplate sand and trees?"

During this dismal night, it may be remarked that a man would conclude that it was really the intention of the seven mad gods to drown him, despite the abominable injustice of it. For it was certainly an abominable injustice to drown a man who had worked so hard, so hard. The man felt it would be a crime most unnatural. Other people had drowned at sea since galleys swarmed with painted sails, but still—

When it occurs to a man that nature does not regard him as important, and that she feels she would not maim the universe by disposing of him, he at first wishes to throw bricks at the temple, and he hates deeply the fact that there are no bricks and no temples. Any visible expression of nature would surely be pelleted with his jeers.

Then, if there be no tangible thing to hoot he feels, perhaps, the desire to confront a personification and indulge in pleas, bowed to one knee, and with hands supplicant, saying: "Yes, but I love myself."

A high cold star on a winter's night is the word he feels that she says to him. Thereafter he knows the pathos of his situation.

The men in the dingey had not discussed these matters, but each had, no doubt, reflected upon them in silence and according to his mind. There was seldom any expression upon their faces save the general one of complete weariness. Speech was devoted to the business of the boat.

To chime the notes of his emotion, a verse mysteriously entered the correspondent's head. He had even forgotten that he had forgotten this verse, but it suddenly was in his mind.

"A soldier of the Legion lay dying in Algiers,
There was a lack of woman's nursing, there was dearth of woman's tears;
But a comrade stood beside him, and he took that comrade's hand,
And he said: 'I shall never see my own, my native land.' "

In his childhood, the correspondent had been made acquainted with the fact that a soldier of the Legion lay dying in Algiers, but he had never regarded the fact as important. Myriads of his school-fellows had informed him of the soldier's plight, but the dinning had naturally ended by making him perfectly indifferent. He had never considered it his affair that a soldier of the Legion lay dying in Algiers, nor had it appeared to him as a matter for sorrow. It was less to him than the breaking of a pencil's point.

Now, however, it quaintly came to him as a human, living thing. It was no longer merely a picture of a few throes in the breast of a poet, meanwhile drinking tea and warming his feet at the grate; it was an actuality—stern, mournful, and fine.

The correspondent plainly saw the soldier. He lay on the sand with his feet out straight and still. While his pale left hand was upon his chest in an attempt to thwart the going of his life, the blood came between his fingers. In the far Algerian distance, a city of low square forms was set against a sky that was faint with the last sunset hues. The correspondent, plying the oars and dreaming of the slow and slower movements of the lips of the soldier, was moved by a profound and perfectly impersonal comprehension. He was sorry for the soldier of the Legion who lay dying in Algiers.

The thing which had followed the boat and waited had evidently grown bored at the delay. There was no longer to be heard the slash of the cut-water, and there was no longer the flame of the long trail. The light in the north still glimmered, but it was apparently no nearer to the boat. Sometimes the boom of the surf rang in the correspondent's ears, and he turned the craft seaward then and rowed harder. Southward, some one had evidently built a watch-fire on the beach. It was too low and too far to be seen, but it made a shimmering, roseate reflection upon the bluff back of it, and thus could be discerned from the boat. The wind came stronger, and sometimes a wave suddenly raged out like a mountain-cat, and there was to be seen the sheen and sparkle of a broken crest.

The captain, in the bow, moved on his water-jar and sat erect. "Pretty long night," he observed to the correspondent. He looked at the shore. "Those life-saving people take their time."

"Did you see that shark playing around?"

"Yes, I saw him. He was a big fellow, all right."

"Wish I had known you were awake."

Later the correspondent spoke into the bottom of the boat.

"Billie!" There was a slow and gradual disentanglement. "Billie, will you spell me?" "Sure," said the oiler.

As soon as the correspondent touched the cold comfortable sea-water in the bottom of the boat, and had huddled close to the cook's life-belt he was deep in sleep, despite the fact that his teeth played all the popular airs. This sleep was so good to him that it was but a moment before he heard a voice call his name in a tone that demonstrated the last stages of exhaustion. "Will you spell me?"

"Sure, Billie."

The light in the north had mysteriously vanished, but the correspondent took his course from the wide-awake captain.

Later in the night they took the boat farther out to sea, and the captain directed the cook to take one oar at the stern and keep the boat facing the seas. He was to call out if he should hear the thunder of the surf. This plan enabled the oiler and the correspondent to get respite together. "We'll give those boys a chance to get into shape again," said the captain. They curled down and, after a few preliminary chatterings and trembles, slept once more the dead sleep. Neither knew they had bequeathed to the cook the company of another shark, or perhaps the same shark.

As the boat caroused on the waves, spray occasionally bumped over the side and gave them a fresh soaking, but this had no power to break their repose. The ominous slash of the wind and the water affected them as it would have affected mummies.

"Boys," said the cook, with the notes of every reluctance in his voice, "she's drifted in pretty close. I guess one of you had better take her to sea again." The correspondent, aroused, heard the crash of the toppled crests.

As he was rowing, the captain gave him some whisky-and-water, and this steadied the chills out of him. "If I ever get ashore and anybody shows me even a photograph of an oar—"

At last there was a short conversation.

"Billie. . . . Billie, will you spell me?"

"Sure," said the oiler.

VII

When the correspondent again opened his eyes, the sea and the sky were each of the grey hue of the dawning. Later, carmine and gold was painted upon the waters. The morning appeared finally, in its splendor, with a sky of pure blue, and the sunlight flamed on the tips of the waves.

On the distant dunes were set many little black cottages, and a tall white windmill reared above them. No man, nor dog, nor bicycle appeared on the beach. The cottages might have formed a deserted village.

The voyagers scanned the shore. A conference was held in the boat. "Well," said the captain, "if no help is coming we might better try a run through the surf right away. If we stay out here much longer we will be too weak to do anything for ourselves at all." The others silently acquiesced in this reasoning. The boat was headed for the beach. The correspondent wondered if none ever ascended the tall wind-tower, and if then they never looked seaward. This tower was a giant, standing with its back to the plight of the ants. It represented in a degree, to the correspondent, the serenity of nature amid the struggles of the individual—nature in the wind, and nature in the vision of men. She did not seem cruel to him then, nor beneficent, nor treacherous, nor wise. But she was indifferent, flatly indifferent. It is, perhaps, plausible that a man in this situation, impressed with the unconcern of the universe, should see the innumerable flaws of his life, and have them taste wickedly in his mind and wish for another chance. A distinction between right and wrong seems absurdly clear to him, then, in this new ignorance of the grave-edge, and he understands that if he were given another opportunity he would mend his conduct and his words, and be better and brighter during an introduction or at a tea.

"Now, boys," said the captain, "she is going to swamp, sure. All we can do is to work her in as far as possible, and then when she swamps, pile out and scramble for the beach. Keep cool now, and don't jump until she swamps sure."

The oiler took the oars. Over his shoulders he scanned the surf. "Captain," he said, "I think I'd better bring her about, and keep her head-on to the seas and back her in."

"All right, Billie," said the captain. "Back her in." The oiler swung the boat then and, seated in the stern, the cook and the correspondent were obliged to look over their shoulders to contemplate the lonely and indifferent shore.

The monstrous in-shore rollers heaved the boat high until the men were again enabled to see the white sheets of water scudding up the slanted beach. "We won't get in very close," said the captain. Each time a man could wrest his attention from the rollers, he turned his glance toward the shore, and in the expression of the eyes during this contemplation there was a singular quality. The correspondent, observing the others, knew that they were not afraid, but the full meaning of their glances was shrouded.

As for himself, he was too tired to grapple fundamentally with the fact. He tried to coerce his mind into thinking of it, but the mind was dominated at this time by the muscles, and the muscles said they did not care. It merely occurred to him that if he should drown it would be a shame.

There were no hurried words, no pallor, no plain agitation. The men simply looked at the shore. "Now, remember to get well clear of the boat when you jump," said the captain.

Seaward the crest of a roller suddenly fell with a thunderous crash, and the long white comber came roaring down upon the boat.

"Steady now," said the captain. The men were silent. They turned their eyes from the shore to the comber and waited. The boat slid up the incline, leaped at the furious top, bounced over it, and swung down the long back of the wave. Some water had been shipped and the cook bailed it out.

But the next crest crashed also. The tumbling, boiling flood of white water caught the boat and whirled it almost perpendicular. Water swarmed in from all sides. The correspondent had his hands on the gunwale at this time, and when the water entered at that place he swiftly withdrew his fingers, as if he objected to wetting them.

The little boat, drunken with this weight of water, reeled and snuggled deeper into the sea.

"Bail her out, cook! Bail her out," said the captain.

"All right, captain," said the cook.

"Now, boys, the next one will do for us, sure," said the oiler. "Mind to jump clear of the boat."

The third wave moved forward, huge, furious, implacable. It fairly swallowed the dingey, and almost simultaneously the men tumbled into the sea. A piece of lifebelt had lain in the bottom of the boat, and as the correspondent went overboard he held this to his chest with his left hand.

The January water was icy, and he reflected immediately that it was colder than he had expected to find it on the coast of Florida. This appeared to his dazed mind as a fact important enough to be noted at the time. The coldness of the water was sad; it was tragic. This fact was somehow so mixed and confused with his opinion of his own situation that it seemed almost a proper reason for tears. The water was cold.

When he came to the surface he was conscious of little but the noisy water. Afterward he saw his companions in the sea. The oiler was ahead in the race. He was swimming strongly and rapidly. Off to the correspondent's left, the cook's great white and corked back bulged out of the water, and in the rear the captain was hanging with his one good hand to the keel of the overturned dingey.

There is a certain immovable quality to a shore, and the correspondent wondered at it amid the confusion of the sea.

It seemed also very attractive, but the correspondent knew that it was a long journey, and he paddled leisurely. The piece of life-preserver lay under him, and sometimes he whirled down the incline of a wave as if he were on a hand-sled.

But finally he arrived at a place in the sea where travel was beset with difficulty. He did not pause swimming to inquire what manner of current had caught him, but there his progress ceased. The shore was set before him like a bit of scenery on a stage, and he looked at it and understood with his eyes each detail of it.

As the cook passed, much farther to the left, the captain was calling to him, "Turn over on your back, cook! Turn over on your back and use the oar."

"All right, sir." The cook turned on his back, and, paddling with an oar, went ahead as if he were a canoe.

Presently the boat also passed to the left of the correspondent with the captain clinging with one hand to the keel. He would have appeared like a man raising himself to look over a board fence, if it were not for the extraordinary gymnastics of the boat. The correspondent marvelled that the captain could still hold to it.

They passed on, nearer to shore—the oiler, the cook, the captain—and following them went the water-jar, bouncing gaily over the seas.

The correspondent remained in the grip of this strange new enemy—a current. The shore, with its white slope of sand and its green bluff, topped with little silent cottages, was spread like a picture before him. It was very near to him then, but he was impressed as one who in a gallery looks at a scene from Brittany or Holland.

He thought: "I am going to drown? Can it be possible? Can it be possible? Can it be possible?" Perhaps an individual must consider his own death to be the final phenomenon of nature.

But later a wave perhaps whirled him out of this small, deadly current, for he found suddenly that he could again make progress toward the shore. Later still, he was aware that the captain, clinging with one hand to the keel of the dingey, had his face turned away from the shore and toward him, and was calling his name. "Come to the boat! Come to the boat!"

In his struggle to reach the captain and the boat, he reflected that when one gets properly wearied, drowning must really be a comfortable arrangement, a cessation of hostilities accompanied by a large degree of relief, and he was glad of it, for the main thing in his mind for some months had been horror of the temporary agony. He did not wish to be hurt.

Presently he saw a man running along the shore. He was undressing with most remarkable speed. Coat, trousers, shirt, everything flew magically off him.

"Come to the boat," called the captain.

"All right, captain." As the correspondent paddled, he saw the captain let himself down to bottom and leave the boat. Then the correspondent performed his one little marvel of the voyage. A large wave caught him and flung him with ease and supreme speed completely over the boat and far beyond it. It struck him even then as an event in gymnastics, and a true miracle of the sea. An over-turned boat in the surf is not a plaything to a swimming man.

The correspondent arrived in water that reached only to his waist, but his condition did not enable him to stand for more than a moment. Each wave knocked him into a heap, and the under-tow pulled at him.

Then he saw the man who had been running and undressing, and undressing and running, come bounding into the water. He dragged ashore the cook, and then waded towards the captain, but the captain waved him away, and sent him to the correspondent. He was naked, naked as a tree in winter, but a halo was about his head, and he shone like a saint. He gave a strong pull, and a long drag, and a bully heave at the correspondent's hand. The correspondent, schooled in the minor formulae, said: "Thanks, old man." But suddenly the man cried: "What's that?" He pointed a swift finger. The correspondent said: "Go."

In the shallows, face downward, lay the oiler. His forehead touched sand that was periodically, between each wave, clear of the sea.

The correspondent did not know all that transpired afterward. When he achieved safe ground he fell, striking the sand with each particular part of his body. It was as if he had dropped from a roof, but the thud was grateful to him.

It seemed that instantly the beach was populated with men with blankets, clothes, and flasks, and women with coffeepots and all the remedies sacred to their minds. The welcome of the land to the men from the sea was warm and generous, but a still and dripping shape was carried slowly up the beach, and the land's welcome for it could only be the different and sinister hospitality of the grave.

When it came night, the white waves paced to and fro in the moonlight, and the wind brought the sound of the great sea's voice to the men on shore, and they felt that they could then be interpreters.

EUDORA WELTY
Petrified Man

"Reach in my purse and git me a cigarette without no powder in it if you kin, Mrs. Fletcher, honey," said Leota to her ten o'clock shampoo-and-set customer. "I don't like no perfumed cigarettes."

Mrs. Fletcher gladly reached over to the lavender shelf under the lavender-framed mirror, shook a hair net loose from the clasp of the patent-leather bag, and slapped her hand down quickly on a powder puff which burst out when the purse was opened.

"Why, look at the peanuts, Leota!" said Mrs. Fletcher in her marvelling voice.

"Honey, them goobers has been in my purse a week if they's been in it a day. Mrs. Pike bought them peanuts."

"Who's Mrs. Pike?" asked Mrs. Fletcher, settling back. Hidden in this den of curling fluid and henna packs, separated by a lavender swing-door from the other customers, who were being gratified in other booths, she could give her curiosity its freedom. She looked expectantly at the black part in Leota's yellow curls as she bent to light the cigarette.

"Mrs. Pike is this lady from New Orleans," said Leota, puffing, and pressing into Mrs. Fletcher's scalp with strong red-nailed fingers. "A friend, not a customer. You see, like maybe I told you last time, me and Fred and Sal and Joe all had us a fuss, so Sal and Joe up and moved out, so we didn't do a thing but rent out their room. So we rented it to Mrs. Pike. And Mr. Pike." She flicked an ash into the basket of dirty towels. "Mrs. Pike is a very decided blonde. *She* bought me the peanuts."

"She must be cute," said Mrs. Fletcher.

"Honey, 'cute' ain't the word for what she is. I'm tellin' you, Mrs. Pike is attractive. She has her a good time. She's got a sharp eye out, Mrs. Pike has."

She dashed the comb through the air, and paused dramatically as a cloud of Mrs. Fletcher's hennaed hair floated out of the lavender teeth like a small storm-cloud.

"Hair fallin'."

"Aw, Leota."

"Uh, huh, commencin' to fall out," said Leota, combing again, and letting fall another cloud.

"Is it any dandruff in it?" Mrs. Fletcher was frowning, her hair-line eyebrows diving down toward her nose, and her wrinkled, beady-lashed eyelids batting with concentration.

"Nope." She combed again. "Just fallin' out."

"Bet it was that last perm'nent you gave me that did it," Mrs. Fletcher said cruelly. "Remember you cooked me fourteen minutes."

"You had fourteen minutes comin' to you," said Leota with finality.

"Bound to be somethin'," persisted Mrs. Fletcher. "Dandruff, dandruff. I couldn't of caught a thing like that from Mr. Fletcher, could I?"

"Well," Leota answered at last, "you know what I heard in here yestiddy, one of Thelma's ladies was settin' over yonder in Thelma's booth gittin' a machineless, and I don't mean to insist or insinuate or anything, Mrs. Fletcher, but Thelma's lady just happ'med to throw out —I forgotten what she was talkin' about at the time—that you was p-r-e-g., and lots of times that'll make your hair do awful funny, fall out and God knows what all. It just ain't our fault, is the way I look at it."

There was a pause. The women stared at each other in the mirror.

"Who was it?" demanded Mrs. Fletcher.

"Honey, I really couldn't say," said Leota. "Not that you look it."

"Where's Thelma? I'll get it out of her," said Mrs. Fletcher.

"Now, honey, I wouldn't go and git mad over a little thing like that," Leota said, combing hastily, as though to hold Mrs. Fletcher down by the hair. "I'm sure it was somebody didn't mean no harm in the world. How far gone are you?"

"Just wait," said Mrs. Fletcher, and shrieked for Thelma, who came in and took a drag from Leota's cigarette.

"Thelma, honey, throw your mind back to yestiddy if you kin," said Leota, drenching Mrs. Fletcher's hair with a thick fluid and catching the overflow in a cold wet towel at her neck.

"Well, I got my lady half wound for a spiral," said Thelma doubtfully.

"This won't take but a minute," said Leota. "Who is it you got in there, old Horse Face? Just cast your mind back and try to remember who your lady was yestiddy who happ'm to mention that my customer was pregnant, that's all. She's dead to know."

Thelma drooped her blood-red lips and looked over Mrs. Fletcher's head into the mirror. "Why, honey, I ain't got the faintest," she breathed. "I really don't recollect the faintest. But I'm sure she meant no harm. I declare, I forgot my hair finally got combed and thought it was a stranger behind me."

"Was it that Mrs. Hutchinson?" Mrs. Fletcher was tensely polite.

"Mrs. Hutchinson? Oh, Mrs. Hutchinson." Thelma batted her eyes.

"Naw, precious, she come on Thursday and didn't ev'm mention your name. I doubt if she ev'm knows you're on the way."

"Thelma!" cried Leota staunchly.

"All I know is, whoever it is'll be sorry some day. Why, I just barely knew it myself!" cried Mrs. Fletcher. "Just let her wait!"

"Why? What're you gonna do to her?"

It was a child's voice, and the women looked down. A little boy was making tents with aluminum wave pinchers on the floor under the sink.

"Billy Boy, hon, mustn't bother nice ladies," Leota smiled. She slapped him brightly and behind her back waved Thelma out of the booth. "Ain't Billy Boy a sight? Only three years old and already just nuts about the beauty-parlor business."

"I never saw him here before," said Mrs. Fletcher, still unmollified.

"He ain't been here before, that's how come," said Leota. "He belongs to Mrs. Pike. She got her a job but it was Fay's Millinery. He oughtn't to try on those ladies' hats, they come down over his eyes like I don't know what. They just git to look ridiculous, that's what, an' of course he's gonna put 'em on: hats. They tole Mrs. Pike they didn't appreciate him hangin' around there. Here, he couldn't hurt a thing."

"Well! I don't like children that much," said Mrs. Fletcher.

"Well!" said Leota moodily.

"Well! I'm almost tempted not to have this one," said Mrs. Fletcher. "That Mrs. Hutchinson! Just looks straight through you when she sees you on the street and then spits at you behind your back."

"Mr. Fletcher would beat you on the head if you didn't have it now," said Leota reasonably. "After going this far."

Mrs. Fletcher sat up straight. "Mr. Fletcher can't do a thing with me."

"He can't!" Leota winked at herself in the mirror.

"No, siree, he can't. If he so much as raises his voice against me, he knows good and well I'll have one of my sick headaches, and then I'm just not fit to live with. And if I really look that pregnant already—"

"Well, now, honey, I just want you to know—I habm't told any of my ladies and I ain't goin' to tell 'em—even that you're losin' your hair. You just get you one of those Stork-a-Lure dresses and stop worryin'. What people don't know don't hurt nobody, as Mrs. Pike says."

"Did you tell Mrs. Pike?" asked Mrs. Fletcher sulkily.

"Well, Mrs. Fletcher, look, you ain't ever goin' to lay eyes on Mrs. Pike or her lay eyes on you, so what diffunce does it make in the long run?"

"I knew it!" Mrs. Fletcher deliberately nodded her head so as to destroy a ringlet Leota was working on behind her ear. "Mrs. Pike!"

Leota sighed. "I reckon I might as well tell you. It wasn't any more Thelma's lady tole me you was pregnant than a bat."

"Not Mrs. Hutchinson?"

"Naw, Lord! It was Mrs. Pike."

"Mrs. Pike!" Mrs. Fletcher could only sputter and let curling fluid roll into her ear. "How could Mrs. Pike possibly know I was pregnant or otherwise, when she doesn't even know me? The nerve of some people!"

"Well, here's how it was. Remember Sunday?"

"Yes," said Mrs. Fletcher.

"Sunday, Mrs. Pike an' me was all by ourself. Mr. Pike and Fred had gone over to Eagle Lake, sayin' they was goin' to catch 'em some fish, but they didn't a course. So we was settin' in Mrs. Pike's car, it's a 1939 Dodge—"

"1939, eh," said Mrs. Fletcher.

"—An' we was gettin' us a Jax beer apiece—that's the beer that Mrs. Pike says is made right in N.O., so she won't drink no other kind. So I seen you drive up to the drugstore an' run in for just a secont, leavin' I reckon Mr. Fletcher in the car, an' come runnin' out with looked like a perscription. So I says to Mrs. Pike, just to be makin' talk, 'Right yonder's Mrs. Fletcher, and I reckon that's Mr. Fletcher—she's one of my regular customers,' I says."

"I had on a figured print," said Mrs. Fletcher tentatively.

"You sure did," agreed Leota. "So Mrs. Pike, she give you a good look—she's very observant, a good judge of character, cute as a minute, you know—and she says, 'I bet you another Jax that lady's three months on the way.' "

"What gall!" said Mrs. Fletcher. "Mrs. Pike!"

"Mrs. Pike ain't goin' to bite you," said Leota. "Mrs. Pike is a lovely girl, you'd be crazy about her, Mrs. Fletcher. But she can't sit still a minute. We went to the travellin' freak show yestiddy after work. I got through early—nine o'clock. In the vacant store next door. What, you ain't been?"

"No, I despise freaks," declared Mrs. Fletcher.

"Aw. Well, honey, talkin' about bein' pregnant an' all, you ought to see those twins in a bottle, you really owe it to yourself."

"What twins?" asked Mrs. Fletcher out of the side of her mouth.

"Well, honey, they got these two twins in a bottle, see? Born joined plumb together—dead a course." Leota dropped her voice into a soft lyrical hum. "They was about this long—pardon—must of been full time, all right, wouldn't you say?—an' they had these two heads an' two faces an' four arms an' four legs, all kind of joined *here*. See, this face looked this-a-way, and the other face looked that-a-way, over their shoulder, see. Kinda pathetic."

"Glah!" said Mrs. Fletcher disapprovingly.

"Well, ugly? Honey, I mean to tell you—their parents was first cousins and all like that. Billy Boy, git me a fresh towel from off Teeny's stack—this 'n's wringin' wet—an' quit ticklin' my ankles with that curler. I declare! He don't miss nothin'."

"Me and Mr. Fletcher aren't one speck of kin, or he could never of had me," said Mrs. Fletcher placidly.

"Of course not!" protested Leota. "Neither is me an' Fred, not that we know of. Well, honey, what Mrs. Pike liked was the pygmies. They've got those pygmies down there, too, an' Mrs. Pike was just wild about 'em. You know, the teeniest men in the universe? Well, honey, they can just rest back on their little bohunkus an' roll around an' you can't hardly tell if they're sittin' or standin'. That'll give you some idea. They're about forty-two years old. Just suppose it was your husband!"

"Well, Mr. Fletcher is five foot nine and one half," said Mrs. Fletcher quickly.

"Fred's five foot ten," said Leota, "but I tell him he's still a shrimp, account of I'm so tall." She made a deep wave over Mrs. Fletcher's other temple with the comb. "Well, these pygmies are a kind of a dark brown, Mrs. Fletcher. Not bad-lookin' for what they are, you know."

"I wouldn't care for them," said Mrs. Fletcher. "What does that Mrs. Pike see in them?"

"Aw, I don't know," said Leota. "She's just cute, that's all. But they got this man, this petrified man, that ever'thing ever since he was nine years old, when it goes through his digestion, see, somehow Mrs. Pike says it goes to his joints and has been turning to stone."

"How awful!" said Mrs. Fletcher.

"He's forty-two too. That looks like a bad age."

"Who said so, that Mrs. Pike? I bet she's forty-two," said Mrs. Fletcher.

"Naw," said Leota, "Mrs. Pike's thirty-three, born in January, an Aquarian. He could move his head—like this. A course his head and mind ain't a joint, so to speak, and I guess his stomach ain't, either—not yet, anyways. But see—his food, he eats it, and it goes down, see, and then he digests it"—Leota rose on her toes for an instant—"and it goes out to his joints and before you can say 'Jack Robinson,' it's stone—pure stone. He's turning to stone. How'd you like to be married to a guy like that? All he can do, he can move his head just a quarter of an inch. A course he *looks* just *terrible*."

"I should think he would," said Mrs. Fletcher frostily. "Mr. Fletcher takes bending exercises every night of the world. I make him."

"All Fred does is lay around the house like a rug. I wouldn't be surprised if he woke up some day and couldn't move. The petrified man just sat there moving his quarter of an inch though," said Leota reminiscently.

"Did Mrs. Pike like the petrified man?" asked Mrs. Fletcher.

"Not as much as she did the others," said Leota deprecatingly. "And then she likes a man to be a good dresser, and all that."

"Is Mr. Pike a good dresser?" asked Mrs. Fletcher skeptically.

"Oh, well, yeah," said Leota, "but he's twelve or fourteen years older'n her. She ast Lady Evangeline about him."

"Who's Lady Evangeline?" asked Mrs. Fletcher.

"Well, it's this mind reader they got in the freak show," said Leota. "Was real good. Lady Evangeline is her name, and if I had another dollar I wouldn't do a thing but have my other palm read. She had what Mrs. Pike said was the 'sixth mind' but she had the worst manicure I ever saw on a living person."

"What did she tell Mrs. Pike?" asked Mrs. Fletcher.

"She told her Mr. Pike was as true to her as he could be and besides, would come into some money."

"Humph!" said Mrs. Fletcher. "What does he do?"

"I can't tell," said Leota, "because he don't work. Lady Evangeline didn't tell me enough about my nature or anything. And I would like to go back and find out some more about this boy. Used to go with this boy until he got married to this girl. Oh, shoot, that was about three and a half years ago, when you was still goin' to the Robert E. Lee Beauty Shop in Jackson. He married her for her money. Another fortune-teller told me that at the time. So I'm not in love with him any more, anyway, besides being married to Fred, but Mrs. Pike thought, just for the hell of it, see, to ask Lady Evangeline was he happy."

"Does Mrs. Pike know everything about you already?" asked Mrs. Fletcher unbelievingly. "Mercy!"

"Oh, yeah, I told her ever'thing about ever'thing, from now on back to I don't know when—to when I first started goin' out," said Leota. "So I ast Lady Evangeline for one of my questions, was he happily married, and she says, just like she was glad I ask her, 'Honey,' she says, 'naw, he isn't. You write down this day, March 8, 1941,' she says, 'and mock it down: three years from today him and her won't be occupyin' the same bed.' There it is, up on the wall with them other dates—see, Mrs. Fletcher? And she says, 'Child, you ought to be glad you didn't git him, because he's so mercenary.' So I'm glad I married Fred. He sure ain't mercenary, money don't mean a thing to him. But I sure would like to go back and have my other palm read."

"Did Mrs. Pike believe in what the fortune-teller said?" asked Mrs. Fletcher in a superior tone of voice.

"Lord, yes, she's from New Orleans. Ever'body in New Orleans believes ever'thing spooky. One of 'em in New Orleans before it was raided says to Mrs. Pike one summer she was goin' to go from State to State and meet some grey-headed men, and sure enough, she says she went on a beautician convention up to Chicago. . . ."

"Oh!" said Mrs. Fletcher. "Oh, is Mrs. Pike a beautician too?"

"Sure she is," protested Leota. "She's a beautician. I'm goin' to git her in here if I can. Before she married. But it don't leave you. She says sure enough, there was three men who was a very large part of making her trip what it was, and they all three had grey in their hair and they went in six States. Got Christmas cards from 'em. Billy Boy, go see if Thelma's got any dry cotton. Look how Mrs. Fletcher's a'drippin'."

"Where did Mrs. Pike meet Mr. Pike?" asked Mrs. Fletcher primly.

"On another train," said Leota.

"I met Mr. Fletcher, or rather he met me, in a rental library," said Mrs. Fletcher with dignity, as she watched the net come down over her head.

"Honey, me an' Fred, we met in a rumble seat eight months ago and we was practically on what you might call the way to the altar inside of half an hour," said Leota in a guttural voice, and bit a bobby pin open. "Course it don't last. Mrs. Pike says nothin' like that ever lasts."

"Mr. Fletcher and myself are as much in love as the day we married," said Mrs. Fletcher belligerently as Leota stuffed cotton into her ears.

"Mrs. Pike says it don't last," repeated Leota in a louder voice. "Now go git under the dryer. You can turn yourself on, can't you? I'll be back to comb you out. Durin' lunch I promised to give Mrs. Pike a facial. You know—free. Her bein' in the business, so to speak."

"I bet she needs one," said Mrs. Fletcher, letting the swing-door fly back against Leota. "Oh, pardon me."

A week later, on time for her appointment, Mrs. Fletcher sank heavily into Leota's chair after first removing a drug-store rental book, called *Life Is Like That,* from the seat. She stared in a discouraged way into the mirror.

"You can tell it when I'm sitting down, all right," she said.

Leota seemed preoccupied and stood shaking out a lavender cloth. She began to pin it around Mrs. Fletcher's neck in silence.

"I said you sure can tell it when I'm sitting straight on and coming at you this way," Mrs. Fletcher said.

"Why, honey, naw you can't," said Leota gloomily. "Why, I'd never know. If somebody was to come up to me on the street and say, 'Mrs. Fletcher is pregnant!' I'd say, 'Heck, she don't look it to me.'"

"If a certain party hadn't found it out and spread it around, it wouldn't be too late even now," said Mrs. Fletcher frostily, but Leota was almost choking her with the cloth, pinning it so tight, and she couldn't speak clearly. She paddled her hands in the air until Leota wearily loosened her.

"Listen, honey, you're just a virgin compared to Mrs. Montjoy," Leota was going on, still absent-minded. She bent Mrs. Fletcher back in the chair and, sighing, tossed liquid from a teacup onto her head and dug both hands into her scalp. "You know Mrs. Montjoy—her husband's that premature-grey-headed fella?"

"She's in the Trojan Garden Club, is all I know," said Mrs. Fletcher.

"Well, honey," said Leota, but in a weary voice, "she came in here not the week before and not the day before she had her baby—she come in here the very selfsame day, I mean to tell you. Child, we was all plumb scared to death. There she was! Come for her shampoo an' set. Why, Mrs. Fletcher, in an hour an' twenty minutes she was layin' up there in the Babtist Hospital with a seb'm-pound son. It was that close a shave. I declare, if I hadn't been so tired I would of drank up a bottle of gin that night."

"What gall," said Mrs. Fletcher. "I never knew her at all well."

"See, her husband was waitin' outside in the car, and her bags was all packed an' in the back seat, an' she was all ready, 'cept she wanted her shampoo an' set. An' havin' one pain right after another. Her husband kep' comin' in here, scared-like, but couldn't do nothin' with her a course. She yelled blood murder, too, but she always yelled her head off when I give her a perm'nent."

"She must of been crazy," said Mrs. Fletcher. "How did she look?"

"Shoot!" said Leota.

"Well, I can guess," said Mrs. Fletcher. "Awful."

"Just wanted to look pretty while she was havin' her baby, is all," said Leota airily. "Course, we was glad to give the lady what she was after—that's our motto—but I bet a hour later she wasn't payin' no mind to them little end curls. I bet she wasn't thinkin' about she ought to have on a net. It wouldn't of done her no good if she had."

"No, I don't suppose it would," said Mrs. Fletcher.

"Yeah man! She was a-yellin'. Just like when I give her perm'nent."

"Her husband ought to make her behave. Don't it seem that way to you?" asked Mrs. Fletcher. "He ought to put his foot down."

"Ha," said Leota. "A lot he could do. Maybe some women is soft."

"Oh, you mistake me, I don't mean for her to get soft—far from it! Women have to stand up for themselves, or there's just no telling. But now you take me—I ask Mr. Fletcher's advice now and then, and he appreciates it, especially on something important, like is it time for a permanent—not that I've told him about the baby. He says, 'Why, dear, go ahead!' Just ask their *advice*."

"Huh! If I ever ast Fred's advice we'd be floatin' down the Yazoo River on a houseboat or somethin' by this time," said Leota. "I'm sick of Fred. I told him to go over to Vicksburg."

"Is he going?" demanded Mrs. Fletcher.

"Sure. See, the fortune-teller—I went back and had my other palm read, since we've got to rent the room agin—said my lover was goin' to work in Vicksburg, so I don't know who she could mean, unless she meant Fred. And Fred ain't workin' here—that much is so."

"Is he going to work in Vicksburg?" asked Mrs. Fletcher. "And—"

"Sure. Lady Evangeline said so. Said the future is going to be brighter than the present. He don't want to go, but I ain't gonna put up with nothin' like that. Lays around the house an' bulls—did bull—with that good-for-nothin' Mr. Pike. He says if he goes who'll cook, but I says I never get to eat anyway—not meals. Billy Boy, take Mrs. Grover that *Screen Secrets* and leg it."

Mrs. Fletcher heard stamping feet go out the door.

"Is that that Mrs. Pike's little boy here again?" she asked, sitting up gingerly.

"Yeah, that's still him." Leota stuck out her tongue.

Mrs. Fletcher could hardly believe her eyes. "Well! How's Mrs. Pike, your attractive new friend with the sharp eyes who spreads it around town that perfect strangers are pregnant?" she asked in a sweetened tone.

"Oh, Mizziz Pike." Leota combed Mrs. Fletcher's hair with heavy strokes.

"You act like you're tired," said Mrs. Fletcher.

"Tired? Feel like it's four o'clock in the afternoon already," said Leota. "I ain't told you the awful luck we had, me and Fred? It's the worst thing you ever heard of. Maybe *you* think Mrs. Pike's got sharp eyes. Shoot, there's a limit! Well, you know, we rented out our room to this Mr. and Mrs. Pike from New Orleans when Sal an' Joe Fentress got mad at us 'cause they drank up some home-brew we had in the closet—Sal an' Joe did. So, a week ago Sat'day Mr. and Mrs. Pike moved in. Well, I kinda fixed up the room, you know—put a sofa pillow on the couch and picked some ragged robbins and put in a vase, but they never did say they appreciated it. Anyway, then I put some old magazines on the table."

"I think that was lovely," said Mrs. Fletcher.

"Wait. So, come night 'fore last, Fred and this Mr. Pike, who Fred just took up with, was back from they said they was fishin', bein' as neither one of 'em has got a job to his name, and we was all settin' around in their room. So Mrs. Pike was settin' there, readin' a old *Startling G-Man Tales* that was mine, mind you, I'd bought it myself, and all of a sudden she jumps!—into the air—you'd 'a' thought she'd set on a spider—an' says, 'Canfield'—ain't that silly, that's Mr. Pike—'Canfield, my God A'mighty,' she says, 'honey,' she says, 'we're rich, and you won't have to work.' Not that he turned one hand anyway. Well, me and Fred rushes over to her, and Mr. Pike, too, and there she sets, pointin' her finger at a photo in my copy of *Startling G-Man*. 'See that man?' yells Mrs. Pike. 'Remember him, Canfield?' 'Never forget a face,' says Mr. Pike. 'It's Mr. Petrie, that we stayed with him in the apartment next to ours in Toulouse Street in N.O. for six weeks. Mr. Petrie.' 'Well,' says Mrs. Pike, like she can't hold out one secont longer, 'Mr. Petrie is wanted for five hundred dollars cash, for rapin' four women in California, and I know where he is.' "

"Mercy!" said Mrs. Fletcher. "Where was he?"

At some time Leota had washed her hair and now she yanked her up by the back locks and sat her up.

"Know where he was?"

"I certainly don't," Mrs. Fletcher said. Her scalp hurt all over.

Leota flung a towel around the top of her customer's head. "Nowhere else but in that freak show! I saw him just as plain as Mrs. Pike. *He* was the petrified man!"

"Who would ever have thought that!" cried Mrs. Fletcher sympathetically.

"So Mr. Pike says, 'Well whatta you know about that,' an' he looks real hard at the photo and whistles. And she starts dancin' and singin' about their good luck. She meant our bad luck! I made a point of tellin' that fortune-teller the next time I saw her. I said, 'Listen, that magazine was layin' around the house for a month, and there was the freak show runnin' night an' day, not two steps away from my own beauty parlor, with Mr. Petrie just settin' there waitin'. An' it had to be Mr. and Mrs. Pike, almost perfect strangers."

"What gall," said Mrs. Fletcher. She was only sitting there, wrapped in a turban, but she did not mind.

"Fortune-tellers don't care. And Mrs. Pike, she goes around actin' like she thinks she was Mrs. God," said Leota. "So they're goin' to leave tomorrow, Mr. and Mrs. Pike. And in the meantime I got to keep that mean, bad little ole kid here, gettin' under my feet ever' minute of the day an' talkin' back too."

"Have they gotten the five hundred dollars' reward already?" asked Mrs. Fletcher.

"Well," said Leota, "at first Mr. Pike didn't want to do anything about it. Can you feature that? Said he kinda liked that ole bird and said he was real nice to 'em, lent 'em money or somethin'. But Mrs. Pike simply tole him he could just go to hell, and I can see her point. She says, 'You ain't worked a lick in six months, and here I make five hundred dollars in two seconts, and what thanks do I get for it? You go to hell, Canfield,' she says. So," Leota went on in a despondent voice, "they called up the cops and they caught the ole bird, all right, right there in the freak show where I saw him with my own eyes, thinkin' he was petrified. He's the one. Did it under his real name—Mr. Petrie. Four women in California, all in the month of August. So Mrs. Pike gits five hundred dollars. And my magazine, and right next door to my beauty parlor. I cried all night, but Fred said it wasn't a bit of use and to go to sleep, because the whole thing was just a sort of coincidence—you know: can't do nothin' about it. He says it put him clean out of the notion of goin' to Vicksburg for a few days till we rent out the room agin—no tellin' who we'll git this time."

"But can you imagine anybody knowing this old man, that's raped four women?" persisted Mrs. Fletcher, and she shuddered audibly. "Did Mrs. Pike *speak* to him when she met him in the freak show?"

Leota had begun to comb Mrs. Fletcher's hair. "I says to her, I says,

'I didn't notice you fallin' on his neck when he was the petrified man—don't tell me you didn't recognize your fine friend?' And she says, 'I didn't recognize him with that white powder all over his face. He just looked familiar,' Mrs. Pike says, 'and lots of people look familiar.' But she says that old petrified man did put her in mind of somebody. She wondered who it was! Kep' her awake, which man she'd ever knew it reminded her of. So when she seen the photo, it all come to her. Like a flash. Mr. Petrie. The way he'd turn his head and look at her when she took him in his breakfast."

"Took him in his breakfast!" shrieked Mrs. Fletcher. "Listen—don't tell me. I'd 'a' felt something."

"Four women. I guess those women didn't have the faintest notion at the time they'd be worth a hundred an' twenty-five bucks a piece some day to Mrs. Pike. We ast her how old the fella was then, an' she says he musta had one foot in the grave, at least. Can you beat it?"

"Not really petrified at all, of course," said Mrs. Fletcher meditatively. She drew herself up. "I'd 'a' felt something," she said proudly.

"Shoot! I did feel somethin'," said Leota. "I tole Fred when I got home I felt so funny. I said, 'Fred, that ole petrified man sure did leave me with a funny feelin'.' He says, 'Funny-haha or funny-peculiar?' and I says, 'Funny-peculiar.'" She pointed her comb into the air emphatically.

"I'll bet you did," said Mrs. Fletcher.

They both heard a crackling noise.

Leota screamed, "Billy Boy! What you doin' in my purse?"

"Aw, I'm just eatin' these ole stale peanuts up," said Billy Boy.

"You come here to me!" screamed Leota, recklessly flinging down the comb, which scattered a whole ashtray full of bobby pins and knocked down a row of Coca-Cola bottles. "This is the last straw!"

"I caught him! I caught him!" giggled Mrs. Fletcher. "I'll hold him on my lap. You bad, bad boy, you! I guess I better learn how to spank little old bad boys," she said.

Leota's eleven o'clock customer pushed open the swing-door upon Leota paddling him heartily with the brush, while he gave angry but belittling screams which penetrated beyond the booth and filled the whole curious beauty parlor. From everywhere ladies began to gather round to watch the paddling. Billy Boy kicked both Leota and Mrs. Fletcher as hard as he could, Mrs. Fletcher with her new fixed smile.

Billy Boy stomped through the group of wild-haired ladies and went out the door, but flung back the words, "If you're so smart, why ain't you rich?"

JOHN CHEEVER

Goodbye, My Brother

We are a family that has always been very close in spirit. Our father was drowned in a sailing accident when we were young, and our mother has always stressed the fact that our familial relationships have a kind of permanence that we will never meet with again. I don't think about the family much, but when I remember its members and the coast where they lived and the sea salt that I think is in our blood, I am happy to recall that I am a Pommeroy—that I have the nose, the coloring, and the promise of longevity—and that while we are not a distinguished family, we enjoy the illusion, when we are together, that the Pommeroys are unique. I don't say any of this because I'm interested in family history or because this sense of uniqueness is deep or important to me but in order to advance the point that we are loyal to one another in spite of our differences, and that any rupture in this loyalty is a source of confusion and pain.

We are four children; there is my sister Diana and the three men—Chaddy, Lawrence, and myself. Like most families in which the children are out of their twenties, we have been separated by business, marriage, and war. Helen and I live on Long Island now, with our four children. I teach in a secondary school, and I am past the age where I expect to be made headmaster—or principal, as we say—but I respect the work. Chaddy, who has done better than the rest of us, lives in Manhattan, with Odette and their children. Mother lives in Philadelphia, and Diana, since her divorce, has been living in France, but she comes back to the States in the summer to spend a month at Laud's Head. Laud's Head is a summer place on the shore of one of the Massachusetts islands. We used to have a cottage there, and in the twenties our father built the big house. It stands on a cliff above the sea and, excepting St. Tropez and some of the Apennine villages, it is my favorite place in the world. We each have an equity in the place and we contribute some money to help keep it going.

Our youngest brother, Lawrence, who is a lawyer, got a job with a

Cleveland firm after the war, and none of us saw him for four years. When he decided to leave Cleveland and go to work for a firm in Albany, he wrote Mother that he would, between jobs, spend ten days at Laud's Head, with his wife and their two children. This was when I had planned to take my vacation—I had been teaching summer school—and Helen and Chaddy and Odette and Diana were all going to be there, so the family would be together. Lawrence is the member of the family with whom the rest of us have least in common. We have never seen a great deal of him, and I suppose that's why we still call him Tifty—a nickname he was given when he was a child, because when he came down the hall toward the dining room for breakfast, his slippers made a noise that sounded like "Tifty, tifty, tifty." That's what Father called him, and so did everyone else. When he grew older, Diana sometimes used to call him Little Jesus, and Mother often called him The Croaker. We had disliked Lawrence, but we looked forward to his return with a mixture of apprehension and loyalty, and with some of the joy and delight of reclaiming a brother.

Lawrence crossed over from the mainland on the four-o'clock boat one afternoon late in the summer, and Chaddy and I went down to meet him. The arrivals and departures of the summer ferry have all the outward signs that suggest a voyage—whistles, bells, hand trucks, reunions, and the smell of brine—but it is a voyage of no import, and when I watched the boat come into the blue harbor that afternoon and thought that it was completing a voyage of no import, I realized that I had hit on exactly the kind of observation that Lawrence would have made. We looked for his face behind the windshields as the cars drove off the boat, and we had no trouble in recognizing him. And we ran over and shook his hand and clumsily kissed his wife and the children. "Tifty!" Chaddy shouted. "Tifty!" It is difficult to judge changes in the appearance of a brother, but both Chaddy and I agreed, as we drove back to Laud's Head, that Lawrence still looked very young. He got to the house first, and we took the suitcases out of his car. When I came in, he was standing in the living room, talking with Mother and Diana. They were in their best clothes and all their jewelry, and they were welcoming him extravagantly, but even then, when everyone was endeavoring to seem most affectionate and at a time when these endeavors come easiest, I was aware of a faint tension in the room. Thinking about this as I carried Lawrence's heavy suitcases up the stairs, I realized that our dislikes are as deeply ingrained as our better passions, and I remembered that once, twenty-five years ago, when I had hit Lawrence on the head with a rock, he had picked himself up and gone directly to our father to complain.

I carried the suitcases up to the third floor, where Ruth, Lawrence's wife, had begun to settle her family. She is a thin girl, and she seemed very tired from the journey, but when I asked her if she didn't want me to bring a drink upstairs to her, she said she didn't think she did.

When I got downstairs, Lawrence wasn't around, but the others were all ready for cocktails, and we decided to go ahead. Lawrence is the only member of the family who has never enjoyed drinking. We took our cocktails onto the terrace, so that we could see the bluffs and the sea and the islands in the east, and the return of Lawrence and his wife, their presence in the house, seemed to refresh our responses to the familiar view; it was as if the pleasure they would take in the sweep and the color of that coast, after such a long absence, had been imparted to us. While we were there, Lawrence came up the path from the beach.

"Isn't the beach fabulous, Tifty?" Mother asked. "Isn't it fabulous to be back? Will you have a Martini?"

"I don't care," Lawrence said. "Whiskey, gin—I don't care what I drink. Give me a little rum."

"We don't have any *rum*," Mother said. It was the first note of asperity. She has taught us never to be indecisive, never to reply as Lawrence had. Beyond this, she is deeply concerned with the propriety of her house, and anything irregular by her standards, like drinking straight rum or bringing a beer can to the dinner table, excites in her a conflict that she cannot, even with her capacious sense of humor, surmount. She sensed the asperity and worked to repair it. "Would you like some Irish, Tifty dear?" she said. "Isn't Irish what you've always liked? There's some Irish on the sideboard. Why don't you get yourself some Irish?" Lawrence said that he didn't care. He poured himself a Martini, and then Ruth came down and we went in to dinner.

In spite of the fact that we had, through waiting for Lawrence, drunk too much before dinner, we were all anxious to put our best foot forward and to enjoy a peaceful time. Mother is a small woman whose face is still a striking reminder of how pretty she must have been, and whose conversation is unusually light, but she talked that evening about a soil-reclamation project that is going on up-island. Diana is as pretty as Mother must have been; she is an animated and lovely woman who likes to talk about the dissolute friends that she has made in France, but she talked that night about the school in Switzerland where she had left her two children. I could see that the dinner had been planned to please Lawrence. It was not too rich, and there was nothing to make him worry about extravagance.

After supper, when we went back onto the terrace, the clouds held that kind of light that looks like blood, and I was glad that Lawrence had such a lurid sunset for his homecoming. When we had been out there a few minutes, a man named Edward Chester came to get Diana. She had met him in France, or on the boat home, and he was staying for ten days at the inn in the village. He was introduced to Lawrence and Ruth, and then he and Diana left.

"Is that the one she's sleeping with now?" Lawrence asked.

"What a horrid thing to say!" Helen said.

"You ought to apologize for that, Tifty," Chaddy said.

"I don't know," Mother said tiredly. "I don't know, Tifty. Diana is in a position to do whatever she wants, and I don't ask sordid questions. She's my only daughter. I don't see her often."

"Is she going back to France?"

"She's going back the week after next."

Lawrence and Ruth were sitting at the edge of the terrace, not in the chairs, not in the circle of chairs. With his mouth set, my brother looked to me then like a Puritan cleric. Sometimes, when I try to understand his frame of mind, I think of the beginnings of our family in this country, and his disapproval of Diana and her lovers reminded me of this. The branch of the Pommeroys to which we belong was founded by a minister who was eulogized by Cotton Mather for his untiring abjuration of the Devil. The Pommeroys were ministers until the middle of the nineteenth century, and the harshness of their thought—man is full of misery, and all earthly beauty is lustful and corrupt—has been preserved in books and sermons. The temper of our family changed somewhat and became more lighthearted, but when I was of school age, I can remember a cousinage of old men and women who seemed to hark back to the dark days of the ministry and to be animated by perpetual guilt and the deification of the scourge. If you are raised in this atmosphere—and in a sense we were—I think it is a trial of the spirit to reject its habits of guilt, self-denial, taciturnity, and penitence, and it seemed to me to have been a trial of the spirit in which Lawrence had succumbed.

"Is that Cassiopeia?" Odette asked.

"No, dear," Chaddy said. "That isn't Cassiopeia."

"Who was Cassiopeia?" Odette said.

"She was the wife of Cepheus and the mother of Andromeda," I said.

"The cook is a Giants fan," Chaddy said. "She'll give you even money that they win the pennant."

It had grown so dark that we could see the passage of light through the sky from the lighthouse at Cape Herion. In the dark below the cliff, the continual detonations of the surf sounded. And then, as she often does when it is getting dark and she has drunk too much before dinner, Mother began to talk about the improvements and additions that would someday be made on the house, the wings and bathrooms and gardens.

"This house will be in the sea in five years," Lawrence said.

"Tifty the Croaker," Chaddy said.

"Don't call me Tifty," Lawrence said.

"Little Jesus," Chaddy said.

"The sea wall is badly cracked," Lawrence said. "I looked at it this afternoon. You had it repaired four years ago, and it cost eight thousand dollars. You can't do that every four years."

"Please, Tifty," Mother said.

"Facts are facts," Lawrence said, "and it's a damned-fool idea to build a house at the edge of a cliff on a sinking coastline. In my lifetime, half the garden has washed away and there's four feet of water where we used to have a bathhouse."

"Let's have a very *general* conversation," Mother said bitterly. "Let's talk about politics or the boat-club dance."

"As a matter of fact," Lawrence said, "the house is probably in some danger now. If you had an unusually high sea, a hurricane sea, the wall would crumble and the house would go. We could all be drowned."

"I can't *bear* it," Mother said. She went into the pantry and came back with a full glass of gin.

I have grown too old now to think that I can judge the sentiments of others, but I was conscious of the tension between Lawrence and Mother, and I knew some of the history of it. Lawrence couldn't have been more than sixteen years old when he decided that Mother was frivolous, mischievous, destructive, and overly strong. When he had determined this, he decided to separate himself from her. He was at boarding school then, and I remember that he did not come home for Christmas. He spent Christmas with a friend. He came home very seldom after he had made his unfavorable judgment on Mother, and when he did come home, he always tried, in his conversation, to remind her of his estrangement. When he married Ruth, he did not tell Mother. He did not tell her when his children were born. But in spite of these principled and lengthy exertions he seemed, unlike the rest of us, never to have enjoyed any separation, and when they are together, you feel at once a tension, an unclearness.

And it was unfortunate, in a way, that Mother should have picked that night to get drunk. It's her privilege, and she doesn't get drunk often, and fortunately she wasn't bellicose, but we were all conscious of what was happening. As she quietly drank her gin, she seemed sadly to be parting from us; she seemed to be in the throes of travel. Then her mood changed from travel to injury, and the few remarks she made were petulant and irrelevant. When her glass was nearly empty, she stared angrily at the dark air in front of her nose, moving her head a little, like a fighter. I knew that there was not room in her mind then for all the injuries that were crowding into it. Her children were stupid, her husband was drowned, her servants were thieves, and the chair she sat in was uncomfortable. Suddenly she put down her empty glass and interrupted Chaddy, who was talking about baseball. "I know one *thing*," she said hoarsely. "I know that if there is an afterlife, I'm going to have a very different kind of family. I'm going to have nothing but fabulously rich, witty, and enchanting children." She got up and, starting for the door, nearly fell. Chaddy caught her and helped her up the stairs. I could hear their tender good nights, and then Chaddy came back. I thought that Lawrence by now would be tired from his journey and his return, but he remained on the terrace, as if he were waiting to see the final malfeasance, and the rest of us left him there and went swimming in the dark.

When I woke the next morning, or half woke, I could hear the sound of someone rolling the tennis court. It is a fainter and a deeper sound than the iron buoy bells off the point—an unrhythmic iron chiming—that belongs in my mind to the beginnings of a summer day, a good portent. When I went downstairs, Lawrence's two kids were in the living room, dressed in ornate cowboy suits. They are frightened and skinny children. They told me their father was rolling the tennis court but that they did not want to go out because they had seen a snake under the doorstep. I explained to them that their cousins—all the other children—ate breakfast in the kitchen and that they'd better run along in there. At this announcement, the boy began to cry. Then his sister joined him. They cried as if to go in the kitchen and eat would destroy their most precious rights. I told them to sit down with me. Lawrence came in, and I asked him if he wanted to play some tennis. He said no, thanks, although he thought he might play some singles with Chaddy. He was in the right here, because both he and Chaddy play better tennis than I, and he did play some singles with Chaddy after breakfast, but later on, when the others came down to play family doubles, Lawrence disappeared. This made me cross—unreasonably so, I suppose—but we play darned interesting family doubles and he could have played in a set for the sake of courtesy.

Late in the morning, when I came up from the court alone, I saw Tifty on the terrace, prying up a shingle from the wall with his jackknife. "What's the matter, Lawrence?" I said. "Termites?" There are termites in the wood and they've given us a lot of trouble.

He pointed out to me, at the base of each row of shingles, a faint blue line of carpenter's chalk. "This house is about twenty-two years old," he said. "These shingles are about two hundred years old. Dad must have bought shingles from all the farms around here when he built the place, to make it look venerable. You can still see the carpenter's chalk put down where these antiques were nailed into place."

It was true about the shingles, although I had forgotten it. When the house was built, our father, or his architect, had ordered it covered with lichened and weather-beaten shingles. I didn't follow Lawrence's reasons for thinking that this was scandalous.

"And look at these doors," Lawrence said. "Look at these doors and window frames." I followed him over to a big Dutch door that opens onto the terrace and looked at it. It was a relatively new door, but someone had worked hard to conceal its newness. The surface had been deeply scored with some metal implement, and white paint had been rubbed into the incisions to imitate brine, lichen, and weather rot. "Imagine spending thousands of dollars to make a sound house look like a wreck," Lawrence said. "Imagine the frame of mind this implies. Imagine wanting to live so much in the past that you'll pay men carpenters' wages to disfigure your front door." Then I remembered Lawrence's sensitivity to time and his sentiments and opinions about our feelings for the past. I had heard him say, years ago, that we and our friends and our part of the nation, finding ourselves unable to cope with the problems of the present, had, like a wretched adult, turned back to what we supposed was a happier and simpler time, and that our taste for reconstruction and candlelight was a measure of this irremediable failure. The faint blue line of chalk had reminded him of these ideas, the scarified door had reinforced them, and now clue after clue presented itself to him—the stern light at the door, the bulk of the chimney, the width of the floorboards and the pieces set into them to resemble pegs. While Lawrence was lecturing me on these frailties, the others came up from the court. As soon as Mother saw Lawrence, she responded, and I saw that there was little hope of any rapport between the matriarch and the changeling. She took Chaddy's arm. "Let's go swimming and have Martinis on the beach," she said. "Let's have a *fabulous* morning."

The sea that morning was a solid color, like verd stone. Everyone went to the beach but Tifty and Ruth. "I don't mind *him*," Mother said. She was excited, and she tipped her glass and spilled some gin into the sand. "I don't mind *him*. It doesn't matter to me how *rude* and *horrid* and *gloomy* he is, but what I can't bear are the faces of his wretched little children, those fabulously unhappy little children." With the height of the cliff between us, everyone talked wrathfully about Lawrence, about how he had grown worse instead of better, how unlike the rest of us he was, how he endeavored to spoil every pleasure. We drank our gin; the abuse seemed to reach a crescendo, and then, one by one, we went swimming in the solid green water. But when we came out no one mentioned Lawrence unkindly; the line of abusive conversation had been cut, as if swimming had the cleansing force claimed for baptism. We dried our hands and lighted cigarettes, and if Lawrence was mentioned, it was only to suggest, kindly, something that might please him. Wouldn't he like to sail to Barin's cove, or go fishing?

And now I remember that while Lawrence was visiting us, we went swimming oftener than we usually do, and I think there was a reason for this. When the irritability that accumulated as a result of his company began to lessen our patience, not only with Lawrence but with one another, we would all go swimming and shed our animus in the cold water. I can see the family now, smarting from Lawrence's rebukes as they sat on the sand, and I can see them wading and diving and surface-diving and hear in their voices the restoration of patience and the rediscovery of inexhaustible good will. If Lawrence noticed this change—this illusion of purification—I suppose that he would have found in the vocabulary of psychiatry, or the mythology of the Atlantic, some circumspect name for it, but I don't think he noticed the change. He neglected to name the curative powers of the open sea, but it was one of the few chances for diminution that he missed.

The cook we had that year was a Polish woman named Anna Ostrovick, a summer cook. She was first-rate—a big, fat, hearty, industrious woman who took her work very seriously. She liked to cook and to have the food she cooked appreciated and eaten, and whenever we saw her, she always urged us to eat. She cooked hot bread—crescents and brioches—for breakfast two or three times a week, and she would bring these into the dining room herself and say, "Eat, eat, eat!" When the maid took the serving dishes back into the pantry, we could sometimes hear Anna, who was standing there, say, "Good! They eat." She fed the garbage man, the milkman, and the gardener. "Eat!" she told them. "Eat, eat!" On Thursday afternoons, she went to the movies with the maid, but she didn't enjoy the movies, because the actors were all so thin. She would sit in the dark theater for an hour and a half watching the screen anxiously for the appearance of someone who had enjoyed his food. Bette Davis merely left with Anna the impression of a woman who has not eaten well. "They are all so skinny," she would say when she left the movies. In the evenings, after she had gorged all of us, and washed the pots and pans, she would collect the table scraps and go out to feed the creation. We had a few chickens that year, and although they would have roosted by then, she would dump food into their trough and urge the sleeping fowl to eat. She fed the songbirds in the orchard and the chipmunks in the yard. Her appearance at the edge of the garden and her urgent voice—we could hear her calling "Eat, eat, eat"—had become, like the sunset gun at the boat club and the passage of light from Cape Herion, attached to that hour. "Eat, eat, eat," we could hear Anna say. "Eat, eat . . ." Then it would be dark.

When Lawrence had been there three days, Anna called me into the kitchen. "You tell your mother," she said, "that *he* doesn't come into my kitchen. If *he* comes into my kitchen all the time, I go. *He* is always coming into my kitchen to tell me what a sad woman I am. He is always telling me that I work too hard and that I don't get paid enough and that I should belong to a union with vacations. Ha! He is so skinny but he is always coming into my kitchen when I am busy to pity me, but I am as good as him, I am as good as *anybody,* and I do not have to have people like that getting into my way all the time and feeling sorry for me. I am a famous and a wonderful cook and I have jobs everywhere and the only reason I come here to work this summer is because I was never before on an island, but I can have other jobs tomorrow, and if he is always coming into my kitchen to pity me, you tell your mother I am going. I am as good as *anybody* and I do not have to have that skinny all the time telling how poor I am."

I was pleased to find that the cook was on our side, but I felt that the situation was delicate. If Mother asked Lawrence to stay out of the kitchen, he would make a grievance out of the request. He could make a grievance out of anything, and it sometimes seemed that as he sat darkly at the dinner table, every word of disparagement, wherever it was aimed, came home to him. I didn't mention the cook's complaint to anyone, but somehow there wasn't any more trouble from that quarter.

The next cause for contention that I had from Lawrence came over our backgammon games.

When we are at Laud's Head, we play a lot of backgammon. At eight o'clock, after we have drunk our coffee, we usually get out the board. In a way, it is one of our pleasantest hours. The lamps in the room are still unlighted, Anna can be seen in the dark garden, and in the sky above her head there are continents of shadow and fire. Mother turns on the light and rattles the dice as a signal. We usually play three games apiece, each with the others. We play for money, and you can win or lose a hundred dollars on a game, but the stakes are usually much lower. I think that Lawrence used to play—I can't remember—but he doesn't play any more. He doesn't gamble. This is not because he is poor or because he has any principles about gambling but because he thinks the game is foolish and a waste of time. He was ready enough, however, to waste his time watching the rest of us play. Night after night, when the game began, he pulled a chair up beside the board, and watched the checkers and the dice. His expression was scornful, and yet he watched carefully. I wondered why he watched us night after night, and, through watching his face, I think that I may have found out.

Lawrence doesn't gamble, so he can't understand the excitement of winning and losing money. He has forgotten how to play the game, I think, so that its complex odds can't interest him. His observations were bound to include the facts that backgammon is an idle game and a game of chance, and that the board, marked with points, was a symbol of our worthlessness. And since he doesn't understand gambling or the odds of the game, I thought that what interested him must be the members of his family. One night when I was playing with Odette—I had won thirty-seven dollars from Mother and Chaddy—I think I saw what was going on in his mind.

Odette has black hair and black eyes. She is careful never to expose her white skin to the sun for long, so the striking contrast of blackness and pallor is not changed in the summer. She needs and deserves admiration—it is the element that contents her—and she will flirt, unseriously, with any man. Her shoulders were bare that night, her dress was cut to show the division of her breasts and to show her breasts when she leaned over the board to play. She kept losing and flirting and making her losses seem like a part of the flirtation. Chaddy was in the other room. She lost three games, and when the third game ended, she fell back on the sofa and, looking at me squarely, said something about going out on the dunes to settle the score. Lawrence heard her. I looked at Lawrence. He seemed shocked and gratified at the same time, as if he had suspected all along that we were not playing for anything so insubstantial as money. I may be wrong, of course, but I think that Lawrence felt that in watching our backgammon he was observing the progress of a mordant tragedy in which the money we won and lost served as a symbol for more vital forfeits. It is like Lawrence to try to read significance and finality into every gesture that we make, and it is certain of Lawrence that when he finds the inner logic to our conduct, it will be sordid.

Chaddy came in to play with me. Chaddy and I have never liked to lose to each other. When we were younger, we used to be forbidden to play games together, because they always ended in a fight. We think we know each other's mettle intimately. I think he is prudent; he thinks I am foolish. There is always bad blood when we play anything—tennis or backgammon or softball or bridge—and it does seem at times as if we were playing for the possession of each other's liberties. When I lose to Ghaddy, I can't sleep. All this is only half the truth of our competitive relationship, but it was the half-truth that would be discernible to Lawrence, and his presence at the table made me so self-conscious that I lost two games. I tried not to seem angry when I got up from the board. Lawrence was watching me. I went out onto the terrace to suffer there in the dark the anger I always feel when I lose to Chaddy.

When I came back into the room, Chaddy and Mother were playing. Lawrence was still watching. By his lights, Odette had lost her virtue to me, I had lost my self-esteem to Chaddy, and now I wondered what he saw in the present match. He watched raptly, as if the opaque checkers and the marked board served for an exchange of critical power. How dramatic the board, in its ring of light, and the quiet players and the crash of the sea outside must have seemed to him! Here was spiritual cannibalism made visible; here, under his nose, were the symbols of the rapacious use human beings make of one another.

Mother plays a shrewd, an ardent, and an interfering game. She always has her hands in her opponent's board. When she plays with Chaddy, who is her favorite, she plays intently. Lawrence would have noticed this. Mother is a sentimental woman. Her heart is good and easily moved by tears and frailty, a characteristic that, like her handsome nose, has not been changed at all by age. Grief in another provokes her deeply, and she seems at times to be trying to divine in Chaddy some grief, some loss, that she can succor and redress, and so re-establish the relationship that she enjoyed with him when he was sickly and young. She loves defending the weak and the child-like, and now that we are old, she misses it. The world of debts and business, men and war, hunting and fishing has on her an exacerbating effect. (When Father drowned, she threw away his fly rods and his guns.) She has lectured us all endlessly on self-reliance, but when we come back to her for comfort and for help—particularly Chaddy—she seems to feel most like herself. I suppose Lawrence thought that the old woman and her son were playing for each other's soul.

She lost. "Oh *dear,*" she said. She looked stricken and bereaved, as she always does when she loses. "Get me my glasses, get me my checkbook, get me something to drink." Lawrence got up at last and stretched his legs. He looked at us all bleakly. The wind and the sea had risen, and I thought that if he heard the waves, he must hear them only as a dark answer to all his dark questions; that he would think that the tide had expunged the embers of our picnic fires. The company of a lie is unbearable, and he seemed like the embodiment of a lie. I couldn't explain to him the simple and intense pleasures of playing for money, and it seemed to me hideously wrong that he should have sat at the edge of the board and concluded that we were playing for one another's soul. He walked restlessly around the room two or three times and then, as usual, gave us a parting shot. "I should think you'd go crazy," he said, "cooped up with one another like this, night after night. Come on, Ruth. I'm going to bed."

That night, I dreamed about Lawrence. I saw his plain face magnified into ugliness, and when I woke in the morning, I felt sick, as if I had suffered a great spiritual loss while I slept, like the loss of courage and heart. It was foolish to let myself be troubled by my brother. I needed a vacation. I needed to relax. At school, we live in one of the dormitories, we eat at the house table, and we never get away. I not only teach English winter and summer but I work in the principal's office and fire the pistol at track meets. I needed to get away from this and from every other form of anxiety, and I decided to avoid my brother. Early that day, I took Helen and the children sailing, and we stayed out until suppertime. The next day, we went on a picnic. Then I had to go to New York for a day, and when I got back, there was the costume dance at the boat club. Lawrence wasn't going to this, and it's a party where I always have a wonderful time.

The invitations that year said to come as you wish you were. After several conversations, Helen and I had decided what to wear. The thing she most wanted to be again, she said, was a bride, and so she decided to wear her wedding dress. I thought this was a good choice—sincere, lighthearted, and inexpensive. Her choice influenced mine, and I decided to wear an old football uniform. Mother decided to go as Jenny Lind, because there was an old Jenny Lind costume in the attic. The others decided to rent costumes, and when I went to New York, I got the clothes. Lawrence and Ruth didn't enter into any of this.

Helen was on the dance committee, and she spent most of Friday decorating the club. Diana and Chaddy and I went sailing. Most of the sailing that I do these days is in Manhasset, and I am used to setting a homeward course by the gasoline barge and the tin roofs of the boat shed, and it was a pleasure that afternoon, as we returned, to keep the bow on a white church spire in the village and to find even the inshore water green and clear. At the end of our sail, we stopped at the club to get Helen. The committee had been trying to give a submarine appearance to the ballroom, and the fact that they had nearly succeeded in accomplishing this illusion made Helen very happy. We drove back to Laud's Head. It had been a brilliant afternoon, but on the way home we could smell the east wind—the dark wind, as Lawrence would have said—coming in from the sea.

My wife, Helen, is thirty-eight, and her hair would be gray, I guess, if it were not dyed, but it is dyed an unobtrusive yellow—a faded color—and I think it becomes her. I mixed cocktails that night while she was dressing, and when I took a glass upstairs to her, I saw her for the first time since our marriage in her wedding dress. There would be no point in saying that she looked to me more beautiful than she did on our wedding day, but because I have grown older and have, I think, a greater depth of feeling, and because I could see in her face that night both youth and age, both her devotion to the young woman that she had been and the positions that she had yielded graciously to time, I think I have never been so deeply moved. I had already put on the football uniform, and the weight of it, the heaviness of the pants and the shoulder guards, had worked a change in me, as if in putting on these old clothes I had put off the reasonable anxieties and troubles of my life. It felt as if we had both returned to the years before our marriage, the years before the war.

The Collards had a big dinner party before the dance, and our family—excepting Lawrence and Ruth—went to this. We drove over to the club, through the fog, at about half past nine. The orchestra was playing a waltz. While I was checking my raincoat, someone hit me on the back. It was Chucky Ewing, and the funny thing was that Chucky had on a football uniform. This seemed comical as hell to both of us. We were laughing when we went down the hall to the dance floor. I stopped at the door to look at the party, and it was beautiful. The committee had hung fish nets all around the sides and over the high ceiling. The nets on the ceiling were filled with colored balloons. The light was soft and uneven, and the people—our friends and neighbors—dancing in the soft light to "Three O'Clock in the Morning" made a pretty picture. Then I noticed the number of women dressed in white, and I realized that they, like Helen, were wearing wedding dresses. Patsy Hewitt and Mrs. Gear and the Lackland girl waltzed by, dressed as brides. Then Pep Talcott came over to where Chucky and I were standing. He was dressed to be Henry VIII, but he told us that the Auerbach twins and Henry Barrett and Dwight MacGregor were all wearing football uniforms, and that by the last count there were ten brides on the floor.

This coincidence, this funny coincidence, kept everybody laughing, and made this one of the most lighthearted parties we've ever had at the club. At first I thought that the women had planned with one another to wear wedding dresses, but the ones that I danced with said it was a coincidence and I'm sure that Helen had made her decision alone. Everything went smoothly for me until a little before midnight. I saw Ruth standing at the edge of the floor. She was wearing a long red dress. It was all wrong. It wasn't in the spirit of the party at all. I danced with her, but no one cut in, and I was darned if I'd spend the rest of the night dancing with her and I asked her where Lawrence was. She said he was out on the dock, and I took her over to the bar and left her and went out to get Lawrence.

The east fog was thick and wet, and he was alone on the dock. He was not in costume. He had not even bothered to get himself up as a fisherman or a sailor. He looked particularly saturnine. The fog blew around us like a cold smoke. I wished that it had been a clear night, because the easterly fog seemed to play into my misanthropic brother's hands. And I knew that the buoys—the groaners and bells that we could hear then—would sound to him like half-human, half-drowned cries, although every sailor knows that buoys are necessary and reliable fixtures, and I knew that the foghorn at the lighthouse would mean wanderings and losses to him and that he could misconstrue the vivacity of the dance music. "Come on in, Tifty," I said, "and dance with your wife or get her some partners."

"Why should I?" he said. "Why should I?" And he walked to the window and looked in at the party. "Look at it," he said. "Look at that . . ."

Chucky Ewing had got hold of a balloon and was trying to organize a scrimmage line in the middle of the floor. The others were dancing a samba. And I knew that Lawrence was looking bleakly at the party as he had looked at the weather-beaten shingles on our house, as if he saw here an abuse and a distortion of time; as if in wanting to be brides and football players we exposed the fact that, the lights of youth having been put out in us, we had been unable to find other lights to go by and, destitute of faith and principle, had become foolish and sad. And that he was thinking this about so many kind and happy and generous people made me angry, made me feel for him such an unnatural abhorrence that I was ashamed, for he is my brother and a Pommeroy. I put my arm around his shoulders and tried to force him to come in, but he wouldn't.

I got back in time for the Grand March, and after the prizes had been given out for the best costumes, they let the balloons down. The room was hot, and someone opened the big doors onto the dock, and the easterly wind circled the room and went out, carrying across the dock and out onto the water most of the balloons. Chucky Ewing went running out after the balloons, and when he saw them pass the dock and settle on the water, he took off his football uniform and dove in. Then Eric Auerbach dove in and Lew Phillips dove in and I dove in, and you know how it is at a party after midnight when people start jumping into the water. We recovered most of the balloons and dried off and went on dancing, and we didn't get home until morning.

The next day was the day of the flower show. Mother and Helen and Odette all had entries. We had a pickup lunch, and Chaddy drove the women and children over to the show. I took a nap, and in the middle of the afternoon I got some trunks and a towel and, on leaving the house, passed Ruth in the laundry. She was washing clothes. I don't know why she should seem to have so much more work to do than anyone else, but she is always washing or ironing or mending clothes. She may have been taught, when she was young, to spend her time like this, or she may be at the mercy of an expiatory passion. She seems to scrub and iron with a penitential fervor, although I can't imagine what it is that she thinks she's done wrong. Her children were with her in the laundry. I offered to take them to the beach, but they didn't want to go.

It was late in August, and the wild grapes that grow profusely all over the island made the land wind smell of wine. There is a little grove of holly at the end of the path, and then you climb the dunes, where nothing grows but that coarse grass. I could hear the sea, and I remember thinking how Chaddy and I used to talk mystically about the sea. When we were young, we had decided that we could never live in the West because we would miss the sea. "It is very nice here," we used to say politely when we visited people in the mountains, "but we miss the Atlantic." We used to look down our noses at people from Iowa and Colorado who had been denied this revelation, and we scorned the Pacific. Now I could hear the waves, whose heaviness sounded like a reverberation, like a tumult, and it pleased me as it had pleased me when I was young, and it seemed to have a purgative force, as if it had cleared my memory of, among other things, the penitential image of Ruth in the laundry.

But Lawrence was on the beach. There he sat. I went in without speaking. The water was cold, and when I came out, I put on a shirt. I told him that I was going to walk up to Tanners Point, and he said that he would come with me. I tried to walk beside him. His legs are no longer than mine, but he always likes to stay a little ahead of his companion. Walking along behind him, looking at his bent head and his shoulders, I wondered what he could make of that landscape.

There were the dunes and cliffs and then, where they declined, there were some fields that had begun to turn from green to brown and yellow. The fields were used for pasturing sheep, and I guess Lawrence would have noticed that the soil was eroded and that the sheep would accelerate this decay. Beyond the fields there are a few coastal farms, with square and pleasant buildings, but Lawrence could have pointed out the hard lot of an island farmer. The sea, at our other side, was the open sea. We always tell guests that there, to the east, lies the coast of Portugal, and for Lawrence it would be an easy step from the coast of Portugal to the tyranny in Spain. The waves broke with a noise like a "hurrah, hurrah, hurrah," but to Lawrence they would say "*Vale, vale.*" I suppose it would have occurred to his baleful and incisive mind that the coast was terminal moraine, the edge of the prehistoric world, and it must have occurred to him that we walked along the edge of the known world in spirit as much as in fact. If he should otherwise have overlooked this, there were some Navy planes bombing an uninhabited island to remind him.

That beach is a vast and preternaturally clean and simple landscape. It is like a piece of the moon. The surf had pounded the floor solid, so it was easy walking, and everything left on the sand had been twice changed by the waves. There was the spine of a shell, a broomstick, part of a bottle and part of a brick, both of them milled and broken until they were nearly unrecognizable, and I suppose Lawrence's sad frame of mind —for he kept his head down—went from one broken thing to another. The company of his pessimism began to infuriate me, and I caught up with him and put a hand on his shoulder. "It's only a summer day, Tifty," I said. "It's only a summer day. What's the matter? Don't you like it here?"

"I don't like it here," he said blandly, without raising his eyes. "I'm going to sell my equity in the house to Chaddy. I didn't expect to have a good time. The only reason I came back was to say goodbye."

I let him get ahead again and I walked behind him, looking at his shoulders and thinking of all the goodbyes he had made. When Father drowned, he went to church and said goodbye to Father. It was only three years later that he concluded that Mother was frivolous and said goodbye to her. In his freshman year at college, he had been very good friends with his roommate, but the man drank too much, and at the beginning of the spring term Lawrence changed roommates and said goodbye to his friend. When he had been in college for two years, he concluded that the atmosphere was too sequestered and he said goodbye to Yale. He enrolled at Columbia and got his law degree there, but he found his first employer dishonest, and at the end of six months he said goodbye to a good job. He married Ruth in City Hall and said goodbye to the Protestant Episcopal Church; they went to live on a back street in

Tuckahoe and said goodbye to the middle class. In 1938, he went to Washington to work as a government lawyer, saying goodbye to private enterprise, but after eight months in Washington he concluded that the Roosevelt administration was sentimental and he said goodbye to it. They left Washington for a suburb of Chicago, where he said goodbye to his neighbors, one by one, on counts of drunkenness, boorishness, and stupidity. He said goodbye to Chicago and went to Kansas; he said goodbye to Kansas and went to Cleveland. Now he had said goodbye to Cleveland and come East again, stopping at Laud's Head long enough to say goodbye to the sea.

It was elegiac and it was bigoted and narrow, it mistook circumspection for character, and I wanted to help him. "Come out of it," I said. "Come out of it, Tifty."

"Come out of what?"

"Come out of this gloominess. Come out of it. It's only a summer day. You're spoiling your own good time and you're spoiling everyone else's. We need a vacation, Tifty. I need one. I need to rest. We all do. And you've made everything tense and unpleasant. I only have two weeks in the year. Two weeks. I need to have a good time and so do all the others. We need to rest. You think that your pessimism is an advantage, but it's nothing but an unwillingness to grasp realities."

"What are the realities?" he said. "Diana is a foolish and a promiscuous woman. So is Odette. Mother is an alcoholic. If she doesn't discipline herself, she'll be in a hospital in a year or two. Chaddy is dishonest. He always has been. The house is going to fall into the sea." He looked at me and added, as an afterthought, "You're a fool."

"You're a gloomy son of a bitch," I said. "You're a gloomy son of a bitch."

"Get your fat face out of mine," he said. He walked along.

Then I picked up a root and, coming at his back—although I have never hit a man from the back before—I swung the root, heavy with sea water, behind me, and the momentum sped my arm and I gave him, my brother, a blow on the head that forced him to his knees on the sand, and I saw the blood come out and begin to darken his hair. Then I wished that he was dead, dead and about to be buried, not buried but about to be buried, because I did not want to be denied ceremony and decorum in putting him away, in putting him out of my consciousness, and I saw the rest of us—Chaddy and Mother and Diana and Helen—in mourning in the house on Belvedere Street that was torn down twenty years ago, greeting our guests and our relatives at the door and answering their mannerly condolences with mannerly grief. Nothing decorous was lacking, so that even if he had been murdered on a beach, one would feel before the tiresome ceremony ended that he had come into the winter of his life and that it was a law of nature, and a beautiful one, that Tifty should be buried in the cold, cold ground.

He was still on his knees. I looked up and down. No one had seen us. The naked beach, like a piece of the moon, reached to invisibility. The spill of a wave, in a glancing run, shot up to where he knelt. I would still have liked to end him, but now I had begun to act like two men, the murderer and the Samaritan. With a swift roar, like hollowness made sound, a white wave reached him and encircled him, boiling over his shoulders, and I held him against the undertow. Then I led him to a higher place. The blood had spread all through his hair, so that it looked black. I took off my shirt and tore it to bind up his head. He was conscious, and I didn't think he was badly hurt. He didn't speak. Neither did I. Then I left him there.

I walked a little way down the beach and turned to watch him, and I was thinking of my own skin then. He had got to his feet and he seemed steady. The daylight was still clear, but on the sea wind fumes of brine were blowing in like a light fog, and when I had walked a little way from him, I could hardly see his dark figure in this obscurity. All down the beach I could see the heavy salt air blowing in. Then I turned my back on him, and as I got near to the house, I went swimming again, as I seem to have done after every encounter with Lawrence that summer.

When I got back to the house, I lay down on the terrace. The others came back. I could hear Mother defaming the flower arrangements that had won prizes. None of ours had won anything. Then the house quieted, as it always does at that hour. The children went into the kitchen to get supper and the others went upstairs to bathe. Then I heard Chaddy making cocktails, and the conversation about the flower-show judges was resumed. Then Mother cried, "Tifty! Tifty! Oh, Tifty!"

He stood in the door, looking half dead. He had taken off the bloody bandage and he held it in his hand. "My brother did this," he said. "My brother did it. He hit me with a stone—something—on the beach." His voice broke with self-pity. I thought he was going to cry. No one else spoke. "Where's Ruth?" he cried: "Where's Ruth? Where in hell is Ruth? I want her to start packing. I don't have any more time to waste here. I have important things to do. I have *important* things to do." And he went up the stairs.

They left for the mainland the next morning, taking the six o'clock boat. Mother got up to say goodbye, but she was the only one, and it is a harsh and an easy scene to imagine the matriarch and the changeling, looking at each other with a dismay that would seem like the powers of love reversed. I heard the children's voices and the car go down the drive, and I got up and went to the window, and what a morning that was! Jesus, what a morning! The wind was northerly. The air was clear. In the early heat, the roses in the garden smelled like strawberry jam. While I was dressing, I heard the boat whistle, first the warning signal and then the double blast, and I could see the good people on the top deck drinking coffee out of fragile paper cups, and Lawrence at the bow, saying to the sea, "*Thalassa, thalassa,*" while his timid and unhappy children watched the creation from the encirclement of their mother's arms. The buoys would toll mournfully for Lawrence, and while the grace of the light would make it an exertion not to throw out your arms and swear exultantly, Lawrence's eyes would trace the black sea as it fell astern; he would think of the bottom, dark and strange, where full fathom five our father lies.

Oh, what can you do with a man like that? What can you do? How can you dissuade his eye in a crowd from seeking out the cheek with acne, the infirm hand; how can you teach him to respond to the inestimable greatness of the race, the harsh surface beauty of life; how can you put his finger for him on the obdurate truths before which fear and horror are powerless? The sea that morning was iridescent and dark. My wife and my sister were swimming—Diana and Helen—and I saw their uncovered heads, black and gold in the dark winter. I saw them come out and I saw that they were naked, unshy, beautiful, and full of grace, and I watched the naked women walk out of the sea.

ROBERT PENN WARREN

The Patented Gate and the Mean Hamburger

You have seen him a thousand times. You have seen him standing on the street corner on Saturday afternoon, in the little county-seat towns. He wears blue jean pants, or overalls washed to a pale pastel blue like the color of sky after a shower in spring, but because it is Saturday he has on a wool coat, an old one, perhaps the coat left from the suit he got married in a long time back. His long wrist bones hang out from the sleeves of the coat, the tendons showing along the bone like the dry twist of grapevine still corded on the stove-length of a hickory sapling you would find in his wood box beside his cookstove among the split chunks of gum and red oak. The big hands, with the knotted, cracked joints and the square, horn-thick nails, hang loose off the wrist bone like clumsy, home-made tools hung on the wall of a shed after work. If it is summer, he wears a straw hat with a wide brim, the straw fraying loose around the edge. If it is winter, he wears a felt hat, black once, but now weathered with streaks of dark gray and dull purple in the sunlight. His face is long and bony, the jawbone long under the drawn-in cheeks. The flesh along the jawbone is nicked in a couple of places where the unaccustomed razor has been drawn over the leather-coarse skin. A tiny bit of blood crusts brown where the nick is. The color of the face is red, a dull red like the red clay mud or clay dust which clings to the bottom of his pants and to the cast-iron-looking brogans on his feet, or a red like the color of a piece of hewed cedar which has been left in the weather. The face does not look alive. It seems to be molded from the clay or hewed from the cedar. When the jaw moves, once, with its deliberate, massive motion on the quid of tobacco, you are still not convinced. That motion is but the cunning triumph of a mechanism concealed within.

But you see the eyes. You see that the eyes are alive. They are pale blue or gray, set back under the deep brows and thorny eyebrows. They are not wide, but are squinched up like eyes accustomed to wind or sun or to measuring the stroke of the ax or to fixing the object over the rifle sights. When you pass, you see that the eyes are alive and are warily and dispassionately estimating you from the ambush of the thorny brows. Then you pass on, and he stands there in that stillness which is his gift.

With him may be standing two or three others like himself, but they are still, too. They do not talk. The young men, who will be like these men when they get to be fifty or sixty, are down at the beer parlor, carousing and laughing with a high, whickering laugh. But the men on the corner are long past all that. They are past many things. They have endured and will endure in their silence and wisdom. They will stand on the street corner and reject the world which passes under their level gaze as a rabble passes under the guns of a rocky citadel around whose base a slatternly town has assembled.

I had seen Jeff York a thousand times, or near, standing like that on the street corner in town, while the people flowed past him, under the distant and wary and dispassionate eyes in ambush. He would be waiting for his wife and the three tow-headed children who were walking around the town looking into store windows and at the people. After a while they would come back to him, and then, wordlessly, he would lead them to the store where they always did their trading. He would go first, marching with a steady bent-kneed stride, setting the cast-iron brogans down deliberately on the cement; then his wife, a small woman with covert, sidewise, curious glances for the world, would follow, and behind her the towheads bunched together in a dazed, glory-struck way. In the store, when their turn came, Jeff York would move to the counter, accept the clerk's greeting, and then bend down from his height to catch the whispered directions of his wife. He would straighten up and say, "Gimme a sack of flahr, if'n you please." Then when the sack of flour had been brought, he would lean again to his wife for the next item. When the stuff had all been bought and paid for with the grease-thick, wadded dollar bills which he took from an old leather coin purse with a metal catch to it, he would heave it all together into his arms and march out, his wife and towheads behind him and his eyes fixed level over the heads of the crowd. He would march down the street and around to the hitching lot where the wagons were, and put his stuff into his wagon and cover it with an old quilt to wait till he got ready to drive out to his place.

For Jeff York had a place. That was what made him different from the other men who looked like him and with whom he stood on the street corner on Saturday afternoon. They were croppers, but he, Jeff York, had a place. But he stood with them because his father had stood with their fathers and his grandfathers with their grandfathers, or with men like their fathers and grandfathers, in other towns, in settlements in the mountains, in towns beyond the mountains. They were the great-great-grandsons of men who, half woodsmen and half farmers, had been shoved into the sand hills, into the limestone hills, into the barrens, two hundred, two hundred and fifty years before and had learned there the way to grabble a life out of the sand and the stone. And when the soil had leached away into the sand or burnt off the stone, they went on west, walking with the bent-kneed stride over the mountains, their eyes squinching warily in the gaunt faces, the rifle over the crooked arm, hunting a new place.

But there was a curse on them. They only knew the life they knew, and that life did not belong to the fat bottom lands, where the cane was head-tall, and to the grassy meadows and the rich swale. So they passed those places by and hunted for the place which was like home and where they could pick up the old life, with the same feel in the bones and the squirrel's bark sounding the same after first light. They had walked a long way, to the sand hills of Alabama, to the red country of North Mississippi and Louisiana, to the Barrens of Tennessee, to the Knobs of Kentucky and the scrub country of West Kentucky, to the Ozarks. Some of them had stopped in Cobb County, Tennessee, in the hilly eastern part of the county, and had built their cabins and dug up the ground for the corn patch. But the land had washed away there, too, and in the end they had come down out of the high land into the bottoms—for half of Cobb County is a rich, swelling country—where the corn was good and the tobacco unfurled a leaf like a yard of green velvet and the white houses stood among cedars and tulip trees and maples. But they were not to live in the white houses with the limestone chimneys set strong at the end of each gable. No, they were to live in the shacks on the back of the farms, or in cabins not much different from the cabins they had once lived in two hundred years before over the mountains or, later, in the hills of Cobb County. But the shacks and the cabins now stood on somebody else's ground, and the curse which they had brought with them over the mountain trail, more precious than the bullet mold or grandma's quilt, the curse which was the very feeling in the bones and the habit in the hand, had come full circle.

Jeff York was one of those men, but he had broken the curse. It had taken him more than thirty years to do it, from the time when he was nothing but a big boy until he was fifty. It had taken him from sun to sun, year in and year out, and all the sweat in his body, and all the power of rejection he could muster, until the very act of rejection had become a kind of pleasure, a dark, secret, savage dissipation, like an obsessing vice. But those years had given him his place, sixty acres with a house and barn.

When he bought the place, it was not very good. The land was rundown from years of neglect and abuse. But Jeff York put brush in the gullies to stop the wash and planted clover on the run-down fields. He mended the fences, rod by rod. He patched the roof on the little house and propped up the porch, buying lumber and shingles almost piece by piece and one by one as he could spare the sweat-bright and grease-slick quarters and half-dollars out of his leather purse. Then he painted the house. He painted it white, for he knew that that was the color you painted a house sitting back from the road with its couple of maples, beyond the clover field.

Last, he put up the gate. It was a patented gate, the kind you can ride up to and open by pulling on a pull rope without getting off your horse or out of your buggy or wagon. It had a high pair of posts, well braced and with a high crossbar between, and the bars for the opening mechanism extending on each side. It was painted white, too. Jeff was even prouder of the gate than he was of the place. Lewis Simmons, who lived next to Jeff's place, swore he had seen Jeff come out after dark on a mule and ride in and out of that gate, back and forth, just for the pleasure of pulling on the rope and making the mechanism work. The gate was the seal Jeff York had put on all the years of sweat and rejection. He could sit on his porch on a Sunday afternoon in summer, before milking time, and look down the rise, down the winding dirt track, to the white gate beyond the clover, and know what he needed to know about all the years passed.

Meanwhile Jeff York had married and had had the three towheads. His wife was twenty years or so younger than he, a small, dark woman, who walked with her head bowed a little and from that humble and unprovoking posture stole sidewise, secret glances at the world from eyes which were brown or black—you never could tell which because you never remembered having looked her straight in the eye—and which were surprisingly bright in that sidewise, secret flicker, like the eyes of a small, cunning bird which surprises you from the brush. When they came to town she moved along the street, with a child in her arms or later with the three trailing behind her, and stole her looks at the world. She wore a calico dress, dun-colored, which hung loose to conceal whatever shape her thin body had, and in winter over the dress a brown wool coat with a scrap of fur at the collar which looked like some tattered growth of fungus feeding on old wood. She wore black high-heeled shoes, slippers of some kind, which she kept polished and which surprised you under that dress and coat. In the slippers she moved with a slightly limping, stealthy gait, almost sliding them along the pavement, as though she had not fully mastered the complicated trick required to use them properly. You knew that she wore them only when she came to town, that she carried them wrapped up in a piece of newspaper until their wagon had reached the first house on the outskirts of town, and that, on the way back, at the same point, she would take them off and wrap them up again and hold the bundle in her lap until she got home. If the weather happened to be bad, or if it was winter, she would have a pair of old brogans under the wagon seat.

It was not that Jeff York was a hard man and kept his wife in clothes that were as bad as those worn by the poorest of the women of the croppers. In fact, some of the cropper women, poor or not, black or white, managed to buy dresses with some color in them and proper hats, and went to the moving picture show on Saturday afternoon. But Jeff still owed a little money on his place, less than two hundred dollars, which he had had to borrow to rebuild his barn after it was struck by lightning. He had, in fact, never been entirely out of debt. He had lost a mule which had got out on the highway and been hit by a truck. That had set him back. One of his towheads had been sickly for a couple of winters. He had not been in deep, but he was not a man, with all those years of rejection behind him, to forget the meaning of those years. He was good enough to his family. Nobody ever said the contrary. But he was good to them in terms of all the years he had lived through. He did what he could afford. He bought the towheads a ten-cent bag of colored candy every Saturday afternoon for them to suck on during the ride home in the wagon, and the last thing before they left town, he always took the lot of them over to the dogwagon to get hamburgers and orange pop.

The towheads were crazy about hamburgers. And so was his wife, for that matter. You could tell it, even if she didn't say anything, for she would lift her bowed-forward head a little, and her face would brighten, and she would run her tongue out to wet her lips just as the plate with the hamburger would be set on the counter before her. But all those folks, like Jeff York and his family, like hamburgers, with pickle and onions and mustard and tomato catsup, the whole works. It is something different. They stay out in the country and eat hog-meat, when they can get it, and greens and corn bread and potatoes, and nothing but a pinch of salt to brighten it on the tongue, and when they get to town and get hold of beef and wheat bread and all the stuff to jack up the flavor, they have to swallow to keep the mouth from flooding before they even take the first bite.

So the last thing every Saturday, Jeff York would take his family over to Slick Hardin's Dew Drop Inn Diner and give them the treat. The diner was built like a railway coach, but it was set on a concrete foundation on a lot just off the main street of town. At each end the concrete was painted to show wheels. Slick Hardin kept the grass just in front of the place pretty well mowed and one or two summers he even had a couple of flower beds in the middle of that shirttail-size lawn. Slick had a good business. For a few years he had been a prelim fighter over in Nashville and had got his name in the papers a few times. So he was a kind of hero, with the air of romance about him. He had been born, however, right in town and, as soon as he had found out he wasn't ever going to be good enough to be a real fighter, he had come back home and started the dogwagon, the first one ever in town. He was a slick-skinned fellow, about thirty-five, prematurely bald, with his head slick all over. He had big eyes, pale blue and slick looking like agates. When he said something that he thought smart, he would roll his eyes around, slick in his head like marbles, to see who was laughing. Then he'd wink. He had done very well with his business, for despite the fact that he had picked up city ways and a lot of city talk, he still remembered enough to deal with the country people, and they were the ones who brought the dimes in. People who lived right there in town, except for school kids in the afternoon and the young toughs from the pool room or men on the night shift down at the railroad, didn't often get around to the dog-wagon.

Slick Hardin was perhaps trying to be smart when he said what he did to Mrs. York. Perhaps he had forgotten, just for that moment, that people like Jeff York and his wife didn't like to be kidded, at least not in that way. He said what he did, and then grinned and rolled his eyes around to see if some of the other people present were thinking it was funny.

Mrs. York was sitting on a stool in front of the counter, flanked on one side by Jeff York and on the other by the three towheads. She had just sat down to wait for the hamburger—there were several orders in ahead of the York order—and had been watching in her sidewise fashion every move of Slick Hardin's hands as he patted the pink meat onto the hot slab and wiped the split buns over the greasy iron to make them ready to receive it. She always watched him like that, and when the hamburger was set before her she would wet her lips with her tongue.

That day Slick set the hamburger down in front of Mrs. York, and said, "Anybody likes hamburger much as you, Mrs. York, ought to git him a hamburger stand."

Mrs. York flushed up, and didn't say anything, staring at her plate. Slick rolled his eyes to see how it was going over, and somebody down the counter snickered. Slick looked back at the Yorks, and if he had not been so encouraged by the snicker he might, when he saw Jeff York's face, have hesitated before going on with his kidding. People like Jeff York are touchous, and they are especially touchous about their women-folks, and you do not make jokes with or about their women-folks unless it is perfectly plain that the joke is a very special kind of friendly joke. The snicker down the counter had defined the joke as not entirely friendly. Jeff was looking at Slick, and something was growing slowly in that hewed-cedar face, and back in the gray eyes in the ambush of thorny brows.

But Slick did not notice. The snicker had encouraged him, and so he said, "Yeah, if I liked them hamburgers much as you, I'd buy me a hamburger stand. Fact, I'm selling this one. You want to buy it?"

There was another snicker, louder, and Jeff York, whose hamburger had been about half way to his mouth for another bite, laid it down deliberately on his plate. But whatever might have happened at that moment did not happen. It did not happen because Mrs. York lifted her flushed face, looked straight at Slick Hardin, swallowed hard to get down a piece of the hamburger or to master her nerve, and said in a sharp strained voice, "You sellen this place?"

There was complete silence. Nobody had expected her to say anything. The chances were she had never said a word in that diner in the couple of hundred times she had been in it. She had come in with Jeff York and, when a stool had come vacant, had sat down, and Jeff had said, "Gimme five hamburgers, if'n you please, and make 'em well done, and five bottles of orange pop." Then, after the eating was over he had always laid down seventy-five cents on the counter—that is, after there were five hamburger-eaters in the family—and walked out, putting his brogans down slow, and his wife and kids following without a word. But now she spoke up and asked the question, in that strained, artificial voice, and everybody, including her husband, looked at her with surprise.

As soon as he could take it in, Slick Hardin replied, "Yeah, I'm selling it."

She swallowed hard again, but this time it could not have been hamburger, and demanded, "What you asken fer hit?"

Slick looked at her in the new silence, half shrugged, a little contemptuously, and said, "Fourteen hundred and fifty dollars."

She looked back at him, while the blood ebbed from her face. "Hit's a lot of money," she said in a flat tone, and returned her gaze to the hamburger on her plate.

"Lady," Slick said defensively, "I got that much money tied up here. Look at that there stove. It is a Heat Master and they cost. Them coffee urns, now. Money can't buy no better. And this here lot, lady, the diner sets on. Anybody knows I got that much money tied up here, I got more. This lot cost me more'n . . ." He suddenly realized that she was not listening to him. And he must have realized, too, that she didn't have a dime in the world and couldn't buy his diner, and that he was making a fool of himself, defending his price. He stopped abruptly, shrugged his shoulders, and then swung his wide gaze down the counter to pick out somebody to wink to.

But before he got the wink off, Jeff York had said, "Mr. Hardin.'

Slick looked at him and asked, "Yeah."

"She didn't mean no harm," Jeff York said. "She didn't mean to be messen in your business."

Slick shrugged. "Ain't no skin off my nose," he said. "Ain't no secret I'm selling out. My price ain't no secret neither."

Mrs. York bowed her head over her plate. She was chewing a mouthful of her hamburger with a slow, abstracted motion of her jaw, and you knew that it was flavorless on her tongue.

That was, of course, on a Saturday. On Thursday afternoon of the next week, Slick was in the diner alone. It was the slack time, right in the middle of the afternoon. Slick, as he told it later, was wiping off the stove and wasn't noticing. He was sort of whistling to himself, he said. He had a way of whistling soft through his teeth. But he wasn't whistling loud, he said, not so loud he wouldn't have heard the door open or the steps if she hadn't come gum-shoeing in on him to stand there waiting in the middle of the floor until he turned round and was so surprised he nearly had heart failure. He had thought he was there alone, and there she was, watching every move he was making, like a cat watching a goldfish swim in a bowl.

"Howdy-do," he said, when he got his breath back.

"This place still fer sale?" she asked him.

"Yeah, lady," he said.

"What you asken fer hit?"

"Lady, I done told you," Slick replied, "fourteen hundred and fifty dollars."

"Hit's a heap of money," she said.

Slick started to tell her how much money he had tied up there, but before he had got going, she had turned and slipped out of the door.

"Yeah," Slick said later to the men who came into the diner, "me like a fool starting to tell her how much money I got tied up here when I knowed she didn't have a dime. That woman's crazy. She must walked that five or six miles in here just to ask me something she already knowed the answer to. And then turned right round and walked out. But I am selling me this place. I'm tired of slinging hash to them hicks. I got me some connections over in Nashville and I'm gonna open me a place over there. A cigar stand and about three pool tables and maybe some beer. I'll have me a sort of club in the back. You know, membership cards to get in, where the boys will play a little game. Just sociable, I got good connections over in Nashville. I'm selling this place. But that woman, she ain't got a dime. She ain't gonna buy it."

But she did.

On Saturday Jeff York led his family over to the diner. They ate hamburgers without a word and marched out. After they had gone, Slick said, "Looks like she ain't going to make the invest-mint. Gonna buy a block of bank stock instead." Then he rolled his eyes, located a brother down the counter, and winked.

It was almost the end of the next week before it happened. What had been going on inside the white house out on Jeff York's place nobody knew or was to know. Perhaps she just starved him out, just not doing the cooking or burning everything. Perhaps she just quit attending to the children properly and he had to come back tired from work and take care of them. Perhaps she just lay in bed at night and talked and talked to him, asking him to buy it, nagging him all night long, while he would fall asleep and then wake up with a start to hear her voice still going on. Or perhaps she just turned her face away from him and wouldn't let him touch her. He was a lot older than she, and she was probably the only woman he had ever had. He had been too ridden by his dream and his passion for rejection during all the years before to lay even a finger on a woman. So she had him there. Because he was a lot older and because he had never had another woman. But perhaps she used none of these methods. She was a small, dark, cunning woman, with a sidewise look from her lowered face, and she could have thought up ways of her own, no doubt.

Whatever she thought up, it worked. On Friday morning Jeff York went to the bank. He wanted to mortgage his place, he told Todd Sullivan, the president. He wanted fourteen hundred and fifty dollars, he said. Todd Sullivan would not let him have it. He already owed the bank one hundred and sixty dollars and the best he could get on a mortgage was eleven hundred dollars. That was in 1935 and then farmland wasn't worth much and half the land in the country was mortgaged anyway. Jeff York sat in the chair by Todd Sullivan's desk and didn't say anything. Eleven hundred dollars would not do him any good. Take off the hundred and sixty dollars he owed and it wouldn't be but a little over nine hundred dollars clear to him. He sat there quietly for a minute, apparently turning that fact over in his head. Then Todd Sullivan asked him, "How much you say you need?"

Jeff York told him.

"What you want it for?" Todd Sullivan asked.

He told him that.

"I tell you," Todd Sullivan said, "I don't want to stand in the way of a man bettering himself. Never did. That diner ought to be a good proposition, all right, and I don't want to stand in your way if you want to come to town and better yourself. It will be a step up from that farm for you, and I like a man has got ambition. The bank can't lend you the money, not on that piece of property. But I tell you what I'll do. I'll buy your place. I got me some walking horses I'm keeping out on my father's place. But I could use me a little place of my own. For my horses. I'll give you seventeen hundred for it. Cash."

Jeff York did not say anything to that. He looked slow at Todd Sullivan as though he did not understand.

"Seventeen hundred," the banker repeated. "That's a good figure. For these times."

Jeff was not looking at him now. He was looking out the window, across the alleyway—Todd Sullivan's office was in the back of the bank. The banker, telling about it later when the doings of Jeff York had become for a moment a matter of interest, said, "I thought he hadn't even heard me. He looked like he was half asleep or something. I coughed to sort of wake him up. You know the way you do. I didn't want to rush him. You can't rush those people, you know. But I couldn't sit there all day. I had offered him a fair price."

It was, as a matter of fact, a fair price for the times, when the bottom was out of everything in the section.

Jeff York took it. He took the seventeen hundred dollars and bought the dogwagon with it, and rented a little house on the edge of town and moved in with his wife and the towheads. The first day after they got settled, Jeff York and his wife went over to the diner to get instructions from Slick about running the place. He showed Mrs. York all about how to work the coffee machine and the stove, and how to make up the sandwiches, and how to clean the place up after herself. She fried up hamburgers for all of them, herself, her husband, and Slick Hardin, for practice, and they ate the hamburgers while a couple of hangers-on watched them. "Lady," Slick said, for he had money in his pocket and was heading out for Nashville on the seven o'clock train that night, and was feeling expansive, "lady, you sure fling a mean hamburger."

He wiped the last crumbs and mustard off his lips, got his valise from behind the door, and said, "Lady, git in there and pitch. I hope you make a million hamburgers." Then he stepped out into the bright fall sunshine and walked away whistling up the street, whistling through his teeth and rolling his eyes as though there were somebody to wink to. That was the last anybody in town ever saw of Slick Hardin.

The next day, Jeff York worked all day down at the diner. He was scrubbing up the place inside and cleaning up the trash which had accumulated behind it. He burned all the trash. Then he gave the place a good coat of paint outside, white paint. That took him two days. Then he touched up the counter inside with varnish. He straightened up the sign out front, which had begun to sag a little. He had that place looking spic and span.

Then on the fifth day after they got settled—it was Sunday—he took a walk in the country. It was along toward sundown when he started out, not late, as a matter of fact, for by October the days are shortening up. He walked out the Curtisville pike and out the cut-off leading to his farm. When he entered the cut-off, about a mile from his own place, it was still light enough for the Bowdoins, who had a filling station at the corner, to see him plain when he passed.

The next time anybody saw him was on Monday morning about six o'clock. A man taking milk into town saw him. He was hanging from the main cross bar of the white patented gate. He had jumped off the gate. But he had propped the thing open so there wouldn't be any chance of clambering back up on it if his neck didn't break when he jumped and he should happen to change his mind.

But that was an unnecessary precaution, as it developed. Dr. Stauffer said that his neck was broken very clean. "A man who can break a neck as clean as that could make a living at it," Dr. Stauffer said. And added, "if he's damned sure it ain't ever his own neck."

Mrs. York was much cut up by her husband's death. People were sympathetic and helpful, and out of a mixture of sympathy and curiosity she got a good starting trade at the diner. And the trade kept right on. She got so she didn't hang her head and look sidewise at you and the world. She would look straight at you. She got so she could walk in high heels without giving the impression that it was a trick she was learning. She wasn't a bad-looking woman, as a matter of fact, once she had caught on how to fix herself up a little. The railroad men and the pool hall gang liked to hang out there and kid with her. Also, they said, she flung a mean hamburger.

BERNARD MALAMUD
The Magic Barrel

Not long ago there lived in uptown New York, in a small, almost meager room, though crowded with books, Leo Finkle, a rabbinical student in the Yeshivah University. Finkle, after six years of study, was to be ordained in June and had been advised by an acquaintance that he might find it easier to win himself a congregation if he were married. Since he had no present prospects of marriage, after two tormented days of turning it over in his mind, he called Pinye Salzman, a marriage broker whose two-line advertisement he had read in the *Forward.*

The matchmaker appeared one night out of the dark fourth-floor hallway of the graystone rooming house where Finkle lived, grasping a black, strapped portfolio that had been worn thin with use. Salzman, who had been long in the business, was of slight but dignified build, wearing an old hat, and an overcoat too short and tight for him. He smelled frankly of fish, which he loved to eat, and although he was missing a few teeth, his presence was not displeasing, because of an amiable manner curiously contrasted with mournful eyes. His voice, his lips, his wisp of beard, his bony fingers were animated, but give him a moment of repose and his mild blue eyes revealed a depth of sadness, a characteristic that put Leo a little at ease although the situation, for him, was inherently tense.

He at once informed Salzman why he had asked him to come, explaining that his home was in Cleveland, and that but for his parents, who had married comparatively late in life, he was alone in the world. He had for six years devoted himself almost entirely to his studies, as a result of which, understandably, he had found himself without time for a social life and the company of young women. Therefore he thought it the better part of trial and error—of embarrassing fumbling—to call in an experienced person to advise him on these matters. He remarked in passing that the function of the marriage broker was ancient and honorable, highly approved in the Jewish community, because it made practical the necessary without hindering joy. Moreover, his own parents had been brought together by a matchmaker. They had made, if not a financially profitable marriage—since neither had possessed any worldly goods to speak of—at least a successful one in the sense of their everlasting devotion to each other. Salzman listened in embarrassed surprise, sensing a sort of apology. Later, however, he experienced a glow of pride in his work, an emotion that had left him years ago, and he heartily approved of Finkle.

The two went to their business. Leo had led Salzman to the only clear place in the room, a table near a window that overlooked the lamp-lit city. He seated himself at the matchmaker's side but facing him, attempting by an act of will to suppress the unpleasant tickle in his throat. Salzman eagerly unstrapped his portfolio and removed a loose rubber band from a thin packet of much-handled cards. As he flipped through them, a gesture and sound that physically hurt Leo, the student pretended not to see and gazed steadfastly out the window. Although it was still February, winter was on its last legs, signs of which he had for the first time in years begun to notice. He now observed the round white moon, moving high in the sky through a cloud menagerie, and watched with half-open mouth as it penetrated a huge hen, and dropped out of her like an egg laying itself. Salzman, though pretending through eyeglasses he had just slipped on, to be engaged in scanning the writing on the cards, stole occasional glances at the young man's distinguished face, noting with pleasure the long, severe scholar's nose, brown eyes heavy with learning, sensitive yet ascetic lips, and a certain, almost hollow quality of the dark cheeks. He gazed around at shelves upon shelves of books and let out a soft, contented sigh.

When Leo's eyes fell upon the cards, he counted six spread out in Salzman's hand.

"So few?" he asked in disappointment.

"You wouldn't believe me how much cards I got in my office," Salzman replied. "The drawers are already filled to the top, so I keep them now in a barrel, but is every girl good for a new rabbi?"

Leo blushed at this, regretting all he had revealed of himself in a curriculum vitae he had sent to Salzman. He had thought it best to acquaint him with his strict standards and specifications, but in having done so, felt he had told the marriage broker more than was absolutely necessary.

He hesitantly inquired, "Do you keep photographs of your clients on file?"

"First comes family, amount of dowry, also what kind promises," Salzman replied, unbuttoning his tight coat and settling himself in the chair. "After comes pictures, rabbi."

"Call me Mr. Finkle. I'm not yet a rabbi."

Salzman said he would, but instead called him doctor, which he changed to rabbi when Leo was not listening too attentively.

Salzman adjusted his horn-rimmed spectacles, gently cleared his throat and read in an eager voice the contents of the top card:

"Sophie P. Twenty-four years. Widow one year. No children. Educated high school and two years college. Father promises eight thousand dollars. Has wonderful wholesale business. Also real estate. On the mother's side comes teachers, also one actor. Well known on Second Avenue."

Leo gazed up in surprise. "Did you say a widow?"

"A widow don't mean spoiled, rabbi. She lived with her husband maybe four months. He was a sick boy she made a mistake to marry him."

"Marrying a widow has never entered my mind."

"This is because you have no experience. A widow, especially if she is young and healthy like this girl, is a wonderful person to marry. She will be thankful to you the rest of her life. Believe me, if I was looking now for a bride, I would marry a widow."

Leo reflected, then shook his head.

Salzman hunched his shoulders in an almost imperceptible gesture of disappointment. He placed the card down on the wooden table and began to read another:

"Lily H. High school teacher. Regular. Not a substitute. Has savings and new Dodge car. Lived in Paris one year. Father is successful dentist thirty-five years. Interested in professional man. Well Americanized family. Wonderful opportunity."

"I knew her personally," said Salzman. "I wish you could see this girl. She is a doll. Also very intelligent. All day you could talk to her about books and theater and what not. She also knows current events."

"I don't believe you mentioned her age?"

"Her age?" Salzman said, raising his brows. "Her age is thirty-two years."

Leo said after a while, "I'm afraid that seems a little too old."

Salzman let out a laugh. "So how old are you, rabbi?"

"Twenty-seven."

"So what is the difference, tell me, between twenty-seven and thirty-two? My own wife is seven years older than me. So what did I suffer?—Nothing. If Rothschild's daughter wants to marry you, would you say on account her age, no?"

"Yes," Leo said dryly.

Salzman shook off the no in the yes. "Five years don't mean a thing I give you my word that when you will live with her for one week you will forget her age. What does it mean five years—that she lived more and knows more than somebody who is younger? On this girl, God bless her, years are not wasted. Each one that it comes makes better the bargain."

"What subject does she teach in high school?"

"Languages. If you heard the way she speaks French, you will think it is music. I am in the business twenty-five years, and I recommend her with my whole heart. Believe me, I know what I'm talking, rabbi."

"What's on the next card?" Leo said abruptly.

Salzman reluctantly turned up the third card:

"Ruth K. Nineteen years. Honor student. Father offers thirteen thousand cash to the right bridegroom. He is a medical doctor. Stomach specialist with marvelous practice. Brother-in-law owns own garment business. Particular people."

Salzman looked as if he had read his trump card.

"Did you say nineteen?" Leo asked with interest.

"On the dot."

"Is she attractive?" He blushed. "Pretty?"

Salzman kissed his finger tips. "A little doll. On this I give you my word. Let me call the father tonight and you will see what means pretty."

But Leo was troubled. "You're sure she's that young?"

"This I am positive. The father will show you the birth certificate."

"Are you positive there isn't something wrong with her?" Leo insisted.

"Who says there is wrong?"

"I don't understand why an American girl her age should go to a marriage broker."

A smile spread over Salzman's face.

"So for the same reason you went, she comes."

Leo flushed. "I am pressed for time."

Salzman, realizing he had been tactless, quickly explained. "The father came, not her. He wants she should have the best, so he looks around himself. When we will locate the right boy he will introduce him and encourage. This makes a better marriage than if a young girl without experience takes for herself. I don't have to tell you this."

"But don't you think this young girl believes in love?" Leo spoke uneasily.

Salzman was about to guffaw but caught himself and said soberly, "Love comes with the right person, not before."

Leo parted dry lips but did not speak. Noticing that Salzman had snatched a glance at the next card, he cleverly asked, "How is her health?"

"Perfect," Salzman said, breathing with difficulty. "Of course, she is a little lame on her right foot from an auto accident that it happened to her when she was twelve years, but nobody notices on account she is so brilliant and also beautiful."

Leo got up heavily and went to the window. He felt curiously bitter and upbraided himself for having called in the marriage broker. Finally, he shook his head.

"Why not?" Salzman persisted, the pitch of his voice rising.

"Because I detest stomach specialists."

"So what do you care what is his business? After you marry her do you need him? Who says he must come every Friday night in your house?"

Ashamed of the way the talk was going, Leo dismissed Salzman, who went home with heavy, melancholy eyes.

Though he had felt only relief at the marriage broker's departure, Leo was in low spirits the next day. He explained it as arising from Salzman's failure to produce a suitable bride for him. He did not care for his type of clientele. But when Leo found himself hesitating whether to seek out another matchmaker, one more polished than Pinye, he wondered if it could be—his protestations to the contrary, and although he honored his father and mother—that he did not, in essence, care for the match-making institution? This thought he quickly put out of mind yet found himself still upset. All day he ran around in the woods—missed an important appointment, forgot to give out his laundry, walked out of a Broadway cafeteria without paying and had to run back with the ticket in his hand; had even not recognized his landlady in the street when she passed with a friend and courteously called out, "A good evening to you, Doctor Finkle." By nightfall, however, he had regained sufficient calm to sink his nose into a book and there found peace from his thoughts.

Almost at once there came a knock on the door. Before Leo could say enter, Salzman, commercial cupid, was standing in the room. His face was gray and meager, his expression hungry, and he looked as if he would expire on his feet. Yet the marriage broker managed, by some trick of the muscles, to display a broad smile.

"So good evening. I am invited?"

Leo nodded, disturbed to see him again, yet unwilling to ask the man to leave.

Beaming still, Salzman laid his portfolio on the table. "Rabbi, I got for you tonight good news."

"I've asked you not to call me rabbi. I'm still a student."

"Your worries are finished. I have for you a first-class bride."

"Leave me in peace concerning this subject." Leo pretended lack of interest.

"The world will dance at your wedding."

"Please, Mr. Salzman, no more."

"But first must come back my strength," Salzman said weakly. He fumbled with the portfolio straps and took out of the leather case an oily paper bag, from which he extracted a hard, seeded roll and a small, smoked white fish. With a quick motion of his hand he stripped the fish out of its skin and began ravenously to chew. "All day in a rush," he muttered.

Leo watched him eat.

"A sliced tomato you have maybe?" Salzman hesitantly inquired.

"No."

The marriage broker shut his eyes and ate. When he had finished he carefully cleaned up the crumbs and rolled up the remains of the fish, in the paper bag. His spectacled eyes roamed the room until he discovered, amid some piles of books, a one-burner gas stove. Lifting his hat he humbly asked, "A glass of tea you got, rabbi?"

Conscience-stricken, Leo rose and brewed the tea. He served it with a chunk of lemon and two cubes of lump sugar, delighting Salzman.

After he had drunk his tea, Salzman's strength and good spirits were restored.

"So tell me, rabbi," he said amiably, "you considered some more the three clients I mentioned yesterday?"

"There was no need to consider."

"Why not?"

"None of them suits me."

"What then suits you?"

Leo let it pass because he could give only a confused answer.

Without waiting for a reply, Salzman asked, "You remember this girl I talked to you—the high school teacher?"

"Age thirty-two?"

But, surprisingly, Salzman's face lit in a smile. "Age twenty-nine."

Leo shot him a look. "Reduced from thirty-two?"

"A mistake," Salzman avowed. "I talked today with the dentist. He took me to his safety deposit box and showed me the birth certificate. She was twenty-nine years last August. They made her a party in the mountains where she went for her vacation. When her father spoke to me the first time I forgot to write the age and I told you thirty-two, but now I remember this was a different client, a widow."

"The same one you told me about? I thought she was twenty-four?"

"A different. Am I responsible that the world is filled with widows?"

"No, but I'm not interested in them, nor for that matter, in school teachers."

Salzman pulled his clasped hands to his breast. Looking at the ceiling he devoutly exclaimed, "Yiddishe kinder, what can I say to somebody that he is not interested in high school teachers? So what then you are interested?"

Leo flushed but controlled himself.

"In what else will you be interested," Salzman went on, "if you not interested in this fine girl that she speaks four languages and has personally in the bank ten thousand dollars? Also her father guarantees further twelve thousand. Also, she has a new car, wonderful clothes, talks on all subjects, and she will give you a first-class home and children. How near do we come in our life to paradise?"

"If she's so wonderful, why wasn't she married ten years ago?"

"Why?" said Salzman with a heavy laugh. "—Why? Because she is *partikiler*. This is why. She wants the *best*."

Leo was silent, amused at how he had entangled himself. But Salzman had aroused his interest in Lily H., and he began seriously to consider calling on her. When the marriage broker observed how intently Leo's mind was at work on the facts he had supplied, he felt certain they would soon come to an agreement.

Late Saturday afternoon, conscious of Salzman, Leo Finkle walked with Lily Hirschorn along Riverside Drive. He walked briskly and erectly, wearing with distinction the black fedora he had that morning taken with trepidation out of the dusty hat box on his closet shelf, and the heavy black Saturday coat he had thoroughly whisked clean. Leo also owned a walking stick, a present from a distant relative, but quickly put temptation aside and did not use it. Lily, petite and not unpretty, had on something signifying the approach of spring. She was au courant, animatedly, with all sorts of subjects, and he weighed her words and found her surprisingly sound—score another for Salzman, whom he uneasily sensed to be somewhere around, hiding perhaps high in a tree along the street, flashing the lady signals with a pocket mirror; or perhaps a cloven-hoofed Pan, piping nuptial ditties as he danced his invisible way before them, strewing wild buds on the walk and purple grapes in their path, symbolizing fruit of a union, though there was of course still none.

Lily startled Leo by remarking, "I was thinking of Mr. Salzman, a curious figure, wouldn't you say?"

Not certain what to answer, he nodded.

She bravely went on, blushing, "I for one am grateful for his introducing us. Aren't you?"

He courteously replied, "I am."

"I mean," she said with a little laugh—and it was all in good taste, or at least gave the effect of being not in bad—"do you mind that we came together so?"

He was not displeased with her honesty, recognizing that she meant to set the relationship aright, and understanding that it took a certain amount of experience in life, and courage, to want to do it quite that way. One had to have some sort of past to make that kind of beginning.

He said that he did not mind. Salzman's function was traditional and honorable—valuable for what it might achieve, which, he pointed out, was frequently nothing.

Lily agreed with a sigh. They walked on for a while and she said after a long silence, again with a nervous laugh, "Would you mind if I asked you something a little bit personal? Frankly, I find the subject fascinating." Although Leo shrugged, she went on half embarrassedly, "How was it that you came to your calling? I mean was it a sudden passionate inspiration?"

Leo, after a time, slowly replied, "I was always interested in the Law."

"You saw revealed in it the presence of the Highest?"

He nodded and changed the subject. "I understand that you spent a little time in Paris, Miss Hirschorn?"

"Oh, did Mr. Salzman tell you, Rabbi Finkle?" Leo winced but she went on, "It was ages ago and almost forgotten. I remember I had to return for my sister's wedding."

And Lily would not be put off. "When," she asked in a trembly voice, "did you become enamored of God?"

He stared at her. Then it came to him that she was talking not about Leo Finkle, but of a total stranger, some mystical figure, perhaps even passionate prophet that Salzman had dreamed up for her—no relation to the living or dead. Leo trembled with rage and weakness. The trickster had obviously sold her a bill of goods, just as he had him, who'd expected to become acquainted with a young lady of twenty-nine, only to behold, the moment he laid eyes upon her strained and anxious face, a woman past thirty-five and aging rapidly. Only his self-control had kept him this long in her presence.

"I am not," he said gravely, "a talented religious person," and in seeking words to go on, found himself possessed by shame and fear. "I think," he said in a strained manner, "that I came to God not because I loved Him, but because I did not."

This confession he spoke harshly because its unexpectedness shook him.

Lily wilted. Leo saw a profusion of loaves of bread go flying like ducks high over his head, not unlike the winged loaves by which he had counted himself to sleep last night. Mercifully, then, it snowed, which he would not put past Salzman's machinations.

He was infuriated with the marriage broker and swore he would throw him out of the room the minute he reappeared. But Salzman did not come that night, and when Leo's anger had subsided, an unaccountable despair grew in its place. At first he thought this was caused by his disappointment in Lily, but before long it became evident that he had involved himself with Salzman without a true knowledge of his own intent. He gradually realized—with an emptiness that seized him with six hands—that he had called in the broker to find him a bride because he was incapable of doing it himself. This terrifying insight he had derived as a result of his meeting and conversation with Lily Hirschorn. Her probing questions had somehow irritated him into revealing—to himself more than her—the true nature of his relationship to God, and from that it had come upon him, with shocking force, that apart from his parents, he had never loved anyone. Or perhaps it went the other way, that he did not love God so well as he might, because he had not loved man. It seemed to Leo that his whole life stood starkly revealed and he saw himself for the first time as he truly was—unloved and loveless. This bitter but somehow not fully unexpected revelation brought him to a point of panic, controlled only by extraordinary effort. He covered his face with his hands and cried.

The week that followed was the worst of his life. He did not eat and lost weight. His beard darkened and grew ragged. He stopped attending seminars and almost never opened a book. He seriously considered leaving the Yeshivah, although he was deeply troubled at the thought of the loss of all his years of study—saw them like pages torn from a book, strewn over the city—and at the devastating effect of this decision upon his parents. But he had lived without knowledge of himself, and never in the Five Books and all the Commentaries—mea culpa—had the truth been revealed to him. He did not know where to turn, and in all this desolating loneliness there was no *to whom,* although he often thought of Lily but not once could bring himself to go downstairs and make the call. He became touchy and irritable, especially with his landlady, who asked him all manner of personal questions; on the other hand, sensing his own disagreeableness, he waylaid her on the stairs and apologized abjectly, until mortified, she ran from him. Out of this, however, he drew the consolation that he was a Jew and that a Jew suffered. But gradually, as the long and terrible week drew to a close, he regained his composure and some idea of purpose in life: to go on as planned. Although he was imperfect, the idea was not. As for his quest of a bride, the thought of continuing afflicted him with anxiety and heartburn, yet perhaps with this new knowledge of himself he would be more successful than in the past. Perhaps love would now come to him and a bride to that love. And for this sanctified seeking who needed a Salzman?

The marriage broker, a skeleton with haunted eyes, returned that very night. He looked, withal, the picture of frustrated expectancy—as if he had steadfastly waited the week at Miss Lily Hirschorn's side for a telephone call that never came.

Casually coughing, Salzman came immediately to the point: "So how did you like her?"

Leo's anger rose and he could not refrain from chiding the matchmaker: "Why did you lie to me, Salzman?"

Salzman's pale face went dead white, the world had snowed on him.

"Did you not state that she was twenty-nine?" Leo insisted.

"I give you my word—"

"She was thirty-five, if a day. *At least* thirty-five."

"Of this don't be too sure. Her father told me—".

"Never mind. The worst of it was that you lied to her."

"How did I lie to her, tell me?"

"You told her things about me that weren't true. You made me out to be more, consequently less than I am. She had in mind a totally different person, a sort of semi-mystical Wonder Rabbi."

"All I said, you was a religious man."

"I can imagine."

Salzman sighed. "This is my weakness that I have," he confessed. "My wife says to me I shouldn't be a salesman, but when I have two fine people that they would be wonderful to be married, I am so happy that I talk too much." He smiled wanly. "This is why Salzman is a poor man."

Leo's anger left him. "Well, Salzman, I'm afraid that's all."

The marriage broker fastened hungry eyes on him.

"You don't want any more a bride?"

"I do," said Leo, "but I have decided to seek her in a different way. I am no longer interested in an arranged marriage. To be frank, I now admit the necessity of premarital love. That is, I want to be in love with the one I marry."

"Love?" said Salzman, astounded. After a moment he remarked, "For us, our love is our life, not for the ladies. In the ghetto they—"

"I know, I know," said Leo. "I've thought of it often. Love, I have said to myself, should be a by-product of living and worship rather than its own end. Yet for myself I find it necessary to establish the level of my need and fulfill it."

Salzman shrugged but answered, "Listen, rabbi, if you want love, this I can find for you also. I have such beautiful clients that you will love them the minute your eyes will see them."

Leo smiled unhappily. "I'm afraid you don't understand."

But Salzman hastily unstrapped his portfolio and withdrew a manila packet from it.

"Pictures," he said, quickly laying the envelope on the table.

Leo called after him to take the pictures away, but as if on the wings of the wind, Salzman had disappeared.

March came. Leo had returned to his regular routine. Although he felt not quite himself yet—lacked energy—he was making plans for a more active social life. Of course it would cost something, but he was an expert in cutting corners; and when there were no corners left he would make circles rounder. All the while Salzman's pictures had lain on the table, gathering dust. Occasionally as Leo sat studying, or enjoying a cup of tea, his eyes fell on the manila envelope, but he never opened it.

The days went by and no social life to speak of developed with a member of the opposite sex—it was difficult, given the circumstances of his situation. One morning Leo toiled up the stairs to his room and stared out the window at the city. Although the day was bright his view of it was dark. For some time he watched the people in the street below hurrying along and then turned with a heavy heart to his little room. On the table was the packet. With a sudden relentless gesture he tore it open. For a half-hour he stood by the table in a state of excitement, examining the photographs of the ladies Salzman had included. Finally, with a deep sigh he put them down. There were six, of varying degrees of attractiveness, but look at them long enough and they all become Lily Hirschorn: all past their prime, all starved behind bright smiles, not a true personality in the lot. Life, despite their frantic yoohooings, had passed them by; they were pictures in a brief case that stank of fish. After a while, however, as Leo attempted to return the photographs into the envelope, he found in it another, a snapshot of the type taken by a machine for a quarter. He gazed at it a moment and let out a cry.

Her face deeply moved him. Why, he could at first not say. It gave him the impression of youth—spring flowers, yet age—a sense of having been used to the bone, wasted; this came from the eyes, which were hauntingly familiar, yet absolutely strange. He had a vivid impression that he had met her before, but try as he might he could not place her although he could almost recall her name, as if he had read it in her own handwriting. No, this couldn't be; he would have remembered her. It was not, he affirmed, that she had an extraordinary beauty—no, though her face was attractive enough; it was that *something* about her moved him. Feature for feature, even some of the ladies of the photographs could do better; but she leaped forth to his heart—had *lived,* or wanted to—more than just wanted, perhaps regretted how she had lived—had somehow deeply suffered: it could be seen in the depths of those reluctant eyes, from the way the light enclosed and shone from her, and within her, opening realms of possibility: this was her own. Her he desired. His head ached and eyes narrowed with the intensity of his gazing, then as if an obscure fog had blown up in the mind, he experienced fear of her and was aware that he had received an impression, somehow, of evil. He shuddered, saying softly, it is thus with us all. Leo brewed some tea in a small pot and sat sipping it without sugar, to calm himself. But before he had finished drinking, again with excitement he examined the face and found it good: good for Leo Finkle. Only such a one could understand him and help him seek whatever he was seeking. She might, perhaps, love him. How she had happened to be among the discards in Salzman's barrel he could never guess, but he knew he must urgently go find her.

Leo rushed downstairs, grabbed up the Bronx telephone book, and searched for Salzman's home address. He was not listed nor was his office. Neither was he in the Manhattan book. But Leo remembered having written down the address on a slip of paper after he had read Salzman's advertisement in the "personals" column of the *Forward.* He ran up to his room and tore through his papers, without luck. It was exasperating. Just when he needed the matchmaker he was nowhere to be found. Fortunately Leo remembered to look in his wallet. There on a card he found his name written and a Bronx address. No phone number was listed, the reason—Leo now recalled—he had originally communicated with Salzman by letter. He got on his coat, put a hat on over his skull cap and hurried to the subway station. All the way to the far end of the Bronx he sat on the edge of his seat. He was more than once tempted to take out the picture and see if the girl's face was as he remembered it, but he refrained, allowing the snapshot to remain in his inside coat pocket, content to have her so close. When the train pulled into the station he was waiting at the door and bolted out. He quickly located the street Salzman had advertised.

The building he sought was less than a block from the subway, but it was not an office building, nor even a loft, nor a store in which one could rent office space. It was a very old tenement house. Leo found Salzman's name in pencil on a soiled tag under the bell and climbed three dark flights to his apartment. When he knocked, the door was opened by a thin, asthmatic, gray-haired woman, in felt slippers.

"Yes?" she said, expecting nothing. She listened without listening. He could have sworn he had seen her, too, before but knew it was an illusion.

"Salzman—does he live here? Pinye Salzman," he said, "the matchmaker?"

She stared at him a long minute. "Of course."

He felt embarrassed. "Is he in?"

"No." Her mouth, though left open, offered nothing more.

"The matter is urgent. Can you tell me where his office is?"

"In the air." She pointed upward.

"You mean he has no office?" Leo asked.

"In his socks."

He peered into the apartment. It was sunless and dingy, one large room divided by a half-open curtain, beyond which he could see a sagging metal bed. The near side of the room was crowded with rickety chairs, old bureaus, a three-legged table, racks of cooking utensils, and all the apparatus of a kitchen. But there was no sign of Salzman or his magic barrel, probably also a figment of the imagination. An odor of frying fish made Leo weak to the knees.

"Where is he?" he insisted. "I've got to see your husband."

At length she answered, "So who knows where he is? Every time he thinks a new thought he runs to a different place. Go home, he will find you."

"Tell him Leo Finkle."

She gave no sign she had heard.

He walked downstairs, depressed.

But Salzman, breathless, stood waiting at his door.

Leo was astounded and overjoyed. "How did you get here before me?"

"I rushed."

"Come inside."

They entered. Leo fixed tea, and a sardine sandwich for Salzman. As they were drinking he reached behind him for the packet of pictures and handed them to the marriage broker.

Salzman put down his glass and said expectantly, "You found somebody you like?"

"Not among these."

The marriage broker turned away.

"Here is the one I want." Leo held forth the snapshot.

Salzman slipped on his glasses and took the picture into his trembling hand. He turned ghastly and let out a groan.

"What's the matter?" cried Leo.

"Excuse me. Was an accident this picture. She isn't for you."

Salzman frantically shoved the manila packet into his portfolio. He thrust the snapshot into his pocket and fled down the stairs.

Leo, after momentary paralysis, gave chase and cornered the marriage broker in the vestibule. The landlady made hysterical outcries but neither of them listened.

"Give me back the picture, Salzman."

"No." The pain in his eyes was terrible.

"Tell me who she is then."

"This I can't tell you. Excuse me."

He made to depart, but Leo, forgetting himself, seized the matchmaker by his tight coat and shook him frenziedly.

"Please," sighed Salzman. "*Please.*"

Leo ashamedly let him go. "Tell me who she is," he begged. "It's very important for me to know."

"She is not for you. She is a wild one—wild, without shame. This is not a bride for a rabbi."

"What do you mean wild?"

"Like an animal. Like a dog. For her to be poor was a sin. This is why to me she is dead now."

"In God's name, what do you mean?"

"Her I can't introduce to you," Salzman cried.

"Why are you so excited?"

"Why, he asks," Salzman said, bursting into tears. "This is my baby, my Stella, she should burn in hell."

Leo hurried up to bed and hid under the covers. Under the covers he thought his life through. Although he soon fell asleep he could not sleep her out of his mind. He woke, beating his breast. Though he prayed to be rid of her, his prayers went unanswered. Through days of torment he endlessly struggled not to love her; fearing success, he escaped it. He then concluded to convert her to goodness, himself to God. The idea alternately nauseated and exalted him.

He perhaps did not know that he had come to a final decision until he encountered Salzman in a Broadway cafeteria. He was sitting alone at a rear table, sucking the bony remains of a fish. The marriage broker appeared haggard, and transparent to the point of vanishing.

Salzman looked up at first without recognizing him. Leo had grown a pointed beard and his eyes were weighted with wisdom.

"Salzman," he said, "love has at last come to my heart."

"Who can love from a picture?" mocked the marriage broker.

"It is not impossible."

"If you can love her, then you can love anybody. Let me show you some new clients that they just sent me their photographs. One is a little doll."

"Just her I want," Leo murmured.

"Don't be a fool, doctor. Don't bother with her."

"Put me in touch with her, Salzman," Leo said humbly. "Perhaps I can be of service."

Salzman had stopped eating and Leo understood with emotion that it was now arranged.

Leaving the cafeteria, he was, however, afflicted by a tormenting suspicion that Salzman had planned it all to happen this way.

Leo was informed by letter that she would meet him on a certain corner, and she was there one spring night, waiting under a street lamp. He appeared, carrying a small bouquet of violets and rosebuds. Stella stood by the lamp post, smoking. She wore white with red shoes, which fitted his expectations, although in a troubled moment he had imagined the dress red, and only the shoes white. She waited uneasily and shyly. From afar he saw that her eyes—clearly her father's—were filled with desperate innocence. He pictured, in her, his own redemption. Violins and lit candles revolved in the sky. Leo ran forward with flowers outthrust.

Around the corner, Salzman, leaning against a wall, chanted prayers for the dead.

JOHN UPDIKE
Who Made Yellow Roses Yellow?

Of the three telephones in the apartment, the one in the living room rested on a tabouret given to Fred Platt's grandmother by Henry James, who considered her, the Platts claimed, the only educated woman in the United States. Above this cherrywood gift hung an oval mirror, its frame a patterned involvement of cherubs, acanthus leaves, and half-furled scrolls; its gilt, smooth as butter in the valleys between figures, yielded on the crests of the relief to touches of Watteau brown. Great-Uncle Randy, known for his whims and mustaches, had rescued the mirror from a Paris auction. In the capacious room there was nothing of no intrinsic interest, nothing that would not serve as cause for a narrative, except the three overstuffed pieces installed by Fred's father—two chairs, facing each other at a distance of three strides, and a crescent-shaped sofa, all covered in spandy-new, navy-blue leather. This blue, the dark warm wood of inherited cabinets, the twilight colors of aged books, the scarlet and purple of the carpet from Cairo (where Charlotte, Uncle Randy's wife, had caught a bug and died), and the dismal sonorities of the Secentistico Transfiguration on the west wall vibrated around the basal shade of plum. Plum: a color a man can rest in, the one toward which all dressing gowns tend. Reinforcing the repose and untroubled finality of the interior were the several oval shapes. The mirror was one of a family, kin to the feminine ellipse of the coffee table; to the burly arc of Daddy's sofa, as they never failed to call it; to the ovoid, palely painted base of a Florentine lamp; to the plaster medallion on the ceiling—the one cloud in the sky of the room—and to the recurrent, tiny gold seal of the Oxford University Press, whose books, monochrome and Latinate as dons, were among the chief of the senior Platt's plum-colored pleasures.

Fred, his only son, age twenty-five, dialed a JUdson number. He listened to five burrs before the receiver was picked up, exposing the tail end of a girl's giggle. Still tittery, she enunciated, "Carson Chemi-cal."

"Hello. Is—ah, Clayton Thomas Clayton there, do you know?"

"Mr. Thomas Clayton? Yes he is. Just one moment please." So poor Clayton Clayton had finally got somebody to call him by his middle name, that "Thomas" which his parents must have felt made all the difference between the absurd and the sublime.

"Mr. Clayton's of-fice," another girl said. "About what was it you wished to speak to him?"

"Well nothing, really. It's a friend."

"Just one moment, please."

After a delay—purely disciplinary, Fred believed—an unexpectedly deep and even melodious voice said, "Yes?"

"Clayton Clayton?"

A pause. "Who is this?"

"Good morning, sir. I represent the Society for the Propagation and Eventual Adoption of the A.D. Spooner Graduated Income Tax Plan. As perhaps you know, this plan calls for an income tax which increases in inverse proportion to income, so that the wealthy are exempted and the poor taxed out of existence. Within five years, Mr. Spooner estimates, poverty would be eliminated: within ten, a thing not even of memory. Word has come to our office—"

"It's Fred Platt, isn't it?"

"Word has come to our office that in recent years Providence has so favored thee as to incline thy thoughts the more favorably to the Plan."

"Fred?"

"Congratulations. You now own the Motorola combination phonograph-and-megaphone. Do you care to try for the Bendix?"

"How long have you been in town? It's damn good to hear from you."

"Since April first. It's a prank of my father's. Who are all these girls you live in the midst of?"

"Your father called you back?"

"I'm not sure. I keep forgetting to look up 'wastrel' in the dictionary."

That made Clayton laugh. "I thought you were studying at the Sorbonne."

"I was, I was."

"But you're not now."

"I'm not now. *Moi et la Sorbonne, nous sommes kaput.*" When the other was silent. Fred added, "*Beaucoup kaput.*"

"Look, we must get together," Clayton said.

"Yes. I was wondering if you eat lunch."

"When had you thought?"

"Soon?"

"Wait. I'll check." Some muffled words—a question with his hand over the mouthpiece. A drawer scraped. "Say, Fred, this is bad. I have something on the go every day this week."

"So. Well, what about June 21st? They say the solstice will be lovely this year."

"Wait. What about today? I'm free today, they just told me."

"Today?" Fred had to see Clayton soon, but immediately seemed like a push. "*Comme vous voulez, Monsieur.* Oneish?"

"All right, uh—could you make it twelve-thirty? I have a good bit to do . . ."

"Just as easy. There's a Chinese place on East Forty-ninth Street run by Australians. Excellent murals of Li Po embracing the moon in the Yalu, *plus* the coronation of Henri Quatre."

"I wonder, could that be done some other time? As I say, there's some stuff here at the office. Do you know Shulman's? It's on Third Avenue, a block from here, so that—"

"Press of work, eh?"

"You said it," Clayton said, evidently sensing no irony. "Then I'll see you then."

"In all the old de dum de dumpty that this heart of mine embraces."

"Pardon?"

"See you then."

"Twelve-thirty at Shulman's."

"Absolutely."

"So long."

"So long."

The first impulse after a humiliation is to look into a mirror. The heavy Parisian looking glass, hung on too long a wire, leaned inches from the wall. A person standing would see reflected in it not his head but the carpet, some furniture, and perhaps, in the upper portion of the oval, his shoes and cuffs. By tilting his chair Fred could see his face, flushed like the mask someone momentarily absent from an enervating cocktail party spies in the bathroom mirror. There, the hot-skinned head, backed by pastel tiles and borrowing imperturbability from the porcelain fixtures, strikes the owner as a glamorous symbol of Man, half angel, half beast; and each eye seems the transparent base of a cone luminous with intuitions, secrets, quips, deviltry, and love. Here, in this overstuffed room, his red face, above his black suit, just looked hot. His excited appearance annoyed him. Between his feverish attempt to rekindle friendship—his mind skidding, his tongue wagging—and Clayton's response an embarrassing and degrading disproportion had existed.

Until now it had seemed foolishly natural for Clayton to offer him a job. Reportedly he had asked Bim Blackwood to jump Harcourt for a publicity job at Carson Chemical. Bim had said, without seeing anything funny in the word, that Clayton had lots of "power" at Carson. "In just three years, he's near the top. He's a *killer*. Really."

It had been hard to gather from Bim's description exactly what Clayton did. As Bim talked on, flicking with increasing rapidity at the stiff eave of brown hair that overhung his forehead with conceited carelessness, he would say anything to round out a sentence, never surrendering his right to be taken seriously. "It's an octopus," he had asserted. "You know *ev*erything is chemicals *ult*imately. Clayton told me the first thing he was given to do was help design the wrapper for an ammoniated chewing gum they were just putting out. He said the big question was whether chalk-white or mint-green suggested better a clean feeling in the mouth. They had a survey on it; it cost thousands and *thousands*—thousands of little men going inside people's mouths. Of course he doesn't draw any more; he consults. Can you imagine doing nothing all day but *consult?* On pamphlets, you know, and 'flyers'—what *are* flyers anyway?—and motion pictures to show to salesmen to show them how to explain the things they sell. He's *ter*ribly involved with *tele*vision; he told me a *hor*rible story about a play about Irish peasants the Carson Chemical Hour was putting on and at the last minute it dawned on everybody that these people were *organic farmers.* Clayton Clayton saw it through. The killer instinct."

Clayton hadn't had to go into the Army. Troubled knees, or something. That was the thing about poor children: they acquired disabilities which give them the edge in later life. It's cruel, to expect a man without a handicap to go far.

Fred's position was not desperate. An honorable office in the investments firm (for Father was of the newest school, which sees no wrong in playing favorites) was not, as Father had said, with his arch way of trotting out clichés as if they were moderately obscure literary quotations, "the fate worse than death." Furthermore—he was a great man for furthermores—anyone who imagined that the publicity arm of Carson Chemical was an ivory tower compared to Braur, Chappell & Platt lived in a fool's paradise.

Yet viewed allegorically the difference seemed great. Something about all this, perhaps the chaste spring greenery of Central Park, which from these windows was spread out with the falcon's-eye perspective of a medieval map, suggested one of the crossroads in *The Faerie Queene.*

Besides, he had been very kind to Clayton—gotten him onto the *Quaff,* really. Sans *Quaff,* where would Clayton be? Not that Clayton need consider any of this. Hell, it wasn't as if Fred were asking for something; he was offering something. He pushed back the chair a few feet, so a full view of himself was available in the tilted mirror: a tall, narrow-skulled, smooth-cheeked youth, tightly dressed in darkest gray. A lapsed Episcopalian, Fred was half in love with the clergy.

Entering, late, the appointed restaurant, Fred instantly spotted Clayton Clayton standing at the bar. That three years had passed, that the place was smoky and crowded with interchangeable men, did not matter; an eclipsing head bowed, and the fragment of cheek then glimpsed, though in itself nothing but a daub of white, not only communicated to

Fred one human identity but stirred in him warm feelings for the *Quaff*, college, his youth generally, and even America. Fred had inherited that trick of the rich of seeming to do everything out of friendship, but he was three generations removed from the making of the money, and a manner of business had become, in him, a way of life; his dealings were in fact at the mercy of his affections. Grotesquely close to giggling, he walked up to his man and intoned, "*Ego sum via, vita, veritas.*"

Clayton turned, grinned, and pumped Fred's hand. "How *are* you, Fred?"

Members of the *Quaff* did not ask one another how they were; Fred had supposed ex-members also did not. Finding they did balked him. He could not think of the joke to turn such a simple attack aside. "Pretty well," he conceded and, as if these words were an exorcism enabling the gods of fatuity to descend and dwell in his lips, heard himself add, in what seemed full solemnity, "How are *you?*"

"I'm doing"—Clayton paused, nodding once, giving the same words a new import—"pretty well."

"Yes, everybody says."

"I was glad I could make it today. I really am up to my ears this week." Confidingly: "I'm in a crazy business."

On one wall of the restaurant were Revolutionary murals, darkened perhaps by smoke and time but more likely by the painter's timidity. "Ah," said Fred, gesturing. "The Renaissance Popes in Hell."

"Would you like one of these?" Clayton touched the glass in front of him; it contained that collegiate brew, beer.

How tender of Clayton still to drink beer! By a trick of vision, the liquid stood on the dark bar unbounded by glass. The sight of that suspended amber cylinder, like his magic first glimpse of Clayton's face, conjured in Fred a sensation of fondness. This time he curbed his tendency to babble and said, anxious to be honest, certain that the merest addition of the correct substance—the simple words exchanged by comrades—would reform the alchemy of the relationship, "Yes. I would like one. Quite a bit."

"I tell you. Let's grab a table and order from there. They'll let us stand here all day."

Fred felt not so much frustrated as deflected, as if the glass that wasn't around the beer was around Clayton.

"There's a table." Clayton picked up his glass, placed a half dollar in the center of the circle its base had occupied, and shouldered away from the bar. He led the way into a booth, past two old men brandishing their topcoats. Inside, the high partitions shielded them from much of the noise of the place. Clayton took two menus from behind the sugar and handed one to Fred. "We had better order the food first, then ask for the beer. If you asked for the drinks first, they'll just run off." He was perfect: the medium-short dry-combed hair, the unimpeachable brown suit, the buttonless collar, the genially dragged vowels, the little edges of efficiency bracing the consonants. Some traces of the scholarship-bothered freshman from Hampton (Md.) High School who had come down to the *Quaff* on Candidates' Night with an armful of framed sports cartoons remained—the not smoking, the tucked-in chin and the attendant uplook of the boyishly lucid eyes, and the skin allergy that placed on the flank of each jaw a constellation of red dots. Even these vestiges fitted into the picture, by lending him, until he learned to feign it, the ingratiating uncertainty desired in New York executives. It was just this suggestion of inexperience that in his genuine inexperience Clayton was working to suppress. "See anything you like," he asked with a firmness not interrogative.

"I think maybe a lamb chop."

"I don't see them on the menu."

"I don't either."

Raising his hand to the level of his ear and snapping his fingers, Clayton summoned a waiter. "This gentleman wants a lamb chop. Do you have them?"

The waiter didn't bother to answer, just wrote it down.

"I think I might try," Clayton went on, "the chopped sirloin with mushroom sauce. Beans instead of the peas, if you will. And I'm having another glass of Ballantine. Shall I make that two, Fred?"

"Do you have any decent German beer? Würzburger? Or Löwenbräu?"

The request materialized the man, who had been serving them with only his skimpy professional self. Now he smiled, and stood bodied forth as a great-boned Teuton in the prime of his fifties, with the square Bavarian skull, a short hooked nose, and portentous ears covered with a diaphanous fuzz that brought to the dignity they already possessed a certain silky glamour. "I believe, sir, we have the Löwenbräu. I don't think we have any of the Würzburger, sir."

"O.K. Anything." Though Fred truly repented stealing Clayton's show, the evidence of his crime refused to disappear. He had called into being a genie—cloying, zealous, delighted to have his cavernous reserve of attentiveness tapped at last. The waiter bowed and indeed whispered, making an awkward third party of Clayton, "I think we have the Löwenbräu. If not, would an English stout do? A nice Guinness, sir?"

"Anything is fine." Trying to bring Clayton back into it, Fred asked him, "Do you want one? Fewer bubbles than Ballantine. Less tingle for more ferment."

Clayton's answering laugh would have been agreeable if he had not, while uttering it, lowered his eyelids, showing that he conceived of this as a decision whereby he stood to gain or lose. "No, I think I'll stick to Ballantine." He looked Fred needlessly in the eyes. When Clayton felt threatened, the middle sector of his face clouded over; the area between his brows and nostrils queerly condensed.

Fred was both repelled and touched. The expression was exactly that worn by the adolescent Clayton at the *Quaff* candidates' punches, when all the dues members, dead to the magazine, showed up resplendent in black suits and collar pins, eager for Martinis, as full of chatter and strut as a flock of whooping cranes bent on proving they were not extinct yet. Fred pitied Clayton, remembering the days when Fred alone, a respected if sophomore member, was insisting that the kid with the gag name be elected to the *Quaff:* The point was he could draw. Wonky, sure. He was right out of the funny papers. But at least his hands looked like hands. Outrageous, of course, to have the drawings framed, but his parents put him up to that—anybody who'd call a helpless baby Clayton Clayton. . . . He wore cocoa-colored slacks and sport shirts. They'd wear out. If he was sullen, he was afraid. The point was, If we don't get anybody on the magazine who can draw we'll be forced to run daguerreotypes of Chester Arthur and the Conkling Gang.

"Do you see much of Anna Spooner?" Clayton asked, referring back, perhaps unconsciously, to Fred's earlier mistake, his mention of the income-tax plan of their friend A. D. Spooner, nicknamed "Anno Domini" and eventually "Anna."

"Once or twice. I haven't been back that long. He said he kept running into you at the Old Grads' Marching Society."

"Once in a while."

"You don't sound too enthusiastic."

"I hadn't meant to. I mean I hadn't meant not to. He's about the same. Same tie, same jokes. He never thanks me when I buy him a drink. I don't mean the money bothers me. It's one of those absurd little things. I shouldn't even mention it."

The waiter brought the beers. Fred stared into his Löwenbräu and breathed the word "Yeah."

"How long *have* you been back?"

"Two weeks, I guess."

"That's right. You said. Well, tell me about it. What've you been doing for three years?" His hands were steadily folded on the table, conference-style. "I'm interested."

Fred laughed outright at him. "There isn't that much. In the Army I was in Germany in the Quartermaster Corps."

"What did you do?"

"Nothing. Typed. Played blackjack, faro, Rook."

"Do you find it's changed you much?"

"I type faster. And my chest now is a mass of pornographic tattoos."

Clayton laughed a little. "It just interests me. I know that psychologically the effect on me of *not* going in is—is genuine. I feel not exactly guilty, but it's something that everyone of our generation has gone through. Not to seems incom*plete*."

"It should, it should. I bet you can't even rev out a Bowling Bunting

H-4 jet-cycle tetrameter. As for shooting a bazooka! Talk of St. Teresa's spiritual experiences—"

"It's impressive, how little it's changed you. I wonder if I'm changed. I do like the work, you know. People are always slamming advertising, but I've found out it's a pretty damn essential thing in our economy."

The waiter came and laid their plates before them. Clayton set to with a disconcerting rapacity, forking in the food as often with his left hand as with his right, pausing only to ask questions. "Then you went back to Europe."

"Then I went back to Europe."

"Why? I mean what did you do? Did you do any writing?"

In recent years Fred's literary intelligence had exerted itself primarily in the invention of impeccable but fruitless puns. Parcel Proust. Or Supple Simon. (Supple Simon met a Neiman/Fellow at the Glee Club, gleamin'./ Said Supple Simon, "Tell me, Fellow/Who made yellow roses yellow?") "Why, yes," he told Clayton. "Quite a bit. I've just completed a three-volume biography of the great Hungarian actress, Juxta Pose."

"No, actually. What did you do in Paris?"

"Actually, I sat in a chair. The same chair whenever I could. It was a straw chair in the sidewalk area of a restaurant on the Boulevard Saint-Michel. In the summer and spring the tables are in the open, but when it gets cold they enclose the area with large windows. It's best then. Everybody except you sits inside the restaurant, where it's warm. It's best of all at breakfast, around eleven of a nippy morning, with your *café* and *croissant avec du beurre* and your copy of *Là-Bas* all on a little table the size of a tray, and people outside the window trying to sell *ballons* to Christmas tourists."

"You must know French perfectly. It annoys hell out of me that I don't know any."

"*Oui, pardon zut!* and *alors!* are all you need for ordinary conversation. Say them after me: *oui*—the lips so—*par-don*—"

"The reason you probably don't write more," Clayton said, "is that you have too much taste. Your critical sense is always a jump ahead of your creative urge." Getting no response, he went on, "I haven't been doing much drawing, either. Except roughing out ideas. But I plan to come back to it."

"I know you do. I know you will."

That was what Clayton wanted to hear. He loved work; it was all he knew how to do. His type saw competition as the spine of the universe. His *Quaff* career had been all success, all adaptation and productivity, so that in his senior year Clayton was president, and everybody said he alone was keeping silly old *Quaff* alive, when in fact the club, with its fragile ethic of ironic worthlessness, had withered under him.

Clayton had a forkful of hamburger poised between the plate and his mouth. "What does your father want?" In went the hamburger.

"My father seems to fascinate you. He is a thin man in his late fifties. He sits at one end of an enormous long room filled with priceless things. He is wearing a purple dressing gown and trying to read a book. But he feels the room is tipping. So he wants me to get in there with him and sit at the other end to keep the balance."

"No. I didn't mean—"

"He wants me to get a job. Know of one?" So the crucial question was out, stated like a rebuke.

Clayton carefully chewed. "What sort?"

"I've already been offered a position in Braur, Chappell & Platt. A fine old firm. I'm looking for something with less pay."

"In publishing?"

Stalling, stalling. "Or advertising."

Clayton set down his fork. "Gee. You should be able to get something."

"I wouldn't know why. I have no experience. I can't use my father's pull. That wouldn't be the game."

"I wish you had been here about six months ago. There was an opening up at Carson, and I asked Bim Blackwood, but he didn't want to make the jump. Speaking of Bim, he's certainly come along."

"Come along? Where to?"

"You know. He seems more mature. I feel he's gotten ahold of himself. His view of things is better proportioned."

"That's very perceptive. Who else do we know who's come along?"

"Well, I would say Harry Ducloss has. I was talking last week with a man Harry works for."

"He said he's come along?"

"He said he thought highly of him."

" 'Thought highly.' Fermann was always thinking highly of people."

"I saw Fermann in the street the other day. Boy!"

"Not coming along?"

Clayton lifted his wrists so the waiter could clear away his plate. "It's just, it's"—with a peculiar intensity, as if Fred had often thought the same thing but never so well expressed it—"*something* to see those tin gods again."

"Would you young men like dessert?" the waiter asked. "Coffee?" To Fred: "We have nice freshly baked strudel. Very nice. It's made right in the kitchen ovens."

Fred deferred to Clayton. "Do you have time for coffee?"

Clayton craned his neck to see the clock. "Eight of two." He looked at Fred apologetically. "To tell the truth—"

"No coffee," Fred told the waiter.

"Oh, let's have it. It'll take just a few minutes."

"No, it doesn't matter to me and I don't want you to be late."

"They won't miss me. I'm not *that* indispensable. Are you sure you don't want any?"

"Positive."

"All right," Clayton said in the dragged-out, musical tone of a parent acceding to a demand that will only do the child harm. "Could I have the check, please, waiter?"

"Certainly, sir." The something sarcastic about that "sir" was meant for Fred to see.

The check came to $3.80. When Fred reached for his wallet, Clayton said, "Keep that in your pocket. This is on me."

"Don't be a fool. The lunch was my idea."

"No, please. Let me take this."

Fred dropped a five-dollar bill on the table.

"No, look," Clayton said. "I know you have the money—"

"Money! We *all* have *money*."

Clayton, at last detecting anger, looked up timidly, his irises in the top of his eyes, his chin tucked in. "Please. You were always quite kind to me."

It was like a plain girl opening her mouth in the middle of a kiss. Fred wordlessly took back his five. Clayton handed four ones and a quarter to the waiter and said, "That's right."

"Thank *you,* sir."

"Thanks a lot," Fred said to Clayton as they moved toward the door.

"It's—" Clayton shook his head slightly. "You can get the next one."

"Merci beaucoup."

"I hope you didn't mind coming to this place."

"A great place. Vy, sey sought I vuss Cherman."

Outside, the pavement glittered as if cement were semiprecious; Third Avenue, disencumbered of the el, seemed as spacious and queenly as a South American boulevard. In the harsh light of the two o'clock sun, blemishes invisible in the shadows of the restaurant could be noticed on the skin of Clayton's face—an uneven redness on the flesh of the nose, two spots on his forehead, a flaky area partially hidden beneath an eyebrow. Clayton's feet tended to shuffle backward; he was conscious of his skin, or anxious to get back to work. Fred stood still, making it clear he was travelling in another direction. Clayton did not feel free to go. "You really want a job in advertising?"

"Forget it. I don't really."

"I'll keep on the lookout."

"Don't go to any trouble, but thanks anyway."

"Thank *you,* for heaven's sake. I really enjoyed this. It's been good."

For a moment Fred was sorry; he had an impulse to walk a distance with Clayton, to forgive everything, but Clayton, helplessly offensive, smiled and said, "Well. Back to the salt mines."

"Well put." Fred lifted his hand in a benign ministerial gesture startling to passersby. "Ye are the salt of the earth. *La lumiére du monde.* The light of the world. *Fils de Saint Louis, montez au ciel!*"

Clayton, bewildered by the foreign language, backed a step away and with an uncertain jerk of his hand affirmed, "See you."

"*Oui. Le roi est un bon homme. Le crayon de ma tante est sur la table de mon chat. Merci. Merci.* Meaning thank you. Thanks again."

JAMES BALDWIN

This Morning, This Evening, So Soon

"You are full of nightmares," Harriet tells me. She is in her dressing gown and has cream all over her face. She and my older sister, Louisa, are going out to be girls together. I suppose they have many things to talk about—they have *me* to talk about, certainly—and they do not want my presence. I have been given a bachelor's evening. The director of the film which has brought us such incredible and troubling riches will be along later to take me out to dinner.

I watch her face. I know that it is quite impossible for her to be as untroubled as she seems. Her self-control is mainly for my benefit—my benefit, and Paul's. Harriet comes from orderly and progressive Sweden and has reacted against all the advanced doctrines to which she has been exposed by becoming steadily and beautifully old-fashioned. We never fought in front of Paul, not even when he was a baby. Harriet does not so much believe in protecting children as she does in helping them to build a foundation on which they can build and build again, each time life's high-flying steel ball knocks down everything they have built.

Whenever I become upset, Harriet becomes very cheerful and composed. I think she began to learn how to do this over eight years ago, when I returned from my only visit to America. Now, perhaps, it has become something she could not control if she wished to. This morning, at breakfast, when I yelled at Paul, she averted Paul's tears and my own guilt by looking up and saying, "My God, your father is cranky this morning, isn't he?"

Paul's attention was immediately distracted from his wounds, and the unjust inflicter of those wounds, to his mother's laughter. He watched her.

"It is because he is afraid they will not like his songs in New York. Your father is an *artiste, mon chou,* and they are very mysterious people, *les artistes.* Millions of people are waiting for him in New York, they are begging him to come, and they will give him a *lot* of money, but he is afraid they will not like him. Tell him he is wrong."

She succeeded in rekindling Paul's excitement about places he has never seen. I was also, at once, reinvested with all my glamour. I think it is sometimes extremely difficult for Paul to realize that the face he sees on record sleeves and in the newspapers and on the screen is nothing more or less than the face of his father—who sometimes yells at him. Of course, since he is only seven—going on eight, he will be eight years old this winter—he cannot know that I am baffled, too.

"Of course, you are wrong, you are silly," he said with passion—and caused me to smile. His English is strongly accented and is not, in fact, as good as his French, for he speaks French all day at school. French is really his first language, the first he ever heard. "You are the greatest singer in France"—sounding exactly as he must sound when he makes this pronouncement to his schoolmates—"the greatest *American* singer" —this concession was so gracefully made that it was not a concession at all, it added inches to my stature, America being only a glamorous word for Paul. It is the place from which his father came, and to which he now is going, a place which very few people have ever seen. But his aunt is one of them and he looked over at her. "Mme. Dumont says so, and she says he is a *great actor, too*." Louisa nodded, smiling. "And she has seen *Les Fauves Nous Attendent*—five times." This clinched it, of course. Mme. Dumont is our concierge and she has known Paul all his life. I suppose he will not begin to doubt anything she says until he begins to doubt everything.

He looked over at me again. "So you are wrong to be afraid."

"I was wrong to yell at you, too. I won't yell at you any more today."

"All right." He was very grave.

Louisa poured more coffee. "He's going to knock them dead in New York. You'll see."

"Mais bien sur," said Paul, doubtfully. He does not quite know what "knock them dead" means, though he was sure, from her tone, that she must have been agreeing with him. He does not quite understand this aunt, whom he met for the first time two months ago, when she arrived to spend the summer with us. Her accent is entirely different from anything he has ever heard. He does not really understand why, since she is my sister and his aunt, she should be unable to speak French.

Harriet, Louisa, and I looked at each other and smiled. "Knock them dead," said Harriet, "means *d'avoir un succès fou*. But you will soon pick up all the American expressions." She looked at me and laughed. "So will I."

"That's what he's afraid of." Louisa grinned. "We have *got* some expressions, believe me. Don't let anybody ever tell you America hasn't got a culture. Our culture is as thick as clabber milk."

"Ah," Harriet answered, "I know. I know."

"I'm going to be practicing later," I told Paul.

His face lit up. *"Bon."* This meant that, later, he would come into my study and lie on the floor with his papers and crayons while I worked out with the piano and the tape recorder. He knew that I was offering this as an olive branch. All things considered, we get on pretty well, my son and I.

He looked over at Louisa again. She held a coffee cup in one hand and a cigarette in the other; and something about her baffled him. It was early, so she had not yet put on her face. Her short, thick, graying hair was rougher than usual, almost as rough as my own—later, she would be going to the hairdresser's; she is fairer than I, and better-looking; Louisa, in fact, caught all the looks in the family. Paul knows that she is my older sister and that she helped to raise me, though he does not, of course, know what this means. He knows that she is a schoolteacher in the *American* South, which is not, for some reason, the same place as South America. I could see him trying to fit all these exotic details together into a pattern which would explain her strangeness—strangeness of accent, strangeness of manner. In comparison with the people he has always known, Louisa must seem, for all her generosity and laughter and affection, peculiarly uncertain of herself, peculiarly hostile and embattled.

I wondered what he would think of his Uncle Norman, older and much blacker than I, who lives near the Alabama town in which we were born. Norman will meet us at the boat.

Now Harriet repeats, "Nightmares, nightmares. Nothing ever turns out as badly as you think it will—in fact," she adds laughing, "I am happy to say that that would scarcely be possible."

Her eyes seek mine in the mirror—dark-blue eyes, pale skin, black hair. I had always thought of Sweden as being populated entirely by blondes, and I thought that Harriet was abnormally dark for a Swedish girl. But when we visited Sweden, I found out differently. "It is all a great racial salad, Europe, that is why I am sure that I will never understand your country," Harriet said. That was in the days when we never imagined that we would be going to it.

I wonder what she is really thinking. Still, she is right, in two days we will be on a boat, and there is simply no point in carrying around my load of apprehension. I sit down on the bed, watching her fix her face. I realize that I am going to miss this old-fashioned bedroom. For years, we've talked about throwing out the old junk which came with the apartment and replacing it with less massive, modern furniture. But we never have.

"Oh, everything will probably work out," I say. "I've been in a bad mood all day long. I just can't sing any more." We both laugh. She reaches for a wad of tissues and begins wiping off the cream. "I wonder how Paul will like it, if he'll make friends—that's all."

"Paul will like any place where you are, where we are. Don't you worry about Paul."

Paul has never been called any names, so far. Only, once he asked us what the word *métis* meant and Harriet explained to him that it meant mixed blood, adding that the blood of just about everybody in the world was mixed by now. Mme. Dumont contributed bawdy and detailed corroboration from her own family tree, the roots of which were somewhere in Corsica; the moral of the story, as she told it, was that women were weak, men incorrigible, and *le bon Dieu* appallingly clever. Mme. Dumont's version is the version I prefer, but it may not be, for Paul, the most utilitarian.

Harriet rises from the dressing table and comes over to sit in my lap. I fall back with her on the bed, and she smiles down into my face.

"Now, don't worry," she tells me, "please try not to worry. Whatever is coming, we will manage it all very well, you will see. We have each other and we have our son and we know what we want. So, we are luckier than most people."

I kiss her on the chin. "I'm luckier than most men."

"I'm a very lucky woman, too."

And for a moment we are silent, alone in our room, which we have shared so long. The slight rise and fall of Harriet's breathing creates an intermittent pressure against my chest, and I think how, if I had never left America, I would never have met her and would never have established a life of my own, would never have entered my own life. For everyone's life begins on a level where races, armies, and churches stop. And yet everyone's life is always shaped by races, churches, and armies; races, churches, armies menace, and have taken, many lives. If Harriet had been born in America, it would have taken her a long time, perhaps forever, to look on me as a man like other men; if I had met her in America, I would never have been able to look on her as a woman like all other women. The habits of public rage and power would also have been our private compulsions, and would have blinded our eyes. We would never have been able to love each other. And Paul would never have been born.

Perhaps, if I had stayed in America, I would have found another woman and had another son. But that other woman, that other son are in the limbo of vanished possibilities. I might also have become something else, instead of an actor-singer, perhaps a lawyer, like my brother, or a teacher, like my sister. But no, I am what I have become and this woman beside me is my wife, and I love her. All the sons I might have had mean nothing, since I *have* a son, I named him, Paul, for my father, and I love him.

I think of all the things I have seen destroyed in America, all the things that I have lost there, all the threats it holds for me and mine.

I grin up at Harriet. "Do you love me?"

"Of course not. I simply have been madly plotting to get to America all these years."

"What a patient wench you are."

"The Swedes are very patient."

She kisses me again and stands up. Louisa comes in, also in a dressing gown.

"I hope you two aren't sitting in here yakking about the *subject*." She looks at me. "My, you are the sorriest-looking celebrity I've ever seen. I've always wondered why people like you hired press agents. Now I know." She goes to Harriet's dressing table. "Honey, do you mind if I borrow some of the *mad* nail polish?"

Harriet goes over to the dressing table. "I'm not sure I know *which* mad nail polish you mean."

Harriet and Louisa, somewhat to my surprise, get on very well. Each seems to find the other full of the weirdest and most delightful surprises. Harriet has been teaching Louisa French and Swedish expressions, and Louisa has been teaching Harriet some of the saltier expressions of the black South. Whenever one of them is not playing straight man to the other's accent, they become involved in long speculations as to how a language reveals the history and the attitudes of a people. They discovered that all the European languages contain a phrase equivalent to "to work like a nigger." ("Of course," says Louisa, "they've had black men working for them for a long time.") "Language is experience and language is power," says Louisa, after regretting that she does not know any of the African dialects. "That's what I keep trying to tell those dicty bastards down South. They get their own experience into the language, we'll have a great language. But, no, they all want to talk like white folks." Then she leans forward, grasping Harriet by the knee. "I tell them, honey, white folks ain't saying *nothing*. Not a thing are they saying—and *some* of them know it, they *need* what you got, the whole world needs it." Then she leans back, in disgust. "You think they listen to me? Indeed they do not. They just go right on, trying to talk like white folks." She leans forward again, in tremendous indignation. "You know some of them folks are *ashamed* of Mahalia Jackson? *Ashamed* of her, one of the greatest singers alive! They think she's common." Then she looks about the room as though she held a bottle in her hand and were looking for a skull to crack.

I think it is because Louisa has never been able to talk like this to any white person before. All the white people she has ever met needed, in one way or another, to be reassured, consoled, to have their consciences pricked but not blasted; could not, could not afford to hear a truth which would shatter, irrevocably, their image of themselves. It is astonishing the lengths to which a person, or a people, will go in order to avoid a truthful mirror. But Harriet's necessity is precisely the opposite: it is of the utmost importance that she learn everything that Louisa can tell her, and then learn more, much more. Harriet is really trying to learn from Louisa how best to protect her husband and her son. This is why they are going out alone tonight. They will have, tonight, as it were, a final council of war. I may be moody, but they, thank God, are practical.

Now Louisa turns to me while Harriet rummages about on the dressing table. "What time is Vidal coming for you?"

"Oh, around seven-thirty, eight o'clock. He says he's reserved tables for us in some very chic place, but he won't say where." Louisa wriggles her shoulders, raises her eyebrows, and does a tiny bump and grind. I laugh. "That's right. And then I guess we'll go out and get drunk."

"I hope to God you do. You've been about as cheerful as a cemetery these last few days. And, that way, your hangover will keep you from bugging us tomorrow."

"What about *your* hangovers? I know the way you girls drink."

"Well, we'll be paying for our own drinks," says Harriet, "so I don't think we'll have that problem. But *you're* going to be feted, like an international movie star."

"You sure you don't want to change your mind and come out with Vidal and me?"

"We're sure," Louisa says. She looks down at me and gives a small, amused grunt. "An international movie star. And I used to change your diapers. I'll be damned." She is grave for a moment. "Mama'd be proud of you, you know that?" We look at each other and the air between us is charged with secrets which not even Harriet will ever know. "Now, get the hell out of here, so we can get dressed."

"I'll take Paul on down to Mme. Dumont's."

Paul is to have supper with her children and spend the night there.

"For the last time," says Mme. Dumont and she rubs her hand over Paul's violently curly black hair. "*Tu vas nous manquer, tu sais?*" Then she looks up at me and laughs. "He doesn't care. He is only interested in seeing the big ship and all the wonders of New York. Children are never sad to make journeys."

"I would be very sad to go," says Paul, "but my father must go to New York to work and he wants me to come with him."

Over his head, Mme. Dumont and I smile at each other. "*Il est malin, ton gosse!*" She looks down at him again. "And do you think, my little diplomat, that you will like New York?"

"We aren't only going to New York," Paul answers, "we are going to California, too."

"Well, do you think you will like California?"

Paul looks at me. "I don't know. If we don't like it, we'll come back."

"So simple. Just like that," says Mme. Dumont. She looks at me. "It is the best way to look at life. Do come back. You know, we feel that you belong to us, too, here in France."

"I hope you do," I say. "I hope you do. I have always felt—always felt at home here." I bend down and Paul and I kiss each other on the cheek. We have always done so—but will we be able to do so in America? American fathers never kiss American sons. I straighten, my hand on Paul's shoulder. "You be good. I'll pick you up for breakfast, or, if you get up first you come and pick me up and we can hang out together tomorrow, while your *Maman* and your Aunt Louisa finish packing. They won't want two men hanging around the house."

"*D'accord.* Where shall we hang out?" On the last two words he stumbles a little and imitates me.

"Maybe we can go to the zoo, I don't know. And I'll take you to lunch at the Eiffel Tower, would you like that?"

"Oh, yes," he says, "I'd love that." When he is pleased, he seems to glow. All the energy of his small, tough, concentrated being charges an unseen battery and adds an incredible luster to his eyes, which are large and dark brown—like mine—and to his skin, which always reminds me of the colors of honey and the fires of the sun.

"Ok, then." I shake hands with Mme. Dumont. "*Bonsoir, Madame.*" I ring for the elevator, staring at Paul. "*Ciao, Pauli.*"

"*Bonsoir, Papa.*"

And Mme. Dumont takes him inside.

Upstairs, Harriet and Louisa are finally powdered, perfumed, and jeweled, and ready to go: dry martinis at the Ritz, supper, "in some *very* expensive little place," says Harriet, and perhaps the Folies Bergère afterwards. "A real cornball, tourist evening," says Louisa. "I'm working on the theory that if I can get Harriet to act like an American now, she won't have so much trouble later."

"I very much doubt," Harriet says, "that I will be able to endure the Folies Bergère for three solid hours."

"Oh, then we'll duck across town to Harry's New York bar and drink mint juleps," says Louisa.

I realize that, quite apart from everything else, Louisa is having as much fun as she has ever had in her life. Perhaps she, too, will be sad to leave Paris, even though she has only known it for such a short time.

"Do people drink those in New York?" Harriet asks. I think she is making a list of the things people do or do not do in New York.

"*Some* people do." Louisa winks at me. "Do you realize that this Swedish chick's picked up an Alabama drawl?"

We laugh together. The elevator chugs to a landing.

"We'll stop and say goodnight to Paul," Harriet says. She kisses me. "Give our best to Vidal."

"Right. Have a good time. Don't let any Frenchmen run off with Louisa."

"I did not come to Paris to be protected, and if I had, this wild chick *you* married couldn't do it. I just *might* upset everybody and come home with a French count." She presses the elevator button and the cage goes down.

I walk back into our dismantled apartment. It stinks of departure. There are bags and crates in the hall which will be taken away tomorrow, there are no books in the bookcases, the kitchen looks as though we never cooked a meal there, never dawdled there, in the early morning or late at night, over coffee. Presently, I must shower and shave but now I pour myself a drink and light a cigarette and step out on our balcony. It is dusk, the brilliant light of Paris is beginning to fade, and the green of the trees is darkening.

I have lived in this city for twelve years. This apartment is on the top floor of a corner building. We look out over the trees and the roof tops of the Champ de Mars, where the Eiffel Tower stands. Beyond this field is the river, which I have crossed so often, in so many states of mind. I have crossed every bridge in Paris, I have walked along every *quai*. I know the river as one finally knows a friend, know it when it is black, guarding all the lights of Paris in its depths, and seeming, in its vast silence, to be communing with the dead who lie beneath it; when it is yellow, evil, and roaring, giving a rough time to tugboats and barges, and causing people to remember that it has been known to rise, it has been known to kill; when it is peaceful, a slick dark, dirty green, playing host to rowboats and *les bateaux mouches* and throwing up from time to time an extremely unhealthy fish. The men who stand along the *quai*s all summer with their fishing lines gratefully accept the slimy object and throw it in a rusty can. I have always wondered who eats those fish.

And I walk up and down, up and down, glad to be alone.

It is August, the month when all Parisians desert Paris and one has to walk miles to find a barbershop or a laundry open in some tree-shadowed, silent side street. There is a single person on the avenue, a paratrooper walking toward École Militaire. He is also walking, almost certainly, and rather sooner than later, toward Algeria. I have a friend, a good-natured boy who was always hanging around the clubs in which I worked in the old days, who has just returned from Algeria, with a recurring, debilitating fever, and minus one eye. The government has set his pension at the sum, arbitrary if not occult, of fifty-three thousand francs every three months. Of course, it is quite impossible to live on this amount of money without working—but who will hire a half-blind invalid? This boy has been spoiled forever, long before his thirtieth birthday, and there are thousands like him all over France.

And there are fewer Algerians to be found on the streets of Paris now. The rug sellers, the peanut vendors, the postcard peddlers and money-changers have vanished. The boys I used to know during my first years in Paris are scattered—or corralled—the Lord knows where.

Most of them had no money. They lived three and four together in rooms with a single skylight, a single hard cot, or in buildings that seemed abandoned, with cardboard in the windows, with erratic plumbing in a wet, cobblestoned yard, in dark, dead-end alleys, or on the outer, chilling heights of Paris.

The Arab cafés are closed—those dark, acrid cafés in which I used to meet with them to drink tea, to get high on hashish, to listen to the obsessive, stringed music which has no relation to any beat, any time, that I have ever known. I once thought of the North Africans as my brothers and that is why I went to their cafés. They were very friendly to me, perhaps one or two of them remained really fond of me even after I could no longer afford to smoke Lucky Strikes and after my collection of American sport shirts had vanished—mostly into their wardrobes. They seemed to feel that they had every right to them, since I could only have wrested these things from the world by cunning—it meant nothing to say that I had had no choice in the matter; perhaps I had wrested these things from the world by treason, by refusing to be identified with the misery of my people. Perhaps, indeed, I identified myself with those who were responsible for this misery.

And this was true. Their rage, the only note in all their music which I could not fail to recognize, to which I responded, yet had the effect of setting us more than ever at a division. They were perfectly prepared to drive all Frenchmen into the sea, and to level the city of Paris. But I could not hate the French, because they left me alone. And I love Paris, I will always love it, it is the city which saved my life. It saved my life by allowing me to find out who I am.

It was on a bridge, one tremendous, April morning, that I knew I had fallen in love. Harriet and I were walking hand in hand. The bridge was the Pont Royal, just before us was the great *horloge,* high and lifted up, saying ten to ten; beyond this, the golden statue of Joan of Arc, with her sword uplifted. Harriet and I were silent, for we had been quarreling about something. Now, when I look back, I think we had reached that state when an affair must either end or become something more than an affair.

I looked sideways at Harriet's face, which was still. Her dark-blue eyes were narrowed against the sun, and her full, pink lips were still slightly sulky, like a child's. In those days, she hardly ever wore make-up. I was in my shirt sleeves. Her face made me want to laugh and run my hand over her short dark hair. I wanted to pull her to me and say, *Baby, don't be mad at me,* and at that moment something tugged at my heart and made me catch my breath. There were millions of people all around us, but I was alone with Harriet. She was alone with me. Never, in all my life, until that moment, had I been alone with anyone. The world had always been with us, between us, defeating the quarrel we could not achieve, and making love impossible. During all the years of my life, until that moment, I had carried the menacing, the hostile, killing world with me everywhere. No matter what I was doing or saying or feeling, one eye had always been on the world—that world which I had learned to distrust almost as soon as I learned my name, that world on which I knew one could never turn one's back, the white man's world. And for the first time in my life I was free of it; it had not existed for me; I had been quarreling with my girl. It was our quarrel, it was entirely between us, it had nothing to do with anyone else in the world. For the first time in my life I had not been afraid of the patriotism of the mindless, in uniform or out, who would beat me up and treat the woman who was with me as though she were the lowest of untouchables. For the first time in my life I felt that no force jeopardized my right, my power, to possess and to protect a woman; for the first time, the first time, felt that the woman was not, in her own eyes or in the eyes of the world, degraded by my presence.

The sun fell over everything, like a blessing, people were moving all about us, I will never forget the feeling of Harriet's small hand in mine, dry and trusting, and I turned to her, slowing our pace. She looked up at me with her enormous, blue eyes, and she seemed to wait. I said, "*Harriet. Harriet. Tu sais, il y a quelque chose de très grave qui m'est arrivé. Je t'aime. Je t'aime. Tu me comprends*, or shall I say it in English?"

This was eight years ago, shortly before my first and only visit home.

That was when my mother died. I stayed in America for three months. When I came back, Harriet thought that the change in me was due to my grief—I was very silent, very thin. But it had not been my mother's death which accounted for the change. I had known that my mother was going to die. I had not known what America would be like for me after nearly four years away.

I remember standing at the rail and watching the distance between myself and Le Havre increase. Hands fell, ceasing to wave, handkerchiefs ceased to flutter, people turned away, they mounted their bicycles or got into their cars and rode off. Soon, Le Havre was nothing but a blur. I thought of Harriet, already miles from me in Paris, and I pressed my lips tightly together in order not to cry.

Then, as Europe dropped below the water, as the days passed and passed, as we left behind us the skies of Europe and the eyes of everyone on the ship began, so to speak, to refocus, waiting for the first glimpse of America, my apprehension began to give way to a secret joy, a checked anticipation. I thought of such details as showers, which are rare in Paris, and I thought of such things as rich, cold, American milk and heavy, chocolate cake. I wondered about my friends, wondered if I had any left, and wondered if they would be glad to see me.

The Americans on the boat did not seem to be so bad, but I was fascinated, after such a long absence from it, by the nature of their friendliness. It was a friendliness which did not suggest, and was not intended to suggest, any possibility of friendship. Unlike Europeans, they dropped titles and used first names almost at once, leaving themselves, unlike the Europeans, with nowhere thereafter to go. Once one had become "Pete" or "Jane" or "Bill" all that could decently be known was known and any suggestion that there might be further depths, a person, so to speak, behind the name, was taken as a violation of that privacy which did not, paradoxically, since they trusted it so little, seem to exist among Americans. They apparently equated privacy with the unspeakable things they did in the bathroom or the bedroom, which they related only to the analyst, and then read about in the pages of best sellers. There was an eerie and unnerving irreality about everything they said and did, as though they were all members of the same team and were acting on orders from some invincibly cheerful and tirelessly inventive coach. I was fascinated by it. I found it oddly moving, but I cannot say that I was displeased. It had not occurred to me before that Americans, who had never treated me with any respect, had no respect for each other.

On the last night but one, there was a gala in the big ballroom and I sang. It had been a long time since I had sung before so many Americans. My audience had mainly been penniless French students, in the weird, Left Bank bistros I worked in those days. Still, I was a great hit with them and by this time I had become enough of a drawing card, in the Latin quarter and in St. Germain des Prés, to have attracted a couple of critics, to have had my picture in *France-soir*, and to have acquired a legal work permit which allowed me to make a little more money. Just the same, no matter how industrious and brilliant some of the musicians had been, or how devoted my audience, they did not know, they could not know, what my songs came out of. They did not know what was funny about it. It was impossible to translate: It damn well better be funny, or Laughing to keep from crying, or What did *I* do to be so black and blue?

The moment I stepped out on the floor, they began to smile, something opened in them, they were ready to be pleased. I found in their faces, as they watched me, smiling, waiting, an artless relief, a profound reassurance. Nothing was more familiar to them than the sight of a dark boy, singing, and there were few things on earth more necessary. It was under cover of darkness, my own darkness, that I could sing for them of the joys, passions, and terrors they smuggled about with them like steadily depreciating contraband. Under cover of the midnight fiction that I was unlike them because I was black, they could stealthily gaze at those treasures which they had been mysteriously forbidden to possess and were never permitted to declare.

I sang *I'm Coming, Virginia,* and *Take This Hammer,* and *Precious Lord.* They wouldn't let me go and I came back and sang a couple of the oldest blues I knew. Then someone asked me to sing *Swanee River,* and I did, astonished that I could, astonished that this song, which I had put down long ago, should have the power to move me. Then, if only, perhaps, to make the record complete, I wanted to sing *Strange Fruit,* but, on this number, no one can surpass the great, tormented Billie Holiday. So I finished with *Great Getting-Up Morning* and I guess I can say that if I didn't stop the show I certainly ended it. I got a big hand and I drank at a few tables and I danced with a few girls.

After one more day and one more night, the boat landed in New York. I woke up, I was bright awake at once, and I thought, *We're here.* I turned on all the lights in my small cabin and I stared into the mirror as though I were committing my face to memory. I took a shower and I took a long time shaving and I dressed myself very carefully. I walked the long ship corridors to the dining room, looking at the luggage piled high before the elevators and beside the steps. The dining room was nearly half empty and full of a quick and joyous excitement which depressed me even more. People ate quickly, chattering to each other, anxious to get upstairs and go on deck. Was it my imagination or was it true that they seemed to avoid my eyes? A few people waved and smiled, but let me pass; perhaps it would have made them uncomfortable, this morning, to try to share their excitement with me; perhaps they did not want to know whether or not it was possible for me to share it. I walked to my table and sat down. I munched toast as dry as paper and drank a pot of coffee. Then I tipped my waiter, who bowed and smiled and called me "sir" and said that he hoped to see me on the boat again. "I hope so, too," I said.

And was it true, or was it my imagination, that a flash of wondering comprehension, a flicker of wry sympathy, then appeared in the waiter's eyes? I walked upstairs to the deck.

There was a breeze from the water but the sun was hot and made me remember how ugly New York summers could be. All of the deck chairs had been taken away and people milled about in the space where the deck chairs had been, moved from one side of the ship to the other, clambered up and down the steps, crowded the rails, and they were busy taking photographs—of the harbor, of each other, of the sea, of the gulls. I walked slowly along the deck, and an impulse stronger than myself drove me to the rail. There it was, the great, unfinished city, with all its towers blazing in the sun. It came toward us slowly and patiently, like some enormous, cunning, and murderous beast, ready to devour, impossible to escape. I watched it come closer and I listened to the people around me, to their excitement and their pleasure. There was no doubt that it was real. I watched their shining faces and wondered if I were mad. For a moment I longed, with all my heart, to be able to feel whatever they were feeling, if only to know what such a feeling was like. As the boat moved slowly into the harbor, they were being moved into safety. It was only I who was being floated into danger. I turned my head, looking for Europe, but all that stretched behind me was the sky, thick with gulls. I moved away from the rail. A big, sandy-haired man held his daughter on his shoulders, showing her the Statue of Liberty. I would never know what this statue meant to others, she had always been an ugly joke for me. And the American flag was flying from the top of the ship, above my head. I had seen the French flag drive the French into the most unspeakable frenzies, I had seen the flag which was nominally mine used to dignify the vilest purposes: now I would never, as long as I lived, know what others saw when they saw a flag. "There's no place like home," said a voice close by, and I thought, *There damn sure isn't.* I decided to go back to my cabin and have a drink.

There was a cablegram from Harriet in my cabin. It said: Be good. Be quick. I'm waiting. I folded it carefully and put it in my breast pocket. Then I wondered if I would ever get back to her. How long would it take me to earn the money to get out of this land? Sweat broke out on my forehead and I poured myself some whiskey from my nearly empty bottle. I paced the tiny cabin. It was silent. There was no one down in the cabins now.

I was not sober when I faced the uniforms in the first-class lounge. There were two of them; they were not unfriendly. They looked at my passport, they looked at me. "You've been away a long time," said one of them.

"Yes," I said, "it's been a while."

"What did you do over there all that time?"—with a grin meant to hide more than it revealed, which hideously revealed more than it could hide.

I said, "I'm a singer," and the room seemed to rock around me. I held on to what I hoped was a calm, open smile. I had not had to deal with these faces in so long that I had forgotten how to do it. I had once known how to pitch my voice precisely between curtness and servility, and known what razor's edge of a pickaninny's smile would turn away wrath. But I had forgotten all the tricks on which my life had once depended. Once I had been an expert at baffling these people, at setting their teeth on edge, and dancing just outside the trap laid for me. But I was not an expert now. These faces were no longer merely the faces of two white men, who were my enemies. They were the faces of two white people whom I did not understand, and I could no longer plan my moves in accordance with what I knew of their cowardice and their needs and their strategy. That moment on the bridge had undone me forever.

"That's right," said one of them, "that's what it says, right here on the passport. Never heard of you, though." They looked up at me. "Did you do a lot of singing over there?"

"Some."

"What kind—concerts?"

"No." I wondered what I looked like, sounded like. I could tell nothing from their eyes. "I worked a few nightclubs."

"Nightclubs, eh? I guess they liked you over there."

"Yes," I said, "they seemed to like me all right."

"Well"—and my passport was stamped and handed back to me—"let's hope they like you over here."

"Thanks." They laughed—was it at me, or was it my imagination? and I picked up the one bag I was carrying and threw my trench coat over one shoulder and walked out of the first-class lounge. I stood in the slow-moving, murmuring line which led to the gangplank. I looked straight ahead and watched heads, smiling faces, step up to the shadow of the gangplank awning and then swiftly descend out of sight. I put my passport back in my breast pocket—*Be quick. I'm waiting*—and I held my landing card in my hand. Then, suddenly, there I was, standing on the edge of the boat, staring down the long ramp to the ground. At the end of the plank, on the ground, stood a heavy man in a uniform. His cap was pushed back from his gray hair and his face was red and wet. He looked up at me. This was the face I remembered, the face of my nightmares; perhaps hatred had caused me to know this face better than I would ever know the face of any lover. "Come on, boy," he cried, "come on, come on!"

And I almost smiled. I was home. I touched my breast pocket. I thought of a song I sometimes sang, *When will I ever get to be a man?* I came down the gangplank, stumbling a little, and gave the man my landing card.

Much later in the day, a customs inspector checked my baggage and waved me away. I picked up my bags and started walking down the long stretch which led to the gate, to the city.

And I heard someone call my name.

I looked up and saw Louisa running toward me. I dropped my bags and grabbed her in my arms and tears came to my eyes and rolled down my face. I did not know whether the tears were for joy at seeing her, or from rage, or both.

"How are you? How are you? You look wonderful, but, oh, haven't you lost weight? It's wonderful to see you again."

I wiped my eyes. "It's wonderful to see you, too, I bet you thought I was never coming back."

Louisa laughed. "I wouldn't have blamed you if you hadn't. These people are just as corny as ever, I swear I don't believe there's any hope for them. How's your French? Lord, when I think that it was I who studied French and now I can't speak a word. And you never went near it and you probably speak it like a native."

I grinned. "*Pas mal. Te me défends pas mal.*" We started down the wide steps into the street. "My God," I said. "New York." I was not aware of its towers now. We were in the shadow of the elevated highway but the thing which most struck me was neither light nor shade, but noise. It came from a million things at once, from trucks and tires and clutches and brakes and doors; from machines shuttling and stamping and rolling and cutting and pressing; from the building of tunnels, the checking of gas mains, the laying of wires, the digging of foundations; from the chattering of rivets, the scream of the pile driver, the clanging of great shovels; from the battering down and the raising up of walls; from millions of radios and television sets and juke boxes. The human voices distinguished themselves from the roar only by their note of strain and hostility. Another fleshy man, uniformed and red faced, hailed a cab for us and touched his cap politely but could only manage a peremptory growl: "Right this way, miss. Step up, sir." He slammed the cab door behind us. Louisa directed the driver to the New Yorker Hotel.

"Do they take us there?"

She looked at me. "They got laws in New York, honey, it'd be the easiest thing in the world to spend all your time in court. But over at the New Yorker, I believe they've already got the message." She took my arm. "You see? In spite of all this chopping and booming, this place hasn't really changed very much. You still can't hear yourself talk."

And I thought to myself, Maybe that's the point.

Early the next morning we checked out of the hotel and took the plane for Alabama.

I am just stepping out of the shower when I hear the bell ring. I dry myself hurriedly and put on a bathrobe. It is Vidal, of course, and very elegant he is, too, with his bushy gray hair quite lustrous, his swarthy, cynical, gypsylike face shaved and lotioned. Usually he looks just any old way. But tonight his brief bulk is contained in a dark-blue suit and he has an ironical pearl stickpin in his blue tie.

"Come in, make yourself a drink. I'll be with you in a second."

"I am, *hélas!*, on time. I trust you will forgive me for my thoughtlessness."

But I am already back in the bathroom. Vidal puts on a record: Mahalia Jackson, singing *I'm Going to Live the Life I Sing About in My Song.*

When I am dressed, I find him sitting in a chair before the open window. The daylight is gone, but it is not exactly dark. The trees are black now against the darkening sky. The lights in windows and the lights of motorcars are yellow and ringed. The street lights have not yet been turned on. It is as though, out of deference to the departed day,

Paris waited a decent interval before assigning her role to a more theatrical but inferior performer.

Vidal is drinking a whiskey and soda. I pour myself a drink. He watches me.

"Well. How are you, my friend? You are nearly gone. Are you happy to be leaving us?"

"No." I say this with more force than I had intended. Vidal raises his eyebrows, looking amused and distant. "I never really intended to go back there. I certainly never intended to raise my kid there—"

"*Mais, mon cher,*" Vidal says, calmly, "you are an intelligent man, you must have known that you would probably be returning one day." He pauses. "And, as for Pauli—did it never occur to you that he might wish one day to see the country in which his father and his father's fathers were born?"

"To do that, really, he'd have to go to Africa."

"America will always mean more to him than Africa, you know that."

"I don't know." I throw my drink down and pour myself another. "Why should he want to cross all that water just to be called a nigger? America never gave him anything."

"It gave him his father."

I look at him. "You mean, his father escaped."

Vidal throws back his head and laughs. If Vidal likes you, he is certain to laugh at you and his laughter can be very unnerving. But the look, the silence which follows this laughter can be very unnerving, too. And, now, in the silence, he asks me, "Do you really think that you have escaped anything? Come. I know you for a better man than that." He walks to the table which holds the liquor. "In that movie of ours which has made you so famous, and, as I now see, so troubled, what are you playing, after all? What is the tragedy of this half-breed troubadour if not, precisely, that he has taken all the possible roads to escape and that all these roads have failed him?" He pauses, with the bottle in one hand, and looks at me. "Do you remember the trouble I had to get a performance out of you? How you hated me, you sometimes looked as though you wanted to shoot me! And do you remember when the role of Chico began to come alive?" He pours his drink. "Think back, remember. I am a very great director, *mais pardon!* I could not have got such a performance out of anyone but you. And what were you thinking of, what was in your mind, what nightmare were you living with when you began, at last, to play the role—truthfully?" He walks back to his seat.

Chico, in the film, is the son of a Martinique woman and a French *colon* who hates both his mother and his father. He flees from the island to the capital, carrying his hatred with him. This hatred has now grown, naturally, to include all dark women and all white men, in a word, everyone. He descends into the underworld of Paris, where he dies.

Les fauves—the wild beasts—refers to the life he has fled and to the life which engulfs him. When I agreed to do the role, I felt that I could probably achieve it by bearing in mind the North Africans I had watched in Paris for so long. But this did not please Vidal. The blowup came while we were rehearsing a fairly simple, straightforward scene. Chico goes into a sleazy Pigalle dance hall to beg the French owner for a particularly humiliating job. And this Frenchman reminds him of his father.

"You are playing this boy as though you thought of him as the noble savage," Vidal said, icily. "*Ça vient d'où*—all these ghastly mannerisms you are using all the time?"

Everyone fell silent, for Vidal rarely spoke this way. This silence told me that everyone, the actor with whom I was playing the scene and all the people in the "dance hall," shared Vidal's opinion of my performance and were relieved that he was going to do something about it. I was humiliated and too angry to speak; but perhaps I also felt, at the very bottom of my heart, a certain relief, an unwilling respect.

"You are doing it all wrong," he said, more gently. Then, "Come, let us have a drink together."

We walked into his office. He took a bottle and two glasses out of his desk. "Forgive me, but you put me in mind of some of those English *lady* actresses who love to play *putain* as long as it is always absolutely clear to the audience that they are really ladies. So perhaps they read a book, not usually, *hélas!*, *Fanny Hill*, and they have their chauffeurs drive them through Soho once or twice—and they come to the stage with a performance so absolutely loaded with detail, every bit of it meaningless, that there can be no doubt that they are acting. It is what the British call a triumph." He poured two cognacs. "That is what you are doing. Why? Who do you think this boy is, what do you think he is feeling, when he asks for this job?" He watched me carefully and I bitterly resented his look. "You come from America. The situation is not so pretty there for boys like you. I know you may not have been as poor as—as some—but is it really impossible for you to understand what a boy like Chico feels? Have you never, yourself, been in a similar position?"

I hated him for asking the question because I knew he knew the answer to it. "I would have had to be a very lucky black man not to have been in such a position."

"You would have had to be a very lucky *man*."

"Oh, God," I said, "please don't give me any of this equality-in-anguish business."

"It is perfectly possible," he said, sharply, "that there is not another kind."

Then he was silent. He sat down behind his desk. He cut a cigar and lit it, puffing up clouds of smoke, as though to prevent us from seeing each other too clearly. "Consider this," he said. "I am a French director who has never seen your country. I have never done you any harm, except, perhaps, historically—I mean, because I am white—but I cannot be blamed for that—"

"But *I* can be," I said, "and I am! I've never understood why, if *I* have to pay for the history written in the color of my skin, *you* should get off scot-free!" But I was surprised at my vehemence, I had not known I was going to say these things, and by the fact that I was trembling and from the way he looked at me I knew that, from a professional point of view anyway, I was playing into his hands.

"What makes you think I *do?*" His face looked weary and stern. "I am a Frenchman. Look at France. You think that I—we—are not paying for our history?" He walked to the window, staring out at the rather grim little town in which the studio was located. "If it is revenge that you want, well, then, let me tell you, you will have it. You will probably have it, whether you want it or not, our stupidity will make it inevitable." He turned back into the room. "But I beg you not to confuse me with the happy people of your country, who scarcely know that there is such a thing as history and so, naturally, imagine that they can escape, as you put it, scot-free. That is what you are doing, that is what I was about to say. I was about to say that I am a French director and I have never been in your country and I have never done you any harm—but you are not talking to that man, in this room, now. You are not talking to Jean Luc Vidal, but to some other white man, whom you remember, who has nothing to do with me." He paused and went back to his desk. "Oh, most of the time you are not like this, I know. But it is there all the time, it must be, because when you are upset, this is what comes out. So you are not playing Chico truthfully, you are lying about him, and I will not let you do it. When you go back, now, and play this scene again, I want you to remember what has just happened in this room. You brought your past into this room. That is what Chico does when he walks into the dance hall. The Frenchman whom he begs for a job is not merely a Frenchman—he is the father who disowned and betrayed him and all the Frenchmen whom he hates." He smiled and poured me another cognac. "Ah! If it were not for *my* history, I would not have so much trouble to get the truth out of you." He looked into my face, half smiling. "And you, you are angry—are you not?—that I *ask* you for the truth. You think I have no right to ask." Then he said something which he knew would enrage me. "Who are you then, and what good has it done you to come to France, and how will you raise your son? Will you teach him never to tell the truth to anyone?" And he moved behind his desk and looked at me, as though from behind a barricade.

"You have no right to talk to me this way."

"Oh, yes, I do," he said. "I have a film to make and a reputation to maintain and I am going to get a performance out of you." He looked at his watch. "Let us go back to work."

I watch him now, sitting quietly in my living room, tough, cynical, crafty old Frenchman, and I wonder if he knows that the nightmare at the bottom of my mind, as I played the role of Chico, was all the possible fates of Paul. This is but another way of saying that I relived the disasters which had nearly undone me; but, because I was thinking of Paul, I discovered that I did not want my son ever to feel toward me as I had felt toward my own father. He had died when I was eleven, but I had watched the humiliations he had to bear, and I had pitied him. But was there not, in that pity, however painfully and unwillingly, also some contempt? For how could I *know* what he had borne? I knew only that I was his son. However he had loved me, whatever he had borne, I, his son, was despised. Even had he lived, he could have done nothing to prevent it, nothing to protect me. The best that he could hope to do was to prepare me for it; and even at that he had failed. How can one be prepared for the spittle in the face, all the tireless ingenuity which goes into the spite and fear of small, unutterably miserable people, whose greatest terror is the singular identity, whose joy, whose safety, is entirely dependent on the humiliation and anguish of others?

But for Paul, I swore it, such a day would never come. I would throw my life and my work between Paul and the nightmare of the world. I would make it impossible for the world to treat Paul as it had treated my father and me.

Mahalia's record ends. Vidal rises to turn it over. "Well?" He looks at me very affectionately. "Your nightmares, please!"

"Oh, I was thinking of that summer I spent in Alabama, when my mother died." I stop. "You know, but when we finally filmed that bar scene, I was thinking of New York. I was scared in Alabama, but I almost went crazy in New York. I was sure I'd never make it back here—back here to Harriet. And I knew if I didn't, it was going to be the end of me." Now Mahalia is singing *When the Saints Go Marching In.* "I got a job in the town as an elevator boy, in the town's big department store. It was a special favor, one of my father's white friends got it for me. For a long time, in the South, we all—depended—on the—*kindness* —of white friends." I take out a handkerchief and wipe my face. "But this man didn't like me. I guess I didn't seem grateful enough, wasn't enough like my father, what he thought my father was. And I couldn't get used to the town again, I'd been away too long, I hated it. It's a terrible town, anyway, the whole thing looks as though it's been built around a jailhouse. There's a room in the courthouse, a room where they beat you up. Maybe you're walking along the street one night, it's usually at night, but it happens in the daytime, too. And the police car comes up behind you and the cop says, 'Hey, boy. Come on over here.' So you go on over. He says, 'Boy, I believe you're drunk.' And, you see, if you say, 'No, no sir,' he'll beat you because you're calling him a liar. And if you say anything else, unless it's something to make him laugh, he'll take you in and beat you, just for fun. The trick is to think of some way for them to have their fun without beating you up."

The street lights of Paris click on and turn all the green leaves silver. "Or to go along with the ways *they* dream up. And they'll do anything, anything at all, to prove that you're no better than a dog and to make you feel like one. And they hated me because I'd been North and I'd been to Europe. People kept saying, I hope you didn't bring no foreign notions back here with you, boy. And I'd say, 'No sir,' or 'No ma'am,' but I never said it right. And there was a time, all of them remembered it, when I *had* said it right. But now they could tell that I despised them—I guess, no matter what, I wanted them to know that I despised them. But I didn't despise them any more than everyone else did, only the others never let it show. They knew how to keep the white folks happy, and it was easy—you just had to keep them feeling like they were God's favor to the universe. They'd walk around with great, big, foolish grins on their faces and the colored folks loved to see this, because they hated them so much. 'Just look at So-and-So,' somebody'd say. 'His white is *on* him today.' And when we didn't hate them, we pitied them. In America, that's usually what it means to have a white friend. You pity the poor bastard because he was born believing the world's a great place to be, and you know it's not, and you can see that he's going to have a terrible time getting used to this idea, if he ever gets used to it."

Then I think of Paul again, those eyes which still imagine that I can do anything, that skin, the color of honey and fire, his jet-black, curly hair. I look out at Paris again, and I listen to Mahalia. "Maybe it's better to have the terrible times first. I don't know. Maybe, then, you can have, *if* you live, a better life, a real life, because you had to fight so hard to get it away—you know?—from the mad dog who held it in his teeth. But then your life has all those tooth marks, too, all those tatters, and all that blood." I walk to the bottle and raise it. "One for the road?"

"Thank you," says Vidal.

I pour us a drink, and he watches me. I have never talked so much before, not about those things anyway. I know that Vidal has nightmares, because he knows so much about them, but he has never told me what his are. I think that he probably does not talk about his nightmares any more. I know that the war cost him his wife and his son, and that he was in prison in Germany. He very rarely refers to it. He has a married daughter who lives in England, and he rarely speaks of her. He is like a man who has learned to live on what is left of an enormous fortune.

We are silent for a moment.

"Please go on," he says, with a smile. "I am curious about the reality behind the reality of your performance."

"My sister, Louisa, never married," I say, abruptly, "because, once, years ago, she and the boy she was going with and two friends of theirs were out driving in a car and the police stopped them. The girl who was with them was very fair and the police pretended not to believe her when she said she was colored. They made her get out and stand in front of the headlights of the car and pull down her pants and raise her dress—they said that was the only way they could be sure. And you can imagine what they said, and what they did—and they were lucky, at that, that it didn't go any further. But none of the men could do anything about it. Louisa couldn't face the boy again, and I guess he couldn't face her." Now it is really growing dark in the room and I cross to the light switch. "You know, I know what that boy felt, I've felt it. They want you to feel that you're not a man, maybe that's the only way they can feel like men, I don't know. I walked around New York with Harriet's cablegram in my pocket as though it were some atomic secret, in *code*, and they'd kill me if they ever found out what it meant. You know, there's something wrong with people like that. And thank God Harriet was here, she *proved* that the world was bigger than the world they wanted me to live in, I *had* to get back here, get to a place where people were too busy with their own lives, *their private lives,* to make fantasies about mine, to set up walls around mine." I look at him. The light in the room has made the night outside blue-black and golden and the great searchlight of the Eiffel Tower is turning in the sky. "That's what it's like in America, for me, anyway. I always feel that I don't exist there, except in someone else's—usually dirty—mind. I don't know if you know what that means, but I do, and I don't want to put Harriet through that and I don't want to raise Paul there."

"Well," he says at last, "you are not required to remain in America forever, are you? You will sing in that elegant club which apparently feels that it cannot, much longer, so much as open its doors without you, and you will probably accept the movie offer, you would be very foolish not to. You will make a lot of money. Then, one day, you will remember that airlines and steamship companies are still in business and that France still exists. *That* will certainly be cause for astonishment."

Vidal was a Gaullist before de Gaulle came to power. But he regrets the manner of de Gaulle's rise and he is worried about de Gaulle's regime. "It is not the fault of *mon général,*" he sometimes says, sadly. "Perhaps it is history's fault. I *suppose* it must be history which always arranges to bill a civilization at the very instant it is least prepared to pay."

Now he rises and walks out on the balcony, as though to reassure himself of the reality of Paris. Mahalia is singing *Didn't It Rain?* I walk out and stand beside him.

"You are a good boy—Chico," he says. I laugh. "You believe in love. You do not know all the things love cannot do, but"—he smiles—"love will teach you that."

We go, after dinner, to a Left Bank discothèque which can charge outrageous prices because Marlon Brando wandered in there one night. By accident, according to Vidal. "Do you know how many people in Paris are becoming rich—to say nothing of those, *hélas!*, who are going broke—on the off chance that Marlon Brando will lose his way again?"

He has not, presumably, lost his way tonight, but the discothèque is crowded with those strangely faceless people who are part of the night life of all great cities, and who always arrive, moments, hours, or decades late, on the spot made notorious by an event or a movement or a handful of personalities. So here are American boys, anything but beardless, scratching around for Hemingway; American girls, titillating themselves with Frenchmen and existentialism, while waiting for the American boys to shave off their beards; French painters, busily pursuing the revolution which ended thirty years ago; and the young, bored, perverted, American *arrivistes* who are buying their way into the art world via flattery and liquor, and the production of canvases as arid as their greedy little faces. Here are boys, of all nations, one step above the pimp, who are occasionally walked across a stage or trotted before a camera. And the girls, their enemies, whose faces are sometimes seen in ads, one of whom will surely have a tantrum before the evening is out.

In a corner, as usual, surrounded, as usual, by smiling young men, sits the drunken blonde woman who was once the mistress of a famous, dead painter. She is a figure of some importance in the art world, and so rarely has to pay for either her drinks or her lovers. An older Frenchman, who was once a famous director, is playing *quatre cent vingt-et-un* with the woman behind the cash register. He nods pleasantly to Vidal and me as we enter, but makes no move to join us, and I respect him for this. Vidal and I are obviously cast tonight in the role vacated by Brando: our entrance justifies the prices and sends a kind of shiver through the room. It is marvelous to watch the face of the waiter as he approaches, all smiles and deference and grace, not so much honored by our presence as achieving his reality from it; excellence, he seems to be saying, gravitates naturally toward excellence. We order two whiskey and sodas. I know why Vidal sometimes comes here. He is lonely. I do not think that he expects ever to love one woman again, and so he distracts himself with many.

Since this is a discothèque, jazz is blaring from the walls and record sleeves are scattered about with a devastating carelessness. Two of them are mine and no doubt, presently, someone will play the recording of the songs I sang in the film.

"I thought," says Vidal, with a malicious little smile, "that your farewell to Paris would not be complete without a brief exposure to the perils of fame. Perhaps it will help prepare you for America, where, I am told, the populace is yet more carnivorous than it is here."

I can see that one of the vacant models is preparing herself to come to our table and ask for an autograph, hoping, since she is pretty—she has, that is, the usual female equipment, dramatized in the usual, modern way—to be invited for a drink. Should the maneuver succeed, one of her boy friends or girl friends will contrive to come by the table, asking for a light or a pencil or a lipstick, and it will be extremely difficult not to invite this person to join us, too. Before the evening ends, we will be surrounded. I don't, now, know what I expected of fame, but I suppose it never occurred to me that the light could be just as dangerous, just as killing, as the dark.

"Well, let's make it brief," I tell him. "Sometimes I wish that you weren't quite so fond of me."

He laughs. "There are some very interesting people here tonight. Look."

Across the room from us, and now staring at our table, are a group of American Negro students, who are probably visiting Paris for the first time. There are four of them, two boys and two girls, and I suppose that they must be in their late teens or early twenties. One of the boys, a gleaming, curly-haired, golden-brown type—the color of his mother's fried chicken—is carrying a guitar. When they realize we have noticed them, they smile and wave—wave as though I were one of their possessions, as, indeed, I am. Golden-brown is a mime. He raises his guitar, drops his shoulders, and his face falls into the lugubrious lines of Chico's face as he approaches death. He strums a little of the film's theme music, and I laugh and the table laughs. It is as though we were all back home and had met for a moment, on a Sunday morning, say, before a church or a poolroom or a barbershop.

And they have created a sensation in the discothèque, naturally, having managed, with no effort whatever, to outwit all the gleaming boys and girls. Their table, which had been of no interest only a moment before, has now become the focus of a rather pathetic attention; their smiles have made it possible for the others to smile, and to nod in our direction.

"Oh," says Vidal, "he does that far better than you ever did, perhaps I will make him a star."

"Feel free, *m'sieu, le bon Dieu*, I got mine." But I can see that his attention has really been caught by one of the girls, slim, tense, and dark, who seems, though it is hard to know how one senses such things, to be treated by the others with a special respect. And, in fact, the table now seems to be having a council of war, to be demanding her opinion or her cooperation. She listens, frowning, laughing; the quality, the force of her intelligence causes her face to keep changing all the time, as though a light played on it. And, presently, with a gesture she might once have used to scatter feed to chickens, she scoops up from the floor one of those dangling rag bags women love to carry. She holds it loosely by the drawstrings, so that it is banging somewhere around her ankle, and walks over to our table. She has an honest, forthright walk, entirely unlike the calculated, pelvic workout by means of which most women get about. She is small, but sturdily, economically, put together.

As she reaches our table, Vidal and I rise, and this throws her for a second. (It has been a long time since I have seen such an attractive girl.)

Also, everyone, of course, is watching us. It is really a quite curious moment. They have put on the record of Chico singing a sad, angry Martinique ballad; my own voice is coming at us from the walls as the girl looks from Vidal to me, and smiles.

"I guess you know," she says, "we weren't *about* to let you get out of here without bugging you just a little bit. We've only been in Paris just a couple of days and we thought for sure that we wouldn't have a chance of running into you anywhere, because it's in all the papers that you're coming home."

"Yes," I say, "yes. I'm leaving the day after tomorrow."

"Oh!" She grins. "Then we really *are* lucky." I find that I have almost forgotten the urchin-like grin of a colored girl. "I guess, before I keep babbling on, I'd better introduce myself. My name is Ada Holmes."

We shake hands. "This is Monsieur Vidal, the director of the film."

"I'm very honored to meet you, sir."

"Will you join us for a moment? Won't you sit down?" And Vidal pulls a chair out for her.

But she frowns contritely. "I really ought to get back to my friends." She looks at me. "I really just came over to say, for myself and all the kids, that we've got your records and we've seen your movie, and it means so much to us"—and she laughs, breathlessly, nervously, it is somehow more moving than tears—"more than I can say. Much more. And we wanted to know if you and your friend"—she looks at Vidal—"your *director*, Monsieur Vidal, would allow us to buy you a drink? We'd be very honored if you would."

"It is we who are honored," says Vidal, promptly, "*and* grateful. We were getting terribly bored with one another, thank God you came along."

The three of us laugh, and we cross the room.

The three at the table rise, and Ada makes the introductions. The other girl, taller and paler than Ada, is named Ruth. One of the boys is named Talley—"short for Talliafero"—and Golden-brown's name is

Pete. "Man," he tells me, "I dig you the most. You tore me up, baby, tore me *up*."

"You tore up a lot of people," Talley says, cryptically, and he and Ruth laugh. Vidal does not know, but I do, that Talley is probably referring to white people.

They are from New Orleans and Tallahassee and North Carolina; are college students, and met on the boat. They have been in Europe all summer, in Italy and Spain, but are only just getting to Paris.

"We meant to come sooner," says Ada, "but we could never make up our minds to leave a place. I thought we'd never pry Ruth loose from Venice."

"I resigned myself," says Pete, "and just sat in the Piazza San Marco, drinking gin fizz and being photographed with the pigeons, while Ruth had herself driven *all* up and down the Grand Canal." He looks at Ruth. "Finally, thank heaven, it rained."

"She was working off her hostilities," says Ada, with a grin. "We thought we might as well let her do it in Venice, the opportunities in North Carolina are really terribly limited."

"There are some very upset people walking around down there," Ruth says, "and a couple of tours around the Grand Canal might do them a world of good."

Pete laughs. "Can't you just see Ruth escorting them to the edge of the water?"

"I haven't lifted my hand in anger yet," Ruth says, "but, oh Lord," and she laughs, clenching and unclenching her fists.

"You haven't been back for a long time, have you?" Talley asks me.

"Eight years. I haven't really lived there for twelve years."

Pete whistles. "I fear you are in for some surprises, my friend. There have been some changes made." Then, "Are you afraid?"

"A little."

"We all are," says Ada, "that's why I was so glad to get away for a little while."

"Then you haven't been back since Black Monday," Talley says. He laughs. "That's how it's gone down in Confederate history." He turns to Vidal. "What do people think about it here?"

Vidal smiles, delighted. "It seems extraordinarily infantile behavior, even for Americans, from whom, I must say, I have never expected very much in the way of maturity." Everyone at the table laughs. Vidal goes on. "But I cannot really talk about it, I do not understand it. I have never really understood Americans; I am an old man now, and I suppose I never will. There is something very nice about them, something very winning, but they seem so ignorant—so ignorant of life. Perhaps it is strange, but the only people from your country with whom I have ever made contact are black people—like my good friend, my discovery, here," and he slaps me on the shoulder. "Perhaps it is because we, in Europe, whatever else we do not know, or have forgotten, know about suffering. We have suffered here. You have suffered, too. But most Americans do not yet know what anguish is. It is too bad, because the life of the West is in their hands." He turns to Ada. "I cannot help saying that I think it is a scandal—and we may all pay very dearly for it—that a civilized nation should elect to represent it a man who is so simple that he thinks the world is simple." And silence falls at the table and the four young faces stare at him.

"Well," says Pete, at last, turning to me, "you won't be bored, man, when you get back there."

"It's much too nice a night," I say, "to stay cooped up in this place, where all I can hear is my own records." We laugh. "Why don't we get out of here and find a sidewalk café?" I tap Pete's guitar. "Maybe we can find out if you've got any talent."

"Oh, talent I've got," says Pete, "but character, man, I'm lacking."

So, after some confusion about the bill, for which Vidal has already made himself responsible, we walk out into the Paris night. It is very strange to feel that, very soon now, these boulevards will not exist for me. People will be walking up and down, as they are tonight, and lovers will be murmuring in the black shadows of the plane trees, and there will be these same still figures on the benches or in the parks—but they will not exist for me, I will not be here. For a long while Paris will no longer exist for me, except in my mind; and only in the minds of some people will I exist any longer for Paris. After departure, only invisible things are left, perhaps the life of the world is held together by invisible chains of memory and loss and love. So many things, so many people, depart! And we can only repossess them in our minds. Perhaps this is what the old folks meant, what my mother and my father meant, when they counseled us to keep the faith.

We have taken a table at the Deux Magots and Pete strums on his guitar and begins to play this song:

> Preach the word, preach the word, preach the word!
> If I never, never see you any more.
> Preach the word, preach the word.
> And I'll meet you on Canaan's shore.

He has a strong, clear, boyish voice, like a young preacher's, and he is smiling as he sings his song. Ada and I look at each other and grin, and Vidal is smiling. The waiter looks a little worried, for we are already beginning to attract a crowd, but it is a summer night, the gendarmes on the corner do not seem to mind, and there will be time, anyway, to stop us.

Pete was not there, none of us were, the first time this song was needed;

and no one now alive can imagine what that time was like. But the song has come down the bloodstained ages. I suppose this to mean that the song is still needed, still has its work to do.

The others are all, visibly, very proud of Pete; and we all join him, and people stop to listen:

Testify! Testify!
If I never, never see you any more!
Testify! Testify!
I'll meet you on Canaan's shore!

In the crowd that has gathered to listen to us, I see a face I know, the face of a North African prize fighter, who is no longer in the ring. I used to know him well in the old days, but have not seen him for a long time. He looks quite well, his face is shining, he is quite decently dressed. And something about the way he holds himself, not quite looking at our table, tells me that he has seen me, but does not want to risk a rebuff. So I call him. "Boona!"

And he turns, smiling, and comes loping over to our table, his hands in his pockets. Pete is still singing and Ada and Vidal have taken off on a conversation of their own. Ruth and Talley look curiously, expectantly, at Boona. Now that I have called him over, I feel somewhat uneasy. I realize that I do not know what he is doing now, or how he will get along with any of these people, and I can see in his eyes that he is delighted to be in the presence of two young girls. There are virtually no North African women in Paris, and not even the dirty, rat-faced girls who live, apparently, in cafés are willing to go with an Arab. So Boona is always looking for a girl, and because he is so deprived and because he is not Western, his techniques can be very unsettling. I know he is relieved that the girls are not French and not white. He looks briefly at Vidal and Ada. Vidal, also, though for different reasons, is always looking for a girl.

But Boona has always been very nice to me. Perhaps I am sorry that I called him over, but I did not want to snub him.

He claps one hand to the side of my head, as is his habit. "*Comment vas-tu, mon frère?* I have not see you, oh, for long time." And he asks me, as in the old days, "You all right? Nobody bother you?" And he laughs. "Ah! *Tu as fait le chemin, toi!* Now you are *vedette,* big star—wonderful!" He looks around the table, made a little uncomfortable by the silence that has fallen, now that Pete has stopped singing. "I have seen you in the movies—you know?—and I tell everybody, I know *him!*" He points to me, and laughs, and Ruth and Talley laugh with him. "That's right, man, you make me real proud, you make me cry!"

"Boona, I want you to meet some friends of mine." And I go round the table: "Ruth, Talley, Ada, Pete"—and he bows and shakes hands, his dark eyes gleaming with pleasure—*"et Monsieur Vidal, le metteur en scène du film qui t'a arrache des larmes."*

"Enchanté." But his attitude toward Vidal is colder, more distrustful. "Of course I have heard of Monsieur Vidal. He is the director of many films, many of them made me cry." This last statement is utterly, even insolently, insincere.

But Vidal, I think, is relieved that I will now be forced to speak to Boona and will leave him alone with Ada.

"Sit down," I say, "have a drink with us, let me have your news. What's been happening with you, what are you doing with yourself these days?"

"Ah," he sits down, "nothing very brilliant, my brother." He looks at me quickly, with a little smile. "You know, we have been having hard times here."

"Where are you from?" Ada asks him.

His brilliant eyes take her in entirely, but she does not flinch. "I am from Tunis." He says it proudly, with a little smile.

"From Tunis. I have never been to Africa, I would love to go one day."

He laughs. "Africa is a big place. Very big. There are many countries in Africa, many"—he looks briefly at Vidal—"different kinds of people, many colonies."

"But Tunis," she continues, in her innocence, "is free? Freedom is happening all over Africa. That's why I would like to go there."

"I have not been back for a long time," says Boona, "but all the news I get from Tunis, from my people, is not good."

"Wouldn't you like to go back?" Ruth asks.

Again he looks at Vidal. "That is not so easy."

Vidal smiles. "You know what I would like to do? There's a wonderful Spanish place not far from here, where we can listen to live music and dance a little." He turns to Ada. "Would you like that?"

He is leaving it up to me to get rid of Boona, and it is, of course, precisely for this reason that I cannot do it. Besides, it is no longer so simple.

"Oh, I'd love that," says Ada, and she turns to Boona. "Won't you come, too?"

"Thank you, mam'selle," he says, softly, and his tongue flicks briefly over his lower lip, and he smiles. He is very moved, people are not often nice to him.

In the Spanish place there are indeed a couple of Spanish guitars, drums, castanets, and a piano, but the uses to which these are being put carry one back, as Pete puts it, to the levee. "These are the wailingest Spanish cats I ever heard," says Ruth. "They didn't learn how to do this in Spain, no, they didn't, they been rambling. You ever hear anything like this going on in Spain?" Talley takes her out on the dance floor, which is already crowded. A very handsome Frenchwoman is dancing with an enormous, handsome black man, who seems to be her lover, who seems to have taught her how to dance. Apparently, they are known to the musicians, who egg them on with small cries of "*Olé!*" It is a very good-natured crowd, mostly foreigners, Spaniards, Swedes, Greeks. Boona takes Ada out on the dance floor while Vidal is answering some questions put to him by Pete on the entertainment situation in France. Vidal looks a little put out, and I am amused.

We are there for perhaps an hour, dancing, talking, and I am, at last, a little drunk. In spite of Boona, who is a very good and tireless dancer, Vidal continues his pursuit of Ada, and I begin to wonder if he will make it and I begin to wonder if I want him to.

I am still puzzling out my reaction when Pete, who has disappeared, comes in through the front door, catches my eye, and signals to me. I leave the table and follow him into the streets.

He looks very upset. "I don't want to bug you, man," he says, "but I fear your boy has goofed."

I know he is not joking. I think he is probably angry at Vidal because of Ada, and I wonder what I can do about it and why he should be telling me.

I stare at him, gravely, and he says, "It looks like he stole some money."

"Stole *money*? Who, Vidal?"

And then, of course, I get it, in the split second before he says, impatiently, "No, are you kidding? Your friend, the Tunisian."

I do not know what to say or what to do, and so I temporize with questions. All the time I am wondering if this can be true and what I can do about it if it is. The trouble is, I know that Boona steals, he would probably not be alive if he didn't, but I cannot say so to these children, who probably still imagine that everyone who steals is a thief. But he has never, to my knowledge, stolen from a friend. It seems unlike him. I have always thought of him as being better than that, and smarter than that. And so I cannot believe it, but neither can I doubt it. I do not know anything about Boona's life, these days. This causes me to realize that I do not really know much about Boona.

"Who did he steal it from?"

"From Ada. Out of her bag."

"How much?"

"Ten dollars. It's not an awful lot of money, but"—he grimaces—"none of us *have* an awful lot of money."

"I know." The dark side street on which we stand is nearly empty. The only sound on the street is the muffled music of the Spanish club. "How do you know it was Boona?"

He anticipates my own unspoken rejoinder. "Who else could it be? Besides—somebody *saw* him do it."

"Somebody saw him?"

"Yes."

I do not ask him who this person is, for fear that he will say it is Vidal.

"Well," I say, "I'll try to get it back." I think that I will take Boona aside and then replace the money myself. "Was it in dollars or in francs?"

"In francs."

I have no dollars and this makes it easier. I do not know how I can possibly face Boona and accuse him of stealing money from my friends. I would rather give him the benefit of even the faintest doubt. But, "Who saw him?" I ask.

"Talley. But we didn't want to make a thing about it—"

"Does Ada know it's gone?"

"Yes." He looks at me helplessly. "I know this makes you feel pretty bad, but we thought we'd better tell you, rather than"—lamely—"anybody else."

Now, Ada comes out of the club, carrying her ridiculous handbag, and with her face all knotted and sad. "Oh," she says, "I hate to cause all this trouble, it's not worth it, not for ten lousy dollars." I am astonished to see that she has been weeping, and tears come to her eyes now.

I put my arm around her shoulder. "Come on, now. You're not causing anybody any trouble and, anyway, it's nothing to cry about."

"It isn't your fault, Ada," Pete says, miserably.

"Oh, I ought to get a sensible handbag," she says, "like you're always telling me to do," and she laughs a little, then looks at me. "Please don't try to do anything about it. Let's just forget it."

"What's happening inside?" I ask her.

"Nothing. They're just talking. I think Mr. Vidal is dancing with Ruth. He's a great dancer, that little Frenchman."

"He's a great talker, too," Pete says.

"Oh, he doesn't mean anything," says Ada, "he's just having fun. He probably doesn't get a chance to talk to many American girls."

"He certainly made up for lost time tonight."

"Look," I say, "if Talley and Boona are alone, maybe you better go back in. We'll be in in a minute. Let's try to keep this as quiet as we can."

"Yeah," he says, "okay. We're going soon anyway, okay?"

"Yes," she tells him, "right away."

But as he turns away, Boona and Talley step out into the street, and it is clear that Talley feels that he has Boona under arrest. I almost laugh, the whole thing is beginning to resemble one of those mad French farces with people flying in and out of doors; but Boona comes straight to me.

"They say I stole money, my friend. You know me, you are the only one here who knows me, you know I would not do such a thing."

I look at him and I do not know what to say. Ada looks at him with her eyes full of tears and looks away. I take Boona's arm.

"We'll be back in a minute," I say. We walk a few paces up the dark, silent street.

"She say I take her money," he says. He, too, looks as though he is about to weep—but I do not know for which reason. "You know me, you know me almost twelve years, you think I do such a thing?"

Talley saw you, I want to say, but I cannot say it. Perhaps Talley only thought he saw him. Perhaps it is easy to see a boy who looks like Boona with his hand in an American girl's purse.

"If you not believe me," he says, "search me. Search me!" And he opens his arms wide, theatrically, and now there are tears standing in his eyes.

I do not know what his tears mean, but I certainly cannot search him. I want to say, I know you steal, I know you have to steal. Perhaps you took the money out of this girl's purse in order to eat tomorrow, in order not to be thrown into the streets tonight, in order to stay out of jail. This girl means nothing to you, after all, she is only an American, an American like me. Perhaps, I suddenly think, no girl means anything to you, or ever will again, they have beaten you too hard and kept you out in the gutter too long. And I also think, if you would steal from her, then of course you would lie to me, neither of us means anything to you; perhaps, in your eyes, we are simply luckier gangsters in a world which is run by gangsters. But I cannot say any of these things to Boona. I cannot say, Tell me the truth, nobody cares about the money any more.

So I say, "Of course I will not search you." And I realize that he knew I would not.

"I think it is that Frenchman who say I am a thief. They think we all are thieves." His eyes are bright and bitter. He looks over my shoulder. "They have all come out of the club now."

I look around and they are all there, in a little dark knot on the sidewalk.

"Don't worry," I say. "It doesn't matter."

"You believe me? My brother?" And his eyes look into mine with a terrible intensity.

"Yes," I force myself to say, "yes, of course, I believe you. Someone made a mistake, that's all."

"You know, the way American girls run around, they have their sack open all the time, she could have lost the money anywhere. Why she blame me? Because I come from Africa?" Tears are glittering on his face. "Here she come now."

And Ada comes up the street with her straight, determined walk. She walks straight to Boona and takes his hand. "I am sorry," she says, "for everything that happened. Please believe me. It isn't worth all this fuss. I'm sure you're a very nice person, and"—she falters—"I must have lost the money, I'm sure I lost it." She looks at him. "It isn't worth hurting your feelings, and I'm terribly sorry about it."

"I no take your money," he says. "Really, truly, I no take it. Ask him"—pointing to me, grabbing me by the arm, shaking me—"he know me for years, he will tell you that I never, never steal!"

"I'm sure," she says. "I'm sure."

I take Boona by the arm again. "Let's forget it. Let's forget it all. We're all going home now, and one of these days we'll have a drink again and we'll forget all about it, all right?"

"Yes," says Ada, "let us forget it." And she holds out her hand.

Boona takes it, wonderingly. His eyes take her in again. "You are a very nice girl. Really. A very nice girl."

"I'm sure you're a nice person, too." She pauses. "Goodnight."

"Goodnight," he says, after a long silence.

Then he kisses me on both cheeks. *"Au revoir, mon frère."*

"Au revoir, Boona."

After a moment we turn and walk away, leaving him standing there.

"Did he take it?" asks Vidal.

"I tell you, I *saw* him," says Talley.

"Well," I say, "it doesn't matter now." I look back and see Boona's stocky figure disappearing down the street.

"No," says Ada, "it doesn't matter." She looks up. "It's almost morning."

"I would gladly," says Vidal, stammering, "gladly—"

But she is herself again. "I wouldn't think of it. We had a wonderful time tonight, a wonderful time, and I wouldn't think of it." She turns to me with that urchin-like grin. "It was wonderful meeting you. I hope you won't have too much trouble getting used to the States again."

"Oh, I don't think I will," I say. And then, "I hope you won't."

"No," she says, "I don't think anything they can do will surprise me any more."

"Which way are we all going?" asks Vidal. "I hope someone will share my taxi with me."

But he lives in the sixteenth arrondissement, which is not in anyone's direction. We walk him to the line of cabs standing under the clock at Odéon.

And we look each other in the face, in the growing morning light. His face looks weary and lined and lonely. He puts both hands on my shoulders and then puts one hand on the nape of my neck. "Do not forget me, Chico," he says. "You must come back and see us, one of these days. Many of us depend on you for many things."

"I'll be back," I say. "I'll never forget you."

He raises his eyebrows and smiles. *"Alors, Adieu."*

"Adieu, Vidal."

"I was happy to meet all of you," he says. He looks at Ada. "Perhaps we will meet again before you leave."

"Perhaps," she says. "Goodby, Monsieur Vidal."

"Goodby."

Vidal's cab drives away. "I also leave you now," I say. "I must go home and wake up my son and prepare for our journey."

I leave them standing on the corner, under the clock, which points to six. They look very strange and lost and determined, the four of them. Just before my cab turns off the boulevard, I wave to them and they wave back.

Mme. Dumont is in the hall, mopping the floor.

"Did all my family get home?" I ask. I feel very cheerful, I do not know why.

"Yes," she says, "they are all here. Paul is still sleeping."

"May I go in and get him?"

She looks at me in surprise. "Of course."

So I walk into her apartment and walk into the room where Paul lies sleeping. I stand over his bed for a long time.

Perhaps my thoughts traveled—travel through to him. He opens his eyes and smiles up at me. He puts a fist to his eye and raises his arms. *"Bonjour, Papa."*

I lift him up. "*Bonjour.* How do you feel today?"

"Oh, I don't know yet," he says.

I laugh. I put him on my shoulder and walk out into the hall. Mme. Dumont looks up at him with her radiant, aging face.

"Ah," she says, "you are going on a journey! How does it feel?"

"He doesn't know yet," I tell her. I walk to the elevator door and open it, dropping Paul down to the crook of my arm.

She laughs again. "He will know later. What a journey! *Jusqu'au nouveau monde!*"

I open the cage and we step inside. "Yes," I say, "all the way to the new world." I press the button and the cage, holding my son and me, goes up.

JOYCE CAROL OATES

How I Contemplated the World from the Detroit House of Correction and Began My Life Over Again

Notes for an essay for an English class at Baldwin Country Day School; poking around in debris; disgust and curiosity; a revelation of the meaning of life; a happy ending. . . .

I. Events

1. The girl (myself) is walking through Branden's, that excellent store. Suburb of a large famous city that is a symbol for large famous American cities. The event sneaks up on the girl, who believes she is herding it along with a small fixed smile, a girl of fifteen, innocently experienced. She dawdles in a certain style by a counter of costume jewelry. Rings, earrings, necklaces. Prices from $5 to $50, all within reach. All ugly. She eases over to the glove counter, where everything is ugly too. In her close-fitted coat with its black fur collar she contemplates the luxury of Branden's, which she has known for many years: its many mild pale lights, easy on the eye and the soul, its elaborate tinkly decorations, its women shoppers with their excellent shoes and coats and hairdos, all dawdling gracefully, in no hurry.

Who was ever in a hurry here?

2. The girl seated at home. A small library, paneled walls of oak. Someone is talking to me. An earnest husky female voice drives itself

against my ears, nervous, frightened, groping around my heart, saying, "If you wanted gloves why didn't you say so? Why didn't you ask for them?" That store, Branden's, is owned by Raymond Forrest who lives on DuMaurier Drive. We live on Sioux Drive. Raymond Forrest. A handsome man? An ugly man? A man of fifty or sixty, with gray hair, or a man of forty with earnest courteous eyes, a good golf game, who is Raymond Forrest, this man who is my salvation? Father has been talking to him. Father is not his physician; Dr. Berg is his physician. Father and Dr. Berg refer patients to each other. There is a connection. Mother plays bridge with. . . . On Mondays and Wednesdays our maid Billie works at. . . . The strings draw together in a cat's cradle, making a net to save you when you fall. . . .

3. *Harriet Arnold's.* A small shop, better than Branden's. Mother in her black coat, I in my close-fitted blue coat. Shopping. Now look at this, isn't this cute, do you want this, why don't you want this, try this on, take this with you to the fitting room, take this also, what's wrong with you, what can I do for you, why are you so strange . . . ? "I wanted to steal but not to buy," I don't tell her. The girl droops along in her coat and gloves and leather boots, her eyes scan the horizon which is pastel pink and decorated like Branden's, tasteful walls and modern ceilings with graceful glimmering lights.

4. Weeks later, the girl at a bus-stop. Two o'clock in the afternoon, a Tuesday, obviously she has walked out of school.

5. The girl stepping down from a bus. Afternoon, weather changing to colder. Detroit. Pavement and closed-up stores; grillwork over the windows of a pawnshop. What is a pawnshop, exactly?

II. Characters

1. The girl stands five feet five inches tall. An ordinary height. Baldwin Country Day School draws them up to that height. She dreams along the corridors and presses her face against the Thermoplex glass. No frost or steam can ever form on that glass. A smudge of grease from her forehead . . . could she be boiled down to grease? She wears her hair loose and long and straight in suburban teenage style, 1968. Eyes smudged with pencil, dark brown. Brown hair. Vague green eyes. A pretty girl? An ugly girl? She sings to herself under her breath, idling in the corridor, thinking of her many secrets (the thirty dollars she once took from the purse of a friend's mother, just for fun, the basement window she smashed in her own house just for fun) and thinking of her brother who is at Susquehanna Boys' Academy, an excellent preparatory school in Maine, remembering him unclearly . . . he has long manic hair and a squeaking voice and he looks like one of the

popular teenage singers of 1968, one of those in a group, *The Certain Forces, The Way Out, The Maniacs Responsible.* The girl in her turn looks like one of those fieldsful of girls who listen to the boys' singing, dreaming and mooning restlessly, breaking into high sullen laughter, innocently experienced.

2. The mother. A midwestern woman of Detroit and suburbs. Belongs to the Detroit Athletic Club. Also the Detroit Golf Club. Also the Bloomfield Hills Country Club. The Village Women's Club at which lectures are given each winter on Genet and Sartre and James Baldwin, by the Director of the Adult Education Program at Wayne State University. . . . The Bloomfield Art Association. Also the Founders Society of the Detroit Institute of Arts. Also. . . . Oh, she is in perpetual motion, this lady, hair like blown-up gold and finer than gold, hair and fingers and body of inestimable grace. Heavy weighs the gold on the back of her hairbrush and hand mirror. Heavy heavy the candlesticks in the dining room. Very heavy is the big car, a Lincoln, long and black, that on one cool autumn day split a squirrel's body in two unequal parts.

3. The father, Dr. ____. He belongs to the same clubs as #2. A player of squash and golf; he has a golfer's umbrella of stripes. Candy stripes. In his mouth nothing turns to sugar, however, saliva works no miracles here. His doctoring is of the slightly sick. The sick are sent elsewhere (to Dr. Berg?), the deathly sick are sent back for more tests and their bills are sent to their homes, the unsick are sent to Dr. Coronet (Isabel, a lady), an excellent psychiatrist for unsick people who angrily believe they are sick and want to do something about it. If they demand a male psychiatrist, the unsick are sent by Dr. ____ (my father) to Dr. Lowenstein, a male psychiatrist, excellent and expensive, with a limited practice.

4. Clarita. She is twenty, twenty-five, she is thirty or more? Pretty, ugly, what? She is a woman lounging by the side of a road, in jeans and a sweater, hitch-hiking, or she is slouched on a stool at a counter in some roadside diner. A hard line of jaw. Curious eyes. Amused eyes. Behind her eyes processions move, funeral pageants, cartoons. She says, "I never can figure out why girls like you bum around down here. What are you looking for anyway?" An odor of tobacco about her. Unwashed underclothes, or no underclothes, unwashed skin, gritty toes, hair long and falling into strands, not recently washed.

5. Simon. In this city the weather changes abruptly, so Simon's weather changes abruptly. He sleeps through the afternoon. He sleeps through the morning. Rising he gropes around for something to get him going, for a cigarette or a pill to drive him out to the street, where the temperature is hovering around 35°. Why doesn't it drop? Why, why doesn't the cold clean air come down from Canada, will he have to go up into Canada to get it, will he have to leave the Country of his Birth and sink into Canada's frosty fields . . . ? Will the F.B.I. (which he

dreams about constantly) chase him over the Canadian border on foot, hounded out in a blizzard of broken glass and horns . . . ?

"Once I was Huckleberry Finn," Simon says, "but now I am Roderick Usher." Beset by frenzies and fears, this man who makes my spine go cold, he takes green pills, yellow pills, pills of white and capsules of dark blue and green . . . he takes other things I may not mention, for what if Simon seeks me out and climbs into my girl's bedroom here in Bloomfield Hills and strangles me, what then . . . ? (As I write this I begin to shiver. Why do I shiver? I am now sixteen and sixteen is not an age for shivering.) It comes from Simon, who is always cold.

III. World Events

Nothing.

IV. People & Circumstances Contributing to this Delinquency

Nothing.

V. Sioux Drive

George, Clyde G. 240 Sioux. A manufacturer's representative; children, a dog; a wife. Georgian with the usual columns. You think of the White House, then of Thomas Jefferson, then your mind goes blank on the white pillars and you think of nothing. Norris, Ralph W. 246 Sioux. Public relations. Colonial. Bay window, brick, stone, concrete, wood, green shutters, sidewalk, lantern, grass, trees, blacktop drive, two children, one of them my classmate Esther (Esther Norris) at Baldwin. Wife, cars. Ramsey, Michael D. 250 Sioux. Colonial. Big living room, thirty by twenty-five, fireplaces in living room, library, recreation room, paneled walls wet bar five bathrooms five bedrooms two lavatories central air conditioning automatic sprinkler automatic garage door three children one wife two cars a breakfast room a patio a large fenced lot fourteen trees a front door with a brass knocker never knocked. Next is our house. Classic contemporary. Traditional modern. Attached garage, attached Florida room, attached patio, attached pool and cabana, attached roof. A front door mailslot through which pour *Time Magazine, Fortune, Life, Business Week, The Wall Street Journal, The New York Times, The New Yorker, The Saturday Review, M.D., Modern Medicine, Disease of the Month* . . . and also. . . . And in addition to all this, a quiet sealed letter from Baldwin saying: *Your daughter is not doing work compatible with her performance on the Stanford-Binet. . . .* And your son is not doing well, not well at all, very sad. Where is your son anyway? Once he stole trick-and-treat candy from some six-year-old kids, he himself being a robust ten. The beginning. Now your daughter steals. In the Village Pharmacy she made off with, yes she did, don't deny it, she made off with a copy of *Pageant Magazine* for no reason, she swiped a roll of lifesavers in a green wrapper and was in no need of saving her life or even in need of sucking candy; when she was no more than eight years old she stole, don't blush, she stole a package of *Tums* only because it was out on the counter and available, and the nice lady behind the counter (now dead) said nothing. . . . Sioux Drive. Maples, oaks, elms. Diseased elms cut down. Sioux Drive runs into Roosevelt Drive. Slow turning lanes, not streets, all drives and lanes and ways and passes. A private police force. Quiet private police, in unmarked cars. Cruising on Saturday evenings with paternal smiles for the residents who are streaming in and out of houses, going to and from parties, a thousand parties, slightly staggering, the women in their furs alighting from automobiles bought of Ford and General Motors and Chrysler, very heavy automobiles. No foreign cars. Detroit. In 275 Sioux, down the block, in that magnificient French Normandy mansion, lives ——— ——— himself, who has the C—— account itself, imagine that! Look at where he lives and look at the enormous trees and chimneys, imagine his many fireplaces, imagine his wife and children, imagine his wife's hair, imagine her fingernails, imagine her bathtub of smooth clean glowing pink, imagine their embraces, his trouser pockets filled with odd coins and keys and dust and peanuts, imagine their ecstasy on Sioux Drive, imagine their income tax returns, imagine their little boy's pride in his experimental car, a scaled-down C——, as he roars around the neighborhood on the sidewalks frightening dogs and Negro maids, oh imagine all these things, imagine everything, let your mind roar out all over Sioux Drive and DuMaurier Drive and Roosevelt Drive and Ticonderoga Pass and Burning Bush Way and Lincolnshire Pass and Lois Lane.

When spring comes, its winds blow nothing to Sioux Drive, no odors of hollyhocks or forsythia, nothing Sioux Drive doesn't already possess, everything is planted and performing. The weather vanes, had they weather vanes, don't have to turn with the wind, don't have to contend with the weather. There is no weather.

VI. Detroit

There is always weather in Detroit. Detroit's temperature is always 32°. Fast falling temperatures. Slow rising temperatures. Wind from the north-northeast four to forty miles an hour, small craft warnings, partly cloudy today and Wednesday changing to partly sunny through Thursday . . . small warnings of frost, soot warnings, traffic warnings, hazardous lake conditions for small craft and swimmers, restless Negro gangs, restless cloud formations, restless temperatures aching to fall out the very bottom of the thermometer or shoot up over the top and boil everything over in red mercury.

Detroit's temperature is 32°. Fast falling temperatures. Slow rising temperatures. Wind from the north-northeast four to forty miles an hour. . . .

VII. Events

1. The girl's heart is pounding. In her pocket is a pair of gloves! In a plastic bag! Airproof breathproof plastic bag, gloves selling for twenty-five dollars on Branden's counter! In her pocket! Shoplifted! . . . In her purse is a blue comb, not very clean. In her purse is a leather billfold (a birthday present from her grandmother in Philadelphia) with snapshots of the family in clean plastic windows, in the billfold are bills, she doesn't know how many bills. . . . In her purse is an ominous note from her friend Tykie *What's this about Joe H. and the kids hanging around at Louise's Sat. night? You heard anything?* . . . passed in French class. In her purse is a lot of dirty yellow Kleenex, her mother's heart would break to see such dirty Kleenex, and at the bottom of her purse are brown hairpins and safety pins and a broken pencil and a ballpoint pen (blue) stolen from somewhere forgotten and a purse-size compact of Cover Girl Make-Up, Ivory Rose. . . . Her lipstick is Broken Heart, a corrupt pink; her fingers are trembling like crazy; her teeth are beginning to chatter; her insides are alive; her eyes glow in her head; she is saying to her mother's astonished face *I want to steal but not to buy.*

2. At Clarita's. Day or night? What room is this? A bed, a regular bed, and a mattress on the floor nearby. Wallpaper hanging in strips. Clarita says she tore it like that with her teeth. She was fighting a barbaric tribe that night, high from some pills she was battling for her life with men wearing helmets of heavy iron and their faces no more than Christian crosses to breathe through, every one of those bastards looking like her lover Simon, who seems to breathe with great difficulty through the slits of mouth and nostrils in his face. Clarita has never heard of Sioux Drive. Raymond Forrest cuts no ice with her, nor does the C—— account and its millions; Harvard Business School could be at the corner of Vernor and 12th Street for all she cares, and Vietnam might have sunk by now into the Dead Sea under its tons of debris, for all the amazement she could show . . . her face is overworked, overwrought, at the age of

twenty (thirty?) it is already exhausted but fanciful and ready for a laugh. Clarita says mournfully to me *Honey somebody is going to turn you out let me give you warning.* In a movie shown on late television Clarita is not a mess like this but a nurse, with short neat hair and a dedicated look, in love with her doctor and her doctor's patients and their diseases, enamored of needles and sponges and rubbing alcohol. . . . Or no: she is a private secretary. Robert Cummings is her boss. She helps him with fantastic plots, the canned audience laughs, no, the audience doesn't laugh because nothing is funny, instead her boss is Robert Taylor and they are not boss and secretary but husband and wife, she is threatened by a young starlet, she is grim, handsome, wifely, a good companion for a good man. . . . She is Claudette Colbert. Her sister too is Claudette Colbert. They are twins, identical. Her husband Charles Boyer is a very rich handsome man and her sister, Claudette Colbert, is plotting her death in order to take her place as the rich man's wife, no one will know because they are *twins*. . . . All these marvelous lives Clarita might have lived, but she fell out the bottom at the age of thirteen. At the age when I was packing my overnight case for a slumber party at Toni Deshield's she was tearing filthy sheets off a bed and scratching up a rash on her arms. . . . Thirteen is uncommonly young for a white girl in Detroit, Miss Brook of the Detroit House of Correction said in a sad newspaper interview for the *Detroit News*; fifteen and sixteen are more likely. Eleven, twelve, thirteen are not surprising in colored . . . they are more precocious. What can we do? Taxes are rising and the tax base is falling. The temperature rises slowly but falls rapidly. Everything is falling out the bottom, Woodward Avenue is filthy, Livernois Avenue is filthy! Scraps of paper flutter in the air like pigeons, dirt flies up and hits you right in the eye, oh Detroit is breaking up into dangerous bits of newspaper and dirt, watch out. . . .

Clarita's apartment is over a restaurant. Simon her lover emerges from the cracks at dark. Mrs. Olesko, a neighbor of Clarita's, an aged white wisp of a woman, doesn't complain but sniffs with contentment at Clarita's noisy life and doesn't tell the cops, hating cops, when the cops arrive. I should give fake names, more blanks, instead of telling all these secrets. I myself am a secret; I am a minor.

3. My father reads a paper at a medical convention in Los Angeles. There he is, on the edge of the North American continent, when the unmarked detective put his hand so gently on my arm in the aisle of Branden's and said, "Miss, would you like to step over here for a minute?"

And where was he when Clarita put her hand on my arm, that wintry dark sulphurous aching day in Detroit, in the company of closed-down barber shops, closed-down diners, closed-down movie houses, homes, windows, basements, faces . . . she put her hand on my arm and said, "Honey, are you looking for somebody down here?"

And was he home worrying about me, gone for two weeks solid, when they carried me off . . . ? It took three of them to get me in the police cruiser, so they said, and they put more than their hands on my arm.

4. I work on this lesson. My English teacher is Mr. Forest, who is from Michigan State. Not handsome, Mr. Forest, and his name is plain unlike Raymond Forrest's, but he is sweet and rodent-like, he has conferred with the principal and my parents, and everything is fixed . . . treat her as if nothing has happened, a new start, begin again, only sixteen years old, what a shame, how did it happen? – nothing happened, nothing could have happened, a slight physiological modification known only to a gynecologist or to Dr. Coronet. I work on my lesson. I sit in my pink room. I look around the room with my sad pink eyes. I sigh, I dawdle, I pause, I eat up time, I am limp and happy to be home, I am sixteen years old suddenly, my head hangs heavy as a pumpkin on my shoulders, and my hair has just been cut by Mr. Faye at the Crystal Salon and is said to be very becoming.

(Simon too put his hand on my arm and said, "Honey, you have got to come with me," and in his six-by-six room we got to know each other. Would I go back to Simon again? Would I lie down with him in all that filth and craziness? Over and over again.

a Clarita is being betrayed as in front of a Cunningham Drug Store she is nervously eyeing a colored man who may or may not have money, or a nervous white boy of twenty with sideburns and an Appalachian look, who may or may not have a knife hidden in his jacket pocket, or a husky red-faced man of friendly countenance who may or may not be a member of the Vice Squad out for an early twilight walk.)

I work on my lesson for Mr. Forest. I have filled up eleven pages. Words pour out of me and won't stop. I want to tell everything . . . what was the song Simon was always humming, and who was Simon's friend in a very new trench coat with an old high school graduation ring on his finger . . . ? Simon's bearded friend? When I was down too low for him Simon kicked me out and gave me to him for three days, I think, on Fourteenth Street in Detroit, an airy room of cold cruel drafts with newspapers on the floor. . . . Do I really remember that or am I piecing it together from what they told me? Did they tell the truth? Did they know much of the truth?

perception

VIII. Characters

1. Wednesdays after school, at four; Saturday mornings at ten. Mother drives me to Dr. Coronet. Ferns in the office, plastic or real, they look the same. Dr. Coronet is queenly, an elegant nicotine-stained lady who would have studied with Freud had circumstances not prevented it, a bit of a Catholic, ready to offer you some mystery if your teeth will ache too much without it. Highly recommended by Father! Forty dollars an hour, Father's forty dollars! Progress! Looking up! Looking better! That new haircut is so becoming, says Dr. Coronet herself, showing how normal she is for a woman with an I.Q. of 180 and many advanced degrees.

2. Mother. A lady in a brown suede coat. Boots of shiny black material, black gloves, a black fur hat. She would be humiliated could she know that of all the people in the world it is my ex-lover Simon who walks most like her . . . self-conscious and unreal, listening to distant music, a little bowlegged with craftiness. . . .

3. Father. Tying a necktie. In a hurry. On my first evening home he put his hand on my arm and said, "Honey, we're going to forget all about this."

4. Simon. Outside a plane is crossing the sky, in here we're in a hurry. Morning. It must be morning. The girl is half out of her mind, whimpering and vague. Simon her dear friend is wretched this morning . . . he is wretched with morning itself . . . he forces her to give him an injection with that needle she knows is filthy, she has a dread of needles and surgical instruments and the odor of things that are to be sent into the blood, thinking somehow of her father. . . . This is a bad morning, Simon says that his mind is being twisted out of shape, and so he submits to the needle which he usually scorns and bites his lip with his yellowish teeth, his face going very pale. *Ah baby!* he says in his soft mocking voice, which with all women is a mockery of love, *do it like this—Slowly*—And the girl, terrified, almost drops the precious needle but manages to turn it up to the light from the window . . . it is an extension of herself then? She can give him this gift then? *I wish you wouldn't do this to me,* she says, wise in her terror, because it seems to her that Simon's danger—in a few minutes he may be dead—is a way of pressing her against him that is more powerful than any other embrace. She has to work over his arm, the knotted corded veins of his arm, her forehead wet with perspiration as she pushes and releases the needle, staring at that mixture of liquid now stained with Simon's bright blood. . . . When the drug hits him she can feel it herself, she feels that magic that is more than any woman can give him, striking the back of his head and making his face stretch as if with the impact of a terrible sun. . . . She

tries to embrace him but he pushes her aside and stumbles to his feet. *Jesus Christ,* he says. . . .

5. Princess, a Negro girl of eighteen. What is her charge? She is close-mouthed about it, shrewd and silent, you know that no one had to wrestle her to the sidewalk to get her in here; she came with dignity. In the recreation room she sits reading *Nancy Drew and the Jewel Box Mystery,* which inspires in her face tiny wrinkles of alarm and interest: what a face! Light brown skin, heavy shaded eyes, heavy eyelashes, a serious sinister dark brow, graceful fingers, graceful wristbones, graceful legs, lips, tongue, a sugar-sweet voice, a leggy stride more masculine than Simon's and my mother's, decked out in a dirty white blouse and dirty white slacks; vaguely nautical is Princess's style. . . . At breakfast she is in charge of clearing the table and leans over me, saying, *Honey you sure you ate enough?*

6. The girl lies sleepless, wondering. Why here, why not there? Why Bloomfield Hills and not jail? Why jail and not her pink room? Why downtown Detroit and not Sioux Drive? What is the difference? Is Simon all the difference? The girl's head is a parade of wonders. She is nearly sixteen, her breath is marvelous with wonders, not long ago she was coloring with crayons and now she is smearing the landscape with paints that won't come off and won't come off her fingers either. She says to the matron *I am not talking about anything,* not because everyone has warned her not to talk but because, because she will not talk, because she won't say anything about Simon who is her secret. And she says to the matron *I won't go home* up until that night in the lavatory when everything was changed. . . . "No, I won't go home I want to stay here," she says, listening to her own words with amazement, thinking that weeds might climb everywhere over that marvelous $180,000 house and dinosaurs might return to muddy the beige carpeting, but never never will she reconcile four o'clock in the morning in Detroit with eight o'clock breakfasts in Bloomfield Hills . . . oh, she aches still for Simon's hands and his caressing breath, though he gave her little pleasure, he took everything from her (five-dollar bills, ten-dollar bills, passed into her numb hands by men and taken out of her hands by Simon) until she herself was passed into the hands of other men, police, when Simon evidently got tired of her and her hysteria. . . . *No, I won't go home, I don't want to be bailed out,* the girl thinks as a *Stubborn and Wayward Child* (one of several charges lodged against her) and the matron understands her crazy white-rimmed eyes that are seeking out some new violence that will keep her in jail, should someone threaten to let her out. Such children try to strangle the matrons, the attendants, or one another . . . they want the locks locked forever, the doors nailed shut . . . and this girl is no different up until that night her mind is changed for her. . . .

IX. That Night

Princess and Dolly, a little white girl of maybe fifteen, hardy however as a sergeant and in the House of Correction for armed robbery, corner her in the lavatory at the farthest sink and the other girls look away and file out to bed, leaving her. God how she is beaten up! Why is she beaten up? Why do they pound her, why such hatred? Princess vents all the hatred of a thousand silent Detroit winters on her body, this girl whose body belongs to me, fiercely she rides across the midwestern plains on this girl's tender bruised body . . . revenge on the oppressed minorities of America! revenge on the slaughtered Indians! revenge on the female sex, on the male sex, revenge on Bloomfield Hills, revenge revenge. . . .

X. Detroit

In Detroit weather weighs heavily upon everyone. The sky looms large. The horizon shimmers in smoke. Downtown the buildings are imprecise in the haze. Perpetual haze. Perpetual motion inside the haze. Across the choppy river is the city of Windsor, in Canada. Part of the continent has bunched up here and is bulging outward, at the tip of Detroit; a cold hard rain is forever falling on the expressways . . . shoppers shop grimly, their cars are not parked in safe places, their windshields may be smashed and graceful ebony hands may drag them out through their shatterproof smashed windshields crying *Revenge for the Indians!* Ah, they all fear leaving Hudson's and being dragged to the very tip of the city and thrown off the parking roof of Cobo Hall, that expensive tomb, into the river. . . .

XI. Characters We Are Forever Entwined With

1. Simon drew me into his tender rotting arms and breathed gravity into me. Then I came to earth, weighted down. He said *You are such a little girl,* and he weighed me down with his delight. In the palms of his hands were teeth marks from his previous life experiences. He was thirty-five, they said. Imagine Simon in this room, in my pink room: he is about six feet tall and stoops slightly, in a feline cautious way, always thinking, always on guard, with his scuffed light suede shoes and his clothes which are anyone's clothes, slightly rumpled ordinary clothes that ordinary men might wear to not-bad jobs. Simon has fair, long hair, curly hair, spent languid curls that are like . . . exactly like the curls of wood shavings to the touch, I am trying to be exact . . . and he smells of unheated mornings and coffee and too many pills coat-

ing his tongue with a faint green-white scum. . . . Dear Simon, who would be panicked in this room and in this house (right now Billie is vacuuming next door in my parents' room; a vacuum cleaner's roar is a sign of all good things), Simon who is said to have come from a home not much different from this, years ago, fleeing all the carpeting and the polished banisters . . . Simon has a deathly face, only desperate people fall in love with it. His face is bony and cautious, the bones of his cheeks prominent as if with the rigidity of his ceaseless thinking, plotting, for he has to make money out of girls to whom money means nothing, they're so far gone they can hardly count it, and in a sense money means nothing to him either except as a way of keeping on with his life. *Each Day's Proud Struggle,* the title of a novel we could read at jail. . . . Each day he needs a certain amount of money. He devours it. It wasn't love he uncoiled in me with his hollowed-out eyes and his courteous smile, that remnant of a prosperous past, but a dark terror that needed to press itself flat against him, or against another man . . . but he was the first, he came over to me and took my arm, a claim. We struggled on the stairs and I said, *Let me loose, you're hurting my neck, my face,* it was such a surprise that my skin hurt where he rubbed it, and afterward we lay face to face and he breathed everything into me. In the end I think he turned me in.

2. Raymond Forrest. I just read this morning that Raymond Forrest's father, the chairman of the board at ———, died of a heart attack on a plane bound for London. I would like to write Raymond Forrest a note of sympathy. I would like to thank him for not pressing charges against me one hundred years ago, saving me, being so generous . . . well, men like Raymond Forrest are generous men, not like Simon. I would like to write him a letter telling of my love, or of some other emotion that is positive and healthy. Not like Simon and his poetry, which he scrawled down when he was high and never changed a word . . . but when I try to think of something to say, it is Simon's language that comes back to me, caught in my head like a bad song, it is always Simon's language:

There is no reality only dreams
Your neck may get snapped when you wake
My love is drawn to some violent end
She keeps wanting to get away
My love is heading downward
And I am heading upward
She is going to crash on the sidewalk
And I am going to dissolve into the clouds

XII. Events

1. Out of the hospital, bruised and saddened and converted, with Princess's grunts still tangled in my hair . . . and Father in his overcoat looking like a Prince himself, come to carry me off. Up the expressway and out north to home. Jesus Christ, but the air is thinner and cleaner here. Monumental houses. Heartbreaking sidewalks, so clean.

2. Weeping in the living room. The ceiling is two storeys high and two chandeliers hang from it. Weeping, weeping, though Billie the maid is *probably listening*. I will never leave home again. Never. Never leave home. Never leave this home again, never.

3. Sugar doughnuts for breakfast. The toaster is very shiny and my face is distorted in it. Is that my face?

4. The car is turning in the driveway. Father brings me home. Mother embraces me. Sunlight breaks in movieland patches on the roof of our traditional-contemporary home, which was designed for the famous automotive stylist whose identity, if I told you the name of the famous car he designed, you would all know, so I can't tell you because my teeth chatter at the thought of being sued . . . or having someone climb into my bedroom window with a rope to strangle me. . . . The car turns up the blacktop drive. The house opens to me like a doll's house, so lovely in the sunlight, the big living room beckons to me with its walls falling away in a delirium of joy at my return, Billie the maid is *no doubt* listening from the kitchen as I burst into tears and the hysteria Simon got so sick of. Convulsed in Father's arms, I say I will never leave again, never, why did I leave, where did I go, what happened, my mind is gone wrong, my body is one big bruise, my backbone was sucked dry, it wasn't the men who hurt me and Simon never hurt me but only those girls . . . my God, how they hurt me . . . I will never leave home again. . . . The car is perpetually turning up the drive and I am perpetually breaking down in the living room and we are perpetually taking the right exit from the expressway (Lahser Road) and the wall of the restroom is perpetually banging against my head and perpetually are Simon's hands moving across my body and adding everything up and so too are Father's hands on my shaking bruised back, far from the surface of my skin on the surface of my good blue cashmere coat (dry-cleaned for my release). . . . I weep for all the money here, for God in gold and beige carpeting, for the beauty of chandeliers and the miracle of a clean polished gleaming toaster and faucets that run both hot and cold water, and I tell them *I will never leave home, this is my home, I love everything here, I am in love with everything here. . . .*

I am home.

JAMES ALAN McPHERSON
Gold Coast

I

That spring, when I had a great deal of potential and no money at all, I took a job as a janitor. That was when I was still very young and spent money very freely, and when, almost every night, I drifted off to sleep lulled by sweet anticipation of that time when my potential would suddenly be realized and there would be capsule biographies of my life on dust jackets of many books, all proclaiming: ". . . He knew life on many levels. From shoeshine boy, free-lance waiter, 3rd cook, janitor, he rose to . . ." I had never been a janitor before and I did not really have to be one and that is why I did it. But now, much later, I think it might have been because it is possible to be a janitor without really becoming one, and at parties or at mixers when asked what it was I did for a living, it was pretty good to hook my thumbs in my vest pockets and say comfortably: "Why, I am an apprentice janitor." The hippies would think it degenerate and really dig me and it made me feel good that people in Philosophy and Law and Business would feel uncomfortable trying to make me feel better about my station while wondering how the hell I had managed to crash the party.

"What's an apprentice janitor?" they would ask.

"I haven't got my card yet," I would reply. "Right now I'm just taking lessons. There's lots of complicated stuff you have to learn before you get your card and your own building."

"What kind of stuff?"

"Human nature, for one thing. *Race* nature, for another."

"Why race?"

"Because," I would say in a low voice looking around lest someone else should overhear, "you have to be able to spot Jews and Negroes who are passing."

"That's terrible," would surely be said then with a hint of indignation.

"It's an art," I would add masterfully.

After a good pause I would invariably be asked: "But you're a Negro yourself, how can you keep your own people out?"

At which point I would look terribly disappointed and say: "*I* don't keep them out. But if they get in it's my job to make their stay just as miserable as possible. Things are changing."

Now the speaker would just look at me in disbelief.

"It's Janitorial Objectivity," I would say to finish the thing as the speaker began to edge away. "Don't hate me," I would call after him to his considerable embarrassment. "Somebody has to do it."

It was an old building near Harvard Square. Conrad Aiken had once lived there and in the days of the Gold Coast, before Harvard built its great Houses, it had been a very fine haven for the rich; but that was a world ago, and this building was one of the few monuments of that era which had survived. The lobby had a high ceiling with thick redwood beams and it was replete with marble floor, fancy ironwork, and an old-fashioned house telephone that no longer worked. Each apartment had a small fireplace, and even the large bathtubs and chain toilets, when I was having my touch of nature, made me wonder what prominent personage of the past had worn away all the newness. And, being there, I felt a certain affinity toward the rich.

It was a funny building; because the people who lived there made it old. Conveniently placed as it was between the Houses and Harvard Yard, I expected to find it occupied by a company of hippies, hopeful working girls, and assorted graduate students. Instead, there were a majority of old maids, dowagers, asexual middle-aged men, homosexual young men, a few married couples and a teacher. No one was shacking up there, and walking through the quiet halls in the early evening, I sometimes had the urge to knock on a door and expose myself just to hear someone breathe hard for once.

It was a Cambridge spring: down by the Charles happy students were making love while sad-eyed middle-aged men watched them from the bridge. It was a time of activity: Law students were busy sublimating, Business School people were making records of the money they would make, the Harvard Houses were clearing out, and in the Square bearded pot-pushers were setting up their restaurant tables in anticipation of the Summer School faithfuls. There was a change of season in the air, and to comply with its urgings, James Sullivan, the old superintendent, passed his three beaten garbage cans on to me with the charge that I should take up his daily rounds of the six floors, and with unflinching humility, gather whatever scraps the old-maid tenants had refused to husband.

I then became very rich, with my own apartment, a sensitive girl, a stereo, two speakers, one tattered chair, one fork, a job, and the urge to acquire. Having all this and youth besides made me pity Sullivan: he had been in that building thirty years and had its whole history recorded in the little folds of his mind, as his own life was recorded in the wrinkles of his face. All he had to show for his time there was a berserk dog, a wife almost as mad as the dog, three cats, bursitis, acute myopia, and a drinking problem. He was well over seventy and could hardly walk, and his weekly check of twenty-two dollars from the company that managed the building would not support anything. So, out of compromise, he was retired to superintendent of my labor.

My first day as a janitor, while I skillfully lugged my three overflowing cans of garbage out of the building, he sat on his bench in the lobby, faded and old and smoking in patched, loose blue pants. He watched me. He was a chain smoker and I noticed right away that he very carefully dropped all of the ashes and butts on the floor and crushed them under his feet until there was a yellow and gray smear. Then he laboriously pushed the mess under the bench with his shoe, all the while eyeing me like a cat in silence as I hauled the many cans of muck out to the big disposal unit next to the building. When I had finished, he gave me two old plates to help stock my kitchen and his first piece of advice.

"Sit down, for Chrissake, and take a load off your feet," he told me.

I sat on the red bench next to him and accepted the wilted cigarette he offered me from the crushed package he kept in his sweater pocket.

"Now I'll tell you something to help you get along in the building," he said.

I listened attentively.

"If any of these sons-of-bitches ever ask you to do something extra, be sure to charge them for it."

I assured him that I absolutely would.

"If they can afford to live here, they can afford to pay. The bastards."

"Undoubtedly," I assured him again.

"And another thing," he added. "Don't let any of these girls shove any cat shit under your nose. That ain't your job. You tell them to put it in a bag and take it out themselves."

I reminded him that I knew very well my station in life, and that I was not about to haul cat shit or anything of that nature. He looked at me through his thick-lensed glasses. He looked like a cat himself. "That's right," he said at last. "And if they still try to sneak it in the trash be sure to make the bastards pay. They can afford it." He crushed his seventh butt on the floor and scattered the mess some more while he lit up another. "I never hauled out no cat shit in the thirty years I been here and you don't do it either."

"I'm going up to wash my hands," I said.

"Remember," he called after me, "don't take no shit from any of them."

I protested once more that, upon my life, I would never, never do it, not even for the prettiest girl in the building. Going up in the elevator, I felt comfortably resolved that I would never do it. There were no pretty girls in the building.

I never found out what he had done before he came there, but I do know that being a janitor in that building was as high as he ever got in life. He had watched two generations of the rich pass the building on their way to the Yard, and he had seen many governors ride white horses thirty times into that same Yard to send sons and daughters of the rich out into life to produce, to acquire, to procreate and to send back sons and daughters so that the cycle would continue. He had watched the cycle from when he had been able to haul the cans out for himself, and now he could not, and he was bitter.

He was Irish, of course, and he took pride in Irish accomplishments when he could have none of his own. He had known Frank O'Connor when that writer had been at Harvard. He told me on many occasions how O'Connor had stopped to talk every day on his way to the Yard. He had also known James Michael Curley, and his most colorful memory of the man was a long ago day when he and James Curley sat in a Boston bar and one of Curley's runners had come in and said: "Hey Jim, Sol Bernstein the Jew wants to see you." And Curley, in his deep, memorial voice had said to James Sullivan: "Let us go forth and meet this Israelite Prince." These were his memories, and I would obediently put aside my garbage cans and laugh with him over the hundred or so colorful, insignificant little details which made up a whole lifetime of living in the basement of Harvard. And although they were of little value to me then, I knew that they were the reflections of a lifetime and the happiest moments he would ever have, being sold to me cheap, as youthful time is cheap, for as little time and interest as I wanted to spend. It was a buyer's market.

II

In those days I believed myself gifted with a boundless perception and attacked my daily garbage route with a gusto superenforced by the happy knowledge that behind each of the fifty or so doors in our building lived a story which could, if I chose to grace it with the magic of my pen, become immortal. I watched my tenants fanatically, noting their perversions, their visitors, and their eating habits. So intense was my search for material that I had to restrain myself from going through their refuse scrap by scrap; but at the topmost layers of muck, without too much hand-soiling in the process, I set my perceptions to work. By late June, however, I had discovered only enough to put together a skimpy, rather naïve Henry Miller novel. The most colorful discoveries being:

(1) The lady in #24 was an alumna of Paducah College.

(2) The couple in #55 made love at least five hundred times a week and the wife had not yet discovered the pill.

(3) The old lady in #36 was still having monthly inconvenience.

(4) The two fatsos in #56 consumed nightly an extraordinary amount of chili.

(5) The fat man in #54 had two dogs that were married to each other, but he was not married to anyone at all.

(6) The middle-aged single man in #63 threw out an awful lot of flowers.

Disturbed by the snail's progress I was making, I confessed my futility to James one day as he sat on his bench chain-smoking and smearing butts on my newly waxed lobby floor. "So you want to know about the tenants?" he said, his cat's eyes flickering over me.

I nodded.

"Well the first thing to notice is how many Jews there are."

"I haven't noticed many Jews," I said.

He eyed me in amazement.

"Well, a few," I said quickly to prevent my treasured perception from being dulled any further.

"A few, hell," he said. "There's more Jews here than anybody."

"How can you tell?"

He gave me that undecided look again. "Where do you think all that garbage comes from?" He nodded feebly toward my bulging cans. I looked just in time to prevent a stray noodle from slipping over the brim. "That's right," he continued. "Jews are the biggest eaters in the world. They eat the best too."

I confessed then that I was of the chicken-soup generation and believed that Jews ate only enough to muster strength for their daily trips to the bank.

"Not so!" he replied emphatically. "You never heard the expression: 'Let's get to the restaurant before the Jews get there'?"

I shook my head sadly.

"You don't know that in certain restaurants they take the free onions and pickles off the tables when they see Jews coming?"

I held my head down in shame over the bounteous heap.

He trudged over to my can and began to turn back the leaves of noodles and crumpled tissues from #47 with his hand. After a few seconds of digging he unmucked an empty paté can. "Look at that," he said triumphantly. "Gourmet stuff, no less."

"That's from #44," I said.

"What else?" he said all-knowingly. "In 1946 a Swedish girl moved in up there and took a Jewish girl for her roommate. Then the Swedish girl moved out and there's been a Jewish Dynasty up there ever since."

I recalled that #44 was occupied by a couple that threw out a good number of S. S. Pierce cans, Chivas Regal bottles, assorted broken records, and back issues of *Evergreen* and the *Realist.*

"You're right," I said.

"Of course," he replied as if there was never any doubt. "I can spot them anywhere, even when they think they're passing." He leaned closer and said in a you-and-me voice: "But don't ever say anything bad about them in public, the Anti-Defamation League will get you."

Just then his wife screamed for him from the second floor, and the dog joined her and beat against the door. He got into the elevator painfully and said: "Don't ever talk about them in public. You don't know who they are and that Defamation League will take everything you got."

Sullivan did not really hate Jews. He was just bitter toward anyone better off than himself. He liked me because I seemed to like hauling garbage and because I listened to him and seemed to respect what he said and seemed to imply, by lingering on even when he repeated himself, that I was eager to take what wisdom he had for no other reason than that I needed it in order to get along.

He lived with his wife on the second floor and his apartment was very dirty because both of them were sick and old, and neither could move very well. His wife swept dirt out into the hall, and two hours after I had mopped and waxed their section of the floor, there was sure to be a layer of dirt, grease, and crushed-scattered tobacco from their door to the end of the hall. There was a smell of dogs and cats and age and death about their door, and I did not ever want to have to go in there for any reason because I feared something about it I cannot name.

Mrs. Sullivan, I found out, was from South Africa. She loved animals much more than people and there was a great deal of pain in her face. She kept little pans of meat posted at strategic points about the building, and I often came across her in the early morning or late at night throwing scraps out of the second-floor window to stray cats. Once, when James was about to throttle a stray mouse in their apartment, she had screamed at him to give the mouse a sporting chance. Whenever she attempted to walk she had to balance herself against a wall or a rail, and she hated the building because it confined her. She also hated James and most of the tenants. On the other hand, she loved the *Johnny Carson Show,* she loved to sit outside on the front steps (because she could get no further unassisted), and she loved to talk to anyone who would stop to listen. She never spoke coherently except when she was cursing James, and then she had a vocabulary like a sailor. She had great, shrill lungs, and her screams, accompanied by the rabid barks of the dog, could be heard all over the building. She was never really clean, her teeth were bad, and the first most pathetic thing in the world was to see her sitting on the steps in the morning watching the world pass, in a stained smock and a fresh summer blue hat she kept just to wear downstairs, with no place in the world to go. James told me, on the many occasions of her screaming, that she was mentally disturbed and could not control herself. The admirable thing about him was that he never lost his temper with her, no matter how rough her curses became and no matter who heard them. And the second most pathetic thing in the world was to see them slowly making their way in Harvard Square, he supporting her, through the hurrying crowds of miniskirted summer girls, J-Pressed Ivy Leaguers, beatniks, and bused Japanese tourists, decked in cameras, who would take pictures of every inch of Harvard Square except them. Once, he told me, a hippie had brushed past them and called back over his shoulder: "Don't break any track records, Mr. and Mrs. Speedy Molasses."

Also on the second floor lived Miss O'Hara, a spinster who hated Sullivan as only an old maid can hate an old man. Across from her lived a very nice, gentle, celibate named Murphy who had once served with Montgomery in North Africa and who was now spending the rest of his life cleaning his little apartment and gossiping with Miss O'Hara. It was an Irish floor.

I never found out just why Miss O'Hara hated the Sullivans with such a passion. Perhaps it was because they were so unkempt and she was so superciliously clean. Perhaps it was because Miss O'Hara had a great deal of Irish pride and they were stereotyped Irish. Perhaps it was because she merely had no reason to like them. She was a fanatic about cleanliness and put out her little bit of garbage wrapped very neatly in yesterday's *Christian Science Monitor* and tied in a bow with a fresh piece of string. Collecting all those little neat packages, I would wonder where she got the string and imagined her at night picking meat-market locks with a hairpin and hobbling off with yards and yards of white cord concealed under the gray sweater she always wore. I could even imagine her back in her little apartment chuckling and rolling the cord into a great white ball by candlelight. Then she would stash it away in her breadbox. Miss O'Hara kept her door slightly open until late at night, and I suspected that she heard everything that went on in the building. I had the feeling that I should never dare to make love with gusto for fear that she would overhear and write down all my happy-time phrases, to be maliciously recounted to me if she were ever provoked.

She had been in the building longer than Sullivan, and I suppose that her greatest ambition in life was to outlive him and then attend his wake with a knitting ball and needles. She had been trying to get him fired for twenty-five years or so and did not know when to quit. On summer nights when I painfully mopped the second floor, she would offer me root beer, apples, or cupcakes while trying to pump me for evidence against him.

"He's just a filthy old man, Robert," she would declare in a little-old-lady whisper. "And don't think you have to clean up those dirty old butts of his. Just report him to the Company."

"Oh, I don't mind," I would tell her, gulping the root beer as fast as possible.

"Well, they're both a couple of lushes, if you ask me. They haven't been sober a day in twenty-five years."

"Well, she's sick too, you know."

"Ha!" She would throw up her hands in disgust. "She's only sick when he doesn't give her the booze."

I fought to keep down a burp. "How long have *you* been here?"

She motioned for me to step out of the hall and into her dark apartment. "Don't tell him,"—she nodded towards Sullivan's door—"but I've been here for thirty-four years." She waited for me to be taken aback. Then she added: "And it was a better building before those two lushes came."

She then offered me an apple, asked five times if the dog's barking bothered me, forced me to take a fudge brownie, said that the cats had wet the floor again last night, got me to dust the top of a large chest too high for her to reach, had me pick up the minute specks of dust which fell from my dustcloth, pressed another root beer on me, and then showed me her family album. As an afterthought, she had me take down a big old picture of her great-grandfather, also too high for her to reach, so that I could dust that too. Then together we picked up the dust from it which might have fallen to the floor. "He's really a filthy old man, Robert," she said in closing, "and don't be afraid to report him to the property manager any time you want."

I assured her that I would do it at the slightest provocation from Sullivan, finally accepted an apple but refused the money she offered, and escaped back to my mopping. Even then she watched me, smiling, from her half-opened door.

"Why does Miss O'Hara hate you?" I asked James once.

He lifted his cigaretted hand and let the long ash fall elegantly to the floor. "That old bitch has been an albatross around my neck ever since I got here," he said. "Don't trust her, Robert. It was her kind that sat around singing hymns and watching them burn saints in this state."

There was never an adequate answer to my question. And even though the dog was noisy and would surely kill someone if it ever got loose, no one could really dislike the old man because of it. The dog was all they had. In his garbage each night, for every wine bottle, there would be an equally empty can of dog food. Some nights he took the brute out for a long walk, when he could barely walk himself, and both of them had to be led back to the building.

III

In those days I had forgotten that I was first of all a black and I had a very lovely girl who was not first of all a black. We were both young and optimistic then, and she believed with me in my potential and liked me partly because of it; and I was happy because she belonged to me and not to the race, which made her special. It made me special too because I did not have to wear a beard or hate or be especially hip or ultra–Ivy Leaguish. I did not have to smoke pot or supply her with it, or be for any other cause at all except myself. I only had to be myself, which pleased me; and I only had to produce, which pleased both of us. Like many of the artistically inclined rich, she wanted to own in someone else what she could not own in herself. But this I did not mind, and I forgave her for it because she forgave me moods and the constant smell of garbage and a great deal of latent hostility. She only minded James Sullivan and all the valuable time I was wasting listening to him rattle on and on. His conversations, she thought, were useless, repetitious, and promised nothing of value to me. She was accustomed to the old-rich whose conversations meandered around a leitmotiv of how well off they were and how much they would leave behind very soon. She was not at all cold, but she had been taught how to tolerate the old-poor and perhaps toss them a greeting in passing. But nothing more.

Sullivan did not like her when I first introduced them because he saw that she was not a hippie and could not be dismissed. It is in the nature of things that liberal people will tolerate two interracial hippies more than they will an intelligent, serious-minded mixed couple. The former liaison is easy to dismiss as the dregs of both races, deserving of each other and the contempt of both races; but the latter poses a threat because there is no immediacy or overpowering sensuality or "you-pick-my-fleas-I'll-pick-yours" apparent on the surface of things, and people, even the most publicly liberal, cannot dismiss it so easily.

"That girl is Irish, isn't she?" he had asked one day in my apartment soon after I had introduced them.

"No," I said definitely.

"What's her name again?"

"Judy Smith," I said, which was not her name at all.

"Well, I can spot it," he said. "She's got Irish blood, all right."

"Everybody's got a little Irish blood," I told him.

He looked at me cattily and craftily from behind his thick lenses. "Well, she's from a good family, I suppose."

"I suppose," I said.

He paused to let some ashes fall to the rug. "They say the Colonel's Lady and Nelly O'Grady are sisters under the skin." Then he added: "Rudyard Kipling."

"That's true," I said with equal innuendo, "that's why you have to maintain a distinction by marrying the Colonel's Lady."

An understanding passed between us then, and we never spoke more on the subject.

Almost every night the cats wet the second floor while Meg Sullivan watched the *Johnny Carson Show* and the dog howled and clawed the door. During commercials Meg would curse James to get out and stop dropping ashes on the floor or to take the dog out or something else, totally unintelligible to those of us on the fourth, fifth and sixth floors. Even after the *Carson Show* she would still curse him to get out, until finally he would go down to the basement and put away a bottle or two of wine. There was a steady stench of cat functions in the basement, and with all the grease and dirt, discarded trunks, beer bottles, chairs, old tools and the filthy sofa on which he sometimes slept, seeing him there made me want to cry. He drank the cheapest sherry, the wino kind, straight from the bottle; and on many nights that summer at 2:00 A.M. my phone would ring me out of bed.

"Rob? Jimmy Sullivan here. What are you doing?"

There was nothing suitable to say.

"Come on down to the basement for a drink."

"I have to be at work at eight-thirty," I would protest.

"Can't you have just one drink?" he would say pathetically.

I would carry down my own glass so that I would not have to drink out of the bottle. Looking at him on the sofa, I could not be mad because now I had many records for my stereo, a story that was going well, a girl who believed in me and belonged to me and not to the race, a new set of dishes, and a tomorrow morning with younger people.

"I don't want to burden you unduly," he would always preface.

I would force myself not to look at my watch and say: "Of course not."

"My Meg is not in the best health, you know," he would say, handing the bottle to me.

"She's just old."

"The doctors say she should be in an institution."

"That's no place to be."

"I'm a sick man myself, Rob. I can't take much more. She's crazy."

"Anybody who loves animals can't be crazy."

He took another long draw from the bottle. "I won't live another year. I'll be dead in a year."

"You don't know that."

He looked at me closely, without his glasses, so that I could see the desperation in his eyes. "I just hope Meg goes before I do. I don't want them to put her in an institution after I'm gone."

At 2:00 A.M. with the cat stench in my nose and a glass of bad sherry standing still in my hand because I refused in my mind to touch it, and when all my dreams of greatness were above him and the basement and the building itself, I did not know what to say. The only way I could keep from hating myself was to talk about the AMA or the Medicare program or hippies. He was pure hell on all three. To him, the medical profession was "morally bankrupt," Medicare was a great farce which deprived oldsters like himself of their "rainy-day dollars," and hippies were "dropouts from the human race." He could rage on and on in perfect phrases about all three of his major dislikes, and I had the feeling that because the sentences were so well constructed and well turned, he might have memorized them from something he had read. But then he was extremely well read and it did not matter if he had borrowed a phrase or two from someone else. The ideas were still his own.

It would be 3:00 A.M. before I knew it, and then 3:30, and still he would go on. He hated politicians in general and liked to recount, at these times, his private catalogue of political observations. By the time he got around to Civil Rights it would be 4:00 A.M., and I could not feel sorry or responsible for him at that hour. I would begin to yawn and at first he would just ignore it. Then I would start to edge toward the door, and he would see that he could hold me no longer, not even by declaring that he wanted to be an honorary Negro because he loved the race so much.

"I hope I haven't burdened you unduly," he would say again.

"Of course not," I would say, because it was over then and I could leave him and the smell of the cats there and sometimes I would go out in the cool night and walk around the Yard and be thankful that I was only an assistant janitor, and a transient one at that. Walking in the early dawn and seeing the Summer School fellows sneak out of the girls' dormitories in the Yard gave me a good feeling, and I thought that tomorrow night it would be good to make love myself so that I could be busy when he called.

IV

"Why don't you tell that old man your job doesn't include baby-sitting with him?" Jean told me many times when she came over to visit during the day and found me sleeping.

I would look at her and think to myself about social forces and the pressures massing and poised, waiting to attack us. It was still July then. It was hot and I was working good. "He's just an old man," I said. "Who else would listen to him?"

"You're too soft. As long as you do your work you don't have to be bothered with him."

"He could be a story if I listened long enough."

"There are too many stories about old people."

"No," I said, thinking about us again, "there are just too many people who have no stories."

Sometimes he would come up and she would be there, but I would let him come in anyway, and he would stand in the room looking dirty and uncomfortable, offering some invented reason for having intruded. At these times something silent would pass between them, something I cannot name, which would reduce him to exactly what he was: an old man, come out of his basement to intrude where he was not wanted. But all the time this was being communicated, there would be a surface, friendly conversation between them. And after five minutes or so of being unwelcome, he would apologize for having come, drop a few ashes on the rug and back out the door. Downstairs we could hear his wife screaming.

We endured and aged and August was almost over. Inside the building the cats were still wetting, Meg was still screaming, the dog was getting madder, and Sullivan began to drink during the day. Outside it was hot and lush and green, and the summer girls were wearing shorter mini-skirts and no panties and the middle-aged men down by the Charles were going wild on their bridge. Everyone was restless for change, for August is the month when undone summer things must be finished or regretted all through the winter.

V

Being imaginative people, Jean and I played a number of original games. One of them we called "Social Forces," the object of which was to see which side could break us first. We played it with the unknown nightriders who screamed obscenities from passing cars. And because that was her side I would look at her expectantly, but she would laugh and say: "No." We played it at parties with unaware blacks who attempted to enchant her with skillful dances and hip vocabulary, believing her to be community property. She would be polite and aloof, and much later, it then being my turn, she would look at me expectantly. And I would force a smile and say: "No." The last round was played while taking her home in a subway car, on a hot August night, when one side of the car was black and tense and hating and the other side was white and of the same mind. There was not enough room on either side for the two of us to sit and we would not separate; and so we stood, holding on to a steel post through all the stops, feeling all the eyes, between the two sides of the car and the two sides of the world. We aged. And, getting off finally at the stop which was no longer ours, we looked at each other, again expectantly, and there was nothing left to say.

I began to avoid the old man, would not answer the door when I knew it was he who was knocking, and waited until very late at night, when he could not possibly be awake, to haul the trash down. I hated the building then; and I was really a janitor for the first time. I slept a lot and wrote very little. And I did not give a damn about Medicare, the AMA, the building, Meg or the crazy dog. I began to consider moving out.

In that same month, Miss O'Hara finally succeeded in badgering Murphy, the celibate Irishman, and a few other tenants into signing a complaint about the dog. No doubt Murphy signed because he was a nice fellow and women like Miss O'Hara had always dominated him. He did not really mind the dog: he did not really mind anything. She called him "Frank Dear," and I had the feeling that when he came to that place, fresh from Montgomery's Campaign, he must have had a will of his own; but she had drained it all away, year by year, so that now he would do anything just to be agreeable.

One day soon after the complaint, the Property Manager came around to tell Sullivan that the dog had to be taken away. Miss O'Hara told me the good news later, when she finally got around to my door.

"Well, that crazy dog is gone now, Robert. Those two are enough."

"Where is the dog?" I asked.

"I don't know, but Albert Rustin made them get him out. You should have seen the old drunk's face," she said. "That dirty useless old man."

"You should be at peace now," I said.

"Almost," was her reply. "The best thing would be to get rid of those two old boozers along with the dog."

I congratulated Miss O'Hara again and then went out. I knew that the old man would be drinking and would want to talk. I did not want to talk. But very late that evening he called on the telephone and caught me in.

"Rob?" he said. "James Sullivan here. Would you come down to my apartment like a good fellow? I want to ask you something important."

I had never been in his apartment before and did not want to go then. But I went down anyway.

They had three rooms, all grimy from corner to corner. There was a peculiar odor in that place I did not want to ever smell again, and his wife was dragging herself around the room talking in mumbles. When she saw me come in the door, she said: "I can't clean it up. I just can't. Look at that window. I can't reach it. I can't keep it clean." She threw up both her hands and held her head down and to the side. "The whole place is dirty and I can't clean it up."

"What do you want?" I said to Sullivan.

"Sit down." He motioned me to a kitchen chair. "Have you changed that bulb on the fifth floor?"

"It's done."

He was silent for a while, drinking from a bottle of sherry, and he offered me some and a dirty glass. "You're the first person who's been in here in years," he said. "We couldn't have company because of the dog."

Somewhere in my mind was a note that I should never go into his apartment. But the dog had not been the reason. "Well, he's gone now," I said, fingering the dirty glass of sherry.

He began to cry. "They took my dog away," he said. "It was all I had. How can they take a man's dog away from him?"

There was nothing I could say.

"I couldn't do nothing," he continued. After a while he added: "But I know who it was. It was that old bitch O'Hara. Don't ever trust her, Rob. She smiles in your face but it was her kind that laughed when they burned Joan of Arc in this state."

Seeing him there, crying and making me feel unmanly because I wanted to touch him or say something warm, also made me eager to be far away and running hard. "Everybody's got problems," I said. "I don't have a girl now."

He brightened immediately, and for a while he looked almost happy in his old cat's eyes. Then he staggered over to my chair and held out his hand. I did not touch it, and he finally pulled it back. "I know how you feel," he said. "I know just how you feel."

"Sure," I said.

"But you're a young man, you have a future. But not me. I'll be dead inside of a year."

Just then his wife dragged in to offer me a cigar. They were being hospitable and I forced myself to drink a little of the sherry.

"They took my dog away today," she mumbled. "That's all I had in the world, my dog."

I looked at the old man. He was drinking from the bottle.

VI

During the first week of September one of the middle-aged men down by the Charles got tired of looking and tried to take a necking girl away from her boyfriend. The police hauled him off to jail, and the girl pulled down her dress tearfully. A few days later another man exposed himself near the same spot. And that same week a dead body was found on the banks of the Charles.

The miniskirted brigade had moved out of the Yard and it was quiet and green and peaceful there. In our building another Jewish couple moved into #44. They did not eat gourmet stuff and, on occasion, threw out pork-and-beans cans. But I had lost interest in perception. I now had many records for my stereo, loads of S. S. Pierce stuff, and a small bottle of Chivas Regal which I never opened. I was working good again and did not miss other things as much; or at least I told myself that.

The old man was coming up steadily now, at least three times a day, and I had resigned myself to it. If I refused to let him in he would always come back later with a missing bulb on the fifth floor. We had taken to buying cases of beer together, and when he had finished his half, which was very frequently, he would come up to polish off mine. I began to enjoy talking about politics, the AMA, Medicare, and hippies, and listening to him recite from books he had read. I discovered that he was very well read in history, philosophy, literature and law. He was extraordinarily fond of saying: "I am really a cut above being a building superintendent. Circumstances made me what I am." And even though he was drunk and dirty and it was very late at night, I believed him and liked him anyway because having him there was much better than being alone. After he had gone I could sleep and I was not lonely in sleep; and it did not really matter how late I was at work the next morning, because when I really thought about it all, I discovered that nothing really matters except not being old and being alive and having potential to dream about, and not being alone.

Whenever I passed his wife on the steps she would say: "That no-good bastard let them take my dog away." And whenever her husband complained that he was sick she said: "That's good for him. He took my dog away."

Sullivan slept in the basement on the sofa almost every night because his wife would think about the dog after the *Carson Show* and blame him for letting it be taken away. He told her, and then me, that the dog was on a farm in New Hampshire; but that was unlikely because the dog had been near mad, and it did not appease her. It was nearing autumn and she was getting violent. Her screams could be heard for hours through the halls and I knew that beyond her quiet door Miss O'Hara was plotting again. Sullivan now had little cuts and bruises on his face and hands, and one day he said: "Meg is like an albatross around my neck. I wish she was dead. I'm sick myself and I can't take much more. She blames me for the dog and I couldn't help it."

"Why don't you take her out to see the dog?" I said.

"I couldn't help it, Rob," he went on. "I'm old and I couldn't help it."

"You ought to just get her out of here for a while."

He looked at me, drunk as usual. "Where would we go? We can't even get past the Square."

There was nothing left to say.

"Honest to God, I couldn't help it," he said. He was not saying it to me.

That night I wrote a letter from a mythical New Hampshire farmer telling them that the dog was very fine and missed them a great deal because he kept trying to run off. I said that the children and all the other dogs liked him and that he was not vicious any more. I wrote that the open air was doing him a lot of good and added that they should feel absolutely free to come up to visit the dog at any time. That same night I gave him the letter.

One evening, some days later, I asked him about it.

"I tried to mail it, I really tried," he said.

"What happened?"

"I went down to the Square and looked for cars with New Hampshire license plates. But I never found anybody."

"That wasn't even necessary, was it?"

"It had to have a New Hampshire postmark. You don't know my Meg."

"Listen," I said. "I have a friend who goes up there. Give me the letter and I'll have him mail it."

He held his head down. "I'll tell you the truth. I carried that letter in my pocket so much it got ragged and dirty and I got tired of carrying it. I finally just tore it up."

Neither one of us said anything for a while.

"If I could have sent it off it would have helped some," he said at last. "I know it would have helped."

"Sure," I said.

"I wouldn't have to ask anybody if I had my strength."

"I know."

"If I had my strength I would have mailed it myself."

"I know," I said.

That night we both drank from his bottle of sherry and it did not matter at all that I did not provide my own glass.

VII

In late September the Cambridge police finally picked up the bearded pot-pusher in the Square. He had been in a restaurant all summer, at the same table, with the same customers flocking around him; but now that summer was over, they picked him up. The leaves were changing. In the early evening students passed the building and Meg, blue-hatted and waiting on the steps, carrying sofas and chairs and coffee tables to their suites in the Houses. Down by the Charles the middle-aged men were catching the last phases of summer sensuality before the grass grew cold and damp, and before the young would be forced indoors to play. I wondered what those hungry, spying men did in the winter or at night when it was too dark to see. Perhaps, I thought, they just stood there and listened.

In our building Miss O'Hara was still listening. She had never stopped. When Meg was outside on the steps it was very quiet and I felt good that Miss O'Hara had to wait a long, long time before she heard anything. The company gave the halls and ceilings a new coat of paint, but it was still old in the building. James Sullivan got his yearly two-week vacation and they went to the Boston Common for six hours: two hours going, two hours sitting on the benches, and two hours coming back Then they both sat on the steps, watching, and waiting.

At first I wanted to be kind because he was old and dying in a special way and I was young and ambitious. But at night, in my apartment, when I heard his dragging feet in the hall outside and knew that he would be drunk and repetitious and imposing on my privacy, I did not want to be kind any more. There were girls outside and I knew that I could have one now because that desperate look had finally gone somewhere deep inside. I was young and now I did not want to be bothered.

"Did you read about the lousy twelve per cent Social Security increase those bastards in Washington gave us?"

"No."

He would force himself past me, trying to block the door with my body, and into the room. "When those old pricks tell me to count my blessings, I tell them, 'You're not one of them.'" He would seat himself at the table without meeting my eyes. "The cost of living's gone up more than twelve per cent in the last six months."

"I know."

"What unmitigated bastards."

I would try to be busy with something on my desk.

"But the Texas Oil Barons got another depletion allowance."

"They can afford to bribe politicians," I would mumble.

"They tax away our rainy-day dollars and give us a lousy twelve per cent."

"It's tough."

He would know that I did not want to hear any more and he would know that he was making a burden of himself. It made me feel bad that it was so obvious to him, but I could not help myself. It made me feel bad that I disliked him more every time I heard a girl laugh on the street far below my window. So I would nod occasionally and say half-phrases and smile slightly at something witty he was saying for the third time. If I did not offer him a drink he would go sooner and so I gave him Coke when he hinted at how dry he was. Then, when he had finally gone, saying, "I hope I haven't burdened you unduly," I went to bed and hated myself.

VIII

If I am a janitor it is either because I have to be a janitor or because I want to be a janitor. And if I do not have to do it, and if I no longer want to do it, the easiest thing in the world, for a young man, is to step up to something else. Any move away from it is a step up because there is no job more demeaning than that of a janitor. One day I made myself suddenly realize that the three dirty cans would never contain anything of value to me, unless, of course, I decided to gather material for Harold Robbins or freelance for the *Realist*. Neither alternative appealed to me.

Toward dawn one day, during the first part of October, I rented a U-Haul truck and took away two loads of things I had accumulated.

The records I packed very carefully, and the stereo I placed on the front seat of the truck beside me. I slipped the Chivas Regal and a picture of Jean under some clothes in a trunk I will not open for a long time. And I left the rug on the floor because it was dirty and too large for my new apartment. I also left the two plates given to me by James Sullivan, for no reason at all. Sometimes I want to go back to get them, but I do not know how to ask for them or explain why I left them in the first place. But sometimes at night, when there is a sleeping girl beside me, I think that I cannot have them again because I am still young and do not want to go back into that building.

I saw him once in the Square walking along very slowly with two shopping bags, and they seemed very heavy. As I came up behind him I saw him put them down and exercise his arms while the crowd moved in two streams around him. I had an instant impulse to offer help and I was close enough to touch him before I stopped. I will never know why I stopped. And after a few seconds of standing behind him and knowing that he was not aware of anything at all except the two heavy bags waiting to be lifted after his arms were sufficiently rested, I moved back into the stream of people which passed on the left of him. I never looked back.

RAYMOND BARRIO
The Campesinos

Dawn.

Outside, the coolest night.

Outside, the soft, plush, lingering sheen of nightlight.

Within his breezy air-conditioned shack Manuel lay half asleep in the middle of the biggest apricot orchard in the world, nothing but apricot trees all around, in one of a long double row of splintered boards nailed together and called a shack. A migrant's shack. He struggled to come awake. Everything seemed to be plugged up. A distant roar closed in steadily. He awoke in a cold sweat. He sat up abruptly in the cold darkness.

The roar grew louder and louder. He leaned forward, hunched in his worn, torn covers, and peered through the grimy window. A huge black monster was butting through trees, moving and pitching about, its headlights piercing the armor of night, then swinging away again as the roaring lessened. Manuel smiled. The roar of a tractor. He rubbed the sleep from his eyes. He stretched his aching arms and shoulders. He thought of Lupe and the kids back in Drawbridge.

On the very brink of the full onslaught of summer's punishing heat, with the plums and pears and apricots fattening madly on every vine, branch, bush, and limb in every section of every county in the country, pickers were needed right now immediately on every farm and orchard everywhere and all at once. The frantic demand for pickers increased rapidly as the hot days mounted. That sure looked good out there. What a cool job that was. Driving a tractor at night. Maybe he could get Ramiro to teach him to drive one.

Manuel well knew what his physical energy was.

His physical energy was his total worldly wealth.

No matter how anxious he was to work, he did have his limit. He had to rest his body. The finger joint he'd injured still hurt. He missed Lupe's chatter. He'd signed up with that shrewd contractor, Roberto Morales, that shrewd, fat, energetic contratista, manipulator of migrating farm workers, that smiling middleman who promised to deliver so many hands to the moon at such and such a time at such and such an orchard at such and such a price, for such a small commission. A tiny percentage. Such a little slice. Silvery slavery—modernized.

Roberto Morales, an organization man, was a built-in toll gate. A parasite. A collector of drops of human sweat. An efficiency expert. Had he had not been Mexican, he would have made a fantastic capitalist, like Turner. He was Turner upside down. Sucking blood from his own people. With the help and convenient connivance of Turner's insatiable greed.

The agricultural combine's imperative need to have its capital personally plucked when ripe so as to materialize its honest return on its critical investment in order to keep its executives relaxed in blue splendor in far-off desert pools, was coupled to the migrant workers' inexorable and uncompromising need to earn pennies to fend off stark starvation.

Good money.

Good dough.

Good hard work.

Pick fast.

Penny a bucket.

Check off.

Get the count right.

Cotsplumsprunespeachesbeanspeas.

Pods.

The seed of life.

And:—don't complain. . . .

Manuel lay back in the blackness. As the darkness receded and the light of day started creeping imperiously across its own land, he thought that these powerful orchard land owners were awfully generous to give him such a beautiful hostel to stop in overnight. The skylight hotel. There the land stood. A heaving, sleeping mother earth. A marvelous land. Ripening her fruit once again. Once more. Ripening it fatly and pregnantly for the thousandth time. It must be plucked said the wise man. For it cannot hang around on limbs a minute extra. At no man's convenience. As soon as the baby's ready. Lush and full of plump juices. Hugging its new seed around its own ripeness. The plum and the cot and the peach and the pear must plummet again to earth. Carrying the seed of its own delicate rebirth and redestruction back home to earth again. A clever mother earth who in her all-but-unbelievable generosity was capable of giving man fivefold, tenfold the quantity of fruit he could himself eat, five times fifty, and yet the pickers were never paid enough to satisfy their hunger beyond their actual working hours. And yet it was called a moral world. An ethical world. A good world. A happy world. A world full of golden opportunities. Manuel simply couldn't figure it out.

What was wrong with the figures?

Why was mother earth so generous? And men so greedy?

You got twenty-five cents a basket for tomatoes. A dollar a crate for some fruit. You had to work fast. That was the whole thing. A frantic lunatic to make your barely living wage. If you had no rent to pay, it was OK. You were ahead, amigo. Pay rent, however, stay in one place, and you couldn't migrate after the other easy pickings. The joy of working was looking over your dreams locked to hunger.

Manuel studied the whorls in the woodwork whirling slowly, revealed in the faint crepuscular light penetrating his shack. His cot was a slab of half-inch plywood board twenty-two inches wide and eight feet long, the width of the shack, supported by two two-by-four beams butted up against the wall at both ends beneath the side window. The shack itself was eight by twelve by seven feet high. Its roof had a slight pitch. The rain stains in the ceiling planks revealed the ease with which the rain penetrated. Except for two small panes of glass exposed near the top, most of the window at the opposite end was boarded up. A single, old, paint-encrusted door was the only entry. No curtains. No interior paneling. Just a shack. A shack of misery. He found he was able to admire and appreciate the simplicity and the strength of the construction. He counted the upright studs, level, two feet apart, the double joists across the top supporting the roof. Cracks and knotholes aplenty, in the wall siding, let in bright chinks of light during the day and welcome wisps of clear fresh air at night. The rough planking of the siding was stained dark. The floor was only partly covered with odd sections of plywood. Some of the rough planking below was exposed, revealing cracks leading down to the cool black earth beneath. A small thick table was firmly studded to a portion of the wall opposite the door. A few small pieces of clear lumber stood bunched together, unsung, unused, unhurried, in the far corner. An overhead shelf, supported from the ceiling by a small extending perpendicular arm, containing some boxes of left-over chemicals and fertilizers, completed the furnishings in his temporary abode.

It was habitable.

He could raise his family in it.

If they were rabbits.

The first rays of a brute new day clinked in through the small rectangle of panes. The ray hovered, then peaked, then rested on the covers pushed up by his knees. He recalled his mountain trips with his uncle to the great forbidding barrancas near Durango in Central Mexico, and stopping to rest in the middle of the wild woods, and coming unexpectedly upon a crumbling, splintered hulk of a shack that was all falling apart. It barely gave them shelter from the sudden pelting storm they were trying to escape, he as a young frightened boy, but shelter it was—and how beautiful that experience was, then, for they were free, daring, adventurers, out there in that wilderness, alone and daring, with nothing between them and God's own overpowering nature, alone. They belonged to nothing. To no one. But themselves. They were dignity purified. No one forced them to go or stay there. They were delighted and grateful to the shack. For the protection it afforded them. Though it was hardly more than a ratty pile of splinters. Far worse than this one he was now occupying . . . but also somehow far more beautiful in his memory.

And now. Here he was. Shut up in this miserable shack. So sturdily built. Thinking how it sickened him inside because it was more a jail cell than a shelter. He didn't care how comfortable and convenient the growers made the shacks for him. They were huts of slavery. What he wanted was an outlet for his pride. A sudden fierce wave of anger made him want to cross the shack with his fists. There had to be some way to cross the ungulfable bridge. Why was necessity always the bride of hunger? To be free . . . ah, and also to be able to eat all one wanted. My heart, mi corazon, why did work always have to blend with such misery? The welcome warmth of the sun's early rays, penetrating more, warmed his frame. But it was a false, false hope. He knew it. The work that lay ahead of him that day would drain and stupify and fatigue him once again to the point of senseless torpor, ready to fall over long before the work day was done. And that fatigue wasn't merely so bad to bear as the deadly repetitious monotony of never changing, never resting, doing the same plucking over and over and over again. But he had to do it. He had no choice. It was all he could do. It had to be done if he wanted the money. And he had to have the money, if he wanted to feed his family. The brain in his arms was his only capital. Not very much, true, but it was the only sacrifice he could offer the money gods, the only heart he could offer on the pyramid of gold.

His life. La gran vida.

Wide awake now, fully refreshed, his whole body lithe and toned, Manuel was ashamed to find himself eager to start in work, knowing that he would do well, but ashamed because he could think of nothing he would rather do more. The final step.

The final the final the final the final the final the final step.

over + over just like picking

To want to work oneself to death. A la muerte. It wasn't the work itself that bothered him. It was the total immersion, the endless, ceaseless, total use of all his energies and spirit and mind and being that tore him apart within. He didn't know what else he was good for or could do with his life. But there had to be something else. He had to be something more than a miserable plucking animal. Pluck pluck pluck. Feed feed feed. Glug glug glug. Dressing quickly, rolling up his blanket roll and stuffing it into a corner to use again that night, Manuel stepped coolly out into the morning sweetness and breathed the honey-scented humidity rinsing air rising from the honied soil, and joined the

contrast to life + shack

thickening throng of his fellow pluckers milling about the large open barn serving as a cookout. Feeding all the pickers was another of the fat man's unholy prerogatives, for he cheated and overpriced on meals too. Roberto Morales, the fat man, the shrewd contratista, was a bully man, busily darting his blob about, exhorting his priceless pickers to hurry, answering questions, giving advice, in the cool half-light, impatiently, pushing, giving orders. Manuel, in order to avoid having to greet him, scowled at his toes when Roberto came trouncing by, saying, "Apurense, compañeros, hurry, hurry, hurry, amigos." Sure. Amigos. Si. Si. Frens. They all gulped their food down hurriedly, standing. Just like home. Paper plates, plastic cups. Wooden spoons. And bits of garbage flying into large canisters. Then in the still cool nightlike morning air, like a flood of disturbed birds, they all picked up their pails and filed into the orchard.

The apricots were plump.

Smooth.

A golden syrupy orange.

Manuel popped two into his mouth, enjoying their cool natural sweetness after the bitter coffee. He knew he could not eat too many. His stomach muscles would cramp. Other pickers started pulling rapidly away from him. Let them. Calmly he calculated the struggle. Start the press sure, slow, and keep it going steady. Piecework. Fill the bucket, fill another, and still another. The competition was among a set of savages, as savage for money as himself, savages with machetes, hacking their way through the thickets of modern civilization back to the good old Aztec days, waiting to see who'd be first in line to wrench his heart out. Savage beasts, eager to fill as many buckets as possible in as short a time as possible, cleaning out an entire orchard, picking everything in sight clean, tons of fruit, delivering every bit of ripe fruit to the accountants in their cool air-conditioned orifices.

The competition was not between pickers and growers.

It was between pickers—Jorge and Guillermo.

Between the poor and the hungry, the desperate, and the hunted, the slave and the slave, slob against slob, the depraved and himself. You were your own terrible boss. That was the cleverest part of the whole thing. The picker his own bone picker, his own willing built-in slave driver. God, that was good! That was where they reached into your scrotum and screwed you royally and drained your brain and directed your sinews and nerves and muscles with invisible fingers. To fatten their coffers. And drive you to your coffin. That sure was smart. Meant to be smart. Bookkeepers aren't dumb. You worked hard because you wanted to do that hard work above everything else. Pickfast pickhard pickfurious pick pick pick. They didn't need straw bosses studying your neck to see if you kept bobbing up and down to keep your picking pace up. Like the barn-stupid chicken, you drove yourself to do it. You were your own money monkey foreman, monkey on top of your own back.

You over-charged yourself.

With your own frenzy.

Neat.

You pushed your gut and your tired aching arms and your twitching legs pumping adrenalin until your tongue tasted like coarse sandpaper.

You didn't even stop to take a drink, let alone a piss, for fear you'd get fined, fired, or bawled out.

And then, after all that effort, you got your miserable pay.

Would the bobbing boss's sons stoop to that?

His fingers were loose and dexterous now. The plump orange balls plopped pitter patter like heavy drops of golden rain into his swaying, sweaty canvas bucket. His earnings depended entirely on how quickly he worked and how well he kept the pressure up. The morning sun was high. The sweet shade was fragrant and refreshing and comfortable under the leafy branches. The soil too was still cool and humid. It was going to be another hot one.

There.

Another row ended.

He swung around the end of the row and for a moment he was all alone, all by himself. He looked out far across the neighboring alfalfa field, dark green and rich and ripe. Then he looked at the long low Diablo Range close by, rising up into the misty pale blue air kept cool by the unseen bay nearby. This was all his. For a flowing, deceptive minute, all this rich, enormous terrain was all his. All this warm balmy baby air. All this healthful sunny breeze. All those hills, this rich fertile valley, these orchards, these tiled huertas, these magnificent farms all, all his . . . for his eyes to feast upon. It was a moment he wished he could capture forever and etch permanently on his memory, making it a part of living life for his heart to feast joyously on, forever. Why couldn't he stop? Why? Why couldn't he just put the bucket down and open his arms and walk into the hills and merge himself with the hills and just wander invisibly in the blue?

What Manuel couldn't really know was that he was completing yet another arc in the unending circle that had been started by one of his Mexican forebears exactly two hundred years before—for even the memory of history was also robbed from him—when Gaspar de Portola, hugging the coastline, nearing present-day San Francisco, climbed what is now Sweeney Ridge, and looked down upon San Francisco's magnificent land-locked Bay, overlooking what is now the International Airport.

Both don Gaspar and don Manuel were landlords and landless at precisely the same instant of viewing all this heady beauty. And both were equally dispossessed. Both were also possessed of a keen sense of pride and natural absorption with the ritual and mystery of all life. The living that looked mighty good in a flash to Manuel lasted a good deal longer for don Gaspar whose stumbling accident swept him into the honored and indelible pages of glorious history.

Manuel was now a mere straw among the enormous sludge of humanity flowing past, a creature of limb and his own driving appetites, a creature of heed and need. Swinging around another end run he placed his ladder on the next heavy limb of the next pregnant tree. He reached up. He plucked bunches of small golden fruit with both hands. He worked like a frenzied windmill in slow motion. He cleared away an arc as far as the circumference of his plucking fingers permitted. A living model for da Vinci's outstretched man. Adam heeding God's moving finger. He moved higher. He repeated another circle. Then down and around again to another side of the tree, until he cleared it, cleared it of all visible, viable, delectable, succulent fruit. It was sweet work. The biggest difference between him and the honey-gathering ant was that the ant had a home.

Several pickers were halfway down the next row, well in advance of him. He was satisfied he was pacing himself well. Most of the band was still behind him. The moving sun, vaulting the sky dome's crackling earth parting with its bronzing rays, pounded its fierce heat into every dead and living crevice. Perspiration poured down his sideburns, down his forehead, down his cheek, down his neck, into his ears, off his chin. He tasted its saltiness with the tip of his dry tongue. He wished he'd brought some salt tablets. Roberto Morales wasn't about to worry about the pickers, and Manuel wasn't worried either. Despite the heat, he felt some protection from the ocean and bay. It had been much, much worse in Texas, and much hotter in Delano in the San Joaquin valley and worst of all in Satan's own land, the Imperial Valley.

No matter which way he turned, he was trapped in an endless maze of apricot trees, as though forever, neat rows of them, neatly planted, row after row, just like the blackest bars on the jails of hell. There had to be an end. There had to be. There—trapped. There had to be a way out. Locked. There had to be a respite. Animal. The buckets and the crates kept piling up higher. Brute. He felt alone. Though surrounded by other pickers. Beast. Though he was perspiring heavily, his shirt was powder dry. Savage. The hot dry air. The hot dry air sucking every drop of living moisture from his brute body. Wreck. He stopped and walked to the farthest end of the first row for some water, raised the dented dipper from the brute tank, drank the holy water in great brute gulps so he wouldn't have to savor its tastelessness, letting it spill down his torn shirt to cool his exhausted body, to replenish his brute cells and animal pores and stinking follicles and pig gristle, a truly refined wreck of an animal, pleased to meetcha. Predator.

Lunch.

Almost too exhausted to eat, he munched his cheese with tortillas, smoked on ashes, then lay back on the cool ground for half an hour. That short rest in the hot shade replenished some of his humor and resolve. He felt his spirit swell out again like a thirsty sponge in water. Then up again. The trees. The branches again. The briarly branches. The scratching leaves. The twigs tearing at his shirt sleeves. The ladder. The rough bark. The endlessly unending piling up of bucket upon box upon crate upon stack upon rack upon mound upon mountain. He picked a mountain of cots automatically. An automaton. A beast. A ray of enemy sun penetrated the tree that was hiding him and split his forehead open. His mind whirred. He blacked out. Luckily he'd been leaning against a heavy branch. His feet hooked to the ladder's rung. His half-filled bucket slipped from his grasp and fell in slow motion, splattering the fruit he'd so laboriously picked. To the ground. Roberto happened by and shook his head. "Whatsamatter, can't you see straight, pendejo." Manuel was too tired even to curse. He should have had some salt pills.

Midafternoon.

The summer's fierce zenith passed overhead. It passed. Then dropped. It started to light the ocean behind him, back of the hills. Sandy dreams. Cool nights. Cold drinks. Soft guitar music with Lupe sitting beside him. All wafting through his feverish moments. Tiredness drained his spirit of will. Exhaustion drained his mind. His fingers burned. His arms flailed the innocent trees. He was slowing down. He could hardly fill his last bucket. Suddenly the whistle blew. The day's work was at last ended.

Ended!

The contratista Roberto Morales stood there.

His feet straddled. Mexican style. A real robber. A Mexican general. A gentlemanly, friendly, polite, grinning, vicious, thieving brute. The worst kind. To his own people. Despite his being a fellow Mexican, despite his torn, old clothing, everyone knew what kind of clever criminal he was. Despite his crude, ignorant manner, showing that he was one of them, that he'd started with them, that he grew up with them, that he'd suffered all the sordid deprivations with them, he was actually the shrewdest, smartest, richest cannibal in forty counties around. They sure couldn't blame the gueros for this miscarriage. He was a crew chief. How could anyone know what he did to his own people? And what did the gueros care? So the anglo growers and guero executives, smiling in their cool filtered offices, puffing their elegant thin cigars, washed their clean blond bloodless dirtless hands of the whole matter. All they did was hire Roberto Morales. Firm, fair, and square. For an agreed-upon price. Good. How he got his people down to the pickings was no concern of theirs. They were honest, those gueros. They could sleep at night. They fulfilled their end of the bargain, and cheated no one. Their only crime; their only soul crime indeed was that they just didn't give a shit how that migratory scum lived. It was no concern of theirs. Their religion said it was no concern of theirs. Their wives said it was no concern of theirs. Their aldermen said it was no concern of theirs. Their—

Whenever Roberto Morales spoke, Manuel had to force himself not to answer. He had to keep his temper from flaring.

"Now," announced Morales at last, in his friendliest tone. "Now. I must take two cents from every bucket. I am sorry. There was a miscalculation. Everybody understands. Everybody?" He slid his eyes around smiling, palms up.

The tired, exhausted pickers gasped as one.

Yes. Everyone understood. Freezing in place. After all that hard work.

"Any questions, men?"

Still grinning, knowing, everyone realizing that he had the upper hand, that that would mean a loss of two or three dollars out of each picker's pay that day, a huge windfall for Morales.

"You promised to take nothing!" Manuel heard himself saying. Everyone turned in astonishment to stare at Manuel.

"I said two cents, hombre. You got a problem or what?"

"You promised."

The two men, centered in a huge ring of red-ringed eyes, glared at each other. Reaching for each other's jugular. The other exhausted animals studied the tableau through widening eyes. It was so unequal. Morales remained calm, confident, studying Manuel. As though memorizing his features. He had the whole advantage. Then, with his last remaining energy, Manuel lifted his foot and clumsily tipped over his own last bucket of cots. They rolled away in all directions around everyone's feet.

Roberto Morales' eyes blazed. His fists clenched. "You pick them up, Gutierrez."

So. He knew his name. After all. For answer, Manuel kicked over another bucket, and again the fruit rolled away in all directions.

Then an astonishing thing happened.

All the other pickers moved toward their own buckets still standing beside them on the ground awaiting the truck gatherer, and took an ominous position over them, straddling their feet over them. Without looking around, without taking his eyes off Manuel, Roberto Morales said sharply, "All right. All right, men, I shall take nothing this time."

Manuel felt a thrill of power course through his nerves.

He had never won anything before. He would have to pay for this, for his defiance, somehow, again, later. But he had shown defiance. He had salvaged his money savagely and he had earned respect from his fellow slaves. The gringo hijos de la chingada would never know of this little incident, and would probably be surprised, and perhaps even a little mortified, for a few minutes. But they wouldn't give a damn. It was bread, pan y tortillas out of his children's mouths. But they still wouldn't give a single damn. Manuel had wrenched Morales' greedy fingers away and removed a fat slug of a purse from his sticky grasp. And in his slow way, in his stupid, accidental, dangerous way, Manuel had made an extravagant discovery, as Don Gaspar had also made two centuries before, in almost exactly the same spot. And that was—that a man counted for something. For men, Manuel dimly suspected, are built for something more important and less trifling than the mere gathering of prunes and apricots, hour upon hour, decade upon decade, insensibly, mechanically, antlike. Men are built to experience a certain sense of honor and pride.

Or else they are dead before they die.

DAVID MADDEN

No Trace

Gasping for air, his legs weak from the climb up the stairs, Ernest stopped outside the room, surprised to find the door wide open, almost sorry he had made it before the police. An upsurge of nausea, a wave of suffocation forced him to suck violently for breath as he stepped into Gordon's room—his *own* two decades before.

Tinted psychedelic emerald, the room looked like a hippie pad, posing for a *Life* photograph, but the monotonous electronic frenzy he heard was the seventeen-year locusts, chewing spring leaves outside. He wondered whether the sleeping pills had so dazed him that he had stumbled into the wrong room. No, now, as every time in his own college years when he had entered this room, what struck him first was the light falling through the leaded, green-stained windowglass. As the light steeped him in the ambience of the early forties, it simultaneously illuminated the artifacts of the present. Though groggy from the pills, he experienced, intermittently, moments of startling clarity when he saw each object separately.

Empty beer can pyramids.

James Dean, stark poster photograph.

Records leaning in orange crate.

Life-size red-head girl, banjo blocking her vagina, lurid color.

Rolltop desk, swivel chair, typewriter.

Poster photograph of a teen-age hero he didn't recognize.

Large CORN FLAKES carton.

Ernest recognized nothing, except the encyclopedias, as Gordon's. Debris left behind when Gordon's roommate ran away. Even so, knowing Gordon, Ernest had expected the cleanest room in DeLozier Hall, vacant except for suitcases sitting in a neat row, awaiting the end-of-ceremonies dash to the car. He shut the door quietly, listening to an automatic lock catch, as if concealing not just the few possible incriminating objects he had come to discover, but the entire spectacle of a room startlingly

"No Trace" originally appeared in *The Southern Review*. Reprinted by permission of the Louisiana State University Press.

overpopulated with objects, exhibits, that might bear witness, like archeological unearthings, to the life lived there.

He glanced into the closet. Gordon's suitcases did not have the look of imminent departure. Clothes hung, hangers crammed tightly together, on the rack above. The odor emanating from the closet convulsed him slightly, making him shut his eyes, see Gordon raise his arm, the sleeve of his gown slip down, revealing his white arm, the grenade in his hand. Shaking his head to shatter the image, Ernest opened his eyes, but saw swift images of young men in academic regalia rising from the ground in the front rows, staggering around, stunned, blinded by blood, shrapnel, burning shreds of skin and cloth. Green leaves falling. The force of the concussion spraying locusts that stuck to the clothes of the parents. Old men crawling on their hands and knees in brilliant sunlight at the back of the platform.

Turning abruptly from the closet, Ernest moved aimlessly about the room, distracted by objects that moved toward him. He had to hurry before someone discovered the cot downstairs empty, before police came to lock up Gordon's room. The green light drew him to the window where the babel of locusts was louder. Through the antique glass, he saw, as if under water, the broken folding chairs below, parodying postures into which the explosion had thrown the audience. The last of the curiosity seekers, turning away, trampling locusts, left three policemen alone among knocked-over chairs.

I AM ANONYMOUS/HELP ME. Nailed, buttons encrusted the window-frame. SUPPORT MENTAL HEALTH OR I'LL KILL YOU. SNOOPY FOR PRESIDENT. As he turned away, chalked, smudged lettering among the buttons drew him back: DOCTOR SPOCK IS AN ABORTIONIST. After his roommate ran away, why hadn't Gordon erased that? Jerking his head away from the button again, Ernest saw a ball-point pen sticking up in the desk top. On a piece of paper, the title "The Theme of Self-Hatred in the Works of—" the rest obscured by a blue circular, a message scrawled in lipstick across it: GORDY BABY, LET ME HOLD SOME BREAD FOR THIS CAUSE. MY OLD LADY IS SENDING ME A CHECK NEXT WEEK. *THE* CARTER. The circular pleaded for money for the Civil Liberties Union. Ernest shoved it aside, but "The Theme of Self-Hatred in the Works of—" broke off anyway. Gordon's blue scrapbook, green in the light, startled him. Turning away, Ernest noticed REVOLUTION IN A REVOLUTION? A TOLKIEN READER, BOY SCOUT HANDBOOK in a bookcase.

As he stepped toward the closet, something crunching harshly underfoot made him jump back. Among peanut shells, brown streaks in the green light. Gordon tracking in smashed guts of locusts. Fresh streaks, green juices of leaves acid-turned to slime. He lifted one foot, trying to look at the sole of his shoe, lost balance, staggered backward, let himself drop on the edge of a cot. If investigators compared the stains—using his handkerchief, he wiped the soles. Dying and dead locusts, *The Alumni Bulletin* had reported, had littered the campus paths for weeks. Everywhere, the racket of their devouring machinery, the reek of their putrefaction when they fell, gorged. Sniffing his lapels, he inhaled the stench of locusts and sweat, saw flecks of—he shut his eyes, raked breath into his lungs, lay back on the cot.

Even as he tried to resist the resurgent power of the sleeping pills, Ernest felt his exhausted mind and body sink into sleep. When sirens woke him, he thought for a moment he still lay on the bare mattress in the room downstairs, listening to the siren of that last ambulance. The injured, being carried away on stretchers, passed by him again: the president, five seniors, several faculty members, a famous writer of the thirties scheduled for an honorary degree, a trustee, a parent of one of the graduates. The Dean of Men had hustled Ernest into a vacated room, and sent to his house nearby for sleeping pills. Sinking into sleep, seeing the grenade go off again and again until the explosions became tiny, receding, mute puffs of smoke, Ernest had suddenly imagined Lydia's face when he would have to telephone her about Gordon, and the urgency of being prepared for the police had made him sit up in bed. The hall was empty, everyone seemed to be outside, and he had sneaked up the narrow back stairway to Gordon's room.

Wondering which cot was Gordon's, which his roommate's, and why *both* had recently been slept in, Ernest sat up and looked along the wooden frame for the cigarette burns he had deliberately made the day before his own commencement when he and his roommate were packing for home. As he leaned across the cot, looking for the burn, his hand grazed a stiff yellow spot on the sheet. The top sheet stuck to the bottom sheet. An intuition of his son's climactic moment in an erotic dream the night before—the effort to keep from crying choked him. "I advocate—" Leaping away from the cot, he stopped, reeling, looked up at a road sign that hung over the door: DRIVE SLOWLY, WE LOVE OUR KIDS. Somewhere an unprotected street. What's-his-name's fault. *His* junk cluttered the room.

Wondering what the suitcases would reveal, Ernest stepped into the closet. Expecting them to be packed, he jerked up on them and jolted himself, they were so light. He opened them anyway. Crumbs of dirt, curls of lint. Gordon's clothes, that Lydia had helped him select, or sent him as birthday or Easter presents, hung in the closet, pressed. Fetid clothes Gordon's roommate—Carter, yes Carter—had left behind dangled from hooks, looking more like costumes. A theatrical black leather jacket, faded denim pants, a wide black belt, ruby studs, a jade velvet cape, and, on the floor, boots and sandals. In a dark corner leaned the hooded golf clubs Ernest had handed down to Gordon, suspecting he would never lift them from the bag. "You don't like to hunt," he had blurted out one evening. "You don't like to fish. You don't get excited about football. Isn't there *some*thing we could do together?" "We could just sit and talk." They had ended up watching the Ed Sullivan Show.

Ernest's hand, paddling fish-like among the clothes in the dim closet, snagged on a pin that fastened a price tag to one of the suits he had bought Gordon for Christmas. Though he knew from Lydia that no girl came regularly on weekends from Melbourne's sister college to visit Gordon, surely he had had some occasion to wear the suit. Stacked on the shelf above: shirts, the cellophane packaging unbroken. His fingers inside one of the cowboy boots, Ernest stroked leather that was still flesh soft. Imagining Lydia's hysteria at the sight of Gordon, he saw a mortician handling Gordon's body, sorting, arranging pieces, saw not Gordon's, but the body of one of his clients on view, remembering how awed he had been by the miracle of skill that had put the man back together only three days after the factory explosion. Ernest stroked a damp polo shirt, unevenly stained pale green in the wash, sniffed it, realizing that Carter's body could not have left an odor that lasting. Now he understood what had disturbed him about Gordon's clothes, showing, informal and ragged, under the skirt of the black gown, at the sleeves, at the neck, as he sat on the platform, waiting to deliver the valedictory address.

Gripping the iron pipe that held the hangers, shoved tightly together, his body swinging forward as his knees sagged, Ernest let the grenade explode again. Gentle, almost delicate, Gordon suddenly raises his voice above the nerve-wearying shrill of the seventeen-year locusts that encrust the barks of the trees, a voice that had been too soft to be heard except by the men on the platform whose faces expressed shock—at *what* Ernest still did not know—and as that voice screams, a high-pitched nasal screech like brass, "I advocate a total revolution!" Gordon's left arm raises a grenade, holds it out before him, eclipsing his still-open mouth, and in his right hand, held down stiff at his side, the pin glitters on his fingers. Frightened, raring back, as Ernest himself does, in their seats, many people try to laugh the grenade off as a bold but imprudent rhetorical gesture.

Tasting again Gordon's blood on his mouth, Ernest thrust his face between smothering wool coats, retched again, vomited at last.

A key thrust into the lock, the door opened.

"You sure this is the one?"

"Don't it look like it?"

"What's that smell?"

"Lock it back and give the Marshal the key."

"This'll lock automatically, won't it?"

"Just push in on that gismo."

The voices and the lock catching roused Ernest from a stupor of convulsion.

As he tried to suck air into his lungs, gluey bands of vomit strangled him, lack of oxygen smothered him. Staggering backward out of the closet, he stood in the middle of the room, swaying. Avoiding Gordon's, he lowered himself carefully onto the edge of Carter's cot by the closet. He craved air but the stained-glass window, the only window in this corner room, wouldn't open, a disadvantage that came with the privilege of having the room with the magnificent light. The first time he had seen the room since his graduation—he and Lydia had brought Gordon down to begin his freshman year—he had had to heave breath up from dry lungs to tell Gordon about the window. Early in the nineteenth century when DeLozier Hall was the entire school—and already one of the finest boys' colleges in the midwest—this corner room and the two adjacent comprised the chapel. From the fire that destroyed DeLozier Hall in 1938, three years before Ernest himself arrived as a freshman, only this window was saved. Except for the other chapel windows, DeLozier had been restored, brick by brick, exactly as it was originally. "First chance you get, go look in the cemetery at the grave of the only victim of the fire—nobody knows who it was, so the remains were never claimed. Probably somebody just passing through." He had deliberately saved that to leave Gordon with something interesting to think about. From the edge of the cot, he saw the bright eruption of vomit on Gordon's clothes.

The chapel steeple chimed four o'clock. The racket of the locusts' mandibles penetrated the room as if carried in through the green light. Photosynthesis. Chlorophyll. The D+ in biology that wrecked his average.

Rising, he took out his handkerchief and went into the closet. When the handkerchief was sopping wet, he dropped it into a large beer carton, tasting again the foaming beer at his lips, tingling beads on his tongue in the hot tent on the lawn as the ceremonies were beginning. He had reached the green just as the procession was forming. "You've been accepted by Harvard Grad School." Gordon had looked at him without a glimmer of recognition—Ernest had assumed that the shrilling of the locusts had drowned out his voice—then led his classmates toward the platform. Ernest was standing on a dirty tee shirt. He finished the job with that, leaving a corner to wipe his hands on, then he dropped it, also, into the carton.

He sat on the edge of the cot again, afraid to lie back on the mattress, to sink into the gulley Carter had made over the four years and fall asleep. He only leaned back, propped on one arm. Having collected himself, he would make a thorough search, to prepare himself for whatever the police would find, tag, then show him for final identification. An exhibit of shocks. The police might even hold him responsible somehow—delinquently ignorant of his son's habits, associates. They might even find something that would bring in the F.B.I.—membership in some radical organization. What was *not* possible in a year like this? He had to arm himself against interrogation. "What sort of boy was your son?" "Typical, average, normal boy in every way. Ask my wife." But how many times had he read that in newspaper accounts of monstrous crimes? What did it mean anymore to be normal?

Glancing around the room, on the verge of an unsettling realization, Ernest saw a picture of Lydia leaning on Carter's rolltop desk. Even in shadow the enlarged snapshot he had taken himself was radiant. A lucid April sunburst in the budding trees behind her bleached her green dress white, made her blond hair look almost platinum. Clowning, she had kicked out one foot, upraising and spreading her arms, and when her mouth finished yelling "Spring!" he had snapped her dimpled smile. On the campus of Melbourne's sister college, Briarheath, locusts riddled those same trees, twenty years taller, forty miles from where he sat, while Lydia languished in bed alone—a mysterious disease, a lingering illness. Then the shunned realization came, made him stand up as though he were an intruder. On this cot, or perhaps the one across the room, he had made love to Lydia—that spring, the first and only time before their marriage. In August, she had discovered that she was pregnant. Gordon had never for a moment given them cause to regret that inducement to marriage. But Lydia's cautionary approach to sexual relations had made Gordon an only child.

Glancing around the room again, he hoped to discover a picture of himself. Seeing none, he sat down again. Under his thumb, he felt a rough texture on the wooden frame of the cot. The cigarette burn he had made himself in 1945. Then *this* had been Gordon's cot. Of course. By his desk. Flinging back the sheets, Ernest found nothing.

He crossed the room to Carter's cot where a dime store reproduction of a famous painting of Jesus hung on the wall. Jerking hard to unstick the sheets, he lay bare Carter's bed. Twisted white sweat socks at the bottom. He shook them out. Much too large for Gordon. But Carter, then Gordon, had worn them with Carter's cowboy boots. Gordon had been sleeping in Carter's bed. Pressing one knee against the edge of the cot, Ernest leaned over and pushed his palms against the wall to examine closely what it was that had disturbed him about the painting. Tiny holes like acne scars in Jesus' upturned face. Ernest looked up. Ragged, feathered darts hung like bats from the ceiling. Someone had printed in Gothic script on the bottom white border: J. C. BLOWS. Using his fingernails, Ernest scraped at the edge of the tape, pulled carefully, but white wall paint chipped off, exposing the wallpaper design that dated back to his own life in the room. He stopped, aware that he had only started his search, that if he took this painting, he might be inclined to take other things. His intention, he stressed again to himself, was only to investigate, to be forewarned, not to search and destroy. But already he had the beer carton containing Carter's, or Gordon's, tee shirt and his own handkerchief to dispose of. He let the picture hang, one edge curling over, obscuring the lettering.

Backing into the center of the room, one leg painfully asleep, Ernest looked at a life-sized girl stuck to the wall with masking tape, holding a banjo over her vagina, the neck of it between her breasts, tip of her tongue touching one of the tuning knobs. His eyes on a sticker stuck to the pane, he went to the window again: FRUIT OF THE LOOM. 100% VIRGIN COTTON. More buttons forced him to read: WAR IS GOOD BUSINESS, INVEST YOUR SON. How would the police separate Carter's from Gordon's things? FLOWER POWER. He would simply tell them that Carter had left this junk behind when he bolted. But Gordon's failure to discard some of it, at least the most offensive items, bewildered Ernest. One thing appeared clear: living daily since January among Carter's possessions, Gordon had worn Carter's clothes, slept in Carter's bed.

From the ceiling above the four corners of the room hung the blank faces of the amplifiers, dark mouths gaping. Big Brother is listening. *1984.* Late Show. Science Fiction bored Ernest. Squatting, he flipped through records leaning in a Sunkist orange crate: MILES DAVIS/ THE GRATEFUL DEAD/ LEADBELLY/ THE BEATLES, their picture red X-ed out/ MANTOVANI/ THE MAMAS AND THE PAPAS/ THE LOVING SPOONFUL. He was wasting time—Carter's records couldn't be used against Gordon. But then he found Glenn Miller's "In the Mood" and "Moonlight Serenade," a 78 rpm collector's item he had given Gordon. "Soothing background music for test-cramming time." TOM PAXTON/ THE MOTHERS OF INVENTION/ 1812 OVERTURE (Gordon's?)/ THE ELECTRONIC ERA/ JOAN BAEZ/ CHARLIE PARKER/ BARTOK.

Rising, he saw a poster he had not glimpsed before, stuck to the wall with a bowie knife, curled inward at its four corners: a color photograph of a real banana rising like a finger out of the middle of a cartoon fist.

Over the rolltop desk hung a guitar, its mouth crammed full of wilted roses. The vomit taste in his own mouth made Ernest retch. Hoping Carter had left some whiskey behind, he quickly searched the rolltop desk, finding a Jack Daniels bottle in one of the cubbyholes. Had Gordon taken the last swallow himself this morning just before stepping out of this room?

Finding a single cigarette in a twisted package, Ernest lit it, quickly snuffed it in a hubcap used as an ashtray. The smell of fresh smoke would make the police suspicious. Recent daily activity had left Carter's desk a shambles. Across the room, Gordon's desk was merely a surface, strewn with junk. The Royal portable typewriter he had given Gordon for Christmas his freshman year sat on Carter's desk, the capital lock key set.

Among the papers on Carter's desk, Ernest searched for Gordon's notes for his speech. Ernest had been awed by the way Gordon prepared his senior project in high school—very carefully, starting with an outline, going through three versions, using cards, dividers, producing a forty-page research paper on Wordsworth. Lydia had said, "Why, Ernest, he's been that way since junior high, worrying about college." On Carter's desk, Ernest found the beginnings of papers on Dryden, *The Iliad, Huckleberry Finn.* While he had always felt contentment in Gordon's perfect social behavior and exemplary academic conduct and achievements, sustained from grammar school right on through college, Ernest had sometimes felt, but quickly dismissed, a certain dismay. In her presence, Ernest agreed with Lydia's objections to Gordon's desire to major in English, but alone with him, he had told Gordon, "Satisfy yourself first of all." But he couldn't tell Gordon that he had pretended to agree with his mother to prevent her from exaggerating her suspicion that their marriage had kept him from switching to English himself after he got his B.S. in Business Administration. Each time she brought up the subject, Ernest wondered for weeks what his life would have been like had he become an English professor. As he hastily surveyed the contents of the desk, he felt the absence of the papers Gordon had written that had earned A's, helping to qualify him, as the student with the highest honors, to give the valedictory address.

Handling chewed pencils made Ernest sense the taste of lead and wood on his own tongue. He noticed a CORN FLAKES box but was distracted by a ball-point pen that only great force could have thrust so firmly into the oak desk. The buffalo side of a worn nickel leaned against a bright Kennedy half-dollar. Somewhere under this floor lay a buffalo nickel he had lost himself through a crack. Perhaps Gordon or Carter had found it. He unfolded a letter. It thanked Carter for his two hundred dollar contribution to a legal defense fund for students who had gone without permission to Cuba. Pulling another letter out of a pigeonhole, he discovered a bright gold piece resembling a medal. Trojan contraceptive. His own brand before Lydia became bedridden. Impression of it still on his wallet—no, that was the *old* wallet he carried as a senior. The letter thanked Carter for his inquiry about summer work with an organization sponsored by SNCC. In another pigeonhole, he found a letter outlining Carter's duties during a summer voter campaign in Mississippi. "As for the friend you mention, we don't believe it would be in our best interests to attempt to persuade him to join our work. If persuasion is desirable, who is more strategically situated than you, his own roommate?" Marginal scrawl in pencil: "This is the *man* talking, Baby!"

As he rifled through the numerous letters, folded hastily and slipped or stuffed into pigeonholes, Ernest felt he was getting an overview of liberal and left-wing activities, mostly student-oriented, over the past five years, for Carter's associations began in high school. He lifted his elbow off Gordon's scrapbook—birthday present from Lydia—and flipped through it. Newspaper photo of students at a rally, red ink enringing a blurred head, a raised fist. Half full: clippings of Carter's activities. AP photo: Carter, bearded, burning his draft card. But no creep—handsome, hair and smile like Errol Flynn in *The Sea Hawk*. Looking around at the poster photograph he hadn't recognized when he came in, Ernest saw Carter, wearing a Gestapo billcap, a monocle, an opera cape, black tights, Zorro boots, carrying a riding crop. When Ernest first noticed the ads—"Blow Yourself Up"—he had thought it a good deal at $2.99. Had Gordon given the scrapbook to Carter, or had he cut and pasted the items himself?

Ernest shoved the scrapbook aside and reached for a letter. "Gordy, This is just to tell you to save your tears over King. We all wept over JFK our senior year in high school, and we haven't seen straight since. King just wasn't where the action's at. Okay, so I told you different a few months ago! How come you're always light years behind *me*? Catch up! Make the leap! I'm dumping all these creeps that try to play a rigged game. Look at Robert! I think I'm beginning to understand Oswald and Speck and Whitman. They're the *real* individuals! They work alone while we run together like zebras. But, on the other hand, maybe the same cat did *all* those jobs. And maybe Carter knows who. Sleep on *that* one, Gordy, Baby." Los Angeles, April 5. Suddenly, the first day back from Christmas vacation, Carter had impulsively walked out of this room. "See America first! Then the world!" That much Gordon had told them when Ernest and Lydia telephoned at Easter, made uneasy by his terse letter informing them that he was remaining on campus to "watch the locusts emerge from their seventeen-year buried infancy into appalling one-week adulthood," adding parenthetically, that he had to finish his honors project. Marriage to Lydia had prevented Ernest's desire, like Carter's, to see the world. Not "prevented." Postponed perhaps. A vice-president of a large insurance company might hope to make such a dream come true—if only after he retired. Deep in a pigeonhole, Ernest found a snap-shot of Gordon, costumed for a part in *Tom Sawyer*—one of the kids who saunter by in the whitewashing scene. False freckles. He had forgotten. On the back, tabs of fuzzy black paper —ripped out of the scrapbook.

Mixed in with Carter's were Lydia's letters. "Gordon, Precious, You promised—" Feverish eyes. Bed rashes. Blue Cross. Solitude. Solitaire. "Sleep, Lydia." Finding none of his own letters, Ernest remembered writing last week from his office, and the sense of solitude on the fifteenth floor, where he had seemed the only person stirring, came back momentarily. Perhaps in some drawer or secret compartment all his letters to Gordon (few though they had been) and perhaps other little mementos —his sharp-shooters' medal and the Korean coin that he had given

Gordon, relics of his three years in the service, and matchbooks from the motels where he and Gordon had stayed on occasional weekend trips—were stored. Surely, somewhere in the room, he would turn up a picture of himself. He had always known that Gordon preferred his mother, but had he conscientiously excluded his father from his life, eliminating all trace? No, he shouldn't jump to conclusions. He had yet to gather and analyze all the evidence. Thinking in those terms about what he was doing, Ernest realized that not only was he going to destroy evidence to protect Gordon's memory as much as possible and shield Lydia, he was now deliberately searching for fragments of a new Gordon, hoping to know and understand him, each discovery destroying the old Gordon who would now always remain a stranger.

But he didn't have time to move so slowly, like a slow-motion movie. Turning quickly in Carter's swivel chair, Ernest bent over the large CORN FLAKES box, brimful of papers that had been dropped, perhaps tossed, into it. Gordon's themes, including his honors thesis in a stiff black binder: "ANGUISH, SPIRITUAL AND PHYSICAL, IN GERARD MANLEY HOPKINS' POETRY. Approved by: Alfred Hansen, Thorne Halpert (who had come to Melbourne in Ernest's own freshman year), Richard Kelp, John Morton." In red pencil at the bottom, haphāzard scrawls, as if they were four different afterthoughts: "*Dis*approved by: Jason Carter, Gordon Foster, Lydia Foster, Gerard Manley Hopkins." Up the left margin, in lead pencil: "PISS ON *ALL* OF YOU!" Ernest saw Gordon burning the box in the community dump on the edge of the village.

Ernest stepped over to Gordon's desk, seeking some sort of perspective, some evidence of Gordon's life before he moved over to the rolltop desk and mingled his own things with Carter's. The gray steel drawers were empty. Not just empty. Clean. Wiped clean with a rag—a swipe in the middle drawer had dried in a soapy pattern of broken beads of moisture. Ernest saw there an image: a clean table that made him feel the presence behind him of another table where Gordon, now in pieces, lay. Under dirty clothes slung aside lay stacks of books and old newspapers, whose headlines of war, riot, murder, assassinations, negotiations seemed oddly remote in this room. The portable tape-recorder Ernest had given Gordon last fall to help him through his senior year. He pressed the LISTEN button. Nothing. He pressed the REWIND. LISTEN. ". . . defy analysis. But let's examine this passage from Aristotle's *De Interpretatione*: 'In the case of that which is or which has taken place, propositions, whether positive or negative, must be true or false.' " "What did he say?" Someone whispering. "I didn't catch it." (Gordon's voice?) "Again, in the case of a pair of contraries—contradictories, that is . . ." The professor's voice slipped into a fizzing silence. "I'm recording your speech, son," he had written to Gordon last week, "so your mother can hear it." But Ernest had forgotten his tape-recorder.

The headline of a newspaper announced Charlie Whitman's sniper slaying of twelve people from the observation tower of the university administration building in Austin, Texas. But that was two summers past. Melbourne had no summer school. Folded, as though mailed. Had Carter sent it to Gordon from—Where *was* Carter from? Had Gordon received it at home?

A front-page news photo showed a Buddhist monk burning on a Saigon street corner. Ernest's sneer faded in bewilderment as he saw that the caption identified an American woman burning on the steps of the Pentagon. Smudged pencil across the flames: THE MOTHER OF US ALL. Children bereft, left to a father, perhaps no father even. Ernest tried to remember the name of one of his clients, an English professor, who had shot himself a week after the assassination of Martin Luther King. No note. Any connection? His wife showed Ernest the Student Guide to Courses—one anonymous, thus sexless, student's evaluation might have been a contributing factor: "This has got to be the most boring human being on the face of the earth." Since then, Ernest had tried to make his own presentations at company meetings more entertaining. Lately, many cases of middle-aged men who had mysteriously committed suicide hovered on the periphery of Ernest's consciousness. It struck him now that in every case, he had forgotten most of the "sensible" explanations, leaving nothing but mystery. Wondering whether those men had seen something in the eyes of their children, even their wives, that Ernest himself had been blind to, he shuddered but did not shake off a sudden clenching of muscles in his shoulders. "When the cause of death is legally ruled as suicide," he had often written, "the company is relieved of its obligations to—" Did Gordon *know* the grenade would explode? Or did he borrow it, perhaps steal it from a museum, and then did it, like the locusts, seventeen years dormant, suddenly come alive? Ernest had always been lukewarm about gun controls, but now he would insist on a thorough investigation to determine where Gordon purchased the grenade. Dealer in war surplus? Could they prove he meant it to go off? "When the cause of death is legally ruled—" Horrified that he was thinking so reflexively like an insurance executive, Ernest slammed his fist into his groin, and staggered back into the bed Gordon had abandoned.

His eyes half-opened, he saw his cigarette burn again on the wooden frame beside his hand. He recalled Gordon's vivid letter home the first week of his freshman year: "My roommate turns my stomach by the way he dresses, talks, acts, eats, sleeps." Ernest had thought that a boy so different from Gordon would be good for him, so his efforts, made at Lydia's fretful urgings, to have Carter replaced, or to have Gordon moved, were slapdash. He very much wanted his son to go through Melbourne in his old room. Books on Gordon's desk at the foot of the cot caught his attention. Some dating from junior high, these were all Gordon's including the Great Books, with their marvelous Syntopicon. As the swelling pain in his groin subsided, Ernest stood up, hovered over the books.

A frayed copy of *Winnie the Pooh* startled him. "To Ernest, Christmas, 1928. All my love, Grandmother." The year he learned to write, Gordon had printed his own name in green crayon across the top of the next page. As Ernest leafed through the book, nostalgia eased his nerves. Penciled onto Winnie the Pooh was a gigantic penis extending across the page to Christopher Robin, who was bending over a daisy. "Damn you, Carter!" Ernest slammed it down—a pillar of books slurred, tumbled onto the floor. He stood still, staring into the green light, trying to detect the voices of people who might have heard in the rooms below. Ernest heard only the locusts in the light. A newspaper that had fallen leaned and sagged like a tent: Whitman's face looked up from the floor, two teeth in his high school graduation smile blacked out, a pencil-drawn tongue flopping out of his mouth. His name was scratched out and YOU AND ME, BABY was lettered in. Ernest kicked at the newspaper, twisted his heel into Whitman's face, and the paper rose up around his ankles like a yellowed flower, soot-dappled.

Ernest backed into the swivel chair, turned, rested his head in his hands on the rolltop desk, and breathed in fits and starts. He wanted to throw the hubcap ashtray through the stained-glass window and feel the spring air rush in upon his face and fill and stretch his lungs. Cigarillo butts, scorched Robert Burns bands, cigarette butts. Marijuana? He sniffed, but realized he couldn't recognize it if it *were*.

Was there nothing in the room but pale emanations of Carter's gradual transformation of Gordon? Closing his eyes, trying to conjure up Gordon's face, he saw, clearly, only Carter's smile, like a weapon, in the draft-card burning photograph. *Wanting* to understand Gordon, he had only a shrill scream of defiance, an explosion, and this littered room with which to begin. He imagined the mortician, fitting pieces together, an arm on a drain board behind him. And when he was finished, what would he have accomplished? In the explosion, Gordon had vacated his body, and now the pieces had stopped moving, but the objects in his room twitched when Ernest touched them. Taking a deep breath, he inhaled the stench of spit and tobacco. He shoved the hubcap aside, and stood up.

Bending his head sideways, mashing his ear against his shoulder, Ernest read the titles of books crammed into cinderblock and pineboard shelves between Carter's cot and the window: 120 DAYS OF SODOM, the Marquis de Sade/ AUTOBIOGRAPHY OF MALCOLM X/ THE POSTMAN ALWAYS RINGS TWICE, James M. Cain/ MEIN KAMPF —He caught himself reading titles and authors aloud in a stupor. Silently, his lips still moving, he read: BOY SCOUT HANDBOOK. Though he had never been a scout, Ernest had agreed with Lydia that, like a fraternity, it would be good for Gordon in future life. FREEDOM NOW, Max Reiner/ NAUSEA, Jean-Paul Sartre/ ATLAS SHRUGGED, Ayn Rand/ THE SCARLET LETTER. Heritage, leather-bound edition he had given Gordon for his sixteenth birthday. He had broken in the new Volkswagen, a surprise graduation present, driving it down. Late for the ceremonies, he had parked it illegally behind DeLozier Hall so it would be there when he and Gordon brought the suitcases and his other belongings down. CASTRO'S CAUSE, Harvey Kreyborg/ NOTES FROM UNDERGROUND, Dostoyevski/ LADY CHATTERLEY'S LOVER, Ernest's own copy. Had Gordon sneaked it out of the house? Slumping to his knees, he squinted at titles he had been unable to make out: Carter had cynically shelved Ernest's own copy of PROFILES IN COURAGE, passed on to Gordon, next to OSWALD RESURRECTED by Eugene Federogh.

There was a book with a library number on its spine. He would have to return that. The Gordon he had known would have done so before commencement. Afraid the police might come in suddenly and catch him there, Ernest rose to his feet. Glancing through several passages, highlighted with a yellow magic-marker, he realized that he was reading about "anguish, spiritual and physical, in Gerard Manley Hopkins' poetry." He rooted through the CORN FLAKES box again, took out Gordon's honors thesis. Flipping through the pages, he discovered a passage that duplicated, verbatim, a marked passage in the book. No footnote reference. The bibliography failed to cite the book that he held in his hand and now let drop along with the honors thesis into the beer carton onto Carter's fouled tee shirt and Ernest's handkerchief.

Why had he cheated? He never had before. Or had he plagiarized *all* those papers, from junior high on up to this one? No, surely, this time only. Ernest himself had felt the pressure in his senior year, and most of the boys in his fraternity had cheated when they really *had* to. Now he felt compelled to search thoroughly, examine everything carefully. The police had no right to invade a dead boy's privacy and plunge his invalid mother into grief.

In Carter's desk drawers, Ernest searched more systematically among letters and notes, still expecting to discover an early draft of Gordon's unfinished speech; perhaps it would be full of clues. He might even find the bill of sale for the grenade. Across the naked belly of a girl ripped from a magazine was written: "Gordy—" Carter had even renamed, rechristened Gordon. "Jeff and Conley and I are holding a peace vigil in the cold rain tonight, all night. Bring us a fresh jar of water at midnight. And leave your goddamn middle-class mottos in the room. Love, Carter."

A letter from Fort Jackson, South Carolina, April 20, 1968. "Dear Gordon, I am being shipped to Vietnam. I will never see you again. I have not forgotten what you said to me that night in our room across the

Dark Gulf between our cots. As always, Carter." Without knowing what Carter meant, Ernest knew that gulf himself. He had tried to bridge it, touch Scott, his own roommate, whose lassitude about life's possibilities often provoked Ernest to wall-pounding rage. He had finally persuaded Scott to take a trip West with him right after graduation. Scott's nonchalant withdrawal at the last minute was so dispiriting that Ernest had accepted his father's offer of a summer internship with the insurance company as a claims adjustor.

A 1967 letter described in detail the march on the Pentagon. "What are you doing down there, you little fink? You should be up here with the rest of us. My brothers have been beaten by the cops. I'm not against the use of napalm in *some* instances. Just don't let me get my hands on any of it when those pig sonofabitches come swinging their sticks at us. We're rising up all over the world, Baby—or didn't you know it, with your nose in Chaucer's tales. Melbourne is about due to be hit so you'd better decide whose side you're on. I heard about this one campus demonstration where somebody set fire to this old fogey's life-long research on some obscure hang-up of his. I can think of a few at Melbourne that need shaking up." Ernest was shocked, then surprised at himself for being shocked. He wondered how Gordon had felt.

As Ernest pulled a postcard out of a pigeonhole, a white capsule rolled out into his hand. For a common cold, or LSD? He stifled an impulse to swallow it. By chance escape what chance might reveal. He flipped the capsule against the inside of the CORN FLAKES box and it popped like a cap pistol. Comic postcard—out-house, hillbillies—mailed from Alabama, December 12, 1966. "Gordy, Baby, Wish you were here. You sure as hell ain't all *there*! Love, till death do us part, Carter." In several letters, Carter fervently attempted to persuade Gordon to abandon his "middle-class Puritan Upforcing" and embrace the cause of world brotherhood, which itself embraced all other great causes of "our time." But even through the serious ones ran a trace of self-mockery. He found Carter's draft notice, his *own* name crossed out, Gordon's typed in. Across the body of the form letter, dated January 1, 1968, was printed in Gothic script: NON SERVIUM.

As Ernest reached for a bunch of postcards, he realized that he was eager not only to discover more about Gordon, but to assemble into some shape the fragments of Carter's life. A series of postcards with cryptic, taunting messages traced Carter's trail over the landscape of America, from early January to the middle of March, 1968. From Carmel, California, a view of a tower and cypress trees: "Violence is the sire of all the world's values." Ernest remembered the card Gordon sent him from Washington, D. C. when he was in junior high: "Dear Dad, Our class went to see Congress but they were closed. Our teacher got mad. She dragged us all to the Smithsonian and showed us Lindbergh's airplane.

It was called THE SPIRIT OF ST. LOUIS. I didn't think it looked so hot. Mrs. Landis said she saved the headlines when she was in high school. Did you? Your son, Gordon."

Ernest found a night letter from Lynn, Massachusetts. "Dear Gordon, Remembering that Jason spoke of you so often and so fondly, his father and I felt certain that you would not want to learn through the newspapers that our dear son has been reported missing in action. While no one can really approve in his heart of this war, Jason has always been the sort of boy who believed in dying for his convictions. We know that you will miss him. He loved you as though you were his own brother. Affectionate regards, Grace and Harold Carter." June 1, 1968, three days ago.

Trembling, Ernest sought more letters from Carter. One from boot camp summed up, in wild, impassioned prose, Carter's opinions on Civil Rights, the war, and "the American Dream that's turned into a nightmare." In another, "God is dead and buried on LBJ's ranch" dispensed with religion and politics, "inseparable." May 4, 1968. "Dear Gordy, We are in the jungle now, on a search and destroy mission. You have to admire some of these platoon leaders. I must admit I enjoy watching them act out their roles as all-American tough guys. They have a kind of style, anyway. In here you don't have time to analyze your thoughts. But I just thought a word or two written at the scene of battle might bring you the smell of smoke." Ernest sniffed the letter, uncertain whether the faint smell came from the paper.

He pulled a wadded letter out of a pigeonhole where someone had stuffed it. As he unwadded the note, vicious ball-point pen markings wove a mesh over the words: "Gordon, I'm moving in with Conley. Pack my things and set them in the hall. I don't even want to *enter* that room again. What you said last night made me sick. I've lived with you for three and a half years because I was always convinced that I could save your soul. But after last night, I know it's hopeless. Carter." Across the "Dark Gulf" between their beds, what could *Gordon* have said to shock Carter? Had Gordon persuaded him to stay after all? Or was it the next day that Carter had "impulsively" run away? Ernest searched quickly through the rest of the papers, hoping no answer existed, but knowing that if one did and he failed to find it, the police wouldn't fail.

"Gordy, Baby, Everything you read is lies! I've been in the field three weeks now. My whole life's search ends here, in this burning village, where I'm taking time to write to you. Listen, Baby, this is life! This is what it's all about. In the past weeks I've personally set fire to thirty-seven huts belonging to Viet Cong sympathizers. Don't listen to those sons-of-bitches who whine and gripe and piss and moan about this war. This is a *just* war. We're on the right side, man, the *right* side. This place has opened my eyes and heart, baby. With the bullets and the blood all around, you see things clearer. Words! To hell with words! All these beady-eyed little bastards understand is *bullets,* and a knife now and then. These bastards killed my buddy, a Black boy by the name of Bird. The greatest guy that ever lived. Well, there's ten Viet Cong that ain't alive today because of what they did to my buddy, and there'll be another hundred less Viet Cong if I can persuade them to send me out after I'm due to be pulled back. Yesterday, I found a Viet Cong in a hut with his goddamn wife and kids. I turned the flame thrower on the sons-of-bitches and when the hut burned down, I pissed on the hot ashes. I'm telling you all this to open your eyes, mister. This is the way it really is. Join your ass up, get over here where you belong. Forget everything I ever said to you or wrote to you before. I have seen the light. The future of the world will be decided right here. And I will fight until the last Viet Cong is dead. Always, your friend, Carter." May 21, 1968, two weeks ago.

Trying to feel as Gordon had felt reading this letter, feeling nothing, Ernest remembered Gordon's response to a different piece of information some kid in grammar school dealt him when he was eleven. Having informed Gordon that Santa Claus was a lie, he added the observation that nobody ever knows who his real father and mother are. Just as Ernest stepped into the house from the office, Gordon had asked: "Are you my real father?" In the living room where colored lights blazed on the tree, Lydia was weeping. It took two months to rid Gordon of the fantasy that he had been adopted. Or had he simply stopped interrogating them? But how did a man know *any*thing? Did that professor ever suspect that one day in print he would be labeled "the most boring man on the face of the earth"? Did Carter ever sense he would end up killing men in Vietnam? Did Gordon ever suspect that on his graduation day—

Now the day began to make sense. After Carter's letter from Vietnam, reversing everything he had preached to Gordon, Gordon had let his studies slide, and then the plagiarism had just happened, the way things will, because how could he really care anymore? Then did the night letter from Carter's mother shock him into pulling the grenade pin? Was "I advocate a total revolution!" Gordon's *own* climax to the attitude expressed in Carter's Vietnam letter? Or did the *old* Carter finally speak through Gordon's mouth? These possibilities made sense, but Ernest felt nothing.

His foot kicked a metal wastebasket under Carter's desk. Squatting, he pulled it out, and, sitting again in the swivel chair, began to unwad several letters. "Dear Dad—" The rest blank. "Dear Dad—" Blank. "Dear Dad—" Blank. "Dear Father—" Blank. "Dear Dad—" Blank.

Ernest swung around in Carter's chair, rocked once, got to his feet, stood in the middle of the room, his hands dangling in front of him, the leaded moldings of the window cast black wavy lines over his suit, the green light stained his hands, his heart beat so fast he became aware that he was panting. Like a dog. His throat felt dry, his tongue swollen, eyes burning from reading in the oblique light. Dark spots of sweat on the floor. "Gordon. Gordon. Gordon."

Whatever Gordon had said in his valedictory address, Ernest knew that certain things in this room would give the public the wrong image of his son. Or perhaps—he faced it—the right image. Wrong or right, it would incite the disease in Lydia's body to riot and she would burn. He rolled the desk top down and began stuffing things into the beer carton. When it was full, he emptied the contents of the CORN FLAKES box onto the desk, throwing only the honors thesis back into it. When he jerked the bowie knife out of the wall, the banana poster fell. He scraped at the clotting vomit on the clothes hanging in the closet, and wiped the blade on the sole of his shoe. Then he filled the CORN FLAKES box with letters and other incriminating objects.

He opened the door and looked out. The hall was dim and deserted. The surviving seniors had gone home, though some must have lingered behind with wounded classmates, teachers, parents. The police would still be occupied with traffic. The back staircase was dark. He stacked the beer carton on top of the CORN FLAKES box, lifted both in his arms, and started to back out the door. But under the rolltop desk in a bed of lint lay a piece of paper that, even wadded up, resembled a telegram. Setting the boxes down, the cardboard already dark brown where he had pressed his forehead, Ernest got on his knees and reached under the desk. Without rising, he unwadded the paper. URGENT YOU RENEW SUBSCRIPTION TO TIME AT STUDENT RATE. STOP. WORLD NEWS AT YOUR FINGERTIPS. STOP. Mock telegram technique, special reply pencil enclosed.

The boxes were heavier as Ernest lifted them again and backed out the door, almost certain that the grenade had not been a rhetorical flourish. Bracing the boxes against the wall, lifting his knee under them, Ernest quickly reached out, pulled at the door knob. When the door slammed, locked, startling him, he grabbed the boxes as they almost tipped over into the stairwell.

He had to descend very slowly. The narrow staircase curved twice before it reached the basement. His shoulder slid along the wall as he went down, carefully, step by step. The bottom of the box cut into his palms, sweat tickled his spine, and his thighs chafed each other as sweat dried on his flesh. He saw nothing until he reached the basement where twilight coming through the window of the door revealed the furnace. As he fumbled for the knob, already the devouring locusts jangled in his ears like a single note quivering relentlessly on a violin.

Locusts had dropped from the ivy onto the black hood of the Volkswagen, parked up tight against the building. He opened the trunk, set the boxes inside, closed the lid, locked it.

As he got in behind the wheel, a glimpse of the cemetery behind the dormitory made him recall the grave that had so awed him during his freshman year. From where he sat, turning the ignition key, the larger tombs of the historic dead obscured the small white stone, but he had not forgotten the epitaph: HERE LIES AN UNIDENTIFIED VICTIM OF THE FIRE THAT RAZED DELOZIER HALL, MAY 16, 1938. Since all the Melbourne students had been accounted for, he (or perhaps she) must have been a visitor.

Pulling off the highway, he drove along a dirt trail, new grass sprouting between the wheel ruts. Here, as visible evidence testified, Melbourne students brought the girls who came down from Briarheath. Parked, he let dusk turn to dark.

Then he left the woods, lights dimmed until he got onto the highway. On the outskirts of the town, looking at this distance like a village erected in one of those elaborate electric train sets, he turned onto a cinder road and stopped at a gate, got out, lifted the latch, drove through, then went back and closed the gate.

Headlights off, he eased over the soft, sooty dirt road, the rough bushes on each side a soft gray blur, into the main lot, where the faculty and other townspeople dumped junk and garbage.

The smell made him aware of the taste at the back of his mouth, the stench of burning rubber and plastic and dead animals made his headache pound more fiercely, his left eyelid beat like a pulse.

He unlocked the trunk, lifted out the CORN FLAKES box, and stumbled in the dark over tin cans and broken tools and springs and tires, set the box down, then went back and got the other box.

The boxes weren't far enough into the dump. He dragged them, one with each hand, backwards, up and over the rough terrain, stumbling, cutting his hand on rusty cans and nails in charred wood, thinking of tetanus, of Lydia without him.

Standing up, he sucked in the night air, feeling a dewy freshness mingled with the acrid smoke and fumes. He reached into his pocket for his lighter. His thumb began to hurt as he failed repeatedly to make the flint catch.

A bright beam shot out over the dump, another several yards beside it, then another—powerful flashlights—and as he crouched to avoid the lights, rifle fire shattered the silence over the dump. Reaching out, grabbing the cardboard flaps to keep his balance, Ernest squatted beside his boxes.

"Get that son-of-a-bitch, Doc!"

Twisting his neck around, Ernest saw the beam swing and dip through oily smoke coiling out of the debris and stop on a rat, crouched on a fire-blackened icebox door. It started to run. But the slick porcelain allowed its feet no traction.

ANN PETRY
The Witness

It had been snowing for twenty-four hours, and as soon as it stopped the town plows began clearing the roads and sprinkling them with a mixture of sand and salt. By nightfall the main roads were what the roadmaster called clean as a whistle. But the little winding side roads and the store parking lots and the private walkways lay under a thick blanket of snow.

Because of that, Charles Woodruff parked his station wagon, brand-new, expensive, in the road in front of the Congregational Church, rather than risk getting stuck in the lot behind it. He was early for the minister's class, so he sat still, deliberately savoring the new-car smell of the station wagon. He found himself sniffing audibly and thought the sound rather a greedy one, and so he got out of the car and stood on the snow-covered walk, studying the church. A full moon lay low on the horizon. It gave a wonderfully luminous quality to the snow, to the church and to the branches of the great elms dark against the winter sky.

He ducked his head because the wind was coming in gusts straight out of the north, blowing snow until it swirled around him, stinging his face. It was so cold that his toes felt as though they were freezing, and he began to stamp his feet. Fortunately his coat insulated his body against the cold. He hadn't really planned to buy a new coat, but during the Christmas vacation he had been in New York City and had gone into one of those thick-carpeted, faintly perfumed, crystal-chandeliered stores that sell men's clothing, and he had seen the coat hanging on a rack—a dark-gray cashmere coat lined with nutria and adorned with a collar of black Persian lamb. A tall, thin salesman who smelled of heather saw him looking at the coat and said: "Try it on, sir—it's toast-warm, cloud-light, guaranteed to make you feel like a prince. Do try it on. Here—let me hold your coat, sir." The man's voice sounded as though he were purring, and he kept brushing against Woodruff like a cat. He managed to sell him the coat, a narrow-brimmed felt hat and a pair of fur-lined gloves.

If Addie were alive and learned he had paid five hundred dollars for an overcoat, she would have argued with him fiercely, nostrils flaring, eyebrows lifted. Standing there alone in the snow in front of the church, he permitted himself a small indulgence. He pretended Addie was standing beside him. He spoke to her aloud: "You always said I had to dress more elegantly than my students so they would respect my clothes even if they didn't respect my learning. You said——"

He stopped abruptly, thinking he must look like a lunatic, standing in the snow, stamping his feet and talking to himself. If he kept it up long enough, someone would call the state police and a bulletin about him would go clattering out over the teletype: "Attention all cruisers, attention all cruisers: A Black man—repeat, a Black man—is standing in front of the Congregational Church in Wheeling, New York. Description follows, description follows: thinnish, tallish Black man, clipped mustache, expensive (extravagantly expensive, outrageously expensive, unjustifiably expensive) overcoat, felt hat like a Homburg, eyeglasses glittering in the moonlight, feet stamping in the moonlight, mouth muttering in the moonlight. Light of the moon we danced. Glimpses of the moon revisited . . ."

There was no one in sight; no cars were passing. It was so still, it would be easy to believe that the entire population of the town had died and lay buried under the snow and that he was the sole survivor. And that would be ironic, because he did not really belong in this all-white community.

The thought of his alien presence here evoked an image of Addie, dark-skinned, intense, beautiful. He had been sixty-five when she died and had just retired as a professor of English at Virginia College for Negroes. He had spent all his working life there. He had planned to write a grammar to be used in first-year English classes, to perfect his herb garden, catalogue his library, tidy up his files and organize his clippings—a wealth of material in those clippings. But without Addie these projects seemed inconsequential, like the busywork that grade-school teachers devise to keep children out of mischief. When he was offered a job teaching in a high school in a small town in New York, he had accepted it quickly.

Everybody was integrating, and so this little, frozen Northern town was integrating too. Someone had probably asked why there were no Black teachers in the school system, and the school board and the superintendent of schools had said they were searching for one—and the search had yielded that brand-new Black widower, Charles Woodruff, eager to escape from his old environment.

So for the past year he had taught English to academic seniors in Wheeling High School. No problems. No hoodlums. All his students were being herded toward college like so many cattle. He thought that what was being done to them was a crime against nature. They were hard-working, courteous, pathetic. He had introduced a new textbook, discarded a huge anthology filled with mutilated poetry, mutilated essays, mutilated short stories. His students liked him and told him so. Other members of the faculty said he was lucky, but just wait—the freshmen and the sophomores coming up were a bunch of hoodlums, a whole new ball game.

Because of his success with his English classes he had been asked by Dr. Shipley, the Congregational minister, to assist (Shipley used words like "assist" instead of "help") him with a class of delinquent boys that met at the church on Sunday nights. Woodruff felt he should make some kind of contribution to the life of this small town that had treated him with genuine friendliness, so he had said yes.

But when he first saw those seven boys assembled in the minister's study, he knew that he could not help the minister with them—they were beyond both his and the minister's reach. They sat silent, motionless, their shoulders hunched as though against some chill they found in the air of that small, book-lined room. Their eyelids were like shutters drawn over their eyes. Their long hair covered their foreheads to the eyebrows in front and reached to the collars of their jackets in back. Their legs, stretched out straight in front of them, were encased in pants that fitted as tightly as the leotard of a ballet dancer.

He kept looking at them, studying them. Suddenly, as though at a signal, they all looked at him. This collective stare was so hostile that he felt himself stiffen, and sweat broke out on his forehead. He assumed that the same thing had happened to Dr. Shipley, because Shipley's eyeglasses kept fogging up, though the room was not overly warm.

Shipley talked for an hour. He began to get hoarse. Though he asked a question now and then and waited hopefully for a reply, there was none. The boys sat mute and motionless.

After they left, filing out one behind another, Woodruff had asked Shipley about them—who they were and why they attended this class in religion.

Shipley said, "They come here under duress. The Juvenile Court requires their attendance at this class."

"How old are they?"

"About sixteen. Very bright. Still in high school. They're all sophomores—that's why you don't know them. Rambler, the tall, thin boy, the ringleader, has an IQ in the genius bracket. As a matter of fact, if they weren't so bright, they'd be in reform school. This class is part of an effort to—well, to turn them into God-fearing, responsible young citizens."

"Are their families poor?"

"No, indeed. The parents of these boys are—well, they're the backbone of the great middle class in this town."

After the third meeting of the class, during which the same hostile silence had prevailed, Woodruff said, "Dr. Shipley, do you think we are accomplishing anything?" He had said "we," though he was well aware that these young outlaws newly spawned by the white middle class were, thank God, Shipley's problem—the white man's problem. This cripplingly tight shoe was usually on the Black man's foot. He found it rather pleasant to have the position reversed.

Shipley ran his fingers through his hair. It was very short hair, stiff-looking, crew-cut.

"I don't know," he said, frowning. "I really don't know. They don't even respond to a greeting or a direct question. It is a terribly frustrating business, an exhausting business. When the class is over I feel as though I had spent the entire evening lying prone under the unrelieved weight of all their bodies."

Woodruff, stamping his feet outside the church, jumped and then winced because he heard sounds like gunshots borne on the wind. He stood still, listening. Then he started moving quickly toward the building that housed the minister's study.

The sounds had been made by the car the boys drove. It had no muffler, and its snorting and backfiring and dreadful condition were like a snarling message aimed at the adult world: Only bald-headed, big-bellied rat finks drive shiny cars. We're left with the junk—the beat-up chassis, the thin tires, the brakes that don't hold, the transmission that's shot to hell. Woodruff had seen them push the car out of the parking lot behind the church. It wouldn't go into reverse.

Bent over, picking his way through the deep snow lest he stumble and fall, Woodruff tried to hurry, and the explosive sounds of that terrible engine came closer and closer. He envisioned himself as a black beetle against the snow, trying to scuttle out of danger. But why should he think he was in danger? By the pricking of my thumbs, something wicked this way comes.

Once inside the building, he drew a deep breath. He greeted the minister, hung his hat and coat on the brass hatrack and then sat down beside Shipley behind the old fumed-oak desk. He braced himself for the entrance of the boys.

There was the sound of the front door opening, followed by the sound of their heavy boots in the hall. Suddenly they were all there in the minister's study. They brought in cold air with them. They sat down with their jackets on—great, dark, quilted jackets that had been designed for European ski slopes. At the first meeting of the class Dr. Shipley had suggested they remove them, and they had simply sat and stared at him until he fidgeted and looked away. He never again made a suggestion that was direct and personal.

Woodruff glanced at the boys and then directed his gaze away from them, thinking that if a bit of gilt braid and a touch of velvet were added to their clothing, they could pass for the seven dark, bastard sons of some old and evil twelfth-century king. Of course, they weren't all dark. Three of them were blond, two had brown hair and one had red hair; only one had black hair. All of them were white. But there was about them an aura of something so evil, so dark, so suggestive of the black horror of nightmares, that he shivered deep inside himself whenever he saw them. Though he thought of them as being black, he did not mean the blackness of human flesh, warm, soft to the touch. It was the blackness and the coldness of the hole from which D. H. Lawrence's snake had emerged.

The hour was almost up when, to Woodruff's surprise, Rambler, the tall boy, the one who drove the ramshackle car, the one Shipley had said was the leader of the group, began asking questions about cannibalism. His voice was husky, low in pitch, and he almost whispered when he spoke. Woodruff found himself leaning forward in an effort to hear.

Rambler said, "Is it a crime to eat human flesh?"

Dr. Shipley said, surprised, "Yes. It's cannibalism. It is a sin and it is also a crime." He spoke slowly, gently, as though he were wooing a timid wild animal that had ventured out of the woods and would turn tail and scamper back if he spoke in his normal voice.

"Well, if the cats who go for this human-flesh bit don't think it's a sin and if they eat it because they haven't any other food, it isn't a sin for them, is it?" The boy spoke quickly, not pausing for breath, running his words together.

"There are many practices and acts acceptable to non-Christians that are sinful. Christians condemn such acts no matter what the circumstances."

Woodruff thought uncomfortably, Why does Shipley have to sound so pompous, so from-the-top-of-Olympus? The boys, bright-eyed, mouths slightly open, long hair obscuring their foreheads, were staring at him. Then Rambler said, in his husky, whispering voice, "What about you, Doc?"

Dr. Shipley said, "Me?" his voice losing its coaxing tone, rising in pitch. "What do you mean?"

"Well, man, you're eatin' human flesh, ain't you?"

Woodruff had no idea what the boy was talking about. But Dr. Shipley was looking down at his own hands with a curiously self-conscious expression, and now Woodruff saw that Shipley's nails were bitten to the quick.

The boy said, "It's self-cannibalism, ain't it, Doc?"

Shipley put his hands on the desk and braced himself preparatory to standing up. His thin, bony face had reddened. Before he could move or speak, the boys got up and began to file out of the room. Rambler leaned over and ran his hand through the minister's short-cut, bristly hair and said, "Don't sweat it, Doc."

Woodruff usually stayed a half hour or more after the class ended. Dr. Shipley liked to talk, and Woodruff listened to him patiently, although he thought the minister had a second-rate mind and rambled But Shipley sat with his head bowed, a pose not conducive to conversation, and Woodruff left almost immediately after the boys, carrying in his mind's eye a picture of all those straight, narrow backs with the pants so tight they were like elastic bandages on their thighs, and the oversized, bulky jackets and the long, frowzy hair. He thought they looked like paper dolls cut all at once, exactly alike, with a few swift slashes of a scissors wielded by a skilled hand.

He walked toward his car, head down, picking his way through the snow, and then he stopped, surprised. The boys were standing in the road. They had surrounded a girl. He didn't think she was a high-school girl, though she was young. She had long blond hair that spilled over the quilted black jacket she was wearing. At first he couldn't tell what the boys were doing, but as he got closer he saw that they were moving toward their ancient car and forcing the girl to move with them, though she was resisting. They were talking to one another and to her, their voices companionable, half playful.

"So we all got one in the oven."

"So it's all right if it's all of us."

"No," said the girl.

"Aw, come on, Nellie—hurry up."

"It's colder'n hell, Nellie. Move!"

They kept pushing her toward the car and she turned on them and said, "Quit it."

"Aw, get in."

One of them gave her a hard shove that sent her closer to the car. She screamed and Rambler clapped his hand over her mouth, and she must have bitten his hand because he snatched it away, and then she screamed again because he slapped her, and then two of them picked her up and threw her onto the front seat and one of them stayed there, holding her.

Woodruff thought, There are seven of them—young, strong, satanic. He ought to go home where it was quiet and safe, mind his own business—Black man's business. Leave this white man's problem for a white man, leave it alone, not his, don't interfere, go home to the bungalow he had rented—ridiculous type of architecture in this cold climate, developed for India, a hot climate, and that open-porch business——

He said, "What are you doing?" He spoke with the voice of authority, the male schoolteacher's voice, and thought, Wait, slow down, cool it; you're a Black man speaking with a white man's voice.

They turned and stared at him; they assumed what he called the stance of the new young outlaw, with shoulders hunched, hands in pockets. In the moonlight he thought they looked like a frieze around a building

—the hunched-shoulder posture repeated again and again, made permanent in stone. Classic.

"What are you doing?" he said again, voice louder, deeper.

"We're standin' here."

"You can see us, can't you?"

"Why did you force that girl into your car?"

"You're dreamin'."

"I saw what happened. And that boy is holding her in there."

"You been readin' too much."

They kept moving in, closing in on him. There was a subtle change in the tone of voice of the next speaker. It was more contemptuous and louder.

"What girl, ho-daddy? What girl?"

One of them suddenly reached out and knocked his hat off his head; another snatched his glasses off and threw them in the road and there was the tinkling sound of glass shattering. It made him shudder. He was half blind without his glasses.

They unbuttoned his overcoat and went through the pockets of his pants and jacket. One of them took his wallet; another took his car keys, picked up his hat and then was actually behind the wheel of his station wagon and moving off in it.

He shouted, "My car! Damn you, you're stealing my car—" His brand-new station wagon! He kept it immaculate, swept it out every morning, washed the windows. He tried to break away but the boys simply pushed him toward their car.

"Don't sweat it, man. You goin' ride with us and this little chick-chick."

"You goin' be our pro-tec-shun, ho-daddy. You goin' be our pro-tec-shun."

They took off his coat and put it around him backward without putting his arms in the sleeves, and then buttoned it up. The expensive coat was just like a strait jacket—it pinioned his arms to his sides. He tried to work his way out of it by flexing his muscles, hoping that the buttons would pop off or a seam would give; and he thought, enraged, They must have stitched the goddamn coat to last for a thousand years and put the goddamn buttons on the same way. The fur collar pressed against his throat, choking him.

Woodruff was forced into the back seat, two boys on either side of him. The boys next to him were sitting half on him. The one holding his wallet examined its contents. He whistled. "Hey!" he said. "Ho-daddy's got one hundred and forty-four bucks! We got us a rich ho-daddy."

Rambler held out his hand and the boy handed the money over without a protest, not even a sigh. Then Rambler got in behind the wheel. The girl was quiet only because the boy beside her had his hand around her throat, and from the way he was holding his arm, Woodruff knew he was exerting a certain amount of pressure.

"Give the man a hat," Rambler said.

One of the boys felt around until he found a cap. "Here you go," he said. He pulled a black wool cap down on Woodruff's head, over his eyes, over his nose.

Woodruff couldn't see anything. He couldn't breathe through his nose; he had to breathe through his mouth or suffocate. The freezing air actually hurt the inside of his mouth. The overcoat immobilized him and the steady pressure of the fur collar against his windpipe was beginning to interfere with his normal rate of breathing. He knew that his whole circulatory system would gradually slow down. He thought how simply and easily a person could be rendered helpless just by means of an overcoat and a knitted cap. Then he thought, alarmed, If they leave me out in the woods like this, I will be dead by morning. What do they want of me, anyway?

He cleared his throat preparatory to questioning them, but Rambler started the car and he could not make himself heard above the engine. He thought the noise would shatter his eardrums and he wondered how these boys could bear it—the terrible roar and cannonade of the engine and the rattling of the doors and windows. Then they were off and it was like riding in a jeep, only worse, because the seat was broken and they were jounced up out of it and then back down into a hollowed-out place, all of them on top of one another. He tried to keep track of the turns the car made but couldn't; there were too many of them. He assumed that whenever they stopped it was because of a traffic light or a stop sign.

It seemed to him they had ridden for miles and miles when the car began to jounce up and down more violently than ever, and he decided they had turned onto a rough, rutted road. Then they stopped. The car doors were opened and the boys pushed him out of the car. He couldn't keep his balance and he stumbled and fell flat on his face in the snow, and they all laughed. They had to haul him to his feet, for his movements were so constricted that he couldn't get up without help.

The cap had worked up a little so that he could breathe more freely than before and see anything that was in his immediate way. They either didn't notice or didn't care. As they guided him along he saw that they were in a cemetery. They were approaching a small building and he saw his station wagon parked beside it. The boy who had driven it opened the door of the building, and Woodruff saw that it was lighted by a big bulb that dangled from the ceiling. Inside were shovels and rakes, a grease-encrusted riding mower, bags of grass seed and a bundle of material that looked like the artificial grass used around new graves.

Rambler said, "Put the witness here."

They stood him against the back wall, facing the wall.

"He's here and yet he ain't here."

"Ho-daddy's here, and yet he ain't here."

"He's our witness."

And then Rambler's voice again: "If he moves, ice him with a shovel."

The girl screamed, and then the sound was muffled, only a kind of far-off moaning sound. They must have gagged her. All the sounds were muffled—it was like trying to see something in a fog or hear something when other sounds overlay the one thing you were listening for. What had they brought him here for? They would go away and leave him with the girl, but the girl would know that he hadn't——

How would she know? They had probably blindfolded her too. What were they doing? He could see shadows on the wall. Sometimes they moved, sometimes they were still, and then the shadows would move again and then there would be laughter. Silence after that, and then thuds, thumps, silence again. Terrible sounds behind him. He started to turn around and someone poked him in the back sharply with the handle of a shovel or a rake. He began to sweat despite the terrible cold.

He tried to relax by breathing deeply; he felt as though he were going to faint. His hands and feet were numb. His head ached. He had strained so to hear what was going on behind him that he was afraid he had impaired his own hearing.

When Rambler said, "Come on, ho-daddy—it's your turn," he was beginning to lose all feeling in his arms and legs.

Someone unbuttoned his coat, plucked the cap off his head. He let his breath out in a long-drawn-out sigh. He doubted that he could have survived much longer with that pressure on his throat. The boys looked at him curiously. They threw his coat on the hard-packed dirt floor and tossed the cap on top of it. He thought that the black knitted cap, like a sailor's watch cap, was as effective a blindfold as could be found—provided, of course, a person couldn't use his hands to remove it.

The girl was lying on the floor, half-naked. They had put some burlap bags under her. She looked as though she were dead.

They pushed him toward her, saying, "It's your turn."

He balked, refusing to move.

"You don't want none?"

They laughed. "Ho-daddy don't want none.'

They pushed him closer to the girl and someone grabbed one of his hands and placed it on the girl's thigh, on her breasts, and then they laughed again. They handed him his coat, pulled the cap down on his head.

"Let's go, ho-daddy. Let's go."

Before he could put his coat back on they hustled him outdoors. One of them threw his empty wallet at him and another aimed his car keys straight at his head. The metal stung as it hit his cheek. Before he could catch them the keys disappeared in the snow. The boys went back inside the building and emerged carrying the girl, half-naked, head hanging limply like the head of a corpse.

"The girl—" Woodruff said.

"You're our witness, ho-daddy. You're our big fat witness."

They propped the girl up in the back seat of their car. "You're the only witness we got," one of them repeated, laughing. "Take good care of yourself."

"She'll freeze to death like that," he protested.

"Not Nellie."

"She likes it."

"Come on, man—let's go, let's go, let's go," Rambler said impatiently.

Woodruff's arms and hands were so numb that he had trouble getting his coat on. He had to take his gloves off and poke around in the snow with his bare hands before he could retrieve his wallet and keys. The pain in his hands was as sharp and intense as that of a burn.

Getting into his car, he began to shake with fury. Once he got out of this wretched cemetery, he would call the state police. Young animals. He had called them outlaws; they weren't outlaws—they were animals. In his haste he dropped the keys, and had to feel around on the floor of the car for them.

When he finally got the car started he was shivering and shaking, and his stomach was quivering so that he didn't dare try to drive. He turned on the heater and watched the tiny taillight on Rambler's car disappear. The explosive sounds of the engine gradually receded. When he could no longer hear them, he flicked on the light in his car and looked at his watch. It was quarter past three. Wouldn't the parents of those godforsaken boys wonder where they were at that hour? Perhaps they didn't care. Perhaps they were afraid of them—just as he was.

Though he wanted to get home as quickly as possible so that he could get warm, so that he could think, he had to drive slowly, peering out at the narrow, rutted road, because he was half blind without his glasses. When he reached the cemetery gates he stopped, not knowing whether to turn right or left, for he had no idea where he was. He took a chance and turned right, following the macadam road, still going slowly. He saw a church on a hill and recognized it as the Congregational Church in Brooksville, the next town, and knew he was about five miles from home.

By the time he reached his own driveway, sweat was pouring from his body; even his eyelashes were wet. In the house he turned on the lights, first in the living room, then in the hall and in his bedroom. He went to his desk, opened a drawer and fished out an old pair of glasses. He had had them for years. They looked rather like Peter Cooper's glasses, which he'd once seen in The Cooper Union Museum in New York—small, with steel frames. They evoked an image of a careful, scholarly man. Addie had made him stop wearing them. She said they gave him the look of another era, made it easy for his students to caricature him—the tall, slender, slightly stooped figure, the steel-rimmed glasses. She said his dark, gentle eyes looked as though they were trapped behind those little glasses.

Having put them on, he went to the telephone and stood with one hand on it, sweating again, trembling again. He turned away, took off his overcoat, hung it on a hanger and placed it in the hall closet.

He began to pace up and down the living room—a pleasant, spacious room, simply furnished. It had a southern exposure overlooking a meadow, and there were big windows on that side. The thought crossed his mind lightly, like the silken, delicate strand of a cobweb, that he would have to leave here, and he brushed it away. Not quite away—a trace remained.

He wasn't going to call the police. Chicken. That was the word his students used. Fink was another one. He was going to chicken out. He was going to fink out.

Why wasn't he going to call the police? Well, what would he tell them? That he'd been robbed? That was true. That he'd been kidnapped? Well, that was true too, but it seemed like a harsh way of putting it. He'd have to think about that one. That he'd been witness to a rape? He wasn't even certain they had raped the girl. No? Whom was he trying to kid—himself? Himself.

So why wasn't he going to the police? He hadn't touched the girl. But those horrible little hoods—toads, rather—those horrible, toadlike hoods would say he had touched her. Well, he had. Hadn't he? They had made sure of that. Would the police believe him? The school board? The PTA? Where there's smoke, there must be fire. "I'm not going to let *my* daughter stay in his class."

He started shivering again. He made himself a cup of tea and sat down on the window seat in the living room to drink it, and then got up and turned off the lights and looked out at the snow. The moonlight was so bright that he could see the tall winter grasses in the meadow, yellow against the snow. Immediately he thought of the long blond hair of that starvation-thin young girl. Bleached hair? Perhaps. It didn't lessen the outrage. She had been dressed just like the boys—big, quilted jacket, skin-tight pants, even her hair worn like theirs, obscuring the face.

There was a sudden movement outside the window and he frowned and leaned forward. He saw a pair of rabbits leaping, running, literally playing games with each other. He had never before seen such free, joyous movement; not even children at play exhibited it.

Watching this joyous, heel-kicking play, he found himself thinking, I cannot continue to live in the same small town with that girl and those seven boys. The boys had known before he did that he would not report this—this incident, these crimes. They were bright enough to know that he would realize quickly how neatly they had boxed him in. If he dared enter a complaint against them, they would accuse him of raping the girl, would say they had found him in the cemetery with her. Whose story would be believed? "Where there's smoke, there's fire."

Right after that he started packing. He put his clothes in a footlocker. He stacked his books on the floor of the station wagon. He was surprised to find among them a medical textbook that had belonged to Addie's brother John.

He sat down and read all the information on angina pectoris. At eight o'clock he called the school and said he wasn't feeling well (which was true) and that he would not be in. Then he called the office of the local doctor and made an appointment for that afternoon.

When he talked to the doctor he described the violent pain in his chest that went from the shoulder down to his fingertips on the left side, causing a squeezing, crushing sensation that left him feeling faint, dizzy.

The doctor, a fat man in an old tweed jacket and a limp white shirt, said after he examined him, "Angina. You'll have to take three or four months off until we can get this thing under control."

"I will resign immediately."

"Oh, no, that isn't necessary. Besides, I've been told you're the best English teacher we've ever had. It would be a great pity to lose you."

"No," Woodruff said, "it is better to resign." Come back here and look at that violated little girl? Come back here? Ever?

He scarcely listened to the detailed instructions he was to follow, did not even glance at the three prescriptions he was handed, for he was eager to be on his way. He composed a letter of resignation in his mind. When he went back to the bungalow he wrote it quickly, and then put it on the front seat of the station wagon to be mailed en route.

He went back into the house just long enough to call his landlord. He said he'd had a heart attack and was going home to Virginia to convalesce, that he had turned the thermostat down to sixty-five and would return the house keys by mail. The landlord said, My goodness, you just paid a month in advance, I'll mail you a refund, what's your new address, so sorry, ideal tenant . . .

Woodruff hung up the receiver and said, "Peace be with you, brother." There was already an echo in the room, although it wasn't empty; all he'd removed were his books and his clothes.

He put on his elegant overcoat. When he got back to Virginia he would give the coat away. His pleasure in it was destroyed now, for he would always remember the horrid feeling of the collar tight across his throat. Even the feeling of the fabric under his fingertips would forever evoke an image of the cemetery, the tool shed and the girl.

He drove down the road slowly. There were curves and he couldn't go fast; besides, he liked to look at this landscape. It was high, rolling land. Snow lay over it—blue-white where there were shadows cast by the birch trees and the hemlocks, yellow-white and sparkling in the great meadow where he had watched the heel-kicking freedom of the rabbits at play.

At the entrance to the highway he stopped. As he waited for an opportunity to move into the stream of traffic he heard close at hand the loud, explosive sound of an engine—a familiar sound. He was so alarmed that he momentarily experienced all the symptoms of a heart attack—the sudden, terrible inability to breathe and the feeling that something was squeezing his chest, kneading it, so that pain ran through him, following the course of his circulatory system.

The car that turned off the highway and entered the same road he was leaving was Rambler's car. In the sunlight, silhouetted against the snow, it looked like a junkyard on wheels—fenders dented, sides dented, chassis rusted. All the boys were in the car. Rambler was driving. Nellie was in the front seat, a terrible bruise under one eye. For a fraction of a second Woodruff looked straight into Rambler's eyes, just visible under the long, untidy hair. His expression was cold, impersonal, analytical.

After Woodruff got on the highway he kept looking in the rearview mirror. There was no sign of pursuit. Evidently Rambler had not noticed that the car was loaded for flight. The books and cartons on the seats, the footlocker on the floor—all this would have been out of his range of vision. Woodruff wondered what they were doing. Wrecking the interior of the bungalow? No, they probably were waiting for him to return so that they could blackmail him. Blackmail a Black male.

On the turnpike he kept going faster and faster—sixty-five miles an hour, seventy-five, eighty. He felt exhilarated by this tremendous speed. It was clearing his mind, heartening him, taking him out of himself.

He began to rationalize what had happened. He decided that Rambler and his friends didn't give a damn that Woodruff was a Black man. They couldn't care less. They were very bright boys, bright enough to recognize him for what he was: a Black man in his sixties, conditioned all his life by the knowledge that "white woman taboo for you," as one of his African students used to say. The moment he attempted to intervene in front of the church, they had decided to take him with them. They knew he wasn't going to the police about any matter that involved sex and a white girl, especially when there were seven of them to accuse him of having relations with the girl. They had used his presence in that tool shed to give an extra, exquisite fillip to their dreadful game.

He turned on the radio for music, any kind of music, thinking it would distract him. He got one of those stations that played what he called thump-and-blare music. A husky-voiced woman was shouting—not singing but shouting:

"I'm gonna turn on the big heat
I'm gonna turn up the high heat
For my ho-daddy, ho-daddy,
For my ho-daddy, ho-daddy."

He flipped the switch, cutting off the sound, and gradually diminished the speed of the car to normal. "We got us a rich ho-daddy." That's what one of the boys had said in front of the church when he plucked the money out of Woodruff's wallet. A rich ho-daddy? A Black ho-daddy. A witness. Another poor scared Black bastard who was a witness.

Index of Authors and Titles*

* Page numbers for stories reprinted in this book are in boldface type.

Index of Critical Terms Defined or Discussed*

* Page numbers for the most important entries are printed in boldface type.

Chronological Index